French Baroque Music

from Beaujoyeulx to Rameau

REVISED EDITION

French Baroque Music

from Beaujoyeulx to Rameau

REVISED EDITION

James R. Anthony

W. W. Norton & Company, Inc.
New York

REVISED EDITION

Library of Congress Cataloging in Publication Data

Anthony, James R.
French baroque music from Beaujoyeulx to Rameau.

Bibliography: p.
Includes index.
1. Music—France—History and criticism.   2.   Music
—History and criticism—16th century.   3.   Music—History and criticism—17th century.   4.   Music—History
and criticism—18th century.   I.   Title.
ML270.2.A6   1978   781.7'44   77–28478

1 2 3 4 5 6 7 8 9 0

to Louise

Contents

Part four : Instrumental Ensemble and Solo Music

Part five : Vocal Chamber Music

Epilogue

Illustrations

Tables

Author's Note

Anyone who has heard Marie-Claire Alain play a Couperin organ mass at Saint-Merri or who has pored over the Charpentier *Meslanges* at the Bibliothèque Nationale and the *grands motets* by Delalande at the Bibliothèque Municipale de Versailles will understand the function of this book. The music of Charpentier and Delalande deserves a better fate than that accorded it by an indifferent history. At its best, like the paintings of Watteau, the wit of Montesquieu, the incisive characterization of Molière, this music along with that by Lully, Couperin, Campra, Leclair and others transcends the heroic pose of the *grand siècle* and the perfumed elegance of the Regency. Even at its most superficial it helps illuminate the society that created it. Guillemain's sonatas 'ou Conversations galantes et amusantes entre une Flûte Traversière, un Violon, une Basse de Viole et la Basse continue' tells us almost as much about 'Rococo hedonism' as does Lancret's 'Le Déjeuner de Jambon'.

Although we must not claim for this music the depth of feeling that characterizes the best German Baroque music from Schütz to Bach, nor the almost visceral passion of the best Italian Baroque music from Monteverdi to Vivaldi, French music of the same time has its own quite different life force, its *raison d'être*. It speaks of the dance in all its guises as does no other music, it gives full play to the imagination and to a flight of fancy that delights the senses, and like all of the best in French art, it develops a high degree of sensitivity to decoration: in short, it merits our attention.

The purpose of this book is to present a style study of the music of the French Baroque against the background of the institutions and practices of the *grand siècle*. In a very general way the outer boundaries of the book are fixed at 1581 and 1733. The former date saw the performance of Beaujoyeulx's *Ballet comique de la Reine,* the first French court ballet in which we may foresee the later *tragédie lyrique.* The latter date has a double significance: it marked the death of François Couperin, the greatest, if not the most representative composer of the later years of Louis xiv; and it was the year of Rameau's *Hippolyte et*

1

Aricie, a work considered by the eighteenth century as having marked a 'revolution in the progress of music in France' (*Almanach des spectacles*, 1765) and which indirectly led to the operatic quarrels of the later eighteenth century.

In commenting on the incredible growth of specialization and the sheer bulk of material now available to the discipline of musicology, Friedrich Blume suggested that the generalized encyclopedia or dictionary of music may well be a thing of the past and that the 'future will belong to specialized reference books' (*Notes*, xxiv 1967, p. 227). The same comment might be made with regard to general histories of music. For years Paul Henry Lang's monumental *Music in Western Civilization* was the only thoroughly competent book of its scope in English. Within the past generation many general music history texts have been published. At the same time more and more books are being written on the various periods of music history. These range from a highly detailed and technical approach to the most popular 'music appreciation' bias. Within the past few years, for example, two books on the Baroque period alone have been printed (Claude Palisca's *Baroque Music*, Englewood Cliffs, 1968, and Edith Borroff's *The Music of the Baroque*, Dubuque, 1970).

A book on the music of a particular country during a particular period is a natural step in the progression starting from the general and moving through period histories. Such a book, with its great advantage of concentrated focus, should aim to synthesize the research conducted over years by specialists in a limited area and as such be considered a 'specialized reference book'. In a modest way, that is what this book purports to do.

Music of the French Baroque lacks a significant body of material printed in English. Take Michel-Richard Delalande, for example, who 30 years ago was named by Lang as 'one of France's greatest musicians' (*Music in Western Civilization*, New York 1941, p. 540). The paucity of material on him dramatically underscores this situation. His *grands motets* are the subject of a few scattered articles, he receives four lines in Bukofzer's *Music in the Baroque Era*, one sentence in Borroff's *The Music of the Baroque* and is totally ignored by Palisca in his *Baroque Music*.

Or were we to choose a genre such as the *opéra-ballet* which Guy Ferchault characterized as marking a 'new step in the history of forms' (*La Musique des origines à nos jours*, ed. Norbert Dufourcq, Paris 1946, p. 186), a point of view agreed with by most French scholars, we would discover that neither *Grove's Dictionary of Music and Musicians* nor the *Harvard Dictionary of Music* has a listing under 'opera ballet' and that Norman Demuth's *French Opera, Its Development to the Revolution* (Sussex, 1963), neglects even to define the genre. This book, then, tries to redress these and similar sins of omission.

2

For this reason special emphasis is given to the period labelled *pré-ramiste* by the French, that is, the period between the death of Lully (1687) and the debut of Rameau as an opera composer (1733). In so doing, we may hope that such composers as André Campra (1660–1744), Jean-Joseph Mouret (1682–1738), Michel de Montéclair (1667–1737) and André Cardinal Destouches (1672–1749) may be vindicated in part from the imputation that all operatic composers between Lully and Rameau were mere 'imitators of Lully' (Martin Cooper. *Gluck*, London and New York, 1935, p. 166).

The task of writing this book was simplified considerably by the number of primary sources from the period now available in facsimile, in reprint or in translation.* At almost any university library a student may research the 1724 edition of Campra's *L'Europe galante* and contrast it with Destouches' *Amadis de Grèce*; he may puzzle over the striking Mediant $\frac{9}{7}_{\sharp 5}$ chord found in so much music of the French Baroque and find it discussed in an obscure MS treatise on composition by Bernier translated into English; he may enjoy the attractive plates that grace the 1582 publication of the *Ballet comique*; he may be a silent observer as Lecerf and his countess debate the merits of French and Italian music; and he may trace Rameau's difficulties with the Subdominant chord from the *Traité de l'harmonie* through the *Génération harmonique* in not one but two facsimiles of the complete theoretical writings of Rameau—surely a most expensive consequence of the lack of any 'union list' of publications-in-progress.

Yet make no mistake, the millennium has not arrived. Much music of Charpentier and Delalande slumbers in the archives of Paris and Versailles libraries. It is shocking that neither the *Oeuvres complètes* of Lully nor of Rameau are 'complete'. We await David Fuller's book on a history of French harpsichord music, Vladimir Féderov's on a history of the Ballard printing monopoly promised us in Volume 1 of the *MGG*,† a Denise Launay anthology and style study of the motet in France *after* Du Mont, a second volume of Madeleine Jurgens' edition of *Documents du Minutier Central* covering the period after 1650.

We would be remiss to conclude this preface without mention of the *crise de conscience* experienced by any non-French writer who couples the words 'French' and 'Baroque'. For many French scholars the words are mutually exclusive when applied to most French art of the seventeenth and eighteenth centuries which, they claim with conviction, was a period in France dominated by classical tradition. Although not

---

* Minkoff Reprints of Geneva has undertaken the ambitious task of reprinting several of the most important sources found at the Bibliothèque Nationale dealing with French Baroque music. The 1977 catalogue entitled 'Musique et Musicologie' includes about 200 titles.

† See p. 389 for abbreviations of journals and periodicals.

submitting to the extreme statements and harsh indictments of Abbé
Pluche who found in 'la musique Barroque' only a concern for the
production of noise 'like animals with no intelligence' (*Le Spectacle de
la nature*, VII, 1746, p. 132), we have the distinct impression that for
many contemporary French scholars the term 'Baroque music' still
carries the pejorative taint left from Rousseau's definition: 'Baroque
Music is that in which the Harmony is confused and filled with Modulation and Dissonance; the Melody is harsh and unnatural, the Intonation difficult; & the Tempo forced' (*Dictionnaire de musique*, 1768,
p. 41). The most convincing spokesman for the French opposition to
the use of 'Baroque' as a description for French musical style in the
seventeenth and eighteenth centuries is Norbert Dufourcq who recognizes two classical eras. The first, and the one that concerns us here,
was led by 'Lully, Couperin, Delalande, Rameau in France; Corelli,
A. Scarlatti in Italy; Purcell in England; Pachelbel following
Schütz in Germany. This classicism largely utilized a contrapuntal
language which Bach carried to its height. . . .' ('Classicism', *Larousse
de la musique*, ed. Dufourcq, 1, Paris 1957, p. 201).[1] The essential logic
of the French opposition is irrefutable if we recognize the colonnade of
the Louvre, the paintings of Poussin and the plays of Racine as mani-
festations of 'classical' tradition. The contradiction implicit in impre-
cise use of these terms may be seen in Bukofzer's acknowledgement of
a French 'classical tradition' where he uses 'baroque' to define an era
chronologically:

> The lucid rationalism of the French classical tradition pre-
> vented French music from succumbing to the turbulent affections
> unleashed by the Italian baroque. The seventeenth century was
> for the French drama the *grand siècle* of the 'classics' in the strict
> sense of the word. Although Corneille, Racine and Molière be-
> longed essentially to the baroque era they showed . . . how deeply
> they were impressed by the purportedly 'classical' concepts of the
> ancient drama.
>
> (*Music in the Baroque Era*, New York, 1947, p. 141)

Within the past decade there appears to have been less resistance
on the part of some French scholars to apply the term 'Baroque' to
French music both as a style concept and as a period designation.
Denise Launay regretted that the French point of view in the 'quarrel
of the Baroque' had not been made the object of a particular study
(Introduction to *Anthologie du motet latin polyphonique en France*,
Paris 1963) although in 1957 some French scholars contributed to a
colloquium on *Le 'Baroque' musical* (vol. IV of *Les Colloques de
Wégimont*) which took place at the University of Liège.[2] With guarded
language, François Lesure addressed himself to the 'problem of the

4

baroque français' at the end of his chapter on the 'Naissance de l'Orchestre' in the *Histoire de la musique* (ed. Roland-Manuel, I, Paris 1960, p. 1570). 'One speaks of the resistance in France to the baroque. However, it cannot be doubted that before Lully there are certain elements in French instrumental music, as well as in the *air de cour*, which ... can pass for a certain type of baroque art, tempered or moderated *à la française*. . . .'

This author has employed the term 'Baroque' in the title of his book in the conviction that there are some 'Baroque' elements in French music of the seventeenth and early eighteenth centuries no matter how 'tempered or moderated *à la française*' they may be. More important, what we have rightly or wrongly come to refer to as 'Baroque techniques' or 'Baroque practices' (which in actuality may have little to do with what we mean by 'Baroque style') are in common use today. Thus, French music, like German, like Italian, like English, will make use of the basso continuo, the stile concertato and will exploit the most 'Baroque' of inventions, the opera.

As is true in any intensive study of music written within a limited period of time, there is much chaff that must be separated from the wheat, much music that deserves to remain undisturbed in the archives. At the same time there are many pleasant surprises in addition to the more obvious ones mentioned earlier: the *chansons à boire* and the *airs sérieux* by Jean Sicard, for example, the *grands motets* by Henry Desmarest, or the three books of *Cantates françoises* by Montéclair. This is music that remains virtually unknown and certainly unavailable in modern editions. It is hoped that whatever interest may be stimulated by the reading of this book may be channelled in the direction of editing and publishing some of this forgotten music by minor masters of the *grand siècle*.

I wish to express my gratitude to the following individuals who have made the undertaking of this study possible: to Franklin B. Zimmerman who first encouraged me to write the book; to François Lesure and Nanie Bridgman at the Bibliothèque Nationale, to André Ménétrat and Nicole Wild at the Bibliothèque de l'Opéra and to Pierre Breillat and Jean-Michel Nectoux at the Bibliothèque Municipale de Versailles; to Denise Launay, Norbert Dufourcq and Marcelle Benoit for their encouragement and warm hospitality; to John Emerson at the music library of the University of California at Berkeley for his invaluable assistance in tracking down some obscure references; to the Graduate College Committee for Faculty Research Support in the Humanities and Social Sciences and to the Graduate College Faculty Research Support Committee, both of the University of Arizona, whose generous grants allowed me a measure of economic stability while on a sabbatical leave in France; to Jeanne Mills-Pont who aided greatly in the translation for the appendix; to my colleague Diran Akmajian, linguist *par excellence*, who read the entire draft with a critical eye; and to my wife, Louise, whose persuasive sense of style brought about many a concession. In addition, acknowledgment is made to the Centre National de la Recherche Scientifique (CNRS) for permission to use copyrighted material in four musical examples.

Preface to the Revised Edition

I am indebted to Claire Brook of W. W. Norton and Company for the opportunity to prepare an edition of *French Baroque Music* which, in the language of the eighteenth century, has been 'revüe, augmentée et corrigée'. Reviewers of the original edition made many invaluable suggestions for which I am grateful.

This 'revised, augmented and corrected' edition adds much new material that was unavailable, overlooked, or not in print at the time of the first edition. The value of the book as a research tool has been substantially increased by the addition of more documentation in footnotes, a more comprehensive Bibliography and a totally revised Index.

Although the chapters on keyboard music and instrumental solo and ensemble music have been expanded, the basic organization and premises found in the original have been maintained. The outer chronological limits are still generally fixed at 1581 and 1733.

Rameau's later operas remain outside its scope. The most superficial treatment of them would require another chapter at least. In any case, I am not convinced that Rameau, like Bach, was a 'living anachronism' in his own period (Julian Rushton, *M&L* [July, 1974], p. 351). There are as many elements in his *tragédies lyriques* that point ahead to Gluck as there are those that derive from Lully. The *Lullistes* and *Ramistes* had little difficulty in recognizing that which separated the established, secure past from an unsettled future represented by *Hippolyte et Aricie*. 'Not until Rameau', writes Paul-Marie Masson, 'do we have the feeling that operatic music has entered a new phase, an impression which, even after his first dramatic venture, was shared by all his contemporaries. After the Regency, Rameau's dramatic music assumed the proportions of a musical revolution' (*NOHM*, V, p. 240).

As before, the Series 1 and 2 of 'La Vie musicale en France sous les Rois Bourbons' (Editions A. and J. Picard) remain the basic repository of studies dealing with the *grand siècle*. New archival research in the great tradition of La Laurencie's *L'Ecole française de violon de Lully à Viotti* has been undertaken in France (see, for example, Marcelle Benoit's *Musiques de cour*). The 1977 catalogue of Minkoff Reprints (Geneva) lists 200 seventeenth and eighteenth century treatises, tutors and journals as well as several out-of-print classics by such early twentieth century scholars as Gérold, La Laurencie and Brenet.

7

At the same time, only one volume has been added to the Lully *Oeuvres complètes* and none to the *Oeuvres complétes* of Rameau. There is still no history of the Ballard printing monopoly, and one still awaits the publication of Bernard Bardet's thesis on the 'Violons de la musique de chambre sous Louis XIV'.

I would like to acknowledge Ann Basart, music librarian at the University of California at Berkeley, for her prompt response to research questions. I would like also to extend my appreciation to Constance Keffer and Deborah Burkhard, graduate students at the University of Arizona. In conclusion, it is my fervent hope that a special place in the Parthenon of music editors be reserved for Hinda Keller Farber of W. W. Norton for the endless hours she spent collating, interleafing and verifying the new material within the body of the original text.

Tucson, Arizona, July, 1977

Chapter 1

⟶⟫ ⟪⟵

Institutions and Organizations
of the Grand Siècle

Any study of the music of the seventeenth and early eighteenth centuries in France must also be a study of the institutions from which much of the music issued. Surely no nation at any time in history has known the all-pervasive 'organizing' that characterized the France of Louis XIV.

On 9 March 1661, Cardinal Mazarin died and Louis XIV at age 23 took unto himself the destiny of France. He chose to become his own first minister, thus eliminating the threat of another power-hungry Cardinal Richelieu or Mazarin. 'Above all', he wrote in his *Mémoires*, 'I was resolved not to have a prime minister . . . there being nothing more shameful than to see on the one hand all the power and, on the other, the mere title of king.'

To help him govern and direct policy, he appointed talented and ambitious men from the middle class among whom were Colbert, Le Tellier and Louvois, thus inaugurating, in Saint-Simon's words, the 'reign of the vile bourgeoisie'. By eliminating the nobility from his councils, he neutralized their power and, in effect, reduced the *princes du sang* to decorative impotency.

In exercising his passion for order at all levels of society, Colbert, between 1661 and his death in 1683, completed the creation of royal academies that were to systematize the artistic and intellectual life of the regime. In 1661 only the Académie Française (established by Cardinal Richelieu in 1635) and the Académie Royale de Peinture et de Sculpture (1648) existed; within the next decade, Colbert approved the founding of five more academies: Académie Royale de Danse (1661), Académie des Inscriptions et Belles Lettres (1663), Académie des Sciences (1666), Académie Royale de Musique (1669) and Académie Royale d'Architecture (1671).

It is hardly surprising that many facets of musical life of the *grand siècle* would also fall under a hierarchal administration which reflected the centralized bias of the regime. The phrase composed or printed 'by express order of His Majesty' graced many scores ranging from

9

pièces d'occasion, such as the *Airs de trompettes, timbales et hautbois fait par Mr. de Luly* for the carrousel of Monseigneur (the *grand Dauphin*) in 1686, to the *grands motets* composed for the royal chapel by Du Mont, Robert and Lully.

The king, except for some ability on the lute and guitar, made little mark as a performing musician. He was, however, at least semi-literate musically and possessed a fair amount of critical acumen.

He was considerably more than an aristocratic abstraction dispensing royal privileges and patents from the splendour of a Versailles council chamber. More than any other monarch of his time, he became personally involved in the music for his court, especially in the years following the final move to Versailles in 1682. He chose the music instructors for his family and relatives with care; he suggested to Quinault and Lully the subject matter of certain *tragédies lyriques*; and, according to Titon du Tillet,[1] he gave Clérambault the texts to several cantatas later performed in the apartments of Mme de Maintenon.

The king's attitude is well expressed by the archival comment apropos of a vacancy among the musicians of his *Chambre*: 'When places become available, His Majesty, in line with his plan to appoint individuals experienced in their profession to his *Chambre*, does not tolerate anyone who lacks these qualities and all the experience necessary to acquit himself of the task perfectly.'[2]

In order to find individuals 'experienced in their profession', he established a series of competitions; the first to choose four *sous-maîtres* for his royal chapel in 1663 (Du Mont, Expilly, Robert, Gobert) was followed 15 years later by another competition for the positions of four organists for the royal chapel (Nivers, Lebègue, Thomelin, Buterne); the most impressive of all was the great *concours* of 1683, again for the royal chapel *sous-maîtres* in which over 35 applicants from all over the realm competed (see Chapter 13, p. 184). In choosing Jean-Baptiste Lully as *Surintendant de la Musique de la Chambre* in 1661 and as *Maître de la Musique de la Famille Royale* in 1662, Louis XIV was assured of an efficient and ruthless agent whose absolutism, in fact, paralleled his own.

The King's Music[3]

Music at the court of Louis XIV was organized, from an administrative point of view, into three large divisions: Music of the Chamber (*Musique de la Chambre*), Music of the Great Stable (*Musique de la Grande Ecurie*), and Music of the Royal Chapel (*Musique de la Chapelle Royale*). In addition, the 24 *Violons du Roi* (referred to also as the *Grande Bande*) and the *Petits Violons du Roi* (referred to as the

Petite Bande and later in the century as the *Violons du Cabinet*), although technically under the administration of the *Chambre*, were, because of their great prestige, virtually autonomous. The approximate total of 120 musicians included in these groups were referred to collectively as 'Musiciens du Roi' or 'Officiers de la Maison du Roi'. Often an instrumentalist was simply called a 'Violon de la Chambre du Roi' or an 'Hautbois du Roi'.

MUSIC OF THE CHAMBER

The source of the music both of the *Chambre* and the *Ecurie* may be traced back to François I. This most pleasure-loving of the Valois kings, who was sensitive both to spectacular *fêtes* and to the more intimate and contemplative arts, created two categories for his court music. For the music of his *Chambre*, he chose soloists: singers (for madrigals and chansons), lutenists and virtuosi cornett players from Italy to which later were added organists, harpsichordists and viol players. For his *Ecurie*, he chose ensemble instruments appropriate for performances *'en plein air'*; they include oboes, sackbuts and violins for the parades and lavish ceremonies that lent colourful accents to his gentle Loire valley.[4]

At some point before 1571, during the reign of Charles IX, the bowed strings, the viols and violins, moved from the *Ecurie* to the *Chambre*. In 1592 under Henri IV, the position of *Surintendant de la Musique de la Chambre* was created. During the seventeenth and eighteenth centuries two men were appointed to this position each of whom served for one term. In addition to administrative functions, they were responsible for the choice of music and for the over-all organization of all non-religious musical performances at court. Aiding the *Surintendant* was the *Maître de Musique de la Chambre* who had the added responsibility for the education of the young musicians (called pages) attached to the *Chambre*. The third administrative division was that of *Compositeur de la Chambre* whose special task was often reflected in such titles as 'Compositeur de la musique instrumentale de la Chambre' or 'Compositeur des entrées des ballets.'

By 1590, discouraged by poor pay and the interminable wars of religion, many Italian violinists who had been brought to the court of Catherine de Medici by Maréchal de Brissac and who had acquitted themselves so nobly in the first court ballet, *Ballet comique de la Reine* (1581), returned home. French performers now formed the nucleus of players who eventually staffed the most important ensemble groups: the *12 Hautbois* and the *24 Violons*. By 1609 there were 22 *Violons ordinaires de la chambre du Roy*; by 1626 this group which then numbered 24 was given official recognition by Louis XIII as the *24 Violons du Roi* and was often referred to as the *Grande Bande*. Some of the best of these violinists (and oboists) came from the Parisian popular orchestras of the Guild (*Confrérie*) of Saint Julien.[5] They traded the 'rough and ready' life of the streets for a more genteel existence as a 'violon de la chambre du Roy'.

Hidden away in the archival records of the *Minutier Central* are many success stories of 'violons de chambre' such as one Jean de La Motte who entered the king's *Chambre* as a 'violon' in 1606 and by 1622 was also dancing teacher of the pages of the *Grand Ecurie*, and who ended up owning five houses in the Paris suburbs.[6]

The *24 Violons*, often reinforced by the *12 Grands Hautbois* of the *Ecurie*, constitute the first formally established orchestra to be built around a group of stringed instruments. The distribution of parts within the typical *a 5* texture of French seventeenth century instrumental music was as follows: six first violins (*dessus*), six basses (probably the *basse de violon*, not the violoncello) and four each of the three inner parts all tuned as the modern viola, but each with its own clef; the inner parts, or the 'parties de remplissage', were known as *haute-contre*, *taille* and *quinte*.

The *Petits Violons* were created by Louis XIV about 1648. The king assigned them to Lully who had found fault with the performance of the *Grande Bande* ostensibly on the grounds of their sloppiness and undisciplined use of ornaments. In actuality, Lully probably wanted a group of his own to test his ideas of orchestral performance techniques which, 20 years later, were to make his opera orchestra the envy of all Europe.

The *Petits Violons* appeared for the first time under Lully's direction in the court ballet *La Galanterie du temps* (1656), and for a six-year period the new group was used almost to the exclusion of the *24 Violons*. After 1661 Lully apparently reconciled his differences with the *Grande Bande* and the ensembles were then combined for the execution of ballets and other special court performances.

The division of labour between the two groups is difficult to determine. However, in an extract from the *Etat de France* for the year 1686, Prunières discovered the following:

> The *Grande Bande* of the *Vingt-quatre Violons*, always so labelled although they are at present twenty-five ... plays for the dinner of the King, for Ballets and for Comedies. The *Petits Violons* which number twenty-four ... follow the King on his journeys to the country, usually play for his supper, for Balls and the Recreation of His Majesty. They also play for Ballets. ...[7]

MUSIC OF THE ECURIE

For the 'man in the street' in the twentieth century the word *stable* evokes a dark and malodorous place. For the seventeenth-century man who gazed at the magnificent semi-circular stables at Versailles built by

Mansart in 1682, the *Grand Ecurie* meant much more than housing for the king's horses. Among the many *officiers du roi* attached to the *Grand Ecurie* were the musicians traditionally associated with military and outdoor pageantry. These were Louis xiv's best wind and brass players who were available for the many ceremonies attending foreign dignities such as the envoys from Siam (1686) and the ambassadors from Persia (1715). They were the chief source of music for parades and outdoor *fêtes*; they accompanied the king to parliament and their fanfares were heard both on the battle field and at the hunt. The people revelled in the sight of the colourful mounted trumpeters whose remote descendants in the Garde Républicaine quicken the pulse of parade watchers today as they play their trumpets at a gallop down the Champs-Elysées on Bastille Day.

From the 1540's, the instrumentalists of the *Ecurie* were already grouped into three categories including 12, 5, and 6 musicians respectively: 1. 'Sackbuts and instrumentalists' ('Saqueboutes et joueurs d'instruments'), 2. 'Fifes and drums' ('Fiffres et tabourins') and 3. 'Trumpets' ('Trompettes').[8]

Although 'joueurs d'instruments' originally referred mainly to wind instruments (oboes and cornetts) violinists were also included in the music of the *Ecurie*, reminding us that the violin was considered especially appropriate for music *'en plein air'*. As we have already seen, however, sometime before 1571 most bowed strings had been transferred from the *Ecurie* to the *Chambre*.[9]

By 1571 the *Ecurie* had at its disposal 12 trumpets, 8 fifes and drums, 15 sackbuts, oboes and cornetts, 1 musette and, according to Ecorcheville, one 'undetermined player'. The divisions remained essentially the same under Louis XIV. In the 'Etat des Officiers de la Maison du Roi' for 1689 (see Benoit, *Musiques de cour*, p. 121) the following administrative units of the *Ecurie* are itemized: 'Trompettes' (12 players); 'Joueurs de violon, hautbois, saqueboutes et cornets' (12 players); 'Hautbois et musettes de Poictou' (6 players); 'Joueurs de fifres et tambour' (8 players); and 'Cromornes et trompettes marines' (6 players).

The four best trumpet players, the 'trompettes ordinaires', were always expected to be available and to precede the royal coach on horseback in uniform. The eight remaining were used for performances of *Te Deums*, funerals, coronations, arrivals of visiting dignitaries and the like.

The third category included some of the best performers who were prepared to play on a variety of wind instruments. In the second half of the seventeenth century the category became known as the *12 Grands Hautbois*, actually 10 instruments of the oboe family and 2 bassoons. They had only three official functions a year to meet: the rising (*lever*) of the king on the first day of January and May, and on

24 August for Saint Louis' day. The remainder of the time they combined with such other groups as the 24 *Violons* for performances of court ballets, *divertissements*, operas, etc.

After 1690 the music of the *Ecurie* entered a long decline. Ecorcheville estimates that by the time of the Regency, there were scarcely six or eight musicians out of 43 who served effectively. Yet even at the end of his long life Louis XIV took some comfort from their music, and 'on Saint Louis' day, 1715, a few days before his death, the drums and oboes (of the *Ecurie*) were in place under his window' (Ecorcheville, *SIMG*, p. 641).

In truth, the significance of the *Ecurie* to a history of French Baroque music does not lie with its spectacular 'orchestration' of the ceremonies, the *carrousels* and *fêtes* performed for the pleasure of the king and the royal family; its historical function, in retrospect, was to provide an invaluable proving ground for the great family dynasties of wind players. Generations of Hotteterres and Philidors were blessed with economic security and with ample opportunities for extensive performance on their chosen instruments. This in turn not only led to the betterment of performance techniques, but also, and most important, it stimulated needed reforms in the construction of the instruments themselves to the point that soon after the turn of the century, French oboes and flutes were the most admired in Europe.

MUSIC OF THE ROYAL CHAPEL

The royal chapel, also first organized by François I (1543), changed little during the late sixteenth and early seventeenth centuries. In principle, it was a stronghold of musical conservatism and thereby merely reflected the state of religious music in France until Louis XIV initiated some reforms after 1679.

As late as 1645, when Guillaume du Peyrat published his formidable *Histoire ecclésiastique de la cour ou les Antiquitez et recherches de la chapelle et oratoire du roy de France depuis Clovis Ier jusques à nostre temps, divisée en trois livres*, the chapel was composed of 'two *sous-maîtres*, ... a first cornettist (*cornet ordinaire*), another cornettist, two boy sopranos, eight basses, eight tenors, eight counter-tenors, eight chaplains, four chapel clerks and two grammar instructors for the children'.

The important post of *sous-maître*, which also could carry the title *Compositeur de la Chapelle*, had comparable authority to the *Surintendant de la Musique de la Chambre*. His responsibility was to train the choir and to choose and compose the music for the king's Mass and other important ceremonies. His immediate superior's position, *Maître de la Chapelle*, was usually an honorary appointment to the royal chapel given to a highly placed ecclesiastic, such as the Archbishop of Paris or of Rheims, rather than to a musician.

14

In 1678 the Treaty of Nijmegen, which made Louis XIV 'master of western Europe for the next ten years',[10] gave him some respite from following his armies. At this time he turned his attention to the transformation of Versailles, which had begun as early as 1661, and to his royal chapel. Versailles had already had two chapels; the first, dating from 1664, was little larger than a *salon*. The second existed from about 1672 to 1682 in the Aile-de-la-reine, a large one-storey *salon*. The third was inaugurated in 1682 when the king and his court made their permanent residence at Versailles. It was designed on two levels and was located in the Aile-du-roi on the site of the present 'Salon d'Hercule'.[11] The magnificent final chapel, begun by Mansart and completed by Robert de Cotte, dates from the end of the ageing monarch's rule (1710).

The *grand motet*, the *ne plus ultra* of French Baroque religious music, owes its very existence to the king's concept of music appropriate for the chapel of Europe's most powerful monarch. By 1708 Delalande, as the most important composer of *grands motets*, had a sizeable working group at the royal chapel. The singers included 11 sopranos and mezzo-sopranos, 18 counter-tenors, 23 tenors, 24 baritones and 14 basses. The sopranos included male sopranos or falsettists (*dessus mues*), castrati (*dessus italiens*) and boy sopranos (*pages*). Women were used towards the end of the reign of Louis XIV. The orchestra in 1708 comprised strings (6 violins and violas, 3 bass violins, 1 double bass or theorbo), 2 flutes, 2 oboes, a bass crumhorn, 2 serpents and one bassoon.[12] The group could, of course, be augmented by singers from the *Chambre* and instrumentalists from the *24 Violons* and the *Ecurie*.

From the sixteenth century to the Revolution, the kings of France were to demand from Paris churches, such as Notre-Dame and the Sainte-Chapelle, the best singers for their own chapel. Often the choir directors of the churches in Paris were themselves members of the royal chapel which brought about an irregularity of service in their own parishes.[13] At the Sainte-Chapelle the responsibility for the direction of the choir and the composition of the music lay with the *Maître de Musique des Enfants*, a position held by Marc-Antoine Charpentier for the last six years of his life.

The broad lines of demarcation placed between institutions constituting the king's music were artificial and served administrative ends only. Members of each institution passed freely from one group to another, and there were several smaller, more nebulous groups also marked for performance. Thus, the oboes that played at balls and *divertissements* might be drawn from the two companies of musketeers quartered at Versailles each of whom boasted four oboists and six drummers. Trumpets could be supplied by the *Ecurie* as well as by the *Trompettes des Menus Plaisirs* who were players drawn from the king's corps of bodyguards.

Performances by combined groups were common, especially for such ceremonies as coronations, royal births and deaths, marriages and so on. Once a year on Saint Louis' Eve, free public concerts were held in the Tuileries gardens. At this time the 24 *Violons*, the trumpets and drums of the *Ecurie* and the orchestra of the Académie Royale de Musique all joined together. In a sense it was the king's gift to the city of Paris, and for the poor of the teeming metropolis it was a rare opportunity to catch a glimpse of delights taken for granted by the rich. The thrust of the crowds was such that on one occasion, we read in the *Mercure* of August 1719:[14]'After the fireworks, the crowd pushing to the gates of the Tuileries was so great that it cost the lives of six or eight women who were suffocated or crushed to death.'

The Town's Music

J'Entends déjà partout les charrettes courir,
Les maçons travailler, les boutiques s'ouvrir:
Tandis que dans les airs mille cloches émues,
D'un funèbre concert font retentir les nues,
Et se mêlant au bruit de la grêle et des vents,
Pour honorer les morts, font mourir les vivans,...

(*Satire VI: Les Embarras de Paris*
Nicolas Boileau-Despreaux)

The music of Paris in the *grand siècle* was more than the sound of Lully's orchestra at the Académie Royale de Musique, more than a Charpentier *Te Deum* at the Sainte-Chapelle or a Couperin organ Mass at Saint Gervais. It was the music of 'mille cloches', the music of the street punctuated by the cries of the hawkers: 'There is not a city in the world', wrote Louis-Sebastien Mercier in his *Tableau de Paris* (1781), 'where the street sellers possess more harsh and piercing voices.... Sounds from their gullets even drown out the noise and confusion of city squares'.[15] For Paris in the seventeenth century was still very much a medieval city: noisy, crowded and malodorous. The stench of refuse from *Les Halles* was no respecter of royalty housed in the dark and uncomfortable apartments of the near-by Louvre. In 1706, according to the king's chief engineer, Vauban, the greater metropolitan area had 856,938 souls, and to Montesquieu's Persian it must have seemed that all of them were concentrated in the centre of town:

...the houses are so high here, that one would judge them to be occupied only by astrologers. You know well that a city built in the air, which has six or seven houses one on top of the other, is

16

extremely crowded, and that, when everybody goes down into the streets, there is great confusion.

(Lettres persanes)

Yet the music of the streets was also heard in the sounds of the king's masons and carpenters at work lifting the face of the old city and creating, for an eternity to admire, the monuments of the age of Louis XIV. There was geometry in Le Nôtre's garden of the Tuileries and in the closed forms of the royal squares (Place des Victoires and Place Louis-le-Grand). The classicism of Perrault's colonnade of the Louvre was softened by Italian decoration. In the church of Val-de-Grâce, the College of Mazarin and the chapel of the Invalides, Italian Baroque exuberance was restrained by the same French classical spirit.

Much of the musical life of the city was centred in an area bounded on the north by *Les Halles*, on the east by Saint Gervais at the entrance to the Marais, on the west by the Tuileries and south across the Seine by Saint-Severin and the Latin Quarter. Here were the most important churches; Saint-Merri, Saint-Gervais, Saint-Germain-l'Auxerrois, the Oratoire, Saint-Jean-en-Grève, Saint-Jacques-de-la-Boucherie, Notre-Dame, the Sainte-Chapelle and Saint-Severin. Within the same area were the Académie Royale de Musique and the home of the *Concert Spirituel* and the *Concerts Italiens*. Here too were the shops of the makers of stringed instruments (*luthiers*) and the builders of harpsichords and organs; and here in Montesquieu's 'city built in the air', bordering on the Rue Saint Martin near the hospital of Saint-Julien-des-Ménétriers, lived most of the musicians of the *Confrérie* of Saint Julien.

CONFRÉRIE OF SAINT-JULIEN-DES-MÉNÉTRIERS

From 1321 when 37 minstrels registered with the Provost of Paris to establish a musicians' guild, there was powerful and paternalistic protection for the 'dancing masters and the players of instruments both loud and soft and the oboes' ('Maîtres à danser et joueurs d'instruments tant haut que bas et les hautbois') of Paris.

During the sixteenth and seventeenth centuries the purpose of the group was to protect its members against exploitation and to assure equal profit sharing. The articles governing the corporation, many of which are found in the documents of the *Minutier Central*, assured a remarkable degree of protection for the members of what was in actuality the first musicians' union. If engaged for an 'aubade' or 'réveil', for example, members were supposed to share their profits with those who did not participate. All were required to give an accurate report of their earnings under pain of expulsion, and the members even enjoyed a type of medical insurance whereby those who were sick would be paid 'as if they had worked' unless the illness were reported to be 'shameful' ('honteuse').[16]

The leader of the *Confrérie* was known as the *Roi des Ménétriers* and later in the seventeenth century as the *Roi des Violons*. The high point of the syndicate, both quantitatively and qualitatively, was reached in the late years of the sixteenth century and the early years of the seventeenth before the exodus of many of the best players from the *Confrérie* to the king's *Chambre*. The pages of the *Minutier Central* are filled with documentation of the syndicate's activities. It is curious that a series of legal papers, couched in the abstruse, archaic language of minor functionaries, can make flesh and blood of the Parisian 'joueurs d'instruments'. The din and clamour of the street life, the hand-to-mouth existence of these often illiterate musicians are all recorded here. One can imagine the torrent of abuse and invective, result of the frustrations of daily living, that must have motivated an item of 17 July 1602 whereby, if any member of the association 'jurent et blasphèment le nom de Dieu par colère et autrement, prenant querelle avecq alcuns d'iceulx, en ce cas sera tenu ledict diffaillant payer aux autres ses associez la somme de deux escus'.

For the town musician who was called upon to perform for weddings, engagement parties, banquets, masquerades, dawn and evening street serenades and formal concerts, the notarized contracts were designed to protect the musicians as much from each other as from any outside exploitation. Thus, the 11 'joueurs d'instruments' who in 1618 formed an association to play together for 13 years, levied a fine of 16 'solzs' should any member miss the Friday afternoon *rendezvous* 'pour consertir entre eulx'. The instruments and their designated performers were also carefully spelled out; in one instance we read that this was done to make sure that no one would change his part 'sans le consentement de tous les autres ses compagnons'.

After the mid-years of the seventeenth century with many of its best players now affluent members of the *24 Violons du Roi*, the *Petits Violons* or the *Ecurie*, the importance of the *Confrérie* declined. It had become fat, lazy and complacent; worse, it had been corrupted by power. Secure behind its impressive array of royal patents and notarized articles, it lashed out in a series of power plays designed to force an even greater number of musicians into its orbit of control.

The 'Roi des Violons', after the death of Louis Constantin in 1657, was the powerful Guillaume Dumanoir (1615–90) who also signed himself as 'joueur de violon du Cabinet de Sa Majesté, l'un des vingt-quatre violons de sa Grande Bande, et pourvu aussi de l'office de Roy des joueurs d'instrumens et des Maîtres à dancer de France'.[17]

In 1660 'Guillaume I', as he was called with heavy sarcasm by Besche l'âiné,[18] was at the height of his power with some 200 performers and composers under his command. He basked in the praise of Louis XIV

('Notre très cher et bien-aimé Guillaume Dumanoir'), and yet, one year later his fortune had begun to turn. The king effectively isolated him by appointing Lully to a position of unprecedented power, and in the same year 13 of the *Maîtres de Danse* of the *Confrérie* were in active revolt against their union. In an *opera-buffa* atmosphere of charge and countercharge (satirized by Molière in the *maître de musique* and the *maître de danse* scenes from *Le Bourgeois gentilhomme*), the dancers succeeded in receiving a royal patent in 1661 to establish an Académie Royale de Danse on the strange grounds that the dance 'has no need of Instruments of Music and that it is totally independent of the Violin'. In a Pyrrhic victory of sorts, Dumanoir had the last word in his polemic of 1664, *Le Mariage de la Musique avec la Dance*: 'In a word, who does not know that the Dance is not, properly speaking, an Art, but only an exercise.'

In 1668 'Guillaume I' relinquished his throne to his son, 'Guillaume II', who had learned little from his father's mistakes. He attempted to blur the lines of distinction found on all patents between, for example, the 'maîtres à danser et joueurs d'instruments...' and the 'compositeurs de musique, organistes et professeurs de clavessin' in order to bring the latter group under the jurisdiction of the *Confrérie*. However, the 'composers of music, organists and professors of harpsichord' had no intention of submitting to the abusive restrictions of the syndicate. In a document quoted by Ecorcheville (*Vingt Suites*, p. 28), entitled *Raisons qui prouvent manifestement que les compositeurs et joueurs d'instruments d'harmonie ne peuvent être de la communauté des ménestriers*, they stated:

> The *maîtres* have taught violin to all the lackeys of Paris. They have played with riff-raff (*racaille*) in order to get out of sharing profits with other *maîtres*. They have allowed most of their *maîtres* to play in cabarets against Article VI of their Statutes. They have accepted as *maîtres* all sorts of vagabonds and even coachmen to whom they have issued false credentials, although they have never filled a term of apprenticeship in the home of a *maître*.

The king's organists, Lebègue, Nivers, Buterne and François Couperin, petitioned the king for *Lettres Patentes* which would remove permanently the threat of coercion and economic privation initiated by the *Confrérie*. The king supported his organists and in a royal patent of 25 June 1707 dealt a crushing blow to the *Confrérie* of Saint Julien. The *Lettres Patentes* read, in part:

> ... wishing to treat favourably the organists of our chapel and others who make their living teaching composition and performers of the above mentioned *instruments d'harmonie*, and to

maintain them in the free exercise of their profession, We have by these presents, signed by our hand . . . forbidden the so-called *maîtres à danser, joueurs d'instruments tant haut que bas et hautbois*, to trouble the petitioners in the exercise of their profession . . .

Ringing words, these, to emanate from an absolute monarch, and in the opinion of Besche, 'The Organists of the King and those of the Capital were the first who undertook the defence of freedom in the Musical Art'. The *Confrérie*, now a butt of musical jokes, was immortalized a few years later (1717) in the satiric programme suite of François Couperin, 'Les Fastes de la grande et ancienne Mxnxstrxndxsx (Ménestrandise)'.

In summary, however, it should be emphasized that the *Confrérie* had served an important role in the history of French instrumental music. In their best days they not only kept their ranks filled by means of a careful system of apprenticeship, but they also trained fine performers who made up the bulk of the king's instrumentalists. By showing instrumental distributions between 1583 and 1625, Lesure has demonstrated that the 24 *Violons* transferred to the court the scoring practices of the *Confrérie* orchestra with their predilection for many treble and bass instruments (*RdM*, xxxvi, 52).

The *Confrérie* of Saint-Julien-des-Ménétriers 'had suffered diverse fortunes' since its founding in the fourteenth century as Ecorcheville points out, 'but its church, its hospital, a concert hall and above all a solid syndical organization still rendered service to those whose métier was music '[19] (*Vingt Suites*, p. 21).

Académie Royale de Musique[20]

In the *Lettres Patentes* of 28 June 1669, Louis xiv accorded 'our well-loved and faithful Pierre Perrin' the sole privilege of establishing 'Académies d'Opéra' in the realm for performances 'en Musique en Vers François' modelled on those academies that had been established in Italy 'for several years'.

Little matter that there were no such royal academies for the performance of opera in Italy or in Germany and England as Perrin had claimed. He had touched a point of national pride in Colbert and manoeuvred the creation of yet another institution. Perrin now had a guaranteed 12 year dictatorship over opera production in France.

The sordid tale of his misadventures (see Chapter 6, pp. 65–66) reached a climax with the unfortunate man's imprisonment for debt. Impatiently awaiting his chance was Jean-Baptiste Lully who had committed one of the few errors of judgment in his career by refusing to believe that the French wanted a national opera. Now acting with dispatch, he purchased the entire privilege from Perrin paying him sufficient funds to allow him to leave jail. The king was informed of this move presumably by Mme de Montespan, and on 13 March 1672 he formally transferred the privilege to his *Surintendant de Musique*. 'In order to assure greater success, we believed it appropriate to give control (of the opera) to an individual whose experience and capacity we know well. . . .' To avoid duplication and perhaps to assure a fresh beginning, the king changed the name of the organization from the Académies d'Opéra to the Académie Royale de Musique, and further, he extended the privilege from a dozen years to the lifetime of Lully and his heirs. In actuality, the privilege passed in and out of the hands of Nicolas de Francine, Lully's son-in-law, until his retirement in 1728 when the opera came under the direction of Destouches.

More clever and more ruthless than Perrin, Lully succeeded in obtaining as well a series of repressive patents that assured him absolute power over French stage music and effectively immobilized potential rivals (see Chapter 5, p. 57).

In Durey de Noinville's *Histoire du Théâtre de l'Académie royale de Musique en France* (2nd ed., 1757), we may read the many articles issued by the king at Versailles and Marly in 1713 and 1714 to assure a more effective administrative control over the Paris opera. These regulations obviously grew from the smooth running and efficient organization that Lully had made of the Académie Royale de Musique. Among other items we learn that free schools of music and dance were established (Article II); a lucrative pension system for singers and dancers was created (Article XIII); and there was even medical coverage that assured a pension to those 'crippled in the service of the Opera' (Article XLI).

For almost 100 years (1674–1763) the home of French opera was the Grande Salle of the Palais Royal that had been occupied by Molière's troupe at the time of that great playwright's death in 1673. The hall was one of two built for Cardinal Richelieu in the Palais Royal. Inaugurated in 1641, it was renovated in 1732 and again in 1749, and destroyed by fire in 1763. It was barely satisfactory for the type of spectacle envisioned by Lully and later by Rameau. It was much longer than wide with a parterre, a gallery (amphitheatre), eight loges and a double balcony. Although it could hold over 2,000 people, it was cramped, and its stage was small. From the English translation (1741) of Luigi Riccoboni's *Réflexions historiques et critiques sur les différens Théâtres de l'Europe* (p. 152) we read:

> The Decorations of the Stage of the Opera are very handsome, but not to be compared with those of Italy, the Smallness of the Stage not admitting of their being either so large or so magnificent as those of the vast Theatres of Venice, Milan, etc.

For Grimm's 'petit prophète de Boehmisch-Broda' (1753), the Paris opera was a marionette theatre. De Brosses after visiting Naples in 1739 commented that the stage alone of San Carlo was larger than the entire Paris opera.[21]

The price remained fairly uniform, and, according to Riccoboni, was 'double that of any other Entertainment, in proportion to the Preference of Places'. At the beginning of the eighteenth century, admission to the balcony or on the stage was 11 *livres*, 10 *sols*; 7 *livres*, 4 *sols* for the first loge and gallery; 3 *livres*, 12 *sols* for the second loge; 1 *livre*, 16 *sols* for the third loge and the parterre.[22]

In his *Séjour de Paris* (1727) an affluent German traveller, J. C. Nemeitz, included in his 'faithful Instruction for Travellers of Means' much information regarding the Paris musical scene of the 1720's as seen through the eyes of a class-conscious young *galant*. Ranking the seating arrangements in the Paris theatres, he wrote:

> At the Comedies (Comédie Française and Comédie Italienne) a man of quality takes his place on the Stage and in one of the first Loges, or in the Parterre, if there are not too many people. But rarely in the second Loge which is for the bourgeois, and never in the Amphitheatre where all sorts of riff-raff are assembled. But the Amphitheatre of the Opera is honourable and has the rank of the first Loge. The second Loge is still passable. But no one would willingly seat himself in the alleged *Paradis*, excepting the Balcony which is on the side. The Balcony, below, to the side of the stage, is for gentlemen of distinction and costs 10 *livres* per person. But the Parterre is sometimes visited by people even of the first quality, since one has the advantage there of being able to enter or to leave freely without disturbing anyone. When one is in the Parterre of the Comédie or the Opera, one takes care to whistle at some Actor or to clap his hands in order to mock him. This gives rise sometimes to disagreements. . . .
>
> (*Le Séjour de Paris*, p. 105)

In general, *tragédies lyriques* and *opéras-ballets* were performed beginning at 5 p.m. on Sundays, Tuesdays, Thursdays and Fridays during the winter; the Thursday performances were cut in the summer months. Out of deference to the wishes of the church, the opera closed 23 days during the Easter season and 11 days annually for solemn religious feasts.

In 1715 permission was granted to the Académie Royale de Musique to sponsor public balls in the theatre from 11 November until Advent and from Epiphany to Shrove Tuesday. The royal patent specifically stated that 'His Majesty very expressly forbade entrance to anyone who is not masked'. According to Durey de Noinville, the balls began at

11 p.m. and ended at 6 or 7 a.m. Thirty musicians assembled one half-hour before the dancing commenced to give a concert 'de grands morceaux de symphonie des meilleurs maîtres' (*Histoire du théâtre*, I, p. 164).

The Concert Spirituel[23]

'The taste for music', we read in the *Mercure de France* (April, 1727), 'has never been so universal. In Paris and in the smallest towns of Provence, there are Concerts and Academies of Music that have been maintained at considerable cost, and there are new ones established each day'. The first permanent concert organization to give series of subscription concerts on a commercial basis came into being in Paris two years earlier.

It was the *Concert Spirituel* founded in 1725 by Anne Danican-Philidor (1681–1728), one of the 21 children of André Danican-Philidor, 'l'âiné' (*d*.1730), a composer and the king's music librarian ('Garde de la Musique'). In order to circumvent the notorious privilege obtained by Lully and passed on to his heirs that prevented anyone from 'singing any piece in its entirety whether in French or other languages' without written permission, Philidor agreed to pay Francine, administrative head of the Académie Royale de Musique and Lully's son-in-law, the sum of 10,000 *livres* annually for a three-year period. Philidor agreed further to prevent the performance of operatic fragments or pieces with French texts.

The concerts took place on religious holidays when the Académie Royale de Musique was closed. Durey de Noinville stated that this amounted to about 24 concerts a year and included the following feast days: Feast of the Purification of the Virgin (2 February), Feast of the Annunciation (25 March), from Passion Sunday to Quasimodo inclusive, Ascension Day, Pentecost, Corpus Christi, Feast of the Assumption of the Virgin (15 August), Nativity of the Virgin (8 September), All Saints Day (1 November), Conception of the Virgin (8 December), Christmas Eve and Christmas Day.

The inaugural concert was held on 18 March (Passion Sunday) 1725 in the Salle des Suisses of the Tuileries Palace. The *salle* was a gift of Louis xv and remained the home of the *Concert Spirituel* until 1784. The first programme included a suite of airs for strings by Delalande, the *grands motets*, *Confitebor* and *Cantate Domino*, also by Delalande and the 'Christmas' Concerto (Opus vi, No. 8) of Corelli.

The performers at the *Concert Spirituel* were usually first rate; the vocal soloists came from the Opera, and the chorus was made up of some of the best singers of the royal chapel and the principal churches of Paris. Motets by Lully, Bernier, Marchand, Destouches, Lalouette,

Gilles, Petouille, Desmarest, Montéclair, Dornel, Colin de Blamont, Campra and many others were performed, but the motets of Delalande remained throughout the history of the *Concert Spirituel* the examples of this genre most in demand.

Like the early history of the *opéra comique*, the story of the *Concert Spirituel* is that of an organization acclaimed by audiences and performers alike, yet beset by financial woes and impossible restrictions brought about, in part, by jealous rivals. Philidor resigned in 1728 a few months before his death, and the enterprise was taken over by Michel de Lannoy, Pierre Simard and the composer Jean-Joseph Mouret. During this administration, the complexion of the concerts changed somewhat. Italian performers and compositions were much in vogue, and instrumental music began to achieve a significance that would contribute substantially to the development of the sonata and the concerto in France. Included among the instrumentalists were such violinists as Jean-Baptiste Anet (1661–1755), a student of Corelli, and Jean-Pierre Guignon (1702–74), the 'Roi des Violons' who specialized in the sonatas and concertos of Vivaldi and who was rivalled at the concerts by the great French composer-performer Jean-Marie Leclair (1697–1764).

Financially, this administration fared no better than that of Philidor, and on 25 December 1734, the Académie Royale de Musique moved in to take control of the *Concert Spirituel*. The musical direction was wisely given to the violinist-composer Jean-Ferry Rebel (1666–1747). Although each concert included at least one *grand motet*, the main significance of the *Concert Spirituel* lay more and more in the domain of instrumental music. Each programme contained at least one sonata or concerto for violin played by Guignon or Leclair, and Italian and German symphonies began to appear on the programmes in the late 1740's.

Under the direction of Pancrace Royer (1705–55) and Jean-Joseph Mondonville (1711–72), the instrumental and vocal forces of the *Concert Spirituel*, according to Durey de Noinville, were as follows: vocal soloists included 4 sopranos, 1 counter-tenor and 3 baritones; and the chorus was made up of 12 sopranos, 14 counter-tenors, 7 tenors and 5 lower voices (basses and baritones). This particular distribution of parts demonstrates the domination of the counter-tenor over the tenor in French vocal writing of the Baroque period. The *Symphonie* consisted of 16 violins, 2 violas (*parties*), 6 basses and 2 double basses, 5 flutes and oboes and 3 bassoons. This too reflects the strong emphasis on treble and bass instruments that characterized French scoring practices at that same time.

The *Concert Spirituel* existed for 66 years. It provided an important forum for new music, vocal and instrumental, religious and secular, and in no small way it thereby contributed to the formation of new musical attitudes on the part of French composers, performers and consumers of music in the eighteenth century.

Co-existing with the *Concert Spirituel* in its early days were two additional concert series: the so-called *Concerts Français* and the *Concerts Italiens*. The *Concerts Français* was established by Philidor just six months before his resignation from the directorship of the *Concert Spirituel*. Its concerts were held in the Tuileries on Saturdays and Sundays during the winter season. The series had a big advantage in having obtained the services of two of the best singers at the Opera: Mlle Le Maure and Mlle Antier. The programmes included mostly French *divertissements* and cantatas. Over 100 concerts were given from 1727 to November, 1730 when, except for scattered concerts, the series terminated.[24]

The *Concerts Français* competed directly with the *Concerts Italiens* which in 1726 also gave subscription concerts in the Tuileries on Thursdays and Saturdays. At the *Concerts Italiens*, we learn from Titon du Tillet:

> ...one performed only Italian music; it was composed almost entirely of Italian musicians with some Frenchmen who had been in Italy. Several *Amateurs de la Musique Italienne*, such as M. Crozat, M. Gaudiori, Guardian of the Royal Treasury, and others, undertook the expenses of these concerts.

Thus was inaugurated the age of the wealthy middle-class *entrepreneur* that reached its height in Rameau's sponsor, the financier La Pouplinière. Antoine Crozat (1655–1738) had already given concerts at his home on the Rue de Richelieu from 1715 to 1724 (Daval, p. 114), and for over 30 years (1731–62) private concerts under the financial direction of Alexandre-Jean-Joseph Le Riche de la Pouplinière (1693–1762) presented to the Parisian musical world some of the most important performers and compositions of the period.

Part one

Stage Music

Chapter 2

≫ ≪

Ballet de Cour I:
From Beaujoyeulx to Lully

On the evening of 15 October 1581 from 10 at night to 3.30 in the morning, *Circé ou le Balet comique de la Royne* (as the title was originally spelled) was performed at the Petit Bourbon palace in Paris. This first court ballet[1] was part of the second day's festivities celebrating the marriage of the Duc de Joyeuse and the queen's sister, Marguerite de Veudemont. There is no evidence that the spectators, estimated by Beaujoyeulx as numbering between 'nine or ten thousand', heard an 'invention nouvelle'[2] in this long performance, nor is there any reason to suppose that the queen mother, Catherine de Medici, realized that her favourite project carried out by Beaujoyeulx at the staggering cost of close to £200,000 was the first attempt in France to unify poetry, dance, music and decor within one continuous action.

To all appearances, *Circé* was one more ambitious *fête* in the tradition of sixteenth-century entertainments at the court of the Valois kings. The mythological personages, the nymphs and satyrs, the political allusions, the eulogies of the monarch and the elaborate machinery had their counterparts in the earlier *fêtes* at Fontainebleau and Bayonne which in their turn had been modelled on Italian masquerades and pastorales.

An immediate forerunner of *Circé* is the *divertissement Le Paradis d'Amour*, presented in August, 1572 as part of the wedding celebration of Henri of Navarre and Marguerite de Valois. In its allegorical character,[3] its vocal solos, its machinery and dancing, it evokes much of the same atmosphere as the later work. Unlike *Circé*, however, it lacks a unified and continuous dramatic action.

By virtue of this unity of action the *Ballet comique*, in the opinion of later aestheticians and historians, deserves a significant place in the development of French dramatic music. Typical is the comment of Daquin de Château-Lyon who described the *Ballet comique* as the first work in France to give 'some idea of the musical theatre' (*Lettres sur les hommes célèbres*, 1752). For some, the *Ballet comique* was not only the first example of a dramatic representation in music, it was also the first work of this genre to demonstrate the ubiquitous, albeit ill-defined, seventeenth and eighteenth century value judgment of 'good taste' ('le bon goût').[4]

How many writers of later generations were actually familiar with the text and music of *Circé* and how many were echoing, often verbatim, the opinions of others, is impossible to determine. The printed score of 1582 was well known in later times. Claude-François Ménestrier summarized the action and included textual fragments from it in his *Des Représentations en musique anciennes et modernes* (1681). Charles Burney owned a copy of the score and Jean-Benjamin de La Borde in his *Essai sur la musique ancienne et moderne* (1780) mentioned its availability in the king's library. Did the brothers Parfaict, those meticulous compilers of all manner of information on the French theatre, write from direct observation when they invited all to 'read again the singing *vers* of the ballet of 1582 . . . you will observe there the birth of *le bon goût*' or were they merely quoting Lecerf de la Viéville's work where the identical sentence is found?[5]

In writing the 1582 preface, Beaujoyeulx was aware that he had indeed created an 'invention nouvelle', for he stated that 'there has never been a ballet printed in which the word "comique" was employed'. He saw the necessity of justifying his coupling of 'ballet' and 'comique'. It follows in this context that 'comique' describes a work containing dramatic unity such as a comedy. In like manner did Saint-Hubert in his *La Manière de composer et faire réussir les ballets* (1641) define ballet as 'comédie muette', an apt description appropriated 40 years later by Père Ménestrier in his *Des Ballets anciens et modernes*.

The *Ballet comique* had a clear relationship to the concept of humanism as formulated by the *Pléiade* and by Baïf's Académie de Poésie et de Musique which had become the Académie du Palais under Henri III. This is not surprising. The Duc de Joyeuse had been a financial supporter of Baïf's Académie, and the chief composer of the *Ballet comique*, Lambert de Beaulieu, was closely associated with the co-founder of the Académie, Thibaud de Courville. The commendatory poem found at the beginning of the printed edition supports the humanistic mystique of the ballet in the lines:

Et la façon tant estimée
De nos poètes anciens,
Les Vers avecques la musique,
Le Balet confus mesuré,
Démonstrant du ciel azuré
L'accord par un effect mystique.

The syllabic choruses bear a clear resemblance to the *vers mesuré à l'antique* (see Example 1) and the Pythagorean-Platonic bias of the Académie was graphically represented by the carefully planned geometric figures of the concluding *grand ballet*. In defining 'ballet' in his preface as a 'geometric mingling of several dancers', Beaujoyeulx clearly considered his project within the humanistic milieu of the Académie.

Circé owes its existence to many hands. The exact role of the Huguenot poet Agrippa D'Aubigny is still in doubt. He claimed to have been the real author of the ballet (see Yates, p. 257). Most scholars, however, credit Beaujoyeulx with the master plan for the ballet. Baltasar de Beaujoyeulx (born Baltazarini da Belgiojoso) arrived in France about 1555. According to Pierre de Bourdeille, seigneur de Brantôme, it was the Maréchal de Brissac who sent Beaujoyeulx from Piedmont with his 'bande de viollons très exquise' to be employed by Catherine de Medici as a *valet de chambre*. Brantôme, who, it should be remembered, was a close personal friend of the musician, also informed us that Beaujoyeulx was the 'meilleur viollon de la chrestienté'.[6] Beaujoyeulx was assisted in the composition of *Circé* by Jacques Salmon and Lambert de Beaulieu who were responsible for the music. La Chesnaye wrote the text, and Jacques Patin, 'peintre du Roy', designed the stage sets and costumes.

A study of the 1582 edition reveals French lyric drama in embryo. There is a single line of dramatic action: to destroy the power of the enchantress, Circé, in order to re-establish harmony, reason and order. This theme is coupled with adulatory references to the king which shows that political propagandists and flatterers, or both, have been finding their own values in art for some time.

The extant music includes eight choruses (one *a* 4, five *a* 5 and two *a* 6), two vocal solos, two duos with choral refrains and two sets of instrumental dances. The accompaniments for the vocal solos and duos were not printed. Beaujoyeulx's *livret*, which gives much detailed information regarding the action and setting, is very vague concerning specific instrumentation. Flageolets, 'orgues doulces', harps, lutes, lyres, oboes, cornetts, sackbuts, recorders, 'violons' (generic term for all strings of the violin family) and 'aultres doux instrumens' are mentioned throughout the score, and we are told that 40 musicians (voices and instruments) performed in the 'voûte dorée' (a cloud machine which was illuminated inside) during the descent of Jupiter. The dances, scored in five-part texture, were performed by ten 'violons' and constitute the earliest known printed violin music.

The intrinsic musical value of the *Ballet comique* is not commensurate with its historical position. The choral music is square and rigidly homophonic with only an occasional cross relation to lend some harmonic interest.

Example 1

Extract from chorus, 'Allez filles d'Achellois', Ballet comique de la Reine *(after ed. of 1582).*

The dances, however, especially the famous 'Son de la clochette' which is too familiar to be reproduced here, have a formal charm despite the almost geometric regularity of phrase groupings. The long dialogue between Glauque and Tethys is one of the earliest examples of declamatory singing in stage music. Yet, the use of long melismas on inconsequential and unaccented words indicates a general lack of concern with either rules of prosody or a dramatic rendering of the text.

The components of a typical seventeenth-century *ballet de cour* are the following: *récits, vers, entrées,* and usually a concluding *grand ballet.* The word *récit* should not be confused with *récitatif.* As a generic term it was used to characterize 'that which is sung by only one voice' (Antoine Furetière, *Dictionnaire universel,* edition of 1691, ii, p. 533). Therefore, a *récitatif* is a particular type of *récit.*[7] In the *ballet de cour* the *récit* had a more specific meaning. At first declaimed and after 1605 sung by a solo voice, *récits* were generally found at the beginning of each act of the ballet and were most often performed by characters who did not dance. Often similar in structure and melodic content to the *air de cour,* they served to comment on the action.

The *vers pour les personnages* were texts distributed among the spectators. They constituted a type of *livret* which often included indiscreet references to the masked performers. The custom of publishing such *livrets,* with their detailed descriptions of the *mise-en-scène* and their summary of the author's intentions, became a normal procedure after 1610. Michel de Pure complained that the *vers* were the 'weakest and least important part of the ballet . . . an ornamental pastiche' (*Idée des spectacles anciens et nouveaux*, 1668, p. 296). The *entrées*, which separated the acts into scenes, were entrances of elaborately costumed and masked dancers identified not only by their pantomime, their dances and characteristic music, but also by the *vers* and *récits*. The *danses de caractère*, which made up many of the *entrées*, were dances believed characteristic of certain countries. Jean-Baptiste Dubos defined the term as referring to a dance whose 'melody and rhythm imitate a specific style and which is, therefore, assumed to be appropriate for certain peoples' (*Réflexions critiques sur la poésie et sur la peinture*, ed. of 1755, III, p. 184). Ménestrier in his *Remarques pour la conduite des Ballets* (1658) commented that 'melody has different characteristics in different countries; it is heavy in Germany, serious and forceful in Spain, lively in Italy and regular in France'.[8]

The *grand ballet*, a forerunner of the operatic finale, concluded the ballet and was danced by the *grands seigneurs* and, at least once each year, by the king himself. It was distinguished from the other *entrées* by an 'atmosphère de luxe',[9] often in marked contrast to the quality of dancing. Michel de Pure, a witness of the collaboration between Lully and Benserade in the composition of court ballets, described the frustration of Lully who was continually embarrassed by the 'stupidity' of most of the noble dancers, many of whom appeared quite incapable of mastering the more rapid steps (*Idée des spectacles anciens et nouveaux*). The dancers, who in general remained masked throughout, were members of the court plus a few professionals in the service of the king. In the 'ballets of the king' men took the roles of female characters; in the 'ballets of the queen' women of the court were permitted to dance.

All court ballets resulted from the collaboration of a royal patron, poets for the *vers* and *récits*, at least two composers responsible for the vocal and instrumental music, and a machinist to plan and execute the elaborate stage machinery. The patron determined the subject matter (*sujet*) and the distribution of labour.

The role of the king in the choice and treatment of the *sujet* must not be underestimated. Louis XIII, himself the composer of at least one court ballet (*Ballet de la Merlaison*, 1635), chose the subject for *La Délivrance de Renaud* (1617) for which he may have created his own role as a demon of fire. The popular theme of deliverance adapted from Tasso's *Gerusalemme liberata* is also the *sujet* of the *Ballet de Tancrède* (1619). It took little imagination to interpret the combat of Tancrède and his cavaliers against the monsters of the enchanted forest as an allegorical representation of Louis XIII and his favourite *grand seigneur*, Charles D'Albert de Luynes, delivering France from her enemies. The Jesuits also were quick to realize the propaganda potential of the ballet, and at Rheims in 1628 they mounted a production of *La Conquête du Char de la Gloire* in which the giants of the black tower (Huguenots of La Rochelle) hold captive the knights who are eventually liberated by the shepherd, Caspis (Richelieu), after Théandre (Louis xiii) has killed the dragon of the tower.[10]

De Gouy in the preface to his *Airs spirituels* (1650) suggests that Louis xiii would have much preferred spending all his time on the preparation and performance of ballets if only the 'cares of governing so many people in such difficult times had allowed him leisure commensurate with his zeal'. I have included an Appendix which gives in translation a description of the preparation of a *Ballet du Roy* danced by Louis xiii at the Hôtel de Ville in Paris on 25 February 1626. The order to prepare the Hôtel de Ville for a performance of the *Grand Bal de la Douairière de Billebahaut* had been given by the king to his *conseiller d'état* at the Louvre on 4 February, and all subordinates in the complex chain of command went feverishly to work to build the elaborate machines, to construct platforms and to prepare the banquet halls and rooms of the Hôtel de Ville. From this description found in the *Histoire de la Ville de Paris* (1725) it is clear that neither labour nor expense were stinted in the preparation of a *ballet de cour*.

Too often poets of second rank composed the verses for the *vers* and *récits* although Bertaut, Malherbe, Sigongnes, L'Estoile, Sorel, Bordier, Racan, Théophile, and Voiture are known to have supplied texts for the music of Guédron, Bataille, Vincent, Boësset (Antoine and Jean), Moulinié, Richard, Chancy, de Mollier, Lambert and Cambefort.

The machinists, usually brought in from Italy, held a position second to none in the creation of *ballets de cour*. Enthusiastic descriptions of complex and quick scene changes are plentiful in seventeenth-century sources. 'In rapid succession one saw the Plain of Casale, the snow-covered Alps, the stormy sea, the yawning pit of Hell and the opening of the sky with Jupiter descending', wrote Michel de Marolles in describing the long (5 acts, 36 *entrées*) *Ballet de la Prosperité des Armes de la France*, 1641 (*Mémoires*, iii, 1645, p. 239). From time to time voices were raised against an opulence that too often indicated 'more of purse than intelligence' (Michel de Pure, *Idée des spectacles anciens et nouveaux*, p. 303). It is refreshing in the midst of such excesses to read both Marolles and Saint-Hubert who singled out the *Ballet des doubles femmes* (1626) as an example of a successful ballet which cost little to produce and which contained none of those 'large machines and long perspectives which rather than adding grace to the setting often acted as detriments to the performers' (Marolles, *Mémoires*, I, p. 133).

Saint-Hubert's *La Manière de composer et faire réussir les ballets* is one of the earliest and most informative sources for a study of the seventeenth-century *ballet de cour*. According to him the ballet, riding and fencing were the three proper forms of exercise for the nobility. He recognized two principal types of ballets, the serious and the grotesque, and he acknowledged the possibility of their co-existing within the same ballet. He classified ballets by their length: a 'ballet royal' ordinarily included 30 *entrées*, a 'beau' ballet had at least 20 *entrées* and a 'petit' had 10 to 12. He enumerated six necessary components for the creation of a worthy ballet: subject, airs, dances, costumes, machinery and organization. Calling attention to the danger of rushing through preparation for a ballet and perhaps admonishing those among the nobility too lazy to 'exercise', Saint-Hubert added:

> It is very necessary to take time to study the steps and the *entrées*. That which is improvised never succeeds well; fifteen days for a *grand ballet* and eight days for a *petit ballet* would not be too much time to spend in preparation.
>
> (*La Manière de composer* . . . , p. 17)

About 1620, Michel Henry, a violinist of the royal chamber, copied an important collection of ballet music. Unfortunately, the music in Henry's hand is not extant, but his list enumerates 96 ballets danced at the court during the first two decades of the seventeenth century and gives, therefore, some gauge of the popularity of the genre.[11] Apparently the structural significance of the *Ballet comique*, with its single dramatic intrigue, had little influence on those responsible for most of the ballets on Henry's list. These works, which borrowed liberally from the 'mascarades à l'Italienne' and the court *fêtes,* included many *entrées* of colourful and grotesque characters with no relationship to any central plot. Such titles as *Ballets des foux* (1596), *Ballet des barbiers* (1598), *Ballet des nègres* (1601), *Ballet des sorciers* (1601), *Ballet des garçons des tavernes* (1603), *Ballet des bouteilles et des dames* (1607) and *Ballet des paysans et des grenouilles* (1607) are illustrative of the preoccupation with burlesque elements at the turn of the century.

Not until 1609 with the *Ballet de la Reyne* (*vers* by Malherbe) and 1610 with the *Ballet d'Alcine* was there a return to the unified dramatic action established 29 years before by Beaujoyeulx. This type of ballet, labelled by Prunières 'ballet mélodramatique', remained fashionable for about a decade. At its best in such works as *Le Triomphe de Minerve* (1615), *La Délivrance de Renaud* (1617), the *Ballet de Tancrède* (1619) and the *Ballet de Psyché* (1619), the *ballet mélodramatique* was a convincing dramatic spectacle. The *récits* composed by Pierre Guédron (1565–1621) for *Renaud* and *Tancrède* at times approach dramatic declamation worthy of a Monteverdi.[12] Although there is little information regarding the use of specific instruments in the ballets mentioned above, the *livret* to *Renaud* (printed by Ballard in 1617) describes the 'concert' at the beginning of the ballet as having been performed by 64 voices, 28 viols and 14 lutes (composed by Jacques Mauduit). By the time of *Tancrède* the large number of treble instruments (4 cornetts, 4 oboes and 6 flutes) that characterized French operatic scoring until the time of Rameau was already in evidence. With its unified plot, use of chorus and spectacular theatrical finales, the *ballet mélodramatique* bordered on opera.

In 1621 with the death of Louis XIII's favourite patron of the ballet, De Luynes, the *ballet mélodramatique* was superseded by the *ballet à entrées* which, as the name implies, was a purely choreographic spectacle: a succession of tableaux and pantomimes and a steady procession of elaborately costumed figures (see Plates 2–5). The unity of plot established by Beaujoyeulx and nurtured by the *ballet mélodramatique* was discarded. The apparent abruptness of this change has perplexed many modern historians who have speculated widely on the causes.

Their attention is perhaps unwarranted, for decorative elements had threatened any tendencies towards dramatic unity in the *ballet de cour* almost from its inception. The structural differences described by Prunières and others apparently escaped the notice of such keen observers as Saint-Hubert or Marolles who could not, of course, have anticipated the significance attached to the *ballet mélodramatique* as an important precursor of French opera by twentieth-century historians.

Yet in point of fact, the *ballet mélodramatique* up to the time of the death of De Luynes and Guédron was pointed towards opera. All the necessary constituents were included, not the least of which was a composer of considerable dramatic talent. Why, indeed, under the patronage of a musically sophisticated monarch was not French opera created some 50 years before Lully's *Cadmus et Hermione?*

The mixture of serious and grotesque elements would not have disturbed the audiences of the time who were used to this 'baroque' juxtaposition in the plays of Jean de Schelandre and Alexandre Hardy. For François Ogier, who condoned the mixture of 'grave things with those less serious', the theatre was created only for 'pleasure and diversion'.[13] Almost 60 years later Père Ménestrier defined his generation's concept of theatre in his *Des Ballets anciennes et modernes* (1682). By then there were distinct differences established, at least in principle, between tragedy, comedy and ballet: 'Tragedy and Comedy were created for instructional purposes . . . and the Ballet for *pleasure and diversion*' (italics mine). Ménestrier's air-tight classifications are perhaps more the product of his Jesuit training than empirical observation. However, the years that separate Ogier from Ménestrier had witnessed the establishment of the French classical drama with its impressive superstructure of rules and regulations and with its seat of authority centred in the Académie Française founded by Richelieu in 1635.

In this rarefied atmosphere of Cartesian rationalism and imagined or real academy control, the *ballet de cour* could only be accepted as 'exercise' or royal 'diversion'. It was understandable that it would relinquish any dramatic pretensions. It had lost, if indeed it had ever possessed, the singlemindedness of purpose rooted in Renaissance humanism of the Florentine Camerata.

Ménestrier shows the distance between the dramaturgical rules of French classical theatre and the ballets of the mid-seventeenth century:

> The subjects of ballets are drawn ordinarily from the Fable, from History, from the properties of natural or moral existence, or from caprice.... The Fable ... need not resemble reality.... It demands no other unity but that of a plan that assures that different *entrées* have some rapport with a Subject. Unity of time and place, which the Tragedy observes with so much care, is almost never found.... The principal condition of the Fable of a Ballet is that it be ingenious and agreeable....
>
> (*Remarques pour la conduite des Ballets*)

For the royal participants and spectators it was sufficient that the ballet entertain on a lavish scale. Through it they could act out the role of ideal courtier and thereby, it was hoped, be noticed by their king. As we have seen, the court ballet was in fact a political arm of the monarchy, a means of 'domesticating' the nobility and praising the centralized power and control of the regime.[14] For king and courtier alike it is doubtful that the fine distinctions of Père Ménestrier and other aestheticians even existed.

A more compelling reason why the *ballet mélodramatique* did not evolve into opera after the death of Guédron was the lack of a composer of dramatic instincts. There was no Monteverdi in France to build on the models of *Tancrède* or *Renaud*. In spite of the melodic gifts of Boësset and Cambefort, it was not until Lully that any real attempt was made to utilize the dramatic potential of the ballet. Marin Mersenne clearly understood this deficiency. In his *Harmonie universelle* (1636) he acknowledged the critical role of Peri in introducing theatrical declamation in music and added: 'our musicians are, it would seem, too timid to introduce this manner of declamation in France'.

The *ballet à entrées* under the aegis of the fat and gout-ridden Duc de Nemours was a choreographic spectacle composed of several parts. Each part had its own subject matter and characters; each part, however, related in some manner to a collective idea expressed in the title. In the *Grand Bal de la Douairière de Billabahaut* (1626) the four corners of the world each send delegates to the Ball of the Douairière. Each part of the world has its own ballet preceded by *récits* and including several *entrées*. The *Ballet des quatres Monarchies Chrestiennes* (1635) is a spectacular ethnographic ballet with Italy, Spain, Germany and France constituting its four sections.

In spite of the fragmentary state of much of the music and the questionable taste of many of the *entrées*, the *ballet à entrées* is worthy of special study. Its influence far exceeded its intrinsic musico-poetic value. Structurally, it is the most important antecedent of the later *opéra-ballet*. André Campra's *L'Europe galante* (1697), although substituting *galanterie* for the *bouffonerie* of the *Grand Bal*, is, nonetheless, in a direct line of descent from this type of ethnographic ballet. Even in its decline, the *ballet à entrées* helped sustain the interest of French audiences in a merger of music, dance and spectacle. Its short binary and simple rondeau airs (their poetic structure based generally on a quatrain or a six-line stanza), the homophonic choruses and variety of dance types contributed to the formation of the *tragédie lyrique*. The history of the French overture may be traced in the scores of pre-Lully *ballets à entrées*. After 1640, most ballets included overtures. In the *Ballet de Mademoiselle* (1640), the *Ballet des rues de Paris* (1647) and the *Ballet de Bacchus* (1651) there are already overtures that suggest the type later standardized by Lully in his ballet *Alcidiane* (1658).[15]

The extant music of the pre-Lully court ballets is scattered among several sources. The vocal music is found in many of the collections of *airs de cour*. In an exhaustive survey of these *recueils*, André Verchaly has succeeded in locating 177 airs or *récits* from 56 ballets all composed before 1643.[16] He insists that no vocal music from court ballets is extant between the *Ballet comique* and Guédron's first book of *Airs de cour à quatre et cinq parties* of 1608.

The sources for instrumental music are equally diffused. Some appear where least expected, for example, in such a collection as Robert Ballard's first book of lute pieces (1611). Volume II of the important Philidor collection now in the Bibliothèque Nationale includes copies made by the king's librarian of dances, overtures and *entrées* from 'Ballets dansés sous le regne du Henry IV et sous celui de Louis XIII'. André Danican-Philidor only copied the treble and bass lines which probably were all that were available to him. Other important sources such as the *Terpsichore Musarum* of Praetorius, the Cassel manuscript (edited by Ecorcheville as *Vingt suites d'orchestre du XVIIᵉ siècle français*), the Uppsala Library manuscript and the *Pièces pour le violon à quatre parties* printed by Ballard in 1665 are discussed in Chapter 19 (pp. 298–300).

In 1651 the *Ballet de Casandre* inaugurated the court ballet of the period of Louis XIV. The 13 year old monarch danced for the first time

36

in this ballet, and Isaac de Benserade (1613–91) made his debut as a poet of superior literary talents.[17] Charles Perrault in his *Les Hommes illustres qui ont paru en France pendant ce siècle* (Paris, 1696) defined the change in concept that Benserade brought to his *vers*. Before him, the *vers* were concerned only with the characters portrayed on stage rather than with those who were performing the roles. 'M. de Benserade', wrote Perrault, 'conceived of the *vers* in such a manner that they applied equally to one as to the other'. Occasionally with a touch of sarcasm, with a suspicion of malice or a raised eyebrow, Benserade in elegant verse illuminated the political and amorous intrigues of those who danced with the king.

After years of stagnation, the *ballet de cour* was given new life by the *Ballet de la Nuit,* performed at the Petit Bourbon on 23 February 1653. The *Ballet de la Nuit* with poetry by Benserade, music by Cambefort and machines devised by Torelli, was divided into 4 parts and 45 *entrées*.

The music by Jean de Cambefort (1605–61) is of interest.[18] The *récit* of Night that constitutes the Prologue resembles more the declamatory style of Guédron than the music of such contemporaries as Jean-Baptiste Boësset (1614–85) or Michel Lambert (1610–96) both of whom contributed *récits* to this ballet. Already present is the insistent anapestic rhythmic formula so characteristic of the recitatives in Lully's ballets and operas.

Example 2
Cambefort: Extract from 'récit de la nuit', Ballet de la Nuit *(after Philidor copy).*

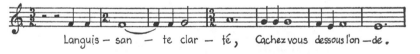

In the second part, which represented the *divertissements* that 'reign between nine in the evening to midnight', the dancers included the king, Mollier, Lambert and Lully. The fourth part ('From three in the morning until the rising of the Sun') introduced the young king in the symbolism of the 'rising sun' for the first time, as may be observed in Plate 6. The ballet ended with:

> Dawn pulls a superb chariot bringing the most beautiful Sun that one had ever seen, which at first dissipated the clouds and then promised the most beautiful and the greatest Day of the World; the Spirits came to render him homage, and that formed the *grand Ballet*. The *sujet* is vast and in all of its Extensiveness completely worthy to exercise the steps of our Young Monarch, without detracting from the scheme. . . .[19]

So it was that a 20-year-old Florentine, Giambattista Lulli (1632–87) found himself on the stage dancing next to the king of France. Less than one month later, on 16 March, Lully was appointed *Compositeur de la Musique instrumentale de la Chambre*, a position left vacant by the death of Lazarini. The year 1653 had double significance for the creator of French opera: it was the beginning of a productive collaboration with the poet Benserade, which lasted until 1681; and more important for Lully, it marked the beginning of his 'plus grande Journée du Monde' in friendship with Europe's most powerful monarch, the 'Roi Soleil'.

Chapter 3

※ ‹‹‹

Ballet de Cour II:
The Period of Lully

Twenty years' apprenticeship as a composer of *ballets de cour* and *comédies-ballets* prepared Lully for his role as creator of the *tragédie lyrique*. *Cadmus et Hermione* is inconceivable without the background of the *Ballet des Muses* or *Psyché*.

Lully[1] was first brought to the attention of the court as dancer and violinist. He had arrived in Paris in 1646, a boy of 14 sent from Florence by the Chevalier de Guise to serve as a *valet de chambre* and teacher of Italian to Mlle de Montpensier, the daughter of Gaston d'Orléans. He requested his release from her staff in 1652 at the time of her exile from Paris, and she acquiesced without protest, 'because he is a great dancer' (*Mémoires*, 1728).

With his appointment in 1653 as a court composer, his position appeared secure, and he gave his full attention to the composition of court ballets.[2] The *ballet de cour* served Lully as a testing ground where he learned to differentiate between the respective styles of his native and adopted lands and where he could observe the reaction of the young king and Cardinal Mazarin to his efforts.

Lully's genuine gift for comedy, which was later snuffed out at the insistence of the Académie Française, became apparent as early as 1655 in the Italian *récit* composed in grotesque style for the *Ballet des Bienvenus* performed at Compiègne in May to celebrate the marriage of Cardinal Mazarin's niece to the Duke of Modena. No French air by Lully can be authenticated before 1657.

In 1656 Cardinal Mazarin commissioned Lully to compose a ballet to be presented before the king and queen at the Louvre during carnival season. For this occasion Lully wrote the *Ballet de la Galanterie du Temps* whose main role, that of a *galant*, was danced by Louis XIV. It is the first ballet for which Lully supplied all the music. It includes Italian airs and dances and, according to Jean Loret, was performed by a 'symphony of more than 25 instruments'.[3] It marks the first appearance under Lully's direction of the *Petits Violons* which soon surpassed its parent organization. Perrault described one of the reforms initiated by Lully and executed by his *Petits Violons:*

> Before him, only the soprano line was considered important in string pieces; the bass and inner parts were a simple accompaniment or a heavy counterpoint composed often on the spot by the performers themselves ... but Lully made all the parts sing together as agreeably as the soprano.

(Les Hommes illustres, i, p. 235)

The *Ballet d'Alcidiane* performed in February, 1658, is the first of Lully's ballets to lead directly to the development of the *tragédie lyrique.* Lully composed all the instrumental music and some of the vocal music. The overture, with its dotted rhythms, its wide melodic profile and its fugal second section, bears the classical stamp of all subsequent French overtures. Loret described it as being played by more than 80 instruments including 36 violins, flutes, viols, harpsichords, guitars, lutes and theorbos (*Muze historique,* letter of 16 February 1658).[4] The 'combat music', with its trumpet-like flourishes and slow harmonic rhythm, prefigures the type of military *divertissement* found in *Thesée* or *Bellérophon.* The 'Chaconne des Maures', which concludes the ballet, assumes the same grand proportions and structural significance of the chaconnes found in the *tragédies lyriques.*

All of the dances, with the exception of the 'petite chaconne', and most of the independent instrumental music of *Alcidiane* employ the five-part texture which Lully later used in the *tragédie lyrique.* There is no reason to look for influences from Venetian opera; as we have observed, five-part texture was used in French dance music at least as early as the *Ballet comique de la Reine.*

The French *récits* in the second and third parts of *Alcidiane* were probably composed by Jean-Baptiste Boësset, but the *récit* 'Que votre empire' is attributed to Lully.[5] It illustrates how well the Florentine had already mastered the style of the French *air de cour* and how he

Example 3
Lully: Extract from 'Que votre empire', Ballet d'Alcidiane (after Philidor copy).

40

had surpassed his French colleagues in dramatic expressiveness. The bass line with its consecutive downward leaps of two major 7ths is bolder than the rather static basses of his contemporaries.

The years 1661 and 1662 marked a turning point in Lully's career. In May, 1661, he was appointed to the important position of *Surintendant de la Musique de la Chambre*; in December 1661 he received *Lettres de Naturalité*. On 16 July 1662 he was appointed *Maître de la Musique de la Famille Royale*, and eight days later at the church of Saint Eustache he completed his naturalization by marrying the daughter of Michel Lambert. The marriage contract gives us an insight into the character of Lully who was not beyond eliminating his humble origins with a stroke of the pen. Thus, the 'son of a miller' by fabrication became 'Jean-Baptiste Lully, Esquire' son of 'Laurent de Lulli, Florentine gentleman'. That Jean-Baptiste was well entrenched at court is evidenced by the fact that Louis xiv, Anne of Austria, Maria Theresa and Colbert were among those who signed the contract.

His musical 'naturalization' kept pace with these events. The French *air de cour* remained his chief model for the vocal music of the ballets composed in the 1660's. Already present, however, were his first attempts to create a synthesis between the Italian laments, modelled in a general way on those of Luigi Rossi, and the French *airs de cour* or *récits* of a more elegiac nature.

The Italian lament of Armide, 'Ah, Rinaldo, e dove sei?' from the *Ballet des Amours déguisés* (1664), is the prototype for the 'plainte' of Venus from the *Ballet de Flore* (1669). Both contain *ritournelles* and utilize a simple *da capo* form. The dramatic use of rests and the presence of such 'affective' intervals as the descending diminished 7th give intensity to the 'plainte' to a degree rarely found in the *récits* of Lambert, Le Camus or Boësset.

Example 4
Lully: Extract from 'Plainte de Vénus', Ballet de Flore (after Philidor copy).

The 'plainte' of Venus quoted above and the earlier 'plainte' of Ariadne from the *Ballet de la Naissance de Vénus* (1665), with its restrained chromaticism, foreshadow the musical language of the great monologues of *Armide* and *Roland* although as late as 1671 in the

41

lament 'Deh piangete al pianto' from the *tragédie ballet, Psyché* (see Chapter 5, p. 60), Lully still appeared more at ease in the Italian lament.

In his dance music Lully quickly assimilated the long heritage of French dances and introduced new dances that were coming into fashion. Abbé Dubos credited Lully with the addition of more fast dances ('airs de vitesse') in the court ballet:

> As the dancers . . . were obliged to move with greater speed and more action than had been common up to that point, and as there were those who maintained that this was a corruption of good taste in the dance . . . Lully himself was obliged to compose the steps that he wished the dancers to execute.
>
> (*Réflexions critiques*, III, p. 167)

In the ballets composed up to 1673 (the year of *Cadmus*), Lully used the following dances in order of priority: bourrées (26), minuets (21), sarabandes (19), gavottes (16), canaries (6), chaconnes (5), courantes (4), galliards (3) and loure (1).[6]

By degrees, however, the purely musical features of the ballet began to usurp the position of the dance. In the words of Pierre Nougaret:

> Only those ballets in which some vocal music was introduced were proper for performance at court (of Louis XIV); but it happened that little by little the musical features dominated the dances to the extent that the latter became only an accessory.
>
> (*De l'Art du Théâtre*, II, 1769, p. 230)

Such ballets as the *Ballet des Muses* (1666) and the *Ballet de Flore* (1669) best illustrate these changes. The impressive choral finale to the prologue of the *Ballet des Muses* expresses the same sentiments found in any number of subsequent operatic prologues: 'Rien n'est si doux que de vivre à la cour de Louis le plus parfait des Roys.' The music for this fatuous text is square and pompous and already tradition-bound. It was to remain the official gesture of adoration throughout the *grand siècle*.[7]

The close liaison between the *Ballet des Muses* and the *tragédie lyrique* was recognized by Sébastien de Brossard who wrote: 'According to all appearances it is this Ballet (*Les Muses*) that gave the idea of composing Operas in French. . . .'[8]

These ballets also show Lully well on the way to the creation of French recitative that approximated the declamatory practices of the French stage. According to Lecerf, he modelled his recitative on the intonation of Racine's mistress, La Champmesle, at the Comédie Française, but the *Ballet des Muses* was composed at least one year

Example 5
Lully: Extract from chorus, 'Rien n'est si doux', Ballet des Muses
(after Philidor copy).

before her first great triumph in *Andromaque*. Example 6a shows the predominantly anapestic rhythmic organization and the division of the alexandrine into hemistiches that characterize the recitatives of the *tragédie lyrique*. By the time of *Cadmus*, Lully had introduced fluctuating metres in order to place the last accented syllable of the line on the first beat of the measure. At that time he would have undoubtedly revised the *Ballet des Muses* recitative as is shown in Example 6b.

Example 6
Lully: 'Recitative' from Ballet des Muses (after Philidor copy).

Lully composed two theatre ballets after the birth of the *tragédie lyrique*. These ballets, *Le Triomphe de l'Amour* (1681) and *Le Temple de la Paix* (1685), bear only a structural resemblance to the earlier *ballet à entrées*. *Le Triomphe de l'Amour*, performed in January at Saint-Germain-en-Laye and repeated in May of the same year in Paris, was the first ballet to be seen at the Académie Royale de Musique. The most important aspect of the Paris performance was the appearance of professional female dancers on stage. Included among these were Mlles de La Fontaine, Pasant, Carré and Leclercq. Mlle de La Fontaine, who remained at the Opéra until 1692, was the outstanding performer of her age. With her began the incredible star system which dominated the French stage throughout the eighteenth century and gave rise to such dancers as Mlles Prévost, Guyot, Subligny, Sallé and Camargo.[9]

Musically, *Le Triomphe de l'Amour* is characterized by a more imaginative approach to instrumentation than is generally the case even in Lully's later works. The 'Prélude de l'Amour' is scored for both transverse flutes and recorders (*taille, quinte, petite basse* and *grande basse*),[10] and there are directions in the edition of 1681 which give precise performance instructions. For example, in the *ritournelle* and the air of Venus in the first *entrée*, the string players are told to play 'gently, almost without touching the strings', and in the 'Prélude pour la Nuit', Lully instructed all players to use mutes and to 'play gently, particularly during the vocal solos'.

The *récits* of *Le Triomphe de l'Amour* lost their independent existence and were carefully integrated into the dramatic action. There are 16 *récits* for the 20 *entrées*, a number far in excess of any earlier ballet. The chorus is given much prominence and includes a large double choir whose two sections remain on opposite sides of the stage throughout the performance. The dance is a mere accessory.

'The Peace', wrote Lully in the preface to his stage ballet *Le Temple de la Paix*, 'which Your Majesty has so generously given to his vanquished Enemies is the subject of this Ballet. . . . Could I find a more fitting subject for which to compose some *chants extraordinaires*?'[11] *Le Temple de la Paix*, then, is a late example of such politically inspired ballets as the *Ballet des quatres Monarchies Chrestiennes* (1635) and the *Grand Ballet de la Prosperité des Armes de France* (1641). In emphasizing his 'chants extraordinaires', Lully gave recognition to non-choreographic elements which dominate this ballet to an even greater degree than in *Le Triomphe de l'Amour*.

Louis XIV appeared on the stage for the last time in 1670 dancing in *Les Amants magnifiques*. Although not so passionately committed to the ballet as his father had been, the king had taken much pleasure in participating in the *ballet de cour*. Whether or not his general education had been neglected as Saint-Simon insisted, he had taken special pains to be well instructed in the dance. The financial account for the year 1660 shows that the king's dancing master received 2,000 *livres* whereas only 300 *livres* were allotted to his writing teacher.[12] By the 1680's, the *ballet de cour* had lost most of its identity with the court; the elaborate procedures of composition and performance detailed by Saint-Hubert and Marolles were already part of the legacy of the past.

By the early years of the eighteenth century, the *ballet de cour* was looked upon as archaic and in questionable taste. Cahusac, writing in the 1750's, stated unequivocally that it was a 'genre which no longer exists' (preface to *La Danse ancienne et moderne*, 1754). It was exhumed at court from time to time for some special occasion. Such is the *Ballet de la Jeunesse* by Delalande performed at Versailles on 28 January 1686. This work, a synthesis between opera and ballet, is an important precursor of the *opéra-ballet* introduced by André Campra with his *L'Europe galante* of 1697. The long poem of about 250 lines is divided into three episodes, devoted to Mercury, to Pallas, and to Philis and Tircis respectively. The music is rich in *symphonies*, recitatives, airs, choruses, and dances. At the centre of the work is the 'Chaconne de la Jeunesse' with a total of 61 variations built on the eight-measure bass line. From Lully, Delalande had learned how to organize an entire scene around the chaconne pattern. The theme and 28 of the variations are instrumental; the balance of the variations are for vocal solo, ensemble and chorus.

Delalande's *L'Inconnu*, a *ballet à entrées*, was danced at the Tuileries in 1720 by Louis xv aged 10. It is one of the last genuine *ballets de cour*, and as if to give a final salute to its glorious past, the ballet is dominated by its dances rather than by its vocal music.

At the Jesuit Collège Louis-le-Grand, the ballet was maintained to 1761, the date of the expulsion of the Jesuits from France. It was part of the annual ceremony marking the end of the year's work. Nemeitz described it as follows:

> The Students of the Jesuits perform a Latin Tragedy at the Collège Louis-le-Grand once a year at the beginning of August. As the Fathers wish to excel in all their actions, they omit nothing to augment the magnificence of their Spectacle. Not content merely to adorn the stage with the most beautiful Decorations and to clothe the Actors in the richest garments, they even bring in the best people of the Opera whether for dancing or for playing in the Orchestra. They mount a Ballet between each act, which is usually directed by Mons. Blondi. The Stage is erected outdoors in the Court of the College.... All the area of this spacious court is full of benches for the Spectators, of which there are such a great number that not only are all places occupied, but all the windows of the College that overlook the court are filled with people from top to bottom. At the conclusion of

the play, some books are distributed to the Students as a prize for their industry.

(Séjour de Paris, pp. 107–8)

All manner of musical performances and ballets served as *intermèdes* that were inserted between the acts of Latin tragedies.[13] Some ballets were closely aligned with the action of their tragedies and may be considered early examples of the *danse en action.* Thus, the tragedy *Aurelius* performed at the College 2 August 1668 included a ballet 'basé sur l'action de la tragédie latine' (Lowe, p. 178). Among the composers who wrote *intermèdes* for the Jesuits were Campra, Charpentier, Clérambault, Colasse, Delalande, Desmarest, Lalouette, Oudot and Royer. Music for 10 ballets composed in the 1680's and performed at the College was copied in 1690 by Philidor in a collection entitled *Les Ballets des Jesuits, composés par Messieurs Beauchant, Desmartins et Collasse.* . . .

Genuine *tragédies en musique* were composed for the College beginning in 1684. These works, which include *Demetrius* (1685) by Claude Oudot (music lost), *Celse martyre* (1687) by Charpentier (music lost) and Charpentier's *David et Jonathan* (1688), developed from the ballets, the *pastorales en musique* and other *intermèdes* and, as such, paralleled in miniature the development of French opera from the *ballet de cour.*

For more than a century, the *ballet de cour* served king and courtier as a luxurious diversion and a legitimate excuse for royal exercise. With the advent of the stage ballet and its professional dancers of great skill, the *ballet de cour* could no longer command the attention of the court. It had served its purpose well; its overtures and prologues, its spectacular finales, its vocal airs, ensembles and choruses, its dances and independent instrumental *symphonies,* and its sense of ceremonial gesture all live on in the *tragédie lyrique.*

46

Chapter 4

»» ««

Italian Opera in France

Italian influence on French art during the sixteenth century was in constant ebb and flow. From their first invasion of Italy, the Valois kings brought back Italian decorators for their châteaux; the gardener Pacello, was at Amboise, Il Boccador contributed much to the decorations of Chambord, Blois and the Hôtel de Ville in Paris, and the great Leonardo da Vinci died in the manor house at Amboise in 1519.

The châteaux of the Loire valley show clearly the happy results of a synthesis between French forms and Italian decoration. The shape of the old medieval fortress can still be discerned underneath the flamboyant decoration of Chambord while the austere keep tempers the elegance of Chenonceaux.

Although a love-hate relationship with Italy persisted throughout the *grand siècle*, there remained constant an assertive French classical spirit. The chronological distance between Du Bellay's *Défense et illustration de la langue française* (1549) and Boileau's *L'Art poétique* (1672) is great, but the order and discipline of French classicism unite them. 'Avoid these excesses', wrote Boileau, 'leave to Italy all this false brilliance and foolish glitter'.

French classical genius tempered and modified Italian baroque exuberance. Lemercier's Sorbonne chapel and Mansart's Val-de-Grâce church owe as much to this spirit as they do to the so-called 'Jesuit style'; the rejection of Bernini's plans for the rebuilding of the Louvre partially reflected the classical bias of both Louis XIV and Colbert.

Partisans of Italian music during the first half of the seventeenth century were much more numerous than we have heretofore believed. The inventories of the music libraries of middle-class Parisians found in the *Minutier Central* reveal that long before the days of the Italophile Nicolas Mathieu, curé of Saint-André-des-Arts, there were impressive private collections of Italian madrigals and motets. In fact, in the collections described by Mme Jurgens, the ultramontane examples far outnumber the French *airs de cour* (*Documents du Minutier Central*, pp. 865–894).

47

Marin Mersenne and André Maugars were among the first in France to attempt a classification of the stylistic difference between French and Italian music. Yet it was still an age of innocence, of peaceful co-existence, and the polemics of Raguenet or Lecerf were far in the future. Probably not too many composers took offence at or even heeded the advice of Maugars found at the end of his *Response faite à un curieux sur le sentiment de la musique d'Italie* (1639) to travel and listen to 'foreign music' in order to 'emancipate themselves from their pedantic rules'.

The role played by seventeenth century Italian opera in the development of the French lyric theatre at mid-century must be seen against this background of a gradually increasing awareness of rival styles. Cardinal Mazarin tried in vain over a 16-year period to establish a permanent Italian opera troupe in Paris. Not even unlimited funds, the support of the queen mother or the glamour of the most prominent names among Italian composers and performers convinced French audiences that this foreign importation could be 'nationalized'.

For Cardinal Mazarin, the wish to promote Italian opera in France was due partly to nostalgia and partly to practical politics. He had formerly been in the service of Cardinal Antonio Barberini in Rome and had witnessed the production of Stefano Landi's *Sant' Alessio* that inaugurated the Barberini palace in 1632. In 1643, after the death of Louis xiii, Mazarin was made a member of the Regency during the minority of Louis xiv. He envisioned opera in France as a political arm of the government with Italian musicians, poets and machinists potentially involved in state intrigues, and the court so diverted by the spectacle that his own political machinations might pass unnoticed.

The first work performed in February of 1645 at the Palais Royal was identified in the *Gazette de Paris* as an Italian comedy and ballet danced by the gentlemen of the court. Prunières conjectured that the work was *Nicandro e Fileno*,[1] but Paul-Marie Masson identified *Nicandro e Fileno*, for which only the libretto remains, as an Italian pastorale composed by Paolo Lorenzani on a poem by the Duc de Nevers and first performed in 1681.[2] During the same year, the composer Marco Marazzoli, the *virtuosa* Leonora Baroni (reputedly a former mistress of Mazarin) and the composer, impressario and secret agent Atto Melani arrived in Paris. By the end of 1646 through the active assistance of the queen mother herself, the French court became a refuge for Cardinal Barberini and his secretary, the poet Francesco Buti, who were escaping the political vicissitudes of the papacy. More important, in June, 1645 the *grand sorcier* among the Italian machinists, Giacomo (or Jacopo) Torelli (1608–78), reached the French capital. (For further information on Torelli's stage machinery see Per Bjurström, *Giacomo Torelli and Baroque Stage Design*, 2nd ed. Stockholm 1961.)

In December, 1645 at the Petit Bourbon palace, there was a performance of *La Finta Pazza* with music by Francesco Sacrati and text by Giulio Strozzi. This was a revised version of a work first heard in Venice in 1641. Torelli adapted the original to suit the tastes of seven-year-old Louis xiv by adding ballets for monkeys, eunuchs, negroes and ostriches. The *livret* and music excited little comment, and the audience appeared less interested in the poetry and music than in the stage sets, machines and rapid scene changes.

Mazarin's next venture, a performance in February of 1646 of Cavalli's *Egisto*, failed precisely because it was mounted with no complicated *mise-en-scène*. This was false economy from the cardinal's point of view, and he was quick to realize that the French audience, except for those few committed to Italian music on its own intrinsic merits, would demand musical productions on a lavish scale. Already unpopular with some powerful members of the royalty, he could ill afford comments similar to those of Mme de Motteville who wrote with reference to *Egisto* that 'we were only twenty or thirty and we almost died of boredom and the cold' (*Mémoires*). Jacques Vanuxem suggests that, because of a conflict in scheduling that cost *Egisto* most of its audience, Mme de Motteville's oft-quoted remarks may have been a reaction to the situation rather than a value judgment,[3] for she immediately added that '*Divertissements* of this nature require a large audience, and solitude has no rapport with the stage'.

Luigi Rossi's *Orfeo* (text by Abbé Buti) provided the image of Italian opera so badly needed by Mazarin. It was performed at the Palais Royal on 2, 3 and 5 March 1647 and was so successful that it was repeated on 25 April and finally on 6 and 8 May. Nuitter and Thoinan quote a contemporary observer who wrote '. . . one does not know which to admire the most, the beauty of its invention, the grace of the solo voices, or the magnificence of the costumes; because by the variety of scenes, the diverse stage decorations and the novelty of the machines, it surpasses all admiration' (*Les Origines de l'opéra française*, p. xxx).

Abbé Buti, well aware of French interest in the dance, attempted a liaison between the subject matter of *Orfeo* and that of its ballet *entrées*. 'From the moment of its appearance in France', wrote Prunières, 'opera was wed to ballet'.[4] The ballet music is missing from the printed score but was presumably written by French court composers.

The poem is a curious mixture of burlesque ballets of owls, tortoises and snails, of clowns and satyrs embellishing the simple tale. The music, however, is Luigi Rossi at his best. The prologue is totally independent of the legend of Orpheus and foreshadows the panegyric prologues of *Alceste* and *Thésée*. A chariot suspended above the French armies holds 'La Victoire' who sings verses in praise of the queen mother, 'Great Anne whose beautiful hands hold the sceptre and hurl thunderbolts'. In the words of Ménestrier, this prologue is a '*pièce détachée* unrelated to the story of Orpheus. . . . We have retained this liberty in France, and almost all Prologues . . . are conceived of as a means of praising the King' (*Des Représentations en musique anciennes et modernes*, p. 196).

In spite of the general approbation that greeted *Orfeo*, there were scarcely disguised rumblings of discontent from two powerful factions: parliament and the church. The parliament, employing Mazarin's tactics, attempted to divert attention from its own grave fiscal problems by emphasizing and distorting the admittedly exorbitant costs of the production of *Orfeo*. Thus, Guy Joli, an historian and adviser to parliament, in his *Memoires* covering 1648–65 (published 1718) estimated the cost of the production to have been as high as 500,000 *écus*, a figure regarded by Nuitter and Thoinan as 'absurd and untruthful' (*Les Origines de l'opéra français*, p. xxxvii). Public opinion as reflected in many of the satirical anti-Mazarin songs, the 'mazarinades', deduced a clear cause-and-effect relationship between the economic miseries of the state and the cost of an Italian opera staged by an Italian machinist and sponsored by an Italian cardinal.

The second faction was the conservative clergy and their supporters at the Sorbonne who were offended by all stage productions. Mme de Motteville in her *Mémoires* mentioned an unidentified curé of Saint-Germain who in 1647 with the support of seven doctors of the Sorbonne warned Anne of Austria that she was in danger of committing a 'mortal sin' should she continue to support this type of 'divertissement'.

The Fronde temporarily upset Mazarin's plans to establish a base in France for Italian opera. Those Italians who remained in France were threatened or, as in the case of Torelli, actually imprisoned. However, with the defeat of the 'frondeurs' and the triumphant return of Mazarin to Paris in February of 1653, plans for a new Italian opera were made.

That inveterate observer, Loret, noted in his *La Muze historique*:

> J'apris hier, en mangeant ma soupe,
> Qu'une belle et gaillarde troupe
> De très rare comédiens,
> Et mesmes grands muziciens,
> Arriva lundy de Mantoue,
> Naples, Turin, Rome et Padoue.

(Letter of 31 January 1654)

The 'belle et gaillarde troupe' was placed under the direction of the composer Carlo Caproli ('Carlo del violino') and on 14 April 1654 at the Petit Bourbon, his opera *Le Nozze di Peleo e di Teti* (libretto by

Abbé Buti) was performed. On the title page we read, 'comédie italienne en musique entremeslée d'un ballet sur le mesme sujet'. This important concession to French taste resulted in a strange and unconvincing attempt to graft French *ballet de cour* on to Italian opera. Each scene of the opera gave rise to a ballet *entrée* with verses by Benserade and music by Lully and other court composers. Young Louis XIV danced in six *entrées*; in one, in the elaborate and completely fanciful costume of an 'indien' he was joined by Jean-Baptiste Lully who had been in his service for one year.

Mazarin was now at the peak of his political power. The Treaty of Paris and the Peace of the Pyrenees were both signed in 1659. Yet he was unable to establish a permanent Italian company in Paris. After each opera, the Italian troupe disbanded, and the musicians went back to Italy. It was often difficult and expensive to plan and execute return trips. The letters that passed between Mazarin and Buti, who was recruiting in Italy during this period, show the extent of the cardinal's stubborn commitment to his *idée fixe*. Money was no object, and in a letter of 8 August 1659 he wrote:

> I ask you only to examine most carefully anyone whom you choose to sing or play the violin and other instruments; because it is necessary that each be outstanding in his métier. . . . I would rather have such performers and spend more money than have those of ordinary talent at a cheaper price.

To celebrate both the marriage of Louis XIV with Maria Theresa and the Peace of the Pyrenees, Mazarin commissioned the famous Francesco Cavalli (1602–1676) to write the opera *Ercole amante* on a *livret* by Abbé Buti. After much bickering, Cavalli arrived in Paris in June of 1660, but neither his opera nor the new 'Théâtre des Machines' at the Tuileries Palace were ready.

A substitution of an earlier Cavalli opera, *Serse*, was hastily arranged. The composer made many alterations and spread the action over five instead of three acts. Mazarin gave Lully the task of supplying ballet music for the *entrées*; Lully, pressed for time, used materials already composed and made no effort to coordinate the subject matter of ballet with opera. He added a typical patriotic prologue and composed a magnificent French overture. It is a more elaborate work than his first essay in this genre (*Alcidiane*) two years earlier; the *fugato* (gai) in triple metre is followed by a concluding section in which the metre (C), tempo (modéré) and general character resemble the opening part of the overture.

The reaction to *Serse* was predictable. The public applauded the dances and the *mise-en-scène* but virtually ignored Cavalli's music. The curious casting, which assigned a castrato, Francesco Maria Melani, to the role of Princess Amastris, lover of King Xerses (also a castrato), and then paraded 'her' in male disguise, may have offended the French audience already ill-disposed towards castrati.

Mazarin did not live to see the performance of *Ercole amante* which finally took place in February of 1662 almost one year after his death. It served as an inauguration piece for the 'Théâtre des Machines' built for Mazarin by the septuagenarian architect Gaspare Vigarani and his two sons, Carlo and Lodovico.[5]

The performance of *Ercole amante* lasted for 6 hours and each act terminated with a spectacular ballet. The final ballet, called the 'ballet de sept planètes', included more than 20 *entrées*. The audience paid little heed to Cavalli's music and revelled instead in the flamboyance of Italian baroque stage design with its long perspectives and its changes in scene. Shown in rapid succession were the rocky coastline, a royal palace, a grotto, an elaborate garden, a fortress, sepulchres midst cypress trees, Hell, the temple of Juno and Mount Olympus with the assembly of gods. Loret devoted 210 lines to *Ercole amante* but dismissed the poem and music in a few words. Undoubtedly the poor acoustics of the new theatre and the audience's general lack of interest in the dramatic intrigue contributed to the failure of an opera which had required three years of preparation and which may have cost as much as 88,700 *livres* to produce. Prunières conjectured that the majority of the audience was not receptive to a work performed in a language that very few understood (*L'Opéra italien*, p. 304), although, as Ménestrier stated, Buti's *livret* 'was translated into French verse for the satisfaction of those who did not understand Italian' (*Des Représentations en musique anciennes et modernes*, p. 205). Musically *Ercole amante* was at the mercy of its own monstrous stage machinery, and it is difficult to imagine even the best voices competing with those gigantic machines that descended from the sky groaning under the weight of 150 persons.

In spite of a consistent history of failures, the influence of Italian opera on the development of the French lyric drama was far from marginal. At the very least, it made clear that a dramatic composition could be sung from beginning to end, and it stimulated the French to seek solutions to the problem more in keeping with their own traditions.

It is difficult to pinpoint the influence of seventeenth century Italian opera on Lully. There is little evidence that he was familiar with the masterpieces of the Venetian or Roman schools other than those Italian operas in France with which he was personally involved. The patina of Italianisms that remained in his compositions after 1673—the *fugati* of the French overtures, the imitative *ritournelles*, the independent comic scenes—was either modified by the predominantly French style, or, in the case of the comic scenes, expunged from all operas subsequent to *Thésée*. Although only 15 at the time of its Paris performance, he was surely familiar with Rossi's *Orfeo*. The *sommeil* trio of *Les Amants magnifiques* (1670), 'Dormez, dormez beaux yeux' (third *intermède*), and the subsequent *sommeils* of the *tragédie lyrique* derive from the trio, 'Dormite, begli occhi', of *Orfeo* (II, 9).[6]

It is less difficult to point out the influence of Italian opera on Lully's librettist, Philippe Quinault (1635–88). The scenes of sacrifice and combat, funeral ceremonies and the evocations of monsters and furies as well as the baroque mixture of comic and pathetic characters come as much from Italian opera as from the *ballet de cour*.[7] In planning the format of the *livret* of the *tragédie lyrique*, Quinault and Lully both must have remembered the applause that greeted the staging of *Ercole amante*.

Perhaps the experience of *Serse* and *Ercole amante* had the effect of strengthening Lully's basically conservative approach to dramatic music. Mazarin's futile attempts should have convinced Lully that French audiences would accept dramatic works with continuous music only if sung in French, but Brossard relates that, even after the impressive success of Perrin and Cambert and the establishment of the Académie d'Opéra, 'Lully railed against Perrin's Académie and affirmed many times that the French language was not proper for these large works . . .' (*Catalogue*, p. 220).

Chapter 5

≫≫ ≪≪

The Comédie-Ballet
and Related Genres

Comédie-Ballet

In August of 1661, Nicolas Fouquet, *Surintendant* of Finance, gave an Italianate *fête* at his palace at Vaux-le-Vicomte to honour 'the greatest king in the world'.[1] For part of the celebration Molière wrote his *comédie-ballet Les Fâcheux* in 15 days. It was the first of 12 such works. In the author's preface he explained that in order to make the most economical use of a limited number of dancers he had decided to relate the *entrées* to the subject of the play and thereby 'make ballet and comedy one'. He added that this *'mélange* is something new for the stage ... and can serve as a plan for other works conceived in more leisure'.

Molière was inaccurate. As we have seen, Abbé Buti had introduced ballet *entrées* into *Orfeo* in 1647, and *Le Nozze di Peleo e di Teti* was described on its title page as an 'Italian comedy in music interspersed with ballets on the same subject'.

The active collaboration of Molière and Lully in the composition of *comédies-ballets* began in 1664 with *Le Mariage forcé* and terminated in 1670 with *Le Bourgeois gentilhomme*.[2] Modern productions of these works cut Lully's music severely—even at the Comédie Française. Yet in their day, 'les deux grands Baptistes' were considered equal partners although there is no doubt but that Lully, by adroit exploitation of Louis XIV's interest in the dance, had a distinct advantage, reflected in a contemporary's description of *Le Bourgeois gentilhomme* as a 'ballet composed of six *entrées* accompanied by comedy' (*Gazette de Paris*, 18 October 1670).

Molière thought of music and dance as complementing the main action of the comedy: through *intermèdes* he introduced sub-plots that emphasized, mirrored or contrasted with the principal intrigue. This concept, first employed as a dramatic principle in the introductory *intermède* of *La Princesse d'Elide*, is the model for the later *opéra comique*. In *Le Sicilien*, Molière and Lully achieved more of a fusion

54

between music and spoken verse than in *La Princesse d'Elide*. Music and dance penetrate the action with natural ease and are not restricted to *intermèdes*. The *intermèdes* of *Le Bourgeois gentilhomme* add an important dimension to the development of the comedy itself although the final *intermède*, the 'Ballet des Nations', is totally independent.

Lully brought to the *comédie ballet* the skills already tested in his *ballets de cour*. He held to the tradition of the burlesque and exotic *entrées* of many of the *ballets à entrées*.[3] The format of the *comédie-ballet* gave him the opportunity to develop further his comic gifts in French and Italian *buffo* scenes. The Italian *buffo* style was a more natural expression for him at first as is evident from such a *ballet de cour* as *L'Amour malade*. The first attempts to create a French *style bouffe* in the bass solos of the magician in *Le Mariage forcé* are stiff and clumsy by comparison. The French comic scenes of *Monsieur de Pourceaugnac* composed five years later show no such awkward self-consciousness. The amusing 'polygamy' duet sung by the two lawyers in the second act illustrates this well developed French comic style.[4]

The *comédie-ballet* is a virtual compendium of musical forms and practices later used by Lully in the *tragédie lyrique*. Monsieur Jourdain's *maître de musique* makes no secret of the fact that the favoured solo voices were the soprano, counter-tenor and bass (*Le Bourgeois gentilhomme*, II, 1). No tenor is mentioned which is further evidence of the lowly status of this voice during the seventeenth century in France.

Scattered throughout the *comédies-ballets* are recitative-like passages that show the predominantly anapestic rhythmic ordering of the fully developed French recitative (see Example 7 below). In fact, according to Etienne Gros, Quinault modelled his poetry for the *tragédie lyrique* on the verse of Molière found in the *comédies-ballets* (*Philippe Quinault*, p. 711).

Example 7
Lully: Extract from Le Bourgeois gentilhomme (*after Philidor copy*).

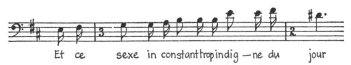

The airs of the *comédie-ballet*, like those of the *ballet de cour*, are in the tradition of the court airs of Lambert, Boësset and others. The relatively restricted range, the discreet 'affective' intervals, frequent cadence points, anapestic rhythms and a syllabic text rendering, all show us a Lully rapidly absorbing the style of his adopted land and consciously removing the last musical vestiges of his Italian origins. Some of his more lively drinking songs became very well known, and we learn from Lecerf that one of these, 'Buvons, chers amis, buvons' (*Le Bourgeois gentilhomme*),was one of the airs that Lully 'loved the most throughout his life'.

One type of binary air cultivated by Lully in the *comédie-ballet* became increasingly popular during the seventeenth century. It is organized as follows: the text, most typically, is a quatrain with the last two lines repeated; the first two lines constitute Part A of the air; in Part B, the textual repetition is never an exact musical repetition although note values and melodic shape may be similar. This particular binary air structure was used many times in the *tragédie lyrique*, and, in terms of frequency, it is the most important binary air in the operas of the generation of composers who followed Lully.[5]

Lully also made use of dance songs in his *comédie-ballets*. Dance songs[6] are songs that are almost literal transcriptions of the dances they precede or follow. They underscore the close relationship between the vocal air and the 'air de danse'. The dance song was absorbed into the *divertissements* of the *tragédie lyrique* and *opéra-ballet* where it often became part of a larger complex in which dance, vocal solo and ensemble were unified thematically (see, for example, the minuets in *Cadmus*, Prologue, scene 5).

In the *comédie-ballet* there are also examples of airs written for bass voice and two obbligato instruments described aptly by Bukofzer as 'double continuo' airs; that is, airs in which the bass voice serves simultaneously as vocal 'melody' and support. In effect, the upper string parts carry the burden of the melody. This curious, but enduring type of bass air may be traced back to the French *airs de cour*[7] and was not restricted to France; it is found in both Venetian opera and in bass solos of Heinrich Schütz.[8] Dialogue airs which often generate duos and trios were used more frequently in the *comédie-ballet* than in the *ballet de cour*. The duos and trios of the *comédie-ballet* are, if anything, less rigidly homophonic than those of the *tragédie lyrique* and are closer to those found in Venetian opera.

The independent instrumental *symphonies* and the dances of the *ballet de cour* have their counterpart in the *comédie-ballet*. In addition to titled dances, there are several *airs de danse* with no fixed choreographic intent. These dances in particular often show a remarkable freedom in phase groupings, and in the use of counter-rhythms in the inner voices (see, for example, the '2e Air' from the Turkish Ceremony of *Le Bourgeois gentilhomme*).

As was true with the *ballet de cour*, the *comédie-ballet* was a haven for all manner of instruments before the relative standardization of the French opera orchestra. At times it was a large, rather heterogeneous orchestra with exotic and colourful instruments. The *livret* of *La Princesse d'Elide* mentions 'several hunting horns and trumpets' in concert with the strings and at one point describes a 'large tree machine in which there are 16 *Faunes* of whom 8 play flutes, the others, violin. ... 30 violins answer them from the orchestra with 6 other harpsichord and theorbo soloists'.

In such *comédies-ballets* as *Georges Dandin* and *Les Amants magnifiques* the musical features tend to dominate, and the link with the dramatic action is compromised. In *Les Amants magnifiques* we are on the very threshold of the *tragédie lyrique*. The book by Molière could substitute as an operatic *livret*; the prologue is sung throughout. Here again the 'kingly' prologue of the *tragédie lyrique* is foreshadowed in the use of more unified musical material; the instrumental introduction to the chorus 'Ouvrons tous nos yeux' engenders the final dance, the 'Menuet des Trompettes'. The finale is a decorative and sumptuous operatic celebration of the Pythian games. Written in the brilliant key of D-Major and scored in part for trumpets and drums, it is climaxed by the entrance of Apollo whose part was danced by the king, thus combining *comédie-ballet* and *ballet de cour*.

The decorative elements in the guise of elaborate stage machinery and costumes remind us that the *comédies-ballets* were originally conceived of as part of court *divertissements*. Félibien in his *Recueil de descriptions de peintures et d'autres ouvrages faits pour le roi* (1689) described Vigarani's machines for *Georges Dandin* with the rapid changes of scene for which the Italian machinists were so well known:

> Here the decoration of the stage is changed in an instant, and one can not imagine how it is that all the real fountains disappear and by what artifice one sees on the stage only large rocks intermixed with trees where several shepherds sing and play all sorts of instruments.

(pp. 209–10)

Open antagonism between Molière and Lully, which ended their collaboration on *comédies-ballets*, may be dated from the extraordinary bid by Lully to obtain the royal privilege for the establishment of the Académie Royale de Musique. It was not in character for Lully to remain on the side lines after observing the successes of Cambert and Perrin with the *Pastorale d'Issy* (1659) and above all with *Pomone* (1671). After buying the royal privilege from Perrin, Lully then managed to obtain a series of patents and ordinances from the king that Molière took as a very real threat to his comedians. The patent of 13 March 1672, which gave Lully the authority to establish an 'Académie Royale de Musique', at the same time forbade the performance of any work which was sung throughout without the written permission of Lully under penalty of a 10,000 *livres* fine and confiscation of the theatre, machines, decorations, costumes, etc. An ordinance of

30 April 1673 reduced to eight (two voices, six instrumentalists) the number of musicians who could appear in productions independent of the Académie Royale de Musique and limited these to musicians (and dancers) not in the employ of the Académie.

Particularly ominous for Molière was the patent of 20 September 1672 in which Lully was given permission to have printed 'all and each of the airs composed by him, as well as the verses, texts, subjects, plans and works for which the above mentioned airs have been composed—with no exceptions'(see Nuitter and Thoinan, *Les Origines de l'opéra français*, p. 281).

Molière countered by collaborating with Marc-Antoine Charpentier (1634–1704) who composed new music for a performance of *Le Mariage forcé* on 8 July 1672.[9] Molière's final work, the *comédie-ballet Le Malade imaginaire*, included *intermèdes* also composed by Charpentier. In order to meet the restrictions of Lully's patents, Charpentier was forced to recast the music three times. Charpentier's struggle is summed up in the titles borne by the three manuscript versions found scattered through the Charpentier *Meslanges* in the Bibliothèque Nationale: 1. 'Le Malade imaginaire avant les deffences'; 2. 'Le Malade imaginaire avec les deffences'; and 3. 'Le Malade imaginaire rajusté autrement pour la 3ième fois'.

The final triumph of Lully's scheming came about fortuitously with the sudden death of Molière following the fourth performance of *Le Malade imaginaire* on 17 February 1673. Lully had been renting a theatre, 'Jeu de Paume de Bel Air' (Rue de Vaugirard, today between the Odéon theatre and the Luxemburg gardens), in which his pastorale-pastiche, *Les Fêtes de l'Amour et de Bacchus*, and his first *tragédie lyrique, Cadmus et Hermione*, had already been performed. Once Molière was out of the way, Lully was able to get the king's permission to take over, at no cost, the hall of the Palais Royal which had formerly served Molière and his troupe (ordinance of 28 April 1673).

A poignant postscript appears in an annotation in La Grange's *Registre* for 1673: 'Those actors and actresses (of Molière's troupe) who remained behind found themselves not only without a troupe but without a theatre as well, which obliged them to seek out another establishment.'[10]

The *comédie-ballet* was sacrificed to Lully's ambition. It had left its mark on the French lyric theatre however. Richard Oliver has illustrated how its general plan shaped *Cadmus*.[11] It bequeathed its basic format to the *opéra comique*, and in the hands of Lully and Molière it was perhaps the only combination of poetry and music that pleased both the partisans of sung and spoken words. Saint-Evremond advised playwrights to return to 'our excellent Comedies, where one may introduce some dances, some Music which detracts nothing from the representation . . . it is thus that you would discover what satisfies both

58

the senses and the mind' (*Sur les opéra* in *Oeuvres meslées,* ed. of 1714, XI, p. 92).

Tragédie-Ballet

Qu'il est vrai que ce grand spectacle,
Qui faisoit la crier: Miracle!
Ce beau spectacle tout royal
Est encore ici sans égal.

(Robinet, *Lettres en vers à Monsieur* August, 1671)

Robinet was describing *Psyché*, a large scale collaborative effort with Lully as composer and Molière, Quinault and Pierre Corneille responsible for the text. In the *livret* of 1671, *Psyché* was labelled 'tragédie ballet'. Of all the works discussed in this chapter, it most closely resembles the *tragédie lyrique*. With minor alterations and the addition of recitatives in 1678, Lully and Thomas Corneille were able to convert the 1671 *tragédie-ballet* into the 1678 *tragédie lyrique* in only three weeks' time.

Psyché owes its existence to the desire of Louis XIV to see Vigarani's machines for *Ercole amante* once more—especially those that represented hell. In 1671 he asked Molière, Racine and Quinault for a subject that would necessarily include the 'hell' machinery. Racine proposed an *Orphée*; Quinault, a *Proserpine*; and Molière, the *Psyché* (see Vanuxem, *Actes des Journées internationales . . .* , p. 40). Vigarani's cloud machinery made a tremendous impression on Robinet and others. Used for the descent of Venus in the Prologue, it is described in the 1671 *livret*:

A large machine descends from the sky in between two smaller machines. All three are enveloped at first in clouds which, in descending, undulate, open and extend themselves until they occupy the entire stage.

Borrowed from the *comédie-ballet* was the conception of music and dance as dramatic agents. The 'pompe funèbre' of Act I, scene 6 with its 'concerts lugubres' and its dances marked by 'violent despair' prefigures the 'pompe funèbre' of *Alceste* (III, 5). The beautiful lament 'Deh piangete al pianto mio' (see Ex. 8) is more natural and spontaneous than its French counterparts, the 'plaintes' of Ariadne from the *Ballet de la Naissance de Vénus* and of Venus from the *Ballet de Flore*. The melodic line is less bound to the strictly syllabic treatment of the text that characterizes the French laments.

The spectacular operatic finale that celebrates the marriage of Love and Psyche was never surpassed by Lully even in his later *tragédies lyriques*. In this final *entrée* Apollo, Bacchus, Momus, Mars and their

59

followers are united. Trumpets and drums combine with voices to orchestrate the closing lines of this unique *tragédie-ballet*:

> Chantons les plaisirs charmants
> Des heureux amants.
> Répondez-nous, trompettes.
> Timbales et tambours;
> Accordez-vous toujours
> Avec le doux son des musettes,
> Accordez-vous toujours
> Avec le doux chant des amours.

Example 8
Lully: Extract from 'Deh, piangete', Psyché (after Ms Vm⁶ 5 in B.N.).

Tragédie à Machines

'The Théâtre du Marais could be considered the cradle of the Académie Royale de Musique', wrote Victor Fournel.[12] If we recognize that machines had played a significant role in many French stage productions dating back to the Italianate pastorales of the late sixteenth century, Fournel's opinion has merit. For it is true that during a 20 year period the taste of the French audience for intricate stage machinery was consistently and skilfully manipulated by impresarios eager to fill the coffers of the Marais theatre which in time became known as the 'Théâtre des Machines'.[13] It is equally true that music and dance under the influence of Italian opera and court ballet invaded the domain of the 'machine tragedy' and in conjunction with the *mise-en-scène* forced it ever closer to opera.

Like the *tragi-comédie*, the *tragédie à machines* was one of the mixed genres that rendered the French stage 'à la fois très riche et très confusé'[14] between the 1640's and 1660's. Always popular with the audiences, if not with the academicians, it only gradually gave way before the law of unities and the establishment of French classical drama.

In 1640 Chapoton's tragedy, *La Descente d'Orphée aux Enfers*, was performed at the Palais Royal. Noting the success of this machine tragedy with interest, the comedians of the Marais performed a new version entitled, *La Grande Journée des Machines ou le mariage d'Orphée et d'Euridice*, in 1648. According to the *livret* the machinist, Denis Buffequin, had contrived the 'most beautiful and most extraordinary machines that the artifice of our century and past centuries could invent'. Much new music was added to the three songs of Orpheus in the original production.

Corneille's machine tragedy, *Andromède*, has more literary merit. It was initially commissioned by Anne of Austria and Cardinal Mazarin and performed at the Petit Bourbon during carnival season in 1650. A reading of the author's preface negates the supposition that by virtue of this work Corneille is an 'initiator of modern opera'.[15] On the contrary, he is aligned firmly on the side of such later critics of opera as Saint-Evremond in stating that sung words are poorly understood and that therefore he had taken care to have nothing sung that was necessary for comprehension. The music by Charles Coypeau (called Dassoucy) was employed only to 'satisfy the ears of the spectators while the eyes are engaged watching the descent or ascent of a machine'. Torelli's machines, however, were far from being 'agréments détachés' like the music. They were considered as essential to the action. Only in choral commentaries found in such scenes as the combat between Persée and the monster ('Le monstre est mort, crions victoire', III, 3) do we come closer to the spirit of opera.[16]

Much nearer to opera is Claude Boyer's *Les Amours de Jupiter et de Sémélé* performed at the Marais in 1666 in which the spoken drama itself is subordinated to the music (by Louis de Mollier), dance and machine. The Prologue describes the rivalry between Melpomène (tragic muse), Thalie (comic muse) and Euterpe (pastoral muse). In the best operatic manner, each muse is assigned her characteristic music. Melpomène enters to the 'grands bruits de clarons et de trompettes'; Thalie plays a 'Tambour de Basque, auquel se mesle un concert de violons'; and Euterpe descends from Mount Parnassus while the musettes and oboes play an air 'fait exprès pour la pastourelle'.[17]

If we allow for exaggeration, Boyer sums up the contribution of the *tragédie à machines* to the French lyric stage in his *Dessein de la tragédie des Amours de Jupiter et Sémélé* (1666):

> Here is a small idea of our Play, which we might call an Aggregation of all that is astonishing in Music and finally, of all that is the most powerful and *galant* in Poetry.

Containing at least as much music as the pastorales of Perrin and Cambert, resembling the subject matter, if not the treatment, of Quinault's *tragédies lyriques*, the *tragédies à machines* may be considered as an 'imperfect and rough reflection of opera'.[18]

Chapter 6

-》》 《《-

The Pastorale

As in the *ballet de cour*, the sources of the French pastorale lay outside of France. The Italian dramatic pastorale, with its love of classical mythology, and the Spanish pastorale, with its conventionalized shepherds and shepherdesses and its chivalrous trappings, come together in the French pastorale.

The first French dramatic pastorales appeared in the late sixteenth century and were based in the main on Italian models. French translations of Tasso's *L'Aminta* (1581) and Guarini's *Il Pastor fido* (1585) had appeared as early as 1584 and 1595 respectively.

In subject matter and in decor, French dramatic pastorales contributed certain elements to the lyric stage that remained constant to the eve of the Revolution. Of central importance was the world of the 'merveilleux', and the magician, so significant in the *livrets* of Quinault, played a leading role. Magic fountains, apparitions, magic potions and rapid metamorphoses were everywhere in evidence. The deities mixed in the affairs of mortals as would the gods of Quinault. Jules Marsan described the dramatic pastorale *Arimène* (1597) by Nicolas de Montreux with its choruses and dances, its monsters and magic and its cloud machines transporting Jupiter and Persée, and one envisions a *mise-en-scène* that had its counterpart 100 years later at the Académie Royale de Musique.[1]

The 5,000 page *roman pastoral L'Astrée* by Honoré d'Urfé exerted considerable influence on the literature and manners of the period. Its first three volumes were in print by 1613. Among the dramatic pastorales based on *L'Astrée* was Racan's *Bergeries* (1625) which bordered on preciousness and further exploited the cult of shepherd and shepherdess that remained a fixed staple of the French lyric stage throughout the seventeenth and eighteenth centuries.

With the appearance of French classical drama, the pastorale was practically eliminated as a dramatic genre—a fate not unlike that of the *ballet mélodramatique*. It sought refuge in the *ballet de cour* and in the tentative beginnings of French opera. In the *ballet de cour* it

62

had been partially absorbed as early as the *Ballet comique de la Reine.* Both the *ballet mélodramatique* and the *ballet à entrées* used the subject matter of the pastorale, and with the sylvan decor of the *Ballet de Tancrède,* we are already 'en plein pastorale'.[2]

The pastorale was well adapted for its role in the creation of French opera. It contributed its symmetrically balanced dialogues which were already a kind of 'music without music' (La Laurencie, *ibid.,* p. 142). Its exploitation of tender, occasionally melancholy subject matter was ideally suited to the lyric stage; and its use of sorcerers, satyrs, buffoons, shepherds and shepherdesses in close proximity to the gods introduced the opportunity for contrast which makes for effective musical theatre.

In 1650 at the height of the Fronde, Charles Dassoucy, who composed the music for Corneille's *Andromède* that year, wrote the pastorale *Les Amours d'Apollon et de Daphné.* This 'musical comedy', which was probably never performed, included about a dozen *chansons* interspersed among the 550 lines of poetry. All of Dassoucy's music for *Andromède, Les Amours d'Apollon et de Daphné* and for his second pastorale, *Le Triomphe de l'Amour sur les bergers et bergères,* is lost; and although we know that Dassoucy played theorbo for the performances of Cavalli's *L'Egisto* and Rossi's *L'Orfeo,* we can only muse on the extent of Italian influence on this first French 'comédie en musique'.

Le Triomphe de l'Amour by Charles de Bey and Michel de La Guerre is the first pastorale that was entirely sung. It was performed, probably in concert version, at the Louvre on 22 January 1655 and was staged two years later with two characters (Tirsis and Philis) added to the original five (Cupid, two shepherds and two shepherdesses). De Bey's dedicatory letter to the king refers to the pastorale as a 'Comédie françoise en Musique' and comments on the 'novelty of this Piece whose format is my invention, and which is, in effect, the first work of its kind ever to have appeared in this Realm'. The 'Argument' from the *Avertissement* of the 1655 version is quoted by Henri Quittard and is a classical example of a pastorale 'plot':

> Climène scorns Lysis who loves her; Philandre scorns Climène who loves him; Cloris loves Lysis; Lysis scorns her; Philandre loves Cloris; Cloris scorns Philandre . . . Lysis, Philandre, Climène and Cloris agree . . . to keep their freedom and to renounce love. Cupid appears with his bow and arrows; . . . all remain together in the Empire of Love.[3]

The talented organist, Robert Cambert (*c.* 1627–77), may have been familiar with de Bey's and La Guerre's 'Comédie en Musique', for in a letter quoted by Nuitter and Thoinan (p. 33) he wrote:

> Having always had the thought of introducing comedies in music as are found in Italy, I began to compose an elegy in 1658

for three contrasting voices in dialogue . . . and this elegy was called the *Muette ingratte*. M. Perrin having heard this piece which was very successful . . . wished to compose a small pastorale.

The first important results of the collaboration between Cambert and Pierre Perrin was the so-called *Pastorale d'Issy*. Ignoring the earlier efforts of Dassoucy and La Guerre, Perrin in the Ballard printed edition of 1659 presumptuously titled his work 'Première Comédie françoise en musique représentée en France. Pastorale. Mise en musique par Monsieur Camber (*sic*), organiste de l'église collégiale de Saint-Honoré à Paris'. Only the *livret* of this pastorale is extant. Although the verses of Perrin are banal, the form is less rigid than the 'comédie françoise' of de Bey. Quite by design and apparently to achieve the greatest possible contrast with Italian opera, the poet 'banished all serious thought' ('raisonnements grave') and even all 'intrigue' from his 5-act, 14-scene pastorale. According to Ménestrier, the work contained songs which were 'linked together following no law but that of expressing beautiful verse and music. . . . All succeeded admirably because the *Symphonie* was beautiful, the performers handsome and everyone was in good voice' (*Des Représentations en musique anciennes et modernes*, p. 208). This blanket approbation accorded the *Pastorale d'Issy* casts some doubts on the Jesuit's critical acumen. Titon du Tillet's comment is perhaps closer to the truth: 'a number of distinguished persons were very satisfied with the work, although the text left much to be desired'.

Certainly it had the 'agrément de la Nouveauté' (Saint-Evremond), for it was performed eight or ten times at the village of Issy in the country home of Monsieur de La Haye, and a performance was arranged in May of the same year at Vincennes before the king, the queen and Cardinal Mazarin. Afterwards in spite of his absorption in Italian opera, Mazarin suggested to Cambert that he compose another pastorale on a larger scale. The result was *Ariane et Bacchus* (music lost) which was only performed in a revised version in London in 1674. If we may trust Saint-Evremond's judgement, we have been deprived of the 'chef d'oeuvre de Cambert'.

On 28 June 1669, Perrin received his privilege to establish an Académie d'Opéra which was inaugurated 3 March 1671 with a performance of *Pomone*. Perhaps under the direct influence of the Lully–Molière *comédie-ballet*, Perrin and Cambert created in *Pomone* a much more ambitious and theatrical work than the *Pastorale d'Issy*. It was well received and was performed 146 times although Cambert, with understandable pique, wrote afterwards that he would have preferred less success, because 'there would not have been so many envious people and I would not have found myself without employment by virtue of having succeeded too well' (Nuitter and Thoinan, p. 157). Saint-

Evremond, in his comedy *Les Opéra* (Act II, sc. 4), has a character describe *Pomone* as follows:

> *Pomone* is the first French Opera to appear on Stage. The Poetry in it is very bad, the Music beautiful. Monsieur de Sourdéac built the Machines; this is enough to give you some idea of their beauty; one observed the Machines with surprise, the Dances with pleasure; one listened to the Songs with delight, to the Words with disgust.

Only the overture, the prologue (subtitled 'à la louange du Roy' and labelled Act I) and five pages of Act II remain. Cambert's scoring is more 'progressive' than Lully's; that is, he avoided throughout the heavy *a* 5 string writing characteristic of the Florentine and preferred an *a* 4 or trio texture. The expressive beginning of the second act, with its bass line rising a diminished 4th to create a poignant dissonant harmony with the melody on the word 'soupire', shows a composer sensitive to the 'affective' nature of Baroque recitative.

Example 9
Cambert: Beginning of Act II, Pomone *(after Ballard Ms ed. in B.N.).*

All the confusing details of Perrin's relationship with his business manager, the talented but unscrupulous Marquis de Sourdéac, and with the Marquis's flunky, the former sergeant, Sieur de Champeron, have been told many times and need not be repeated here.[4] Because of the intrigues of Sourdéac and Champeron, Perrin found himself in debtor's prison, and in June, 1672 the theatre was closed. Robinet in his *Lettres en vers à Monsieur* of 20 June sums up this sorry state of affairs:

Le Grand Opéra plus n'opère,
Dont maint ici se desespère.
La Discorde aux poils couleuvrins,
Qui se nourrit de noirs chagrins
Et de Plaisir est l'ennemie,
En a troublé l'Académie,
Les Intendants et les Acteurs,
Tous sont tombez en guerre atroce,
En guerre incivile et féroce.

Although Perrin continued to languish in jail, a partial resolution of economic difficulties saw the doors of the Académie open again in the winter of 1672 for a performance of a *pastorale héroïque*, *Les Peines et les Plaisirs de l'Amour*, which Cambert wrote to a *livret* by Gabriel Gilbert. The performances must have ended by 1 April on which date the Académie was again closed by royal decree due to the fact that Sourdéac and Champeron had failed to pay any wages. As we have seen, Lully chose this moment to secure the royal privilege for himself. In buying it from Perrin, he made it possible for the librettist to gain his freedom, and he effectively barred Cambert from any further employment in France as a dramatic composer. Cambert followed his former student, Louis Grabu, to London where he established a short-lived 'Royall Academy of Musick' and where he died in 1677.[5]

Les Peines et les Plaisirs de l'Amour shows a marked advance over *Pomone*. Although scarcely superior to Perrin as a poet, Gilbert realized certain dramatic advantages in having the gods involve themselves in the affairs of men; Apollo's love for a mortal shepherdess is rendered in a genuinely pathetic tone.

Unfortunately, as is the case with *Pomone*, Cambert's dramatic talents must be evaluated on the basis of the fragments that remain: the overture, prologue and 14 pages of Act I. The overture, unlike that to *Pomone*, is not 'à la française'. It is more like a multi-sectioned Italian *canzona*.

Based on the extant bits of recitative, Cambert appeared to have been well on the way to the creation of a French recitative which, if less

Example 10
Cambert: Extract from Asterie's recitative, Les Peines et les plaisirs de l'amour (after Ballard Ms ed. in B.N.).

concerned with textual elements than that of Lully, is more genuinely musical. The expressive melismas found in the example above almost never occur in the syllabic recitatives of Lully.

Armed with his new royal patent 'our dear and well-loved Jean-Baptiste Lully' lost no time in activating the new Académie Royale de Musique. The inaugural choice was a pastorale in three acts, *Les Fêtes de l'Amour et de Bacchus*, performed on 15 November 1672. Evidently thrown together in great haste, this pastiche of several earlier works shows no advance over the pastorales of Cambert. In fact, it is less developed from the dramatic point of view due to its lack of a consistent plot. According to the *Avant-Propos*, it was Quinault's task to 'connect these diverse fragments'; Vigarani was responsible for the decor and Des Brosses, for the ballets.

For Etienne Gros, *Les Fêtes de l'Amour et de Bacchus* 'marks the end of the pastorale in music rather than the advent of the *tragédie lyrique*' (*Philippe Quinault*, p. 517). He added that Lully did not favour the 'genre bucolique' and that while pastorale elements were dispersed in the prologues and *divertissements* of the *tragédies lyriques*, the 'pastorale in music disappeared from the stage of the Académie Royale de Musique' (*ibid.*).

Surely this is too harsh a judgment. Lully's final completed work, *Acis et Galathée* (1686), is a *pastorale héroïque*, a genre which also had particular appeal for Regency composers.[6] The third *intermède* of *Les Amants magnifiques* is a masterpiece totally in the 'genre bucolique' with Molière reducing the confusing pairs of lovers and rejected suitors often found in pastorales to one shepherd and one shepherdess. The *divertissement* in Act IV of the *tragédie lyrique Roland* is dramatically integrated into the plot and is effective precisely because it *is* a pastorale (see Chapter 7, pp. 75–76).

The pastorale in the generation between Lully and Rameau continued to play an important role in French opera. It was not by accident that Campra chose a pastorale to represent 'La France' in his *opéra-ballet L'Europe galante*. From the beginning of the pastorale, poets had used its maxims to comment on the social mores of their time. The musical pastorales found in the *opéras-ballets* of the Regency also make use of the unreal world of shepherd and shepherdess to illuminate the all too real world of the last days of Louis XIV and the Regency. An accusing finger is pointed at the innumerable intrigues and deceits that plagued the court at Versailles. In a simple air from Campra's *opéra-ballet Les Muses*, Silvi sings:

> Parmy les grandeurs de la Cour,
> A taire ses secrets, chacun sçait se contraindre;
> Mais, dans ce tranquile séjour,
> Nous n'aprenons point l'art de feindre.

The most famous dancers of the post-Lully operatic world were often given solo roles as shepherds and shepherdesses. In 1729 Le Sieur Dumoulin and Mlle Camargo, two of the most popular dancers of the period, were featured as 'berger et bergère' in Jean-Baptiste Quinault's *Les Amours des Déesses*; 18 years later the same pair starred as 'berger et bergère' in Mouret's *Les Amours des Dieux*.

In a brief summary of the literary pastorale, Joseph Mervesin in 1706 described how the French poets

> ... imitated the Italian and Spanish poets, learning from them how to compose *villanelles*; these are songs in which Shepherds and Shepherdesses speak with tenderness. They soon became very much *à la mode* and since that time have been used in France to express maxims of love, morality and all that is motivated by gentleness and tenderness.

> (*Histoire de la poésie françoise*, p. 137)

This summary serves also for the musical pastorale, for from the *Ballet comique de la Reine* to the beginnings of French opera, from the *tragédie lyrique* to the *opéra-ballet*, from the magic scenes in Rameau's *Dardanus* (1739) to the shepherd Lysis wearing his *carmagnole* and red turban in Grétry's *La Rosière républicaine* (1794), the pastorale is the Ariadne's thread of the French lyric theatre.

Chapter 7

⇥⇥⇥ ⇥⇥⇥

Tragédie Lyrique I: Dramatic Organization and Vocal Music

Avant toute sa pompe & son riche appareil,
La Musique en nos jours ne fait rien de pareil,
Ce bel Art tout divin par ces douces merveilles,
Ne se contente pas de charmer les oreilles,
N'y d'aller jusqu'au coeur par ces expressions,
Emouvoir à son gré toutes les passions.

(Perrault, *Le Siècle de Louis le Grand*)

The *Gazette de France* of 29 April 1673 described the first performance of the first *tragédie en musique* as follows:

> On the 27th, His Majesty, accompanied by Monsieur, Mlle and Mlle d'Orléans went to the Faubourg Saint-Germain to hear the *divertissement de l'Opéra* of the Académie Royale de Musique established by Sieur Batiste Lully, so celebrated in this Art; the group left very satisfied with this superb spectacle in which the Tragedy of Cadmus and of Hermione, a fine work by Sieur Quinault, was performed with machines and surprising decorations invented by Sieur Vigarani, gentleman of Modena.[1]

Thus, 92 years after the performance of the *Ballet comique de la Reine*, French stage music had come full circle. *Cadmus et Hermione* is a large-scale work which synthesized elements borrowed from the court ballet, pastoral, comedy and tragedy ballet, the machine tragedy and Italian opera and, at least in principle, subordinate all to an over-all dramatic unity. In so doing, it eclipsed the earlier attempts of Perrin and Cambert to establish a national opera. 'The *grand Opéra* of *Cadmus* that everyone wished to see', wrote De Tralage in 1687, 'made it easy to forget the operas of *Pomone* and *Les Peines et les Plaisirs de l'Amour'.*[2]

Cadmus opens with a French overture, familiar by 1673, followed in routine fashion of the day by an allegorical-political prologue. The Prologue, loosely based on Ovid (8th Fable of the *Metamorphoses*),

69

alludes to the successful conclusion of the Dutch wars. Shepherds and shepherdesses mix with nymphs and such pastoral deities as Pales, Melisse and the god Pan. 'Le Soleil' destroys the monstrous serpent, and the chorus sings 'Répandons le bruit de sa gloire, Jusques au bout de l'Univers'. The score informs us that the 'allegorical meaning of this subject is so clear that it is pointless to explain it'.

A pair of lovers, a powerful rival, and the critical mingling of gods in the affairs of their mortal protégés formed a ground plan that with minor variants served Quinault for all subsequent *livrets*. The conspicuous use of the chorus, Vigarani's spectacular machinery for the *merveilleux*, the inclusion of a *divertissement* of songs and dances in each act, the use of short binary and rondeau airs and the domination of the recitative illustrate how carefully Lully had 'built-in' a national style designed to please both court and academy.

Livret

From 1673 to 1687, the year of his death, Lully composed an annual opera[3] for which Quinault furnished 11 *livrets*. Each *livret* resulted from a three-fold collaboration between poet, composer and the French Academy. In spite of the generous 4,000 *livres* that Quinault received for each *livret*, there is evidence to suggest that the division of labour was far from equitable. Lecerf's comments illuminate what must have been a complex relationship between an intelligent, imperious composer and his more malleable librettist against the impersonal dicta of the French Academy.

> Quinault wrote out a plan of the action of the Piece. He gave one copy to Lully.... As soon as he had finished writing some scenes, he presented them to the *Académie Françoise*; after having profited by the judgments of the Academy, he brought the rewritten scenes to Lully ... who examined them word by word making further corrections and even cutting half the scene when he deemed it necessary. He sent *Phaëton* back 20 times and demanded that entire scenes be rewritten. Quinault, with Academy approval, had conceived of Phaëton as excessively harsh.... Lully wished Quinault to make Phaëton ambitious but not brutal.
>
> (*Comparaison*, II, pp. 196–98)

Although he rarely attended performances in Paris, the king became an enthusiastic partisan of opera. Mme de Maintenon, to whom the *galant* maxims of Quinault seemed a direct threat to Christian morality, conceded that Louis XIV was interested only in the beauty of the music and that, because of his pleasure in an air, he would go so far as to 'sing his own praises as though they had been written for another' (Ecorcheville, *Vingt Suites*, p. 27). He was said to have preferred *Atys* to all others, but he personally chose the subject matter for *Roland, Armide* and *Amadis*. The dedication found in the first edition of *Phaëton* (1683) suggests that the king's interest embraced even the *mise-en-scène*. Lully thanked his benefactor for having given some attention to all his worries even 'down to the costumes, one of the principal parts of this type of Spectacle'.

Most commonly, Quinault's *livrets* were judged first and foremost as poetry quite apart from any musical merit. The works were often referred to as Quinault's *tragédies en musique* or Quinault's *Opéra*.[4] In principle, there was no question but that poetry should be the dominant force no matter how modified to fit its lyric setting. '. . . Although the Musician may have more talent than the Poet; although by the force of his genius he may assure the success of an Opera, his art is regarded in France as always secondary to that of poetry. . .' (De Rochemont, *Réflexions d'un patriote sur l'opéra françois et sur l'opéra italien*, 1754, p. 25). The concept of operatic music's becoming popular *qua* music was similarly dismissed by Abbé Mably:

> . . . Some are still persuaded that the success of an Opera depends only upon the Music. . . . An excellent Poem is absolutely essential for the long range success of an Opera. The Music, considered by itself, can only have a passing vogue.
>
> (*Lettre à Madame la marquise de P. . . . sur l'Opéra*, 1741, p. 6)

In actuality as Saint-Evremond complained, 'one thinks 100 times more of Baptiste (Lully) than of Thésée or Cadmus' (*Sur les opéra*, p. 94), and although Quinault's verse was praised by many for its adaptability to music, Boileau, no friend to opera, found that it was the very weakness of the verses that 'rendered them suitable for the musician' (*Réflexions critiques*, No. III, 1694).

In the tight compartmentalization of dramatic genres characteristic of the *grand siècle*, there was no niche ready-made to accommodate the lyric tragedy. Gradually an aesthetic was developed that conceived of opera as having its own laws independent from tragedy and comedy. It must be emphasized, however, that this aesthetic was not accepted by all. Perrault wrote:

> The *Opéra* or *Pièce de Machines* not having been invented at the time of Horace, could hardly be subjected to laws made in his time. . . . Nothing is less bearable in a Comedy than to resolve the intrigue by a miracle or the arrival of a god in a machine; and nothing is more beautiful in Opera than these sorts of miracles and appearances of Divinities.
>
> (*Critique de l'Opéra*, 1674, pp. 69–70)

Ménestrier wrote that because opera was 'designed to please and divert rather than to instruct, one seeks there the *merveilleux* more than verisimilitude. It is for this reason that the machines and the extraordinary decorations are appropriate' (*Des Représentations en musique anciennes et modernes*, p. 170). For others, the idea of tragedy as a form of instruction was too strongly ingrained for them to accept any compromises. Samuel Chappuzeau admitted the 'agréable meslange' of Vigarani's machines, of dances and music, and then complained that these 'beautiful spectacles are only for the eyes and ears but do not touch the depths of the soul.... One can say that he has seen and heard but that he has not been instructed' (*Le Théâtre françois*, I, 1674, p. 53).

The *merveilleux* were rejected by such professional opera haters as Saint-Evremond, Boileau and La Bruyère. For the latter, machines were only 'amusements for children, appropriate for Marionettes' (*Des Ouvrages de l'Esprit*, 1688). Saint-Evremond, somewhat in the position of a secular latter-day Saint Augustine, admitted to having enjoyed the *merveilleux* and having been moved by the music of opera, but he was forced to conclude that as long as the mind went unchallenged, it was to no avail to flatter the ears or charm the eyes. 'It (opera) is nonsense. Nonsense', he added, 'filled with music, dance, with machines and decorations, a magnificent nonsense, but nonsense nonetheless' (*Sur les opéra*, p. 83).

The pre-eminent position of the *merveilleux* was not seriously challenged until the mid-eighteenth century when it became a natural focal point for the attacks of partisans of the Italian *opera buffa* who wished to banish 'the demons and the shades, and the fairies and the genii, and all the monsters...' from the stage.[5]

There was general agreement that the unities, those imperious handmaidens of classical drama, could be overlooked in opera if for no other reason than to justify the introduction of the *merveilleux*. However, Quinault was expected to observe unity of action. Few objected to the successive scene changes in *Isis* from the 'pleasant meadows' of Greece to the 'most frozen places of Scythia'. The scene changes in *Thésée* from a 'frightful desert' to an 'enchanted island' offended no one whereas the double intrigue between two minor characters, Arcas and Cléone, that paralleled the main action between Thésée and Aeglé, was 'un peu puérile' according to Rémond de Saint-Mard (*Réflexions sur les opéra*, 1741, p. 28).

Sacrificed to the demands of unity of action was the development of comic scenes along the lines of those found in *Cadmus, Alceste* and *Thésée*. This mixture of genres, a direct derivative of Roman and Venetian opera, was anathema to most academicians. The scene between Charon and the unfortunate shades who must pay tribute to cross the river Styx (*Alceste*, IV, 1) is as fine a piece of comic writing and sharp social satire as exists anywhere in French stage music. A remarkably fluid scene, it is constructed around three short, highly contrasted airs separated by *ritournelles*, dialogue recitatives and choral responses. The scene pivots around the second air in which Charon, singing only 'Donne, passe, donne, passe', resembles the ticket taker at a cinema box-office.

Such a scene forces the conclusion that, by silencing Lully's comic muse, official French taste delayed the development of any indigenous *opéra bouffe*. In fact, as late as 1715 many were scandalized when Mouret chose the stage of the Paris opera house as the setting of the prologue to his *opéra-ballet Les Fêtes de Thalie* and had the comic muse, Thalie, usurp the position of the tragic muse, Melpomène. (See Chapter 10, p. 138.)

Quinault's subject matter derived either from mythology (*Cadmus, Alceste, Isis, Atys, Persée, Proserpine, Thésée* and *Phaëton*) or from the familiar legends of chivalry (*Amadis, Armide, Roland*). The dramatic format of the *tragédie lyrique* remained fairly constant: the intrigue of an amorous couple and one or more rivals often including at least one god or goddess, a parallel intrigue involving personages of lesser rank, a complex system of confidants and followers. Gods and goddesses, magicians and enchantresses compete among themselves and interfere in mortal affairs. When these miraculous interventions bring about a dénouement, there is a resemblance to the later 'rescue opera'. Minerva arrives in Act v of *Thésée* just in time to break the spell of Médée, and the enchantress Urgande in *Amadis* appears in the nick of time to save Amadis and Oriane from the clutches of Arcabonne.

In time-honoured fashion most prologues are divorced from the subject matter of the tragedies. The prologue to *Thésée* jumps into its own time to take place before the palace of Versailles. The prologue to *Isis* glorifies the naval victories of Jean Bart and Duquesne, and that of *Persée* alludes to the king's victories in the Dutch wars. Perhaps towards the end of their collaboration, Lully and Quinault had thoughts of modifying the purely panegyric and decorative prologues and linking them closer to the dramas. In *Amadis* the two main characters of the prologue, Urgande and Alquif, also appear in the tragedy. The death of Amadis is mentioned and precipitates the fatuous comment that the destiny of the world now depends on a hero 'encore plus glorieux'.

The scenes of sacrifice, of combat, sleep scenes, funeral ceremonies and the evocation of monsters, serpents and furies all stem from a variety of sources including dramatic pastorals, court ballets and Italian opera. Quinault was not averse to 'borrowing' Abbé Buti's dancing statues (*Ercole amante*) for his second act of *Cadmus*. However, in giving the whole a greater dramatic unity and in conceiving of the *divertissement* as a possible dramatic agent, Quinault 'nationalized' these heterogeneous and 'baroque' elements.

There is little that is genuinely heroic or tragic in a Quinault *livret*. The famous monologue from Act II of *Armide* ('Enfin il est en ma puissance') was the subject of much contemporary comment precisely because it is a unique example of heightened dramatic intensity achieved by the perfect union of text and music. Only in some of the later operas did Quinault emphasize the more tragic and heroic elements inherent in his subjects. The conflict between 'gloire et devoir' on the one hand and 'amour' on the other is the dramatic core of *Roland* and *Armide*. The political implications for the nobility of this Corneillian theme were of sufficient importance to receive full didactic treatment in each prologue:

> *Du célèbre Roland renouvellons l'Histoire.*
> *La France luy donna le jour.*
> *Montrons les erreurs ou l'Amour peut engager*
> *   un coeur qui néglige la Gloire.*
>
> —Roland

> *Nous y verrons Renaud malgré la volupté,*
> *Suivre un conseil fidèle & sage,*
> *Nous le verrons sortir du Palais enchanté,*
> *Où par l'amour d'Armide il étoit arresté,*
> *Et voler où la gloire appelle son courage.*
>
> —Armide

The amorous intrigues of gods and men are generally more *galant* than heroic in tone, a condition which precipitated many of the later attacks on Quinault's operas by the clergy and the conservative Sorbonne. Ironically, Quinault himself apparently succumbed to this repressive moral climate. After *Armide* he retired from the stage and wrote a long poem on the extinction of heresy in the realm which begins:

> *Je n'ai que trop chanté les Jeux & les Amours*
> *Sur un ton plus sublime, il faut me faire entendu:*
> *Je vous dis adieu, Muse tendre*
> *Je vous dis adieu, pour toujours.*

Musico-Dramatic Organization

The *divertissements* of their *tragédies lyriques* had two functions for Lully and Quinault. First, a decorative, but non-essential and dramatically neutral ornament; and second, a decorative but integral part of the dramatic action itself. These functions could be, but were

74

not necessarily, mutually exclusive. Both shared the spectacle of dance, chorus, songs and machines. In a sense this double function of the *divertissement* is an amalgamation of the *ballet mélodramatique* and *ballet à entrées* under the protective canopy of the *tragédie lyrique*. The second function is a feature of the musico-dramatic organization of the *tragédie lyrique* too often overlooked or minimized by contemporary scholars. During the *grand siècle* and much of the eighteenth century, this Lullian fusion of the arts, a virtual pre-Wagnerian *Gesamtkunstwerk*, was often cited as a model to be emulated.

Lully had learned much from his long association with Molière, and his own court ballets show close liaison between dance and intrigue, but there was no purely operatic model for composer and librettist to follow. The alignment of dance with action in the Italian operas performed during the time of Mazarin was sporadic, and it is unlikely that Lully had any knowledge of the dramatic 'wholeness' of the operas of Monteverdi. 'There were no written rules', wrote the librettist, Pierre-Charles Roy, who continued:

> If only Quinault had followed the example of the great Corneille and left us some reflections on the art he invented and perfected. . . . We must tear from Quinault his secret and by analysis of his dramatic art, we must *décomposer* all his operas in order to examine the inner workings, the development of the intrigue . . . in order to appreciate the skill with which his expositions always turning around a clear action . . . in order to sense the liaisons of *divertissement* and intrigue. . . .
>
> (Lettre sur l'Opéra in vol. ii of
> Lettres sur quelques écrits de ce tems, Geneva 1749)

Perhaps the most notable example of a *divertissement* that combines both functions of spectacle and dramatic agent is the 'village wedding' encompassing scenes 3 to 5 of Act IV of *Roland*. This even won the approbation of Grimm and was considered by Marmontel as a masterpiece 'unique in this genre' ('Pantomime' in *Eléments de littérature*, 1787). The *divertissement* is anticipated in scene 2 where Roland wanders alone in a secluded glade looking for his beloved Angelique. He hears the distant sounds of a 'musique champestre' composed of a *trio des hautbois* (two oboes plus a bassoon) which is actually the trio of the minuet to be heard in its entirety in the following scene. Scene 3 is the 'Nopces de Village', a pastoral *divertissement* including a march, chorus, minuet, dance songs and *entrées* of shepherds and shepherdesses. In scene 4, two shepherds sing a duo commenting on the happy departure of the bridal pair identified as Angelique and Médor. By means of this innocent revelation, Roland confirms the identity of his rival and his betrayal by his mistress.

The contrast between the mounting anger of the distraught hero and the bucolic levity of the *fête* is heightened in scene 5 where the chorus 'Bénissons l'Amour d'Angelique, Bénissons l'Amour de Médor' is interrupted by Roland's cries, 'Taisez-vous, malheureux'. The pastoral mood is shattered, and the end of the *divertissement* 'Ah fuyons, fuyons tous' merges with Roland's 'vengeance' air, 'Je suis trahi' of scene 6. The act ends on a note of despair with the accompanied recitative 'Ah! Je suis descendu dans la nuit du tombeau'. Lully's scheme of tonalities throws this conflict of mood into high relief. The act opens in C-Major and closes in B-flat-Major. Scene 4, the critical scene dramatically, also serves as a harmonic pivot, shifting the tonality from C-Major to B-flat through the Dominant minor key of G.

In most instances, however, the *divertissement* is used to sustain a prevailing mood rather than to contrast two opposing moods. This is true of the bellicose, military-type *divertissements* with trumpet and drum of *Thésée, Bellérophon, Cadmus,* and *Amadis,* described so vividly by La Fontaine:

> *Ses concerts d'instrumens ont le*
> *bruit du tonnerre,*
> *Et ses concerts de voix ressemblent*
> *aux éclats.*
> *Qu'en jour du combat font les cris*
> *des soldats.*

> (*Epître à M. de Niert,* 1677)

It is true of the *divertissement* in Act III (scenes 4 to 8) of *Thésée* in which the 'habitans des Enfers' are catapulted into the action to dramatize the power of Medée against her rival, Aeglé. It is true of the 'Sommeil' from *Atys* and the impressive funeral cortèges of *Psyché* and *Amadis.* In the 'Pompe Funèbre' of *Alceste* (Act III, Scenes 5 and 6), prelude and dramatic symphony substitute for titled dances, and the chorus of 'femmes affligées' and 'hommes désolez' acts out its grief in pantomime.

Following a dramatic composer's natural inclination, Lully often used a *divertissement* to conclude his opera in a blaze of spectacle and sound. This practice was not universally admired, and even an arch supporter such as Lecerf characterized as a 'malheur' those operas such as *Amadis, Persée, Atys* or *Acis et Galathée* that end with 'a *divertissement,* a chaconne, or passacaille'. For contrast, he singled out the final act of *Armide*: 'there is nothing so perfect. It is an Opera in itself. The *divertissement* occurs at the mid-point and leaves the attention of the listener free for the events which follow'. By virtue of its contrast, its economy, and its directness of action, this act deserves the approbation accorded it during the eighteenth century.

The recall of previously used musical material is a musico-dramatic device employed by Lully that has gone unnoticed. Although used sparingly and generally in a non-systematic manner, this primitive leitmotiv technique undoubtedly served as a model for further development at the hands of such *préramiste* composers as Campra and Mouret.

A short vocal phrase of distinctive melodic shape, a 'motto' *ritournelle* or a choral fragment may be subject to later recall. In *Thésée* the refrain 'Revenez, Revenez, Amours revenez' from Venus's air in the prologue is first stated in the *ritournelle* and is interpolated within the recitative that follows the air. In the same opera, a fragment of the chorus 'Il faut périr, Il faut vaincre ou mourir' first used in Act I, scene 1 penetrates Aeglé's recitative in scene 2 and is used at the conclusion of both scenes 3 and 5.

In Act I of *Atys*, the opening *ritournelle* generates much of the ensemble music of scenes 1 to 3. In *Persée*, the entire first scene of Act V is organized around Mérope's opening phrase 'O Mort! Venez finir mon destin déplorable'. In Act I of *Alceste*, the choral fragment 'Vivez, vivez, heureux Epoux' in scene 1 is interlaced with recitatives and recurs in scene 6 of the same act.

Act III of Alceste illustrates the most systematic use of musical recall in the operas of Lully. Each scene builds to the 'Pompe funèbre' of scenes 5 and 6. Each scene is effectively organized around a few short ensemble or choral fragments which recur between *ritournelles*, recitatives and short airs. The fragment 'Alceste est morte' from scene 4 was often parodied and is certainly the source for Rameau's similar 'Hippolyte n'est plus' from Act IV, scene 4 of *Hippolyte et Aricie*.

Example 11
(*a*) Alceste, III, *4* (*after ed. of 1708*). (*b*) Hippolyte, IV, *4* (*after Ballard Ms ed. of 1742*).

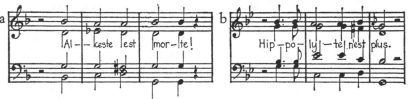

Related to musical recall is Lully's exploitation of an ostinato bass-line pattern as a means of musical organization. In *Persée*, dialogue airs between Mérope and Andromède are built over the same chaconne bass. In this instance the musical and dramatic function of the bass coincide and mirror the meaning of the text 'Unissons nos regrets, le même amour nous lie'.

In his last three operas, Lully employed a chaconne or passacaille

bass pattern to create an inner musical unity for an entire scene. In
Roland much of scene 4 of Act II is composed of a series of dialogue
airs built over a chaconne pattern. In the *divertissement* of the
final act of *Armide*, a passacaille serves as the organizational source
for the entire scene. It generates three songs, a dance and three
choruses and is dramatically silenced by Renaud's recitative 'Allez,
éloignez-vous de moy' that terminates the scene. Finally, in his last
complete opera, *Acis et Galathée*, Lully used a chaconne (Act II) and
passacaille (Act III) to generate solos, ensembles and choruses.

Solo Voice Distribution

All soloists at the Académie Royale de Musique were known as *acteurs*
and *actrices pour les rolles*. Solo parts were identified as the *parties
récitants* to distinguish them from the *parties du choeur*. Lecerf sum-
marizes the association of vocal range with dramatic role as follows:

> A third of the leading roles in the Operas of Lully are those of
> ordinary tenors ('simple tailles'); Our women are always women:
> our basses sing the roles of Kings, Magicians, solemn and older
> Heroes, and our tenors and counters tenors . . . are the young,
> *galant* Heroes and amorous Gods. . . .
>
> *(Comparaison*, II, p. 112)

Evidence from the scores themselves and from contemporary references to performers, however, make it difficult to sustain Lecerf's comments regarding the percentages of roles assigned to 'simple tailles'.
The majority of the leading roles for high male voice in the operas of
Lully are written in the alto clef, the normal clef for the counter-
tenor, although, to be sure, Brossard identified this clef (as well as the
tenor clef) as appropriate for the 'Hautes ou Premières Tailles'. Singers
such as Clédière and Du Mesny, who sang leading roles in *Alceste*,
Thésée, *Bellérophon*, *Proserpine*, *Persé* and *Acis et Galathée*, were normally described as counter-tenors. 'Du Mesny', wrote Parfaict, 'had the
voice of a very high tenor ('haute-taille') which enabled him to pass for
a counter-tenor ('haute-contre'). It is certain that, no matter what
Lully's intention may have been, eighteenth-century revivals of his
operas used only the counter-tenor voice in the leading roles for high
male voices.[6]

The royal ordinance issued at Versailles on 11 January 1713, which
gives the annual salary in *livres* for the first, second and third lead
singers at the Opera, is a measure of a long-standing tradition of the
French lyric stage. The favoured high male voice was the counter-
tenor as seen in the table below (adapted from Durey de Noinville,

Histoire du Théâtre); judging from the salary scale and the distribution of leading roles, however, the bass was equally favoured. The table clearly exposes the subordinate role of Lecerf's 'simple tailles' in French classical opera; there is no subdivision into a first and second singer, and both tenors received less money than the lowest paid soprano!

Table 1

Annual salary in livres *for the first, second, and third* acteurs *and* actrices pour les rolles

Acteurs pour les Rolles	Actrices pour les Rolles
Basses-tailles (basses)	Dessus (sopranos)
1 à 1500	1 à 1500
1 à 1200	1 à 1200
1 à 1000	1 à 1000
	1 à 900
Haute-contres (counter-tenors)	1 à 800
1 à 1500	1 à 700
1 à 1200	
1 à 1000	
Tailles (tenors)	
1 à 600	
1 à 600	

The contralto voice is absent from the *actrices des rolles* in this table. The role of Clorinde in André Campra's *tragédie lyrique Tancrède* (1702) is exceptional and was created by the composer to capitalize on the celebrated low notes of Mlle Maupin.

In terms of preferred vocal timbre and range, there was obviously a great difference between French and Italian taste in the period from Lully to Gluck. Rousseau wrote:

> In France, where the bass and the counter-tenor are preferred and where one makes no use of the contralto (*bas-dessus*), variation is possible in the male voice, but there is only one female voice; in Italy, where they make as much use of a good contralto as they do of a higher voice, . . . there is only one characteristic male voice.
>
> (*Dictionnaire*, p. 545)

Although one may concur with Masson that the French concept 'remains more dramatic than the Italian' (*L'Opéra de Rameau*, p. 261), the tradition that rejected the contralto brought about a convention almost as bizarre as that of the castrato. In almost every instance in the generations following Lully, those nurses and confidantes, ideally designed for the contralto voice, were given to the counter-tenor. (See, for example, the role of Nérine in 'L'Amour saltimbanque' from Campra's *Les Fêtes vénitiennes.*)

Recitative

The central position of recitative in French opera from its inception in Lully throughout the eighteenth century is amply attested to by many contemporary sources. Le Brun wrote for many when he expressed horror at the thought of those 'capricious and ignorant ones' who would destroy the recitative. 'Without recitative,' he questioned, 'how is it possible to expose and develop a dramatic situation?' (*Théâtre lyrique*, 1712, p. 18.)

Recitatives from Lully to Gluck most clearly differentiate French from Italian opera. The careful distinction found in Italy between *recitativo secco* and the aria did not exist in France where lines of demarcation blur. There, the recitative was nourished by the restrained melodic patterns of the air, and the air never completely abandoned the declamatory bias of the recitative. 'Our recitative sings too much; our airs, not enough', wrote de Blainville (*L'Esprit de l'art musical*, 1754, p. 52).

As we have seen, Lully was well on his way to creating a convincing French declamatory style in music before he began his visits to the Comédie Française to hear La Champmesle declaim the lines of Racine. Certainly because of this exposure, the composer attempted to render in music the declamatory practices in vogue at the theatre. There is some reason to believe that the Alexandrine couplets of Racine's verse may have approached a musical line in La Champmesle's performance. If Abbé Dubos' description is accurate, Racine himself instructed his mistress to 'lower the pitch of her voice in pronouncing the following lines (from *Mithridate*) in order to be able to reach a tone one octave above easily . . .' (*Réflexions critiques*, III, p. 144).[7] In any case, declamatory practices grafted on to the recitative by Lully remained sacrosanct throughout much of the eighteenth century.

When Lully adhered too rigidly in his recitative to the anapestic rhythms and the two symmetrical hexameters of the French Alexandrine, the result is monotonous. The following example from *Alceste* shows the most routine application of this declamatory principle.

One way to break up this symmetry was to introduce a changing number of feet per line. This in turn necessitated the use of fluctuating metres to assure that the important accented syllables—particularly the last syllable of the line—would fall on the first beat of the measure. 'The recitative has neither a uniform rhythm nor melody', wrote Marmontel, 'it is ruled exclusively by the caesura and the text phrases' ('Récitatif' in Diderot, *Encyclopédie*). Curiously, in spite of its shifting metres, this type of recitative was called unmeasured by the French, the better to distinguish it from the Italian recitative which was 'measured' throughout by the use of a single metre sign.

Example 12
Lully: Extract from recitative, Alceste (after ed. of 1708).

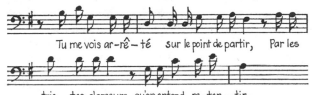

There remains some confusion over the exact metrical relationships to be observed between the constantly shifting meters of French Baroque recitative. Michel de Saint-Lambert in his *Les Principes du clavecin* (Paris, 1702) and Etienne Loulié in the manuscript supplement to his *Eléments ou Principes de musique* (Paris, 1696) clearly document the principle that 'the time value of a beat in one meter should be equal to that of a beat in the other (meter), even though the note values are not the same' (Loulié). That is, that a quarter note in C equals a half note in ₵.

There is some evidence that, as long as the 'built-in' conditions of correct prosody were respected, there was little attempt made to force rhythmically precise rendering of the recitative in performance. Grimarest commented that during the most dramatic moments of a recitative 'one must not beat time, because the Actor must be the master of his song and allow it to conform to his expression' (*Traité du récitatif*, 1707, p. 196).

During Lully's lifetime his recitative was probably performed crisply—'quickly without appearing bizarre' (Lecerf). Unlike eighteenth-century performances, little ornamentation was used. Lecerf quoted Lully as stating 'no embellishments; my recitative is made only for speaking'.

The *récitatif simple* or *ordinaire* is the most common type of recitative found in the operas of Lully. Characterized by changing metres, it was generally used along with short dialogue airs to expedite the action, and it is accompanied only by the basso continuo. 'In the *récitatif ordinaire*', wrote Chastellux, 'the Musician must not be concerned about charming the ear.' He noted three characteristics of this type of recitative which remained constant from Lully until Gluck: '1. It must not employ a constant rhythm or metre; 2. It must not make use of an accompaniment that in a natural and rapid dialogue would prevent the comprehension of the text; and 3. It must not tire the actor by exploiting his most brilliant vocal sounds' (*Essai sur l'union de la poésie et de la musique*, 1765, pp. 21–2).

Beginning with *Atys*, his recitative becomes more expressive, more fluid and better able to mirror the text without sacrificing the laws of prosody. Example 13 below presents several recitative fragments from the later operas of Lully. Yet despite the greater flexibility, increase in range and more deliberate attempts to dramatize the text (see, for example, the rare use by Lully of text painting in the *Proserpine* extract), much even of his later *récitatif ordinaire* seems to lack spontaneity and genuine dramatic sense. The 'filled-in' descending melodic diminished 7th becomes a cliché formula generally serviceable for the most impassioned outbursts, and what composer with a natural gift for dramatic expression would have sanctioned the neutralizing effect of two descending diminished 7th chords from the same pitch level within as many measures?

Example 13
(a) Atys (*after ed. of 1689*). (b) Bellérophon (*after ed. of 1679*).
(c) Proserpine (*after ed. of 1680*). (d) Armide (*after ed. of 1686*).

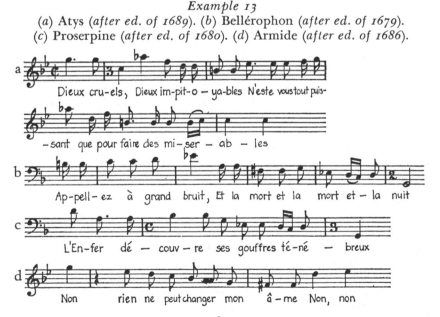

At its best, Lully's *récitatif ordinaire* both stimulates action and defines character. In the great monologue from *Armide* (ii, 5, reprinted in *GMB*, pp. 318–21), Armide's inner conflict is rendered by music and not seen merely in terms of standard seventh-century declamatory practice. Here, the use of rests is not only a result of text caesurae, but more important, is a means of dramatizing Armide's hesitation and confusion. Here, too, wider melodic profile and greater awareness of harmony produce a telling dramatic effect.

The eighteenth century rightfully considered this scene as a model for the best in French recitative. Rameau printed the entire monologue in his *Nouveau système de musique théorique* (1726, pp. 80–90), used it again in his *Observations sur notre instinct pour la musique* (1754, pp. 69–122) to combat Rousseau's criticism of French recitative and finally, in his *Code de musique pratique* (1760, pp. 168–70), he included a detailed harmonic analysis of its opening measures.

Armide's monologue was also considered a testing ground for the performer. If we may accept Titon du Tillet's description, few could equal the performance of Mlle Marie Rochois who created the role in 1686.

> When she began to move and sing, she alone dominated the stage. This struck me above all in the opera *Armide*, in which she played the greatest, the most powerful role in our Opera. . . . What rapture to see her in the 5th scene of the 2nd Act—sword in hand ready to pierce the breast of Renaud. . . . Rage animated her features, love took possession of her heart; first one then the other acted upon her in turn. . . . What true and beautiful poses! How many different movements and expressions in her eyes and on her face during this monologue of 29 lines. . . . One can say that it is the greatest piece in all our Opera and the most difficult to perform well. . . .
>
> (*Le Parnasse françois, pp.* 790–93)

Lully's musical inventiveness may be seen to best advantage in his concept of the accompanied recitative (*récitatif obligé*) first found in *Bellérophon*. During these moments, textual declamation, while not neglected, is subordinated to a heightened musical expression. The accompanied recitative borrows from the air its greater melodic amplitude and often its tighter musical organization. The orchestra is an ever-present background which, after establishing the mood in a *ritournelle* or prelude, freely interpenetrates the recitative itself.

The second scene of Act iv of *Roland* and the third scene of Act ii of *Armide* are composed entirely of long accompanied recitatives with the orchestra having prime importance as a mood determinant. The difference between accompanied air and accompanied recitative becomes more and more difficult to define. As if to confound classification, there are extended passages of accompanied recitative that lack the typical metre fluctuation of simple French recitative. Often reserved for the most expressive or dramatic moments, this type of recitative is a musical hybrid for which there is no adequate term in French. At the time of Rameau, it was classified as a 'récitatif mesuré'. Perhaps the Italian term 'arioso', already defined by Brossard as 'in the same *mouvement* as though singing an air', is the most appropriate term.

In *Amadis* the orchestra is the main protagonist in the accompanied recitatives sung by the magician Arcalaus (ii, 3) and the enchantress Arcabonne (iii, 2, end of scene). In both instances strong rhythms and upbeat *tirades* borrowed from the French overture are used to characterize the supernatural powers of the magicians. Such scenes are the point of departure for the magician Ismenor's accompanied recitative at the beginning of Act ii of Rameau's *Dardanus*.[8]

Air

The lack of clear distinctions between the recitative and air in French classical opera is nowhere better illustrated than in the following description in Carlo Goldoni's *Mémoires* of his first visit to the Académie Royale de Musique:

> I waited for the aria. . . . The dancers appeared: I thought the act was over, not an aria. I spoke of this to my neighbour who scoffed at me and assured me that there had been six arias in the different scenes which I had just heard. How could this be? I am not deaf; the voice was always accompanied by instruments . . . but I assumed it was all recitative.
>
> (*Mémoires*, iii, 1787, p. 38)

Similar was the reaction of Quantz who, in summing up impressions of his visit to France during 1726–27, wrote: 'Their recitatives sing too much, and their arias, too little, so that it is not always possible to divine in their operas whether a recitative or an arioso is being heard.'[9]

The air found in French opera from Lully to Rameau owes nothing to Italy. It was born of the *air de cour* and nurtured in the court and comedy ballets. Lully learned from Lambert, who may have learned from François Richard, François de Chancy and others, how to organize a small 'scene' around a series of short dialogue airs. As early as 1637 in Richard's *Airs de cour avec la tablature de luth* there is such a miniature 'scene' ('Cloris attends un peu') which even culminates in an 'operatic' duo.

Ménestrier, writing only eight years after *Cadmus*, unequivocally stated that the dialogues of Lambert, Boësset, Camus and others served as models for what he called 'Musique d'action & de Théâtre' (*Des Représentations en musique*). In order to illustrate how such 'petites chansons' prefigure the operatic dialogue airs, he quoted the text of a dialogue between Silvie and Tyrsis by Lambert.

From Lully to Gluck, the French operatic air may be classified by function into four main types: the dialogue air, the monologue air, the maxim air and the dance song (see Masson, *L'Opéra de Rameau*, pp. 202–37). A further classification may be made on the basis of formal structure. Most are in the tradition of short binary and rondeau airs, with the binary structure far outnumbering the rondeau. In some binary airs, Parts A and B are approximately the same length with both parts or either one repeated. Others are in the binary formal design first noted in Lully's comedy ballets (see Chapter 5, p. 56) in which Part B includes a textual but not a musical repetition of the last two lines of poetry. In no other air structure is the alliance between binary dance and binary air so clearly revealed. Both share the characteristically longer Part B, itself subdivided by means of a 'secondary' cadence in a related key.

The dialogue air was skilfully used by Lully as a substitute for recitative. Entire scenes were constructed around short dialogue airs interlaced with recitatives. Thus, the first scene of Act 1 of *Amadis* is organized around seven dialogue airs that sum up the various types of binary and rondeau airs found in all French opera until Rameau.

Because of the shortness of the dialogue air, there is little chance for genuine characterization. The strength of 'affective' intervals placed at the beginning of a phrase tends to dissipate rapidly in what is too often a routine cadence formula (see Example 14 below). This is certainly due to the characteristic use of short-breathed vocal lines with a syllabic treatment of text and the concomitant avoidance of melismas that might give more amplitude to the vocal line. The continuo reflects this practice in rapid modulations to closely related keys achieved by short, stereotyped cadential progressions.

Example 14
Lully: *Beginning of Idas' air, 'Amants qui vous plaignez', Atys (after ed. of 1689).*

The static, monologue air was reserved for moments of deep feeling when the 'actor is alone and speaks only with himself' (Rousseau). In function if not in style, it approaches most closely the Italian aria, although in French opera it usually introduces a scene, and in Italian opera, the scene builds towards the aria. It is based on a single 'affection' and is normally accompanied by the orchestra which gave Lully a legitimate opportunity to exploit such purely musical devices as long 'motto' preludes and instrumental interludes.

The celebrated monologue air 'Bois épais' (*Amadis*, ii, 4) is a simple binary air with each part repeated and introduced by a lengthy prelude. Its source may be traced back to the many elegiac court airs, and it is one of the few Lully melodies that has the melodic refinement and naturalness of the best airs of Moulinié, of Antoine Boësset or of Michel Lambert.

Much has been conjectured concerning the influence of Lambert on the formation of his son-in-law's vocal style. Certainly the relationship was a close one, and Lully appeared to have had genuine respect for the older man's musical attainments. As is so often the case, it is conceivable that the influence worked both ways. The monologue 'Atys est trop heureux' (*Atys*, i, 4), interspersed with recitatives and constructed over a chaconne bass, may well have been the source for Lambert's 'Ma Bergère est tendre et fidelle' from his collection of court airs of 1689.

Freer in form than 'Bois épais' and closely modelled on the accompanied recitative is Renaud's monologue 'Plus j'observe ces lieux' from *Armide* (ii, 3).[10] The long prelude, based on an 8th note accompaniment figure that also dominates the air, must be played with mutes and is one of Lully's most enchanting 'nature' scenes.

Most maxim airs make general observations and practical comments on the art of amorous dalliance. Normally sung by secondary characters, they relate more to lovers' intrigues at court than to the mythological personages on stage; they may be considered, therefore, as a commentary upon the *galant* mores of the *grand siècle*. In this they are like the old *vers* of the court ballet. It is not surprising that Mme de Montespan recognized herself in the character of jealous Junon in *Isis* and because of this brought about a temporary halt in the collaboration between Quinault and Lully.

Such *galant* sentiments as 'mais la pluspart des Amants sont sujet à faire bien des faux sermens' (*Thésée*, i, 5) or 'Mais rien n'est si charmant qu'une inconstance mutuelle' (*Thésée*, ii, 2) incurred the enmity of the clergy and the conservative professors of the Sorbonne who in the late seventeenth century mounted their attacks against 'tous ces lieux communs de Morale lubrique, Que Lully rechauffa des sons de sa musique' (Boileau, *Satire* x, 1692). Bossuet railed against 'corruption reduced to maxims . . . in the operas of Quinault with all their false tenderness and misleading invitations to enjoy one's youth . . .' (*Maximes et réflexions sur la comédie*, 1694). Mme de Maintenon contemplated the bad effects of continual exposure to the 'detestable maxims' found in operatic airs.[11] It did not seem to matter that sprinkled throughout Quinault's poetry were also moral maxims such as 'Un hymen qui peut plaire, Ne coûte guère. . . . Rien n'est plus aisé que de faire Un époux d'un amant aimé' (*Alceste*, 11,1). Nor did it matter that 'Perseus teaches us to respect the Gods; Phaeton teaches us to moderate our ambition, Alceste is an example of the duties of conjugal love' (Le Brun, *Théâtre lyrique*, p. 23).

The dance songs in Lully's *tragédies lyriques* form part of each *divertissement*. It is a truism that they constitute the clearest example of the close alliance between dance and song. Their roots lie in the *brunettes*, the *airs tendres* and in the many airs based on dance rhythms found in the collections of seventeenth century *airs de cour*.

Lully had learned how to use his dances as models for dance songs in the *comédie-ballet*. In the *tragédie lyrique* as in the *comédie-ballet*, the simplest treatment is an addition of text to a direct repetition of the instrumental dance. There are, however, several examples of dance songs in which the dance model is freely varied in the vocal version. This often leads to a subtle, well-developed paraphrase technique. Lully accomplished this through altering the phrase structure by contraction or elongation or by retaining the model's phrase grouping and rhythmic structure but changing the melodic and/or harmonic organization.

On occasion there is a reversal of the 'normal' procedure, and the dance song itself becomes the model. The prologue of *Cadmus* closes with a minuet which is an instrumental version of a preceding dance song and chorus.

Vocal Ensembles

The duo was long the favoured small vocal ensemble in French opera. It did not come under direct criticism until a later generation when, spearheaded by Grimm and Rousseau, an attack was levelled against the 'unnaturalness' of the duo. According to Rousseau, 'Nothing is less natural than to see two people speaking at the same time'. This allegation is comparable to the attacks on the use of song instead of speech by Saint-Evremond, Boileau, Fénelon and by La Bruyère who also laboured the obvious by claiming that it was not 'natural' to die singing. In all such comments the critics were judging opera, which by its very nature is 'unnatural', by the standards reserved for spoken drama.

The duo reached French opera by the same route as the air. There are dialogues which include duos in many court air collections, and the duo was employed in pastorales, court and comedy ballets.

In the operas of Lully the duos range from brief fragments and simple strophic dance songs or maxim airs to a duo-air-recitative complex that may dominate an entire scene. Most are strictly homophonic with the points of imitation found often at the beginning of phrases—a type of sham polyphony that by the second measure has already stabilized into a note-against-note style. This lack of polyphony is consistent with a 'word-born' style and predictably dominates all ensemble writing in Lully's operas.

Chorus

Along with dance, the chorus had been an important part of French stage music since the *Ballet comique de la Reine*. In the panegyric prologues of court ballets and the spectacular finales of many comedy and tragedy ballets, it served an essentially decorative function.

In the *tragédie lyrique*, in addition to being the crowning embellishment of the *divertissement*, the chorus also could be involved in the dramatic action either as a direct participant or as a passive commentator.

There is a vivid description of an attacking monster and the attempts to escape him in the chorus 'Toute est perdue' from *Bellérophon*. Metre changes in themselves generate tempo changes thereby creating exciting musical contrast. This is intensified by orchestral interjections that overlap but do not coincide with the chorus, resulting in a rare use of independent, non-doubling orchestral accompaniment (see Example 15).

In Act IV, scene 4 of *Atys*, the chorus witnesses the murder of Sangaride by Atys, and its haunting refrain 'Atys, Atys luy même Fait périr ce qu'il aime' comments on the deed in the manner of an ancient Greek chorus. Act III of *Isis* is almost entirely made up of choruses, some of which employ antiphonal and echo devices. Chorus and orchestra with trumpets and drums combine in the 'Choeur des Combatans' from *Thésée* (I, 1) in which the primitive use of speech rhythms and repeated notes creates an impressive, bellicose sound-painting.

Choral fragments made up of cries of exhortation or supplication are everywhere in evidence. Along with bits of ensemble, recitatives and short airs, they virtually deny the use of any closed musical forms and make difficult the definition of structural divisions. As fragments, they are elements in a scene complex in which they are subordinated to the dramatic flow. They illustrate the dramatist in Lully dominating the musician. The 'through-composed' as opposed to the 'set piece' concept in organizing an operatic scene shows Lully making a virtue of his limitations. That he accomplished what he did in the creation of French opera was due more to superior musical intelligence than to natural, spontaneous musical genius. The long, non-functional choruses of the *divertissements* and the sung 'chaconnes' (see, for example, the finale of *Amadis*), like the sustained choruses of the *grands motets*, are too often repetitive and monotonous.

Example 15
Lully: Extract from chorus, 'Toute est perdue', Bellérophon (after ed. of 1679).

French operatic chorus from Lully to Rameau was divided into a *grand* and a *petit choeur*—a concept based on the *coro concertato* and *coro ripieno* division of much seventeenth century religious choral writing. The *petit choeur*, described by Brossard as a chorus of the best singers, used less than four vocal parts. Trio texture was favoured, and the combination of two sopranos and a counter-tenor became the norm. Indeed, the *Encyclopédie* definition states firmly that the *petit choeur* 'is composed only of three parts; namely, two sopranos and the counter-tenor. . . .'

The composition of the *grand choeur* scarcely varied in seventeenth and eighteenth century French choral writing. The male voices included counter-tenor, tenor and bass; the female, only the soprano. This disposition of voices had already occurred in the early *Miserere* (1664) of Lully and in most of the large choruses of the court ballets. When in the *grands motets* the texture thickened to five voices, the added part was normally a baritone.

The disproportion resulting from this domination by male voices is a musical fact of life which must be faced in modern editions and performances of French choral music of the period. It indicates the lack of interest in the contralto voice in France. Modern substitution of a female alto for the counter-tenor is no solution, for in fact the 'softer' blend achieved by an alto is a distinct distortion of the penetrating, shrill quality, the 'voix aiguë', of the counter-tenor. A possible compromise suggested by some modern editors is the use of at least one tenor singing in falsetto among the contraltos.[12]

Predictably, the texture of most Lully choruses is homophonic; rigid note-against-note, syllabic choral writing, when doubled by the orchestra, gives a massive sound complex appropriate for the many apotheoses to 'Louis le plus parfait des Roys'. There are brief excursions into the neighbourhood of polyphony which never achieve the inner tension and independent part writing necessary in true polyphony. These few measures when they do occur are the result of the use of certain words ('volez', 'fuyons', 'brillez', 'coulez', etc.) rendered musically by an extended melisma that invites imitative treatment.

The routine and often dull part-writing in some choral and instrumental extracts from Lully's operas may be explained by his use of students to fill in the inner voices, although Lecerf insisted that 'Lully himself composed all the parts of his principal choruses and important Duos, Trios and Quartets'. He added, however, that outside of these large pieces, Lully 'only composed the treble and the bass and left for his *Secrétaires* the inner parts. However, when the chorus was fugal, Lully always marked the entrances. . . (*Comparaison*, II, p. 119).

It is difficult to fix the exact number of musicians who sang in the opera chorus at any given time. One can say with certitude that the number proliferated during the eighteenth century and ranged from a chorus of 15 in the earliest days of the Académie d'Opéra to 50 in 1778. Royal Ordinances and printed *livrets* are the source of most of the available information. The chorus of the Académie Royale de Musique in 1713, according to the Royal Ordinance of that year, included 22 men and 12 women (Durey de Noinville, *Histoire du Théâtre*, I, p. 120). This probably did not represent maximum strength, however, as Article 21 adds that 'All the actors and actresses, with the exception of those who hold the 8 *premiers rôles*, must sing in the chorus'.

There seems to be unanimity of opinion in most contemporary sources with regard to the importance of the chorus in French classical opera. It is the one point of agreement between the partisans of French and Italian opera. Even Rousseau, in his letter to Grimm written in 1750 three years before the much better known *Lettre sur la musique française*, admonishes the Italians because of their lack of a genuine chorus: 'Those little choruses, which are sung only by the principal performers, are not worthy of the name' (quoted by Albert Jansen, *Jean-Jacques Rousseau als Musiker*, Berlin, 1884, pp. 445–63).

The same observation was made by Lecerf almost 50 years earlier when he wrote: 'Those marvellous opera companies in Venice, Naples and Rome consist of seven or eight voices' (*Comparaison*, II, p. 75).

Chapter 8

⇛ ⇚

Tragédie Lyrique II:
Instrumental Music and the Dance

Instrumental Music

La Première fois que vous irez à l'Opéra de Paris, lorsque ce nombreux Orchestre commence à jouer, appliquez-vous un peu à cette harmonie, également pleine, douce, éclatante: vous conclurez, en y songeant bien, qu'il n'y a toute apparence que rien en Europe ne vaut l'Orchestre de l'Opéra de Paris.

(Lecerf de La Viéville)

The term *symphonie* was employed in French music of the *grand siècle* to refer to *all* 'compositions written for instruments' (Brossard, *Dictionnaire*, 'Symphonie'); thus, in French classical opera, all instrumental music, whether used independently or in conjunction with the voice, comes under the generic heading of *symphonie*. Predictably, all operatic instrumental music, except for the overture, was expected to have some link with the dramatic or choreographic action, for the concept of an independently conceived instrumental music was anathema to most French aestheticians and critics far into the eighteenth century. The fear that Lully's *symphonies* might be considered as abstract instrumental music must have precipitated Lecerf's comment that, because it could not express the meaning and sentiment of the tragedy, the *symphonie* was the 'least essential part of the Music'.

Lully's dramatic *symphonies* are far in advance of such compositions in Venetian or Roman opera. These instrumental works accompany stage action or help to establish mood. They stand at the beginning of a development that reached a high point in the operas of Rameau. As such they conform to the all-embracing theory of 'imitation' that dominated the aesthetics of the eighteenth century—an aesthetic that viewed the operatic *symphonie* as an example of the expressive power of music when used to imitate nature or, by extension, states of mind.

Perhaps the most complete statement of this doctrine is found in the *Réflexions critiques sur la poésie et sur la peinture* by Dubos. His definition of *symphonie* emphasizes its descriptive potential.

> Music uses only instruments to imitate these sounds (of nature) . . . and we commonly call these imitations, *symphonies*. . . . The true measure of the imitation of a *symphonie* consists in its resemblance to the sound which it pretends to imitate.
>
> *(Réflexions critiques,* III, p. 472)

A psychological dimension was added to the doctrine by Dubos when he suggested that these *symphonies* 'are able to agitate us, calm us, move us; in short, they act upon us in the same manner as the verses of Racine and Corneille'. Dubos, always the *arbiter elegantiae*, left little doubt as to where his sympathies lay, without seeming to attack abstract music:

> These same pieces which move us so perceptibly when they are allied with dramatic action, perhaps would only please us moderately were we to hear them played as Sonatas, . . . and consequently we might judge them without knowledge of their greater merit; that is, their relationship to the action, where, so to speak, they play a role.
>
> *(Réflexions critiques,* III, p. 486)

Lully's opera orchestra seems to have been born full grown in *Cadmus* and scarcely ever varied thereafter. It was institutionalized from its inception, and in its rigid structuring, it parallels other institutions conceived during the reign of Louis XIV. It was conservative, predictable, hierarchal, with little room for trial and error or experimentation. It exploited strong, rather primitive primary colours and rarely, if ever, attempted to realize the individuality of its families of instruments; oboes, flutes, violins, bassoons and even trumpets all share like material.

The court and comedy ballets gave Lully an ideal proving ground where he learned how to deal with a wide variety of instruments. His opera orchestra may be seen as a simplification and refinement of his earlier efforts. It was a double process of eliminating several of the more exotic instruments for which the court ballet had been the traditional repository, and seeking to improve both the performance level of his musicians and, in some cases, the instruments themselves. Inevitably, the keen interest shown by Lully in the woodwinds and the availability of some of the best players in the *Grand Ecurie* stimulated the development of more flexible and pleasing instruments. Thus, the modern oboe owes its existence to the improvements made on the ancient shawm (called *hautbois de Poitou*) by two of the *Grand Ecurie*'s best players, Jean Hotteterre and Michel-Danican

93

Philidor. The new instrument was probably first heard in the ballet of *L'Amour malade* (1657), although the first clear reference to its use is in the 'marche de Hautbois pour le dieu Pan et sa Suite' from the *Plaisirs de l'Ile Enchantée* some five years before Perrin and Cambert's *Pomone*.

Unfortunately, specific information on the exact composition of the Paris opera orchestra under Lully is lacking. We are, therefore, forced to turn to the various 'privileges' and Royal Ordinances dating from the early eighteenth century while constantly modifying these 'official' sources with information found in *livrets* and in the writings of contemporary observers. According to the Royal Ordinance of 1713, the orchestra of the Académie Royale de Musique consisted of 48 members—a number which scarcely varied over the period of a half century. Like the chorus, it was divided into a *grand choeur* and a *petit choeur*.

The *grand choeur* included 12 violins, 7 violas (3 *haute-contre*, 2 *tailles*, 2 *quintes*), 8 basses, 8 oboes, flutes or bassoons, 1 kettledrum, 1 harpsichord and a *batteur de mesure*. The *grand choeur* was used for all *symphonies* designated as 'tous' as well as all accompaniments to large choruses. The common appellation 'violons' undoubtedly also implied the doubling of the outer voices by oboes and bassoons in most cases, the string choir being reserved for those pieces designed for 'violons seuls'.

The *petit choeur* was composed of 10 of the best instrumentalists who formed their own orchestra around their own harpsichord. They accompanied solo airs and alternated with the *grand choeur* in *concertato* passages. The 1713 ordinance is silent on the composition of the *petit choeur*, but the *Privilège . . . pour l'Académie Royal de Musique pour l'année 1712–1713* reveals that there were 2 *dessus de violon*, 2 *flûtes allemandes*, 2 *basses de violon*, 2 *theorbes* and 1 *clavecin*.[1]

Both in terms of the numbers and of the specific kinds of instruments used, the above documents raise more questions than they answer especially when an attempt is made to apply them indiscriminately to Lully's opera orchestra of the 1670's and 1680's. Parts for trumpets, for example, abound in the Lully scores, yet the instruments are not included as a part of the *grand choeur*; they were probably played by two of the wind players. Similarly, there is no mention of such special instruments as the musettes and cromornes—the 'Instruments champestres' called for in the *livrets* of *Thésée* and *Atys*. Obviously these instruments must have been performed by supernumeraries hired for the occasion. At times it is quite possible that the Paris opera orchestra approached the 50 or 60 members described by Lecerf. In fact, for some listeners the opera orchestra dominated the voices. François de Callières wrote, 'one hears only weak voices

94

almost completely covered by the accompaniment of the *clavecin*, or of *Theorbes* and other instruments of the orchestra; because of this, part of an air is lost and almost all the words . . .' (*Histoire poétique de la guerre nouvellement, déclamée entre les anciens et les modernes*, 1688, p. 127).

The five-part string orchestra formed the basis of the *grand choeur*. The three 'filler' parts, the 'parties de remplissage' of the *grand choeur* were the *haute-contre, taille* and *quinte*. All three were tuned a fifth below the violin and therefore correspond to the modern viola. The *haute-contre* used the C-clef on the first line; the *taille*, the C-clef on the second line; and the *quinte*, the C-clef on the third line. This cumbersome system was not simplified until after 1750 when they were reduced to one or two parts and labelled 'alto' (see Masson, *L'Opéra de Rameau*, p. 517). Documentation that the *haute-contre* part was not played by violins is provided by Georg Muffat who, drawing on his first-hand experience as a performer in Lully's opera orchestra, informs us that the *haute-contre* ('called *violetta* in Italian') sounds better played on a medium-sized viola than on a violin (preface to *Florilegium secundum*, 1698).

Evidence seems to support Eppelsheim's conclusions that the string orchestra of the *grand choeur* was made up of members of the violin family and that the bass viol with its greater flexibility and range was restricted to the *petit choeur*.

The question of the *basse de violon* points up the looseness of terminology characteristic of the seventeenth century. Corrette in his *Méthode . . . pour apprendre . . . le violoncelle* (1741) described it as a 'grosse basse de violon'; Muffat in the preface to his *Florilegium secundum* identified it as the 'petite basse à la Française' and equated it with the Italian 'violoncino'; Mattheson, however, confused the *basse de violon* with the Italian *violone* or double bass (*Das neu-eröffnete Orchestre*, 1713); and finally, Brossard in his dictionary article 'Violone' described the double bass as 'our Basse de Violon', but, as though pained by his own ambiguity, he immediately added 'or better, it is a Double Bass and sounds one octave lower than the ordinary *Basses de Violons*'.

The *basse de violon* resembled a violoncello although it was a larger instrument and was tuned a whole tone lower than the 'cello. If we may believe Corrette, the *basse de violon* was replaced by the violoncello some 20 or 30 years before the date of his treatise; that is, sometime between 1710 and 1720, and by 1736 it was considered by Rameau to be the normal bass instrument of the *symphonie* (see Masson, *L'Opéra de Rameau*, p. 516).

Corrette in his *Méthode pour apprendre à jouer de la contrebasse à trois, à quatre, à cinq cordes* (1781) stated that 'Messers Montéclair and Sagioni were the first to play the *contrebasse* at the Paris opera'. This must have occurred soon after the turn of the century. Recent research has uncovered documentation for the use of this instrument by both Gatti (*Scylla*, 1701) and Campra (*Tancrède*, 1703) before its heretofore supposed first appearance in the famous tempest from Marais' *Alcyone* (1706).[2]

Lully's writing for the string orchestra is extremely conservative when compared to his contemporaries in Italy and Germany. The violin part remains in the first position, and the rare use of a c''' was achieved by extending the little finger on the *chanterelle*. The wide leaps, double stops and typically violinistic figurations that appear in Italian music as early as Biagio Marini are foreign to the French style. The many dramatic symphonies by Lully and his successors seem restricted to conjunct motion in the main, with little or no crossing of voices. More violent action is expressed by the kinetic sense suggested by dotted rhythms and *tirades* as opposed to the Italianate mechanical rhythmic pulsation.

It is obvious that for Lully the problems of technique and virtuosity were totally subordinated to the problems of rhythmic accuracy and finesse in performance. How else can one explain the choice of the 'Entrée des songes funestes' (*Atys*, III, 4) as a 'test piece' for potential orchestra members? Technically there are few problems, but rhythmic accuracy and an intimate knowledge of performance practices were clearly a requirement.

Example 16
Lully's 'test piece', the 'Entrée des songes funestes'. Atys (after ed. of 1689).

The problems of recreating the exact instrumentation of a score by Lully are manifold when we consider the writing for winds either independently or in conjunction with the string choir. In only a few instances did the composer clearly indicate the specific use of the transverse flute instead of recorders; it is reasonable to assume that when the score calls for 'flûte' it refers only to recorders. The prestigious position of the two transverse flutes in the *petit choeur* in the Royal Ordinance of 1713 reflects the increased popularity of the improved transverse flute in the early eighteenth century and bears out Jacques Martin Hotteterre's description of the instrument as one of the 'most agreeable and most *à la mode*' (preface to *Principes de la flûte traversière*, 1707).

During Lully's time both instruments co-existed in the opera orchestra. This is borne out by the carefully delineated instrumentation

96

of the famous 'Prélude pour l'Amour' from *Le Triomphe de l'Amour* in which transverse flutes (*flûtes d'Allemagne*) are supported by tenor recorders (*quinte de flûtes*), bass recorders (*petite basse de flûtes*) and great bass recorders (*grande basse de flûtes*).

The writing for recorders is indistinguishable in range and melodic shape from that of the violin. At first glance the use of two flutes (recorders) in dialogue and in concert with the string choir, as found in the prelude to the 'Sommeil' from *Atys* (III, 4), appears almost 'modern' from the point of view of orchestral scoring. Yet, if one consults the *livret* of 1676, one learns that six flutes were employed in this prelude in what was obviously a three plus three combination. This would of course result in a sound complex quite different from that suggested by the score and is but one example of how the *livret* for a specific revival of a Lully opera may throw light on actual performance practices that are scarcely evident from a reading of the score.

The oboes and bassoons were the 'work horses' of the opera orchestra. Not only did they function independently in dance episodes and *concertato*-like alternations with the strings, but they also apparently doubled the outer voices of the string choir. The improved tone of Hotteterre's oboe no longer resembled the instrument described by Mersenne as having the 'strongest and most *violent* tone of all instruments with the exception of the trumpet', yet, when used in substantial numbers, they must have dominated the string timbre. '. . . We have the hautboys,' wrote Raguenet, 'which by their sounds, equally mellow and piercing, have infinite advantage over the violins in all the brisk, lively airs. . . .' (Raguenet quoted in Strunk, *Source Readings*, p. 475).

The 'hautbois, flûte ou Basson' of the 1713 ordinance is not clear with regard to the distribution of parts. Presumably there were eight performers who could double on the three wind instruments and perhaps on the trumpet as well when required to do so. According to Vincent d'Indy (preface to Michaelis edition of Destouches' *Les Eléments*), the woodwinds of the *grand choeur* in 1725 comprised five oboes, five bassoons and two flutes; in 1756 they included four oboes, five bassoons and two flutes (see Masson, *L'Opéra de Rameau*, p. 513). If the members of the *petit choeur* doubled the *grand choeur* in tutti sections, an 'extreme disproportion of sonorities' (D'Indy) would have been the result. Melody instruments (14 violins, 2 flutes, 4 [?] oboes) and bass instruments (10 *basses de violon*, 1 bass viol, 2 theorbos) would have totally dominated the three 'parties de remplissage' of only 7 violas and the harpsichord.

The popular 'trio des hautbois' (two oboes and bassoon) is ideal for pastoral scenes and for achieving a marked colour contrast when used in alternation with the string orchestra. Example 17 below shows

Lully's rare use of more than two oboes in a solo group. This extract from *Atys* also illustrates how clear Lully could be on occasion in indicating exact instrumentation. It is, therefore, disconcerting to consult the *livret* of 1676 and learn that the *a* 4 episode was performed by five oboes and three cromornes, a testimony which lends credence to Joseph Marx's observation that 'To determine the instrumentation of Lully's scores is a very complicated and often impossible task'.[3]

Example 17
Lully: Extract from the 'Entrée des Zephirs', Atys (after ed. of 1689).

Categories of Usage

The *symphonies* of French Baroque opera may be divided into the following three categories: 1. overtures, 2. dramatic *symphonies*, and 3. dances.

The overture in most French stage music from Lully to Rameau is the typical 'Ouverture à la française' whose sharply pointed rhythms (*rythmes saccadés*) and dramatic upbeat *tirades* soon transcended national boundaries. It reached the *tragédie lyrique*, via court and comedy ballets, with its two principal components intact; that is, it retained its pompous introduction in duple or quadruple metre with dotted rhythms and kept its lightly fugal and faster contrasting section loosely modelled on the Venetian *canzona*. It was the 'kingly' introduction *par excellence* and was usually repeated after the prologue as if to suggest that the requisite encomium to Louis XIV had ended and the drama itself might now unfold.

Frozen by tradition, the overture remained in French opera long after its *raison d'être* had ceased to be. It was elevated to a rarified atmosphere by Lecerf. ('Lully's overtures contain beauties that will be new and admirable in all centuries.') D'Alembert's comment that there 'was only one overture at the opera' for a sixty year period is barely an overstatement (*De la liberté de la musique*, 1758).

The overture's formal rigidity and aristocratic bearing were anachronisms in the days of the Regency, and it remained for Rameau to bring a more dramatic as well as musical significance to the genre (see Girdlestone, *Jean-Philippe Rameau*, p. 307).

When Rameau suppressed the prologue to his *tragédie lyrique* *Zoroastre* in 1749, the way was opened to justify a strong dramatic liaison between overture and the following drama. In the *livret* we read that the 'Overture serves as prologue'. However, unlike the typical operatic prologue, the overture to *Zoroastre* relates dramatically (though not musically) to the drama. It is a true 'programme overture', the details of which were carefully spelled out by the composer himself.

The influence of the French overture beyond the boundaries of France far exceeded its intrinsic musical worth in the operas of Lully and his successors. It was introduced into Germany by Johann Sigismund Kusser who spent most of a decade, 1672–1682, in Paris. His *Composition de musique, suivant la méthode françoise contenant six ouvertures de théâtres accompagnées de plusieurs airs* was printed in Stuttgart in 1682. The preface acknowledges the composer's debt to Lully 'whose works at present give pleasure to all the courts of Europe'.

Agostino Steffani, who may have witnessed the first performance of *Bellérophon* in Paris in 1679, used the French overture for most of his operas composed for Munich and Hanover. Overtures and dances from six of his Hanover operas were arranged by him as *Sonate da Camera* and published later by Etienne Roger in Amsterdam (1710).

Not surprisingly, Georg Muffat used the French overture to begin five of his orchestral suites in the *Florilegium primum* of 1695, and before the turn of the century Georg Böhm had already transferred the orchestral overture to the keyboard thus anticipating the three keyboard overtures by J. S. Bach (BWV 822, 820, 831). Handel favoured the French overture from the time of his first Hamburg opera, *Almira* (1705). For Bach it had no limitations of medium or genre; it served as an introduction to a keyboard partita (No. 4 in D-Major), as a prelude (No. 5 in D-Major, *WTC*, II), a fugue (No. 5 in D-Major, *WTC*, I), as an important structural division in a set of variations (Var. 16 from the *Goldberg Variations*) and it even combined with a German chorale tune, this time in praise of a heavenly King (Cantata No. 61, *Nun komm der Heiden Heiland*).

In England it was heard perhaps as early as the 1660's in the repertory of Charles II's band of 24 violins modelled on Louis XIV's *Vingt-Quatre Violons*. In any case, the overture to John Blow's *Venus and Adonis* dates from the lifetime of Lully and is a highly developed French overture harmonically much richer than its models and even exhibiting a thematic liaison with the final chorus of the opera.

In Italy its influence was felt in the Concerti Grossi of Corelli's Opus VI. Rousseau, writing in the 1750's, stated that the French overture had been introduced into Italy 50 years before. He claimed to have been familiar with 'several old Italian operas that were preceded by a Lully overture'. After 1700, however, the conservative French overture was gradually superseded in Italy by the more homophonic *Sinfonia*, although Handel used the French overture for two operas produced during his two-year Italian sojourn. *Rodrigo* (1707) includes an overture followed by a dance suite; *Agrippina* (1709) is introduced by an elaborate 'Sinfonia' that combines the French overture and elements borrowed from the Baroque concerto in the manner of Bach's orchestral overtures.

The *grave* opening section of the French overture could still be heard in the late eighteenth century in yet another role, that of introducing the first movement of the high classical symphonies of Haydn and, more rarely, of Mozart. On into the time of Beethoven, it was recalled in the introduction to his early 'Pathétique' sonata and again in the introduction to his last sonata, Opus 111. By then, it was a dimly remembered echo from a remote past with its double dotted rhythms, its precisely measured *tirades* and its formality lost in overwhelming personal expression.

Dramatic Symphonies

The preludes and *ritournelles* found in French classical opera serve two functions: they may be used in a purely musical way to introduce a scene, an act, an air or an ensemble; or they may be linked dramatically to the action on stage.

Both functions show up clearly in as late an opera as *Amadis*. The preludes to the popular airs, 'Amour que veux-tu de moi?' and 'Bois épais', simply state the entire air in an instrumental version with no discernible dramatic function, but the two preludes in scene 2 of Act III are conceived of as true dramatic symphonies used to accompany specific stage action clearly defined in both score and *livret*. In the first prelude Arcabonne is 'carried into the air by demons and descends onto the ruined palace', and in the second, 'The jailors open the cells and the captives leave'.

There was little distinction made during the seventeenth century between the two terms *prélude* and *ritournelle*. In the broadest possible manner, Brossard defined a prelude as a '*Symphonie* that served to introduce or to prepare what follows'. He included both overture and *ritournelle* under this generic heading.

In terms of musical function, however, the word *ritournelle* may have three meanings. It may refer to the instrumental episodes that recur between sections of extended airs or vocal ensembles; it may be used 'en manière de prélude' (Rousseau) where it is usually scored for strings in trio texture; and it may conclude an air or ensemble.

Independent dramatic symphonies that 'imitate' stage action are found in the operas of Lully under such titles as 'Bruit de trompettes', 'Bruit de Combat', 'Les Vents', 'Entrée des Aquilons', 'Pompes funèbres' and 'Sommeil'. It remained for the *préramiste* period and, above all, for Rameau to develop such imitations of natural phenomena as thunder, storms (especially at sea), tempests and earthquakes.

Dances[4]

All Europe knows what a Capacity and Genius the French have for dancing, and how universally it is admired and followed.

(Riccoboni, *Reflections upon Declamation*)

Lully brought to the dances of his *tragédies lyriques* the fruitful results of a long apprenticeship both as a dancer and a composer of court and comedy ballets. He had always considered the dance an expressive medium and a legitimate dramatic agent. Quinault's *livrets* forced a modification of the non-dramatic and purely decorative *entrées* of the *ballet à entrées*. No 'Sauvages Américains' or 'Ballet des Autruches' interrupt the intrigue; and loosely organized, random samplings of characteristic dances and 'danses du bal' are rare in the *tragédies lyriques*. Often the 'jeux champêtres', the 'fêtes marines' or the 'noces de village' function dramatically if only because of their heightened contrast with the plot material.

This liaison between dance and drama provoked the most comment by contemporaries close enough to have witnessed or heard about its implementation. Even the Italophile François Raguenet conceded French superiority in the domain of the dance. He gave scenes from *Isis* and *Atys* as examples in which dance and action are closely linked.

Lecerf informs us that Lully had as much to do with the choreography as did Pierre Beauchamp who from 1673 to 1687 was responsible for the 'composition des ballets' at the Académie Royale de Musique. In commenting that 'Lully reformed the *entrées* and con-

ceived the expressive steps (*pas d'expression*) that related to the subject . . .', Lecerf implies that it was Lully rather than Beauchamp who
was primarily concerned with the dramatic aspects of the dance. This
is confirmed by Abbé Dubos who wrote that Lully gave a lot of attention to pantomime and drew upon the talents of Louis Hilaire
d'Olivet, a 'maître de danse particulier', for this purpose, using Des
Brosses and Beauchamp to compose the 'ballets ordinaires'.

Untitled dances, less bound by choreographic conventions, afforded
the best opportunity to link dance with plot. Surely many preludes
and *ritournelles* were also converted into genuine dramatic symphonies by means of dance pantomimes although the scores and even
the *livrets* are singularly uncommunicative in this regard.

We have only the word of such a keen observer as Abbé Dubos who
gives us just enough information to tantalize and make us regret all
the more the lack of some choreographic source that would throw
light on the innovative 'danse en action' as conceived of by Olivet
and Lully.

> I have heard tell of some ballets almost without dance, but
> rather composed of gesture and of demonstrations; in a word, a
> pantomime ('jeu muet'), that Lully had created for the funeral
> ceremonies in *Psyché* and *Alceste*, in the second act of *Thésée*
> where the Poet had introduced the dancing old men, in the
> ballet of the fourth act of *Atys* ('Songes funestes') and in the first
> scene of the fourth act of *Isis* ('Choeur de Peuples des climats
> glacez. . . .')
>
> (*Réflexions critiques*, III, p. 265)

Dubos added that the 'shivering chorus' and presumably the preceding *ritournelle* were composed 'uniquely of the gestures and demonstrations of people seized with cold. Not a single dance step from
our ordinary dance was employed'.

By the time of the first edition of the *Réflexions critiques* (1719),
Dubos had 'heard tell' of Lully's use of dramatic pantomime. Already
the innovation had been lost in the proliferation of characteristic
dances and titled dances during the *préramiste* period. It is, therefore,
not surprising that later eighteenth century aestheticians of the dance
often indiscriminately lumped together the dances of the court ballet,
the *tragédie lyrique* and the *opéra-ballet* of the *préramiste* period and
labelled them all examples of 'danse simple'. Louis de Cahusac fancied
himself to have been the first to have 'mis la danse en action' in
Rameau's *Fêtes de l'Hymen et de l'Amour* (1747). Noverre in his
Lettres sur la danse (1760) considered the dances of Lully as 'devoid
of any expression and sentiment. The languid music of Lully rules the
dancers' movements and conveys a feeling of sadness calculated more
to bore the public than to interest it.' This sentiment is echoed by

Charles Compan who, writing 100 years after Lully's death, characterized his music and dances as 'cold, monotonous, without character . . .' (*Dictionnaire de Danse*, 1787).

Table 2 below sums up Lully's use of titled dances in his court and stage ballets and in his *tragédies lyriques*.[5]

Table 2
Titled dances in Lully's ballets and tragédies lyriques

Titled Dances	Ballet Categories	*Tragédies lyriques*
Bourrée	28	6
Gavotte	19	17
Sarabande	24	4
Minuet	36	47
Passepied	2	2
Gigue	5	10
Canarie	10	5
Loure	3	2
Galliard	3	0
Chaconne	9	8
Passacaille	0	4

If it is recalled that the ballet categories generally precede the *tragédies lyriques* in chronology, the above table clearly indicates the changing taste in court and stage dances over more than 30 years. It shows the remarkable growth in popularity of the minuet and gigue and conversely the rapid decline of the galliard. Lully's first minuet was written in 1664 for the *comédie-ballet Le Mariage forcé*. One year later four minuets were included in the *Ballet de la naissance de Vénus*, and by 1681 in the stage ballet *Le Triomphe de l'Amour*, this latter number had doubled. In 1668 de Pure still thought of the minuet, along with the bourrée, as a 'new invention' (*Idée des Spectacles*). Ten years later it had become the most popular operatic dance; *Cadmus, Alceste, Atys, Isis, Bellérophon* and *Roland* each have four minuets, and *Phaëton* has six.

To give specific information on the tempo of Lully's stage dances is not feasible on the basis of our present knowledge. Too often seventeenth and eighteenth century sources themselves give conflicting information as do the attempts of modern scholars to supply fixed metronome markings.[6] Not only did tempos change depending on time and place, but also an idealized dance for lute or keyboard could differ markedly from both a stage dance with its complex choreography and a less involved ballroom dance.

In discussing each of Lully's dances found in his *tragédies lyriques* and listed in the outline below, it seems best, therefore, to adopt a classification based on metre and relative tempo, moving from slow to fast.

Loure: A rather slow dance normally in 6/4 metre usually beginning with an anacrusis. Some sources refer to it as a 'slow gigue' although it may include a shift of pulse from 6/4 to 3/2 as in the 'Loure pour les Pêcheurs' from *Alceste*.

Gavotte: In both the gavotte and the bourrée, the beat is normally the half note. The first section begins with two quarter notes or one half note before the first complete measure. According to Brossard, it is sometimes *gai*, and sometimes *grave*. This lack of consistent tempo is also mentioned by Rousseau who described the dance as 'ordinarily graceful, often gay, and sometimes rather slow and tender'.

Bourrée: A dance of popular origins used less frequently than the gavotte on the operatic stage and often replaced by the rigaudon in the post-Lully period. This association with the rigaudon is mentioned as early as 1699 in Charles Masson's *Nouveau traité des règles de la la composition de la musique*. Masson also comments that the bourrée should carry the word *vite* to indicate a faster tempo than the gavotte or galliard. Each of the 34 bourrées of Lully begins with an upbeat equal to one quarter note.

Gigue: A dance 'full of dotted notes and syncopations' (Brossard) described by D'Alembert as a 'type of accelerated loure' (*Encyclopédie*). A distinction between the 'gigue française' and the 'gigue italienne' was made by Rameau in his *Traité de l'harmonie*; the latter may be in 9/8 or 12/8 whereas the French gigue is most often found in 6/8. Some gigues display a sham polyphony with staggered points of imitation often resulting in longer and more asymmetrical phrase lengths than normally found in French stage dances. The gigue remained popular throughout the Regency but gradually passed from favour. Rousseau in 1767 observed simply that it had 'entirely passed out of fashion; it is not found at all in Italy and scarcely in France'.

Canarie: This dance may be found in both triple metre (3 or 3/8) and compound metre (6/8 or 6/4). According to Masson, the 'Canaries and the Gigue that have a 6/8 metre sign are conducted in 2 equal beats: it is well to note that the Canarie is a bit faster than the gigue.'

For these, it seems reasonable to turn to the classification by Masson found in his *Nouveau traité*. Throughout the short treatise, Masson draws upon extracts from Lully's operas for illustrative purposes. He writes:

> In triple metre there are five sorts of tempo; that is, very slow (*fort grave*), slow (*grave*), moderate (*léger*), quick (*vite*) and

very quick (*très vite*). . . . The Sarabands, Passacaille and Courante must be slow. The Chaconne, moderate; the Minuet, quick; and the Passepied, very quick.

(*Nouveau traité*, p. 7)

Sarabande: According to Brossard, the sarabande is only a minuet whose tempo is slow and whose mood is serious. Rémond de Saint-Mard adds that it is 'always melancholy and exudes a delicate yet serious tenderness (*Réflexions sur l'Opéra*). Typically the sarabande is structured in four-measure phrases with a hemiola occasionally found in the measures preceding a cadence. A faster type of sarabande sometimes labeled 'sarabande legère' was related to the chaconne (see, for example, the 'Sarabande legère' marked 'Mouvement de Chacone' in Montéclair's *Principes de musique divisez en quatre parties*, 1736).
Passacaille: Brossard confirms Masson's ordering of the passacaille by writing that the 'only difference between this dance and the chaconne is that the tempo is usually slower and the melody more expressive and tender'. Both dances are organized in phrases of four or eight measures and are composed of continuous variations over a repeated bass line pattern. Typically, both use the diatonic and chromatic versions of the descending tetrachord pattern often in close juxtaposition; both contain contrasting episodes in trio combination in which the bass line may be altered or missing altogether (see, for example, the chaconne from *Thésée*, IV, 8); and both exploit hemiola patterns at cadence points. Montéclair claimed that the passacaille 'always begins on the first beat of the measure' and that the chaconne 'always begins on the second beat of the measure' (*Principes de musique*). When applied to Lully, this observation holds true in the four passacailles (all late works) and in all but one of the eight operatic chaconnes composed after *Psyché* (1678). Like the French overture, the chaconnes and passacailles of Lully remained a fixed entity in French opera until Gluck, and they too were rapidly assimilated beyond the borders of France.
Chaconne: See above.
Minuet: Masson's 'quick' tempo designation for the minuet is supported by most early eighteenth century sources. For Brossard, the minuet was a 'very gay dance that originated in Poitou. We should imitate the Italians and use a 3/8 or 6/8 metre sign, which always means very gay and very fast; but we employ instead the simple 3.' Lacombe in 1752 wrote that the minuet was in a 'moderate triple metre' (*Dictionnaire portatif des beaux-arts*). By 1768, Rousseau found the tempo to be 'more moderate than quick, and it is the least gay of dances used at balls'. He added, however, that 'it is something else again on the stage' which may imply that the faster stage dance may have persisted throughout the eighteenth century. In any case, under-

standing of these comments would prevent modern interpreters of the early eighteenth century from using the ponderous, slower *Don Giovanni* minuet as the prototype for all such dances.[7] The late seventeenth-century stage minuet already reveals the uniform four-measure phrase structure commonly found in the following century. However, some of the minuets from Lully's early operas are organized in three-measure phrase groupings more typical of the so-called 'menuet de Poitou' (see, for example, the minuet from *Atys*, III, 4).[8]

Passepied: For Brossard the passepied was merely a '*menuet* with a very fast tempo'. It is normally in 3/8 metre, and the dance patterns themselves are similar to those used in its slightly slower sister dance. Phrases of the passepied are typically extended by a characteristic hemiola pattern. Lully only used the title 'passepied' in the ballet *Temple de la Paix*, but there are untitled dances from *Persée* and *Phaëton* that exhibit all the characteristics of this dance. It reached its greatest popularity during the *préramiste* period and after the middle of the century was already in decline. Rousseau flatly stated that 'it is no longer in use'.

In addition to the above named titled dances, it is necessary to add the Lully *marche*. The *marche* is closely related to the dance and was often used as an *entrée* to move dancers and singers on stage. It is found in both triple and duple metre. Often scored with trumpets (doubling the violins) and drums, it is a primitive, but nonetheless effective musical expression of the pomp and ceremony of the *grand siècle*.

As is true for the vocal air, the dance structure favoured by Lully and his followers is binary with either or both of its two parts repeated. Helen Ellis (see Bibliography) estimates that 80 per cent of the dances of Lully are in binary form while the remaining dances are in rondeau or some other type of formal organization.

It is not always possible to determine the exact scoring of Lully's dances. In the opinion of Prunières, the 'harpsichord and wind instruments, unless precisely indicated, did not take part in the execution of the *airs de ballet* . . . as may be seen by examining the separate part books for *Isis* published in 1677 by Ballard' (*Oeuvres complètes*, 'Operas', II, p. xxii). If true, it would seem that the five-part string orchestra with occasional contrasting episodes in trio texture served as the basic scoring principle. The trio episodes are usually scored for recorders and viola, oboes and bassoon or three solo strings from the *petit choeur*. The scoring of the minuet from the prologue to *Armide* is an interesting deviation from the norm with the opening measures of the dance a trio of recorders and viola followed by the five-voiced string ensemble.

Our knowledge of the specific choreography used in French court dances and, by extension, stage dances comes from certain choreographic manuals dating from the turn of the century. They graphically printed the steps appropriate for each dance and included collections of dances in score as well. The most important and most comprehensive notational system was developed by Raoul-Auger Feuillet for his *Chorégraphie ou l'art de décrire la danse par caractères, figures et signes démonstratifs* (first edition, 1700; later editions, 1701, 1709 and 1713). He developed an ingenious system for notating all dance steps in diagram and illustrating the position of the feet and the direction of their movement.[9] The word 'figures' in the title of Feuillet's *Chorégraphie* was explained by him as follows: 'The "figure" is the route *(chemin)* one follows in dancing. . . . The route is a line along which one dances'. Plate 7 was taken from the 1713 edition of the treatise and affords the modern reader some idea of the complexity of his system, which was widely disseminated and was the basis of most choreographic notation of the eighteenth century.

Throughout the seventeenth and eighteenth centuries, French music was increasingly dominated by the dance. It spread from court ballet and opera stage to the lute and harpsichord and even the organ. The rhythm of the minuet, the sarabande, the bourrée or passepied invaded chamber and chapel alike.

Georg Muffat, who went so far as to give detailed rules for bowing his 'Airs de Balet à la Françoise' (see Appendix E in Mellers, *François Couperin*), concluded that in order to understand better the real *mouvement* of each piece, he found that 'a knowledge of the art of the dance is a great aid: most of the best violinists in France understand (the dance) very well, and it is not surprising that they are able to find and maintain the *mouvement* of the measure' (*Florilegium secundum*).[10]

Chapter 9

❯❯❯ ❮❮❮

Tragédie Lyrique III:
From Lully to Rameau

At the time of his death on 22 March 1687, Lully's position as a key candidate for the French Parnassus seemed secure. In France outside Paris, his opera *Phaëton* had inaugurated a royal academy in Lyons in 1687 thanks to an ordinance of 17 August 1684 that gave only Lully permission to 'establish operas in France'. Beyond the borders of France, he was considered to be the composer most representative of French music.

In England, Roger North praised his *entrées* and observed that 'all the compositions of the towne were strained to imitate Baptist's vein' (*Memoires of Musick*, 1728). Charles II, during the heyday of his aping French institutions and manners, sent Pelham Humfrey to France as well as to Italy presumably to absorb their national styles. Although evidence is lacking, Humfrey may have heard some of Lully's court ballets and the 1664 *Miserere*; in any case according to Pepys, he returned to England 'an absolute Monsieur'. *Cadmus et Hermione* was performed in London in February 1686 by a French company, and the music was considered 'indeed very fine'.[1] Among the listeners may have been young Henry Purcell who many years later 'borrowed' the 'Entrée de l'envie' from the prologue for his own instrumental music in *The Tempest*.

By Purcell's time, however, the influence of French music was on the wane in England. English music according to Purcell was 'yet but in its Nonage. . . . Tis now learning *Italian*, which is its best Master, and studying a little of the *French* air, to give it somewhat more of Gayety and Fashion' (preface to *Dioclesian*, 1690). It should be stated that in addition to 'Gayety and Fashion' Purcell found in Lully's *Isis* the model for his famous 'Frost Scene' in Act III of *King Arthur* and undoubtedly learned from Lully the technique of using a chaconne or passacaglia to give structural unity to an entire scene (see, for example, the passacaglia, air, duo, trio and chorus from *King Arthur* Act IV).

We have already discussed the role of J. S. Kusser and others in introducing French overtures and dances into Germany. It was only to be expected that many German princely courts of the late seventeenth century would mimic Versailles and show a strong predilection for French language and culture. The excellent theatre at Wolfenbüttel housed the first recorded performances of Lully's operas in Germany. The court at Celle became a bastion of French taste and manners after 1675 when Georg Wilhelm, Duke of Braunschweig-Lüneberg, married Eléanore Desmier d'Olbreuse of Poitou. There was refuge there for French Huguenots fleeing their native land after Louis xiv revoked the Edict of Nantes. The court boasted a theatre and orchestra which during its best days numbered 16 players, 7 of whom were oboists in the tradition of the Paris opera orchestra.

The extent to which French style had penetrated German music by the early years of the eighteenth century may be seen from Telemann's comment that 'French airs have replaced here the vogue that was formerly held by the Italian cantata. I have known German, English, Russians, Poles and even Jews who know by heart whole passages from *Bellérophon* and *Atys* by Lully' (quoted by Mellers in *François Couperin*, p. 280, translation mine).

In Italy it was French dance music and *symphonies* that were absorbed into chamber sonatas, and characteristically the Italian composers expressed little interest in French vocal music. Titon du Tillet tells us that the Italian composer Theobaldo di Gatti decided to go to France because he had been so charmed by some of the instrumental music from the first operas of Lully to reach Florence, and he 'wished to meet the composer'. Titon also quotes a French cardinal who claimed that Corelli himself responded to the cardinal's praise for his sonatas with the remark that 'it is because I have studied Lully'.[2]

The geographic spread of Lully's operas in the closing years of the seventeenth century is remarkable considering the relative lack of mobility of opera at that time. By the year of Lully's death, *Cadmus* had already been performed in London (1686) and Amsterdam (1687); *Thésée* in Brussels (1682), in The Hague (1682) and in Wolfenbüttel (1687); *Proserpine* in Anvers (1682), in Antwerp (1682) and Wolfenbüttel (1685); *Psyché* in Wolfenbüttel (1686) and Modena (1687); *Atys* in The Hague (1687); *Persée* in Brussels (1682); *Amadis* and *Cadmus* in Amsterdam (1687). *Armide* was the first French opera performed in Rome (1690), and *Acis et Galatée* (1689) the first opera by a non-German composer to be heard at the Hamburg opera.[3]

In France the period following Lully's death saw most important French composers attempting a rapprochement with the invading Italian style. Even the performances of Lully's operas in the eighteenth century must be understood in the context of this situation. All the modifications introduced into his *tragédies lyriques* and into those of his followers, in order to make the genre more palatable to Parisian audiences, must be interpreted with the Italo-Franco style conflict in mind.

Italian music only appeared to have been driven underground during the time of Lully's iron-clad control of the French lyric theatre. Lully was unable or unwilling to prevent the performance of an Italian pastorale at Fontainebleau in 1681 before the king. It was *Nicandro e Fileno* by the popular Paolo Lorenzani who had been in France since 1678 and who by 1683 had been named *maître de chapelle* at the Paris chapel of the Théatins.[4]

In the very heart of Paris, Italian music was performed and disseminated by a small but active group surrounding the dilettante priest of Saint-André-des-Arts, Nicolas Matthieu. Serré de Rieux described this milieu: 'M. Matthieu, curé of Saint-André-des-Arts, established a weekly concert at his home during several years of the last century where only Latin music, composed in Italy since 1650 by the greatest masters, was performed' (*Les Dons des enfants de Latone*, 1734, p. 112). Helpfully, de Rieux included the names of the following masters: Luigi Rossi, Cavalli, Cazzati, Carissimi, Legrenzi, Colonna, Alessandro, Melani, Stradella and Bassani—a cross section of the most important composers of the early and middle Italian Baroque. He added that 'It was through the curé of Saint-André that these great works were first known in Paris'.

The library of Abbé Matthieu included some 200 compositions over two-thirds of which were by Italian composers.[5] Unfortunately, the majority of the Italian holdings were catalogued simply as 'paquets de motets à 1, 2 ou 3 voix, de differens autheurs d'Italie' or 'plusieurs pièces de simphonies de diverse autheurs d'Italie'.

Passing in and out of this heady Italianate atmosphere just across the city from Lully's Académie Royale de Musique were the composer-monks Claude Nicaise and René Ouvrard, both of whom had made Italian tours, Claude Oudot, who was the musical director of the Académie Française, and the composers Marc-Antoine Charpentier, back from his Italian sojourn by 1672, and Michel-Richard Delalande, to whom Abbé Matthieu bequeathed several Italian motets and cantatas.

By 1699 Ballard published his first *Recueil des meilleurs airs italiens* followed by four more *recueils* (1701, 1703, 1705, 1708); in 1699 André Campra composed a short, self-contained Italian opera, *L'Orfeo negl' inferni*, as part of his continuous action ballet, *Le Carnaval de Venise*; in 1701 Corelli's Opus v was first printed in Paris; and in 1706 the first book of *Cantates françaises* by Jean-Baptiste Morin began the fashion for French adaptations of the Italian cantata.

Soon after the turn of the century, Brossard not only organized his *Dictionnaire* around Italian terms but included as well a 'Traité de la manière de bien prononcer les Mots Italiens' which opens: 'Never has there been more taste and passion for Italian music than exists now in France'. By 1713 the *Mercure galant* admitted that 'hardly a Musician arrives here without sonatas or cantatas in his pocket', and the following year the same journal blamed the 'cantatas and sonatas that have flooded all Paris' for a marked change in taste from the 'rich simplicity that is the true character of our language and our genius' (November 1714, p. 201).

With Louis xiv rarely attending the theatre or the opera, with the court at Versailles taking on more and more the 'demeanour of a con-vent' (Gros, *Philippe Quinault*, p. 142) under the puritanical aegis of Mme de Maintenon, with such powerful members of the royalty as Philippe d'Orléans, the future Regent, declaring a 'definite taste for Italian music' (Raguenet, *Défense du Parallèle*, 1705, p. 51) and with the barriers down to let in cantata, sonata and concerto from across the Alps, it was not surprising to find partisans of French music prepared to mount a counter-attack.

So it was that Lully, a living legend during his lifetime, was rapidly canonized after his death as the patron saint of French music. Just as Palestrina had been seen by a later generation through the eyes of Baini as the saviour of Catholic church music (a bias which we are still struggling to overcome), so Lully through the writings of Lecerf de la Viéville emerges as the very symbol of French style. In reading Lecerf one must try to discriminate constantly between anecdote, per-ceptive analysis and mythology, for certainly the life of the Florentine miller's son, who became the most powerful and wealthy musical dic-tator of the *grand siècle*, contains all the raw materials from which legends are spun.

For Lecerf there was assuredly a Lully 'mystique' which conceived of the composer as the very centre of a concentric system, to remain immutable and above the storms of controversy. The system tolerated co-existence but could never concede the presence of a serious rival.

Lecerf on the one hand found himself committed to criticize those who were inclined to deviate from the centre, those who heard the transalpine call and became 'ardent imitators of the Italian manner of composition'; yet in the same breath, he was obliged to admit that such composers as Charpentier, Collasse, Campra and Destouches had been 'reduced' to seeking 'bizarre effects' by the very fact that they wished to avoid the accusation of being mere imitators or plagiarizers of Lully so soon after his demise. The thought that the above com-posers may have wished to 'imitate' the Italian manner because of intrinsic musical merits was apparently anathema to the stubborn Norman.

We should not, however, assume from Lecerf's studied admiration that there was no criticism of Lully in France during his lifetime or soon after his death. There were of course the professional opera haters, Boileau and Bossuet, backed by the conservative clergy; there were those like Louvois who feared that Lully's rapport with Louis XIV might result in political pressures detrimental to their own interests; there was also La Fontaine who, although admitting that on the days Lully's operas were performed coaches lined the Faubourg Saint-Honoré (*Epître à M. de Niert sur l'Opéra*), was not above mounting a savage personal attack against Lully in *Le Florentin* of 1674: 'He is lewd and evil-minded, and he devours anything. . . . His wife, children and all others large and small recite morning and night in their prayers "Lord in your bountiful goodness, Deliver us from the Florentine".'

There were others, less concerned with Lully's rancour and weaknesses of character and more interested in his musical legacy, who sought deliverance. As early as 1688, one year after the composer's death, François de Callières discreetly attacked the sacred Lully recitative: '. . . if you were to hear those long, dull recitatives which in these Operas take up the greatest part of the spectacle, you would be surprised at the complaisance and patience of this good Nation' (*Histoire poétique*, p. 229).

In spite of the rumblings of discontent, coaches continued to fill the Faubourg Saint-Honoré carrying their aristocratic burdens to performances of *Alceste*, *Thésée* or *Armide*, and Lully's name was 'sloganized' in rapidly forming battle lines against the strong Italian penetrations. That Lully received adulation and treatment as 'larger than life' was due more to his usefulness as a symbol of the highest attainments of French music than to the intrinsic merits of his music itself.

Titon du Tillet described Lully as the 'father of our beautiful French music, which he carried to its perfection, abandoning completely any taste for Italian music'. In their over-simplified view of the matter, French aestheticians described French music over and over again with key words or phrases whose antonyms, tainted with partisan bias, were reserved for describing Italian music. The list of adjectives and nouns found below was gathered at random from sources stretching back in time to Mersenne's *Harmonie universelle* (1636) and Maugars' *Response faite à un curieux* (1639) and to Mermet's *De la corruption du goust dans la musique françoise* (1746). With a tiresome uniformity the words recur in source after source for over a hundred years. As it is easier and greater sport to hurl invective than to engage in self-appraisal, the Italian list is longer than the French. From the French point of view, it goes without saying that the sum of the parts under the French column equal 'le bon goût' and, under the Italian column, equal 'la corruption du goût'.

French	Italian
beauté	baroque
calme	bizarre
charme	brilliant
délicate	bruit
douceur	chargé
élégant	colère
grâce	défiguré
intelligent	dépit
naturel	détourné
netteté	diversité
noble	excès
régularité	extravagance
(la belle) simplicité	fureur
tendresse	gaieté
touchant	licence
	peu naturel
	rage
	recherché
	savant
	singulier
	variété
	vif
	violence
	vivacité

The term 'savant' as a term of deprecation perhaps needs an explanation. In his oft-quoted letter to Houdar de La Motte soliciting an operatic *livret*, Rameau defined a 'savant musicien' as one who 'neglects nothing in the different combinations of notes; but he is thought to be so completely absorbed by these combinations that all else is sacrificed including sentiment and the spirit of the work' (quoted in *Oeuvres complètes*, VI, p. xxxiii). Ironically, the same charge was hurled by the *Lullistes* against the *Ramistes* in the continuation of the interminable polemic between the ancients and the moderns and between French and Italian styles that was brought to a boil by the performances of Rameau's *tragédies lyriques* and *opéras-ballets*. One *Lulliste* even complained that Rameau's harmonies 'take on a geometrical tone which frightens the heart' (quoted by Girdlestone, *J. P. Rameau*, p. 481).

In general it was the aestheticians, the arbiters of 'le bon goût', and not the more discriminating among the *préramiste* composers or performers who were opposed to the concept of a discreet 'goûts-réunis'. Whereas André Campra wrote that he had tried to 'mix the vivacity of Italian music with the gentleness of the French' (preface to *Cantates françaises*, I, 1708), and Jacques Aubert admitted to adding some lively and gay touches to the 'graceful' and 'beautiful simplicity' of French melody (preface to *Suites de Symphonies en Trio*, 1730); whereas Couperin with awkward bluntness recalled that Italian and French tastes had 'shared the Republic of Music in France for a long time' and that he always 'esteemed those things that merited it without regard to composer or nation' (preface to *Les Goûts réunis*, 1724), the critics from Lecerf to Louis Bollioud de Mermet found this mixture displeasing. 'It is apparent' wrote the latter, 'that Taste is increasingly degenerating! That which is strange and bizarre, which surprises and astonishes is admired. . . . The most natural and complete Harmony moves less . . . than a composition filled with intellectual trappings, bristling with obstacles, which in the last analysis makes more noise than an impression' (*De la corruption du goust dans la musique françoise*, 1746, pp. 14–15).

It is against this background that we must view the changes in performances of Lully's operas after his death and throughout the eighteenth century. That these changes were considerable is a matter of record. There was much contemporary concern at the broadening of tempo and the introduction of what many considered excessive ornamentation into the airs and recitatives. Abbé Dubos remarked that this slowing down of tempo rendered Lully's recitatives 'soulless' and increased the length of his operas (*Réflexions critiques*).

Many extant Ballard scores of Lully's operas served as actual performing scores for various eighteenth century revivals. These scores, many housed today in the Bibliothèque de l'Opéra, are mute testi-

Example 18

(*a*) Bellérophon (*after ed. of 1679*). (*a*) (*part II*). Bellérophon (*after Bibl. de l'Opéra, A.11a*). (*b*) Bellérophon (*after ed. of 1679*). (*b*) (*Part II*). Bellérophon (*after Bibl. de l'Opéra, A.11a*).

mony to the lack of reverence accorded the printed page of even such a revered master as Lully. The full score of *Alceste* printed by Ballard in 1708 (A. 5a, Bibliothèque de l'Opéra) added a new overture, cut scene 3 of Act I, and eliminated pages of recitatives. Upholding Lecerf's observation that in contrast to opera in Lully's day, opera 'at present is composed one-fourth of dance . . .', the effective choral exclamation 'Triomphez, triomphez' that concludes *Alceste* was excised and a sarabande, musette, march, ariette and chaconne, substituted.

The 1679 Ballard full score of *Bellérophon* at the Bibliothèque de l'Opéra (A. 11a) is also a 'copy used for performances'. Could this have been utilized for the revival of April 1728 about which Parfaict wrote:

'For this *reprise* there were several changes. . . . A new *divertissement* was substituted in the ivth act that appeared more satisfactory than the original' (*Histoire de l'Académie*, p. 45)? Example 18a and 18b above illustrates the many additions of ornaments and the complete re-writing and re-scoring of the prelude to Act I, scene 4.

Other non-structural changes in the performances of Lully operas were a natural by-product of the sudden release of Académie performers from years of disciplined behaviour demanded by Lully. Lecerf, longing for the halcyon days when the director would break a violin over the back of an errant musician, wrote that '. . . under Lully's control the female singers did not have colds for six months out of the year and the male performers were not drunk four days out of the week' (*Comparaison*, II, p. 212). The fact that stringent rules governing the deportment of members of the Académie Royale were drawn up as part of the Royal Ordinance of 1713 documents Lecerf's observations.

Disenchantment with Lully's *tragédie lyrique* became more and more evident as the eighteenth century progressed in spite of the many changes discussed above. Parfaict, referring to the December 1705 revival of *Bellérophon*, wrote: 'This opera which had such a brilliant success when new was received rather poorly at this revival' (*Histoire de l'Académie*, p. 114). The revival of *Roland* in 1709 'was not a happy one, in spite of a small Italian air performed by Mlle Dun' (*ibid.*). In commenting on the season of 1709, Parfaict concluded that 'It is necessary to confess that this year was not a good one for the revivals of old operas'. To be fair, it should be recalled that 1709 was a particularly unsettled year. In Kafka-like fashion, Lully's gods and heroes acted out their *galant* roles in counterpoint against the rioting, hungry street mobs of Paris. The Duchesse d'Orléans, we read in the *Journal* entry for 24 August 1709, 'returns to Versailles from the opera just ahead of the revolt brought about by the scarcity of bread—a revolt in which 40 persons perished'.[6]

In the pages of the *Mercure* for November 1714 we read:

> It is incontestable that no one has succeeded better than Lully in writing this genre of music (*tragédie lyrique*), nor is it any less true that in the area of poetry, Quinault is superior to all who have worked after him. Yet, how many of the works of these two great masters have sustained their initial brilliance; one can easily count them, and I know no others save *Armide*, *Roland*, *Alceste* and *Phaëton*. It isn't that *Bellérophon*, *Thésée* and *Atys* are inferior to the above, but . . . *Bellérophon* nowadays appears too tragic, *Thésée* too listless. . . .'

To read these words is to conclude that the days when the 'soul' of a Mme de La Fayette was 'allarmée' by the 'prodigious beauty' of a

Lully opera had passed.[7] Predictably the *Mercure* writer attributed this state of affairs to the change of taste brought about by the influence of Italian music.

We must beware of such comments, for in spite of the increasing popularity of an attractive new genre such as the *opéra-ballet*, Lully's *tragédies lyriques* continued to hold the stage with remarkable tenacity throughout the eighteenth century. In terms of the longevity of certain Lully operas, our writer was a poor prophet, for *Thésée* 'listless' or not was performed until 1779, for a period of 104 years. *Armide* was performed for 78 years until 1764, just 13 years before Gluck's opera on the same Quinault *livret*; *Amadis*, an opera not even mentioned by the *Mercure* author, remained in the repertory of the Paris opera for 87 years.

Perhaps it is just this remarkable staying power of Lully's *tragédie lyrique* through all the buffeting cross-winds of change in taste and manner that lured the *préramiste* composer into trying his luck with the same genre. How else can one explain why André Campra and Jean-Joseph Mouret, for example, continued to compose *tragédies lyriques* even after the popular successes of their *opéras-ballets*? It is clear that the pleasure-loving Regency audience was not in itself powerful enough to overthrow the aesthetic dogmas of a glorious past age.

Sought-after librettists such as Danchet and La Motte understood the controversial nature of comedy at the Académie Royale de Musique. Certainly they knew that, like Quinault, they would be judged on their tragedies. The prestige of the *tragédie lyrique* carried over into a period basically antithetical to it. Certain administrative procedures reflect this. Articles xvi and xviii from the 1713 ordinances state that the author and composer of a five-act tragedy would receive 100 *livres* for each of the first ten performances, whereas the author and composer of 'ballets' (*opéra-ballet*) would only receive 60 *livres*.[8]

In the light of the above, Danchet quite possibly convinced Campra that it was worth more to them in prestige and remuneration to repeat the success of *Hésione* and *Tancrède* rather than those of *L'Europe galante* or *Les Fêtes vénitiennes*.[9]

In the 46 years that separate Lully's last opera, *Acis et Galatée* (1687), from Rameau's first, *Hippolyte et Aricie* (1733), the lure of the *tragédie lyrique* was such that 59 were performed at the Académie Royale de Musique—15 more than all other types of stage works combined. That this was a chimera for most composers and librettists is evident from the fact that out of the 59 *tragédies lyriques* only 14 enjoyed 3 or more revivals and none could match the longevity of Lully's 8 most popular operas.

In the preface to his *Recueil de Cantates* (1728), Bachelier reports that he questioned a Parisian with regard to the failure of two *tragédies lyriques* written by the violoncellist Batistin Stuck. The answer, if it be a typical Parisian response, illustrates that the hedonistic Regency audience was more interested in a pretty air and its *agréments* than in the high-flown poetry and one-dimensional characters of the *tragédie lyrique*:

> In so far as the *Parterre* cannot sing the short airs which are part of the Opera, these works will always fail. Someone should suggest to M. Batistin that he give his little airs all the *agrémens* of which he is capable in order to heighten the beauty of a scene which might otherwise put us to sleep. . . . If these gentlemen wish to please, they must give us tunes such as 'Qui sert la fierté dans ces belles', 'Nos plaisirs seront peu durable'. . . . This way, the least attractive Soubrette can step out of character . . . and with side glances create a hubbub in the *Parterre* who judge the beauty of a Piece only by the simperings of those who execute it & who give it the seal of their approval by singing through the same air in chorus.

Without a doubt the desultory performance record of most *tragédies lyriques* between Lully and Rameau was due largely to the vacuum created by the death of Lully. Among his students only Pascal Collasse (1649–1709) succeeded in mounting a *tragédie lyrique* that was an unqualified success (*Thétis et Pélée*, 1689), and poor Collasse must have grown desperate to repeat this initial triumph. His *Enée et Lavinie* of 1690 had no revivals; nor did his *Astrée*, 1692; nor *Jason ou La Toison d'Or*, 1696; nor *Canente*, 1700 nor *Polyxène et Pyrrhus*, 1706. He ended by abandoning music for alchemy and dying 'poor and half insane' in 1709.[10] Even Lully's most talented pupil, Henry Desmarest, after a promising debut with *Didon* (1693), knew only dismal failures followed by one moderate success, *Vénus et Adonis*, 1697.

Through the scheming that removed all possible rivals, Lully had indeed created an empire, but an empire which did not provide for heirs. The most important composers of the day had, perforce, chosen to follow other routes to success. Until the turn of the century and the appearance of Destouches and Campra, there were simply no composers trained in the milieu of the lyric stage who could successfully sustain a Lullian *tragédie lyrique*. Delalande, as the most successful court and chapel composer, wisely restricted his stage music to ballets and *divertissements, pièces d'occasion* performed in the gardens of Versailles until, at the end of his career, he collaborated with Destouches in the composition of the *opéra-ballet Les Eléments* (1721). François Couperin was essentially a miniaturist and instrumental composer.

Marc-Antoine Charpentier's situation was more complicated. He was Lully's strongest potential rival and no stranger to stage music.

After the death of Molière, he continued to compose for the Comédie Française and the Hôtel de Bourgogne.

One year after Lully's death, on 25 February 1688, a *tragédie lyrique* by Charpentier was performed in the theatre of the Jesuit College, Louis-le-Grand, where Charpentier had been a *maître de musique* since 1684. This sacred opera, *David et Jonathan*, was written 44 years before Montéclair's more popular *Jephté* and incurred the displeasure of Lecerf who was already ill-disposed towards Charpentier as an 'ardent imitator of the Italian manner'. In proselytizing for the idea of an 'Opéra Chrétien', Lecerf concluded that Charpentier's *Jonathan* 'only half merited the name Opera . . . for it was too dry and too denuded of sentiments of morality and piety'.

It is true that in common with the later *Médée*, it suffers from a poor libretto, but the score, copied by Philidor in 1690, reveals that *David et Jonathan* is a product of Charpentier's most mature period. The many choruses are more polyphonically conceived than those of Lully, the instrumental texture is predominantly *a* 4 (in contrast to the *a* 5 texture found in *Médée*) and there is a rich-part writing and harmonic audacity as opposed to the note-against-note style and simple diatonicism of Lully. The examples below are taken from the moving aria of David 'Ciel, quel triste combat' in scene 3, Act 1. The long aria is in reality an aria 'complex' freely organized in three sections preceded by a prelude. Example 19a shows the opening of the prelude and 19b, an extract from the concluding measures of Part C. The dissonant part writing and parallel 5ths in measure 2 of Example 19b are common in the music of Charpentier.

Charpentier did not attempt a breakthrough at the Académie de Musique until 1693 with *Médée*. Although containing some fine music (see, for example, Médée's monologues in scenes 3 and 5 of Act III), *Médée* cannot compare with the *tragédies lyriques* of Lully from the dramaturgical point of view. Damned by Lecerf as 'le méchant Opéra de Médée', over-praised by Brossard as the opera 'of all operas, without exception, from which one can learn the most essential things regarding the art of composing well' (*Catalogue*), it had only ten performances at the Académie Royale de Musique in December of 1693.

A careful study of *tragédies lyriques* composed between Lully and Rameau convinces me that there is much worthwhile music in such works as Campra's *Tancrède* and *Idoménée*, in Desmarest's (and Campra's) *Iphigénie en Tauride*,[11] in Destouches' *Omphale* and *Amadis de Grèce*, Marais' *Alcyone* and Montéclair's *Jephté*. To be sure, there are pages and pages of imitation-Lully, of 'hack' music written to tired formulae. Yet the tendency to group all *préramiste* composers together as 'pale imitators of Lully'[12] or to consider all the *tragédies lyriques* of Collasse, Desmarest, Campra and Destouches

Example 19
Charpentier: Extracts from 'Ciel, quel triste combat', David et
Jonathan *(after Philidor copy).*

19(a) Prelude. 19(b) Conclusion of Part C of air.

indiscriminately in one brief paragraph and to find them 'slavishly imitative' of Lully[13] seems excessive.

Simply stated, the weakess of most of these *tragédies lyriques* is their near total subordination of the dramatic to the decorative aspects —a change in emphasis that parallels somewhat the change in Venetian opera after the death of Monteverdi. The domination of composer over librettist did much to break down the clean dramatic lines of *livrets* even though their subject matter scarcely differs from that of their Quinault antecedents.

On the positive side, this departure from the restrictions of the dramatist released some purely musical forces that contributed to the operatic vocabulary of Jean-Philippe Rameau.

A more expanded use of the orchestra is apparent in many *tragédies lyriques* of the *préramiste* period. The great musical frescoes of nature in turmoil, the tempests and earthquakes of Rameau stem from the first timid use of programme music in Collasse's *Thétis et Pélée*. This model was followed by Campra in *Hésione* and *Idomenée*, by Desmarest in *Iphigénie en Tauride* and by Marin Marais (1656–1728) in *Alcyone*. The classical prototype of all operatic tempests seems to have been the 'Tempête' from Marais' *Alcyone* (IV, 4). Brossard observed that it inspired a 'prodigious number of others: not only in Opera, but also in Cantatas and even in Church Music' (*Catalogue*, p. 243). The Marais orchestral storm, an extended descriptive *symphonie* of almost 100 measures interrupted from time to time by choral exclamation, was described by Titon du Tillet:

> One cannot avoid speaking of the tempest in the opera (*Alcyone*), which is so praised by Connoisseurs and which makes such an astounding effect. Marais' concept was to have the bass performed not only by bassoons and *basses de violons*, but also by loosely strung drums which were rolled continually, forming a muffled and lugubrious sound that contrasted with the high-pitched, piercing notes coming from the oboes and the *chanterelle* string of the violins. . . .
>
> (*Le Parnasse françois*, p. 626)

As may be seen from the photocopy below taken from a Ballard manuscript edition of *Alcyone* in the Bibliothèque de l'Opéra, contrebasses and bassoons are found on the line below Titon du Tillet's *basses de violons*.

Préramiste scores show the orchestra employed as a mood determinant even more than it was by Lully. At times it dominates a scene. In Act I, scene 4 of Campra's *Tancrède* the orchestral writing is totally independent of the chorus and used to describe the noise of an earthquake. A motive heard in the orchestra dominates the big 'storm'

Example 20
Marais: Beginning of 'Tempeste', Alcyone (Bibl. de l'Opéra, Ms A.69a).

choruses in Campra's *Idomenée*, and the prelude to Act III shows the same orchestral motive characterizing the 'storm' raging in the hearts of Idomenée and Arcas. In Act II, scene 1 of the same opera, the orchestra participates actively in the shipwreck scene and penetrates the recitative of Neptune 'Vents orageux, Cessez'. This scene includes an off-stage chorus of 'shipwrecked people who are heard but not seen'—a device used many years later by Rameau in his *Zoroastre* (1749).

Greater awareness of the colouristic possibilities of the orchestra is also evident in some *tragédies lyriques* of the *préramiste* period.[14] The range of the violins was increased; there was a modest attempt to exploit the idiomatic features of solo instruments and a greater use of obbligato instruments—an influence from the Italian concertos heard in France with greater frequency during the early years of the eighteenth century. Composers became increasingly sensitive to colour combinations. Independent lines for bassoon and violoncello began to appear, and in *Tancrède*, Campra, despite the popularity of the counter-tenor, wrote all male roles for the bass voice and the main female role for the alto.

In vocal writing, the recitative closely follows the model established by Lully, with some small differences worth noting. There is a freer use of the anapestic formula; more rests and sudden changes of tempo emphasize the action or state of mind; expressive use of orchestral *ritournelles* helps establish continuity or contrast of mood; melodic range is greater and there is dramatic use of 'affective' intervals and dissonant harmonies.

Example 21a, b, and c below shows extracts from Destouches' *Omphale* and *Amadis de Grèce* (p. 167) and Campra's *Tancrède*. The

Example 21
(a) *Destouches:* Omphale (*after ed. of 1701*). (b) *Destouches:* Amadis de Grèce (*after ed. of 1712*). (c) *Campra:* Tancrède (*after ed. of 1702*).

ascending minor 6th, the ascending diminished 7th and the diminished octave are melodic intervals not found in Lully.

Destouches particularly reveals a highly developed expressive and dramatic sense in his recitatives. Zoroaster's recitatives from Act III of *Semiramis* wih their dramatic pauses and orchestral interpolations prefigure Rameau's own *Zoroastre* composed 30 years later. Perhaps taking Lully's late accompanied recitatives as models, Destouches fashioned a flexible, 'singing' type of musical declamation which approached the Italian *arioso*. Even F. W. von Grimm in his attack against Destouches' *Omphale* (*Lettre sur Omphale*, 1752) admitted that the composer's recitatives were 'still esteemed'.[15]

Ironically, some of the best examples of *péramiste* recitative are not found in a five-act *tragédie lyrique* but rather in the one-act 'La Tragédie' from Campra's *opéra-ballet Les Muses* (1703). Superficially, this tragic tale, taken from Ovid's *Metamorphoses*, resembles a Lully–Quinault opera in miniature. Danchet simplified the action and reduced the number of characters to those essential to plot development. Example 22a and b below contrasts Althée's recitative 'Vous noires Déitez' from scene 2 of 'La Tragédie' with Phèdre's 'Dieux cruels' from Act IV, scene 5 of Rameau's *Hippolyte*. If anything, Campra's example makes more conspicuous use of 'affective' intervals. The main female character's calling upon the 'black' and 'cruel gods' in both extracts and the striking use of a diminished 7th chord superimposed over a pedal tone establishes a close relationship in subject as well as in musical treatment.

Taken as a whole, *préramiste* stage music presents a more daring harmonic language than was evident in Lully. The static basses and slow harmonic rhythm characteristic of Lully gave way gradually before a more extensive use of chromaticism and more rapid modula-

Example 22
(a) Campra: *Althée's recitative*, Les Muses (*after ed. of 1703*).

(b) Rameau: *Phèdre's recitative*, Hippolyte (*after the De Gland engraved ed. of 1733*).

Example 23
Montéclair: *Extract from accompanied recitative*, Jephté (*after ed. of 1733*).

tions. Diminished and half-diminished 7th and secondary Dominants such as are found in the accompanied recitative from Montéclair's *Jephté* (I, 6) above were common.

Examples similar to Example 24 below from the *ritournelle* of scene 1, Act IV of Destouches' *Amadis de Grèce*, with its suspension chains and its circle of 5ths, are unthinkable in the music of Lully and are clearly a by-product of the Italian trio sonatas. As such, the *ritournelle* would have been considered 'bizarre' and 'peu naturel' by those committed to the 'simple', 'naturel' style of Lully. Also considered too 'recherché' and 'savant' would have been the occasional excursions into rare tonalities such as the D-flat Major and B-Minor coupling of keys used in Campra's *Idomenée* (V, 5).

Example 24

Destouches: Extract from ritournelle, Amadis de Grèce *(after ed. of 1712).*

Although most *préramiste* airs are in the Lully tradition of short binary and *rondeau* structures, there is a tendency towards a more expressive vocal line with greater melodic range. The melodies 'sing' more, and textual fragments repeated for musical reasons are not uncommon. The Italian *aria da capo* and its French progeny, the *ariette*, were found more and more in the *divertissements*.

In no other vocal form of this period is the Italian influence more clearly marked than in the *ariette*. In fact, the *ariette* is the French *aria da capo*. In French hands, the Italian model was stripped of dramatic significance and, as a merely decorative element, was relegated to the dramatically impotent *divertissement*. In that capacity it gave the composer his best chance to write virtuoso vocal music.

The *ariette* made its appearance in French opera about the same time that the cantata in the Italian style came into vogue in France. Thus, the *aria da capo* reached French opera not through direct contact with the Neapolitan opera but by the circuitous route of the cantatas. It is not surprising to find in Campra's *opéra-ballet Les Fêtes vénitiennes* of 1710 three cantatas so labelled in the score.

The word *ariette*, a French diminutive, is totally inadequate to describe this large formal structure—an anomaly well recognized by most eighteenth century writers. Cahusac, describing the Italian *aria da capo*, wrote: 'We title them, improperly, *ariette*. The true translation is *air*' (*La Danse ancienne et moderne*, III, p. 60). Nougaret, however, was careful to make a clear distinction between *ariette* and *air* in France.

> The French word, *Ariette*, comes from the Italian *Aria*. One means by this term a certain number of lines which are sung and of which the melody is extremely ornate. The piece of music which in France is called *Air* is a unified and gentle melody. The French musician uses the *Ariette* to show off the voice of a singer in contrast to an *Air* which he uses to express a sentiment.
>
> (*De l'Art du Théâtre*, II, p. 297)

For Rousseau, ambiguous terminology was just one more weapon in his arsenal. '... One may judge the idea our musicians have of the nature of an opera by the singularity of their nomenclature. Those grand pieces of Italian music which ravish the soul, those masterpieces of genius which draw tears ... the French call *ariettes*' (from 'Lettre sur la musique française', quoted by Strunk, *Source Readings*, p. 649).

The most critical differences between the Lully–Quinault *tragédie lyrique* and its *préramiste* counterpart are the proliferation of dances and the increased emphasis given to what became increasingly a purely decorative *divertissement*. Campra in his *Achille et Déidame* (1735) was accused by one of his contemporaries of 'completely drowning the subject in the *divertissements*. No one wished to honour it [the opera] by calling it a Tragedy' (quoted by Barthélemy, *André Campra*, p. 147).

Table 3
Use of dance in tragédies lyriques

Amadis		Tancrède	Dardanus
Prologue	3	6	7
Act I	3	2	4
Act II	2	4	2
Act III	2	4	7
Act IV	2	2	4
Act V	1	5	6
Totals	13	23	30

That Rameau continued and even expanded the use of the dance in his *tragédies lyriques* is shown in the table above which indicates the number of dances in Lully's *Amadis* (1684), Campra's *Tancrède* (1702) and Rameau's *Dardanus* (revival of 1744).

In the closing years of the *préramiste* period, the Paris opera house became a veritable graveyard for the *tragédie lyrique*. This trend was checked in 1732, one year before *Hippolyte*, with an opera whose prologue is set on the stage of the Académie Royale de Musique itself: Michel Pignolet de Montéclair's *Jephté*, a 'Tragedy taken from Holy Scripture', which in spite of, or perhaps because of, the condemnation of the opera by the Archbishop of Paris, was a great success. From the standpoint of musical and dramatic treatment of the subject, the opera has much to recommend it. 'Tout tremble devant le Seigneur' (Act I), a large chorus in which both Jephté and Phinée participate, was highly regarded by Rameau. The same act also includes an unaccompanied chorus, rare for the period, 'O Gloire! O force d'Israël'. In the final act there is an interesting example of musical recall: the opening music that accompanies the mother of Jephté as she approaches the sacrificial altar recurs in scene 6 as Iphise walks towards the same altar.

'My Lord, there is enough music in this opera to make ten of them; this man will eclipse us all' (quoted by Girdlestone, *Jean-Philippe Rameau*, p. 193). So the ageing André Campra prophesied to the Prince de Conti after the first performance of Jean-Philippe Rameau's *Hippolyte et Aricie* on 1 October 1733. This then is the date that precipitously concludes the *préramiste* period, and this is the date that fixes the outer chronological and stylistic boundaries of our study.

The break with the past sensed by Campra was not lost on other contemporary observers. 'They found the music of this opera a little difficult to execute.... In his (Rameau's) first work for the lyric stage, he has created an harmonious and virile Music of a new character' (*Mercure de France*, October 1733, quoted in *Oeuvres complètes*, vol. VI, p. lv). In point of fact, the singers and members of the orchestra were incapable of performing the magnificent second 'Trio des Parques' from Act II with its exciting enharmonic modulation that shifts the music in semitones from G-minor to D-Minor.[16] Rameau was aware that he had pushed far beyond the harmonic limitations of his predecessors. In his *Génération harmonique* (1737), he discusses this trio and his disappointment at having been forced to change it for the stage performance. One part prophetic visionary, one part practical musician with the traditional limitations of his performers in mind, he concluded sadly that because of indifference towards those who invent and because of lack of sufficient research, the 'infinite variety to which Music is susceptible, is as yet unknown'.

Giving a backward glance on Rameau's career as a dramatic composer, the *Almanach des spectacles* of 1765, one year after his death, viewed *Hippolyte* as marking the date of the 'revolution made in the progress of music in France'. There was at first astonishment over music so much more complex and fertile in image than was customary at that time on the stage. Nonetheless, the audience found it to their taste and ended by applauding it' (quoted in *Oeuvres complètes*, vol. VI, p. lix).

There is little question, then, that Rameau's contemporaries saw *Hippolyte et Aricie* as bringing about a 'sea change' in French music of the period. It is well to acknowledge that much of the 'originality' of *Hippolyte* was created out of a greatly expanded and enriched musical vocabulary employed by the *préramiste* composers. 'The great Rameau', writes Renée Viollier, 'is only the logical and magnificent issue of the labour and researches of his immediate predecessors.'[17] He parallels Bach in that he culminates a style, in his case, that of the *grand siècle*; more than Bach, however, he portends and in places even creates the sound of the future. In the *tragédies lyriques* and *opéras-ballets* of Rameau, the old and the new co-exist sometimes gracefully, sometimes, as the bitter attacks of the *Lullistes* reveal, to the detriment of their Lullian models.

The *récitatif simple*, although given more melodic and harmonic significance, remains essentially unchanged in Rameau's music as do certain scoring practices such as the *trio des hautbois* and the 'double continuo' air. New concepts in French music were his use of independent second violin and viola parts (see prelude to Act I, scene 1) and his use of sustained winds in pairs to support the strings (see prelude to scene 5, Act II and the 'Tonnerre' from Act I). It is in such accompanied recitatives as Phèdre's 'Quelle plainte en ces lieux m'appelle' that closes Act IV that we may observe Rameau's progressive features to best advantage. In this scene, we are on the threshold of high classical opera. Rameau's Phèdre and Gluck's Iphigénie and Clytemnestra speak the same language and it is no longer the language of Lully's Armide.

Rameau's orchestra participates more directly with the vocal music to form entire scene complexes. The orchestra of the second 'Trio des Parques' is the true unifying agent. The motifs first heard in the opening *ritournelle* form a relentless, almost symphonic, counterpoint to the vocal trio that emphasizes the 'sudden horror' of the text. *Préramiste* tempests pale beside the chorus 'Quel bruit! Quels vents!' in scene 3, Act IV where angry strings are punctuated by shrill wind passages. The orchestra sounds curiously 'Viennese' and looks ahead to the sea monster scene in Mozart's *Idomeneo*.

It is music like this that represents the supremacy of musician over poet that was the core of the often bitter arguments between the *Lullistes* and *Ramistes* that divided the Paris musical scene after 1733. In Masson's words, whether Rameau was attacked for his too complicated harmonies, his difficult melodies, his lack of interest in the *livret*, or for his Italianisms, 'all this could be reduced to one basic reproach: too much music'.[18]

In the last analysis, the reputation of Rameau in the galaxy of great composers must be based on his stage works.[19] In terms of musical statement, there is no question but that he is the greatest composer of the French eighteenth century; there is also no question that, among all the first line composers of that century of giants, he is the one least performed today. This neglect is explained by Donald Grout on the grounds that Rameau's opera 'cannot be revived as a living art without reviving the age of Louis XV' (*A Short History of Opera*, 1965, p. 173). Yet, is Rameau's operatic style actually more 'dead' than that of Handel, any more frozen in time than that of Gluck? Anyone who has listened to Anthony Lewis' performance of *Hippolyte* (recorded by L'Oiseau-Lyre) must, I believe, conclude that questions concerning a 'dead operatic style' are curiously irrelevant when viewed face-to-face with the 'living art' that is Rameau's music.

Chapter 10

⇉ ⇇

The Opéra-Ballet

Ce sont de jolis Watteau, des miniatures piquantes, qui exigent toute la précision du dessin, les grâces du pinceau et tout le brillant du coloris.

(Cahusac, *La Danse ancienne et moderne*)

The *grand siècle* of Louis xiv had reached its apogee by 1689. The years 1690 to the end of the king's reign in 1715 were marked by endless wars, economic and social crises ('All of France is no more than a large poorhouse, desolated and without provisions'—Fénelon, *Lettre à Louis XIV*, 1694), and a mood of grim austerity at the court brought about in part by the appalling personal losses sustained by the ageing monarch. The court *divertissements* and chapel *Te Deums* designed to commemorate a happy event, a victory or a royal birth had an increasingly hollow ring. There were few happy events to commemorate; no *Te Deums* were sung for the humiliating French defeats at Blenheim (1704), Ramillies (1706) and Oudenarde (1708); and with the loss of three Dauphins in eleven short months, the pall of death hung over Versailles.[1]

The very concept of the divine right of kings was under attack, and contemporary *chansons* reflected the general mood of discontent and disenchantment with the *grand monarque* and his family:

> Le grand-père est un fanfaron,
> Le fils un imbécile,
> Le petit-fils un grand poltron,
> Ohé! la belle famille!

More and more Louis xiv withdrew from active social life at Versailles. Perhaps in so doing he followed the wishes of the pious Mme de Maintenon and her confessors more than his own natural inclinations. Entries in the *Journal* of the Marquis de Dangeau, begun in 1684 and terminated by his death in 1720, give a vivid picture of the daily life at court. It is clear from the quotations below[2] that the king never totally relinquished his love of music and the theatre but that the days of public display, the pomp and ceremony connected with court performances of *tragédies lyriques* attended by royalty, were a thing of the past. It is also clear that Mme de Maintenon, although desirous that the king take an interest in religious music, arranged *musicales* almost every evening for him in the intimacy of her own apartments.

2 October 1694: After dinner in his chamber the King heard some paraphrases by Racine based on some verses from Saint Paul. Moreau composed the music.

14 October 1703: Fontainebleau. During the evening, the new opera of Destouches, the subject of which is the marriage of Carnival and Madness (*Le Carnaval et la Folie*) was performed. As the King rather likes the music of Destouches, it had been hoped that His Majesty would attend. But he has almost entirely renounced such performances.

9 October 1704: The King never attends public concerts or the Theatre.

5 November 1712: In the evenings there is always music at Mme de Maintenon's on the days when the King is not working with his ministers.

21 December 1712: This evening there was much music at Mme de Maintenon's. The King had some of his musicians perform scenes from *Le Bourgeois gentilhomme*. They were even in the costumes of actors, and the King found that they played the parts very well.

It was inevitable, with the diminishing role of the king as arbiter of fashion, that Versailles itself became less important to the nobility and even to members of the royal family. Gradually Paris took the place of Versailles; it was the town house or the country château that now substituted for the centralized court. Among the king's family the Princesse de Conti, Comte de Toulouse and the Duc d'Antin (all avid music lovers) bought town houses, and the famous 'grandes nuits' at Sceaux at the château of the Duchesse du Maine reached their climax in 1714–15.

It was also inevitable that the style of the *grand siècle* succumbed to modifications more in keeping with the tastes of a pleasure-living public. The austerity and grandeur of Versailles were happily changed for more comfort and intimacy. The *petits appartements* and the *salons*, often conceived in oval and circular shapes, decorated with mirrors and with furniture arranged for intimate conversaton, contrasted markedly with the cold, formal *grandes galeries* of the palace about which even Mme de Maintenon complained: '... there is only grandeur, magnificence and symmetry. One must suffer the draughts

131

from under doors that must face one another. *Il faut périr en sym-métrie'* (quoted by Louis Réau, *Le Rayonnement de Paris au XVIII siècle*, Paris 1946, p. 46).

In painting, the mode of the theatre in amorous dalliance or in *fête galante* rivalled the heroic poses and big battle pieces of the king's official painter, Charles Lebrun. The new style is best seen in the feminine arabesques and *chinoiseries* of Claude Audran, in painted scenes from the *comédie italienne* by Claude Gillot and above all in the *fêtes galantes* of Watteau. Indeed, if the painting of Watteau may be considered the quintessence of the so-called Regency style and the antithesis of the style of Louis XIV, it should be emphasized that the major part of his work was completed before the death of Louis XIV. 'In reality', wrote Louis Réau, 'the art that we call Louis the Four-teenth was dying well before the actual setting of the Sun King' (*Le Rayonnement*, p. 17). Réau dates the beginning of this change from the end of the 'dictatorship of the king's first painter, Lebrun' (died 1690).

Similarly in music, the style of Louis XIV underwent several modi-fications following the end of the 'dictatorship' of the king's first composer, Jean-Baptiste Lully. In the preceding chapter we have dis-cussed the ramifications of these changes as they affected Lullian *tragédie lyrique*. In the *opéra-ballet*, however, we come face-to-face with Regency style during Louis XIV's reign. It is the André Campra of *L'Europe galante* and *Les Fêtes vénitiennes* rather than of *Tancrède* or *Aréthuse*, it is the Jean-Joseph Mouret of *Les Fêtes de Thalie* rather than of *Ariane* that most clearly reveal a Regency style before the chronological beginning of the Regency itself.

A study of the writings of the aestheticians and encyclopedists, a perusal of the influential *Mercure de France*, and a careful reading of *livret* prefaces attest that, in the opinion of the eighteenth century, André Campra and Houdar de La Motte had created a genre 'tout neuf' (Cahusac, 'Ballet', Diderot *Encyclopédie*) with their *opéra-ballet L'Europe galante* of 1697. For Cahusac the new genre differed from the *tragédie lyrique* as follows:

> The opera conceived by Quinault is composed of one central, dramatic action over the course of five acts. It is a vast concept, such as that of Raphael and Michelangelo. The spectacle created by La Motte is composed of several different acts, each repre-senting a single action and including *divertissements* of song and dance. These are pretty Watteaus, piquant miniatures that de-mand precision of design, grace of brushstroke and brilliance of colour.
>
> (*La Danse ancienne et moderne*, III, p. 108)

A contemporary of André Campra, the librettist and poet Pierre-Charles Roy, best summed up the wide gulf that separates the Lullian

132

tragédie lyrique and the *opéra-ballet*: 'This sort of Drama which assembles three or four acts in the same cadre and which presents a different subject for each act with a *divertissement* ... pleases by its variety and sympathizes with French impatience' ('Lettre sur l'Opéra'). Roy concluded that Regency audiences were bored by having to follow a continuous five-act plot and preferred to be amused and diverted. In the preface to Destouches' *Les Eléments* (1725), he wrote that 'separate plots are less fatiguing for the attention than a piece in several acts and make the introduction of *divertissements* easier'.

In his preface to Destouches' *Le Carnaval et la Folie* (1703), La Motte admitted that the title of the work announces only 'a *bagatelle*, and perhaps all Opera is really nothing else...'—an unthinkable comment if applied to a Quinault *tragédie lyrique*.

The confusing, vague and contradictory attempts to define the *opéra-ballet* in many nineteenth and twentieth century sources make it necessary to turn to the eighteenth century for a clear definition. Typical is the definition by Marmontel in the *Encyclopédie*: 'The *opéra-ballet*, that is, a spectacle composed of acts independent from one another as regards action, but united under a collective idea such as the Senses, the Elements.' Nougaret wrote: 'Observe that the *opéras-ballets* are composed of several acts with no connection one with the other ..' (*De l'Art du Théâtre*, II, p. 230). Rousseau defined the *opéra-ballet* as a 'bizarre type of opera ... the Acts each form a different subject related to one another only in a general way' (*Dictionnaire*, p. 38).

Most eighteenth century definitions emphasized two structural features of the *opéra-ballet*: First, each act or *entrée* has its own independent action which relates very loosely to an over-all idea expressed in the titles of the *opéra-ballet* (the terms 'acte' and 'entrée' were used interchangeably when referring to the *opéra-ballet*); and second, each act includes at least one *divertissement* of songs and dances. Therefore, the roots of the genre may be traced to both the opera and the seventeenth century *ballet à entrées* in which each act developed its own plot.

The single source of confusion may be found in the term 'opéra-ballet' itself. It seems to have been rarely employed in the early eighteenth century and was not used consistently even after 1750. Because of the increased emphasis on *divertissements* and the basic relationship between the new genre and the *ballet à entrées*, it is not surprising to find many eighteenth century writers using the generic term 'ballet' to include the new form.

The term 'opéra-ballet' came into more general use in the nineteenth century, and the distinctions which characterize the genre, so carefully delineated by eighteenth century writers, were quickly forgotten. Thus, in the eighteenth century a general, ambiguous title was accorded a precise definition; in the nineteenth century, a title inherently precise was used by most writers in a general and ambiguous way. The basic structural distinction—that of an independent dramatic action for each *entrée*—was seldom recognized. The twentieth century inherited the careless application of the term that had plagued the preceding century. Perhaps the most important and successful attempt to classify the term 'opéra-ballet', as well as such related genres as the 'ballet héroïque', 'acte de ballet', and 'fragments', is founded in Paul-Marie Masson's brilliant study of the *ballet héroïque*. Quite properly, Masson insisted that the term 'opéra-ballet' be reserved for works that lack continuous dramatic action and have 'as many different plots as there are acts'.[3]

Eighteen *opéras-ballets* conforming to the eighteenth century definition were performed at the Académie Royale de Musique between 1697 (*L'Europe galante*) and 1735 (*Les Indes galantes*). The following table lists these *opéras-ballets* in chronological order by title, first

Table 4
Chronology, title, composer and librettist of opéras-ballets
(1697–1735)

	Title	First Performance	Composer	Librettist
1	*L'Europe galante*	24.10.1697	Campra	La Motte
2	*Le Triomphe des Arts*	16. 5.1700	La Barre	La Motte
3	*Les Muses*	28.10.1703	Campra	Danchet
4	*Les Fêtes vénitiennes*	17. 6.1710	Campra	Danchet
5	*Les Amours déguisés*	22. 8.1713	Bourgeois	Fuzelier
6	*Les Fêtes de Thalie*	19. 8.1714	Mouret	La Font
7	*Les Fêtes de l'été*	12. 6.1716	Montéclair	Pellegrin
8	*Les Ages*	9.10.1718	Campra	Fuzelier
9	*Les Plaisirs de la Campagne*	10. 8.1719	Bertin	Pellegrin
10	*Les Fêtes grecques et romaines*	13. 7.1723	de Blamont	Fuzelier
11	*Les Eléments*	29. 5.1725	Destouches	Roy
12	*Les Stratagèmes de l'Amour*	28. 3.1726	Destouches	Roy
13	*Les Amours des Dieux*	14. 9.1727	Mouret	Fuzelier
14	*Les Amours des Déesses*	9. 8.1729	Quinault	Fuzelier
15	*Le Triomphe des Sens*	5. 6.1732	Mouret	Roy
16	*L'Empire de l'Amour*	14. 4.1733	de Brassac	Moncrif
17	*Les Grâces*	5. 5.1735	Mouret	Roy
18	*Les Indes galantes*	23. 8.1735	Rameau	Fuzelier

performance at the Paris Opéra, composer and librettist. Although the *préramiste* period ends with Rameau's *Hippolyte* in 1733, *Les Indes galantes* of 1735 is his first *opéra-ballet*.

A sub-classification of these *opéras-ballets* is possible on the basis of subject matter. The first nine, with the exception of *Le Triomphe des Arts*, substituted at least some believable contemporary characters for the mythological deities and heroes of the *tragédie lyrique*. Genuine comic intrigue, as opposed to occasional comic scenes, was introduced to the French lyric theatre. The *petits-maîtres*, the amorous ladies and the watchful confidantes lightly engaged in superficial banter thus giving to the Regency a medium through which it could observe, in ideal reflection, its own hedonistic pursuits.

By virtue of its subject matter *L'Europe galante* may rightly be considered the first *opéra-ballet*. It opened in 1697. Two years earlier, Pascal Collasse's *Ballet des Saisons* (*livret* by Abbé Jean Pic) was performed at the Paris Opéra in October 1695. This work, which held the stage until 1722, contains a separate intrigue for each act and was undoubtedly the immediate structural model for *L'Europe galante*. Collasse's *opéra-ballet* restricts its material to the mythological-allegorical personages so characteristic of the period, and unlike *L'Europe galante*, its Prologue includes a 40-page panegyric addressed to 'Louis le plus parfait des Roys'—a chorus which was actually lifted from an earlier chorus by Lully in the Prologue to his *Ballet des Muses* (see Chapter 3, p. 43).

The real innovation of Campra and his librettists was to take the formal structure of the *Ballet des Saisons* and the earlier *ballets à entrées* but to dethrone the deities and shopworn characters from mythology. Only the prologues and an occasional *entrée* remained for the odd assortment of characters borrowed by French librettists from allegory and from their *galant* version of classical mythology.

The action of *L'Europe galante* does not take place in ancient times, nor is it rooted in myths. On the contrary, Campra and La Motte rendered precise, contemporary stereotypes of love as practised in four European nations. In the full score of *L'Europe galante* (Ballard, 1724) following the Prologue, La Motte summarized his plan for the opera as follows:

> We have chosen those Nations which are most contrasting and which offer the greatest potential for stage treatment: *France, Spain, Italy* & *Turkey*: We have followed what is normally considered to be characteristic behaviour of their Inhabitants.
>
> *The Frenchman* is portrayed as fickle, indiscreet & amorous.
> *The Spaniard* as faithful and romantic.
> *The Italian* as jealous, shrewd & violent.

Finally, we have expressed, within the limitations of the stage, the haughtiness and supreme authority of the *Sultan* and the passionate nature of the *Sultanas*.

These innovations were not lost on contemporary audiences. A letter of the Princess Palatine written on 10 November 1697 noted: 'It is in truth only a Ballet, but it is charming. It is called *L'Europe galante*. They show how the French, Spanish, Italians and Turks make love; the character of these nationalities is so properly expressed that one is amused' (quoted in Barthélemy, *André Campra*, p. 49).

The comments of Dr Martin Lister in his amusing and informative *A Journey to Paris in the Year 1698* not only reveal the esteem with which Campra's first *opéra-ballet* was held, it also substantiates the audience 'participation' in the singing of some of the popular tunes from the work:

> I was at the Opera, called *l'Europe galante*, several times, and it is lookt upon as one of the very best. It is extremely fine, and the Musick and Singing admirable: The Stage large and magnificent, and well filled with Actors: The Scenes well suited to the thing, and as quick in the removal of them, as can be thought: The dancing exquisite, as being performed by the best Masters of that Profession in Town: The clothing rich, proper, and with great variety.
>
> It is to be wondered, that these Operas are so frequented. There are great numbers of the Nobility that come daily to them, and some that can Sing them all. And it was one thing that was troublesome to us Strangers, to disturb the Box by these voluntary Songs of some parts of the Opera or other.
>
> (*A Journey to Paris*, pp. 170–71)

In eschewing mythological or allegorical subject matter in the body of the work, La Motte and Campra also had reasonable grounds for avoiding the elaborate machinery and the concomitant paraphernalia of the *merveilleux*. In so doing they helped introduce some degree of verisimilitude into the French lyric theatre. That the tradition of the *merveilleux* was too powerful to allow *opéra-ballet* continued exemption is obvious in the modification of *opéra-ballet* subject matter that resulted in 1723 in the creation of the *ballet héroïque*. Even Cahusac, although a partisan of La Motte, felt that perhaps 'La Motte made one mistake in the creation of the *ballet*. Quinault sensed that the *merveilleux* was the very basis of opera. Why could it not also serve as the basis of the Ballet?' ('Ballet' in *Encyclopédie*).

At the same time Cahusac recognized the innovatory nature of *L'Europe galante*. In 1754 he stated categorically that 'La Motte in

136

creating a completely new genre gained the advantage of being copied in turn. . . . *L'Europe galante* is the first of our works for the lyric stage that bears no resemblance to the operas of Quinault' (*La Danse moderne et ancienne*, III, p. 108). The key words 'completely new' and 'no resemblance to the operas of Quinault' must have referred to more than just the formal structure of *opéras-ballets*. Are they not a musical parallel to Cahusac's own happy image of 'pretty Watteaus'? Watteau did not people his canvases with mythological or heroic figures nor did Campra, Mouret or Montéclair in their *opéras-ballets*.

Both the *opéra-ballet* and its sister, the continuous-action ballet, gave French opera its first introduction to comedy. It is not a question here of unrelated, comic episodes similar to those that Lully had already employed in his first *tragédies lyriques*, but rather of a fully developed comic opera. The continuous-action ballets *Aricie* (La Coste and Abbé Pic, 1697), *Les Fêtes galantes* (Desmarest and Duché, 1698) and *Le Carnaval de Venise* (Campra and Regnard, 1699) all had contemporary subject matter and comic plots; all were abject failures and are noted here only because of their distinction in being the first comic operas performed at the Académie Royale de Musique. To be sure there are comic implications in *L'Europe galante*, such as Silvandre's efforts in 'La France' to extricate himself from Céphise's accusations of fickleness, but a continuous comic intrigue is not found in the first *opéra-ballet*.

'La Comédie', the fourth *entrée* from Campra's and Danchet's *opéra-ballet Les Muses* of 1703, is the first comedy to have had a measure of success. A one-act comic opera of considerable charm, 'La Comédie' is an improbable pastiche made up of elements from Molière's *L'Amour médecin* (1665) and an episode described in Plutarch's *Lives* between Antiochus and his beautiful stepmother, Stratonice.

In the minds of most eighteenth century observers, however, it was Campra's *Les Fêtes vénitiennes* of 1710 that first exploited comedy on the lyric stage. 'Danchet', wrote Cahusac, 'in following the plan given by La Motte (*L'Europe galante*), imagined comic *entrées*; it is to him that we owe this genre. . . . Les Fêtes vénitiennes opened a new course for those poets and musicians who had the courage to believe that the theatre of the *merveilleux* could also be the theatre of comedy' (*Encyclopédie*). *Les Fêtes vénitiennes* with its artful combination of comedy and fantasy was a great success throughout the eighteenth century in France, causing Voltaire to complain that whereas Corneille's tragedy *Cinna* was performed one or two times, *Les Fêtes vénitiennes* played for three months (*Dissertation sur la Tragédie ancienne et moderne*, 1749).

From June to December of 1710, a prologue and a total of eight *entrées* had been composed on a trial-and-error basis for *Les Fêtes vénitiennes*, making this *opéra ballet* a most kaleidoscopic translation of 'French impatience'.

Critics of the *opéra-ballet*, including those aestheticians who held that the *tragédie lyrique* was the only legitimate genre for the lyric stage, were spoiling for a fight. The opportunity came on 19 August 1714 with the first performance of Jean-Joseph Mouret's and Joseph de La Font's *Les Fêtes de Thalie*. The humiliating defeat of Melpomène (muse of tragedy) at the hands of Thalie (muse of comedy) in the prologue of this *opéra-ballet*, which the librettist had boldly set on the stage of the Paris Opéra itself, resulted in a *succès de scandale*. Apollo, however, as arbiter of the quarrel between his tragic and comic muses, asks Melpomène why she could not co-exist with Thalie 'as formerly'. Is this an oblique reference to Lully's comic scenes in *Cadmus* and *Alceste*? Apollo continues with a topical reference to contemporary Italian opera: 'This *mélange* still charms Italy today.' Pressure was such that the authors were obliged to change the original title of *Les Fêtes ou le Triomphe de Thalie* to *Les Fêtes de Thalie* and to add a new *entrée*, 'La Critique des Fêtes de Thalie', for the 25th performance on 9 October 1714 in order to justify their audacity.

Rémond de Saint-Mard clearly understood the significance of the subject matter of the *opéra-ballet* for a public suddenly grown tired of the heroic gestures and pretensions of the *grand siècle*:

> We have reached the point, Monsieur, where people want only Ballets (*opéras-ballets*). . . . There is no longer any need for the strong and pathetic action demanded by the tragic. In the Ballet, all laughs. . . . Each act must be made up of a fast moving, light, and, if you wish, a rather *galant* intrigue. . . . Two or three short scenes and the rest of the action in *Ariettes, Fêtes, Spectacles* and other such agreeable things. . . . these small *divertissements* are much better executed than our Operas (*tragédies lyriques*). . . . take (for a model) *L'Europe galante, Les Eléments, Les Fêtes vénitiennes*, and you will find there some *galante* ideas, some graceful melodies, and . . . many agreeable words (*maxims*) that never cease to be natural and simple. . . . You also will find there the portrait of our mores. They are to be sure rather unpleasant (*vilaines*), but they are, nonetheless, ours. . . . Thus, Monsieur, you can see that the Ballet is an extremely agreeable spectacle for us. Nothing is better made for our lightness of spirit, nothing agrees better with our character.
>
> (*Réflexions sur l'Opéra*, 1741, pp. 94–6)

Playful *maxims* and *galanteries* abound in *Les Fêtes vénitiennes*, *Les Fêtes de Thalie* and *Les Fêtes de l'été*. These works are concerned in part with a pragmatic approach to the art of love. There is a touch of cynicism and an almost total lack of sentimentality in librettists La Font's and Danchet's acute observations. Although turns of phrase borrowed from the vocabulary of *préciosité* are found, there is no need here for Mme de Scudéry's metaphorical *carte de tendre*. Rather, there seems to have been an attempt to mirror the world of the country *seigneur* and the *petits-maîtres*, the elegant ladies and their amorous confidantes. There was an effort to render with some accuracy the social and cultural mores, no matter how 'vilaines', of the final years of the reign of Louis XIV and the Regency of Philippe d'Orléans.

The flesh and blood characters of *opéra-ballet* are found in recognizable contemporary settings. 'L'Opéra' from *Les Fêtes vénitiennes* takes place in the theatre of the Grimani Palace in Venice; 'Les Ages rivaux' of *Les Ages* is set in Hamburg; and Marseilles is the location of the first *entrée* of *Les Fêtes de Thalie*.

Campra's *Les Fêtes vénitiennes* also included some topical musical references to certain popular operas performed at the Académie Royale de Musique in the first decade of the eighteenth century. In 'L'Opéra', the Neapolitan soldier Damire is an opera buff who describes with vivid intensity the performance of his adored Léontine as Armide in the famous scene from Act II of Lully's *tragédie lyrique*. In the amusing informative second scene of 'Le Bal', Campra parodied well-known extracts from famous operas of the time. Unlike Mozart in the finale to *Don Giovanni*, Campra did not identify his borrowed material but simply stated in his *Avertissement* to the 1710 edition that he had employed 'some melodies and Symphonies of our most skilful composers'.[4]

Significantly, as we move into the years of the Regency, more and more emphasis is placed on the allegorical role assigned to 'La Folie' (Madness) in the prologues and *divertissements* of many *opéras-ballets*. In his *avertissement* to Destouches' *Le Carnaval et la Folie*, La Motte defined 'La Folie' as a goddess who 'although she did nothing reasonable, at the same time did nothing for which one could not find examples in human behaviour'. In the prologue to *Les Fêtes vénitiennes* she joins forces with 'le Carnaval' and together they triumph over 'severe reason'. However, in *Les Ages* of 1718, the only *opéra-ballet* by Campra written after the beginning of the Regency, 'La Folie' is deified and placed above love in the hierarchy of pleasures. In fact, musical excesses such as the reckless proliferation of dances and airs in *Les Ages* are commensurate with the extravagant tastes of the Regency. The 'fête galante' of *Les Ages* bears approximately the same relationship to *Les Fêtes vénitiennes* as does the grimace of a Lancret to the smile of a Watteau.

The *opéras-ballets* written from 1697 to 1723 constitute the 'first period' of *opéra-ballet* by virtue of their subject matter and musical content. First period *opéra-ballet* gave composer and librettist alike the opportunity to experiment with new and varied forms. The introduction of comic intrigue and characters drawn in part from French and other European society stimulated this experimentation. The opportunity apparently ended with the death of the Regent in 1723. Young Louis xv was at 13 years of age officially king of France. On 13 July 1723 the first performance of Colin de Blamont's *ballet héroïque Les Fêtes grecques et romaines* took place at the Académie Royale de Musique. The end of the first period *opéra-ballet* and the end of the Regency followed closely one upon the other.

The structure of the *ballet héroïque* is the same as that of the *opéra-ballet*; therefore, it may legitimately be considered as a type of *opéra-ballet*, a 'second' or final period of the genre.[5]

One may only speculate on the reasons for the sudden demise of the first period *opéra-ballet*. Was it because of the continued opposition of many aestheticians to comedy on the French lyric stage; was it the return of a king, albeit a boy king, to the French throne; or was it the elusive tragic muse that diverted librettist and composer alike? The revealing discussion by Cahusac of La Motte's defection from the *opéra-ballet* to the tragedy suggests the latter consideration:

> It is indeed strange that he (La Motte) has not given us a greater number of works in such a charming genre. Only *L'Europe galante* among his works holds the stage today. He undoubtedly believed that that which is called the *grand opéra* (*tragédie lyrique*) was alone worthy of his consideration. However, his originality was better served in a genre completely of his own making.
>
> ('Ballet' in *Encyclopédie*)

In any case the *ballet héroïque* with all the trappings of monarchical opera evicted the Don Pedros, the Léonores, the fickle Léandres from the banks of the Seine, the lively *petits-maîtres*, and the watchful confidantes of the first period *opéra-ballet* who were forced to seek refuge in parodies, *vaudevilles* and the budding *opéra comique*.

Fuzelier wrote in his preface to Colin de Blamont's *Les Fêtes grecques et romaines*:

> *Les Fêtes grecques et romaines* is a completely new type of Ballet (*opéra-ballet*). . . . France has up to now only used the Fable as subject matter appropriate for music (*sic*). In a more daring manner, Italy has taken events from History for her operas. The Scarlattis and Bononcinis have already allowed their Heroes to sing that which Corneille and Racine would have declaimed. . . .
>
> Brought together in this Ballet are the best-known Festivals of Antiquity which appeared to be most adaptable to the stage and to music. . . .

We have neglected in this Ballet the use of the *merveilleux* which deals with magic and the descent of Gods. We have thus deviated from a well-worn and not always well-followed path; we shall learn only too soon whether or not we have lost our way.

In Fuzelier's second *ballet héroïque, Les Amours des Dieux* (music by Mouret) of 1727, all pretence of avoiding the return to mythological subject matter is cast aside. Somewhat apologetically as though to convince himself, Fuzelier wrote in the *Avertissement* that, in spite of the use of mythological characters, 'the work . . . is absolutely in the heroic genre'.

The list of *ballets héroïques* performed at the Académie Royale de Musique between 1723 and 1735 (see page 134) testifies to the end of the first period of *opéra-ballet*. Out of the nine *opéras-ballets* all but one are clearly in the format of the *ballet héroïque*. In Destouches' *Les Stratagèmes de l'Amour* of 1726, the librettist, Roy, succeeded in introducing comic intrigues into his *opéra-ballet*. However, he found it necessary to justify this audacity in his *Avertissement*: 'The public has decided that if Comedy is allowed on the stage, it may only be a noble Comedy which bears the character of Antiquity.'

The first period of *opéra-ballet* at its best far exceeds the second in dramatic originality and freshness of musical idiom. Of the nine examples, the four by André Campra, Mouret's *Les Fêtes de Thalie* and Montéclair's *Les Fêtes de l'été* contain much that is worth reviving.[6] Only Destouches' *Les Éléments* among the second period *opéra-ballet* has sufficient musical merit to warrant revival. By virtue of the date of its first performance (22 December 1721 at the Tuileries), *Les Éléments* is a first period *opéra-ballet*. At the same time in its subject matter it clearly prefigures the *ballet héroïque*. The music of *Les Éléments* with its occasional use of unprepared dissonances and parallel seventh and ninth chords gives further evidence of Destouches' sensitivity to harmonic colour. However, efforts to make of him a harbinger of musical impressionism show a lack of familiarity with other *préramiste* composers in whose scores similar harmonic effects occur. Lionel de La Laurencie, for example, in describing Leucosie's air 'La mer était tranquille' (*Entrée* II, scene 1), singled out the chord in bar three as 'altogether extraordinary for the period'. Yet, this chord is none other than the mediant $\frac{9}{7}_{\sharp5}$ chord found also in the music of Charpentier, Delalande and others (see p. 193).[7]

The main problem that confronts the modern scholar in dealing with the *opéra-ballet* is the lack of printed editions in full score (*partition générale*). With the exception of the full score of *L'Europe galante* printed by Ballard in 1724 as an *édition de luxe*,[8] all others exist only in the notorious reduced score (*partition réduite*) favoured by the Ballard printing monopoly for *opéras-ballets* of the *préramiste* period. In preparing a reduced score the general practice seems to have been to eliminate the inner voices. However, this principle was far from universally applied. Vocal and instrumental extracts in trio, for example, were printed in full. Thus, although the 'trio des hautbois' contained three printed parts, the dance for which it served as a 'trio' was printed with only melody and bass!

Yet armed only with reduced scores and a few manuscript copies in full score, one may still explore the musical *terra incognita* that is the first period *opéra-ballet*. It is clear that originality of subject matter may well have stimulated originality in the musico-dramatic devices employed by Campra, Mouret and Montéclair in the *opéra-ballet*.

The repetition of thematic fragments for dramatic ends may be found in the *opéras-ballets* of Campra and his followers. The device was used in the following three ways: 1. the repetition of a general melodic shape and rhythmic organization; 2. the repetition of a phrase of music and text from a particularly important air or ensemble; and 3. the repetition of an instrumental fragment or an entire instrumental composition.

The most striking example of the first type is found in the last scene of *L'Europe galante* (*Entrée* IV, scene 6). It is an abridged version of the 'Prélude pour la Discorde' which was first used to interrupt the *divertissement* of the second scene of the prologue. This is the one extract from the dramatic music of Campra singled out by La Laurencie as an example of a 'germ of the leitmotif'.[9] The D-Major key of the prelude becomes D-Minor; the harmonic underpinning is simplified; the dotted rhythms and string *tirades* remain. There is also a striking parallel between the musical and textual elements that make up Discord's words in both scenes. By converting the authoritative ascending 4th in the prologue (Example 25a) to the more pathetic ascending minor 6th in the last *entrée* (Example 25b) and by changing Discord's defiant 'C'est en vain' to a resigned 'c'en est fait', Campra maintained the textual and general melodic shape but totally altered their meaning. However, judging from copies of the 1724 full score of *L'Europe galante* that served as editions for actual performances, this innovation was lost on the audiences and impresarios of the later eighteenth century. The copies in the Bibliothèque de l'Opéra (A. 45[1]) and the Bibliothèque de Versailles (MSD. 78) have excised the entire final scene of the opera!

The second device, the recurrence of musical and textual fragments, has gone virtually unnoticed, Yet it occurs in *Les Muses, Les Fêtes vénitiennes, Les Fêtes de Thalie* and *Les Fêtes de l'été*. Here the composers of these *opéras-ballets* have given greater dramatic focus to a device already introduced by Lully in certain of his *tragédies lyriques*. Typical is scene 2 from 'L'Amour saltimbanque' (*Les Fêtes vénitiennes*) in which Nérine, the confidante of a young Venetian girl,

Example 25
Campra: *Thematic recurrences in* L'Europe galante *(after ed. of 1724).*
(a) Prologue. (b) Final scene.

Léonore, tries to poison her mistress' mind against all lovers. Nérine
has a recurring phrase first used in the prelude to the scene (Example
26a). This phrase, which forms the main theme of her air 'Songez,
songez' (Example 26b), always returns with the same accompaniment
as is found in the air. It comes back in the recitative following the air
(Example 26c), and it interrupts the recitative of Léonore to close the
scene (Example 26d).

Example 26
Campra: *Thematic recurrences in 'L'Amour saltimbanque', Les Fêtes
vénitiennes (after ed. of 1714).*
(a) Prelude. (b) Air. (c) Recitative. (d) Recitative.

143

One of the best examples of the recurrences of an instrumental fragment or an entire instrumental extract is found in scenes 3 and 4 of 'Les Devins de la Place St Marc' (*Les Fêtes vénitiennes*). The *ritournelle* that begins scene 3 is presented only in fragments, each fragment interrupted by recitatives. The entire composition, with its fragments connected, becomes the 'Marche' used as entrance music for scene 4. The same device was utilized in the attractive 'horoscope' scene from the same *entrée*, a scene which must have influenced Mouret who used the same device and closely related melodic material for Thalie's entrance music in the Prologue to *Les Fêtes de Thalie*.

The increased power of musician over poet shows up in the monologues and Italianate *ariettes* of the *opéra-ballet*. Undoubtedly the lack of continuous plot and the general, non-dramatic subject matter encouraged the writing of these purely decorative yet often musically sophisticated airs.

Italian influence may be seen not only in the increased use of vocal melismas, repeated texts and concerto-like driving rhythms, but even in the use of the cantata itself as an organizational medium. Thus, the *divertissement* of 'Les Devins de la Place St Marc' (*Les Fêtes vénitiennes*) was carefully built around what Campra labelled a *cantate*.[10] Campra's cantata is a nice synthesis between Italian *aria da capo* and French recitative and ballet. The components were carefully organized into the following large diptych: recitative, *ariette*, dance; recitative, *ariette*, dance. In each case the dance is based on the preceding *ariette*. Campra framed the entire cantata with two dances which relate it to the action of the previous scene and help, therefore, to unify the entire *entrée* musically and dramatically.

The *divertissement* of songs and dances was of central importance in the structure of the *opéra-ballet*. Every *entrée* was designed to build towards its *divertissement*. The fact that each *entrée* had its own set of characters helped bring about a measure of contrast between *divertissements*.

The *divertissement* of the *opéra-ballet* and the *tragédie lyrique* of the *préramiste* period is a repository of the most popular dance types of the early eighteenth century. Sometimes with ennui, often with kaleidoscopic brilliance, it offers to following generations a summary of those dances which formed an integral part of the operatic milieu of the Regency. The rigaudon, the forlana, the contredanse and the musette, although well known in the seventeenth century, were not used on the operatic stage until this period, when they joined the dances of Lully discussed in Chapter 8.

The rigaudon was first danced at the Paris Opéra in Desmarest's *tragédie lyrique Circé* (1694). It is a fast dance in duple metre which according to Compan was 'very popular in Provence' (*Dictionnaire de danse*). Campra in *L'Europe galante* (1697) was the first to use the forlana, a Venetian dance that may be thought of as a fast loure. In *Les Muses* (1703) Campra also introduced the contredanse to the lyric stage three years after Feuillet had included it in his *Recueil des dances* (Paris, 1700). This lively dance of English origin is often in compound duple metre and, like the bourrée, it begins on the second beat of the measure. We learn from Rousseau that the contredanse was danced by 'four, six or eight people' at balls (*Dictionnaire*). Perhaps the idea of involving so many dancers transferred to the stage where the dance often served to conclude a final *divertissement* (see, for example, the contredanse from *Les Fêtes vénitiennes* by Campra).

The musette, a French bagpipe, had been a popular folk instrument throughout the seventeenth century. The first tutor dates from 1672 (Borjon de Scellery, *Traité de la musette*). In the late seventeenth century the name of the instrument became the name of the dance which simulated the sound of the bagpipe's drone. The musette appears to have been first used on the stage in Destouches' *tragédie lyrique Callirhoe* (1712).

In the stage music of the period, the number of dances, including those that bear descriptive titles or are simply designated as 'Airs', staggers the imagination. In the four *opéras-ballets* by Campra there is a total of 123 dances! Faced with such information the reader can only wonder how this plethora of dances was used. Were they all grouped indiscriminately in the *divertissements* or was some attempt made to relate them to the dramatic action?

Simply stated, the dance in the *opéra-ballet*, as in the *tragédie lyrique*, functioned in two ways: as a decorative 'agrément' with no discernible relationship to the action; and as a valid dramatic agent either to expedite the action or to lend some emphasis to a salient feature of the scene.

Faced with an audience primarily interested in light diversion, the *préramiste* composer stressed the dance as 'agrément'. As Cahusac pointed out with some irritation, 'La Motte only knew the simple Dance. . . . There are only *divertissements* in which one dances just to dance' (*La Danse ancienne*, III, p. 153).

Sometimes, however, the dance as 'agrément' and the dance as dramatic agent converge in a manner not usually associated with the *opéra-ballet*. The dramatic action of the third *entrée* of *L'Europe galante* ('L'Italie') focuses on the *divertissement* during which the identity of the secret suitor of Olimpia is revealed to his jealous rival, Octavio.

The dance underscores a prevailing mood in several first period *opéras-ballets*. In scene 1 of the Prologue to Mouret's *Les Fêtes de Thalie*, the 'Air des Suivants de Melpomène' emphasizes the severe dignity of the tragic muse. Example 27a below shows the typical dotted rhythms and upbeat *tirades* borrowed from the *tragédie lyrique*. Example 27b shows an extract from the dance associated with Thalie. This dance, which appears in its entirety in scene 5, is introduced in fragments in scene 2 and offers the greatest possible contrast to the stern measures of Melpomène's dance.

Example 27
Mouret: Extracts from Prologue to Les Fêtes de Thalie (*after ed. of 1714*).
(a) *Melpomène*. (b) *Thalie*.

Campra's dances bear out Wilfrid Mellers' observation that he was 'perhaps the most enchanting of dance composers' (*François Couperin*, p. 78). Witness the gestic directness of the minuets with their strong rhythms and triadic melodies that almost suggest Haydn, the unbuttoned humour of the rigaudons with their unabashed parallel 5ths reflecting perhaps the rustic dances of his meridional homeland, the kinetic energy of the contredanses and forlanas with an extra measure thrown in here and there to break up symmetrical phrase grouping.

The *opéra-ballet* after *L'Europe galante* became a kind of *pièce d'occasion* directed towards the specific taste of a specific audience. It is to the credit of Campra, Mouret, Montéclair and Destouches that, although totally committed to this aesthetic, they were able to transcend the limited, superficial pleasures of the Duc d'Orléans and his entourage. These are minor masters, poets in miniature who at their best, like Watteau, created a world half real, half fantasy in the first period of *opéra-ballet*.

Chapter 11
➤➤ ◀◀

From Divertissement to Opéra Comique

Divertissement

No single definition of a *divertissement* is possible within the context of the seventeenth and early eighteenth centuries. As we have noted, one use of the term refers to that portion of the *tragédie lyrique* or *opéra-ballet* composed primarily of songs and dances. For a period that could scarcely claim consistency of terminology as a virtue, it is amusing to find some authors insisting with semantic righteousness that the term 'fête' be reserved for the *opéra-ballet* whereas 'divertissement', be employed for the *tragédie lyrique* (see, for example, Compan, *Dictionnaire de Danse*). *Divertissements* were also found between the acts of pastorales, productions of the Fair Theatres, parodies and *opéras comiques*. They were often closely aligned with the action in spoken drama, whether within or between the acts, where they were sometimes labeled 'intermèdes'. Campra, Charpentier, Collasse, Desmarest, Clérambault and Blainville composed *divertissements* to insert between the acts of Latin tragedies performed at the Jesuit college Louis-le-Grand.

Once we have left the stage we must abandon any attempts to classify *divertissements* by types. A simple pastorale could be labelled a *divertissement,* and an entire week's or even month's entertainment of which the pastorale was but one modest part could be labelled collectively a *divertissement*; a chamber cantata might be sub-titled 'Divertissement', and all six volumes of Mouret's music composed for the New Italian Theatre are grouped generically under the term 'Divertissements'.

During the height of the *grand siècle,* so-called *grands divertissements* were ordered by Louis XIV in 1664, 1668 and 1674.[1] These *divertissements* commemorated welcome events such as victories, royal births or even a yen on the part of king or nobleman to parade his affluence. As such they were a natural outgrowth of the elaborate type of court ballet traditionally presented during the carnival season.

The pages of Félibien's *Relation de la Feste de Versailles* (1676) and his *Les Divertissemens de Versailles* (1676) with engravings by Chauveau bring to life as do no other sources the extravagant pomp thought appropriate for the court of the Roi Soleil. A hierarchy of labour comparable to that required for the production of a court ballet existed also for the preparation of a court *divertissement*. Regarding the *Divertissement* of 18 July 1668, we read that the Duc de Créqui, as first gentleman of the chamber, was charged with everything concerning the comedy; Maréchal de Bellefond, as first minister of the 'Hôtel du Roi', took charge of the food; even the great Colbert, as Superintendent of Buildings, was responsible for outdoor platforms and decorations plus preparations for the fireworks; Vigarani was instructed to build a theatre for the comedy; and Le Vau, the king's first architect, was to erect another large edifice for the Court Ball.

That men of this calibre trained in the arts of fortification, architecture or government should at the same time be pressed almost whimsically into service to supervise and build the trappings and symbols of a king's idle pleasure, should come as no surprise. The progenitors of the Versailles *divertissements* are found in the elaborate *fêtes* of Renaissance Italy and may be traced back to the courts of the Dukes of Burgundy.

According to Félibien, Louis xiv had chosen well:

> One of the things to be considered in the *Fêtes* and *Divertissements* with which the King entertains his court is the promptitude that accompanies their magnificence: these orders are executed with so much diligence, by the care and application particularly on the part of those in direct command, that all believe a miracle to have occurred; so, in a moment without having even noticed it, we are surprised to see a Theatre erected, glades embellished with figures and fantasies; tables of food ready and a thousand other things. . . .
>
> (*Les Divertissemens de Versailles*, p. 4)

Félibien described the outdoor tables groaning with food—conspicuous consumption at its worst:

> One of the tables represented a mountain, where within the various caves one might find diverse sorts of cold meats; another was a façade of a Palace built with marzipans and other pastries. . . . In the centre of these tables was a fountain, the water reaching more than thirty feet in height. . . . After Their Majesties had spent some time in this charming place and after the Ladies had finished eating, the King abandoned the Tables to the men; the destruction of such beautiful arrangements served also as an agreeable *divertissement* for the entire Court in the

pushing and confusion of those who demolished the pastry palace and the mountains of preserves.

(Relation de la feste de Versailles, p. 7)

Versailles, 1668, or Las Vegas, 1968? The *divertissement* given by the king for all his court after the triumphant return from the Franche-Comté campaign (1674) lasted from 4 July to 31 August! Included in the *divertissement* were Lully's *Alceste* (4 July, see Plate 8), Molière's *L'Eglogue de Versailles* (11 July) and *Le Malade imaginaire* (19 July), Lully's *Les Festes de l'Amour et de Bacchus* (28 July) and the inevitable fireworks over the Grand Canal. Félibien was silent concerning the entertainment of the last day (31 August) except to mention that the insatiable king wanted to be shown 'beauties that had never been seen up to this point'.

Félibien's account of the performances of *Les Festes de l'Amour et de Bacchus* demonstrates once again that Lully's conception of the ballet as a *danse en action* came long before Mouret's and La Motte's creations for the Duchesse du Maine (see below) and long before Cahusac introduced it in the operas of Rameau:

> One can say that in this work, Lully has found the secret to satisfy and to charm everyone. . . . If one observes the dances, there is not a step that, accompanied by gestures, does not do as much as words to make us understand. . . .
>
> *(Relation de la feste de Versailles, p. 22)*

Félibien's poetic description of a nocturnal *fête* on the Grand Canal strangely predicts the language and imagery of a *Fête galante* by Verlaine:

> . . . the King followed by all his Court embarked on the great expanse of water where, in the deep of the night, the sound of violins following the vessel of His Majesty could be heard. . . . The half light and the music of the instruments seemed to animate the Statues. . . . the water, partially illuminated by so many shining statues, resembled the long *galeries* and large *salons* . . .
>
> *(Les Divertissemens de Versailles, p. 33)*

The elaborate court *divertissements* described above suffered an eclipse as the reign of Louis xiv entered its long decline. The shift from month-long *divertissements* of the 1660's and 1670's to a series of playful court masquerades anticipated the shift from the *tragédie lyrique* to the *opéra-ballet* in the *préramiste* period.

The *Mercure galant* of March 1688 relates the genesis and fall of the court *divertissement* in a few short pages and in so doing gives us a capsule history of the stage music of the *grand siècle*:

Formerly at the Court a *grand divertissement* would last during an entire carnival season. It was usually a *Grand Ballet en machines*, mixed with vocal solos all relating to some subject such as the *Ballet des Arts*, the *Ballet de la Nuit*. . . . Then, the famous Molière introduced his Comedies mixed with songs and dances. These *divertissements* still give more pleasure than the Ballets. Opera succeeded the Comedies; I will not speak of these spectacles, they are presently *à la mode*. . . . However, for some years, the Court has not presented these *divertissements* during carnival season; It is not to avoid expense, but merely that the same *divertissements* seen over the period of a month resulted in too uniform a pleasure. Substituted for these works were small Masquerades which scarcely cost less but whose diversity . . . made them more agreeable and touching. This has been the pattern for the last three or four years.

As entertaining shifted its centre of gravity from the court at Versailles to Parisian town houses or country châteaux, musical patronage shifted from the king to noblemen and even wealthy middle-class gentlemen who became patrons of *divertissements*.

Pastoral, mythological and allegorical themes dominated most *divertissements*. The stag hunt was also favourite subject matter. *La Chasse du Cerf*, a *divertissement* in seven scenes performed before the king at Fontainebleau on 25 August 1708 with music by Morin, was published by Ballard in 1709. The *Avis*, as is so often the case, tells us much about the practical considerations of achieving maximum results from minimal means!

Although the music must be fast and light, it is very easy; I have reduced everything to a simple Trio. . . . It is a group easy to assemble in any country; the singing roles are composed for *Dessus*, *Haute-contre* or *Haute-taille*, which are the most common voices. . . . I have marked the places where the hunting horns or trumpets may play; but as it is rare that these instruments are heard in Concert, the oboes or violins do just as well. I have used the hunting calls and trumpet fanfares most often heard during a stag hunt and have even allowed them to permeate the chorus.

The magnificent château at Sceaux built by Claude Perrault and acquired by Louis-August de Bourbon, the Duc du Maine, was the scene in the closing years of Louis xiv's reign of a series of *divertissements* known as the 'Grandes Nuits de Sceaux'. Anne-Louise-Bénédicte de Bourbon, the Duchesse du Maine, who had taken up residence at the château in 1700, surrounded herself with a *pléiade* of well-known musicians and poets. Writing in 1712 two years before the 'Grandes Nuits', Abbé Charles Genest described her *divertisse-*

ments at that time as 'pure amusement, unrehearsed . . . a type of impromptu entertainment appropriate only for the occasion' (Preface from *Les Divertissements de Sceaux*, 1712). We are told that these playful charades were devised by and for the Duchesse to help endure insomnia.

The famous 'Grandes Nuits' of 1714 and 1715 were on a much larger scale and involved well-known composers: Mouret, Bernier, Marchand (probably one of the 'Versailles Marchands' rather than Louis), Bourgeois, Colin de Blamont and Courbois. It is difficult to ascertain the programme of each of the 16 'Grandes Nuits'. Lyric comedies, plays, dramatic *divertissements, ballets en action,* even cantatas were performed in an enchanting garden setting designed by Le Nôtre. For the thirteenth night, Mouret's and Néricault Destouches' lyric comedy *Les Amours de Ragonde* was performed, and on the fourteenth night Mouret and La Motte with the help of two of the best dancers of the Paris Opéra (Le Sieur Balon and Mlle Prévost) presented a pantomime, a true *ballet en action* based on the murder of Camille by Horace in the fourth act of Corneille's *Horace.*

Nicolas Bernier's fifth book of French cantatas was dedicated to the Duchesse du Maine. Significantly, its title page reads: '*Les Nuits de Sceaux*//Concerts de chambre//ou Cantates françoises//à plusieurs voix//En manière de divertissements//meslez d'airs de violon et autres symphonies//.'

The cantatas of the collection show a clear link with stage music. They include independent instrumental music such as overture, dances and even a *sommeil*; they have vocal airs, ensembles, recitatives, and one (*L'Aurore*) ends with a large chorus. It is conceivable that as part of the 'Grandes Nuits', these cantatas may actually have been staged 'in the manner of *divertissements'.*

Lyric Comedy

The seven continuous-action ballets performed at the Paris Opéra during the *préramiste* period also may be considered as the first examples of lyric comedy to appear on the French stage; that is, these works are all based on one continuous comic intrigue and are sung throughout. Most were failures and only Campra's *Le Carnaval de Venise* has some interest as a study for his later *opéra-ballet Les Fêtes vénitiennes.* One need not be taken in by the title page of the Ballard 1699 edition that asserts that the music of *Le Carnaval de Venise* is by 'M. Campra le Cadet'. The composer at the time was *maître de musique* at Notre-Dame cathedral, and given the repressive climate at court, it is not surprising that he tried to mask his success as a stage composer and pass off his secular works as compositions by his younger brother Joseph, a violinist in the opera orchestra.[2]

Rameau's *Platée* (1745) was characterized by Grimm as the 'sublime work in a genre which M. Rameau created in France' (*Lettre sur Omphale*), but in addition to the continuous-action ballets there are four other lyric comedies that appeared before *Platée*. These are: *Le Carnaval et la Folie* by Destouches (1704); *La Vénitienne* by La Barre (1705); *Les Amours de Ragonde* by Mouret (1714); and *Don Quichotte chez la duchesse* by Boismortier (1743).[3]

Of these works, the most significant musically is Mouret's *Les Amours de Ragonde* created for the 'Nuits de Sceaux' in 1714 and not performed at the Paris Opera until 1742. Although a genuine lyric comedy, it is labelled a 'comédie-ballet' in the score, a 'comédie en musique' in the Ballard *livret* of 1742 and a 'divertissement comique' by Moncrif in his *Approbation* found at the end of the same *livret*, thus pointing up the looseness of terminology apparent in so many stage media at this time.

Musically, *Les Amours de Ragonde* is a charming, though slight score. In eliminating the non-essential prologue, it antedates Rameau's *Zoroastre* by 35 years. In its use of a concluding *vaudeville* and popular tunes that resemble *timbres*, it owes much to the music of the contemporary Fair Theatres. One such melody in which each of three characters sings a different story is reproduced below.

Example 28
Mouret: Extract from vaudeville *from* Les Amours de Ragonde
(after ed. 'chez la veuve Mouret', n.d.).

Opéra Comique[4]

Both the *tragédie lyrique* and the *opéra comique* in France are indebted to imports from across the Alps. Italian operas mounted in Paris during the time of Mazarin demonstrated that the French would accept, albeit with many modifications, a spectacle with continuous music. At the same time the use of songs and dances as incidental music in a spoken comedy never lost its appeal. The popularity of the Molière–Lully *comédie-ballet* has already been discussed. Even more in demand were the Italian comedians who, with Scaramouche at their head, appeared at the Palais Royal in 1660 and soon became a permanent troupe sharing the hall with Molière.

From the pay scale it is quite obvious that the king favoured the

Italians; Scaramouche's troupe received 16,000 *livres* annually in contrast to the 6,000 allotted Molière and the 12,000 for the home of French tragedy, the Hôtel de Bourgogne.

The repertory of the Ancien Théâtre Italien from 1682 to 1687 is preserved in the six volume *Recueil général de toutes les comédies et scènes françoises jouées par les comédiens italiens du Roy* published in 1700 by Evaristo Gherardi. The author's informative preface reveals that the Italian comedians as in the old *commedia dell'arte* 'learn nothing by heart, and that to play a Comedy, it suffices to have read the plot outline (*sujet*) a moment before going on stage'.

French scenes, apparently written by several hands, were inevitably woven with the Italian and gradually replaced the latter. In the later volumes of the collection, music is much more important although, due to Lully's monopoly, the performers were restricted for several years to six instrumentalists, two singers and two dancers. Out of the 55 plays found in Gherardi's *Recueil*, 43 use music extensively.

The music of the Italian Comedy was of three types: *vaudevilles*, parodies of operas and original compositions. A *vaudeville* was any song whose melody had long since passed into public domain. It was identified textually by a *timbre* which was a title usually based on the first line of the refrain by which the original tune was generally known. The entire melody of the song, tagged by this *timbre*, was known as a *fredon*. The tunes were folk-like with repeated, simple rhythmic patterns and a narrow melodic range; they were popularly called 'Pont Neuf tunes' after the famous bridge over the Seine which, because of its great width, was a favourite meeting-place for local minstrels. Any tune that caught the public's fancy was a likely candidate for the growing stockpile of *fredons*. Many of the simpler tunes from Lully's operas, such as 'Dans ces lieux tout rit sans cesse' from *Phaëton*, lived on far into the eighteenth century as *fredons*.

The Italian Comedy by no means originated the *vaudeville*. The first use of the term goes far back into the early years of the sixteenth century. It was known by such terms as 'voix de ville', 'vau de ville' and 'vau de vire', and it became one of the principal antecedents of the court air. There is no compelling documentation for the statement found in many eighteenth century sources that a certain Olivier Basselin, a fuller from Vaudevire in Normandy, invented the *vaudeville*.

Typical is the definition by Mersenne: 'the *chanson* that we call *vaudeville* is the simplest of all Airs that adapts to any kind of Poetry and that is sung note-against-note'. 'Along with the *ariette* and *villanelle*' for Brossard, it exemplified the 'natural style that everyone can sing almost without art'. It was summed up by Boileau in his *L'Art poétique* of 1674 as follows:

D'un trait de ce poème, en bon mots si fertile,
Le Français, né malin, forma le Vaudeville,

Agréable, indiscret, qui, conduit par le chant,
Passe de bouche en bouche, et s'accroit en marchant;

In the Ancien Théâtre Italien, opera airs were used primarily in parody. Naturally, the operas of Lully and Quinault were chosen and certain scenes, already popular in their original versions, were great favourites. Although the use of such cliché themes as the conflict between 'l'amour' and 'la gloire' plus the general pomposity of the *tragédies lyriques* made them ideal targets for satire, the parodies themselves underscored the popularity of the originals. Not only were the texts and music parodied, but the best-known performers of the Opéra were mimicked as well.

After having enjoyed many years of success in the healthy art of parody, the Ancien Théâtre Italien overstepped the bounds of decorum and on 8 January 1696 produced a satire called *La Fausse prude*, a thinly disguised attack on Mme de Maintenon who was already over-sensitive. The king eventually closed the Italian Comedy on 13 May 1697 and expelled the players from the realm. They were gone for nearly 20 years to return under the more tolerant and relaxed atmosphere of the Regency.

The vacuum created by their departure was rapidly filled by the Fair Theatres (Théâtres de la Foire) which continued the Italians' tradition of satire and parody against seemingly insurmountable odds.

The two important fairs, the 'Foire Saint-Germain' and the 'Foire Saint-Laurent', had been the scene of popular farces and acrobatic displays since the Middle Ages. Scarron's description of the 'Foire Saint-Germain' in 1643 gives us the confusion of jostling mobs, the air punctuated by shrill voices of hawkers and sounds of music. He documented the wide use of musical instruments in the days before Lully's restrictive ordinances:

Le bruit des pénétrants sifflets,
Des flûtes et des flageolets,
Des cornets, hautbois et musettes
Des vendeurs et des archeteurs,
Se mêle à celui des sauteurs
Et des Tambourins à sonnettes,
Des joueurs de marionettes
Que le peuple croit enchanteurs.

The impresarios of the first Fair Theatres were themselves often acrobats or tight-rope walkers. In fact, the important theatre of the Foire Saint-Germain was under the direction of two jumpers, Claude and Pierre Alard in 1678.

In 1697 with the closing of the Ancien Théâtre Italien, the Fair Theatres took over the repertory of the Italian Comedy. This brought them in direct competition with the French Comedy. Among the important playwrights for the Fair Theatres were Alain Le Sage and D'Orneval who from 1724 to 1737 collaborated in publishing a collection of ten volumes of plays including musical extracts (*Théâtre de la Foire ou l'opéra comique*). Let Le Sage's preface sum up the genealogy of the *opéra comique* and review the frustrations in the Fair Theatres' struggle to stay alive:

> The Fair Theatre began with the farces that the tight-rope dancers mixed with their acrobatic feats. Following this, we presented fragments from the old Italian comedies. The French comedians, however, forced us to stop these performances . . . and obtained orders to prevent any of the Fair actors from giving any comedy by monologue or by dialogue. The Fair performers, having been forbidden to speak, resorted to the use of large placards, that is, each Actor wrote his text in large letters on the cardboard that he then showed to the Spectators. These inscriptions were at first in prose. Later, they were set to tunes that the orchestra played and the audience sang. . . . The Actors observing that the audience took pleasure in this *Spectacle en chansons* assumed, correctly, that if they (the actors) were to sing the *vaudevilles* themselves, it would be even more pleasing. They entered into an agreement with the Opera which, by virtue of its patents, allowed them to sing (December 1714). We then began to compose pieces purely *en vaudeville*; and it was at this time that the Spectacle took the name of *Opéra-Comique* (term first used on the publicity posters of 1715). We began little by little to mix prose with poetry. . . . It was so when the *Opéra-Comique* finally succumbed under the blows of its enemies.

We learn from the pages of the *Mercure* (July 1715) that the new *opéra comique* had a popular success that could only bring about retaliatory action from its powerful, jealous rivals: 'On this same day, (25 July 1715, opening of the "Foire Saint-Laurent"), the Comedy and the Opera were deserted. . . .'

In 1719, the Comédie Française suppressed all performances at the Fair Theatres with the exception of tight-rope dancers and marionettes. The Nouveau Théâtre Italien took advantage of this new repression and filled the gap at the 'Foire Saint-Laurent' with regular performances from 1721 to 1723.

In spite of such vicissitudes, the *opéra comique* managed to survive and even to expand. In 1743 its director, Jean Monnet, hired a first class literary talent, Charles-Simon Favart, who brought the genre to its highest point of development from literary and musical points of view.

The subject matter of the *opéra comique* and the new Italian comedy was based on crude realities of daily life, opera parodies and, especially after 1717, the conflicts between the 'deux comédies' and the tribulations of the Fair Theatres. In *La Désolation des deux Comédies* (1718) by Riccoboni and Dominique, the character 'Opéra' communicates only by singing; 'Opéra-Comique', by means of *vaudevilles*; and 'Comédie Française', in verses declaimed in Alexandrine couplets. *Funérailles de la Foire* (1718) parodies the well-known 'Alceste est morte' from the funeral ceremony in *Alceste* (III, 4, see page 77), substituting the words 'La Foire' for 'Alceste'.

Example 29
Alceste *parody from* Funérailles de la Foire *(after Le Sage, Vol.* III*).*

The play was so successful that it was performed at the Palais Royal before the Regent who, according to Parfaict, commented that the *opéra comique* resembled a swan 'who never sings so melodiously as when he is about to die' (*Mémoires à l'histoire du Spectacle de la foire*, Paris 1743, p. 215).

It would be foolish to claim for the *opéra comique*, before the days of Duni, Philidor and Monsigny, a musical significance comparable to that of the earlier *comédie ballet* or the *opéra-ballet* of the *préramiste* period. The plays in the ten volumes of Le Sage's *Le Théâtre* lean heavily on the system of *vaudevilles* taken over from the Ancien Théâtre Italien although descriptive *symphonies*, dances, overtures and *vaudeville* finales became common in the later plays of the collection. There are more than 1,500 tunes reproduced in *Le Théâtre*, 1,100 of them serving as *vaudevilles*.

Le Sage and above all Favart were very skilful in choosing among the vast stockpile of *vaudeville* tunes. A specific *fredon* was often employed in the same situation from one play to the next and functioned somewhat as a primitive leitmotif technique. Speaking of Favart's gift for *fredon* selection, Parfaict noted:

These *vaudevilles* translate with a minute exactitude successive degrees of the same sentiment and the most rapid, minute
shifts within one action. Thus, the sleep of a shepherdess and
the pursual of a kiss could scarcely be rendered with such delicate truth by newly composed music.

(*Dictionnaire des Théâtres de Paris*, VI, p. 69)

Some airs from contemporary *tragédies lyriques* or *opéras-ballets*
were rapidly absorbed into the *opéra comique* as *fredons* each with
its own timbre. Such an air as the rondeau from the end of the second
entrée of Mouret's *Les Fêtes de Thalie* was a popular *fredon* for more
than 40 years. Example 30 below shows its first use in the Mouret
opéra-ballet of 1714 and selected later appearances up through Gluck's
opéra comique Le Diable à quatre, of 1756.

Example 30
(*a*) Les Fêtes de Thalie (*1714*). (*b*) Arlequin traitant (*1716*).
(*c*) L'Ecole des Amans (*1716*). (*d*) La Querelle des théâtres (*1718*).
(*e*) Diable à quatre (*1756*).

Originally composed tunes were used more and more. These were
labelled *ariettes* to distinguish them from the pre-existent *fredons*.
Although Favart encouraged the composition of new music, Parfaict
spoke for many when he wrote:

No matter how agreeable Music composed expressly (for a play)
may be, it is not possible that it be considered the equivalent

of the *Vaudevilles* whose words are known by all . . . and which tunes . . . consecrated by usage . . . explain to the Spectators what the Actor seeks to communicate by gesture and even up to his innermost thoughts.

(*Dictionnaire des Théâtres*, VI, p. 71)

Among the composers of *ariettes* and dances for the *opéra comique* were Jean-Claude Gillier (1667–1737), Jacques Aubert (1689–1753) and the great Rameau himself. Collaborating with the librettist Alexis Piron, Rameau apparently wrote four works for the Fair Theatre, most of the music for which has not survived: *L'Endriague* (1723), *L'Enrôlement d'Arlequin* (1726), *La P[ucelage], ou la Rose* (1726) and *La Robe de dissension ou le faux prodigue* (1726).[5]

From 1717 until his death in 1738, Jean-Joseph Mouret was the most important composer attached to the Nouveau Théâtre Italien. His active collaboration with the Italians began in 1718 with the French comedy *Le Naufrage au port à l'anglais*, which was also the first French language comedy to be performed on the stage of the Nouveau Théâtre Italien. The success of this production convinced Luigi Riccoboni, the director, that only works performed in French with occasional Italian scenes would succeed. Six volumes of *Divertissements du Nouveau Théâtre Italien* include all the 'simphonies, accompagnemens, airs de violons et de flûtes, hautbois, de musettes, airs italiens' composed by Mouret. The 140 'divertissements' found in this collection attest to the industry of the 'musicien des grâces'.

It is fitting to close this chapter with an extract from *Le Procès des Théâtres* (1718), text by Riccoboni and Dominique, in which, in a manner reminiscent of the prologue to *Les Fêtes de Thalie*, Mouret cleverly characterizes the quarrelsome protagonists in the battle for supremacy in the theatrical world. The musical fragments assigned to each 'theatre' are but six or eight measures long and elide almost imperceptibly one with the other.

Example 31
Mouret: Fragments from Le Procès des Théâtres

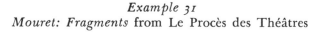

Part two

Religious Music

Chapter 12
→≫ ≪←
From Du Caurroy to Du Mont

Any study of sacred polyphony in France from the death of Eustache
Du Caurroy (1609) to the death of Cardinal Mazarin (1661) and the
beginning of the personal rule of Louis XIV[1] is plagued by an appalling
lack of primary sources. The modern scholar is placed in the frus-
trating position of being able to document, through seventeenth century accounts, the existence of an impressive amount of religious music
from this period and then, because of a staggering mortality rate, be
unable to have direct contact with the music itself. Implicated in this
sad state of affairs is the Ballard family's printing monopoly. Pierre and
his son Robert Ballard were more interested in printing musical settings of psalms, the fashionable paraphrases by Godeau and Desportes'
translations of the many religious parodies of *airs de cour* than they
were in printing Masses or motets.

Where are the three Masses of Du Caurroy described by Mersenne?
What has happened to the Cambrai Masses and motets for double
choir composed between 1612 and 1647 by Gonet, Solon or Penne for
which the music for only one choir is extant? Where are the motets
by Cambert mentioned by Robinet and Loret? And the late motets
of Moulinié? Where are the motets by Jean Mignon which La Borde
informs us were 'judged excellent'? Because not one note of music by
Eustache Picot survives, we are at a loss to know whether or not he carried on some of the innovations of Nicolas Formé whom he succeeded
in 1638 at Sainte-Chapelle. Where and what are the 'antiennes
récitatives' for two voices and continuo by Thomas Gobert mentioned

in his 1646 correspondence with Constantin Huygens? Do the dialogues between solo and chorus in the motets of Guillaume Bouzignac reflect the assimilative power of one man exposed to Roman and Catalan church music, or was Bouzignac the leader of a provincial school whose existence was ignored by the Ballards in Paris?

Based on a study of the extant music, it is clear that the conflict between the religious *stile antico* and *stile moderno*, which took place in Italy soon after the turn of the century, was slow to materialize in France. French composers writing for the church in the first 50 years of the seventeenth century were conservative as a group.

Much of the extant music of Eustache Du Caurroy (1549–1609) praised by Mersenne for its 'impressive harmony and rich counterpoint' is in the tradition of the international Franco-Netherlands school. Many of the 23 motets (from *a* 4 to *a* 7) found in Book I of his *Preces ecclesiasticae* (1609) utilize double choruses of equal voices which dialogue and then unite from time to time. Each choir tends to be developed in the high Renaissance tradition treating text phrases in imitative counterpoint. In the *Victimae paschali* (Book II of *Preces ecclesiasticae* found in Launay, *Anthologie*, pp. 22–27) there are two choirs: one composed of soprano, counter-tenor, tenor and bass; and the other composed of soprano, counter-tenor and tenor. They come together at the conclusion in seven independent parts of real Netherlandish polyphony that may have stimulated Mersenne's comment that 'All the composers of France take him (Du Caurroy) for their master'. Du Caurroy's *a* 5 *Missa pro defunctis*[2] was printed by Ballard in 1636 (privilege date) and performed for the funeral of Henry IV murdered in 1610. Its performance became a tradition which Brossard tells us remained in effect at Saint Denis for the obsequies of kings and princes in the eighteenth century (*Catalogue*).

It is quite likely that the use of double choruses in France at the time of Du Caurroy was still somewhat of a novelty. Our specific sources of information on the *concertato* use of a *grand choeur* and a *petit choeur* come from a later time—nearly mid-century. Thomas Gobert in a letter to Constantin Huygens differentiated the two groups as follows: 'The *grand choeur*, which is *a* 5, is always sung by many voices. The *petit choeur* is composed only of solo voices' (letter of 17 October 1646).[3] The archaic, equal-voiced form of double chorus and the *concertato* treatment of double chorus co-existed as late as 1670. René Ouvrard, *maître des enfants* at the Sainte-Chapelle, wrote in his *La Musique rétablie depuis ses origines*:

When one composes for two, three or more choirs, these choirs may be equally voiced, that is, they may have the same quantity and quality of voice parts; however, one may choose to have one chorus composed of the ordinary soprano, counter-tenor, tenor and bass which is reinforced by a multiplicity of voices and is called the *grand* or *gros choeur*, the other (chorus) . . . may have fewer voices or may have no doubling at all, and this we title . . . the *petit choeur* or the *voix de récit*.[4]

French composers were also conservative in the use of instruments accompanying the chorus although eye-witness accounts of performances often seem to contradict official documents and printed editions. Unlike Italian scores of the period, no separate instrumental parts were printed. As late as 1645, the instrumentalists employed in the royal chapel consisted of two cornett players. The serpent gradually replaced the cornett, and solo instruments made a timid appearance at the Sainte-Chapelle in the 1680's. It was not until the very end of the century, however, that André Campra was allowed to introduce violins at Notre-Dame cathedral some 20 years after he had successfully used them at Saint-Etienne in Toulouse. As late as 1689 influential members of the clergy were opposed to the use of a *symphonie* for ceremonies at the Cathedral of Senlis; and far into the eighteenth century the 24 Masses of Henri Hardouin (1727–1808), *maître de musique* at Reims from 1748 to 1791, were performed *a cappella*.

In contrast, the Cathedral of Rouen soon after 1626 purchased three bass viols, a serpent, bassoon, cornett, sackbut and violins to accompany the *Lamentations*.[5] By 1655, Chartres had a serpent, bassoon and double-bass.

It is difficult to say why some churches and some religious orders were musically progressive and why others remained bastions of conservatism. Did the pockets of Italian influence in Provence enrich the musical resources of some of the Toulouse churches? Certainly in Paris, the chapel of the Theatines, whose priests were called the 'Pères du chant' and whose music was for a time under the direction of Paolo Lorenzani, welcomed musical elements borrowed from secular sources, as did the conventual chapels of the Feuillants, and the Augustinians in the Place des Victoires, and the Jesuits in the Faubourg Saint-Antoine.

These bare facts do not always present a realistic picture of performance practices. For special occasions there is no question but that many instruments were used and that court musicians as well as town musicians augmented the meagre resources of the churches. We are told by Claude Binet that Jacques Mauduit's (1557–1627) *Requiem* performed at the funeral of Ronsard in 1586 was 'animated by all sorts of instruments' (*Oeuvres complètes* of Ronsard, 1587), and we remember that this is the same Mauduit who conducted music 'composed of sixty-four voices, twenty-eight viols and fourteen lutes' for the 1617 performance of the *Ballet de la Délivrance de Renaud*. A description of a ceremony at the Cathedral of Notre-Dame celebrating the Peace of Vervins in 1598, mentions the musicians 'borrowed' from the king's Chamber to augment the musicians of the chapel: 'Those from the chamber with soft and low voices, joined by lutes, viols and other gentle instruments were placed on the right side (of the altar) in order to be better heard. . . . Those from the chapel, blended their stronger, fuller voices with the cornetts and trumpets on the other side.'[6]

The *Mercure galant* described another ceremony at Notre-Dame almost 100 years later in celebration of the birth of the Duc de Bourgogne: 'A concert of trumpets, oboes and violins began the Vespers which was sung by an excellent group composed of all the best voices of the two chapters (of St Etienne and St Saturnin) and of the town' (October 1682). Note that this took place some 12 years before Campra's modest request for violins at Notre-Dame was granted.

The musical conservatism of France in the first half of the seventeenth century is nowhere more dramatically displayed than in the reluctance of her composers to make use of the basso continuo. The first printed work in France in which the continuo is used throughout is not even by a Frenchman; it is Constantin Huygens' *Pathodia Sacra et Profana*, printed by Ballard in 1647, although there are some isolated continuo-like passages for lute in an *air de cour* by Guédron as early as 1617. Etienne Moulinié's *Meslanges de sujets Chrestiens . . . avec une basse continue* was printed by Ballard in 1658 but was in circulation before 1650 and therefore has priority over the Du Mont publication described below. It was not until 1652 that Ballard printed Du Mont's *Cantica sacra*. In the preface the publisher wrote: 'This sort of music with the basso continuo has not been printed before in France. . . . My plan was to join the Motets and one Mass with the *Basse continue*; however, I was advised to print them separately. . . .' Thus, although not initiating the use of the basso continuo, Du Mont through Ballard was the first to use figures and to print separate continuo parts.

The concomitant practice of adding continuo parts to earlier polyphonic vocal music was also slow to develop in France. Brossard chose to ignore the musical conservatism of the 1640's and blamed Ballard for this. Writing about the Ballard edition of Le Jeune's *Octonaires de la Vanité* printed in 1641, Brossard commented: 'It is surprising that in the year 1641, Ballard in his second or third edition (of *Octonaires*), did not include a *Basse continue* that certainly would not have damaged this work. . . . But it is typical of Printers to be lazy and often the fear of spending money prevents them from improving their Work . . .' (*Catalogue*, p. 271).

Settings of the Ordinary of the Mass remained the stronghold of the *stile antico* throughout the seventeenth century. Stylistically static, these Mass settings had their origins in Flemish *a cappella* and Roman polychoral Masses. This conservative bias was reflected by Ballard who, when he deigned to print Masses, generally chose the most archaic examples by Charles d'Helfer, Henri Frémart, François Cosset and others as opposed to those written in *concertato* style. The Renaissance tradition in liturgical music was also supported by the official documents regulating church ceremonies especially in the Paris area. The stern voice of the Council of Trent is heard again in the 1662 *ceremoniale parisiense* admonishing against the use of any instruments other than the organ: 'neither trumpets, winds, or horns'.[7] Denise Launay quotes from an ordinance of the Archbishop of Paris in 1674 that strictly forbade singing 'profane or secular music' in any church or chapel, 'playing on the organ any *chansons* or other airs unworthy of the modesty and gravity of the church, singing in chorus or playing any onstrumental music during Tenebrae . . . or inviting, by means of tickets or publicity announcements, others to come to hear the music as though it were a spectacle or a theatre performance'.

The list of conservative Mass composers in France in the first 60 years of the seventeenth century is a long one. Beginning with Du Caurroy, it includes the Cambrai and Arras composers J. Solon, Antoine Penne and Valérien Gonet whose extant double-choir music is rooted in the Franco-Netherlands tradition. The peripatetic Jean de Bournonville (1580?–1632), *maître de chapelle* at Rouen, Evreux, Saint-Quentin, Abbeville and Amiens, left us 14 Masses and 8 Magnificats. Eight of Pierre Lauverjat's Masses were printed by Ballard between 1612 and 1623 and the Jesuit Charles d'Ambleville included two Masses in his *Harmonia sacra* (1636). Artus Auxcousteaux (1590–1656), *maître de musique* at the Sainte-Chapelle from 1643 to 1651, composed eight Masses using each of the ecclesiastical modes, of which only three survive.[8] According to Brossard, Auxcousteaux's conservative nature was such that he wished 'never to hear the suggestion of adding *Basses continues* to his works' (*Catalogue*, p. 215). Annibal Gantez (1600–68) whose charming *L'Entretien des Musiciens* (1643) gives us such a lively picture of his musical peers, remained conservative in his four and six part Masses. However, he wrote that he found the progressive music of Jean Veillot 'most pleasing' in contrast to the conservative music of André Péchon which he found 'most serious'. Péchon, who was at Saint-German-l'Auxerrois in 1640, favoured the archaic use of a cantus firmus in augmented note values in his motets. Henri Frémart (*d.* after 1646) and François Cosset (*d.* 1673) both left several Masses some of which were printed by Ballard. Brossard himself added a *symphonie* to Cosset's *Missa Gaudeamus a 5* for a performance at the royal chapel in 1688. The *Missa pro defunctis a 4* (1656) by Charles d'Helfer, *maître de chapelle* at Soissons in the 1650's, was performed at the funeral of Delalande in 1726 and again at Saint-Denis for the repose of the soul of Louis xv on 27 July 1774.[9] From the early years of the eighteenth century, instrumental parts were grafted on to these museum pieces to make them palatable to the contemporary listener.

An opinion attributed by Brossard to Pierre Tabart, his immediate predecessor at Meaux, shows awareness of the reaction late in the seventeenth century against this conservative style: 'in spite of his cleverness in writing counterpoint . . . he (Tabart) confessed to me many times that in the end, this sort of writing pleased only the eyes and not the ears, and that he was astonished to find those with such magnificent preparation composing pieces that pleased so few people' (*Catalogue*, p. 491).

Much earlier, Etienne Moulinié, in his preface to the *Meslanges de sujets Chrestiens* (1658), was already an outspoken partisan of the 'agrémens' of the 'new manner' as opposed to the 'austerity' of the old, and in 1659 Thomas Gobert wrote new music for the *Paraphrase des Psaumes de David en vers françois* although these verses by Antoine Godeau, dilettante bishop of Vence, had been set to music by Auxcousteaux in 1654. Why a new setting only five years later? Gobert's printer took the trouble to justify the new effort in his preface on grounds that the old version "did not have all the grace desirable for such admirable verses'.

It is clear then that we must turn to the motet, to the psalm paraphrases, the sacred hymns and spiritual odes, to the noëls and *airs de cour* parodies instead of to the Masses to trace the development of the *stile moderno* in France. The *airs de cour* and *solo récits* as well as elements from the Italian *concertato* style served as models for the 'new style' in France. Also discreetly admired and imitated were early seventeenth century Italian motets for solo voice and continuo by Pietro Pace, Girolamo Marinoni, Antonio Burlini, Severo Bonini and others. The Bibliothèque Nationale is rich in such collections, and documents of the *Minutier central* from 1600 to 1650 in its funerary inventories show the amazing extent to which Italian music permeated private libraries.

Nicolas Formé (1567–1638) was first to move the double chorus motet and Mass in the direction of the Baroque *concertante* motet. He was Du Caurroy's successor as *sous-maître* at the royal chapel (1609). A curious contract dated 30 January 1638 reveals that he gave Pierre and Robert Ballard three double-chorus Masses in the new style to publish in return for a promise that they would print 'no other music (than his) similar to that of the aforementioned three Masses . . . during the lifetime of Sieur Formé'.[10] Unfortunately, these three Masses are not extant, but another double chorus Mass, composed the same year and dedicated to Louis xiii, is clearly in the Venetian *stile concertato* with a *grand choeur a* 5 and a *petit choeur a* 4 made up of soloists. This distribution of vocal parts conforms' to the description of double choruses found in the letter to Huygens by Formé's successor, Thomas Gobert, in 1646. Thus, one generation removed from Du Caurroy and only three years later than the Ballard publication of Charles d'Ambleville's conservative double-chorus motets (*Harmonia sacra*), Nicolas Formé tried to corner the market on the 'new' manner of composing religious music. Undoubtedly by virtue of Louis XIII's approval and the subsequent performances of these works, Formé was looked upon by later generations as the originator of the double chorus motet in France. Contributing to this myth was Sauval's account in his *Histoire et recherches des antiquités de Paris*:[11]

> . . . (Formé) invented the double chorus Motets that the *Maîtres de Musique* have imitated since that time. He surpassed all those who had preceded him in Counterpoint and fine *invention*. . . . the King appreciated the Works of Formé so much that after his death . . . he had them performed often. They have since been locked in a cabinet which the King ordered built for this purpose and for which he alone had the key. . . . at the death of the King, they passed to Jean de Souvre (first gentleman of the chamber) . . . and a few days later they fell into the hands of Jean Villet (Veillot), *sous-maître de la chapelle*, who made much progress because of them.
>
> (*Histoire et recherches*, I, p. 326)

Rarely has the direct influence of an important stylistic change been so clearly documented; the more's the pity that in spite of such precautionary measures, only two Formé motets for double chorus have survived (one of these, *Ecce tu pulchra es*, is in Launay, *Anthologie*, p. 106).

Jean Veillot (Villot, Villet, d. 1662) who alternated with Thomas Gobert as *sous-maître* of the royal chapel, was one of the first to add *symphonies* to Formé's plan of *grand choeur* and *petit choeur*. The 'plus agréable' (Gantez) music of Veillot prefigures the *grand motet* of the next generation and thereby is an important link between Formé and Henry Du Mont, Veillot's successor at the royal chapel. Two motets were copied by Philidor, perhaps because of their popularity. They are *O filii et filiae* and *Sacris solemniis* conceived in a grand manner suitable for royalty. The orchestra is given independent *ritournelles* in addition to music doubling the voices of the *grand choeur*; the soloists of the *a 6 petit choeur* are sustained by a continuo.

Unfortunately, the *Te Deum* composed by Veillot and performed in April 1660 for the double celebration of the Peace of the Pyrenees and the marriage of Louis XIV is not extant. It is tempting, though fruitless, to conjecture a direct bearing of this motet, which drew upon the *24 Violons* as well as 'all the best instrumentalists of Paris', upon the *Miserere* of 1664, the first of Lully's *grands motets*.

Thomas Gobert (died 1672), along with Formé and Veillot, was a composer of the *avant-garde* in France. He admitted to admiring the many 'belles et bonnes choses' in Monteverdi's madrigals, and he did much to stabilize the double chorus motet. His lost *Antiennes recitatives* may have used the basso continuo before Huygens' *Pathodia sacra* of 1647. His peers and superiors alike thought well of him. Gantez noted his 'good jump into the employ of Monsieur le Cardinal (Richelieu) and a better jump yet to the service of the King, since he is now *maître* of his chapel'.

Gobert's *Paraphrase des Psaumes de David*, first printed in 1659, was reprinted in 1661, 1672, 1676 and 1686. Antoine Godeau's translations of the psalms of David were immensely popular and were even recited and sung at the Hôtel de Rambouillet, the headquarters of *préciosité* itself. For this elegant and worldly Catholic milieu, the old-fashioned settings of Auxcousteaux would not do, and it remained for Gobert to realize the 'original intention of the Monseigneur of Vence which was to render them in simple counterpoint for the convenience of those who only know a bit of music' (preface). The 'simple counterpoint' of Gobert is far removed from the archaic Renaissance polyphony of Auxcousteaux. Gobert conceived of the paraphrases as ideally suited for two voices and a continuo which could for the 'convenience' of the performer be reduced to solo voice and continuo.

Etienne Moulinié was *maître de musique* for Gaston d'Orléans, Louis XIII's brother, from 1628 until 1660. Better known today as the composer of *airs de cour* (from 1624 to 1635), he also has significance as a composer for the church. His *Missa pro defunctis* printed by Ballard in 1636 is in the austere style of Du Caurroy, but the influence of the *airs de cour* as well as the Italian solo motets may be seen in the *Meslanges de sujets chrétiens, cantiques, litanies et motets, mis en musique à 2, 3, 4 & 5 parties avec une basse continue* (Ballard, 1658).

In his preface to the *Meslanges*, Moulinié felt it necessary to defend his use of daring intervals and cross relations: '. . . I am obliged to remark here concerning my particular manner of composing. There are some places where I have employed certain passages . . . which are rather bold and which may pass for licence in the opinion of those who prefer the austerity of the old style to the *agrémens* of the new.' Certainly to ears accustomed to Monteverdi, or even Cavalli and Rossi, the few harmonic 'audacities' of Moulinié simply serve to emphasize the conservative nature of French religious music in the mid-seventeenth century. More significant is the importance accorded the solo voice in the *Meslanges*. The motet was then well on the way to becoming a concert piece with solo passages that at times approached true airs.

Lost, unfortunately, are the late motets of Moulinié mentioned in his preface to the *Airs à 4 parties* of 1668; also gone are the motets (?) he presumably wrote to texts by Abbé Perrin. Perrin, to whom we owe many religious texts, was quite specific in indicating voice parts and even the names of composers and performers. Moulinié's name appears at the head of a number of poems which appear to have been arranged by Perrin with a sacred cantata or even an oratorio in mind.

Included among the many pieces copied by Brossard and found today in the Bibliothèque Nationale (Rés Vma Ms 571) are three Masses (*a* 3, *a* 4 and *a* 5), four motets with continuo and a Magnificat for two sopranos, counter-tenor and continuo by Boësset. Brossard stated that he believed the Masses were probably works of Jean-Baptiste Boësset (1614–1685) and not by his father, Antoine (*c.* 1585–1643). We have not progressed beyond Brossard in assigning these works definitely to one Boësset or the other. Launay supports Brossard primarily on the basis of internal stylistic evidence and attributes the music to Jean-Baptiste. Certainly the unequivocal tonal direction of the harmony, the symmetrical phrase groupings, the frequency of cadences and above all the use of a continuo, albeit unfigured, of viols and organ would be more appropriate for a work composed in the 1660's than in the 1630's. However, most French scholars treat the above as an example of a 'new esthetic' (Verchaly) and follow the lead of Henri Quittard in assigning the works to Antoine Boësset.[12]

More remarkable and even more mysterious is the music presumably written by a Languedoc composer, Guillaume Bouzignac, conserved today in two manuscripts.[13] There are many lacunae in the biography of Bouzignac.[14] We know that in 1609 he was *maître de musique des enfants* at the Cathedral of Saint-André in Grenoble. Although we know neither the dates of his birth nor death, certain textual references in some of his motets place him in Carcassonne, Rodez, Angoulême and Tours at different times in his life. Most of the music in the two manuscripts dates from 1628 to 1643. There are 45 works common to both manuscripts with minor variants, but only 9 compositions carry his name. On stylistic grounds, however, most of the remaining anonymous works may be attributed to him.

There is a degree of individuality in his music altogether remarkable in a period of general conformity within a prescribed genre. Simply stated, there is no other music of the time that looks the same on the page or sounds the same as the motets of Bouzignac. This in itself argues against the music's having been composed by a Provençal 'school' with Bouzignac as musical mentor. Ignored by the Ballard presses, it is unlikely that Bouzignac's manuscripts reached Paris; therefore, although he may be considered legitimately as one of the precursors of Marc-Antoine Charpentier in the introduction of the oratorio in France, it seems doubtful that Charpentier was familiar with his music.

Bouzignac is the first composer of religious music in France with a real dramatic flair, nurtured by his exposure to Italian and possibly to Catalan influences which penetrated the Midi to a much greater degree than the north. The use of speech rhythms (see Example 32a) and the repetition of short text fragments give a mosaic-like quality to some of the music that recalls Giovanni Gabrieli. Certain two-syllable words obviously suggested certain rhythmic dialogues to the composer, for these passages recur throughout the motets (Example 32b–c).

Madrigalisms and word painting are used to a greater degree than is normally found in French music of the period. The *petit choeur* is sometimes reduced to one soloist who dialogues with the *grand choeur*. In the *a* 5 motet *Alleluya, Deus dixit*, the *grand choeur* acts as a unifying agent through its music and text ('et factum est ita, ita Alleluya') —a procedure similar to that used by Giovanni Gabrieli in his famous *In Ecclesiis*. In such a motet as *Ex ore infantium* (1628), Bouzignac exploited the sound of a solo baritone in dialogue with the chorus. This embryonic oratorio antedates the *histoire sacrée* of Charpentier by some 70 years.

Bouzignac is representative of many composers who thrived on the rich musical soil of Provence and whose names today are no more than footnotes in a history of French music.[15] Music was performed on a regular basis at the church of Saint-Sauveur in Aix-en-Provence as early as the thirteenth century. It was there that Jacques Cordier as *maître de musique* (1638–53) introduced *violes*; there Guillaume Poitevin (1646–1706), himself a composer of Masses and motets, held the position of *maître de musique* for 35 years (1667 to 1702) and served as a teacher and inspiration to generations of composers: André Campra, Jean Gilles, Jacques Cabassol, Laurent Belissen, Claude-Mathieu Pellegrin and Esprit Blanchard.[16] With Michel Mazarin (brother of the Cardinal) Archbishop in 1644 and with Jérôme de Grimaldi succeeding him in 1655, the music of Rossi, Cavalli and Carissimi must have formed an important part of the repertoire of the church choir.

The progressive trends described on the last several pages were consolidated and systematized in the religious music of a Northerner, Henry de Thier (1610–84), born near Liège, and who, in the 1630's replaced his Walloon family name 'Thier' with the French equivalent, 'Mont'. Du Mont gave us the earliest printed example in France of the *petit motet* for two or three voices and continuo in his *Cantica sacra*; later in his life he created the classical model for the *grand motet* that was rapidly elevated by the royal imprimatur of Louis xiv to the favoured position among all religious genres—a position it kept throughout the remainder of the *grand siècle*.

Music in Flanders was infused with Italianisms during Du Mont's youth. The *stile recitativo* was welcomed by Belgian composers, and

Example 32
Extracts from motets of Bouzignac
(a) Alleluya, Deus dixit. (b) Cantate Domino. (c) Ibid.

the assimilation of the basso continuo in Belgium antedated its adoption in France by some 30 years. Du Mont was surely acquainted with the motets for two, three and four voices, continuo and occasional independent violin parts by Alessandro Grandi, Antonio Cifra, Felice and Giovanni Francesco Anerio and other Venetian and Roman composers which formed part of the repertory of the Flemish churches. He may also have known the Italian prototype for the *petit motet*, the *Concerti ecclesiastici* (1602) of Viadana or the dramatic dialogues found in Vecchi's *Dialoghi* of 1608. This exposure acted as an effective antidote to combat the conservative bias the young composer found when he arrived in France in 1638.

Du Mont exploited the use of the trio texture (two solo voices and continuo) in his *Cantica sacra* first printed by Ballard in 1652. Only 11 of the 35 motets are scored for 4 voices. In his preface he not only explains the use of a second printed part for the basso continuo, he also states that he added an optional treble viol or violin part (found in 9 of the motets). *Cantate Domino* (No. 28) is a *concertato* motet in which 4 solo voices alternate rigidly with a four-part chorus labelled 'omnes'. Many of the motets exhibit the short, highly contrasting and mosaic-like structural divisions so typical of the early Italian Baroque. *Tristitia vestra* (No. 5) and *Alleluia haec dies* (No. 8) are examples of the multi-sectional motets unified through the use of recurring sections and Alleluia refrains, while *O Gloriosa Domine* (No. 26) is a long motet with each of its two large sections introduced by a 12 measure *symphonie*.

In their creative apposition of contrasting rhythms, in their treatment of dissonance, in their restrained use of 'affective' melodic intervals and text painting, the *petits motets* of the *Cantica sacra* show how well Du Mont had assimilated many features of contemporary Italian religious music.

The *petits motets* following the *Cantica sacra* include hymns, antiphons, settings of Godeau's psalms of David and some works in dialogue form. The latter are perhaps Du Mont's most original and far-reaching musical contributions. In the Brossard collection at the Bibliothèque Nationale there is a *Dialogus de anima* (1668) which is a dialogue between God, a sinner and an angel. Its organization into three scenes, each preceded by a *symphonie*, and its use of a *petit* and *grand choeur* as well as solo *récits* justify Brossard's description of this work as a 'type of oratorio'.

Five of the 30 motets included in the *Motets à deux voix* are also organized as dialogues for specific characters such as sinners or angels or brides and bridegrooms. *O fideles miseremini* (No. 30) shows Du Mont's exploitation of the technique of dramatic monody. The 'affective' intervals and repeated text fragments owe a debt to Carissimi and mark this work along with the dialogues as an important precursor of Charpentier's *histoires sacrées*.

Example 33
Du Mont: Extract from O fideles miseremini *(after ed. of 1668).*

With the *Motets à II, III et IV parties* (Ballard, 1671), Du Mont moved the *petit motet* closer to the French models. Co-existing with Italianate dialogues and pieces with echo effects are motets in the style of popular airs based on French dance rhythms. The collection includes a 'double continuo' bass air 'accompanied' by two violins (*Sub ombra noctis*). In his *Airs à quatre parties* (Ballard, 1663) Du Mont joined the company of Lardenois, de Gouy, Auxcousteaux and Gobert in providing music for the psalm paraphrases of Antoine Godeau. With their binary structure, asymmetrical phrases, occasional metre shifts and syllabic settings, the *Airs* are French to the core.

To conclude the survey of the development of religious music in France prior to the majority of Louis XIV (1661), some attention should be given to the music written and arranged in great quantities for use in convents and monasteries.

If the seventeenth century was the century of Antoine Godeau, bishop of Vence and 'maître de la galanterie', it was also the century of François de Sales and Vincent de Paul. If it was the century of the dissolute Abbess of Metz who incurred the wrath of Bossuet, it was also the century of Mme Accarie who introduced the cult of Saint Theresa and the order of the Carmelites. The founding of new orders and the reform of old ones in a spirit of penitence and austerity was characteristic of the century. In 1618 the Jesuits (recalled to France in 1603) founded their Collège de Clermont, called, after 1683, the Collège Louis-le-Grand.

To meet the needs of so many new convents, the Ballards printed many collections of music designed primarily for performers of limited ability and modest means. The necessity of supplying simple music for the Mass gave rise to the so-called *plain-chant musical* composed for choirs singing in unison. In 1634 Pierre Ballard began the publication of François Bourgoing's versions of liturgical chants (*Brevis Psalmodiae Ratio ad usum Presbyterorum Congregationis Oratorii* . . .). These simple melodies have nothing in common with the infinite variety and long melismas of Gregorian chant. Henry Du Mont's five *Messes en plain-chant*, inexplicably called 'messes royales', first appeared in 1669 and were the most popular of what Brenet called these 'grotesque caricatures of true liturgical chant.'[17] They were reprinted three times (1685, 1701, 1711) and were used in country churches into the twentieth century. There exists a Guilmant edition, 'harmonisées à 4 voix'. The Bibliothèque Nationale contains one of them 'arranged for military band'.

The liturgical books by Guillaume Gabriel Nivers help round out any study of the seventeenth century view of the *plain-chant musical*. His *Graduale romanum juxta missale* (1658) and *Antiphonarium romanum juxta breviarium* (1658) predate the 1662 *Ceremoniale parisiense*. Nivers' most important ideas concerning the performance of chant are found in two tutors, *Méthode certaine pour apprendre le pleinchant de l'Eglise* (1698) and *Dissertation sur le chant grégorien* (1683). In his chant books Nivers uses two note values, the *longa* and the *breve*. He sanctions the use of such ornaments as the *port de voix* if performed 'naturally and without being affected'.[18]

Collections of psalm translations were available to composers throughout the seventeenth century. The most popular were by Philippe Desportes, whose translations, some in *vers mesuré*, were given musical settings until mid-century.[19] Beginning in the 1630's, as we have seen, such composers as Jacques de Gouy, Antoine Lardenois, Auxcousteaux, Moulinié and Du Mont chose the psalm paraphrases by Godeau in preference to the literal translations of the earlier generation.

Many simple pieces were collected with an eye to their potential performance possibilities and their adaptability to the requirements of individual institutions. In the *Airs sur les hymnes sacrez, odes et Noëls pour chanter au catechisme* (Ballard, 1623), the soprano 'being the subject may be sung alone, but it is also possible to sing in four parts using the several excellent *fauxbourdons* on the ones found within . . . '

Parodies of *airs de cour* were especially popular. As an example, the collection *La Despouille d'Aegipte* (1629) includes 50 tunes for one voice only, of which over half are by Antoine Boësset and 15 are by Guédron. Not all of this simple music performed at convents was necessarily sterile. A contemporary witness, the Sieur Du Buisson, thought the music he heard at the Abbey of Montmartre in 1641 was 'as excellent as that of the King'. Later in the century and in the century to follow, composers of the calibre of Charpentier, Couperin, Nivers and Clérambault all composed works of the highest musical integrity 'propres pour toutes sortes de Religieux et Religieuses'.

Chapter 13

❖❖❖

The Motet:
From Du Mont to Delalande

Generation of Du Mont, Lully and Robert

'Printed by the express order of His Majesty' we read on the title pages of the collection of fifty *grands motets* composed by Henry Du Mont, Pierre Robert and Jean-Baptiste Lully and printed by Ballard from 1684–86. Designed as much to glorify the King of France as the King of Heaven, these motets became the officially sanctioned models for works in the same genre that formed the basic repertory of the royal chapel, the *Concert Spirituel* and provincial music academies up to the eve of the Revolution. Composed and printed as they were on the 'express order of His Majesty', they are a musical by-product of the passion for order and uniformity that dominated the *grand siècle*.

As early as 1663, the King had appointed four *sous-maîtres* of the royal chapel: Henry Du Mont, Gabriel Expilly, Pierre Robert and Thomas Gobert. However, Loret's carefully chosen words show that in the minds of many it was Du Mont and Robert who carried the burden of composing for the royal chapel:[1]

> *Le Roy, dont l'oreille est scavante*
> *En cette science charmante,*
> *Par un vray jugement d'expert*
> *a choizi Du Mont et Robert.*

> (7 July 1663)

By 1671, the last of the royal academies, that of architecture, had been created; by 1682, the king had taken up permanent residence at Versailles; also in 1682, the 'Eglise Gallican' declared its virtual independence from Rome, and the revocation of the Edict of Nantes was but three short years away. The church marched in willing lockstep with all other institutions, subservient to the will and manner of the Roi Soleil. The year 1682 saw the completion of a new royal chapel at Versailles, a chapel that could draw upon as many as 80 musicians to perform a *grand motet* for a special occasion or for the celebration of the king's Mass.

Louis XIV had been impressed by the opulence and heroic mien of such early Lully *grands motets* as the *Miserere* (1664) and the *Te Deum* (1677). He had also enjoyed the *Motets à 1, 2, 3, 4 et 5 parties avec symphonies et basse-continue* by Paolo Lorenzani heard at the court as early as 1678. It was only to be expected that he would want similar music for his chapel.

The king preferred to attend low Mass (*Messe basse solennelle*) in his chapel; for high Mass, he went to a royal parish in Paris, to Saint-Germain-en-Laye or, after 1690, to Notre-Dame of Versailles. The format of the low Mass gave him a chance to hear at least one *grand* and perhaps two *petits motets*. Abbé Perrin described the arrangement of motets in the service in the preface to his valuable *Cantica pro Capella Regis* (Ballard, 1665), a collection of his motet texts for use at the royal chapel. He wrote as follows:

> . . . there are ordinarily three (motets), one *grand*, one *petit* for the elevation and a *Domine salvum fac Regem*.[2] I have made the *grands* of such a length that they take up a quarter of an hour . . . and they may be worked in from the beginning of the Mass to the Elevation. Those of the Elevation are smaller works and can be performed [at any point] up to the Post-Communion where the *Domine* begins.

Perrin, who supplied the text for Lully's *petit motet Ave coeli munus supernum* and his *grands motets Plaude laetare* and *O lachrymae fideles*, is the source of one of the earliest definitions of the motet in France. Found in the *Cantica*, this definition, in common with all later ones, does not attempt to differentiate between a *grand* or *petit motet* but does emphasize the sectional nature of the genre:

> . . . the Motet is a piece in which several varied and different musical sections are linked together. . . . the variety of the piece will be even greater and the composition easier for the Composer, when there is variation in the stanzas and *versets* and when they are composed with a continual change in mind. . . . I have followed such a method in my motet texts for the King's Mass in his Royal Chapel.

The Brossard definition, in its vagueness, is all-inclusive:

> It (the motet) is a composition of Music, with various movements, which is enriched with all that is most excellent in the art of composition. It is written for 1, 2, 3, 4, 5, 6, 7, 8 and even more Voices or soloists, often with Instruments, and almost always with at least a *Basse-continue*. . . . At present, the term embraces all pieces set to Latin words no matter on what subject,

such as praises of the Saints, Elevations, etc. One even composes entire Psalms in the form of a motet.

('Motet' in *Dictionnaire*)

The *grands motets* of the generation of Du Mont, Lully and Robert are extensions of the earlier works in this form written for the royal chapel by Veillot. Although published posthumously in 1686, the 20 *grands motets* by Henry Du Mont were probably written over the 20-year period during which he served in the royal chapel, A dedication to the king shows the composer embroiled in a stylistic conflict that resulted in a change from the simpler and expressive style of the *petits motets* to the pompous 'official' style of the *grand motet*:

> Sire, several years ago I had the honour of presenting to your Majesty my motets for two voices. . . . I have since ascertained that two voices are assuredly too weak to allow me to be heard on a subject on which I wished to express myself better: and I imagined that Your Majesty would permit me to employ three or four voices. . . . But, Sire, I begin to see that I have scarcely succeeded any better. . . .

To 'succeed better', Du Mont greatly enlarged upon the models of Formé and Veillot. Perhaps he was influenced by Lully's *Miserere* of 1664. At any rate, he created a type of extended cantata employing recitatives, polyphonic and homophonic choruses, *récits*, duos and trios, *symphonies* and *ritournelles*. In so doing, Du Mont achieved a position in French religious music 'somewhat comparable to that of Haydn in the symphony and string quartet'.[3]

The distribution of parts in Du Mont's *grands motets* remained more or less standard throughout the seventeenth century. It was described by Brossard as follows:

> To perform them (Du Mont's motets) it is necessary to have five solo voices that constitute the *petit choeur* including Soprano, Alto, two Tenors, Bass;[4] five parts of the same distribution for the *grand choeur* and five instrumental parts including Violins I and II, Haute-contre and Taille (violas), *Basse de violon* and *basse continue*. Thus, one should have a rather large group of performers. . . . however, five solo voices, two violins, a *basse de violon* and a *basse continue* would suffice.

(*Catalogue*, p. 140)

Structurally, a motet was conceived of as a series of unbroken episodes in which solo voice (or voices) was interspersed between music for the *grand* and *petit choeurs*. These episodes occasionally border on the autonomous but more often merge or elide, one with the next.

The whole is usually preceded by a *symphonie* while *ritournelles* may define structural points of division in the body of the motet. Du Mont's introductory *symphonies* present considerable variety and are themselves worthy of a separate study. *Quemadmodum desiderata* (No. 19) and *O Dulcissima* (No. 16) are closed binary forms somewhat like allemandes and have little to do with what follows. *Confitebimur tibi Deus* (No. 4) begins with a *symphonie* of 35 measures, whereas *Domine in virtute tuo* (No. 6) commences with a tutti chorus instead of a *symphonie*. Perhaps most impressive is the beginning of the *Magnificat* (No. 13) in which Du Mont employed a

Example 34
Du Mont: Opening of Magnificat *(after ed. of 1686).*

symphonie of 21 measures with a motto beginning. The voices of the orchestra weave a contrapuntal fabric rich in dissonance which exposes genuinely independent part writing relating more to the composer's Flemish heritage than to the music of seventeenth century France. The basses, who enter in measure 11 singing the ancient Gregorian formula in unison, are absorbed into the polyphonic web of sound.

Du Mont achieved more independence than Lully or Robert in the instrumental accompaniments to the choruses. Normally the first violin doubles the soprano vocal line, leaving the second violin to embroider in free counterpoint. Notable also are the accompaniments to the *petit choeur* where the strings occasionally introduce an independent motif to be treated later by chorus and orchestra.

Du Mont's inspiration flagged from time to time under the necessity of filling such a breadth of musical space, for he was essentially a miniaturist. Some of the large syllabic choruses are dull and lack the compensatory drive of Lully's finest work in the genre. On the other hand, the five-part polyphony of the 'Gloria Patri' from the *Magnificat* is worthy of Delalande. Du Mont's *grands motets* were impressive models for the next generation. Many of their devices were used by Charpentier and the young Delalande, whose first motets were certainly contemporary with the last of Du Mont's.

Between 1664 and 1685, Lully composed 26 motets of which 11 are *grands motets*. In 1684 'by express order of His Majesty', Ballard printed six of the *grands motets* (*Miserere*, 1664; *Plaude laetare*, 1668; *Te Deum*, 1677; *Dies irae*; *De profundis*, 1683; and *Benedictus Dominus*, 1685). The five additional *grands motets* (*Domine salvum fac regem; Exaudiat te Dominus*, 1685; *Notus in Judea; O lachrymae fideles*; and *Quare fremuerunt*, 1685) remain in manuscript copies which may be found today in such diverse places as the Bibliothèque Nationale in Paris, the Bibliothèque Royale in Brussels, St. Michael's College at Tenbury Wells and the Westdeutsche Bibliothek in Marburg.

Lully used a six-part orchestra including first and second violins, three *parties de remplissage* (*haute-contre, quinte* and *taille*), a *basse de violon* and continuo. In practice, however, this results most often in the typical five-part texture of the opera orchestra with the first and second violins doubling. The distribution of parts for the *grand* and *petit choeur* builds in contrasting sonorities: the *petit choeur*, with its two sopranos, counter-tenor, tenor and bass, emphasizes the higher voices, whereas the *grand choeur* is organized to include a baritone (*basse-taille*) and eliminates the second soprano.

The early *Miserere mei Deus*, which probably dates from 1664, is the most impressive of all the *grands motets* of Lully. According to the *Mémoires* of Marie Dubois, gentleman of the king's chamber, it was a great favourite of Louis xiv.[5] It was performed in 1666 and again in 1672 at the Church of the Oratoire. The latter performance for the funeral of the Chancellor Séguier was heard by Madame de Sévigné who wrote that during the 'Libera me', 'all eyes were filled with tears. I do not believe any other music to exist in heaven.'[6]

When it is not supplying independent *symphonies* or *ritournelles*, the orchestra in the motets of Lully rigidly doubles the choral voice parts. It is unusual to find in these works any of the independent instrumental counterpoint that was timorously used by Du Mont and later exploited by Delalande. A notable exception occurs in the final chorus of the *Miserere* where the first violins, more inspired probably by practical considerations of range than by any artistic principle, initiate the final stretto-like entrance of the subject.

Example 35
Lully: Extract from the récit *'Ecce enim',* Miserere *(after Ms Res F.663 in B.N.).*

The year 1664 was also the year of *Le Mariage forcé, Les Amours déguisés* and *La Princesse d'Elide.* The supple melodic lines found in the *récits* of the *Miserere* owe something to the vocal solos and ensembles of these *comédies-ballets.* The *récit en duo,* 'Amplius lava me', with its sham polyphony and parallel thirds, has the same sensuous quality as the duo of Climène and Philis from the fifth *Intermède* of *La Princesse d'Elide.* The sequence of descending 7th chords, the melodic diminished 7th in 'et in peccatis concepit me' (Example 35 above), as well as the melodic diminished 4th on the word 'iniquitate', in 'Amplius lava me', clearly stem from an Italianate vocabulary of 'affections'.

Composed at some time before 1677, the *Te Deum* was first heard at Fontainebleau on 8 September of that year to celebrate the baptism of Lully's eldest son (then aged 13). It was subsequently performed in October 1679 at Versailles and again on that fateful 8 January 1687 at the Paris chapel of the Feuillants (a religious order of St. Bernard), where Lully, beating the measure with a long stick to keep hundreds of performers together, received the injury to his foot which resulted in his death from blood poisoning two months later.

This work, in common with most of the *grands motets* of Lully, is too long and has many musically arid moments; but the sound of trumpets and drums and the kinetic drive of the big double choruses, with their relentless speech rhythms wedded to massive blocks of homophony, give voice to the real spirit of Versailles. It is a secularized 'concert spirituel' and is the source for such bellicose operatic choruses as are found later in *Bellérophon* and *Thésée*. Surprisingly, in only one other *grand motet, Exudiat te Dominus,* do some of the manuscripts specify trumpets, bassoons and drums. From the description of the 1679 performance of the *Te Deum* found in the *Mercure galant* of October of the same year, it is clear, however, that the manuscripts and printed editions indicated only minimum performance possibilities:

> The musicians were placed in the tribune before a large amphitheatre raised up near the vault; those from the chamber were at the right, and those from the chapel at the left. There were oboes, flutes, trumpets and drums along with the 24 Violins. At least 120 persons sang or played instruments.[7]

Like those of Du Mont, the *grands motets* of Lully were conceived of as loosely organized sections. In the *Te Deum*, the large structural divisions are defined by extended *symphonies*. In the opening section, elements from the *symphonie* serve to unify the structure in rondo fashion. Shorter divisions, which are seldom autonomous units in themselves, are created within the larger units by dividing textual phrases, sentences or lines into solo *récits*, recitatives or a *concertato*-like treatment of the *petit* and *grand choeur*. Thus the text acts as a form-determinant. The contrast achieved by such fragmentation had appeal if we are to believe the report of the *Mercure galant* of September 1677: 'What was particularly admired was that each couplet was of different music. The king found it so beautiful that he wished to hear it again.'[8]

The vertical sonorities in Lully's *grands motets*, coupled with a predominantly syllabic rendering of the text, invite a rather simple, even static, harmony for long stretches at a time. Chromatic inflections, when they occur, are usually the result of secondary Dominant chords used to effect a transitory modulation to a closely related key. Yet, the Lully pieces, although far less imposing from a harmonic point of view than the motets of Delalande and Charpentier, are not totally devoid of harmonic interest. The borrowing of chords from the opposite mode results in a type of 'bi-modality' not uncommon in French music of the Baroque period. An entire section may exploit a 'region' of the opposite mode which, when combined with a dramatic tempo change, is an effective means of underscoring the text. Such a passage is the four-measure 'Sanctus' from the *Te Deum* (see Example 36 below). Set within a larger harmonic frame of C and G-Major, this three-fold 'Sanctus' in G-Minor forms the structural centre of the first section of the motet and affords needed relief from the driving speech rhythms by which it is surrounded.

In outward appearances, the 24 *grands motets* by Pierre Robert (*c.* 1618–99), printed in 1684 by Ballard, differ little from those of Lully and Du Mont. The *grand choeur* has the same distribution of

Example 36
Lully: Extract from Te Deum *(after Ms Res F.666 in B.N.).*

voices, and the orchestra has the six-part division found in the Lully motets although, according to Brossard, 'it is necessary to have seven instrumental parts, namely First and Second violins, *Haute-contre, Taille, Quinte,* a *Basse-continue* for the Viol and Bassoon and finally, a figured *Basse-continue* for the organ, harpsichord and theorbo' (*Catalogue*). This is an interesting quotation that points up again the variance between printed editions or manuscripts and actual performance practices.

It is in his organization of the *petit choeur* that Robert differs most markedly from his contemporaries. His *petit choeur* includes the following eight solo voices in combinations labelled *récits* by the composer: first and second sopranos, first and second counter-tenors, first and second tenors, baritone and bass. More than either Lully or Du Mont, Robert exploited the contrast of sonorities in his 'ensembles de récits' derived from the combinations listed above. For example, within 16 short measures in the verse, 'Testimonium in Joseph', from *Exultate Deo adjutori nostro* (Number 9 of the motets), Robert juxtaposed solo, duo, trio and quartet with soloists including the baritone, first counter-tenor, first tenor, first and second soprano.[9]

There is little evidence that Robert used this wide range of sonorities for textual painting. The *récits*, in contrast to those of Du Mont, seem austere and impersonal. Indeed, with a change of sonority often occurring every few measures, the effect is that of textual fragmentation, and one can only conclude that purely musical features of the sonorities justified their use for Robert.

Freed from the compulsion of heroic posturing, the *petits motets* of Lully and Robert are intrinsically more musical than the *grands motets*. Several are included in a Bibliothèque Nationale manuscript copied in 1688 by Philidor bearing the title *Petits motets et elevations de MM Carissimi, de Lully, Robert, Danielis et Foggia à 2, 3 et 4 parties et quelquefois unes avec des violons*. This important manuscript adds to the testimony pointing to the use of Italian music at the royal chapel during Lully's lifetime. Out of 72 *petits motets*, 32 are by Carissimi, 13 by Daniel Danielis, 7 by Francesco Foggia and 10 each by Robert and Lully.

Both Robert and Lully were more sensitive in their *petits motets* to the expressive power of dissonance, 'affective' intervals and modulation. It would be difficult to find, in any of the *récits* of Robert's *grands motets*, a melodic line so at one with the text and so Italianate in its use of textual repetition, melodic sequence and chromaticism as in the extract from his *petit motet O Flamma*, found in Example 37 below. If the vocal scoring practices of the two composers are compared, it is clear that here, as in the *grands motets*, Robert is more concerned with a contrast of sonorities; seven of the Lully motets are scored for three high voices (*dessus*) and three for two high voices and bass; four of the Robert motets are for various combinations of three voices, five are for combinations of two voices and one is for a second tenor, two violins and continuo.

Example 37
Robert: Extract from O Flamma *(after Philidor copy).*

[desiderio, et ar-de-re   ar – de – re   ar-de-re   et ar-de —   re

Generation of Charpentier and Delalande

In 1683 after twenty years of service at the king's chapel, Du Mont and Robert, well advanced in years, took their retirement. This left the prestigious post of *sous-maître* to be filled. The king, undoubtedly eager to dramatize his personal interest in the music of his chapel, established a solemn competition for the position of four *sous-maîtres*. Thirty-five musicians from all over the realm competed. Among them were Jean Mignon of Notre-Dame, Guillaume Minoret of Saint-Germain-l'Auxerrois, Jacques Lesueur from Rouen, Nicolas Coupillet from the Cathedral of Meaux, Mallet from Avignon, Paolo Lorenzani, *maître de musique* for the queen, and Guillaume-Gabriel Nivers, the king's organist, Daniel Danielis, Jean Rebel, Pascal Collasse, Henry Desmarest, Marc-Antoine Charpentier and Michel-Richard Delalande.

Each had a motet of his own composition performed after which the king eliminated 20 from the competition. Those that remained were kept in isolation for several days during which each composed a motet to the text of Psalm 31, *Beati quorum remissiae sunt*. From this final competition, four *sous-maîtres* were chosen: Coupillet, Collasse, Minoret and Delalande. Charpentier who, the *Mercure galant* informs us, was 'extremely ill at the time of the isolation of the musicians' (April 1683) did not take part in the final test and was awarded a 'consolation prize' by the king in the form of a generous pension.

From the results of the competition, it is all too clear that outside influences determined the choice of most of the *sous-maîtres*. The first three were 'safe' composers who offered no threat to Lully. Nicolas Coupillet was a mediocre composer from Senlis whose subsequent *grands motets* for the royal chapel were actually ghost written for him by Henry Desmarest. Coupillet's ruse was discovered in a scandal which cost him his job in 1693.[10] Fortunately, the king insisted on his choice for the fourth *sous-maître*. 'I have accepted, Messieurs, those whom you have chosen; it is only right that I choose one who conforms to my taste. It is Lalande whom I choose to be responsible for the quarter beginning in January.'[11]

The *grand motet* in France reached full flower at the hands of two composers who led totally dissimilar lives. The one, Michel-Richard Delalande (1657–1726), received all but one of the possible official court appointments available to musicians, and the other, Marc-Antoine Charpentier (c. 1634–1704), never received a direct court appointment. Between them, these two composers produced more than 150 *grands motets*, those of Delalande forming the basic repertoire of the royal chapel and later the *Concert Spirituel*, those of Charpentier serving the Sainte-Chapelle or the Jesuit church of Saint-Louis where Charpentier was employed after 1684.

If one may judge by over 500 compositions (sacred works, instrumental music, *divertissements*, pastorales, stage music and court airs) found in the 28 volumes of manuscripts called *Meslanges* now preserved on microfilm at the Bibliothèque Nationale, Charpentier certainly flourished without recourse to direct court patronage. Undoubtedly, Lully considered Charpentier, an Italian-trained composer possibly aspiring to the lyric stage, as his most serious rival. Had Charpentier participated in the finals of the competition, Lully might have tried to block his appointment as *sous-maître*. Baptiste, however, seems to have made no overt attempts to prevent Charpentier from receiving lucrative musical employment from a variety of Parisian sources. Nor did Charpentier lack royal favour. The king in many ways made it known that he was aware of Charpentier's worth as a composer and teacher. He saw to it that Charpentier was employed as the teacher of both his nephew, Philippe d'Orléans (the future Regent), and his oldest son, the Dauphin, for whose chapel Charpentier also served as *maître de musique*; in addition, the king offered no resistance to Charpentier's serving as a 'composer-in-residence' for his cousin, Mlle de Guise (Marie de Lorraine).

How often did the paths of Charpentier and Delalande cross? What was their professional relationship at the Jesuit college, Louis-le-Grand, during the two years (1683–85) of Delalande's employment? Was it Charpentier who, fresh from his sojourn in Italy and from his lessons with Carissimi, introduced Delalande to the coterie surrounding Abbé Mathieu in Paris? Was it this introduction that led eventually to Delalande's inheriting the Italian cantatas and motets, prize possessions of the *curé* of Saint-André-des-Arts?

Both Delalande and Charpentier enjoyed popular success although little of their music was published in their lifetime. Delalande's motets were considered 'masterpieces of the genre' (Rousseau) and were known beyond the boundaries of France. 'Delalande always enjoys a reputation of which nothing dims the *éclat*', wrote Nougaret in 1769. He added, 'they even perform most of his motets in Italy'.

Charpentier's reputation survived the vitriol of Lecerf ('I do not understand by what miracle Charpentier could be considered an expressive composer of Latin music') and received the warm approbation of Brossard and the begrudging admiration of Parfaict ('a harmony and science [of composition] up to now unknown in France') and Serré de Rieux ('In beautiful Harmony he pointed the way, Ninths and tritones shimmer under his hand').

It is ironic, then, that for all practical purposes, both composers have barely survived the eighteenth century. Many of the 71 motets of Delalande and the greater part of the religious music of Charpentier slumber today undisturbed in the archives of the Bibliothèque Nationale and the Bibliothèque Municipale of Versailles. A study of these sources has convinced this author that Charpentier and Delalande are the most neglected first-rank composers of the *grand siècle*. It is true that within the past three decades there has been a reawakening of interest in the music of Charpentier brought about by the pioneering work of Brenet (as early as 1899), Gastoué and Crussard in France, American doctoral dissertations by Hitchcock, Barber and Dunn, some well-edited performing editions by Crussard, Guy-Lambert, Hitchcock, Launay and others and an impressive discography,[12] but what is really needed is a systematic assault on the formidable 28 volumes of the *Meslanges*. With the Lully and Rameau *Oeuvres complètes* far from 'complètes', it is unlikely that a Charpentier 'monument' is contemplated at present.

For Delalande, the situation is even more bleak in spite of several performing editions edited by Roussel, Cellier and others. One dissertation, a few articles and encyclopedia references[13] and the *Michel-Richard Delalande—Notes et Références pour servir à son histoire* (Paris, 1957) compiled under the direction of Norbert Dufourcq, are practically the sum total of his bibliography. It is a cruel fate that Delalande, who two years before his death was knighted a *Chevalier de Saint-Michel* by Louis xv, receives, as a motet composer, almost the same space (six lines) as Brossard in Prunières' *A New History of Music* (trans. Lockspeiser), that he receives four lines in the standard English language text on the Baroque period (Bukofzer) and is totally neglected in Claude Palisca's *Baroque Music*.

More than the motets of the royal chapel composers, the motets of Charpentier offer the widest spectrum of the use of the genre during the *grand siècle*. They group naturally into three divisions: hymns of praise to the Virgin or a Saint; psalms; and lessons of Tenebrae and Holy Week responses.

The *grands motets* were undoubtedly composed for the Dauphin's chapel, for the Sainte-Chapelle and for the most important Jesuit church, the Eglise Saint-Louis. Some of the simpler *grands motets* and many *petits motets* were destined for convents, others for performances at Mlle de Guise's Hôtel du Marais; still others served as music for the many processionals that were a regular feature of religious life in seventeenth century Paris. Most common among the processionals was the ceremony of the Benediction of the Blessed Sacrament (*Salut de Saint Sacrament*) during such feasts as Corpus Christi, Rogations and Assumption. Those in the procession visited a series of street altars (*reposoirs*) where the Sacrament was exposed. At each 'rest' altar, a motet or a portion thereof would be performed.

Unfortunately, we are in the dark concerning the chronology of most of Charpentier's motets. Occasionally, the composer himself has aided us by having left on his manuscript the names of the performers of a specific composition. Often they may be identified as having been among the six male and six female singers employed by Mlle de Guise during Charpentier's residency at the Hôtel du Marais (*c.* 1675–88). The names of some performers, included among the known musicians at the Sainte-Chapelle, are occasionally noted; and of course, certain 'pièces d'occasion', such as the *In Obitum* (vol. xx)[14] composed for the death of Maria Theresa in 1683, are datable.

Gregorian chant and popular Noël, Italian oratorio and cantata, French overture and dance measure, archaic polyphony and regal Versailles motet—all combine in the religious music of Charpentier and document the composer's advice to his student, Philippe d'Orléans: '. . . diversity gives it (music) all its perfection, as uniformity renders it insipid' (*Règles de Composition*).[15]

Charpentier's *grands motets* are a middle ground between those of Du Mont and Lully, on the one hand, and those of Delalande, on the other. Some are almost without sectional divisions and employ constant elision between different instrumental and vocal media; others are virtual cantatas including some autonomous sections in the style of the later Delalande motets. Many make use of the type of structure already exploited by Du Mont in which an extended section is composed of episodes of motto-prelude, solo, ensemble and chorus—all following one another without breaks. From time to time, Charpentier employed a rondo form of organization, rare in French religious music of the period and perhaps based on the rondo-cantatas popular in Rome. In *Epithalamio* (vol. vii), set in Italian, the opening chorus recurs at the end, and alleluia refrains unify *O Filii et filiae* (vol. viii). Some motets are loosely organized into a chain of contrasting sections conforming more or less to Perrin's definition (see page 175); others show remarkably tight organization similar to that found from time to time in Charpentier's own oratorios and Masses. The *Magnificat* (vol. xi) for eight voices and eight instruments is a symmetrical structure with a double chorus in the centre flanked on both sides by solo or ensemble, the whole being framed by two double choruses.[16]

In vocal and instrumental distribution of parts, Charpentier exhibits more imagination and sense of colour than his predecessors. In many of the double-chorus motets, the *grand* and *petit choeur* are both *a* 4 with the composer favouring the soprano, counter-tenor, tenor and bass combination. We have already mentioned that Charpentier's work avoids the *a* 5 vocal and instrumental texture so prevalent in French music of his day. Such motets as the *Miserere* (vol. vii) and the antiphon *Salve Regina* (vol. iii) build up large choral sonorities unusual even for French music. In contrast, such a motet as *Sub tuum* (vol. xxiii), obviously written for a convent, bears the subtitle 'Antiphona sine organo ad virginem', and is a rare example in the late seventeenth century of an *a cappella* motet. Its tender, personal intimacy is completely different from the official sound of the four extant *Te Deums* written in the style of Lully during the last five years of Charpentier's life when he held the position of *maître de musique des enfants* at the Sainte-Chapelle.

In some manuscripts, Charpentier was specific in his demands down to the last oboe; others are maddeningly incomplete. In the *Te Deum* (vol. xv), edited by Denise Launay ('Le Pupitre', 1969), the title reads: '*Te Deum* à 8 voix, avec fl. et violons'. There is no indication whether or not one choir is a *petit choeur* of soloists, nor is there much specific information regarding instrumental scoring. Yet, in the couplet 'Judex crederis esse venturus', for bass solo, Charpentier specified unequivocally, 'Tous les Violons du 2 choeurs sans Flutes ny Hautbois' and carefully directed the violinists to play with mutes.

More than any other French composer of his generation, Charpentier was a colourist in his use of harmony. At the same time, like Purcell, he represents a transition from modality to tonality, and his cross-relations and other dissonant clashes are usually the result of the same tonal-modal conflict that so enriches the music of his English contemporary.

The theoretical basis for Charpentier's treatment of dissonance is found in his *Règles de Composition* written for Philippe d'Orléans. He gives as a rule: 'Several consecutive 4ths or 5ths are permissible

Example 38
Extracts from Charpentier's Règles de Composition.

between upper voices providing they move in conjunct motion and are of different types', but his example (Example 38a above) shows three consecutive perfect 5ths followed by a diminished 5th. He gives examples of augmented octaves and an augmented 6th chord (Example 38b) adding that 'The augmented octave may only be used as in A and B and may be accompanied by the augmented 6th ('6e plusque majeur) as is shown in C.[17] The treatise also gives examples of cross-relations as seen in Example 38c.

Charpentier, in his little treatise, asked the question, 'Why [have] changes of key?' He gave two reasons: the first, and less important, is to accommodate vocal ranges; the second, and principal, is 'for the expression of different passions, for which the different key properties ("energies") are appropriate'. He included a list of keys, each followed by its appropriate 'affection'.

Properties of the Modes

C-Major	Gay and warlike
C-Minor	Obscure and sad
D-Minor	Grave and pious
D-Major	Joyous and very warlike
E-Minor	Effeminate, amorous and plaintive
E-Major	Quarrelsome and peevish
E♭-Major	Cruel and severe
F-Major	Furious and quick tempered
F-Minor	Obscure and plaintive
G-Major	Quietly joyful
G-Minor	Serious and magnificent
A-Minor	Tender and plaintive
A-Major	Joyous and pastoral
B♭-Major	Magnificent and joyous
B♭-Minor	Obscure and terrifying
B-Minor	Lonely and melancholy
B-Major	Severe and plaintive

This chart, which precedes by 30 years Rameau's 'De la propriété des Modes & des Tons' from the *Traité de l'harmonie,* has significance also in illustrating the wide range of keys that Charpentier obviously felt were available to the composer.

Turning to two motets based on the Marian antiphon *Salve Regina,* we observe a striking example of Charpentier's use of harmony to dramatize the text. One *Salve Regina* (vol. III) is scored for triple chorus and orchestra; the other, found in volume II, is a *petit motet* for '3 like voices'. In both settings, at the words, 'Ad te clamamus, exsules, filii Hevae. Ad te suspira, gementes et flentes in hac lacrymarum valle' (To thee we cry

out, exiled children of Eve; to thee we sigh, we mourn and weep
in this vale of tears), Charpentier made use of the same material, well
pleased with the musical formula he had chosen for these words. In
the *petit motet*, he extended by four measures the chromatically moving, parallel augmented triads found in the *grand motet* (Example
39a and b). As if to compensate for this audacity, he conventionalized
the descending, chromatic harmonization of the concluding text phrase
(Example 39c). Perhaps nowhere in French Baroque music is there as
striking an example of text painting as Charpentier's setting of this

Example 39
(*a*) Grand motet *version (after the* Meslanges, *vol.* III).

(*b*) Petit motet *version (after the* Meslanges, *vol.* II).

(c) Petit motet *version.*

(d) Grand motet *version.*

last phrase, 'In hac lacrymarum valle', in the *grand motet* version (Example 39d). An almost Gesualdo-like series of descending augmented triads finally reaches a 'very plaintive' augmented 6th chord just before the final A-Major triad. It is easy to understand how this would have chilled the heart of Lecerf.

In addition to augmented triads, parallel 5ths and augmented octaves occur in Charpentier's music. As is always true, however, the dissonant intervals are by-products of complex part writing. The example below, taken from the *Te Deum* (vol. xv), illustrates a build-up of eight independent vocal lines that results in some dissonance as well as in parallel 5ths in the closing measures of the opening chorus.

Example 40
Charpentier: Extract from a Te Deum *(after the* Meslanges, *vol.* xv).

A favourite sonority of Charpentier was the use of a 9th chord, constructed on the third degree of a minor scale, with its components including a major 7th and an augmented 5th. This Mediant 9th chord, which often served as a Dominant substitute, was far from unique to Charpentier. Striking examples may be found in the motets of Delalande and in the vocal and instrumental music of Couperin. Its wide use was recognized by Nicolas Bernier who mentioned it in his manuscript treatise, *Principes de composition*, as one type of augmented 5th that 'can be used only on the mediant in the minor mode and then only when one is able to make thereby a ninth occurring on a strong beat'.[18]

Charpentier was always careful to let the text dictate the use of so dissonant a combination of tones. The example, below, from the six-part *Miserere* (vol. VII) shows a typical use of this harmony with the
$\begin{smallmatrix}9\\7\\ \sharp5\end{smallmatrix}$ chord reserved for the 'a peccatis meis' ('from my sins').

Example 41
Charpentier: Extract from Miserere *(after the* Meslanges, *vol.* VII*).*

Rapid, expressive modulations, as well as chains of suspensions over a circle of 5ths, are found in Charpentier's motets, yet surprisingly for someone with Charpentier's interest in Italian music, he made little use of the diminished 7th or Neapolitan 6th chords.

Charpentier was never more Italian, however, than in his use of harmony to dramatize the texts of his motets. Although nourished at the source of opera itself, he was more sensitive to the dramatic possibilities of words in his motets than in his opera *Médée*, written for the Académie Royale de Musique. His harmonic palette was certainly richer and more varied than that of his teacher, Carissimi. At the same time, he was no French Gesualdo or even a Monteverdi. It would be a serious error to assume that the practices described above dominate his music stylistically. If anything, their judicious and sparing use increase their effectiveness. Charpentier's Italianism was tempered and restrained by the French tradition to which he adhered in most of his music. For him, this embraced a melodic style derived from the court air and the dance. Although more contrapuntally oriented than Lully, his polyphony is often more suggested than real; points of imitation tend to line up in vertical sonorities after the initial entrances. The penetration of this tradition by influences from across the Alps gives Charpentier's motets their characteristic sound which justifies their being considered as an ideal example of 'goûts-réunis'.

Of all the composers discussed thus far, Michel-Richard Delalande (La Lande or de Lalande—the spelling used by the composer on legal documents was Delalande) was the most at home in the idiom of the *grand motet*. He was able to bring together totally dissimilar elements in a convincing manner and with an unprecedented depth of feeling. Co-existing in Delalande's motets are the official Versailles style and *galant* airs borrowed from opera; cantus-firmus treatment of Gregorian melodies in finely wrought polyphony are juxtaposed with homophonic 'battle' choruses worthy of a *Bellérophon*, as though, for him, there were no other way to praise his God and, incidentally, his king.

Like the music of Bach, the motets of Delalande are imbued with an over-all spirituality that transcends chapel and concert hall alike. Their eloquent message touched the favoured few who attended the King's Mass at Versailles and the crowds who applauded them after 1725 at the *Concert Spirituel* in Paris. Far from just representing the 'most conservative spirit of the period' (Bukofzer, *Music in the Baroque Era*, p. 259), they exhibit certain progressive tendencies in orchestral scoring, treatment of harmony and form, and attention to text. More restrained than Charpentier in their use of Italianism, they nonetheless succeeded in humanizing what was in danger of becoming cold formulas of obeisance in the late Lully motets.

In an *Avertissement* to the posthumous, printed edition of 40 motets (1729) by Delalande, a former student, Colin de Blamont, gave a succinct summary of his teacher's style that is more perceptive than many present-day analyses. Blamont aptly labelled Delalande a 'Latin Lully' and continued:

> His great merit . . . consisted in a wonderful choice of melody, a judicious choice of harmony, and a nobility of expression. He always sustained the value of the words he chose to treat and rendered musically their true meaning, their majesty and the holy enthusiasm of the Prophets. . . . Profound and learned on the one hand, simple and natural on the other, he applied all his study to touch the soul by a richness of expression, and a vivid pictorialism; the mind is refreshed by the pleasing variety

not only from one work to the next, but within the same piece
. . . by the ingenious disparities with which he ornaments his
works, by the graceful melodies that serve as contrasting episodes
to the most complex choral sections.

The fact that none of Delalande's 71 motets was printed during his
lifetime seems to suggest that a composer of his stature, completely
secure in the paternalism of the regime, had no need to publish.
Unfortunately, the 1729 edition is only complete with regard to the
vocal and obbligato instrumental parts. The *a* 5 orchestra is reduced
to a trio texture for two first violins and bass—a less than satisfactory
arrangement for a composer whose inner voice writing was generally
more independent than that of his contemporaries.

In form, Delalande's later motets call to mind the German cantata
at the time of Bach. Most include autonomous movements, which are
a succession of airs and ensembles, often with obbligato instruments,
interspersed between choral sections. All have opening *symphonies*,
and most have concluding *ritournelles*. In some motets, such as *Sacris
solemnis* (1709), the use of a Gregorian hymn, treated in cantus-firmus
style in the opening chorus, even resembles a chorale 'fantasia' typical
of the opening movement of a Bach cantata. At the same time, many
Delalande motets look back to Du Mont and Lully in basing an
opening section on a motto-prelude, followed by solo *récit*, ensemble
and chorus. Generally. however, each episode is considerably expanded
and may be self-contained. In choosing psalms in preference to all
other texts, Delalande was able to let the versets of the psalms dictate
the musical form: some are organized in recitative and air combinations; others, as solo and ensembles; others, as choral movements.

More than any other composer of *grands motets*, Delalande placed
solo instruments in dialogue with vocal solos and ensembles. The air
'Anima nostra', from Psalm 123, *Nisi quia Dominus* (1703), is accompanied by a recorder and solo violin that weave counterpoint around
the vocal line.

The *récit* 'Ad vesperum', from Psalm 29, *Exaltabo te, Domine*
(1704), juxtaposes transverse flutes and recorders, and the *récit*
'Noctes recolitur', from *Sacris solemnis*, uses a bassoon line that is
independent from the continuo. Borrowed from opera are airs such as
'Ut eruat a morte' from Psalm 32, *Exsultate* (1710), in which a solo
counter-tenor supports melodic material delicately scored for two
flutes and violins.

Delalande's use of counterpoint, both melodic and rhythmic, was
not pedantic. A favourite device was to present the subject and
counter-subject separately, in the sinfonia and following solo *récit*,
and then to combine them in a large fugal chorus. In the hymn *Veni
Creator Spiritus* (before 1689), the text of the fifth verset, 'Hostem
repellas longius, Pacemque dones protinus' ('Repel afar our earthly

foes, Let us dwell henceforth in peace'), is first set for solo *récit* (tenor) in which two clearly differentiated musical ideas are assigned to 'Hostem repellas longius' and to 'Pacemque dones protinus'. These two ideas are then combined in a double-chorus setting of 10 different voice parts with the first choir being predominantly homophonic and the second polyphonic.

Example 42

Delalande: Extract from Veni Creator Spiritus *(after Philidor copy).*

In spite of an occasional subordination of textual clarity to musical devices as in Example 42 above, Delalande understood Latin prosody better than his contemporaries, and he took pains to choose the musical motives best suited for individual words or phrases. Single key words, such as 'non', 'portantes', 'mors', 'ploremus', are given dramatic impetus by means of repetition and above all by the effective use of rests. Triadic motives appropriate for certain words recur with those words in several motets.

Example 43
Use of triadic motives in selected motets of Delalande.

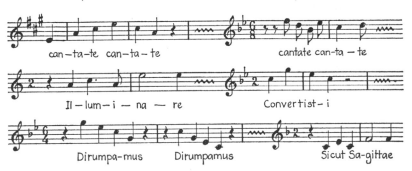

Delalande sought maximum musical contrast between textual ideas in apposition. This is generally achieved either through the choice of melodic materials that, because of built-in rhythmic differences, combine effectively in counterpoint, or it is achieved through a clear contrast of mood resulting from the direction and choice of intervals and change in modality.

Example 44
Delalande: Extract from Pange lingua *(after the ed. of 1729).*

Delalande's use of harmony undoubtedly owes something to his exposure to the music of Charpentier. The $\frac{9}{7}_{\sharp5}$ chord on the Mediant, found so often in the music of Charpentier, is no stranger to the motets of his younger contemporary. Perhaps more than any other French composer before Rameau, Delalande viewed the diminished 7th chord as vested with a compelling dramatic quality. In Example 44, from *Pange lingua*, the careful choice of diminished 7th chords, coupled with a dramatic 'silence' (the word is found in the score), is yet another example of the great care taken by the composer to find the most effective musical setting for the text.

Delalande's orchestra plays both a supportive and an independent role in his *grands motets*. Usually, it functions in both capacities at the same time. That is, some of the voices support (double) the choral lines, while others weave an independent counterpoint around the voice parts as we see in the chorus 'Et ipse redimet Israël', from *De profundis* (Example 45a below). Example 45b shows the first violins and sopranos in 'Desiderium peccatorum peribit' from Psalm 111,

Example 45
(a) *Extract from* De profundis (*after ed. of 1729*).

(*b*) *Extract from* Beatus vir (*after ed. of 1729*).

(*c*) *Extract from* De profundis.

Beatus vir qui timet Dominum, using a simple and an adorned version of the same melody simultaneously which results in a kind of heterophony. In contrapuntal choruses, the orchestra often contributes a fugal entrance, independent of the voices. In *De profundis,* the subject of the 'Requiem aeternam' is treated in imitative entrances spaced one measure apart and shared by voices and instruments (Example 45c).

In Psalm 45, *Deus noster* (1699), the orchestra with ostinato rhythms ($\flat$ ♫ ♫♩) supports the double chorus "Conturbatae sunt gentes', creating an 'operatic' battle scene of great power. Forming contrasting episodes are the 'graceful melodies' noted by Blamont in his *Avertissement.* Borrowed from the opera, they probably served as performance vehicles for Delalande's two daughters, both of whom had excellent voices, or for his wife, Anne Rebel, who was the sister of composer-performer Jean-Ferry Rebel, and who was one of the best singers of the king's *Chambre.* Like the *da capo* arias of Bach cantatas, they are 'ingenious disparities' when placed in apposition to large double choruses. Some were written in a virtuoso and bravura style; others are more restrained in the manner of a Lully operatic

199

air. In the air 'Illumina oculos meos', from Psalm 12, *Usquequo, Domine* (1692), the use of an arpeggiated accompaniment pattern prefigures the *style galant* of the later eighteenth century.

Example 46
Delalande: Extract from Usquequo Domine (*after the ed. of 1729*).

The majority of Delalande's motets are found in three large collections: 1. The manuscript copy of 27 motets made by Philidor in 1689 and 1690, now located at the Bibliothèque Municipale de Versailles (Mss 8–17); 2. The posthumously printed edition of 40 motets mentioned above; and 3. The manuscript copy of 41 motets and some shorter pieces made for, or by, a certain Gaspard-Alexis Cauvin and now housed, except for the last volume, at the Bibliothèque Municipale de Versailles (Mss 216–35).[19] The Cauvin manuscript seems to be a later eighteenth century copy of the 1729 printed edition with a changed sequence of motets and the addition of one motet, *Exaudi Deus*. It has the great advantage of including the instrumental 'parties de remplissage' in contrast to the printed edition which reduces Delalande's large orchestra to two violins and continuo. Eight motets in the early Philidor copy also appear in the Cauvin manuscript and, with one exception, in the printed edition.[20]

A comparison of the same motets in the above sources gives insight into Delalande's development. Changes in the different versions stem partly from his increased maturity and control over the idiom and partly from his wish to conform to the changing tastes of audiences in the closing years of Louis XIV's reign.

In general the changes take the following forms: 1. Creation of elaborate concert arias or duos out of simple *récits* (see, for example, 'Tibi omnes angeli' from *Te Deum*); 2. Change of a predominantly homophonic chorus into one that is more polyphonic (see, for example, 'Et laudamus' from *Te Deum*); 3. Change from an orchestra that is used primarily to double the voices of a chorus to one that is genuinely independent of the voices (see, for example, 'Averte faciem' from *Miserere mei*); 4. Greater economy in the use of some material while other material is expanded.

A fine example of the fourth category is the 'Requiem aeternam' from *De profundis*. The Philidor copy includes a *symphonie* of 14 measures, a solo *récit* of 8 measures, a second *symphonie* of 6 measures and a chorus of 31 measures up to the 'Et lux perpetua'. The chorus is basically homophonic with clear separation of textual elements (Example 47a). In the later and best known version, there is only one *symphonie* of 9 measures that merges with a 53 measure chorus up to 'Et lux perpetua'. The chorus, this time, unifies textual elements and is written in dense, five-part polyphony of Bach-like intensity in which both voices and instruments participate (Example 47b).

Example 47
Delalande: Two versions of De profundis.
(a) First version (after Philidor copy).

(b) Second version (after the ed. of 1729).

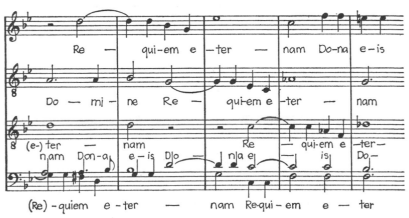

The bond between Michel-Richard Delalande, the 15th son of a Parisian tailor, and his king, the favoured scion of the Bourbon dynasty, was a strong one, apparently nourished by adversity. Blamont in his *Avertissement* relates that, following the loss of the Dauphin in the same year as the death of Delalande's two daughters (1711), Louis xiv told Delalande, 'You have lost two daughters who were deserving of merit. I have lost Monseigneur. Lalande, it is necessary to submit (to the will of God).'

In 1710, Robert de Cotte, working from the plans of his late brother-in-law, Jules-Hardouin Mansart, finished a project that was dear to the heart of the ageing Sun-King—the building of the new and final Versailles chapel. In a figurative and literal sense, it was the *grands motets* of Delalande that gave to the new chapel its most eloquent voice. The grand conception now could be realized with a choir and orchestra totalling close to 90 members and with the magnificent organ of Robert Clicquot possessing 4 manuals and 36 stops.

Out of her vast knowledge of French religious music of the *grand siècle*, Michel Brenet penned a moving tribute to the new chapel, to its composer, its musicians and its king:

The old sovereign crosses by foot the *galeries* of Versailles to come to his recently finished chapel, brilliant with gold and light; 100 Swiss guards line the way of his passage; the bodyguards await him at the Tribune, the chaplain at the holy water basin, the priests in the choir, the ladies in the balcony, the courtiers in the nave, the musicians behind their stands: he passes, noble, handsome, always the king; . . . the celebrant begins the Office, and Lalande lifts his baton; the music, indifferent to any liturgical chronology, is a motet for large chorus. . . . At first there is a *symphonie* played by all the musicians of the *chambre*; then the two daughters of Lalande, the Italian Favalli or Sieur Borel de Miracle, sing some *récits* and duos accompanied by Philibert Rebillé on the transverse flute or Marais playing a bass viol solo; singers and virtuosi compete; there are the *gracieux*, the *tendrement*, the *légers* and the *loure* . . . all the *agréments* that suggest French melody; all this, set off by the overwhelming effect of the choruses . . . that follow the instruments and prepare for the end of the ceremony and the departure of the King. . . .

(*La Musique sacrée sous Louis XIV*, 1899, pp. 12–13)

Chapter 14

-»» «-

The Motet in the Eighteenth Century

Because of its function as the chief decorative element in the king's Mass, the *grand motet* in France, even from its inception, took on the aspects of a sacred concert. Its composers favoured musical settings of non or para-liturgical texts, as opposed to the words of the liturgy, and apparently Delalande himself made no effort to coordinate his *grands motets* with the liturgical year.

No one pretended that the motet was an integral part of the liturgy. This should not imply that somehow it was less 'religious' than a polyphonic Mass, for example. What makes a composition 'religious' instead of merely 'liturgical' is impossible to define unless one arbitrarily chooses Gregorian chant or Palestrina Mass as the only true measure. The *grand motet* could not isolate itself from the aggressive state religion it served. The 'battle' chorus of Delalande's *Deus noster* expresses the tone of the church of a Bossuet as much as Handel's 'Hallelujah Chorus' speaks for the 'muscular protestantism' of eighteenth century England.

It should come as no surprise to find an acceleration in the secularization of religious music as the *grand siècle* gave way to the Regency. Thus, the motets of Brossard and Morin include Alleluia finales organized as instrumental gigues, and a *petit motet* by Mouret (*O sacrum convivium*) even allows the soprano soloist a cadenza. Only the musical integrity of a Couperin allows us to accept Gregorian melodies which, at first glance, seem over-laden with *tremblements* and *ports de voix*, and the motets of Campra and Gilles are permeated by the popular tunes of their meridional homeland.

Secularization was inevitable especially in a religion that used all its musical resources to parade its opulence and to orchestrate its power. The *Mercure* of June 1716 described a religious procession *de luxe* that made use of an altar of repose (*reposoir*) near the palace of Versailles:

All the court had been decorated with the most beautiful and richest tapestries of the Gobelins; in the Marble Court even the pavements were covered. . . . On the left, a stage had been built for the musicians among whom were some of the best voices of the Opera and several players on all kinds of instruments. . . . As soon as the banner of the procession approached, the Duchesse de Berry left the door of the palace . . . to welcome the procession and adore the Holy Sacrament which she then accompanied to the *reposoir*. During this time, the trumpets, drums, oboes and bassoons sounded on the balcony. Following this, a motet composed by M. Destouches was performed by all the musicians.

Undoubtedly, the convents of the *Théatins* and the *Feuillants* and the Abbey of Longchamp had long deserved the admonition of Mme de Maintenon that they had 'made of their church an opera house'. Lecerf has left us a vivid description of performances at convents by popular singers followed by groups of their fashionable admirers:[1]

They are paid to perform the most pious and solemn Motets! Singers, who are placed behind a curtain that they draw apart from time to time to smile at friends among the listeners, are praised for singing a Lesson on Good Friday or a solo motet for Easter. One goes to hear them at an appointed convent: in their honour, the price that would be charged at the Opera is charged, in order to purchase a seat at the Church. One recognizes *Urgande* and *Arcabonne* (characters in Lully's *Amadis*) and claps his hands. (I have even heard applause at the Tenebrae and Assumption Services although I cannot now recall whether it was for *La Moreau* or for *Madame Cheret*.)

(*Comparaison*, III, p. 162)

And yet secularization is no stranger to religious music. At its best, it results in a healthy cross-fertilization, beneficial to both the secular and the religious. *Trouvère* melodies softened the harsh contours of the Gothic motet; 'motet-chanson', as a term, belies its dual origins; and the secular musical world of Baroque opera, dance suite, French overture, Italian concerto and sonata is synthesized in the church cantatas of J. S. Bach. In France, secularization was more a symptom than a cause of the decline of religious music in the eighteenth century. It was the reflection of an age grown tired of heroic posturing and a King-God.

Lacking any firm liturgical base, deprived of a ruling monarch, and purely on stylistic grounds, the *grand motet* should never have survived the *grand siècle*. It was out of joint with the frivolous and feminine world of the Regency; its grandiloquent gesture, hollow; its form, an empty shell. Yet, survive it did—a monolithic vestige of the age of the 'Sun-King' now, it seemed, permanently stabilized as part of the repertory of the royal chapel and the *Concert Spirituel*.

This of itself need not have precipitated a decline had there been composers of the calibre of Delalande who might have infused the *grand motet* with new life; but who now would revive the *grands motets* of Philippe Courbois, François Pétouille, of Guignard, or the Abbé Gaveau?

French composers of the rank of Rameau or Leclair were almost totally committed to stage or instrumental music from the 1730's on. Perhaps they had the instinct, or good sense, to realize that the frivolity of the times, coupled with a strong anti-clericalism—the natural issue of the repressive religious atmosphere at the close of the *grand siècle*—was not the best intellectual or moral climate in which to promote significant religious music.

Henry Desmarest (1661–1741),[2] had he not become involved in an amorous imbroglio resulting in his expulsion from the realm,[3] might have enjoyed a more prosaic but secure career as composer for the court and royal chapel. From Titon du Tillet, we learn that the motet by Desmarest, performed for Louis XIV at the time of the 1683 competition, was 'one of the most beautiful . . . but the King thought him to be too young to hold one of the appointments . . . and gave him a 900 *livres* pension instead' (*Le Parnasse françois*, p. 755).

As a student or follower of Du Mont, Robert and Lully and as a successor to Charpentier at the Jesuit College, Desmarest, by training and, it appears, inclination, would have been ideally suited to work with Delalande at the royal chapel. Of all Delalande's younger contemporaries, he was the best able to fill the large dimensions of the *grand motet* with convincing music.

Motets in manuscript now at the Bibliothèque Nationale and at St Michael's College, Tenbury Wells, show Desmarest's style at its best. Four of those at the Bibliothèque Nationale are psalm settings, each averaging over 100 pages! From Delalande, he had learned how to treat his orchestra independently from the chorus. From the *petit choeur* of the opera chorus, he took the popular sonority of two sopranos and counter-tenor. More than any other composer of his generation in France, Desmarest 'thought' polyphonically. The *grand motet* setting of Psalm Six, *Domine, ne in furore*, composed about 1707 for the Duc de Lorraine, includes a vocal quartet (two sopranos, counter-tenor, bass) accompanied by flutes and strings for the verse 'Laboravi in gemitu meo'. Here is dense polyphony, involving voices and instruments, in which individual lines maintain their direction and tension. Without any linear clogging, all parts share in the overlapping descending motif on the words, 'Lacrymis meis stratum meum rigabo' ('My couch is wet with tears').

All that remains of the *grands motets* of Guillaume Minoret (*c.*

Example 48
Desmarest: Extract from Domine, ne in furore *(after Ms Res F 928 in B.N.).*

1650–1717), one of the winners of the 1683 competition, are six motets copied by Philidor in 1697. On the basis of these works, Minoret's style appears conservative; the instrumental accompaniment is reduced to a continuo in some double choir motets. Yet, remarks by Titon du Tillet provoke interest and point up the dangers of generalizing from such a small sample. In *Le Parnasse françois*, Titon wrote as follows:

Some pieces have singular beauty and may be labelled master-pieces . . . including the third verset of the psalm *Nisi Dominum,* for which Minoret composed a piece for four different voices with independent accompaniment for Violins and Basses resulting in a very beautiful composition that one might say is almost unique.

(*Le Parnasse françois,* p. 754)

Jean Gilles (1668–1705)[4] directed successively the choir schools at Aix-en-Provence, Agde, Avignon and at Saint-Etienne of Toulouse, where he reamined from 1697 to his death. His known music consists of 11 *grands motets,* a *Te Deum,* three Lamentations, two Masses and several *petits motets* all of which are conserved today in manuscripts at the Bibliothèque Nationale and the Bibliothèque Méjanes at Aix.

Gilles, a student of Poitevin at Toulouse, was far away from the direct influence of the royal chapel and consequently from the dominant note of composing 'official' religious music. His motets are more personal and intimate. The melodic line of the *récits,* although heavy with ornament, is often of a popular nature, reflecting the irregular phrase length of Provençal melody.[5]

At the close of the seventeenth century, the *petit motet* had not as yet succumbed to the virtuoso elements stemming from the Italian cantata and opera. The *Motets à voix seule avec la basse continue* by Guillaume-Gabriel Nivers (1632–1714) are typical. These motets were written in 1689 for the young women of the Maison Royale de Saint-Louis at Saint-Cyr where the composer served as organist and choir director. They are intimate works, obviously composed with the resources of the 'Dames de Saint-Louis' in mind, and include 61 motets of which 13 contain dialogues for solo voices and unison chorus. Nivers eschewed both vocal virtuosity and overt dramatic expression, although Mme de Maintenon, who had founded Saint-Cyr three years before for the education of young noble women, forbade the performance of one of the motets, *Adjuro Vos,* because it was 'too tender'.

The motets are short. Some are in binary and some in Rondeau form with an Alleluia acting as refrain. French vocal *agréments,* especially the *port de voix* and the *coulé,* inundate the melodic line. Short vocalises, sometimes placed rather arbitrarily on unimportant words, contribute to creating a 'busy' melody (see Example 49).

Louis-Nicolas Clérambault (1676–1749), who along with Nivers served as *maître de chapelle* at Saint Cyr, also contributed several *petits motets* for one or two solo voices alternating with a unison or two-part chorus.[6] In addition, Jean-Baptiste Moreau (1656–1733), Delalande, Collasse and Louis Marchand (1669–1732) all furnished settings of Racine's *cantiques spirituels* for the young ladies of Saint Cyr.[7]

Daniel Danielis (1635–96),[8] like Du Mont a Walloon born near

Liège, was named in 1684 *maître de chapelle* at Saint-Pierre at Vannes where his motets remained popular throughout the eighteenth century. He left us 72 motets ranging from one to four voices which are scattered today in various manuscript copies at the Bibliothèque Nationale (fonds du Conservatoire) and in the University library at Uppsala. With their textual repetitions, vocalises, rapid and frequent modulations, chromaticism and text painting it is not surprising that Lecerf thought him to have been an Italian and coupled his name with that of Lorenzani as rare examples of Italian composers 'worthy of commendation'.

Example 49
Nivers: Extract from Magnificat *(after ed. of 1689).*

Among Sébastien de Brossard's most important religious compositions are the eight *petits motets* for solo voice of his *Elevations et Motets* of 1695 (republished in 1698 and 1702). Musically, they stem more from Lully than from Charpentier and appear almost devoid of any real Italian influence—surprising in a composer so aware of and so partisan to the Italian musical penetration of France. Their main interest lies in their formal structure in which the music is divided into several autonomous, contrasted sections often terminating with an Alleluia or an Amen finale. The latter are well-developed compositions in their own right which, we are informed by the composer, could be performed as separate pieces.

Typical in its sectionizing is number six of the set, *Angele sancte*, which has the following movement and metre scheme:

'Adagio e affettuoso' / 'Presto e Allegro' / 'Adagio'
(3/2) (C) (3/4)
'Largo' / 'Allegro e Presto' / 'Presto e Allegro'
(C) (C) (12/8)

The final 'Presto e Allegro', amounting to an 'Amen, Alleluia', is, in truth, an instrumental gigue with words added.

Example 50
Brossard: Extract from Angele sancte *(after ed. of 1695).*

That there was a practical reason for such clearly defined sections is suggested by Brossard's *Avertissement*:

Although these Motets may appear to be a little too long, one need only perform as much of each one as is desired; they were conceived so that where the sign ⌒ is found over a note, the section may be terminated at that point.

As early as 1701 in his edition of the motets of Jacques-François Lochon, Ballard clearly anticipated the fad of a fusion of Italian and French taste in the French cantata and other genres. In an *Avertissement*, the printer promoted his publication:

> Persuaded that what is new always pleases, I give these Motets to the Public; the well-informed (sçavants) have found them in such good taste and the Nuns (Dames Religieuses) have found them to be so appropriate for the choir, that I dare to hope for a pleasant reception, all the more because . . . the composer by his genius has found the secret of uniting Italian design and expression with French delicateness and gentleness.

The motets include a profusion of repeated text fragments, worked into long vocal melismas, and Italian terms taken from Brossard. This undoubtedly convinced Lecerf that he could 'expect nothing good from the *nouveaux motets dans le goût françois italien* by Lochon'. He objected:

> I would never display a professed intention of half-copying Italian composers. I cannot emphasize too often that their use of dissonance, changes of key, broken melodic lines (*chants rompus*) *etc.* do not conform to our Music. . . .

By 1703 Campra let it be known in the title to his third book of motets that the collection included a motet 'à la manière italienne'. In fact, the modification of the French motet in the wake of the Italian cantata may be best observed through a study of the first four books of motets by André Campra. Coming from Aix-en-Provence, Campra surely was no stranger to Italian religious music, and it is quite possible that, soon after his arrival in Paris (1694), he became familiar with the popular motets of Paolo Lorenzani in print the previous year.

Significantly, all four books[9] appeared before the first book of Campra's *Cantates Françoises* in which he elevated the combining of French 'delicatesse' and Italian 'vivacité' to a guiding principle. As such, his *petits motets* appear to have been preliminary studies in 'la manière italienne'. As the eighteenth century progressed, the *petit motet* and the *cantate françoise* tended to differ only in subject matter and language. They employed almost identical melodic formulas shaped by French ornamentation and Italian melisma. Both make use of recitatives and share *da capo* airs, and in both genres the driving rhythms of the Italian concerto and the gentle homophony of a French 'sommeil' co-exist.

Campra's first book of *Motets à I, II et III voix avec la basse continue* was printed by Ballard in the same year as Brossard's *Elevations*. Three of the 14 *petits motets* include parts for two violins—instruments, it will be remembered, that Campra introduced at Notre-Dame Cathedral where, in 1694, he had replaced Jean Mignon as director of the choir school.

The melodies of this first set still have some of the simplicity and freshness that spring from the sun-drenched soil of Provence. These melodies are similar to those Campra composed two years later for his *opéra-ballet L'Europe galante*. Vocal melismas are restrained, but the harmony is richer, the modulations are more rapid and often move to more distant keys than is true in the motets of Brossard. *Tota pulchra es* from the *Song of Songs* is an Italian chamber duet wed to a French passacaille. A sensuous melody moving predominantly in parallel thirds creates attractive double suspensions with the rigid bass line; the identical bass was used later by Campra to support the magnificent air 'Sommeil qui chaque nuit' from the second *entrée* ('*L'Espagne*') of *L'Europe galante*.

Example 51
Campra: Extract from Tota pulcra es *(after ed. of 1695).*

Books II and III show more variety than the earlier set in terms of instrumental accompaniment (flutes and violins) and musical forms. *Immensus es Domine* from Book II uses two flutes and includes a 32 measure *ritournelle*. *O Jesu amantissime*, from the same collection, includes a passage bristling with cross-relations and stark chromaticism over a Dominant pedal (see Example 52).

Book III is closer yet to the Italian cantata. *O Dulcis amor* (No. 3) is framed by two *da capo* arias. There are more *airs de vitesse* and demanding vocalises. The third book was less successful than the earlier two, and Lecerf lost no time in placing the blame for this on

Example 52
Campra: Extract from O Jesu amantissime *(after ed. of 1699).*

Campra's 'imitation of the Italians', adding smugly that the 'price and power of true and false beauty are quite different'. With Book IV of 1706, the process of 'Italianizing' the *petit motet* was completed. *Da capo* airs dominate, and the frequent textual repetitions give rise to sequential patterns and long melismas that do little to illuminate the text and much to tire the listener.

Campra returned to the motet after 14 years (Book V, 1720; Psalms, Book I, 1737; Psalms, Book II, 1738). The 16 motets of these three collections are supplemented by many autograph and manuscript copies at the Bibliothèque Nationale (fonds du Conservatoire) and the Bibliothèque Méjanes at Aix-en-Provence. These late works by Campra are all *grands motets* written for the royal chapel. They borrow indiscriminately from the style of the composer's own *tragédies lyriques* and *opéras-ballets*. Bravura passages for soloists abound often accompanied by virtuoso instrumental obbligatos; there are duos and trios sometimes unified by recurring *ritournelles*; there are exciting, warlike choruses set against a background of rapid violin figurations; and Psalm 75, *Notus in Judea Deus*, includes an operatic 'sommeil'. As in the earlier motet collections and in his stage music, Campra shows great skill in constructing large-scaled movements over emphatic ostinato patterns such as the double fugue 'Et lux perpetua' from *De profundis* and the opening of the *Magnificat* in the Aix collection.

More Italian than the motets of Campra are the two books (1704, 1709) by Jean-Baptiste Morin (1677–1745) who, like Campra and Bernier, was in the employ of the Duc d'Orléans. *Da capo* arias include sequences of 7ths and circles of 5ths. Like the *Elevations* of Brossard, many contain 'detachable' Alleluia finales, of which one is also a vocal 'gigue'.

The twelve *Motets à I, II et III voix* of 1711 by Edme Foliot (dates unknown) are in the tradition of Nivers. Even though more French than Italian, these motets include some sentimental duos with paired voices creating chains of suspensions (for example, 'Ora pro nobis' from the *Regina coeli*). As though to dispel fears that his motets were other than a type of *Gebrauchsmusik* for the convent, Foliot wrote in his *Avertissement*: 'I have had no other purpose in mind in composing these works than to render them useful to the Nuns. . . . I have restricted myself to a flowing and natural melody, so sought after by all people of good taste.' Like Brossard's, the motets of Foliot are also designed so that they may be abridged 'in order not to prolong the Divine Office'.

The motets of Nicolas Bernier (1665–1734)[10] are more important musically. His first book, which appeared in 1703, was criticized by Lecerf who found his duos and trios 'disagreeably marked with the stamp of Italy'. A total of 45 *petits motets* was printed in three volumes widely spaced in time (1703, 1713, 1741). Most (30) are for solo voice, and some include violin, two violins or flute *ritournelles*. The restrained vocalises and the use of motto beginnings are discreetly 'Italian'. Most conform to Perrin's 'several pieces loosely strung together', although there are a few that use a rondo structure.

Bernier's 11 *grands motets*, composed for the royal chapel where he was employed with Campra, Delalande and Gervais from 1723 until his death, are all in manuscript. Less 'operatic' than those of Campra, they are clearly in the tradition of the Versailles motet. The orchestra of five part strings doubles the *grand choeur*. The *petit choeur* emphasizes the high voices of sopranos and counter-tenor. The harmonic language is conservative when compared with that of Charpentier or Delalande although there is considerably more harmonic interest than is found in the later motets of Lully.

Virtually ignored by Lecerf, who considered him only as a 'serviteur passionné de l'Italie', François Couperin, of all his contemporaries, succeeded best in the creation of a musical language compounded of French and Italian elements. As applied to the *petits motets*, this *goût réuni* appears to have been a natural musical expression for Couperin whose personal style is rarely lost in self-conscious imitation of 'la manière italienne'. French are the short phrases and many perfect cadences and the melodic *formulae* derived from 'airs serieux' or dance measures. French too is the ornamentation carefully calculated here, as in the keyboard works, for maximum expressiveness—used now as an accent, now as a built-in rubato, placed here to lend a sense of harmonic urgency, there to serve as decorative arabesque. Italian are the vivid musical images that underscore the text and the ability to paint a dramatic scene albeit in miniature. Italian also are the infusion of vocalises in the melodic line, the use of abrupt changes of tonality and the frequent chromaticism.

Most commonly, elements of both styles co-exist harmoniously in the same composition. However, there are examples of pure Italian vocal and instrumental style in immediate apposition with what is unmistakably French. Such are the first two movements of the *Motet de Sainte-Suzanne*. The opening counter-tenor solo, 'Veni, Veni sponsa Christi', with its light polyphony, its use of an introductory phrase that generates small rhythmic cells later employed in counterpoint, could be by Vivaldi or Handel. It is followed by a duet for soprano and counter-tenor, 'Date serta', that, with its note-against-note style, its lack of melisma and its short phrases, could be by Lully.

Although they borrow freely from opera, the *petits motets* and *Elevations* of Couperin are not 'operatic'.[11] An over-riding sense of balance and propriety subordinate virtuoso elements to purity of expression. Only in some of the large-scale works, the *Motet pour le jour de Pâques* or the *Magnificat*, is there a straining for effect and a surface brilliance that appears somewhat contrived.

As a miniaturist, Couperin wisely left to others the setting of complete psalm texts. Rather, he chose verses that seemed to him best suited for musical rendering. He often purposely selected the more lyric sentiments rather than those of the 'blood and thunder' variety. The three collections of Psalm verses of 1703, 1704 and 1705 composed 'by order of the King' and performed at Versailles are among Couperin's most intimate and finely wrought motets. These and the *Leçons de Ténèbres* were the only sacred works by the composer to be printed in his lifetime.

The three collections of psalm extracts are very different in their vocal and instrumental sonorities. The 'sound' of the *Quatre versets d'un motet*, of 1703, is the sound of two high sopranos, one of whom was Mlle Marguerite-Louise Couperin, daughter of François 'the elder', and cousin of François 'the Great'; it is the sound of violins in the role of continuo supporting voice and recorders. The verses are the 11th, 12th, 13th and 14th of the psalm *Mirabilia testimonia tua*. It is a tender, gentle work in which the characteristic sound of the two sopranos is heard at the very beginning before any *symphonie* in a highly original duo, 'sans Basse Continue ny aucun Instrument'. Verse 13 for soprano solo opens with a *ritournelle* scored for recorders and accompanied by 'all the first violins'. The motet closes, as it began, with a duo for two sopranos; this time, however, they are supported by violins, some of whom double the voices on alternate strophes, while others take over the function of the continuo.

Part of the refinement of Couperin's melodic style comes from the infinite variety, yet economy, of his vocalises. Such an example is the four-fold repetition of 'in aeternum' from the final duo. The entire passage is only 17 measures in duration, yet each of the four melismas has its own character—the inner two being allowed to expand through totally different sequential patterns.

Sept versets du motet of 1704, on the other hand, is dominated by the male voice although its last two verses were written for the voice of Mlle Couperin. It exploits the more brilliant sound of transverse flute and oboe as opposed to the gentler recorder. It is the sound of tenor and bass in recitatives and duos and triple metre dance measures. It includes verses 4, 5, 7, 8, 11, 12 and 13 of the psalm *Benedixisti Domine terram tuam.* Verse 5 is a lively choral duet scored for 'all tenors' and 'all basses' in the style of Handel. The penultimate verse provides one of the most striking examples of a 'bi-modality' common in French music of the period, that is, the use of chords borrowed from the parallel minor mode.

Example 53
Couperin: Extract from Verset 12 of Benedixiste Domine *(after ed. of 1704).*

The final verse is scored for oboe and transverse flute, each doubling a melodic line which resembles a thinly scored dance song. There is no continuo, and flute and oboe continue to double after the entrance of the solo soprano.

The *Sept versets du motet* of 1705, based on verses 1, 3, 9, 10, 11, 12 and 15 of Psalm 80, *Qui Regis Israel, intende,* is the most elaborate of the three sets. It is dominated by the sound of its instrumental *symphonies* and obbligato accompaniments. Elements from the concerto, overture and dance merge to create short *symphonies* of great variety. Again, all is expressed in the musical space of a few measures. The central point in the motet, the seventh verse, is defined by a 'Symphonie à deux choeurs' where oboes and flutes play in animated dialogue, and the strings continue to support the bass solo, 'Dux itineris fuisti', in *concertato* fashion. It is also the central point of the psalm, the description of the vine from Egypt which, when planted by God, took root and spread over the land. In dramatic contrast, the next verse uses the *tirades*, dotted rhythms and wide melodic profile of the French overture, with leaps of diminished 7ths and minor 10ths, as well as melodic tritones, to serve as an introduction to the soprano monologue, 'O peruit montes umbra ejus'. Verse 12, marked 'gratieuse-ment', is a gentle nature scene. Extended melismas on 'flumen', echoed in the string accompaniment, suggest the murmuring of waters described in the text.

The final verse, which includes the longest *symphonie* (24 measures), features continuous light counterpoint between a flute and oboe melody and an independent bass line scored for bass viols that supports a counter-tenor solo. The variety between verses is also reflected in the choice of tonalities which move abruptly from C-Minor (Verses 1 and 3) to Bb-Major (Verses 9 and 10) to F-Minor (Versus 11, 12) and back to C-Minor (Verse 15).

Couperin's last religious work is also his best. The three *Leçons de Ténèbres* for Good Friday were composed between 1713 and 1717 'at the request of the Nuns of L.' (undoubtedly, the Abbey of Long-champ near Paris). The *Tenebrae* lessons were among the most popular texts for musical settings during the Baroque period in France. They are part of an extended service that includes psalms, antiphons, readings, responses and canticles that takes place during the first Nocturn of Matins of the three days preceding Easter. Each office includes three 'lessons' selected from the Lamentations of Jeremiah. A vocalise on ritualistic Hebrew letters introduces each verse, and the whole is preceded by the Gregorian melody for the 'Incipit Lamentatio Jeremiae Prophetae' (*Liber Usualis*, 631). Each lesson concludes with 'Jerusalem convertere ad Dominum Deum tuum' (Jerusalem turn back to your Lord God'). A second Gregorian source is the austere *formulae* for the Hebrew letters themselves (*Liber Usualis*, 631–37) to which Couperin added French ornamentation and vocal melismas.

Decorative and graceful melodies have given way in the lessons to expressive recitative born of the *arioso* and dramatic monologue of the *tragédie lyrique*. The moving words of the prophet have a musical intensity rare for Couperin. Amidst the recitatives there are heightened moments in which closed musical forms are introduced. Such are the loosely organized rondeau 'airs' that close the first two lessons. Such is the great 'lament', 'Plorans ploravit in nocte', of the first lesson organized in an ABACC form. The pathetic opening line of this lament describing Jerusalem as a poor widow weeping in the night, makes its way inexorably from f'' down to a minor 10th to d', its passage impeded by repeated notes, expressive ornaments and pauses.

Couperin reserves the wrenching chord of the Mediant 9th for two places that portray desolation in the lessons. The first (Example 54 below) occurs in the above mentioned 'lament' on the words 'ex omnibus charis ejus' ('of all her lovers, she hath none to comfort her'); the second is found in the third lesson on the words 'posuit me desolatam' ('He hath made me desolate').

Example 54
Couperin: Extract from first Leçon de Ténèbres *(after F. du Plessy ed., n.d.).*

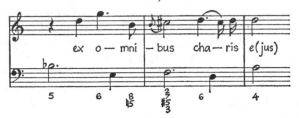

In such a manner does Couperin unite French and Italian practices even in his use of dissonance. The chains of suspensions and the chromaticism are Italian, but the selective use of the chord described above and the stacking up of dissonant tones over a pedal (see the verse 'Omnis populus ejus gemens', from the third lesson) were relatively common post-Lully harmonic procedures in France.

The first two lessons are scored for high voice and continuo; the third adds a second high voice. These are minimum requirements, however, as Couperin stated in his informative *Avertissement* which also illuminates some performance practices of his time; *viz.* the organist's ability to transpose could be assumed, and the harpsichord as well as the organ might be used in church performances. Couperin wrote:

> The first and second Lessons of each day will always be performed by one voice and the third, by two: thus, two voices will suffice to execute all three; although the melody has been notated in the soprano clef, all other types of voices can sing it in as much as most persons today who accompany know how to transpose. . . . It is desirable if one can add a bass viol or a bass violin to the accompaniment of the organ or the harpsichord.

The third lesson is the most impressive from the point of view of consistency of mood and setting. It is a deeply felt and almost continuous recitative and recitative *en duo* whose origins stretch back from the *tragédie lyrique* to Carissimi or even Monteverdi. Yet, it is a recitative in which French ornamentation is an organic part of the melodic line and a critical means of rendering the music expressive (see Example 55).

The long, undulating vocal melismas that make up the initial Hebrew letters afford the greatest possible contrast to the sections in recitative. Their point of departure is the Gregorian formula now

Example 55
Couperin: Extract from third Leçon de Ténèbres *(after du Plessy ed.)*.

O vos o — mnes,qui tran — si — tis per vi — am

extended to an expressive *cantilena*. They are closer to Corelli than Bach, and their polyphony is that of a portion of a slow movement of a trio sonata with its chain of suspensions, evasions of cadence and its improvised ornaments now, however, written in full.

Example 56
Couperin: Extract from third Leçon de Ténèbres *(after du Plessy ed.)*.

Important in sustaining the tradition of the *grand motet* as a concert piece far into the eighteenth century are the motets by Rameau, Charles-Hubert Gervais (1691–1755), Joseph Bodin de Boismortier (1689–1755), Esprit Blanchard (1696–1770), Henri Madin (1698–1748), and Jean-Joseph Cassanea de Mondonville (1711–72). The motets of Rameau deserve to be better known. That they are uneven in quality and lack the unity of expression found in Couperin's best religious music should be obvious to all but the most partisan *Ramistes*. With careful selection, however, certain solos, ensembles and choruses may be performed today with good results in church and concert hall. Unevenness of quality, after all, was common to most *grands motets* after the death of Delalande—a fact recognized by Marmontel who made the practical suggestion that one should have the liberty of choosing to perform an 'attractive collection of pieces with verses taken from here and there' (Article, 'Concert Spirituel', in the *Encyclopédie*). If we may believe Marmontel, the *auctoritas* of the *grand motet* at the *Concert Spirituel* was such that even late in the century no deletions were permitted: 'The difficulty (in performing separate movements) is the necessity of conquering tradition and perhaps (changing) public opinion.'

There are four *grands motets* which may be attributed, with a fair degree of certainty, to Rameau: *Laboravi, In convertendo, Quam dilecta* and *Deus noster refugium*.

Laboravi, which consists of a musical setting of the fifth verse from Psalm 69, was printed in the *Traité de l'harmonie* (Book IV) to illustrate 'fugue'. 'A fugue', wrote Rameau, 'consists of a certain continuous melodic idea that one may repeat as he wishes and in whatever voice part he wishes . . .'. This definition is followed by 12 general rules of fugue writing after which Rameau concluded that the fugue is essentially an 'ornament in Music. which has good taste as its only principle'.

The illustrative motet scored for five part chorus (two sopranos, counter-tenor, tenor and bass) is in one movement. The two sentences of the verse are divided into four clauses, and each is assigned a fugue subject. Rameau combined all this in a rather academic fashion with little attention to textual clarity. With the exception of the final *stretto*, there is not much use made of the contrapuntal complexities described in some of his rules. There is little real tension or pull between the parts, and voices line up in homophony for measures at a time. Thus, by observing the music itself, rather than by the rules it claims to illustrate, we can see how far Rameau was from the fugal procedures of, for example, J. S. Bach.

More typical of a *grand motet* is Psalm 46, *Deus noster refugium*, whose parallel verses are divided into nine autonomous parts including four airs, one duo, one trio, one quartet and two choruses. The third verse, 'Sonuerunt, et turbatae sunt aquae eorum', is a large four-part chorus with string orchestra. As Girdlestone has observed, it is organized as a *concerto grosso* with the orchestra carrying the burden of the recurring *ritournelles*. It is, in reality, a 'storm scene' marked 'vivement' and uses the forward motion and mechanical pulsations of the Italian concerto to describe the roar of waters and mountains that 'shake with the swelling thereof'. The chorus appears distinctly subordinate to the orchestra which continually penetrates the voices with the main thematic material.

Rameau's vocal writing in the solos and ensembles tends to be more brilliant and more melismatic than that of Couperin or Delalande. Descriptive passages abound and, in the trio 'Propterea non timebimus', result in virtuoso lines more appropriate for instruments than voices. The voices of the trio are accompanied by string tremolos describing the mountains borne down to the sea in the upheaval of the earth. This is part of the raw material from which the 'storm symphonies' emerge in the stage music of Rameau.

The air 'Fluminis impetus laetificat civitatem Dei', for soprano solo with obbligato violin and bass viol, includes some difficult rhythmic counterpoint which at times is terraced in simultaneous triplets, 8th note and 16th note patterns.

Example 57
Rameau: Extract from air 'Fluminis impetus', Deus noster refugium (after Ms Rés Vm¹ 507 in B.N.).

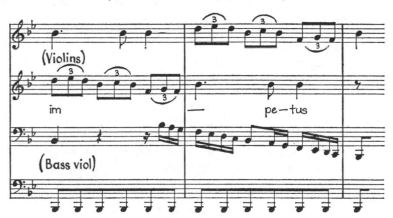

In spite of its uneven quality, the *grand motet In convertendo* is Rameau's religious masterpiece. It is based on verses 1, 2, 4, 5, 6 and 7 of Psalm 126. The date of composition is not known, but it was performed during Holy Week of 1751 at the *Concert Spirituel* where it was coolly received. The *Mercure* attempted to justify its poor reception on the shaky grounds that it was composed 40 years before. Girdlestone suggests that 'between 30 and 40 would have been a truer statement'.

The opening counter-tenor solo, 'In convertendo, Dominus', is an elegiac monologue worthy to stand beside its operatic counterparts: 'Ah faut-il' from *Hippolyte* (IV, 1), 'Coulez mes pleurs' from *Zaïs* (III, 3) or 'Séjour de l'éternelle paix' from *Castor et Pollux* (IV, 1). It employs the shifting metre of French recitative which is rarely found in

Latin music. Its profuse ornamentation is organically shaped to the melodic line to assure the greatest expressivity. Although it seems freely declamatory, it is, in fact, a rondeau air preceded and followed by a *ritournelle*.

On the contrary, the bass solo, 'Converte, Domine', is stiff and mechanical with abstract, sequential vocalises indiscriminately placed on words that are sometimes appropriate ('torrens') and sometimes unimportant ('austro'). The *récit* and chorus, 'Laudate nomen Dei cum cantico', superimposes an extremely melismatic soprano solo over a simple, almost folk-like chorus somewhat reminiscent of the style cultivated by Jean Gilles. The animated trio, 'Qui seminant in lacrimis', for soprano, counter-tenor and bass accompanied by unison violins and continuo, is a dance movement with the greatest concentration of motivic material.

Girdlestone is probably correct in rating the concluding chorus of the motet, 'Euntes ibant et flebant', as the 'greatest piece in all Rameau's church music'. It is a setting of the seventh verse, 'Euntes ibant et flebant, mittentes semina sua. Venientes autem venient cum exultatione, portantes manipulos suos' ('He that goeth forth and weepeth, bearing precious seed, shall doubtless come again with rejoicing, bringing his sheaves with him'). Rameau used two contrasting motifs (Example 58a below) to express the initial textual idea ('Euntes ibant et flebant'). The affective descending chromaticism on the word 'flebant' is often used independently of the first musical idea. The third motif (Example 58b), a predominantly 16th note scalar melody, is ideally suited to the expression of 'come again rejoicing'. During the remainder of the chorus, these three motives are expanded and combined with great skill as is shown in Example 58c.

With Boismortier and Blanchard, the orchestra of the *grand motet* was accorded more importance. Boismortier's setting of Psalm 19, *Exaudiat te Dominum*, of 1730 includes parts for two oboes, trumpet and timpani in addition to the usual strings. The use of more 'operatic' orchestration and long *da capo* airs was an attempt to bring the *grand motet* up to date without basically altering its format. At the same time, the search for novelty resulted in the incorporation of popular elements into the motet which, if anything, emphasized the archaic nature of the genre. Thus, Boismortier's *Fugit nox* of 1741 included several well-known Noëls and was so well received that it was programmed traditionally each December 25th at the *Concert Spirituel* for over 20 years. Late in the century, it was praised by La Borde: 'Boismortier had the secret of interspersing (in his motet) ' Noëls whose melodies combined pleasantly with the *récits*, choruses and *symphonies* with which they appeared to have nothing in common' (*Essai sur la musique ancienne et moderne*, III, p. 393).

Example 58
Rameau: Motivic use in final chorus of In Convertendo *(after autograph Rés Vm¹ 248 in B.N.).*

Blanchard was yet another pupil of Poitevin who, following a series of appointments at Marseilles, Toulon, Besançon and Amiens, served at the royal chapel after the death of Bernier (1734). More than 30 of his motets are preserved in manuscript at the Bibliothèque Nationale. The voice of Delalande can be heard again in some of the large polyphonic choruses. Blanchard's technique of orchestration derives from the Italian concerto and he was the first to introduce the clarinet into the orchestra of the royal chapel.

Henri Madin,[12] *maître de musique* at the royal chapel (1738) was described by Titon du Tillet as an 'Irish gentleman and one of the best motet composers of this century'. Titon added that because of their musical value and popularity, the motets 'merited being printed'; and, indeed, the motet *Diligam Te*, Brenet informs us, was in the repertory at the *Concert Spirituel* as late as 1762.

The 26 *grands motets* of Madin in manuscript at the Bibliothèque Nationale show some of the same technical workmanship found in Delalande and Rameau, at least in the creating of musical motives that may be used in apposition or in combination. A good example is the theme that opens Psalm 130, *De profundis*. Madin divides the text, 'De profundis clamavi', into two strikingly different motives that underscore the meaning of the words and, at the same time, present material that is effective in vertical combination (see Example 59).

The 12 *grands motets* of Mondonville sum up the history of the genre in France. They received much extravagant praise when first heard at the *Concert Spirituel* in the 1740's. They appeared to be the *dernier cri* in the *grand motet* idiom although their superficial pictorialism was attacked by Marmontel who wrote: 'Musicians, who compose pretty tunes and light choruses on the words of David, appear to me to profane his harp' ('Concert Spirituel' in *Encyclopédie*). The *grands motets* of Mondonville point up the superiority of the one composer of religious music in France whose *grands motets* did not seem to date or suffer from style shifts—Delalande. In spite of their fashionable Italianate airs and Mondonville's keen sense of orchestral sonorities, they are anachronisms and seem, today, tired exercises in the 'old style'. There is no question that the repertory of the Chapelle Royale to the very eve of the Revolution was dominated by the *grands motets* of those composers, mostly from the early and middle years of the century, who had mastered the 'old style'. For example, the 1792 volume of the *Livre de motets pour la Chapelle du Roy* (Ballard, 1787–92) gives the titles and texts of motets performed from January to June of 1792 at the Chapelle Royale. Included are 25 by Madin, 14 by Delalande, 13 by Campra, 5 by Gervais and 4 by Bernier.

Example 59
Madin: Motivic use in De profundis *(after Ms H.453 in B.N.).*

Chapter 15

-»»·«««-

Mass and Oratorio: The Domain of Marc-Antoine Charpentier

The Mass

During the reign of Louis XIV, there were no musical settings of the Ordinary of the Mass whose title pages were graced by the caption, 'printed by the express order of His Majesty'. By showing a marked preference for the motet, the king virtually doomed the composition of Masses by composers connected with his chapel. Regal taste became official policy, and many composers not directly involved with composing music for the royal chapel quite naturally took the Delalande motet as the accepted model for their religious music.

There is no known polyphonic setting of the Mass by Delalande, although a plainsong *Messe des deffuns* by him does exist in a manuscript collection in the Bibliothèque Nationale which also includes plainsong Masses and Mass fragments by Henry Du Mont, André Campra, Jean-François Lalouette, François David and Charles Piroye.

Yet as we have seen, Masses continued to be written in France in substantial numbers. With few exceptions,[1] however, they are by provincial composers caught in a musical backwater far from the centre of activity. Even less receptive to change than the *grand motet*, the double-chorus Masses with instruments, the *a cappella* Masses, the *cantus firmus* Masses and the plainsong Masses formed an important part of the repertory of many a provincial church and convent.

François Couperin, in company with Nicolas Grigny and Nicolas Lebègue, preferred to write organ Masses, a Renaissance genre that continued to be popular in France (see Chapter 18). André Campra left us two Masses: an early *a cappella* Mass *a 4*, 'Ad majorem Dei gloriam', printed by Ballard in 1699 and again in 1700, and a *Messe de Requiem*, in manuscript, that Barthelemy conjectures to be a late work (*André Campra*, p. 159). In contrast, Jean Mignon (1640–1710), Campra's predecessor at Notre-Dame, composed primarily Masses, six of which were published between 1676 and 1707.

One of the most popular Masses of the entire eighteenth century, and a work still performed in Paris churches, was actually composed in the closing years of the seventeenth century. It is a *Messe des Morts* by Jean Gilles who, at the time, was director of the choir school at Saint-Etienne of Toulouse. This work by an obscure Provençal composer (he is not listed, for example, in *Grove's*, in *Baker's* or even in the 'French Riemann') caught the fancy of *Concert Spirituel* audiences when it was first performed there in the 1760's, almost 60 years after Gilles' premature death (1705). By this date, the Mass was undoubtedly 'pepped-up' with many instruments added to make it more appealing to late eighteenth century tastes. Michel Corrette (1709–95) even composed a Carillon part 'pour la fin de la Messe'.

It was so popular that it was chosen for performances at the obsequies of Rameau and Louis xv, and it may have been known outside of France, since Sir John Hawkins wrote of it as 'the capital work' of Gilles.

The reasons for its success are not hard to find. It has a melodic freshness, or even sweetness, that cuts through its stiff Lullian exterior. This gives it an immediacy of appeal—a characteristic of a much later Requiem by Gabriel Fauré. Its freshness springs, in part, from the folk music of Gilles' Provençal heritage. Dance-like melodies in triple metre, organized in asymmetrical phrases, are juxtaposed with *a* 4 and *a* 5 choral homophony and with string symphonies reminiscent of Du Mont. Typical is the 'Et tibi' with its alternation of four and five-measure phrase groupings. The first Kyrie Eleison, a tenor solo, contrasts its irregular phrases and syncopated bass line (see Example 60 below) with the short, second Kyrie scored for an *a* 5 chorus. There is little real polyphony, and, as in his motets, Gilles often began his choruses with a florid soprano line superimposed over the remaining voice parts in note-against-note style.

Example 60
Gilles: Extract from Requiem (after Ms Vm¹ 1375 at B.N.).

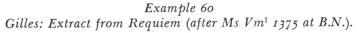

The only composer who made a significant contribution to the Mass in the French Baroque period is a man who, we have noted, had no official connection with the court or the royal chapel—Marc-Antoine Charpentier. The twelve Masses of Charpentier[2] serve as a glossary of Mass-types cultivated during the Baroque period. They range from a simple, straight-forward Mass, predominantly for solo voice and unison chorus, to one for four *a 4* choruses; they range from one that parodies popular Noëls to another built over a Gregorian *cantus firmus*.

As is so often the case with the music of Charpentier, it is difficult to determine the chronology of his Masses. Claude Crussard believes most to have been composed between 1679 and 1689.[3] Only the *Missa Assumpta est Maria* may be definitely dated from the Sainte-Chapelle period (1698–1704), because its manuscript includes the names of singers known to have been at the Sainte-Chapelle during Charpentier's tenure there. As may be observed by the titles, many are *pièces d'occasion* and must have been performed at the Dauphin's chapel or at the Jesuit church of Saint-Louis, and one, we learn from the title, was written for the nuns of Port Royal, the headquarters of Jansenism.

Clarence Barber suggests that the *Messe à quatre choeurs* may be an early work written when the sounds of Roman polychoral music were still fresh in Charpentier's ear.[4] If so, it would be a natural implementation of the composer's careful analysis ('Remarques sur les Messes à 16 parties d'Italie') found on his copy of Francesco Beretta's 16 part *Missa mirabilis elationes maris*, also in four choirs, which Charpentier brought back from Italy.

This large *concertato* Mass is perhaps the only one of its kind in seventeenth century France, and it is even conjectural whether or not it was ever performed. Another Mass for which there are few French precedents is the *Messe pour plusieurs instruments au lieu des orgues.* The words 'instead of organs' tell us that this Mass, with its alternation of verses for instruments and sung plainsong, is a substitute for the traditional organ Mass. Charpentier used a variety of instruments that afford much colour contrast. It is scored for four recorders, three transverse flutes, four bass flutes, two oboes, one cromorne and four-part strings. Exceptional, in music of this late date, is the lack of a continuo.

The organization of the Kyrie Eleison shown below demonstrates how Charpentier aimed for maximum colour contrast in his ensembles. The numbering duplicates that of the original where the Kyrie-Christe-Kyrie complex was labelled Kyrie I to Kyrie IX. The even numbered Kyries, not found below, are simply labelled, 'for the priests'.

Kyrie I:	For all instruments
Kyrie III:	For oboes
Kyrie V:	For violins of the *petit choeur*
Kyrie VII:	For recorders
Kyrie IX:	For all instruments

Kyries I, VII and IX, as well as sections of the Gloria, all make use of the Gregorian *cantus firmus Cunctipotens Genitor Deus* (*Liber*

Usualis, p. 25). There is no Credo, and the Agnus Dei is incomplete. The *cantus firmus* is presented in whole notes and restricted to the bass, which undoubtedly rendered a basso continuo superfluous. The upper parts employ rhythmic, as opposed to melodic, counterpoint and often resemble an 'air serieux'. As in Couperin's organ Masses, elements from the dance are introduced, and the Offertory for a wind and string choir is a French overture in its organization

In spite of their popularity and their use as a basis for organ and instrumental ensemble pieces, French Noëls appear not to have been cultivated as 'parody' tunes for Masses or motets. The earliest extant example of one of these rare Masses may well be the *Messe de minuit pour Noël* of Charpentier. Perhaps this served as a model for Brossard's *Missa Quinta Toni pro nocte ad die Festi Natalis Domini* of 1700. In addition to these two examples, only a Boismortier *grand motet, Fugit nox* of 1741, and the much later *Messe-Oratorio de Noël* of 1786 by Jean-François Le Sueur (1760–1837) use Noël tunes.

Charpentier chose twelve Noëls for his Mass, including two for which no music was provided, but which were to be performed independently after the Credo and during the Offertory.[5] The Mass is scored for solo voices, an *a* 4 chorus, flutes, strings, and organ. Short orchestral interludes introduce the Noëls to be employed subsequently in the vocal settings. Example 61 below, illustrates Charpentier's use

Example 61
Charpentier: Parody technique in the Messe de Minuit *(after the* Meslanges, *vol.* xxv*).*

of parody technique. The opening phrase of the second part of the Noël, 'Où s'en vont ces gais bergers', is lightly exchanged between the voices before lining up in vertical sonorities.

The whole is a tender, moving work in which popular elements lend exactly the right amount of naïveté and simple wonder appropriate to the subject.

Although generally less interesting than some of the other Masses of Charpentier, the *Messe à quatre voix et instruments*[6] is less conservative from the point of view of harmonic practices. The series of descending cross-relations, staggered between the voices in the 'Passus et sepultus est' from the 'Crucifixus', is a vivid example of text painting. Another is the astonishing augmented octave in close apposition to the often used Mediant ninth chord in the 'Miserere nobis' of the Agnus Dei.

Example 62
Charpentier: Use of harmony in the Messe à quatre voix (*after the* Meslanges, *vol.* xiv).

In no other work do the compositional skills of Charpentier's late years show to better advantage than in the *Missa Assumpta est Maria*. There is achieved here a balance between chorus and orchestra, be-

tween polyphony and homophony, and between a prayerful introspection and a dramatic sense of musical characterization. Its dimensions illustrate the healthy state of the performance groups at the
Sainte-Chapelle at the turn of the century. A chorus *a* 6 is used
(sopranos I and II, counter-tenor, tenor, baritone, bass); the orchestra
is *a* 4 and includes two flutes, strings, and organ.

Co-existing with age-old practices, such as the use of 'familiar style'
for the setting of the 'Et Incarnatus est', are the melodic diminished
fourths and augmented fifths, and the searing harmonies of the
'Miserere nobis' section of the 'Qui tollis'. Charpentier uses vocal
range and timbre, in addition to harmony, to delineate contrasting
moods. Thus, only solo tenor, baritone and bass are employed for the
'Crucifixus' with the voices entering in that order, whereas the 'Et
Resurrexit' employs only the high voices of counter-tenor, second and
first sopranos, in that order.

Refined melodic style characterizes the *Missa Assumpta est Maria.*
Many melodies are quiet and move with the predominantly conjunct
motion of liturgical chant (Kyrie and Agnus Dei); others include joyful and quite vocal melismas on such words as 'gratias', 'amen', and
'resurrexit'; others are 'fort et guay' dances (Laudamus te); and still
others are well-suited for their extended fugal treatment ('Cum sancto
spiritu').

Although the orchestra most commonly doubles the voices in the
choral movements, the first and final Kyries, the first Sanctus and the
first and final Agnus Dei are long, autonomous symphonies. This is
instrumental music of high seriousness which, with its contrapuntal
lines, stems from the idiom of the ensemble fantasies and *ricercare* of
the earlier seventeenth century.

Oratorio

In terms of musical significance, the most telling result of Charpentier's three year (?) sojourn in Italy and studies with Carissimi was
his introduction of oratorios, or as he labelled them, *historiae*, into
France. Charpentier's oratorios appear to have been antedated by certain *histoires en musique* composed by the theorist René Ouvrard
(1624–94)[7] and described briefly in letters written to Claude Nicaise
(1623–1701), canon at the Cathedral of Dijon. Albert Cohen has
found references to the following titles: *Histoire du Publicain et du
Pharisien* (letter of 1 September 1664); *Histoire en musique de Jericho* (letter of 29 October 1674); and *Histoire de Joseph* (letter of 24
February 1665). Unfortunately, none of Ouvrard's music for these
works has survived.

According to H. Wiley Hitchcock, the oratorios of Charpentier represent 'exactly the midpoint between those of Carissimi and those of

Handel'.[8] By a wry twist of fate, these impressive compositions, which in some ways surpass those of Charpentier's teacher, were without musical issue in France, and therefore, what has much musical merit is of little importance historically.

Over 130 years separate André Maugars' ecstatic description, of the 'admirable et ravissante' music of the 'Comédie Spirituelle' as he called Italian oratorios heard on his Rome journey, from Marmontel's oblique suggestion, in his 'Concert Spirituel' article (*Encyclopédie*), that French composers might consider the Italian oratorio as an alternative to the *grand motet*. Except for Charpentier, the French during this period were unwilling to attempt any naturalization of the Italian genre in spite of the fact that copies of some Carissimi oratorios found their way into Parisian collections.

It would be ridiculous to accept Rousseau's hypothesis that some in-born deficiency made the French 'ill-suited to the dramatic genre' (*Dictionnaire*, p. 353). More likely, as Marmontel observed, most composers (and audiences) were habit-bound to the officially sanctioned vehicle for religious expression in music—the *grand motet* of the *Concert Spirituel* or the royal chapel.

Marmontel defined Italian oratorios as 'small sacred dramas, not staged but only executed in concert'. He added parenthetically that some 'weak essays in this genre have been performed at the *Concert Spirituel* in Paris'. His 'weak essays' must refer to the two sacred oratorios of Mondonville entitled 'motets français'. The first, *Les Israélites à la montagne d'Horeb*, was performed at the *Concert Spirituel* in 1758; its success was immediate and precipitated a second essay, *Les Fureurs de Saul*, performed the following year. From the *livret* of *Les Israélites*, we read that Monsieur Mondonville 'has enriched our music with a *new genre* . . .' (italics mine).

In his *Present State of Music in France and Italy* (1773, p. 23), Charles Burney wrote: 'The French have never yet had . . . a regular oratorio of any sort performed in their country.' It is clear that neither Burney, Marmontel nor Mondonville knew of the existence of the oratorios of Charpentier,[9] and it is possible that the only works that may stem from direct contact with them are a short *Oratorio à 4 voix . . . pour la Naissance de l'enfant Jésus* by Lochon and the *Histoire de la femme adultère* by Clérambault found in an undated copy owned by Brossard. Lochon's oratorio,[10] which includes chorus, dialogues and a *symphonie* for two violins and continuo, bears little resemblance to the nativity *cantica* of Charpentier. Donald Foster, however, finds several similarities between the Clérambault oratorio and those by Charpentier.[11]

It is clear that the lack of historical 'follow-through' on Charpentier's oratorios has blinded some to their intrinsic merits, in spite of important studies mostly by French and American scholars. How else can one explain the single sentence allotted Charpentier's oratorios in the aricle 'Oratorio' from *Grove's Dictionary* or the two sentence entry at the conclusion of 'Das Oratorium in Italien im 17. Jahrhundert' in the *MGG* article 'Oratorium'.[12]

Using Charpentier's own terminology, his 34 Latin oratorios may be further classified into three categories: *historiae, cantica* and *dialogi*. The 14 *historiae* are large-scale works in the manner of Carissimi's *Jephté* or *Judicium Extremum* employing a narrator (*historicus*), solo *récits*, ensembles, chorus and orchestra. The eight *cantica* are shorter, demand fewer performers and include some works that are less dramatic and more introspective. The term 'cantica' is included by Brossard in his dictionary as a synonym for 'motet'. Similar to the *cantica* are five short *Méditations pour le Carême* scored for three male voices and continuo The seven *dialogi*, like the *cantica*, are modest works written for two protagonists which are either two individuals or two groups.[13] Charpentier may have been familiar with the *Dialogus de anima* of Du Mont as well as the dialogues of Carissimi.

Only the *historia Judicium Salomonis*[14] may be dated. It was performed 11 November 1702 'pour la messe rouge du Palais'. The 'Red Mass' was an annual occurrence in the *grande salle* of the Palais de Justice to observe the convening of the *Parlement*.

It is reasonable to assume that other oratorios were composed for the Jesuit church of Saint-Louis and some we know were composed for the private chapel of the Duchesse de Guise at her Hôtel du Marais.

In Hitchcock's words, the oratorios of Charpentier combine Italian and French traits 'almost in equal measure'. The basic format of a sequence of *symphonies*, solo *récits* and airs, ensembles and choruses with the dramatic narrative controlled by an *historicus* is familiar to us from the oratorios of Carissimi. There also is similarity in subject matter. Generally, although not exclusively, they are based on Old and New Testament stories, and three Charpentier *historiae* treat subjects already used by Carissimi: *Extremum Dei Judicium, Sacrificium Abrahae* and *Judicium Salomonis*.

In his choral writing, Charpentier employed both the *concertato* principle of the *grands motets* of Lully and Delalande and the Roman polychoral style exploited with such telling results in Carissimi's *Judicium extremum.* Although basically homophonic, some choruses have a polyphonic integrity that is worthy of Delalande. A good example is 'Flevit amare' which closes *Le Reniement de St Pierre.* In contrast, there are choruses from some of the nativity *cantica* (see 'Pastores undique' from *In Nativitate Domini Canticum*) that are labelled 'chansons' and resemble popular Noëls.

Much of the solo vocal music is simple or accompanied recitative or arioso. Although more expansive, Charpentier's recitative resembles its Italian model—perhaps because of the Latin text. The airs are few and are relatively insignificant from the dramatic point of view. Some are modelled on French dance measures and a few even resemble the Italian *aria da capo* with extended vocalises and *ritournelles* (see Solomon's air, 'Benedictus es' from *Judicium Salomonis*).

It is in the recitatives and the dialogues cast in ensembles that Charpentier exhibited a dramatic gift never fully realized in his operas. Certainly no French seventeenth century opera taught him how to achieve the high level of musical characterization found in the 'denial' scene from *Le Reniement de St Pierre* where the repeated denials of Peter cut through the persistent questioning of the maids and the relatives of Molchus.[15]

Like Carissimi, Charpentier utilized harmony to underscore the meaning of the text. As in the motets, there are examples of augmented triads and cross-relations. Rests, harmony (Neapolitan sixth chord) and a vocal line that terminates before the final resolution, are all used as agents of dramatic characterization in the death scene from the *historia Caecilia Virgo et Martyr*.

Example 63
Charpentier: Extract from 'death scene' in Caecilia *(after the Meslanges, vol.* III*).*

The oratorios of Charpentier may be most clearly differentiated from those of his teacher in the domain of instrumental music. Carissimi normally employed only two violins and continuo for his symphonies; Charpentier preferred a larger orchestra. *Caecilia Virgo et Martyr* is scored for two four-part string orchestras and even includes a *concertante* part for solo organ in the final section. *Extremum Dei Judicium* uses two trumpets to 'play a fanfare' announcing the Last Judgment, and *Judicium Salomonis* employs a string orchestra with flutes, oboes and bassoons.

The operas of Lully and *préramiste* composers influenced Charpentier's descriptive symphonies which have no counterpart in the Italian oratorio. 'Sommeils', called 'Nuit', are found in the nativity oratorios as well as in such large works as *Judith* and *Judicium Salomonis*. Typical is the Prelude to the second part of *Judicium Salomonis* which resembles the 'Sommeil' from Lully's *Atys* (Act III, Scene 4). The Charpentier 'sommeil' is richer in harmony and more thinly scored, but both use paired flutes and strings (muted in Charpentier) and similar melodic patterns.

Part three

Music for the Lute and Keyboard Instruments

Chapter 16
-》》 《《-
The Lute

You make the lute speak as you wish, and you control your audience as you wish. When a good player picks up his lute and fingers its strings, when from his end of the table, chords are heard seeking out a *fantaisie*, and when he has plucked three chords and sent a tune into the air, then all eyes and ears are drawn to him. If he chooses to let the sound die away under his fingers, all are transported by a gay melancholy; one lets his chin fall on his chest, another sits head in hand . . . still another with mouth wide open and one with his mouth half opened as though all his attention were riveted on the strings. One could believe that all the senses had fled except that of hearing . . . but if in changing his manner of playing, he awakens again the strings, life is returned to his audience and he who had stolen heart and soul returns them and again does what he wants with men.

(René François, *Essais des Merveilles de Nature*, 1621, p. 474)

With such language that has the clean ring of true observation rather than the euphemisms of *préciosité*, François described the power of that most *précieux* of instruments, the lute, to move the listeners of his day. The seventeenth century inherited the previous century's mystique with regard to the lute as a superior social instrument. Nobleman and *bourgeois* alike sought the secrets of its elusive language. With demonstrable skill as lutenist, one might indeed enhance his social position. It was no accident that François I, in creating the division between the music of the *Chambre* and that of the *Ecurie*, at first accepted only the lute among stringed instruments for his *Musique de Chambre*.

The notarial archives of the *Minutier Central* contain many references to 'maistre joueurs de luth' up to 1640. Here, a Parisian merchant hires a teacher to instruct his 13 year old son in the arts of 'writing, arithmetic, music and lute playing'; there, a nobleman and member of Parliament, engages a 'maistre joueur de luth' to teach him 'how to play the lute as perfectly as possible' over a five-year period.

Marie de Medici in 1612 appointed Robert Ballard as 'Maistre joueur de luth', and he lost no time in beginning to teach the child, Louis XIII. When Ennemond Gaultier was chosen by Anne d'Autriche as her private lute teacher, everyone at the court felt called upon to follow her example, and the 'vieux Gaultier' became the most sought-after of teachers. Even Richelieu tried his hand at a few lessons although Tallemant des Réaux confides that 'it would be difficult to imagine anything more ridiculous than to see him (Richelieu) take his lessons from Gaultier' (*Historiettes*, I). By 1636 Mersenne could write that the lute 'has taken such a lead over other stringed instruments, either because honest men gave it this advantage or because of its own excellence and perfection, that one hardly notices the other instruments' ('Livre Second des Instruments', *Harmonie universelle*, p. 56).

The lute was at its peak of popularity during the reign of Louis XIII. Professional performers and lute makers were in great demand. Mersenne mentioned the Vosmeny (Vaumesnil) brothers, Charles and Jacques Hedington from Scotland, Julien Perichon, the 'Polonais' (Jacob Reys), the Gaultiers, Enclos, Marande, René Mésangeau and Vincent among those who excelled in playing the lute. In addition there were Charles Bocquet, Mercure, Merville, Bouvier, Jacques, Sieur de Belleville, François, Sieur de Chancy, Nicolas Chevalier, Estienne Houselot (called Dubuisson), Vignon, the Pinel dynasty, and many others. Several of these composer-performers have left no trace of their music or, in some cases, their identity.[1]

This hue-and-cry for lutenists was not to endure. The vogue for the lute had reached its peak by 1640, and the instrument was already into its long decline even at the time Denis Gaultier was composing his *La Rhétorique des Dieux*. For only a few years did it enjoy harmonious co-existence with the harpsichord whose music had already taken over many of the characteristic features of lute styles. The increasing demand for more bass instruments in the later seventeenth century brought about the construction of double-necked lutes, or archlutes, that included a second pegbox for bass courses. The lute competed in vain with its stronger cousin, the theorbo (a 'short' archlute), and at the end of the century suffered the indignity of being 'converted' into a theorbo by the addition of supplementary strings and an enlargement of its neck.

The eventual adoption of the basso continuo in France hastened the downfall of the lute. The theorbo and the harpsichord, by virtue of their greater carrying-power, became the preferred 'realization' instruments. In 1660, Ballard printed a *Méthode pour apprendre facilement à toucher le théorbe sur la basse continue* by Nicolas Fleury, counter-tenor in the service of the Duc d'Orléans. In the preface to Denis Delair's *Traité d'accompagnement pour le théorbe et le clavecin* of 1690, we read that by following the rules one may gain a 'perfect knowledge of this art as much on the theorbo as on the harpsichord, which are the two instruments most in use for accompanying'.

However, by the third decade of the eighteenth century, lute, theorbo and guitar had virtually disappeared in France although as late as 1759 a Sieur Marlière held an administrative post at court entitled 'joueur de petit luth de la chambre'. Perhaps the last lutenist to be heard in public performance in Paris was Wenzel Josef Kohault who played some duos for lute and violoncello with Jean-Pierre Duport at the *Concert Spirituel* in 1763 and 1764.

If we believe Abbé Carbasus, the lute was a victim of the public's mania for musettes, vielles and other *instruments champêtres* that struck Paris in the 1720's. In his satirical polemic in the form of a *Lettre . . . sur la mode des instruments de musique*, he wrote with heavy sarcasm: 'You are not then informed as to the sole use made today of theorbos, lutes and guitars? These gothic and contemptible instruments have been metamorphosed into *vielles*: that is their tomb.'

Lecerf and Titon du Tillet were probably closer to the truth in blaming the disappearance of the lute on the difficulty of mastering the instrument. Titon wrote in 1732: 'I do not believe that one would find in Paris today more than three or four old and venerable men who play the instrument.'

The limited sonority of the instrument may have contributed to its decline in a period increasingly sympathetic to the brilliant sound of the violin, and François Campion, theorbo player at the Opéra, in his 1716 *Traité d'accompagnement*, blamed the 'pernicious' tablature for the downfall of the lute. This theory was expressed as early as Perrine's *Livre de musique pour le lut* of 1680 that included a 'new and easy Method for playing the lute with notes of music'. Perrine was the first lutenist to discard the tablature and write in keyboard score. In his preface he explained: '. . . it is only because of the great difficulty of learning the tablature of A.b.c. that has been in use up to now . . . that has in the main, caused the abandonment of this Royal instrument . . . '.

Unfortunately, the entire repertory of sixteenth and early seventeenth century lute music was abandoned with the instrument in the closing years of the seventeenth century. The composers, who created the *style brisé* and bequeathed to the Chambonnières and Couperins a very important element in their harpsichord style, sank into oblivion.

Jean Jacquot has commented on the curious phenomenon whereby there were two distinct schools of lute composers in France in the seventeenth century.[2] There were those who wrote primarily autonomous instrumental music, and those who composed *airs de cour* with lute accompaniments. This appears to have been a traditional division of labour, and with few exceptions, composers did not cross these boundaries. The *air de cour* composers were, in the main, more conservative and stuck with the 'old tuning' ('vieil ton') whereas the instrumental composers were more adventurous with tunings and other modifications of their instruments.

The sixteenth century lute was normally an 11-stringed instrument; 5 strings were paired together in 'courses' and there was one solo string, the *chanterelle*. The lute was expanded in the seventeenth century to include more courses. Antoine Francisque's *Le Trésor d'Orphée*, coming at the very turn of the century, for example, was written for a 9 course instrument. That lively source of information on French lutenists, Miss Mary Burwell,[3] reports that Mésangeau used a lute with 19 strings. In addition, up to six bass-courses with a fixed pitch (generally G-F-E-D . . .) were added.

The 'old tuning' (G-c-f-a-d'-g') dating back at least to Attaingnant's two 1529 publications (*Dixhuit basses dances garnies de recoupes et tordions* . . . and *Très breve et familière introduction* . . .) was commonly used through the first 20 years of the seventeenth century. In time, the same spirit of experimentation, which modified the instrument itself, justified the use of new tunings. Ballard's 1623 *Tablature de luth de différents autheurs sur l'accord ordinaire et extraordinaire* is an early result of this experimentation in new tunings. Unfortunately only the title page is extant. Mersenne in his *Harmonie universelle* includes both the 'Accord ordinaire' and 'Accord nouveau, ou extraordinaire' (G-c-f-a-c'-e'). A subsequent publication of Pierre Ballard, *Tablature de luth de différents autheurs sur les accords nouveaux* (1638) is perhaps the first to introduce the tuning that eventually superseded all others in France and ended up as the favoured tuning in the culmination of lute music in eighteenth century Germany. This is the so-called 'nouveau-ton' (A-d-f-a-d'-f') which was *not* introduced by Denis Gaultier. It was exploited first by Denis' cousin, Ennemond Gaultier, and brought by him to England where Mary Burwell quaintly referred to it as 'Old Gaultier's new tuning, called the

236

"goat tuning", because the first lesson he made upon that tuning is called The Goat'.

The first seventeenth century collection of lute music is *Le Trésor d'Orphée* (1600) by Antoine Francisque (*c.* 1570–1605). The complete title gives us much information concerning the contents and also demonstrates the willingness of the composer-arranger to experiment with some new tunings ('cordes avalées'): *Le Trésor d'Orphée, livre de tablature de luth contenant une Suzanne un jour, plusieurs fantaisies, préludes, passemaises, gaillardes, pavanes d'Angleterre, pavanes Espagnolles, fin de gaillarde, suittes de bransles, tant à cordes avallées qu'austres, voltes et courantes.*

There are about 70 pieces, the great majority of which are dances. Only two are transcriptions of vocal works, the 'Suzanne un jour' of Lassus and 'La Cassandre' from Arbeau's *Orchésographie*. Thus, at the very beginning of the century the transcriptions of vocal chansons, so important a part of the Renaissance lute repertory, was virtually abandoned.

More important musically and more international in scope is the *Thesaurus harmonicus* (1603), printed in Cologne, of Jean-Baptiste Besard (*c.* 1567–1625), a Frenchman schooled in Italy and employed in Germany. The 403 compositions arranged by genres in 10 books represent music by 21 different composers and give a good cross-section of all types of lute music composed in Europe at the turn of the century. Here, as in Francisque, we find the newer dances, the allemandes, courantes and even the gavottes appearing in substantial numbers. Besard published a second collection of lute music, *Novus partus, sive concertationes musicae* (1617) that, as part of its 'musical concerts', includes several lute duos and other ensemble pieces for three lutes and voices or viols.[4]

In Amsterdam, Nicolas Vallet (*c.* 1583–*c.* 1642) published his *Secret des Muses* in two books (1615/1616 in Dutch, 1618/1619 in French). The *Secret des Muses* contains a total of 109 pieces for one lute and 7 pieces for four lutes. Although the preludes and fantasies are in Renaissance style, the collection also includes 19 courantes, 3 bourrées, and one example each of a sarabande, allemande and chaconne.[5]

The 'Balardus parisiensis', included in Besard, is Robert Ballard (*c.* 1575–after 1640), son of the founder of the Ballard printing dynasty. He dedicated his first book of compositions for the lute (1611) to Marie de Medicis.[6] This is the first lute tablature printed in France after Francisque. In many ways the collection of 9 *entrées de luth*, 16 ballets, 12 courantes, 10 'Angéliques', 2 'autres' courantes, and 6 voltes is prophetic. Gone completely are the transcriptions of vocal pieces and the polyphonically oriented fantasies. The dances are graceful and homophonic with short, ornamental figures supplanting the fuller chords of the previous century and the texture is dominated by the *style brisé*. The *style brisé* is a classic example of a musical style that exploited the very limitations of the instrument that created it. Chords are arpeggiated and inner voices shredded so that any linear writing is more implied than actual. Consecutive notes from different octaves pass freely in and out of the texture only to disappear in thin air. Ornaments help in sustaining a melodic line, and a constant thinning and thickening of the texture is apparent. This style may already be observed in lute pieces by Francisque and in those of the Besard collection. It is not an innovation of the seventeenth century; in actuality, it is no more than an extension of a technique in evidence from the earliest French lute tablatures.[7]

Some of the dances in Ballard's Book 1 are grouped together in miniature suites. The 'Ballet de la Reine', for example, includes four dances terminating with a courante. Of special significance is the number of courantes included in this collection. In addition to the 14 titled courantes, the '10 Angéliques' are all courantes called 'Favorite d'Angélique' after Angélique Paulet, a lute virtuoso who first appeared at the court in 1609 when she was aged 18.

We have reached the point, now, where the direction of development is away from purely choreographic considerations of the dance and towards an abstraction or idealization of certain characteristic features. The hemiola, which was characteristic of the French courante throughout the Baroque period, may be clearly seen in the example below.

Example 64

Ballard: Hemiola formula in Première Courante (*after Souris*).

... many musical lights have risen in France, Amongst whom a single one—as the sun among the stars—hath drawn the admiration and praise of all the world. It is the first Gaultier (who is named, in regard of his age and his merit, 'old' Gaultier).

Such is the simple homage rendered by Miss Burwell to Ennemond Gaultier, Sieur de Nèves (c. 1575–1651), who was the first lutenist bearing this illustrious name.

In spite of the prestige accorded him as court lutenist to both the queen mother, Marie de Medicis, and later to Anne d'Autriche, nothing by him was published in his lifetime. André Souris has collected, from a wide variety of sources, 85 compositions for the lute (or harpsi-chord) composed by the 'Vieux Gaultier'.[8]

Although bordering on the precious, these miniatures have a charm and sophistication that should make them a source of pleasure to performer and listener alike. The melodic writing shows a great diversity in range and above all in asymmetrical phrase groupings. The use of written-out *ports de voix* and *coulés* (see measures 1 and 3 respectively of Example 65 below) with simultaneous ornament and resolution, add pungency to the music.

Example 65
Gaultier: Use of 'written out' ornamentation in a courante (after Perrine).

There is no better evidence of the transference of media, or perhaps more accurately, the sharing of a common stylistic identity, than in the two chaconne extracts found below. Example 66a is the *Chaconne, ou Cascade de Mᵣ de Launay* for lute by Gaultier; Example 66b is the

Example 66
(a) Gaultier: chaconne (after Souris).

(b) Chaconne (after Bauyn MS in Bibliothèque Nationale).

Chaconne for harpsichord attributed to Jacques Champion de Chambonnières (*c.* 1601–72), considered the father of the French seventeenth century harpsichord school. Both examples exploit the lower range of the instrument and both make use of similar ornamental and nonharmonic tones absorbed into the chords themselves.

The transcriptions of six Gaultier compositions from lute tablature to keyboard score made by Perrine in his *Pièces de luth en musique avec des règles pour les toucher parfaitement sur le luth, et sur le clavessin* (1680) appear to be quite literal except for some rhythmic changes. On the other hand, the twelve Gaultier compositions that found their way into a manuscript of harpsichord pieces now at the Bibliothèque Nationale (*Pièces de clavecin de différents auteurs*) show how the texture of the original lute pieces could be thickened, the syncopations ironed out and the ornaments proliferated.

Example 67
Gaultier: A comparison of 'La Superbe' in lute original and harpsichord transcription.
(a) Lute (after Souris). (b) Harpsichord (after Souris).

Over half of Gaultier's compositions are courantes with many bearing such descriptive titles as 'La Belle Homicide', 'Cléopatre Amante', 'La Petite Bergère', 'L'Adieu', 'La Pleureuse', 'Rossignol', etc. There are 12 allemandes, 11 gigues, 8 sarabandes, and two chaconnes. Also, there are some of the earliest examples of 'tombeaux' among the allemandes including one for Gaultier's teacher, Mésangeau, and one for the lutenist, L'Enclos, mentioned by Mersenne. Although there is a tendency to favour René François' 'gay melancholy', it would be a mistake to read into these idealized dances any pictorialism other than that of an overall mood.

Typical of the problems besetting André Souris and others who would rescue for us some of the lute repertoire from the period of Louis XIII is the case of one Dufaut (Dufault, du Fault) about whom Miss Burwell wrote, 'Mr Dufault would have made a good organist because his way is heavy and affects too much the pedantic rules of music'. Who was Dufaut? According to Titon du Tillet, he was a student of Gaultier but beyond that we have no information regarding his life or work or even his approximate dates of birth and death. Yet music by him kept turning up in various publications such as the two Ballard collections of lute tablatures of 1631 and 1638. The extant music reveals Dufaut to have been an experimenter who never used the 'old tuning' and who enjoyed some of the complexities of phrasing already noted in the music of his teacher. More important, he may have introduced the type of prelude later known as the 'free' or 'non-measured' prelude. There are six semi-measured preludes scattered throughout the lute pieces of Dufaut. The first of these, labeled 'Recherche', found in the *Airs de différents auteurs mis en tablature sur les accords nouveaux* (Ballard, 1631),[9] lacks bar lines and gives only an occasional suggestion of rhythmic values. Born of improvisation and the necessity of testing or 'seeking out' the new tunings, the non-measured preludes reached an apogee in the harpsichord music of Louis Couperin and persisted through the third decade of the eighteenth century.

Denis Gaultier (*c.* 1603–72), or 'le jeune Gaultier', or 'Gaultier de Paris', was a younger cousin of 'Le vieux Gaultier'. The 'young Gaultier' was one of the first composers to take some important steps towards the creation of the Baroque dance suite, that is, the grouping together of a number of different dances unified through a single tonality. His important *La Rhétorique des Dieux* was composed sometime between 1650 and 1655.[10] It includes 56 short dances grouped by tonality into 12 'suites'. The 'suites' generally open with a non-measured prelude, a pavane or an allemande, and include a varied number of dances in random order.

Like his cousin, Denis excelled in writing music marked by a tender melancholy. Unlike the 'old Gaultier', he attempted, from time to time to relate a descriptive title to descriptive music. In this, he pointed the direction towards the late seventeenth century composers of French lute music, Jacques Gallot and Charles Mouton. As examples of this tendency, consider the courante 'La Coquette virtuose' with its 'coquettish' skips in the melody line, or the gentle lyricism of the *tombeau* for his wife in the rarely used key of F-sharp minor.

Along with Gallot and Mouton, Denis was a master of the *tombeau*. Concluding *La Rhétorique des Dieux* are three compositions that form a kind of programme suite. The 'Tombeau du Sieur Lenclos' which opens the 'suite' is an 'Allemande Grave' filled with the dotted rhythms and syncopations that often characterize this dance; this is followed by a 'Consolation des amis de Sieur Lenclos', a courante in a much simpler style; and, the 'suite' concludes with a 'Résolution sur sa mort' called by the composer a 'Chaconne ou Sarabande'.

The seventeenth century school of lute composers in France closes with the lute collections of the Gallot dynasty and Charles Mouton (1626–99). Jacques Gallot (after 1600–85), called 'le Vieux' or 'Gallot de Paris', was a teacher of Brossard; his son also Jacques (*c.* 1640–1700), called 'Gallot le jeune', was a student of Denis Gaultier.

The *Pièces de luth composées sur differens modes* (*c.* 1673–75) by 'Gallot le jeune' is divided into two sections each preceded by a prelude. The dances affect literary titles sometimes lifted from La Rochefoucaud and from the *Caractères* of La Bruyère. The attempt at musical characterization is more marked than in earlier lute composers. Most of the gigues are comic pieces such as the 'Dogue d'Angleterre' or 'La grande Virago'.

Charles Mouton,[11] another protégé of Denis Gaultier, moved the loose ordering of dances even closer to the suite. He published four books of dances of which only two have survived. The two books make up the *Pièces de luth sur différens modes* (1699) and contain eight suites. Each suite has a variable number of dances ranging from four to eleven but each begins with a prelude followed by an allemande or pavane. Most of the dances carry descriptive titles and Mouton, unlike Gaultier and his predecessors, attempted to use the idealized dance movements to suggest miniature portraits of 'La Belle Iris', 'La Complaisance', or 'La Belle Angélique'. In addition to dances favoured by earlier composers, Mouton also used minuets and the Italian type of courante.

More than any other lute composer, Mouton aimed for a unity of style within the same composition. The 'Tombeau de Gogo' that opens Book I; the Allemande, 'Le Dialogue des grâces sur Iris'; and the Courante, 'Le Changeant' all have a continuous flow rare in lute music. Part of this search for unity is also reflected in the number of binary dances with both sections in exact balance.

In considering the music of a sister instrument, the guitar, it is important to realize that in the early years of the seventeenth century, the guitar was no longer considered along with the lute as 'appropriate for musicians' as it had been throughout the sixteenth century. Pierre Trichet in his *Traité des instrumens de musique* (*c.* 1640)[12] considered it little better than a 'Spanish monkey' adding that all knew that for the French the lute was 'the most agreeable of instruments'.

However, the fortunes of the guitar improved later in the century perhaps aided by Louis xiv's partiality for the instrument. Jacques Bonnet, in fact, went so far as to declare that it was the king's 'favourite instrument' (*Histoire de la musique et de ses effets*, 1715).

We owe to Robert De Visée (*c.* 1660–after 1720) two books of dances written for the guitar. The first book, *Livre de Guittarre dédié au Roy* (1682), includes eight dance 'suites'; the second book, *Livre de Pièces pour la Guittarre* (1686), has four 'suites'.[13]

More clearly than any of the lute pieces, or indeed the harpsichord pieces to this date, these two books present a consistent ordering of dances within each suite. Most of the suites are structured in the order of prelude, allemande, courante, sarabande, and gigue with such optional dances as gavottes, bourrées, minuets, chaconnes and passacailles following the gigue in a random order.

In summary, French lute music of the seventeenth century is mannered, precious, even decadent; its melodies are surcharged with ornaments, its rhythms fussy, its harmony often aimless, and its texture without unity. Yet at the same time, it is never pretentious, it never demands more from the instrument than the instrument can give. In its own fragile way, it is honest to itself.

Chapter 17

—»» «««—

The Harpsichord

It would do little but labour the obvious to further document the transference of the *style brisé* from lute to harpsichord in the mid-seventeenth century in France. Examples cited by Bukofzer (*Music in the Baroque Era*, pp. 169–70), Quittard (*Encyclopédie de la Musique et Dictionnaire du Conservatoire*, Part I, vol. III, pp. 1230–40), Apel (*Geschichte der Orgel und Klaviermusik*, p. 542) and many others attest beyond any doubt that this occurred. Further, this style reached Germany and was assimilated into the high Baroque dance suite because of the intimacy of Johann Jakob Froberger with the music of Denis Gaultier, Chambonnières and Louis Couperin during his sojourn in Paris in 1652. It is possible to trace its final flowering in the allemandes of the Bach French Suites, for example. Here, elements of the *style brisé* have been so absorbed that what in the lute pieces was a 'brisé' style, pretending to be linear, has become a linear style 'pretending' to be 'brisé'.

Example 68
Bach: Extract from Allemande of French Suite in C-Minor.

What is more difficult and perhaps more significant, in any style study of seventeenth century French harpsichord music, is to discover why this transfer took place. Why did the sharp distinction between lute and keyboard music that exists in many of the *recueils* of the sixteenth century all but disappear in the seventeenth century? In

244

the words of Daniel Heartz: 'The *style brisé* is already present in the *recueil* of Attaingnant, the first monument of French music for the lute. Keyboard music maintained at this time its own stylistic characteristics and only appropriated the *style brisé* of the lutenist at a much later date.'[1]

The earliest examples of French seventeenth century harpsichord music antedate by many years the collections of Chambonnières. Perhaps as early as 1630, French keyboard music had already settled into a style that was to serve it with few modifications throughout the century. The preludes, allemandes, courantes and sarabandes, presumably of French authorship although written, oddly enough, in German organ tablature in the so-called Copenhagen MS, date from about 1626–39.[2] These allemandes and sarabandes, as well as those written for harpsichord by the lutenist Mésangeau (died 1638),[3] clearly show all the features of the lute style neatly transferred to the harpsichord.

Yet, is it a transference or is it rather a parallel development and subsequent co-existence of the same style in two media? Is it not, perhaps, part of the same movement that saw Renaissance humanism converted into a *fin de siècle* preciousness? Do not the lutenist and the harpsichordist both speak a musical language that has its literary counterpart in the *galant* and frivolous Voiture at the Hôtel de Rambouillet who with his coterie had begun by 1620 to play a role in the Parisian world of letters?

With a few changes of words, Pirro's description of the lute-harpsichord style might also describe the literary conceits stemming from the Hôtel de Rambouillet:

> Instead of saying all, scrupulously and laboriously, the musician (lutenist and harpsichordist) tries to suggest what he has neglected to explain. Inconsistency, doubt, prodigious promises, the delights of a vaporous style, with its flashes of light that surprise or trouble. . . . Lutenist and harpsichordist made a virtue of their fragility.[4]

The first generation of seventeenth century harpsichordists were probably lutenists as well, and for them there was no inconsistency in a stylistic uniformity especially when the style was a modish one that had earned their modest instrument great social prestige.

The question raised above cannot in all probability be answered until we fill in the many gaps in our knowledge of the century between Attaingnant's Parisian keyboard publications and the first appearance of Chambonnières' harpsichord pieces.

Our knowledge of the instrument for which Chambonnières and Louis Couperin wrote their *Pièces de Clavecin* is hampered because of the high mortality rate of seventeenth (and eighteenth) century French harpsichords. Very few signed instruments from the seventeenth century are left. With the help of Mersenne and the few remaining instruments, we can, however, deduce the following: whereas the normal range of the sixteenth century harpsichord was four octaves from C to c''', the seventeenth century extended the compass downward to GG and later to FF. This was accomplished at first by using a bass 'short octave'; that is, the lowest bass note, which appeared to be BB, was tuned down to GG; and the C♯, to AA; the D♯, to BB. By such a bass re-tuning, the instrument lacked certain notes (GG♯, AA♯, for example) that were rarely called for in the music of the period. By the late seventeenth century, the 'short octave' had become obsolete, and by the turn of the century, the compass of the instrument had more or less stabilized. By the 1760s, a five octave compass (from FF to f''') was normal.[5] The French harpsichord was a two manual instrument of about eight feet in length with three sets of strings, and two registers of 8' and one of 4' pitch. The best instruments from the workshop of the Blanchets or Taskin, preferably Flemish instruments 'refait par Pascal Taskin', had clarity of tone, a lightness of touch and a contrast of timbres that was highly prized.

The most important dynasty of harpsichord makers was the Blanchet family whose members spanned a 150 year period, and included Pascal Taskin who married the widow of François-Etienne Blanchet II in 1766. Very few instruments from the Blanchet–Taskin workshop survive. Incredible though it may seem, many French harpsichords belonging to the royalty and surviving the Terror were chopped up for firewood to warm the Conservatory classrooms during the bitter winter of 1816. In addition, much of the work of Blanchet and Taskin was in the enlargement and general restoration (known as 'ravalement') of older Flemish instruments among which the Ruckers was most in demand. 'It is in this art of enlarging the harpsichords of the Ruckers,' we read in Diderot's *Encyclopédie*, 'that the Blanchets succeeded so incomparably well.'

The vast repertory of seventeenth century harpsichord music (over 700 compositions) is almost entirely made up of binary dances, the only exceptions being the preludes, the chaconnes or passacailles and the keyboard transcriptions of instrumental music and airs from the Lully operas.

Albeit with much freedom, the broad outlines of the principal dance types that make up the nucleus of the Baroque dance suite received a measure of standardization at the hands of the French *clavecin* composers. The allemande, usually placed near the beginning of the 'suite', is the most serious, the most 'learned' dance employing points of imitation and a busy texture. The courante, most popular of all French seventeenth century dances, is the most complex rhythmically and, along with the allemande, the most irregular in phrase organization. The sarabande is the most predictable and most unified due to its persistent use of standardized rhythmic patterns. The gigue, even though it carried a number of different metre signatures (3; 6/4; 12/8), was unified by some use of dotted rhythms and a relatively fast tempo. Generally, it is the longest of the seventeenth century dances and the one most likely to use imitation.

From the lute chaconnes of the Gaultiers, Chambonnières and Louis Couperin fashioned their own chaconnes or passacailles which became the prototypes for the monumental works in the same genre by François Couperin, Gaspard Le Roux and Jacques Duphly. Other 'optional' dances found in the repertory of seventeenth century harpsichord music are minuets, galliards, gavottes, pavannes, bourées, canaries and voltes. Dances carrying descriptive titles are numerous and, unlike later examples, rarely deviate from a recognizable dance type.

In spite of a clear attempt to highlight certain characteristic features of each dance type, this music, like that for the lute, remains one step removed from improvisation. In spite of a unity that unavoidably exists between dances of the same type (all allemandes and all courantes, for example) there is almost an insistence on dis-unity within in the individual dance which is achieved through a constant change of texture, avoidance of melodic sequence, lack of harmonic stability and a perverse reluctance to have Part A of any dance share its motivic material and melodic shape with Part B.

Five composers dominated the scene and created the bulk of the seventeenth century harpsichord repertory. They are Jacques Champion de Chambonnières (1602–72), Louis Couperin (1626–61), Jean-Henri D'Anglebert (*c.* 1628–91), Jean-Nicolas Geoffroy (*d.* 1694) and Nicolas-Antoine Lebègue (1631–1702). Although all shared in the creation of a common language, there are some individual differences worth noting. Louis Couperin was certainly the most adventurous harmonically; Chambonnières, the greatest melodist; Lebègue, the most academic and predictable; and D'Anglebert, the most 'difficult'.

For all practical purposes, we may consider Chambonnières to be the founder of the French school of harpsichordists. He numbered, among his students and disciples, Louis Couperin and Couperin's brothers—François ('the elder') and Charles—as well as Cambert, D'Anglebert, Lebègue, Hardel and Nivers.

We have much evidence from his contemporaries concerning his manner of playing. Mersenne comments on his beauty of touch, the lightness and rapidity of his hand and adds that in Chambonnières the harpsichord had 'met its finest master'. More specific is the account of Le Gallois in his *Lettre de Mr le Gallois à Mlle Regnault de Solier touchant la musique* (Paris, 1680) which describes how, each time he played a piece, Chambonnières would add *ports de voix, passages* (probably filled-in skips), *double cadences* (according to the composer's table, these are turns) and explains that one can always find new 'graces' in such diversified performances. Already, the battle lines are drawn between those who favour a more virtuoso, brilliant style and the adherents of the 'coulant' style exemplified by Chambonnières' performance. Le Gallois condemns, in others, the proliferation of ornaments, complaining that 'only a perpetual trill ("cadence") can be heard in their playing which prevents the melody from being distinctly perceived: And they continually employ "passages" particularly between one pitch and its octave'.

Chambonnières' harpsichord music in two books,[6] both published in 1670, appeared only at the end of his career, although the music was presumably composed over a 30-year period. Perhaps in need of some fillip after his 'falling-out' with the king (or with Lully)[7] in 1662, Chambonnières wrote in his Preface that his music had been disseminated among the 'personnes les plus augustes de l'Europe' and had reached 'all cities of the world where there is some knowledge of the harpsichord'. Chambonnières also related the by then familiar story of breaking into print because of the wide distribution of faulty copies of his music.

The two books, each including 30 pieces, are divided into suites usually of four or five and never more than eight separate dances. Each suite begins with an allemande or pavane which is usually followed by a series of courantes, although in some instances, gigues are inserted between the allemandes and courantes, showing how far we are from any consistent standardization of dance order. Courantes make up almost one-half (28 out of 60) of all the dances.

In addition to the printed sets above, some music of Chambonnières remains in manuscript. There are 123 of his compositions in volume I of the Ms *Bauyn*, named after Bauyn d'Angervilliers who copied harpsichord music by Chambonnières, Louis Couperin and other French *clavecinistes* as well as compositions by Frescobaldi and Froberger. Brunold and Tessier, in their edition of the *Oeuvres complètes* of Chambonnières, point out that the Ms *Bauyn* is to the French harpsichord school of the seventeenth century what the *Fitzwilliam Virginal Book* is to late Renaissance English keyboard music.

Example 69 below illustrates Chambonnières' melodic gift. It is from Part B of a D-Minor sarabande and shows a rare appearance, in French harpsichord music of the time, of a melodic sequence used to shift tonal centres (from D-Minor to F-Major) with a clear consolidation of the new harmony following the sequence.

This example is atypical of much seventeenth century harpsichord music whose harmony operates, in part, in a pre-tonal shadow zone. It is both an irritant, to those of us who unfortunately began life with a built-in tonal bias, and at the same time a constant delight to have one's tonal compass totally disoriented. Perfect cadences, often built around secondary chords, follow rapidly one upon the other with little time in between to consolidate key centre. The wonder is that Chambonnières' melodies succeed so well in becoming air-borne in spite of the gravitational pull of so many cadences.

Example 69
Chambonnières: Extract from Part B of a Sarabande (after ed. of 1670).

The dances that carry descriptive titles rarely deliver more than a general musical mood corresponding with the title, such as the Allemande 'dite l'affligée' in G-Minor with a 'Lentement' indicated by the composer. There are flashes of humour from time to time, however, especially in some gigues, and at least one composition is purely descriptive with no relationship to any recognizable dance-type. It is 'La Drollerie' in which the nine measures of Part A are tightly organized around one descending conjunct motive treated in close imitation, whereas Part B introduces two metre changes, alludes briefly to the motive of Part A and engages in sudden changes of texture all within the brief span of 13 measures!

Titon du Tillet tells the story of the three sons of Charles Couperin (Louis, François 'the elder', and Charles) who played some of Louis' pieces for viol for Chambonnières at his château near Chaumes. Chambonnières was reported to have told Louis that 'a man such as he was not made to stay in the provinces and that he should absolutely come with him (Chambonnières) to Paris'. In any case, Couperin was introduced at court by Chambonnières and, by 1657, was already an 'Ordinaire de la musique du Roy'.

Much of the keyboard music of Couperin[8] is conserved in the second volume of the Ms *Bauyn*. It is music that, when compared with Chambonnières', is filled with surprises. He is less conservative than his master in his choice of keys, using E-Minor, B-Minor, C-Minor and A-Major in addition to the more usual ones. The key of F♯-Minor, found in a pavane, is most unusual for an instrument utilizing mean-tone tuning. This may be the only keyboard piece of the French seventeenth century to tempt the cry of the 'chèvre' ('goat'), as the lutenists called it.

The 15 non-measured preludes[9] of Louis Couperin constitute the greatest number of such pieces written by any harpsichord composer. He lavished much care on these compositions borrowed from the lute repertory. He introduced sections labelled 'changement de mouvement' which are actually measured sections within a prelude. Some preludes are in three distinct sections with an imitative, *ricercar* type of middle section sandwiched between non-measured sections; one has two sections with no 'free' final part; others are entirely non-measured. Most interesting is the Prelude in F-Major conceived of as one large unit: its 'free' sections merging without break into the measured, and its final section composed of a long, free melisma decorating an F pedal. Is it possible that Rameau may have known this prelude? His only example of a non-measured prelude opens his *Pièces de Clavecin* of 1706 and uses the same device of a merger between 'free' and measured sections. In both instances, the measured section is organized around a gigue-like rhythm.

In common with most seventeenth century harpsichord composers, Couperin made little effort to unify the two sections of his dances. Sometimes, the disparity is considerable as in Example 70 below, taken from a C-Major allemande; other times, however, a unity of sorts is achieved especially in some allemandes which are based primarily on continuous 16th note movement.

Example 70
Louis Couperin: Extracts from two sections of an Allemande (after the Ms Bauyn in B.N.).

The expressive power of Louis Couperin comes, in part, through richer harmonic language than that of Chambonnières. This is especially true in the cross-relations of the allemande in G-Minor, in the alternating couplets of the chaconnes which reminded Pirro of bass viol solos and oboe duos, and in the 7th and 9th chords of the multi-sectioned 'Tombeau de Mr de Blancrocher', surely the most moving of all the many 'tombeaux' to the dead lutenist.

The ordering of dances in the two books of *Pièces de Clavecin* (1677, 1687)[10] of Nicolas-Antoine Lebègue is more consistent than in the 'suites' of Chambonnières and Couperin. In fact, it is this very uniformity, carried down into the individual dances themselves, that robs this music of the charm and whimsy of a Louis Couperin.

In the second book, Lebègue, for the first time in France, used the word 'suitte', followed by its binding tonality (for example, 'Suitte en de la ré') to identify each of the six orderings of dances. These suites are much closer to what we generally consider the 'norm' of the Baroque dance suite. The optional dances are gavottes, minuets, canaries, bourées, passacailles and chaconnes. Gone are the archaic pavanes and galliards, the voltes and branles. The 'air de hautbois' from the 6th suite is an early example of the transfer of a dance from an operatic *divertissement*. Progressive also is the number of minuets which were the most popular of the optional dances. Only two suites contain no minuets. Several include minuet pairs which are occasionally written in opposing modalities.

Key schemes are also of some interest. Lebègue planned some of his suites so that the last four or five dances would be in the parallel modality. The second suite in G-Minor ends curiously with a gavotte and minuet in the relative major key, which raises the question as to whether or not the order of performance is necessarily governed by the order found in the printed editions.

Jean-Henri D'Anglebert, who succeeded Chambonnières in 1664 as Louis xIV's harpsichordist, brought out in 1689 his *Pièces de Clavecin*[11] wisely dedicated to the king's daughter, the Princesse de Conti. In the Preface, D'Anglebert seems to be apologizing for only using four keys (G and D-Major and their parallel minors) insisting that he had already 'composed in all the others'; he added that he hoped to bring out the 'others' in a second book which apparently never appeared.

The book contains a curious hodge-podge of four long suites, five rather academic organ fugues, a quartet on plainsong material appropriate for performance on the organ or on multiple harpsichords, and a short treatise on the 'Principes de l'Accompagnement'.

Compared to the neat ordering of the suites of Lebègue, D'Anglebert's work seems chaotic. Mixed in with normal dance components are such grandiose works as keyboard 'reductions' of Lully overtures (*Cadmus, La Mascarade, Proserpine*) and other instrumental works from Lully operas such as the chaconnes from *Acis et Galatée* and *Phaëton* and the passacaille from *Armide*.[12] In contrast, short *vaudevilles* in popular style are included 'principally to fill up the ends of pages'. This fact in itself, plus the inordinate length of the suites, makes one suspect that the order and choice of pieces was a matter of personal whim. The 'horror vacui' that forced D'Anglebert to fill up all available space transferred to the music itself as well. The pages are black with notes, and the music, extremely *travaillée*. The ornaments, both those indicated by symbols and those written out, are excessive and thicken the texture. An example of this style may be observed in Apel and Davison's *Historical Anthology of Music* (vol. II, pp. 96–98) which quotes the prelude, allemande and sarabande from the G-Minor suite. The prelude is an impressive piece that derives its particular quality from the melodic interval of the tritone. This interval recurs many times and in many different guises (see Example 71 below) which, when the notes are held down as indicated, gives a wash of sound that one would imagine as stemming more from Fauré or even Debussy than from a seventeenth century harpsichord composer.

Example 71
D'Anglebert: Use of melodic tritone in prelude to the G-Minor suite.

D'Anglebert retained the heavy, five-voiced texture of Lully in his keyboard transcriptions, and there is evidence that D'Anglebert was influenced by this 'orchestral' style in his dances as well. The allemandes and gigues often make use of full, five-voiced chords and busy inner parts that, in terms of the latter dance, would preclude a fast tempo. The two 12/8 gigues are among the first of their type in France. They are both reasonably polyphonic and are unified by means of a concentrated use of motivic material.

Included is a set of 22 variations 'sur les folies d'Espagne', labelled 'bien pauvres' by Pirro. They have historical interest as the only examples of keyboard variations on the 'Folia' tune in seventeenth century France, and they may have been a model for the only eighteenth century Folia variations for the keyboard known to this author: the 'Folies françoises' of Couperin[13] and the 'Folies amusantes' of Dandrieu.

Although known to André Tessier and Paul Brunold, the 255 pieces contained in Jean-Nicolas Geoffroy's *Livre des pièces de clavessin de tous les tons* have only recently been the object of a serious study.[14] Martine Roche suggests 1689 to 1702 as the possible chronological limits for this manuscript collection (Fonds du Conservatoire, Res. 475) by the organist of Saint Nicolas du Chardonnet in Paris.

Geoffroy's book opens with 14 suites in parallel modes on the diatonic scale degrees from C to A with suites 13 and 14 in the keys of B♭-Major and B-Minor respectively. The dances within each suite with few exceptions follow the order of allemande, courante, sarabande, gavotte and minuet with a concluding dance chosen from the following: rondeau, gigue, canarie or chaconne.

In addition to the wide range of keys, heretofore unprecedented in French keyboard music, Geoffroy's dances exhibit such harmonic audacities (see, for example, Roche, pp. 56–57) as to make one wonder whether they are 'experiments, spoofs, or very wrongly copied'.[15]

French harpsichord music of the eighteenth century[16] follows the tradition established by the composers of the previous century as discussed above. The stabilization of the dance suite, begun by Lebègue and Geoffroy and continued by Gaspard Le Roux and Louis Marchand, was never completed in France—the only true 'text book' examples being the six 'Suittes' of Dieupart composed not in France, but in England.

The effect of Couperin's first publication, *Pièces de Clavecin* of 1713, was electrifying. The genre piece rapidly assumed the important level of the established dance types and brought into general notice the concept of descriptive music as an end in itself rather than as an agent of the dance.

Inevitably, French harpsichord music came to terms with the Italian influences that 'flooded' Paris at the turn of the century in the form of cantatas and sonatas. Italian 'vivacité' co-existed with French 'douceur' in the keyboard works of Couperin and Rameau as it did in the cantatas and *opéras-ballets* of André Campra. At first this was felt in matters of tempo and textures, and only to a lesser degree in melodic shape and harmony. It exists in the kinetic drive of the Italian *giga* in 12/8 with its continuous 8th note movement; Italian 'vivacité' is in the sprightly and unsophisticated character pieces such as Couperin's 'L'Etincelante ou La Bontems' (Book II, Ordre II) or his 'L'Atalante' (Book II, Ordre 12) with their clean two-part writing and their mechanical rhythmic pulsations deriving from the Italian sonata and concerto.

The early eighteenth century harpsichord composers gradually modified the *style brisé* with more continuous part writing. They also brought about the gradual unification of the two sections of the binary dance, although striking examples of dissimilar sections endure throughout the period of Couperin and Rameau. In addition to binary dances and character pieces, the rondeau became increasingly popular. Its possibilities for contrast and unity were exploited with telling effect by both Couperin and Rameau. Sixty out of over 240 compositions by Couperin are in this form.

Harmonically, French eighteenth century harpsichord music remained essentially conservative. Such a well known 'avant-garde' example as Rameau's 'L'Enharmonique' is really a demonstration piece and cannot be considered typical. Most of the pre-tonal edges of the previous century were smoothed out as tonal direction became more stable and tonal centres were used as important determinants in the musical architecture. This, however, was in the order of things: it was, after all, the century of Rameau's *Traité de l'harmonie*.

The harmonic outlook of the first part of the century with regard to keyboard music remained essentially French; the practices of an earlier age were given direction and more depth. Italian chromaticism, as an expressive device, is relatively rare although beautiful examples of its use may be found in Couperin's last two books (see particularly, 'La Mistérieuse' and 'Les Ombres errantes' of Book iv) and in Rameau's Courante in A-Minor from the *Nouvelles Suites de Pièces de Clavecin* of 1728. Dissonance resulting from the use of non-harmonic chord tones in French ornamentation and dissonance which results from Italianate chains of suspensions or 7th chords in sequence co-exist.

The use of melodic sequence as a means of expanding motivic material is much more common in the eighteenth century, reaching such proportions in the Rameau A-Minor courante, mentioned above, that the entire piece is built on interlocking sequences. Curiously, even the most adventurous and startling sequences, such as the sudden drop from A-Major to G-Major in the Rameau sarabande from the 1728 *Nouvelles Suites*, have a way of leading nowhere harmonically.

Example 72
Rameau: Use of sequence in Sarabande in A-Major (after the Roussel engraved ed., n.d.).

The physical production of harpsichord music in the eighteenth century in France was enormous. Fuller catalogued 127 titles of extant harpsichord collections by single composers from 1701 to 1782. To be sure, the musical highpoint was reached early in the century with the four books of Couperin and the collections of Rameau. Hosts of imitators inevitably led to mannerism; Couperin's engaging 'programme'

ordres, such as the 'Folies françoises' or the 'Fastes de la grande et ancienne Mxnxstrxndxsx', led to 'Pièces de Clavecin contenant plusieurs Divertissemens' (Dandrieu); and Rameau's powerfully descriptive pieces, such as 'Les Cyclopes' or 'Les Tourbillons', degenerated in the hands of his imitators into 'the Sea agitated by Winds and Storm' (Daquin).

Yet, the well of inspiration that had sustained the French harpsichord school through Couperin and Rameau did not completely dry up in manneristic 'Coo-coo' and other bird lore or in empty virtuoso display pieces like Daquin's 'Les Trois Cadences' with its double and triple trills. Nor was French invention and imagination restricted to the making of folding harpsichords ('clavier brisé'), which 'can be torn down and put together so easily that one can carry (them) on a voyage' (*Encyclopédie*), or that ancestor of the colour organ, Pierre Castel's colour harpsichord ('clavecin oculaire') of 1725 which, the *Encyclopédie* assures us, 'gives to the soul through the eyes the same agreeable sensation of melody and harmony of colour as are communicated through the ears by the ordinary harpsichord'.

French composers, always sensitive to quality of sound, continued to experiment with the harpsichord not only in combination with another harpsichord but also as an equal partner with other instruments. On the outer reaches of our survey are the innovative *Pièces de Clavecin en Sonates avec accompagnement de Violon* of 1734 by Mondonville that not only ushered in the keyboard sonata in France but also continued the development of the keyboard sonata with violin 'accompaniment' which became extremely popular later in the century.

The very first decade itself opened the eighteenth century with a flourish. Ten collections of harpsichord pieces were published within those ten years. This remarkably productive period bridges the gap between the 1689 collection of D'Anglebert and the appearance of Couperin's first book in 1713. It undoubtedly contains much music that was actually composed in the last two decades of the seventeenth century which, of course, makes it virtually impossible to attempt to postulate influences and priorities on the basis of publication dates. Included are collections by François (not Charles) Dieupart (1702), Louis Marchand (two books in 1702), Nicolas Clérambault (1704), Jean-François Dandrieu (three books, about 1705), Gaspard Le Roux (1705), Jean-Philippe Rameau (1706) and Elisabeth Jacquet de La Guerre (1707).

Dieupart (*c.* 1670–1740), who spent the last 40 years of his life in England, is consequently, somewhat outside the mainstream of development of the French eighteenth century harpsichord school. His *Six Suittes de Clavessin*,[17] published in Amsterdam in 1701, are among the very few examples of French dance suites that adhere to the consistent order of overture, allemande, courante, sarabande, optional dances (for Dieupart, these were minuets, passepieds, and gavottes), and gigue. It is also one of the earliest collections to be 'mise en concert', that is, to include alternate performance possibilities with separately available parts for violin, flute, bass viol and archlute.[18]

The music is more 'through-composed' than much French music of the period and shows careful attention paid to part writing that obviously impressed Bach who copied Suites I and VI. The similarity between the Gigue of Dieupart's first suite in A-Major and Bach's Prelude to his first English Suite in the same key has been observed by Dannreuther and others (see Example 73a and c below).

Just as interesting in this link up of influences is the role of Gaspard Le Roux (died *c.* 1707) about whom we have practically no concrete information.[19] Much of the music of Le Roux's *Pièces de Clavessin* was undoubtedly composed many years before the 1705 engraved edition, and some of it may even be contemporaneous with

Example 73
(a) Dieupart: Gigue from A-Major suite.

(b) Le Roux: Gigue from A-Major suite.

(c) Bach: Prelude to English suite in A-Major.

J. Bapt. Lully Surintendant de la Musique du Roy

Ses Ouvrages Brillants de charmes inoüis | Quelle gloire! il la doit a son rare genie,
L'ont fait prendre icy bas pour Dieu de l'harmonie: | Mais pouvoit il moins faire? il chantoit pour Loüis.

1   Jean-Baptiste Lully (from the Ballard 1715 edition of Atys)

2   Ballet des Fées des Forêts de Saint-Germain, *1625* (*Bibliothèque Nationale, Cabinet des Estampes*)

3   Ballet de la Douairière de Billabahaut, *1626* (*Bibliothèque Nationale, Cabinet des Estampes*)

4   Ballet du Château de Bicêtre, *1632* (*Bibliothèque Nationale,*
Cabinet des Estampes)

5   Ballet du Château de Bicêtre, *1632* (*Bibliothèque Nationale,*
Cabinet des Estampes)

6 *Louis XIV as the Sun in the* Ballet de la Nuit, *1653 (Bibliothèque Nationale, Cabinet des Estampes)*

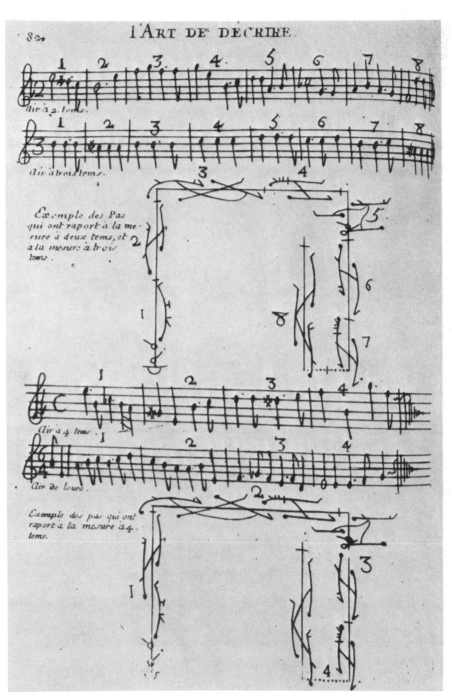

7 *Example of choreography relating to measures of music from Feuillet's* Chorégraphie, ou l'art de Décrire, *1713 edition*

8   *Performance of Lully's* Alceste *on 4 July 1674 in the* Cour de Marbre *at Versailles (Bibliothèque Nationale, Cabinet des Estampes)*

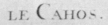

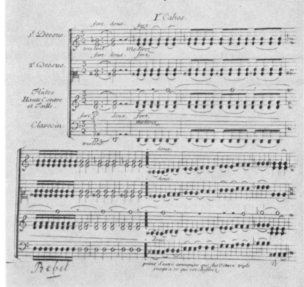

9 *Opening page of Rebel's* Les Elemens *in the score of* 1737

o *Adagio of the sonata,* pus IX, no. 5 from Book IV f *the violin sonatas by* Leclair

11 *Adagio of the sonata, opus V, no. 12 from Book III of the violin sonatas by Leclair*

12 *Handwritten* inégales *found in the Ballard edition of Marais'* Alcyone *at the Bibliothèque de l'Opéra*

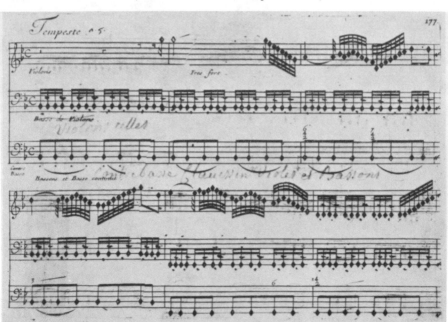

the D'Anglebert collection. In this respect, Le Roux may be thought of as a connecting link between Louis Couperin and his nephew, François 'le grand'. The relatively strict ordering of his suites—prelude, allemande, courante, sarabande followed by optional dances—stemmed perhaps from Lebègue and may have been an influence on Dieupart. An alliance with Dieupart is even more dramatically suggested by the comparison of their two gigues in A-Major and the subsequent Bach copy first noticed by André Pirro.[20]

There are certain progressive tendencies in the keyboard music of Le Roux that make him an important transitional composer in the development of eighteenth century keyboard style. The 'Courante luthée' (Suite I in D-Minor) is an early example of a binary dance with both sections unified by means of a tiny four-note motivic cell that, at various pitch levels, is almost always present in the texture. Also 'progressive' is the use of a rounded-binary form found in the sarabande of Suite VI in F♯-Minor; this apparently appeared so novel to Le Roux that he labelled it 'sarabande grave en rondeau', although its structure remains unequivocally binary with each section repeated. Le Roux's music exhibits a discreet use of melodic sequence, sometimes combined with dissonant harmony that clearly foreshadows Rameau.

Example 74
(a) Le Roux: Extract from Courante in D-Major (after ed. of 1705).

(b) Rameau: Extract from Courante in A-Minor (after Roussel ed. of 1706).

The *Pièces de Clavecin*[21] by the organist Louis Marchand (1669–1732) includes two suites (in D-Minor and G-Minor) which, as in those of Le Roux, maintain the consistent order of prelude, allemande, courante, sarabande and, in the case of Marchand, a gigue which is then followed by optional dances. The consistent part writing of the organ-

257

ist results, inevitably, in a greater unity between sections of the binary dances; in the gigue of the first suite, this even extends to the use of a free inversion technique whereby the direction of the opening melodic material is inverted at the beginning of Part B. This, of course, became standard practice in the gigues of the high Baroque dance suite in Germany.

In 1707, Elisabeth Jacquet de La Guerre, the wife of the Saint Severin and Sainte-Chapelle organist Marin de La Guerre and a protégée of Mme de Maintenon, brought out her second collection of harpsichord pieces (the first book of 1687 is not extant). The 1707 publication is a double volume, to be sold as a pair or separately, consisting of *Pièces de Clavecin* 'that can be played on the Violin' and *Sonates pour le Viollon et pour le Clavecin.*

The fourteen harpsichord pieces fall naturally into two suites with the order: allemande, courante, sarabande, gigue and optional dances. Only the opening allemande bears a descriptive title, 'La Flammande'. The fact that the treble line of the harpsichord may be doubled by a violin places this collection at the very beginning of the development of keyboard music with violin 'accompaniment'. There is nothing in the music itself which suggests that, should this performance option occur, the harpsichordist would then, perforce, consider the bass line as a continuo and supply a 'realization'. By the same token, the lack of a figured bass does not, in itself, preclude the possibility of this manner of performance.

It is most likely, however, that the violin, played softly, added another sound dimension to the melodic line. Edith Borroff quotes an early reference to this practice that appeared in the *Mercure* of August 1729 describing a performance at the court by Marguerite-Antoinette Couperin, François' daughter, who was 'accompanied' on the violin by Sieur Besson: 'Besson . . . has made a particular study in order to play perfectly this sort of piece, softening his violin extremely.'[22]

The music has some harmonic imagination and a nice blend of traditional features (note the extreme *style brisé* of the allemande, 'La Flammande') with more progressive traits. It lacks the excitement that Mlle de La Guerre was apparently able to bring to her *ex tempore* performances: '. . . she had, above all, a marvellous talent for on the spot playing of preludes and fantasies. Sometimes during an entire half hour, she would follow a prelude and fantasy with melodies and harmonies that were extremely varied and in excellent taste' (Titon du Tillet, *Le Parnasse françois*, pp. 636–37).

The paucity of our analytical vocabulary in music is nowhere more evident than in an attempt to deal adequately with the four books of *Pièces de Clavecin* by François Couperin. To label this music collectively as 'Rococo worldliness' (*Harvard Dictionary*, 1969, p. 331) eliminates from consideration such magnificent 'baroque' pieces as the Passacaille (Book II, Ordre 8), 'La Ténébreuse' (Book I, Ordre 3) or 'La Logivière' (Book I, Ordre 5). It ignores the poetry and depth of feeling in 'La Couperin' (Book IV, Ordre 21) or 'La Convalesente' (Book IV, Ordre 26), and it is somewhat akin to Schumann's description of Mozart's G-Minor Symphony as 'Grecian lightness and grace'.

The *Pièces de Clavecin* is an immense corpus of keyboard music embracing over 240 pieces distributed unequally among 27 Ordres. In point of fact, were we to follow Couperin's own suggestion that his four *Concerts Royaux* are appropriate for solo harpsichord as well as violin, flute, oboe, viol and bassoon (*Avertissement*) and that the trios of *Les Nations*, the *Apothéose de Corelli* and the *Apothéose de Lulli* could be performed on two harpsichords as 'I perform them in my family and with my students with great success', we would add more than 80 pieces to the four books of *Pièces de Clavecin*.

The music of these four books has been classified and codified by dance types and structural organization, by melodic and harmonic analysis and by a systematic review of each Ordre (the term is the composer's).[23] The meaning of the often ambiguous and enigmatic titles has been ferreted out when possible by Mèllers (see pp. 356–62). Couperin's musical language has been compared to the verse of Racine and the brushstrokes of Watteau.

All of this has value, but, unfortunately, it gives us little of the essence of the music and tells us almost nothing of the mysterious alchemy that makes Couperin's harpsichord pieces so elusive yet so compelling. For in the company with some of Chopin's Mazurkas and Debussy's Preludes, much of Couperin's keyboard music is more a communication between instrument and performer in the intimacy of his music-room than it is between performer on the stage and an unseen audience. It reveals itself only gradually and only after repeated playings; it is wed to its instrument as is no other music. Only through such intimate acquaintanceship with the music do the many dimensions of Couperin's art unfold.

There are, indeed, an abundance of examples that express 'rococo worldliness' and 'hedonism'; witness the contrived fifes and *tambours* of 'La Basque' (Book II, Ordre 7) or the burlesque pieces that climax in the 'Troisième Acte' of the satiric 'Les Fastes de la grande et ancienne Mxnxstrxndxsx' (Book II, Ordre 11) with its travelling circus of jugglers, jumpers, mountebanks, bears and monkeys. Rococo is the unpretentious grace of 'Soeur Monique' (Book III, Ordre 18) and the well-named 'Les Graces natureles' (Book II, Ordre 11), the playfulness of 'Les Bagatelles' (Book II, Ordre 10), the charming 'nothingness" of 'Le Petit-Rien' (Book III, Ordre 14). This is music far removed from either Baroque exuberance or the classical grandeur of the *grand siècle*.

259

It breathes the spirit of the Regency, and, at the same time, its genre pieces have the effective immediacy and the accurate commentary of some Watteau sketches.

But there is also the Couperin of 'La Ténébreuse' (Book I, Ordre 3) whose explosive utterances almost break out of its narrow, formal boundaries. Part A is a French overture; Part B, a continuous variation that gains in power by a thickening of the texture until it achieves an almost Beethovenian urgency at its climax.

Similar use of contrasting sections within binary structures may be seen in 'La Logivière', whose Part B is made up of unravelling figurations over pedal points that resemble the North German toccata, or in 'La Visionaire' which opens Ordre 25 of Book IV. Although it occupies the place normally accorded the allemande, 'La Visionaire' has severed its connection with the dance; its two sections are complete contrasts in tempo and texture.

In contrast, there is the Couperin who can organize his material with the greatest economy, deriving all from a single motif. (See 'La Laborieuse' and 'Les Idées heureuses', both from Order 2 of Book I.) Often this tight organization is combined with a refined part writing that would do honour to J. S. Bach, himself. It should be emphasized that Couperin did not carry this contrapuntal play consistently through an entire composition except in a very few cases where it is the result of his attempt to transfer the particular texture of the Italian sonata to the harpsichord. Proof of this comes in the allemande, bearing the performance direction 'Légèrement', which the composer included in his *L'Art de toucher le Clavecin* to demonstrate an alternative to the *style brisé*—an alternative style, born of the sonata, in which 'the melody and bass work together throughout the piece'. This is a fine example of two-part writing and of the expansion of motivic material unimpeded by too many regularly recurring cadences.

Couperin was not an innovator nor did he seek to experiment unduly with the binary and rondeau forms he had inherited. He did, however, enrich these simple forms in a wide variety of ways. Rameau may have learned from him the art of having each contrasting couplet of a rondeau move from the simple through the more complex where complexity is achieved by a change in texture or increased harmonic activity. Such is the final couplet of 'Les Baricades mistérieuses' (Book II, Ordre 6) which, in its broken chord spacing and in its delayed resolutions of suspensions, has the sound of Fauré or even Schumann.[24]

Like other harpsichord composers around him, Couperin from time to time singled out certain pieces for multiple performance possibilities. For the popular 'Le Rossignol-en-amour' (Book III, Ordre 14), he suggested a performance on transverse flute; for the two musettes of Ordre 15 of Book III, he supplied both a 'sujet' and a 'contre partie' and added that they would be appropriate for 'all sorts of equal pitched instruments'. In the preface to his third book, he described his 'Pièces-croisées' as suitable for 'two flutes or oboes, as well as two violins, two viols and other instruments of equal pitch'.

This freedom to choose among several instruments contrasts markedly with Couperin's insistence that what he wrote must be scrupulously observed in performance. It is clear that, for him, keyboard ornamentation was not merely decorative but also a means of deepening the expressive content of the piece. That he was aware of the limitations of the harpsichord as an expressive instrument is evident from his preface to the first book. 'The harpsichord', he wrote, 'is perfect with regard to its compass and its brilliance; but as one can neither swell nor diminish the sound, I am always grateful to those who, by an art sustained by taste, are able to render the instrument susceptible to expression.'

He detailed (not always too clearly) his performance wishes with regard to ornamentation more than any other composer; yet apparently, these instructions were not followed to the degree that he wished. In the preface to Book III, he observed with some annoyance:

> After taking such care to mark the ornaments suitable for my pieces (to which end I have published separately a fairly intelligent explanation in my Method entitled *L'Art de toucher le Clavecin*), I am always surprised to hear of those who have learned them with no heed to my instructions. This is unpardonable negligence, the more so as it is no arbitrary matter to put in any ornament that one may wish. I declare, therefore, that my pieces must be executed as I have marked them, and that they will never make an impression on those persons of real taste unless one observes to the letter all that I have marked without any additions or deletions.

Couperin's wish to assure performances of musical integrity may have accounted for his measuring the eight preludes placed at the end of *L'Art de toucher le Clavecin*. Beginning with Dandrieu's 1705 collections, the 'free' preludes were more commonly measured, although the 'non-measured' type did persist here and there through Durocher's collection of 1733. Couperin justified measuring the preludes for a pedagogical reason, *viz.*, they are easier to learn and to teach; but one suspects from his opening remarks that he had little faith in the ability of most performers to sustain the non-measured prelude successfully.

For Couperin, as for any opera composer, parodies were a measure of the success of his work. André Tessier has found examples of parodies of Couperin's harpsichord pieces as early as the Ballard *Recueil d'Airs sérieux et à boire* of 1711, two years before the first book had even been printed.[25] Couperin, in the preface to his third book acknowledged the parodies and offered the broad suggestion that his 'obliging associates' would find in his most recent book 'a vast field for exercising their Minerva'.

The impact of Couperin's four harpsichord books was such that the genre piece was catapulted to a position of prominence and the dance suite, as conceived of by most French harpsichord composers of the first decade of the eighteenth century, appeared doomed.

Significantly, there was an appreciable drop in the number of collections published between the year of Couperin's Book I (1713) and his Book IV (1730). Only the collections of Nicolas Siret (1716, 1719), Rameau (1724, *c.* 1728) and Dandrieu (1724, 1728, 1734) were printed.

Jean-François Dandrieu (1682–1738), organist at St Merri and, after 1721, at the royal chapel, had already written three collections of *Pièces de Clavecin* dating from about 1705. All three contain suites that bear no descriptive titles. His three books of 1724, 1728 and 1734, on the other hand, comprise mostly descriptive pieces. Further, he labelled them 'Premier Livre', 'Second Livre' and 'Troisième Livre'[26] thus appearing to wish to obliterate his earlier efforts. Paul Brunold discovered that many pieces from the 'Troisième Livre' were actually taken from the earlier books and given descriptive titles.[27] It may be that Dandrieu wished to capitalize on Couperin's successes and, in particular, to exploit the 'programme' suite suggested by 'Les Fastes de la grande et ancienne Mxnxstrxndxsx' and others.

The *Premier Livre de Pièces de Clavecin*, actually his fourth book, carries the sub-title 'contenant plusieurs Divertissemens dont les principaux sont les Caractères de la Guerre, ceux de la Chasse et les Fêtes de Vilage'. The 'Caractères de la Guerre', which follows the first suite, is descriptive music with a vengeance. What was suggested in Couperin is here pounded home with little attention to the sensibilities of performer or listener. The 'charge' with its 53 measures af tonic harmony includes cannon shots that, we are told in the preface, are marked only by four notes forming a 'perfect chord. But in order to express the noise of the cannon better, instead of these four notes, one may strike the lowest notes of the Harpsichord with the entire flat of the hand as many times as one wishes.' Thus, a type of aleatory music two hundred years before Charles Ives!

In the *Second Livre de Pièces de Clavecin* of 1728, which also included two *divertissements*, 'La Pastorale' and 'L'Aubade', Dandrieu 'borrowed' Couperin's concept of the 'goût-réuni'. The first suite opens with a French overture appropriately titled 'La Lully'[28] followed immediately by a 'La Corelli' with a double that is a clever parody of the style of the great Italian.

François Dagincour (1684–1758), in his collection of 1733,[29] aimed only to give as good an imitation of Couperin as possible. Louis-Claude Daquin (1694–1772), in his first book of 1735,[30] included one *divertisse-ment*, 'Les Plaisirs de la Chasse', which, we learn, may be performed with 'hunting horns, oboes, violins, flutes, musettes and vielles'. The vogue for keyboard *divertissements* continued throughout the century, reaching a nadir with Michel Corrette's *Divertissement pour le clavier ou le forte piano*, 'containing echoes from Boston and a naval victory won by a frigate against several assembled privateers; the harmony expresses the noise of arms, of cannon, cries of the wounded, plaints of the prisoners in this combat . . .'.

Daquin's 1735 collection also includes some virtuoso descriptive pieces highlighted by a 'storm at sea' with crossed-hand passages representing the 'fury of the waves and the brilliance of the lightning'. In such pieces with their veneer of 'special effects', we are, just two years after the death of Couperin, already far removed from his concept of the genre piece as 'espèces de portraits' (Preface, Book 1) and even farther removed from his attitude toward performance: '. . . I prefer much more that which moves me to that which surprises me' (Preface, Book 1).

Of the composers who published collections under the very nose of Couperin, only Nicolas Siret and Rameau were able to keep their identities and not succumb to the fashion of the moment. Siret (*c*. 1664–1754), who was a student of Couperin's, adhered to the older practice of titled dances in his books of harpsichord suites. They follow in the traditional order of prelude (or overture), allemande, courante, sarabande and optional dances. He also retained the by then archaic, 'non-measured' preludes, although to some he gave a symmetrical form that compromised their improvisatory nature.

Every page of Rameau's first book of *Pièces de Clavecin* of 1706 bears the personal stamp of its composer. The young (23) Rameau already was equipped to deal effectively with the most progressive musical language. Most of the binary dances are titled and in the traditional order. The only descriptive piece is a rondeau, 'La Vénitienne', inserted between the second sarabande and the gavotte. Most of the dances achieve a unity of texture and melodic material rare for this early date. Rameau's use of bold harmonies, both to lend colour and for structural purposes, is evident from the first piece, a prelude, that, in the tradition of Louis Couperin, combines an opening 'free' section with a measured, gigue-like conclusion. In the measured section, are some strikingly dissonant cross-relations culminating in the diminished octave (see below) that apparently so offended the timorous editors of the *Oeuvres complètes* that it was expurgated from their edition.[31]

The first allemande is clearly a sketch, in miniature, for the great allemande in the same key (A-Minor) composed about 20 years later

Example 75
Rameau: Use of dissonance in prelude from Pièces de Clavecin *(after Roussel ed. of 1706).*

and included in the *Nouvelles Suites des Pièces de Clavecin*. In addition to the unity of texture and motive already alluded to, the piece is an interesting study of Rameau's harmonic practices at this date. The diminished 7th chord is given special prominence by its placement in the measure (see, for example, Part A, measures 7 and 12; Part B, measure 13). The use of sequence to extend musical space is already an adumbration of his later music.

The courante, in addition to its striking sequence of 7ths and bass-line chromaticism, uses the diminished 7th chord, this time to delay the final cadence in Part A.

The *Pièces de Clavecin* of 1724 (re-edited in 1731) includes a manual 'On the Technique of the Fingers on the Harpsichord'. In contrast to the first collection, character pieces and dances of a popular nature (rigaudons, musettes, and tambourins) far outnumber the traditional dance members. Here also, for the first time, Rameau used virtuoso elements for such character pieces as 'Les Niais de Sologne', 'Les Tourbillons' and 'Les Cyclops'. Quite different from these are many gentle pieces in the Couperin tradition such as 'Les Soupirs', 'L'Entretien des Muses' and 'Les Tendres plaintes'. 'Les Cyclops' is probably unique in the French harpsichord repertory. A brilliant piece, it makes its effect through the Scarlatti technique of rapid crossed-hand passages[32] and a driving, pulsating rhythm broken dramatically here and there by sudden stops.

The big, aggressive dances, represented by 'Les Cyclops' and 'Les Sauvages', with their bursts of kinetic energy, as well as the popular tambourines and musettes, suggest all manner of choreographic treatment, and it is no accident that Rameau transcribed them for orchestra many years later in the *divertissements* of his *tragédies lyriques* and *opéras-ballets*.[33]

Rameau was able, in certain of his descriptive pieces, to capture the essence of the 'espèce de portrait' with the greatest economy. In just 16 measures, we are given a shocking picture of a cripple ('La Boiteuse') that is cruel in its incisiveness; undoubtedly, a later century

264

would have viewed as social criticism what Rameau saw as simply a descriptive piece in the burlesque genre.

The later collections are those of the *Nouvelles Suites de Pièces de Clavecin* of about 1728 and the *Cinq Pièces* extracted by the composer from his ensemble *Pièces de Clavecin en concerts* of 1741. The Allemande that opens the *Nouvelles Suites* is one of the longest allemandes in the repertory; one section is the appropriate length of most other allemandes. Its length is achieved in part by a series of sequences that flow into one another with great ease. Characteristic of Rameau's later harpsichord writing is the total assimilation of earlier techniques, such as the *style brisé* and textual shifts, into an overall unity. There is an occasional thinning of texture (see, especially, the nearly linear quality of the triplet passages at the end of each section), but the whole appears to be consistent three-part writing with the *style brisé* hidden in the inner voice syncopations (see, for example, measures 8 and 9 of Part A).

In his later rondeaux, there is a greater attempt to diversify the contrasting couplets, moving, as in Couperin, from the simpler to the more complex. This is climaxed by the final couplet of the second rondeau from 'La Timide' (*Cinq Pièces*). This couplet is in itself an excellent example of unity and diversity. Here, in three-measure units, is a real 'patchwork' of harmonies and textures that range from thickly voiced sequential chords, which would not be out of place in a French café tune of today (Example 76a), to Beethoven-like arpeggios that range over three octaves and slow the harmonic rhythm down to one chord change per measure (Example 76b). Unification is achieved by means of the arpeggio figuration, which is never completely absent from the texture, and by the surprising transformation of the beginning of the first rondeau in the first three-measure unit (Example 76c).

The last harpsichord piece by Rameau is 'La Dauphine' which was extemporized for the marriage of the Dauphin to Maria-Josepha of

Example 76
Rameau: Extracts from final couplet to 'La Timide' (after Walsh ed., London, c. 1755).

Saxony in 1747 and did not appear in print until 1895. It bristles with harmonic audacities and revels in the 'forbidden'. Are there any more blatant, more exposed parallel 5ths in the period of common practice than those implied by the trills that close the first measure?

The first publication of keyboard sonatas appeared in France in 1734 and bore the equivocal title of *Pièces de Clavecin en Sonates avec accompagnement de Violon*, Opus III. These six sonatas by Mondonville[34] were written for harpsichord solo or for harpsichord with the accompaniment of the violin. Unlike the earlier attempts by Elisabeth Jacquet de La Guerre (1705), Mondonville's sonatas include an obbligato line for the violin that only doubles the treble line of the harpsichord in the slow part of the French overture that opens the set and in the 'tutti' sections of the first movement of Sonata VI.

Mondonville's preface tells us something about the vogue for the sonata in France at the time of his writing:

> It is rash perhaps to give instrumental music to the public today: there have been such a prodigious number of Sonatas of all types in the past few years, that everyone believes the genre to be exhausted. Therefore . . . I have attempted something new.

The sonatas generally show a nice balance between the two instruments with, however, none of the tight polyphony that characterizes the violin-harpsichord sonatas of J. S. Bach. All six sonatas are cast in a three movement format of F S F with the last movement often a gigue and the middle movement a type of aria in moderate tempo. Sonata vi, labeled 'Concerto' by the composer, exhibits a clear contrast between tutti and solo groups. In terms of variety of textures and techniques these sonatas anticipate much future chamber music with obbligato keyboard.[35]

In 1748 Mondonville printed another set of innovative harpsichord pieces, *Pièces de Clavecin avec Voix ou Violon*, Opus v.[36] In his *Avertissement*, he wrote:

It is composed of pieces for the *Clavecin*, with a part that may be sung by a high voice, or played on a Violin. I believed that this format would particularly interest those who joined a talent for voice to that of playing the harpsichord, since they could then perform this genre of music alone. . . . It is necessary to begin with one of the pieces bearing the words, 'Paratum cor meum' or 'Benefac, Domine', and to learn the vocal line first, distinguishing above all the phrases which are in *le goût François* and those in *le goût Italien*. Afterwards, learn the harpsichord piece which serves as an accompaniment. . . . For those who play the *Clavecin* and who do not have a voice; they may have the vocal lines played on a Violin, or if lacking a violinist and a voice, the accompaniment will stand alone.

When the voice, violin and Harpsichord are all performing, it is necessary to proportion the sound of the voice and of the Violin to the strength of the Harpsichord in order that each part be distinctly heard.

There are nine *petits motets* in the collection, all based on psalm texts. All but one use the violin, and the keyboard part is a true obbligato with no continuo.

The concept of a sonata for keyboard with violin accompaniment was not long in taking hold. By mid-century, Corrette (*Sonates pour le Clavecin avec accompagnement de Violon, c.* 1741) and Louis-Gabriel Guillemain (*Pièces de Clavecin en Sonates avec accompagnement de Violon*, 1745) had collections in print. The preface to the collection of Guillemain (1705–70) reflects the stylistic conflict engendered by the new genre and confirms the paramount role of the keyboard instrument:

In composing my *Pièces en Sonates*, my first idea had been to leave them for Harpsichord without any accompaniment, having often noticed that the Violin would cover [the harpsichord] a bit too much; this made it difficult for me to distinguish the true subject. But in order to conform to the present taste, I believed myself unable to dispense with the part [accompaniment] which demands a great gentleness in performance, in order that the Harpsichord may be heard with ease.

Clearly in the same tradition is Rameau's only example of chamber music, a set of five 'Concerts' for harpsichord with the accompaniment of violin (or flute) and viol (or second violin), called *Pièces de Clavecin en concerts* (1741). In his *Avis*, the composer insisted that these pieces 'leave nothing to be desired if played as harpsichord solos'. While this comment is generally true, in some pieces the harpsichord switches roles with the other instruments and serves as an accompaniment (see, for example, 'La Livri' and 'La Timide').

Italian influence increasingly modified the more traditional keyboard elements stemming from France. The *Sonates et Pièces pour le Clavecin* of 1739 by Jean Barrière (died *c*. 1751) are characteristic of this trend. The collection includes six sonatas in which typical string figurations, coupled with elaborate broken octaves, scales and arpeggios divided between the hands, do little to disguise the basic poverty of the music.

On the other hand, the two styles co-exist with some harmony in the first two books of Jacques Duphly (1715–89) written before mid-century[37] and in the six books of Christophe Moyreau, all published after 1750. The first book of Duphly includes 15 pieces with some musical 'portraits' and some traditional dances. The Courante below clearly juxtaposes elements from the Italian corrente (the 2 metre sign may be thought of as two measures of 3/8) and the *style brisé*.

Example 77
Duphly: Extracts from a courante (after Vandome ed., c. 1744).

The last piece labelled simply 'Legèrement' resembles the *Sonates pour le Clavessin sur le Goût Italien* by Giovanni Benedetto Platti published in Nurnberg in 1742. It is an Italian sonata movement with an embryonic second theme in the Dominant key, a 'development' that begins with the main theme transposed to the Dominant, and an incomplete 'recapitulation' of secondary thematic material transposed back to the Tonic key.

This sonata, like those of Platti, with its thin texture and lively tempo, its repeated notes and 'patter' sequence, all stem from the same source, that is, the Italian *opera buffa*. Thus, two years before the first performance of Pergolesi's *La Serva padrona* in France and many years before the 'Querelle des Bouffons' we observe that the fashionable 'goût Italien' has become a part of French keyboard music.

Chapter 18

-»» «-

Organ Music of the Grand Siècle

It was in Normandy that the French organ school of the *grand siècle* was born. It was in Normandy that the prototype of the French classical organ was created despite the fearful ravages of the religious wars that included wholesale destruction of church organs. In 1580 at Gisors Nicholas Barbier finished the organ for the church of Saint-Gervais et Saint-Protais. This superbly designed instrument with its *Grand Orgue* of 48 keys, its *Positif* and pedal, exhibited the general form of the later French classical organ.

It was to Normandy, to the cathedral of Rouen that young Jehan Titelouze (1563–1633) came in 1588, and it was Titelouze, the organ specialist, who had the foresight to bring the builder Crespin Carlier from Paris to restore the cathedral organ and make of it an instrument worthy of Titelouze, the composer.

In 1623 Ballard printed the first collection of organ compositions by Titelouze, *Les Hymnes pour toucher sur l'Orgue avec les fugues et recherches sur leur plain-chant*;[1] three years later his *Magnificat ou cantiques de la Vierge pour toucher sur l'orgue suivant les huits tons de l'église* appeared. These two collections contain 38 and 56 versets respectively, designed to alternate with the *plain-chant musical*. The musical language is that of Renaissance polyphony. However, the occasional use of free dissonance and some chromaticism remind us that this is also the period of the Italian *ricercare,* labelled 'recherche' by Titelouze, and that Frescobaldi's *Ricercari e Canzoni Francese* had appeared in print only eight years before.

Drawing upon the full resources of his organ, Titelouze required the first verse of each hymn to be performed on the *plein-jeu* (foundations and mixtures of full organ).[2] In such versets the plainsong melody was often given to the trumpet and clarion of the pedal to contrast with the *plein-jeu*. In the best 'learned' fashion, material from the other voices is often derived from the cantus firmus as in the example below extracted from the first verse of *Iste Confessor*.

270

Example 78
Titelouze: Extract from first verset of Iste Confessor *(after ed. of 1624).*

It is difficult to believe that the musically rewarding and technically refined compositions by Titelouze existed in a vacuum, yet very little French organ music survives between Attaingnant's publications of 1530–31 and Titelouze's hymns of almost 100 years later. There are the nine *chanson* intabulations for organ dating from the mid-sixteenth century and found today in the Bayerische Staatsbibliothek of Munich (Ms Mus. 2987).[3] There is a *Fantaisie* by Nicolas de La Grotte on de Rore's *Ancor che col partire* and there is a short *Fantaisie sus orgue ou espinette* by Guillaume Costeley in Bibliothèque Nationale (Ms fr. 9152) which scarcely represents the best work of this 'organiste et vallet de Chambre du Roy'. There are the three *Fantaisies* for organ or viols by Claude Le Jeune printed posthumously in 1612, the third of which is based on the Gregorian melody *Benedicta est coelorum Regina*. Also posthumous are the *Fantaisies à III, IV, V et VI parties* by Du Caurroy, of which 14 are based on plainsong and 4 paraphase a Huguenot psalm.[4] In addition, Ballard in 1610 printed the 24 *Fantaisies à quatre parties* by the Flemish composer Charles Guillet (died 1654) designed for 'those who study Music as well as those who are learning how to play the Organ'.

Even more surprising is the sparsity of collections of organ music from Titelouze's *Magnificat de tous les tons* to François Roberday's *Fugues et Caprices* of 1660. Surprising, because of the number of excellent organs in Paris and in the provinces that presupposes a certain body of original literature; surprising, because of the names that recur in the archives of organists such as Florent Bienvenu at the Sainte-Chapelle, Jean Lesecq at Saint Eustache, Marin Deslions at Saint Etienne-du-Mont, Pierre Chabanceau de La Barre, royal organist, and Charles Racquet at Notre Dame.[5]

Florent Helbic, called Le Bienvenu (1568–1623), was, according to his student, Jean Denis, 'the most excellent organist of his day',[6] yet no music by him has survived although Denis also mentioned his monothematic fugues. Of the organ music of Charles Racquet (1597–1664), from whom Mersenne acquired so much information for his study of the organ, a fantasy in manuscript found in Mersenne's personal copy of his *Harmonie universelle*[7] and 12 *Versets de psaumes en duo sur les 12 modes* (in 'De la composition' from *Harmonie universelle*) are all that survive.

The *Fugues et Caprices* (1660) of François Roberday fils (1624–1680), *valet de chambre* of Anne d'Autriche and Maria Theresa and organist at the Petits-Pères in Paris, are among the last examples of organ music in France that make a conscious effort to be 'learned'. At the same time they show Roberday to have been receptive to influences from outside of France. He based certain of his fugues on themes by Robert Cambert, Pierre Chabanceau de La Barre, Louis (or Charles ?) Couperin, Jean D'Anglebert, Johann Jacob Froberger, Antonio Bertalli and Francesco Cavalli.

Unlike Titelouze, he employed the scoring found in Scheidt's *Tabulatura Nova* (1624): that is, a separate line for each of the four parts, in order, he tells us, to facilitate performance on 'viols or other similar instruments'. Along with fugues that are conservative and academically competent, there are others in which Roberday appears to wish to convince that he is able to change with the changing times. Such a fugue is extracted below with its three sections of the Caprice 'sur le mesme sujet'.

Of more significance than Roberday are Etienne Richard, Henry Du Mont and Louis Couperin who, as transitional composers between Titelouze and Nivers, helped forge a new style of organ music oriented

Example 79
Roberday: Extracts from a fugue and three sections of a caprice
(after Guilmant).

Fugue

(a) Caprice sur le mesme sujet

more towards homophony and to the rhythms of the dance and less towards continuous polyphony. Du Mont was organist at Saint-Paul's church in the fashionable Marais quarter, from 1643 until the year of his death (1684). That he was a fine performer is attested to by the inscription on his tomb at Saint-Paul's. Both church and tomb were destroyed in 1802, but the words can be clearly read in a drawing of the tomb found in the Gaignières collection at the Bibliothèque Nationale: 'It was a delight to hear him play the organ as he did in this church for more than 45 (*sic*) years. He was admired by all the most illustrious persons of his time.' It is, therefore, surprising that there are only scattered compositions (preludes and allemandes)[8] that are specified for organ among the works of Du Mont. From Etienne Richard (*c*. 1620–69), organist at Saint-Jacques-de-la-Boucherie, we have 4 allemandes, 3 courantes, 2 sarabandes, 2 gigues, and 2 preludes for organ. The prelude in D-Minor, found in Pirro's 'L'Art des Organistes',[9] is interesting. Its contrapuntal writing is more natural and supple than that of Roberday and the middle section is composed of a graceful, dance-like piece in triple metre as appropriate for the harpsichord as for the organ.

A final judgement of the role of Louis Couperin in this move away from polyphonic forms to a dance-oriented homophony must await the publication of the recently discovered London Ms which includes 70 pieces by Couperin for organ dating from 1650 to 1659[10] consisting of preludes, fantasies, *basses de trompettes* (possibly the first examples of this genre), duos and versets. Some of the titles of these pieces include the registrations desired by Couperin which resemble those required by Nivers in his first book of organ pieces of 1665.

Among Couperin's pieces in the Ms *Bauyn* are a *Fantaisie sur une basse de trompette* and a duo in G-Minor. The duo with its 'nervous and capricious' counterpoint may reflect Couperin's admiration for the music of Frescobaldi.[11] Philidor copied a *Carillon* 'composed by M. Couperin to imitate the *carillons* of Paris'. Philidor added the information that on All Saint's Day this *Carillon* 'was always played on the organ of Saint Gervais'. The style of the *Carillon* (see below) is totally different from that of Titelouze or Roberday. It is homophonic and closely modelled on dance rhythms.

Example 80
Louis Couperin: Extract from a Carillon *(after Philidor copy).*

During this transition period from Titelouze to Nivers, some of the organ music of a Richard, Du Mont or Louis Couperin appears to be equally adaptable for the harpsichord, and it should come as no surprise that all these composers were known as harpsichordists with Du Mont and Richard both holding court appointments. At the same time, the music remains close in spirit to an earlier generation; its general mood of sobriety, even in the dances, worked against a transference of idiom from harpsichord to organ similar to that which occurred between the lute and the harpsichord. Even so, Jean Denis, organist at Saint-Barthélemy and Saint-Severin, as early as 1650 felt it necessary to warn the organist against 'too much movement and wriggling of fingers . . . that prevent the hearing of the consonances and the (correct) tempos' (*Traité de l'accord de l'espinette*, p. 40). He added that those who make suitable use of such ornaments as trills and mordents must be considered as 'very learned'.

The *Premier Livre d'Orgue* (1665) of Guillaume Gabriel Nivers (1632–1714) is the first extant organ book after Titelouze's *Magnificat de tous les tons* (1626). What occurred stylistically between these two musical landmarks determined the direction of organ music in France for over 100 years. Up to this point it might have been possible to have postulated a development of organ music in France that would have run parallel to that of her northern neighbours. That this did not take place is due in large part to two factors: (1) the stabilization of the French classical organ with its unique built-in colour components; and (2) the predominant influence on organ repertory of such secular genres as the *air de cour*, the dance, vocal *récits* and dialogues, the harpsichord suite and even the sound-complex of Lully's opera orchestra.

There is no other organ music before that of the nineteenth century in which instrument and music are so clearly related as that of the French *grand siècle*. A prelude and fugue of Bach will not lose its musical integrity even when performed on an electric organ or transcribed for the piano; a trio of Lebègue 'scored' for a *dessus de cromorne, tierce en taille* and *récit de voix humaine* was composed with particular colours in mind and loses much of its *raison d'être* if performed with a substitute registration—a fact which prompted Lebègue in the preface to his *Premier Livre d'Orgue* to state baldly that there were several pieces in his collection that were of little use to organists whose instruments lacked the necessary stops to perform them.

The French classical organ developed largely from the Norman instruments described earlier. Even by the time of Mersenne's *Harmonie universelle* it had reached a level of standardization that would remain constant except for minor changes until Dom Bedos de Celle's *L'Art du facteur d'orgues* (1776–70).[12] Between 1660 and 1690 the building of organs in France was in the hands of relatively few masters. It was de Héman, Claude de Villiers, Delaunay, Pierre and Alexandre Thierry, Etienne Enoc, Pierre Desenclos and Robert Clicquot who received the commissions and they who 'built-in' the degree of standardization mentioned above.[13] By 1670 it was normally found with four keyboards and pedal; the *Grand Orgue* and the *Positif* both had 48 keys; the *Echo* and the *Récit* keyboards had a restricted compass of from two to three octaves; and the pedal had about 24 keys. The *Positif* or *Positif à dos* (so-called because its case was at the back of the player) was a copy in miniature of the *Grand Orgue* to which it could be coupled. It was the most important second manual and served the *Grand Orgue* in the capacity of an antiphonal instrument or as a solo group. The *Récit* and the *Echo*, whose chests were above and below the Grand Orgue respectively, were utilized mainly for solo *récits*.

Thus, the French classical organ had manuals devoted entirely to one or two solo stops, unlike the German instruments of the same period where normally every manual controlled a complete division. The standardization of stops (*jeux*)[14] and the concomitant standardization of registration called for in the prefaces of most organ books beginning with Nivers bring a consistency of sound to French organ music of the period that is unique in Europe. It is the sound of the reeds of the *Grand Jeu*, of the *cornets* of the *Récits*, the *cromornes* of the *Positif* and the shrill *trompette* of the Pedal. It is the sound of duos of *cromorne en taille* and *basse de trompette*, of the solo *récits* of the *voix humaine*, the *nasard* and, above all, the *tierce en taille* labeled by Williams as 'the great French contribution to organ music'.[15] It is the understanding that the *Plein Jeu* of the *Positif* is played with 'vitality and includes trills with a touch as light as that of the harpsichord' (Correte, 1703), whereas, the *Plein Jeu* of the *Grand Orgue* is 'majestic with a great harmonic sweep' (Dom Bedos de Celles, 1766). It is, in short, a common legacy of sound uniting the organists of Saint-Louis-des-Invalides with Notre-Dame, of Saint-Germain-des-Prés with Saint-Gervais, of Saint-Merri with Saint-Paul.[16]

The uniformity of content of the seventeenth century organ books of Guillaume-Gabriel Nivers (1665, 1667, 1675), Nicolas Lebègue (1676, 1678, c. 1685), Nicolas Gigault (1685), André Raison (1688), Jacques Boyvin (1689), François Couperin (1690), Gilles Jullien (1690) and Nicolas Grigny (1699) can best be explained against the background of the important *Ceremoniale parisiense*, the so-called 'Ceremonial of the Bishops', drafted in 1622 by a Parisian priest, Martin Sonnet, and published by order of the Archbishop of Paris, J. F. P. de Gondy. In the hierarchical spirit of the age, this document laid down the ground rules for all aspects of the celebration of the Divine Office in the Paris diocese.

The *Ceremoniale* carefully detailed the use of the organ during the Mass and the Office. The organist was instructed to utilize the appropriate Gregorian melodies in alternation with the choir, for Kyries I and III, portions of the Gloria, Sanctus I, the Agnus Dei and the Domine Salvum. For the remaining portion of the Ordinary, the organist was permitted to perform short *récits*, duos, trios and other suitable compositions.[17]

It becomes clear that there was considerable incentive for the organists of the Paris churches to compose a body of original music and music based on Gregorian chant, to supply the formidable demands of the church year. Altogether typical are the three books of Nivers, organist at St Sulpice from 1654 to 1714 and, from 1678, one of the four organists at the royal chapel.

Nivers' first *Livre d'Orgue* (1665) consists of '100 Pieces on all the church modes'.[18] In addition to the first extensive instructions for registration since Mersenne, there are some observations on hand positions and fingering, which bear comparison with those supplied by Couperin some 50 years later in his *L'Art de toucher le clavecin*.

Nivers emphasized the importance of a flowing style ('bien couler les notes') and offered the suggestion that performers 'consult the method of singing, because in this manner of playing, the Organ should imitate the Voice'.

The 100 pieces, which include no Gregorian melodies, are organized into 12 suites unified by key. Each suite opens with a prelude, which we learn from the preface should be played on the *plein jeu*. Two suites include ten versets and the remainder include eight versets which were designed to alternate with the sung chant.

The new style is particularly evident if we examine the fugues which have become almost totally disassociated from polyphony! There is little tension or independence in the part writing, and many sections line up in a type of harpsichordic homophony in which shifts of texture act to destroy any linear integrity.

The dialogues and *récits* exploit solo effects (there are 10 *récits de cromorne*) and clearly show the transfer of vocal melody and harpsichord ornamentation to the organ.

276

The second *Livre d'Orgue* 'including a Mass and Hymns of the Church' (1667)[19] is restricted to the alternating liturgical comments of the organist on the Ordinary of the Mass followed by 26 hymns. The essence of the style shift from Titelouze to Nivers is epitomized in Example 81a and b below. Extracted are two settings of the same Gregorian hymn, 'Pange lingua'; Example 81a comes from the beginning of the third verse of Titelouze's setting (*Les Hymnes pour toucher sur l'Orgue*), Example 81b is a couplet 'en Récit de Voix humaine' from Nivers' second *Livre d'Orgue*.

Nivers' third *Livre d'Orgue* 'on the 8 churches modes'[20] is similar to the first book. Its 105 compositions are grouped in 8 suites all of which have the same symmetrical architecture, a diptych composed of:

Example 81
(a) *Titelouze:* Pange lingua (*after ed. of 1624*).

(b) *Nivers:* Pange lingua (*after ed. of 1667*).

prelude, fugue, *récit,* duo, *basse,* echo, dialogue for two choirs; fugue grave, *récit,* duo, *basse, dialogues de récits,* dialogue for two choirs.

It is more for his extra-musical contributions than for the intrinsic merit of his music that Nivers is a significant figure in the history of French organ music. It was he who showed the way, he who established the basic format of the organ book, and he who utilized to full capacity the colour potential of the new organs.

Of some interest is an anonymous *Livre d'orgue* found today in the Bibliothèque Nationale (fonds du Conservatoire, Res. 476) that was probably collected between 1670 and 1675. The manuscript has been attributed falsely, it is believed, to Jean-Nicolas Geoffroy, organist at Saint-Nicolas du Chardonnet.[21] The collection illustrates a variety of ways of alternating the *plain-chant musical* (here supplied with accompaniments) with short versets that often paraphrase the chant melody. The music of Nicolas Lebègue is more important. He was organist for 40 years at Saint-Merri and a colleague of Nivers at the royal chapel. Acknowledgment of the uniformity of registration in the Paris area comes in the sub-title of Lebègue's *Les Pièces d'Orgues* (1676, new editions in 1678 and 1685) '. . . the present manner of playing the Organ with all stops and particularly those which are little in use in the provinces such as the *Tierces* and *Cromornes en taille*'.

Each of the suites of Lebègue's first book opens with a prelude and closes with a *Plein Jeu*. Occasionally, Lebègue inserts a trio with a nice feeling for independent line. He is a master of *récits* and dialogues that exploit the sounds of the *tierce* or *cromorne en taille* 'the most beautiful (sounds) and most distinctive' on the instrument (Preface).

The *Second Livre d'Orgue* (1678) is an example of *Gebrauchsmusik* which contains 'short and easy pieces based on the 8 modes of the church and the Mass of solemn feasts'. No pedal is necessary; the music may have been intended for Lebègue's own use on the rather primitive instrument at the royal chapel.

In both the first and second books there is a wealth of popular-type melodies that, it must be confessed, owe more to the *divertissements* of the opera than to the '8 modes of the church'. They have a charm and natural grace that influenced most French organ composers to follow.

Example 82

Lebègue: Popular-type melodies found in Book I of Pièces d'Orgues, *1676.*

In the sub-title of the third book (1685) there is tacit acknowledgment of the secularization of the organ repertory as well as the transference of the harpsichord medium to the organ keyboard: *Troisième Livre d'Orgue* 'containing large Offertories and Elevations; And all the best known Noëls, Symphonies and carillons that one can play on the Organ and the Harpsichord'.

The four Symphonies are large preludes in binary form. They are clearly modelled on the French overture and one resembles the type of allemande with dotted rhythms and *tirades* already familiar in the harpsichord collections of D'Anglebert and others. The popular Noëls probably inspired by those already printed by Gigault (1682) include elements from the *style brisé* transferred to the organ for the first time. Nicolas Gigault (1626–1707), organist at Saint-Nicolas-des-Champs, Saint-Honoré and Saint-Martin-des-Champs and Lully's composition teacher, published a *Livre de Musique* dedicated to 'la très Sainct Vierge' in 1682. The collection is entirely made up of popular Noëls each treated in a variety of ways ranging from dialogues *a* 2 to full organ choir. Taking a leaf from some of the harpsichord books, Gigault suggested alternate performance possibilities on 'lute, viols, violin, flute and other instruments'.

Included in the 1682 collection is a demonstration piece, an Allemande, written for those who wished to achieve a certain 'tendresse' in their manner of playing. 'Tendresse' here obviously refers to keyboard ornamentation labelled generically as 'ports de voix' by Gigault. The allemande is presented first in its simple version and then in order to give an idea of how ornaments 'might be applied to all other types of pieces', an ornamented version is included. It is more important as an historical document than as a living piece of music. Its ornamented version is singularly awkward with the incessant, dotted 'ports de voix' tending to work at cross-purposes with the melodic frame.

In 1685, Gigault published his *Livre de Musique pour l'Orgue* that is a compendium of all genres of the French organ repertory in the last quarter of the seventeenth century. The collection contains more than 180 compositions that 'may be played on 1, 2, 3 and 4 keyboards'. There are several Masses and hymns along with some fugues 'treated in the Italian manner'. Like the motets of Brossard that have optional points of conclusion, these compositions were so designed that 'one might finish in several places'.

Many pieces are very short indeed. There is a 'Glorificamus Te' of 7 measures and a 'Benedicamus Te' of 10 measures. Others, however, are overlong including a Fugue of 60 measures based almost exclusively on a ♪♪ ♪♪ ♪♪ rhythmic formula. In fact, Gigault seemed curiously bound to patterns of dotted rhythms. Sequences, circles of fifths and some dissonances 'treated according to the Modern practice' (Preface) dominate the fugues composed 'à la manière Italienne'. In one two-voice fugue, Gigault anticipates the fashionable 12/8 Italian *Giga* used later by both Couperin and Grigny in their organ pieces as well as in many harpsichord collections of the later seventeenth century.

The strong connection between dance rhythms and much of the organ music of the late seventeenth century is acknowledged by André Raison (died 1719) in his *Livre d'Orgue* of 1688. As an aid in interpreting this collection of five Masses and an Offertory for the 'happy convalescence of the King in 1687', Raison stated that 'It is necessary to observe the metre of the Piece that you are to play and to consider whether it has some rapport with a sarabande, gigue, gavotte, bourrée, canarie, passacaille, chaconne or the tempo of the Blacksmith dance (a characteristic dance of *divertissements*). You must give it the same Air that you would were you performing it on the Harpsichord except that you should play the trills a little slower because of the sanctity of the Place.'[22] Unlike most of his contemporaries, Raison allowed for more latitude in the registration of his pieces observing, sensibly, that he himself greatly varied the choice of stops and manuals in performance.

Jacques Boyvin (1649–1706) in his two organ books of 1690 and 1700 is less bound by the dance rhythms that so intrigued his contemporaries. Even the shorter preludes such as the 'Prélude facile' in the fourth mode have achieved a greater amplitude by less static harmony and evasion of cadence. In the *Avis* from his *Premier Livre d'Orgue*, Boyvin justified the by now routine explanations of stop combinations and registration, which he assumed were well known by all his readers, by the fact that his book might fall into the hands of foreign musicians not acquainted with the style.

Gilles Jullien's (*c.* 1650–1703) *Premier Livre d'Orgue* of 1690[23] includes 80 pieces on the 8 church modes. Because the subject of stop combinations had been dealt with so often, he stated that it would be 'of little use to discuss it further here'. Nonetheless, he proceeded to give much valuable information on registration.

Jullien is primarily a colourist who in his *Avis* admitted to some freedom from the 'sense of ordinary chords'. The example below with its three parallel 7th chords is perhaps an illustration of this 'freedom'.

Example 83
Jullien: Extract from a 'Prélude du Quatrième Ton' (after ed. of 1690).

Harpsichordist Jean-Henri D'Anglebert in his *Pièces de Clavecin* of 1689 included five fugues all utilizing the same subject and a *Quatuor sur le Kyrie* for the organ. The quartet, based on Gregorian melodies (*Cunctipotens* and *Salve Regina*), is written in open score with each part designed for a different keyboard.

The French organ school of the seventeenth century reaches its highest musical level with the works of two composers—François Couperin, organist at St Gervais from 1685 to 1723, and Nicolas de Grigny. The amount of music for organ left by each is modest when compared with the depressing weight of numbers found in the collections of their contemporaries. Both composers were concerned with the liturgical considerations spelled out in the *Ceremoniale*; but more important, their music has a sincerity and depth of expression too often lacking in that of their contemporaries. The popular elements, the operatic influences, the profusion of ornamentation are all there with no loss of charm, but there is a greater sense of continuity and more evidence of control over the musical forms.

The royal privilege permitting François Couperin to have his *Pièces d'Orgue* published was given 2 September 1690 with Delalande certifying that 'I have found (them) very fine and worthy of being given to the Public'. A routine matter, it would seem. Delalande had replaced Charles Couperin, the composer's father, as organist at Saint Gervais after Charles' death in 1679; François had in turn replaced Delalande only five years before the privilege date at the age of 18 years.

Yet for some reason Ballard never published the Couperin *Pièces d'Orgue* and the music remained in manuscript copies. Until the earlier years of this century when the research of Pirro, Bouvet, Tessier, Brunold and Tiersot proved otherwise, the music was credited to François Couperin 'the elder', uncle of François 'le Grand'. It seemed to Danjou and Fétis and others that this music was simply too mature, too refined for such a young composer, and that the 'F. Couperin, Sieur de Crouilly, Organiste de l'Eglise St Gervais de Paris' must be the elder François Couperin of whom Titon de Tillet wrote: 'He was a little man who loved good wine'.

The *Pièces* consist of two Masses; one for parishes for everyday use as well as for solemn feasts, and the other suitable for use in convents or monasteries. Although both contain 21 pieces in the identical ordering of Kyrie (5), Gloria (9), Offertory (1), Sanctus-Benedictus (3), Agnus Dei (2) and Deo Gratias (1), the convent Mass is considerably shorter and less demanding for the performer.

Whereas the Masses reveal Couperin's absorption of the tradition of Nivers, Lebègue, Raison and Gigault, they also show the personal mark of the young composer in what may be his first compositions. It is a style nurtured at this point more by French than by Italian elements. The trios lack the crossing of parts, the chains of suspensions and circles of 5ths borrowed from the Italian trio sonata. They resemble more the homophonic trios of Lully's operas. Couperin creates a noble cantilena in the Benedictus of the parish Mass and the 5th couplet of the Gloria of the convent Mass, both scored for

cromorne en taille. The ♩♩.♪|♩ rhythmic pattern, the generally re-
stricted range, the discreet ornamentation and the use of affective
intervals speak the language of Lully's monologues.

The Gregorian melodies of the parish Mass are taken from the
Cunctipotens Genitor Deus. In accordance with the *Ceremoniale* they
are not ornamented and are treated in a sober manner, usually as a
whole note cantus firmus in the tenor or bass. The contrapuntal writing in the fugues and elsewhere strikes a nice balance between the
continuous polyphony of Titelouze and the 'homophonic' fugues of
Lebègue. In general, Couperin's contrapuntal line is not compromised
by the too regularly recurring internal cadences that give a short-
breathed quality to so much French music of the period. The part
writing engenders some cross-relations, and dissonant harmony colours
the music without distracting from the general sobriety of mood. Such
are the major 7th, the augmented 5th and the melodic diminished 4th
in the example below extracted from the 'Fugue sur les jeux d'anches',
the second couplet of the Kyrie of the parish Mass.

Example 84
Couperin: Extract from the Messe pour les paroisses *(after Guilmant).*

The Offertories of both Masses gave Couperin a chance to create a
larger musical structure. The Offertory of the Mass of the convent
resembles a set of free variations on a popular type dance melody.
Chaconne-like, the middle section is in the tonic minor key. The
Positif and *Grand Orgue* are in constant juxtaposition as *ripieno* and
concertino with the texture of the *Positif* usually restricted to three
voices. In the parish Mass, the Offertory is a large tripartite structure
beginning with a French overture in C-Major; following is a trio-
quartet combination in C-Minor.

Popular dance forms invade several of the non-Gregorian pieces.
The 3rd couplet of the Gloria in the parish Mass is a gigue with the
continuous 8th note movement of the Italian form of the dance; the
4th couplet of the same Gloria is a large march—a virtual *entrée* for
an operatic *divertissement* dominated by its trumpet-like melody.

Nicolas de Grigny (1672–1703) dwelt outside the sphere of most
Parisian organists. Although a student of Lebègue's and organist from

1693 to 1695 at Saint-Denis, he lived most of his life in Reims as organist, like his father and grandfather before him, at the cathedral. Little known in the eighteenth century, although Bach accorded him the greatest compliment by copying his *Livre d'Orgue* at Luneburg, practically ignored by Fétis in the nineteenth century, he had to wait until Guilmant and Pirro in volume v of their *Archives des Maîtres de l'Orgue* placed him in his own particular pantheon.

The *Premier Livre d'Orgue* (1699) includes a Mass (based on the *Cunctipotens Genitor Deus*), and in the tradition of Titelouze, it is followed by paraphrases on Gregorian hymns. The scarcely 50 pieces of this collection show Grigny, more than any other French organ composer of his time, able to synthesize the archaic polyphony of a Titelouze with the grace of a Lebègue *récit*.

He often chose a five-part texture with the pedal acting as an harmonic support for the busy inner voices. Six of the eight fugues in the collection are for five voices. Grigny's part writing is generally consistent, and he avoided the shifts of texture that are so much a part of the French keyboard tradition.

It is this consistency and sense of logical development combined with a depth of feeling that may have attracted Bach to the organ music of Grigny. This is especially evident in some of the hymn paraphrases such as the *Ave Maris Stella*. Indeed, certain paraphrases have a similarity to some of the chorale preludes of the German master's *Orgelbüchlein*.

Grigny, like Couperin, built from the French tradition. The dotted rhythms and *tirades* of the French overture are prominent, and the trios often pair the upper voices in thirds or sixths.

The dialogues and offertories 'sur les grands jeux' are more powerful statements than the offertories and symphonies of Lebègue from which they derive. Along with those of Couperin, they are superb musical illustrations for Dom Bedos de Celle's description of what is appropriate for the *Plein Jeu*: 'great harmonic sweep, interlaced with syncopations, dissonant chords, suspensions and harmonic audacities' (Part iii, Chapter 4, *L'Art du facteur d'orgues*).

Grigny's harmonic audacities are also more French than Italian although there is an increased use of modulation and some effective chromatic writing. Again it is a question of using ornamentation to deepen the harmonic expressiveness of the music. Along with this, however, is a frequently powerful use of cross-relations that stems from principles of voice leading. The final measures of the *Point d'Orgue*, a large, fantasy-type composition that closes the collection, are a striking example of passages in double counterpoint that combine the major and minor mode of E simultaneously.

Long before the French harpsichord school reached its climax in the music of Couperin and Rameau, the French organ school had slipped into mannerisms and decadence. To be sure there were composers such as Louis Marchand (1669–1732), Gaspard Corrette (dates unknown), Guillaume Freinsberg (called Guilain, dates unknown), Pierre Du Mage (1674–1751), Jean-François Dandrieu (1682–1738) and Louis-Nicolas Clérambault (1676–1749) who continued to compose books of liturgical suites in the tradition of the seventeenth century masters. Even their music shows the inroads of secular elements that do little to improve the musical content and much to detract from the legitimate purpose of a musical comment on the liturgy.

Few composers were tempted to write in the 'learned' style so out of joint with the mode of the Regency. A study of the few labelled fugues by Clérambault or Marchand, for example, shows how far removed we are in spirit and technique from a fugue *a 5* of Grigny. The subject of the Clérambault fugue from his first Suite (*Livre d'Orgue*, 1710) is totally submerged in a profusion of non-functional ornaments that cannot help but impede its forward motion. The Marchand fugue, although devoid of any indicated ornamentation, makes no pretence of guarding a linear texture; all voices line up in homophony after the second entrance of the subject.

At the same time, there are some fine pages in the organ music of the above composers. Louis Marchand[24] was much in demand as an organist and held posts at three Paris churches (St Benoit, St Honoré, convent of the Cordeliers) as well as at the royal chapel. His music and performing ability were recognized outside of France, and Bach seemed to have held him in high regard in spite of the Frenchman's inglorious last minute defection in the Dresden 'contest' of September 1717. Some of the music of his five short organ books has a dramatic sweep and a sense of harmonic daring that demands attention. As a study in dissonant counterpoint within a chordal frame, the E-Minor piece in the second book is perhaps unprecedented in French music of the period. The constant evasion of cadences and feints towards B-Minor, G-Minor and D-Major help sustain tension throughout the 34 measure piece.

The two Suites, each with seven numbers, that constitute Clérambault's *Livre d'Orgue* contain much music with an unpretentious charm and even naïveté implied in tempo designations such as 'Gayement et gratieusement'. A Lullian chaconne, a real French overture with its two sections (Fort grave) and (Gay) in clear apposition, and an Italian 'Sicilienne' are all found in these suites by the organist of St Sulpice (1714) who also served at Mme de Maintenon's convent at Saint-Cyr.

Italian violin sonatas and concertos inevitably left their mark on French organ music of the eighteenth century. The trio below extracted from the *Pièces d'Orgue pour le Magnificat* (1706) by Guilain, a composer of German origins who reached Paris after 1702 shows clearly the influence of Corelli with its chains of suspensions and its crossing of voices. The *Grand Jeu* from the same collection has the mechanical rhythmic pulsations and the wide melodic profile of the Italian concerto. The piece is constructed around one motive and structured like a short concerto movement with the *Grand Jeu* serving as *ripieno* in rapid alternation with solo cornet passages.

Example 85
Guilain: Extract from an organ trio (after Guilmant).

Dandrieu probably felt the stylistic conflict that could exist between what was appropriate in liturgical music and what was popular when he wrote in the *Avertissement* to his *Premier Livre des Pièces d'Orgue* (1739): 'The difficulty of composing *Pièces d'Orgue* in order that they be worthy of the majesty of the Place where the instrument is played . . . made me reluctant for a long time to undertake this work.'

The collection includes six suites each followed by a Magnificat. The 'noble and elegant simplicity' that Dandrieu decided was appropriate for organ music results in overall ennui for performer and listener. The collection includes two 'Muzetes' bearing the performance directions 'Naivement et loure' and a Duo 'en cors de chasse sur la Trompete'. The Offertory 'pour le jour de Pâques' is similar to a set of harpsichord variations with the eighth variation using an Alberti bass formula.

No such compunctions concerning suitability bothered Louis-Claude Daquin (1694–1772), François d'Agincour (1684–1758), Antoine Dornel (c. 1685–1765), Nicolas Siret (c. 1664–1754), Guillaume-Antoine Calvière (1700–55), Michel Corrette (1709–95) or Claude-Benigne Balbastre (1727–99), all of whom became increasingly concerned with virtuoso effects and the use of the French classical organ as a concert instrument. Elements from the theatre and the dance, already present in organ suites, were exaggerated, and a new dimension was added: the colour potential of the organ was thought of as a vehicle for descriptive music second only to that of the orchestra itself.

In the *Premier Livre d'Orgue* (1737) by Michel Corrette there is, in addition to four magnificats 'for the use of the nuns', a 'Table of pieces from my *Livre de Clavecin* that may be played on the organ'. Corrette gives the titles of six harpsichord pieces and subverts the sacrosanct registration of the French Classical organ to descriptive ends. Thus, 'Les Giboulées de Mars', 'Le Courier', 'Les bottes de sept Lieiues', 'Les Fantastiques' and 'La Prise de Jericho' all are to be played on the *Grand Jeu* whereas 'Les Amants enchantés' belongs on the flutes and 'Les Etoiles' on the *Tierce* of the *Positif*.

Louis-Claude Daquin, a virtuoso at the age of 12 at the church of the Petit Saint-Antoine, was the successor of Marchand at the Cordeliers and of Dandrieu at the royal chapel. Daquin had no rivals as an organ virtuoso after the death of Marchand. His major publications of organ music consist of collections of Noëls which were conceived of not only for organ but for harpsichord and in most instances for violin, flute, and oboe as well. The *Nouveau Livre de Noëls pour l'Orgue* includes 12 Noëls with extensive and difficult variations.

Foreign observers of the French musical scene as far removed in time as J. C. Nemeitz and Charles Burney commented on the introduction of popular elements into the organ music of the liturgy in France. Concerning a midnight Mass, Nemeitz wrote that 'the music that is performed in the churches is not too devout since the organ plays minuets and all types of worldly tunes' (*Séjour de Paris*, p. 232). Years later Burney made essentially the same observations with regard to Balbastre's playing at Saint-Roch: 'When the Magnificat was sung, he played likewise between each verse several minuets, fugues, imitations and every species of music, even to hunting pieces and jigs, without surprising or offending the congregation' (*Present State of Music in France and Italy*, p. 38).

The installation of a large organ at the hall of the *Concert Spirituel* in 1748 was a final step in this process of secularization. Little by little from Nivers to Daquin, the French school of organists had compromised the liturgical functions of their instrument. They had made of an organ that could reveal the introspection of an Agnus Dei of Grigny, an organ that could 'faire l'orage et la tonnerre'.

The critical time for forming a new and vital literature was at the turn of the century. Yet the most important composers were already occupied elsewhere. The organ composer and the harpsichord composer did no more than reflect the tastes of the Regency and the period of Louis xv. Couperin, had he chosen to write a series of *Livres d'Orgue* of the calibre of his *Pièces de Clavecin* might have been the catalyst for a new generation of organ composers in France with something musically significant to say. The harpsichord, not the organ, was the preferred instrument at the court and Couperin must have known it. Why else would the royal chapel have only a mediocre positive organ? By the time the final chapel at Versailles with its magnificent Robert Clicquot organ was finished, it was already too late.

Part four

Instrumental Ensemble and Solo Music

Chapter 19

⇒⇒-⧽⧼-

Instrumental Ensemble and Orchestral Music of the Seventeenth Century

There were many opportunities for ensemble performances in the France of Henri III, Henri IV and Louis XIII. Performance in groups was a natural by-product of the musical division of labour at court; it was a means of livelihood for the town musicians of the Confrérie of Saint-Julien, and in the guise of private concerts, it was the happy companion of the leisure hours of some of the most famous composers and musicians of the time.[1]

The literature of the period is rich in descriptions of concerts some of which were organized on a more or less regular basis. The earliest concerts may have been those at Baïf's and Thibaut de Courville's Académie de Poésie et de Musique, founded in 1570. The statutes of the Académie show that the weekly concerts at Baïf's home might give a twentieth century impresario reason for envy.[2]

It is not certain whether the performances at the Académie included independent instrumental ensemble music during Baïf's lifetime or whether instruments were used exclusively to support the voices. In 1589, Baïf died and Jacques Mauduit (1557–1627) took over direction of the concerts from this date until long after the Académie itself had ceased functioning as an organized group.

If Sauval, writing perhaps 50 years later, was accurate, the concerts directed by Mauduit were no modest undertaking: 'All sorts of things were sung in dialogues and in choirs; sometimes by vocal soloists, sometimes by performers on instruments and singers together. Ordinarily there were from 60 to 80 people (performing), often up to 120' (*Histoires et recherches*, II, p. 492). Instrumental music independent of the voices is suggested by Sauval's observation that 'In the Concerts of Mauduit there were not only these instruments (flutes, lutes, pandoras) but also spinets and viols that he (Mauduit) made fashionable' (*Histoire et recherches*, II, p. 493). The Protestant poet Agrippa d'Aubigné described in a letter having heard 'an excellent concert in Paris of guitars, 12 viols, 4 spinets, 4 lutes, 2 pandoras and 2 theorbos'. (See Reese, *Music in the Renaissance*, p. 566.) The large number of performers suggests that some works were performed with more than one player on a part.

The use of viols and harpsichords together in ensemble music is also confirmed by Mersenne in his description of concerts given by Maugars, Lazarin, La Barre (Pierre) and Du Buisson. In addition to concerts of voices and instruments and concerts of viols and harpsichord, Mersenne mentioned concerts 'of sieur Ballard (Pierre) in which 5 or 6 Lutes play together'. Mersenne's concept of an ideal concert shows the catholicity of the great Jesuit thinker at the very outset of the heated debate on national styles that would preoccupy French aestheticians and musicians for a 150 year period:

> If one wishes to have all the pleasures of which Music is capable, it would be necessary to have all types of singing and to hear one follow the other, in order to judge which surpasses the other: for example, we should hear one of the Madrigals or other Italian airs performed by a dozen good Italian singers, as well as Sarabandes by Spaniards, Courantes and Airs by Frenchmen, and then there would be performed the best pieces of Music available for Instruments, so that 6 Lutes might begin followed by a concert of Viols, and finally there would be a concert of Violins like the 24 of the King.
>
> ('Embellissement des chants', *Harmonie Universelle*, p. 394)

For Jacques de Gouy (died about 1650), the 'first concerts' were some 'concerts spirituels' given before 1650 at the home of Pierre de Chabanceau de La Barre (1592–1656), organist of the royal chapel. In the preface of his *Airs à 4 parties sur les paraphrases des psaumes de Godeau* (1650), he wrote: 'The first concerts were those at the home of M. de La Barre, organist of the King, . . . the renown of these *concerts spirituels* . . . was such that several Archbishops, Bishops, Dukes, Counts, Marquis and many others honoured them by their presence.'

In 1655 Christian Huygens, travelling in France, wrote his father describing the concerts given by the 'Assemblée des honestes curieux' instituted by Chambonnières. Chambonnières' group had apparently been in existence officially 14 years when Huygens first heard them. A notarial entry in the *Minutier Central* (see pp. 435–36 in *Documents*) of 17 October 1641 obliged seven musicians to present themselves before 'Messire Jacques de Champion, Chevallier, seigneur de Chambonnières, gentilhomme ordinaire de la chambre du Roy'. They were to arrive at a hall 'that pleases sieur de Chambonnières punctually at the hour of noon two times weekly on Wednesday and Saturday . . . in order to give a concert of music . . .'. Confirmation of the success of Chambonnières' amusingly titled 'Assemblée des honestes curieux' comes in a notarial entry for the following 13 December which authorized the group to perform in the 'large hall of the Maison de Mandosse'. At this time the Assemblée must have already received royal patronage since in the minutes it is referred to as the 'accademye instituée par le roy'.

Huygens also wrote his father in glowing terms about the concerts given by 'Monsieur Lambert and Mlle Hilaire, his sister-in-law, who sings like an angel'. Michel Lambert (*c.* 1610–96) was Lully's father-in-law and a renowned teacher. According to Titon du Tillet, he used his best students in concerts held at his country house at Puteau near Paris.

Descriptions in the memoirs and letters of Mlle de Scudéry, Mlle de Montpensier and Mme de Sévigné, scattered references in the *Mercure* or Dangeau's *Journal* show a proliferation of private concerts during the reign of Louis XIV. We learn through the pages of the *Mercure*, for example, that Sainte-Colombe, who was a violist and the teacher of Marais, gave family concerts in which he and his two daughters all played bass viols; that Jacques Gallot, of the dynasty of lutenists, gave a concert at his home every Saturday; and that a certain Monsieur Medard had a concert at his home every 15 days. (See Brenet, p. 71.) In fact, the wealthy bourgeoisie, prototypes for the eighteenth century financier La Pouplinière, found it a distinct social advantage to present concerts in their salons—an attitude recorded in Molière's *Le Bourgeois gentilhomme* where Monsieur Jourdain is told that in order to be a person of quality he must have a concert at his home 'every Wednesday or Thursday' (Act II, scene I).

The private concert situation in the early years of the eighteenth century was such that if one were fortunate enough to be a young gentleman of means visiting Paris, as was J. C. Nemeitz, one could not only perfect his performance skills which would assure en '*entrée* into the *grand monde*', but one could also hear a concert every day. Nemeitz lists some of the concerts attended during his Paris sojourn: 'at the homes of the Duc d'Aumont, Ambassador to England . . . Abbé

Grave, Mlle de Maes, who ordinarily gave one a week; and then at the home of Mons Clérambault, who gave one about every 15 days or three weeks. All these Concerts were performed by the best masters of Paris' (*Séjour de Paris*, p. 69).

By the last years of the Grand Monarch's reign, the normal routine of concerts designed to accompany his rising and his dining was augmented by Mme de Maintenon who, in spite of her prudery, had some musical sensitivity. She arranged almost daily performances in her apartments by such well-known musicians as De Visée (guitarist), René Descoteaux (flutist), Antoine Forqueray (bass viol player) and Jean Butern (organist).

The instruments favoured for private concerts through the first half of the seventeenth century were, as we have seen, lutes, viols and harpsichords with occasional use of guitar or flute. These were the 'instruments of repose destined for serious and tranquil pleasures whose languid harmony is the enemy of all action and who demand only sedentary Auditors' (Michel de Pure, *Idée des spectacles*, p. 273). Much of the time these instruments were used to support the voice, although the large number of extant fantasies suggests that there was a considerable body of independent literature available for ensemble performances. In fact, the existence of independent literature for viols in conjunction with other instruments is confirmed by Trichet who wrote:

> Viols . . . are very suitable for consorts of music, whether used with voices, or whether one allows them to be joined by other instruments.
>
> (*Traité des instrumens de musique*)

It was only in the later seventeenth century that flutes, recorders, oboes and violins began to supplant the viols as treble instruments and we arrive at the combination of instruments suggested by the Music Master to M. Jourdain for his weekly concerts: 'bass viol, a theorbo and a harpsichord for the *basse-continue* with the violin to play the *ritournelles*'.

The nature of ensemble performances at court was determined in large part by the categories of the 'King's music' discussed in Chapter One. As has been noted, these divisions were often more semantic than actual.

The *24 Violons* and the *Petits Violons* with some of the best wind players from the *Ecurie* made up the orchestra for the big court ballets, at least after 1661 when Lully had made his peace with the *Grande Bande*. All the king's musicians joined forces for special ceremonies such as coronations, entries of foreign dignitaries, royal births and marriages and the like. In his *Traité des tournois, joustes, carrousels, et autres spectacles publics* (Lyon, 1669), Père Ménestrier discussed the musical resources required for these affairs. According to his specifications, most members of the 'King's music' must have been involved. Ménéstrier tabulated the instruments appropriate for each type of ensemble. For his first category, he included trumpets, cornetts, oboes, cromornes, fifes, transverse flutes, *dulcines* (soft-voiced, double-reed instruments) and *clairons* (high-pitched trumpets) and an entire *batterie* of percussion instruments. For his second category, he listed lutes, theorbos, guitars, musettes, harpsichords and spinets, small organs, violins, viols, harps and recorders.

Apparently after the band of *24 Violons* had officially been established as a separate administrative unit by Louis XIII about 1626, violins were no longer found in the music of the king's *Chambre*. The *Chambre* was an élite group dominated by solo performers including singers, lutenists, violists, harpsichordists and organists. It was natural that the violin should have been excluded, for as early as Philibert Jambe-de-Fer's *Epitôme musical* (Lyon, 1556) the French considered the violin ideally suited to accompany the dance. Trichet in 1630 wrote: 'Violins are principally destined for dances, balls, ballets, masquerades, serenades, morning songs (*aubades*), festivals and all joyous pastimes, having been judged more suitable than any other instrument for this type of recreation'. Writing in 1668, Michel de Pure recognized the violin as capable of sustaining a *grand ballet* 'with equity and justice'. 'The glory of the Violin', he stressed, 'is only to play the measure and tempo accurately as soon as the *Entrée* commences.' His repeated warnings to performers to avoid 'a thousand *coup d'archets* and excessive ornamentation seem to vindicate Lully's distress at the performance practices of the *24 Violons*.[3]

Thus being considered the instrument 'most suitable of all to accompany dance' (Mersenne) and being deemed appropriate for all manner of outdoor music,[4] the violin was not accorded the recognition and prestige that it received in Italy where it was also viewed as a potential concert instrument.

Rather, the violin was considered the instrument of street fiddlers, an attitude that the imperious demands of the Confrérie of Saint Julien did little to dispel. Even after the appearance of the first French sonatas, Lecerf could write that 'The instrument (the violin) is not *noble* in France. . . . That is, Mademoiselle, that one sees few gentlemen of means who play it and many lowly Musicians who make their living by it.' His sentiment echoes almost word-for-word that of Jambe de Fer about 150 years earlier: 'There are few people who perform it (violin) except those who make a living from it.'

Striking documentation of the extent to which the deprecation of the violin had slipped into common speech is offered by the *Diction-naire de Trévoux* (1743). One of the meanings found under the heading 'Violon' follows:

Violin is also a term of abuse and scorn which means fool, impertinent fellow. To consider a man a *Violon* is as if one were to place him in the ranks of the *Ménestriers* who go from cabaret to cabaret playing a violin and increasing the pleasure of the drunkards.

(Vol. VI, p. 814)

Violins which were used in great numbers for court functions were rarely used in private concerts before the late seventeenth century. There was a decided preference for the viol as the chamber instrument *par excellence* both for independent ensemble performance and for the accompaniment of voices. Any twentieth century performer on instruments of the *viola da gamba* family understands as did his forebears that the sonorities of these instruments only superficially resemble those of the violin family. Any substitution of violas or violins for viols (or flutes for recorders) in Bach's Cantata 106, the *Actus Tragicus*, for example, completely changes the desired sound complex, brightens what was dark, makes heavy what was thin. Any modern performer could confirm the words of Trichet who, in discussing the preference for viols, wrote that it was the 'cleanness of their sound, the ease with which they are handled, and the gentle harmony that results, that makes them more willingly employed than other instruments'.

The arbitrary functional division that saw viol as chamber instrument and violin as dance instrument inevitably contributed to the slowness of the French to develop a technique of violin playing comparable to that of the Italians. The French violin literature until the time of Lully rarely leaves the first position, and the wide leaps and rapid arpeggios associated with typical violin figurations are conspicuously absent from seventeenth century French solo and ensemble music.

André Maugars was quick to notice during his Italian sojourn that there were '10 or 12' violinists in Rome who performed marvels on their instruments; whereas he discovered no one in Italy who excelled on the viol and that it was 'little used in Rome'. In contrast, French virtuoso viol players, beginning with Maugars and extending through Antoine Forqueray (died 1745), formed a strong, closed group which had no wish to see the violin in a position of supremacy. Time was against the viol, however, although this unequal rivalry endured into the eighteenth century even as French composers borrowed more and more techniques from the Italian violin sonatas and concertos. The final, rather desperate, attempt to bolster the fading fortunes of the viol was the treatise by Hubert Le Blanc, *Défense de la basse de viole contre les entreprises du violon et les prétensions du violoncel* (1740). The polemical tone of the treatise (the violoncello is described as a 'miserable canker') with its tired shibboleths (a person of quality and of noble education would find the sound of the violin displeasing) did little to sustain the viol against the onslaught of the violin sonatas and concertos of Corelli, Vivaldi and Geminiani played at the *Concert Spirituel* by popular French and Italian virtuosi.

The repertory performed at private concerts during the first half of the seventeenth century is difficult to trace. The bulk of independent ensemble music may have been fantasias for viols (and/or keyboard), since over 130 examples remain.[5] The French and English fantasies reached the height of their popularity at about the same time. Although any direct influence is conjectural, it is a fact that the French were acquainted with English examples of the genre. In Mersenne, for instance, there is a fantasia *a* 6 for viols 'composed by an excellent viol player, English by nationality'.[6]

In 1610, 15 years after the first important set of English fantasias appeared, two collections were printed in France: the *Fantaisies à III, IV, V et VI parties* by Eustache Du Caurroy and the *Vingt-quatre fantaisies à quatre parties* by Charles Guillet. These were followed two years later by three *Fantaisies* by Claude Le Jeune included in the posthumous *Second livre des meslanges*. It is certainly possible that the fantasias by Du Caurroy, Guillet and Le Jeune may be considered as chamber music *and* as compositions designed for performance on the organ (see Ch. 18, p. 271). There must have been fantasias before the appearance of these collections, but only a few for lute and guitar are left. They date from the middle of the sixteenth century. Du Caurroy's and Guillet's collections form a sizeable body of highly competent, refined examples. How could they have been composed in a vacuum? This question also continues to plague us with respect to the *Hymnes de l'église* for organ by Titelouze and the *Pièces de Clavecin* by Chambonnières. Undoubtedly, an important link in the development of the viol fantasia in France was the very man responsible for the introduction of the large, six-stringed bass viol—Jacques Mauduit. He wrote fantasies which may have been part of the repertoire of his concerts at the Académie. Mersenne confirmed their existence but, unfortunately, did not preserve them for posterity as he did with so many other compositions.

The set of Du Caurroy includes 42 fantasias ranging in texture from *a* 3 to *a* 6. The four-part texture is favoured with almost half of the total number in this category. Du Caurroy's contemporaries held him in high esteem and would not have agreed with Charles Burney who found his fantasias 'extremely dry and destitute of idea'—a comment that tells us more about the late eighteenth century approach to the 'learned style' than it does about Du Caurroy's music.

For, 'learned' they are, but in the best sense of the word. Most of the fantasias are based on pre-composed material used as a cantus firmus or employed in paraphrase technique. In classical motet style, some fantasias break up the cantus firmus and let each fragment serve as the subject of a small fugal exposition; in others, the cantus firmus in long note values acts as a source for imitative material in the surrounding voices; in still others, the melodic shape of the cantus firmus shows no relationship to the free counterpoint exhibited in the other voices.

The *24 Fantaisies* by the Bruges composer Charles Guillet are pedagogical compositions designed to give those who would play them on the organ an opportunity to 'exercise their fingers on the keyboard' and in addition to have a means of understanding the church modes. Guillet's ordering and nomenclature of the modes is part Zarlino, part Glareanus. That is, the Zarlino disposition of the modes with the finals on C, D, E, F, G, A are given the Glareanus titles of Dorian through Aeolian.

There are two sets of 12 fantasias each. The music lacks the contrapuntal suppleness of Du Caurroy, and linear tension is often decreased through over-use of parallel motion between voices. Some ingenious structural devices are employed, however, such as the seven-note cantus firmus, in number 10 of the first set, that migrates in turn from the soprano, alto, tenor and bass. Number 12 of the first set resembles a variation canzona with eight short but highly contrasting sections all employing different mensuration signs.

The three fantasias of Claude Le Jeune are extended compositions that are generally less conservative than those of Du Caurroy and Guillet. Each fantasia is divided into two unequal parts. Each of the first two fantasias has a metre change and new material introduced into its second part. There are more modulations, some cross-relations, and the rhythmic activity is rather complex. The many examples of crossing parts, especially between the *cinquiesme* or *haute-contre* and the *taille*, suggest viols rather than a keyboard instrument as an appropriate medium of performance.

Composers of fantasias during the reign of Louis XIII, such as Jehan Henry, called Henry le Jeune (1560–1635), Antoine De Cousu (*c.* 1600–58), Etienne Moulinié (died *c.* 1670) and Nicholas Métru (died *c.* 1670), all wrote fantasias that, especially in the case of Henry and Moulinié, derived as much from the *air de cour* and the dance as from the older imitative style of writing. Jehan Henry, 'violon ordinaire du Roy', composed fantasias ranging in texture from *a 2* to *a 6*. Two of these compositions, apparently designed for court performances, are found in Mersenne ('Livre des Instruments', pp. 186–89 and 277). They are there to illustrate compositions well-suited for violins and cornetts respectively. Both are stylistically removed from

296

the viol fantasias discussed above. The heavy *a* 5 texture allows little breathing space in the music, and although points of imitation occur occasionally between two voices, there is none of the pervading imitation that characterizes the fantasias of the earlier generation.

Etienne Moulinié composed three *Fantaisies à quatre pour les violes* and included them in his *Cinquiesme Livre d'airs de cour* (Paris, 1639). Each fantasia is divided into short and highly contrasting sections, some imitative, some homophonic, but most stemming from the rhythms of the dance and the melodic formulae found in Moulinié's own court airs.

The 'golden age' of the French ensemble fantasia closes with the collection of 36 *Fantaisies à deux parties pour les violles* (Paris, 1642) by Nicolas Métru.[7] These short, unpretentious works conceal some masterful two-part writing, the more so because it appears so effortless. The fantasias are monothematic with the subject answered at the fifth and constantly set off by independent counterpoint. Some of the tunes have a fresh, almost folk-like sound that makes for clear tonal direction in the music.

Example 86
Metru: Selected 'subjects' from the Fantasias (after ed. of 1642).

By the time of Louis Couperin, the older concept of the imitative fantasias was already a thing of the past. Couperin's fantasias are given a figured bass and are binary structures that include French overture and dance measures.

At the end of the seventeenth century, any distinction that served earlier to delineate the genre is lost. For Brossard, *fantaisie* is synonymous with *capriccio* or even *sonata*; common to all three definitions is the idea of a creation 'according to the *fantaisie* of the composer, who, unfettered by general rules of counterpoint, or fixed numbers and types of measure, lets the fire of his genius dictate the change of measure and mood . . .'.

Dances constitute the earliest printed examples of ensemble music in France. The 12 volumes of *Danceries* brought out between 1530 and 1557 by Attaingnant, with their basses danses, branles, pavanes, galliards and tordions, form the bulk of this repertory. (See Reese, *Music in the Renaissance*, p. 563.) After Thoinot Arbeau's *Orchésographie* of 1588, which included some dance tunes as illustrative material, there was a hiatus in the printing of French dance music for ensemble until the *Terpsichore* of Praetorius in 1612. Yet, this was a period rich in the production of court ballets and a time that saw some of the better composer-performers of the Confrérie of Saint Julien accepted into the *violons du chambre du Roy*—musicians who would form the nucleus of the first generation of the *24 Violons* of the king.

Perhaps one reason for the dearth of printed collections of dance music in the early seventeenth century may be attributed to the compositional techniques of the members of the Confrérie. Like modern jazz musicians with their 'lead sheets' or 'fake books', many of the men simply worked from a dance melody to which the bass and inner voices were added, hopefully, in rehearsal. It is conceivable that much of the repertory served both the Confrérie and the court and was committed to memory much the same as the standard 'pop' tunes of today.

A small amount of the total repertory of the 'joueurs d'instruments tant haut que bas' of the Confrérie and the first generation of the *24 Violons* survives in the 312 dances and *airs de ballet* collected and harmonized by Michel Praetorius (1571–1621) and Pierre-Francisque Caroubel (died *c.* 1619) and printed at Wolfenbüttel in 1612 under the title of *Terpsichore Musarum*.

According to the dedicatory page, Antoine Emaraud, dancing master of Duke Friederich Ulrich of Brunswick, gave Praetorius the melodies for certain dances. Praetorius and Caroubel, a *violon du chambre* sojourning at Brunswick, were faced with the not inconsiderable task of harmonizing these tunes in four and five parts. Other dances were collected which had both melody and bass, and a few, identified in the collection by composer, had all parts extant.

Among the composers represented in this important source are Pierre de La Grène, Jean Perrichon, Claude Nyon, called La Fons or De La Font, Pierre de Beauchamps, Jean de La Motte, François Richomme, Jean Lebret and Caroubel, most of whom were members of both the Confrérie and musicians of the king's Chamber.[8]

The dances, arranged by category, give a good cross-section of the most popular dance types at the turn of the century. As found on the title page, the number of examples in each category is as follows: branles (21), other dances with special names (13), courantes (162), voltes (48), ballets (37), passamezzi (3), galliards (23) and doubles (4).

The characteristic features of the dances that will make up the constituent members of the Baroque dance suite clearly emerge from time to time. However, the courante category, by far the largest, illustrates how distant we are from a consistent courante 'type'. Along with the courantes that exploit the shift of accent from 2 to 3, thought of as a marked characteristic of courantes, there are some that closely resemble the canarie, some that borrow from the sarabande the rhythmic pattern ♩.♪♩ and even a few that are programmatic tone paintings (see, for example, 'Courante de Bataglia'). In spite of the inevitable monotony due to grouping so many dances together, the artistry of the harmonizers is evident on many pages. The inner voices often have a melodic integrity of their own, and the rhythmic counterpoint seldom allows the dances to become static.

For the second generation of the *24 Violons*, the richest source is the so-called manuscript of Cassel edited by Jules Ecorcheville as *Vingt Suites d'orchestre du XVIIe siècle Français*. The manuscript includes 200 pieces, grouped into 20 'suites' and collected between 1650 and 1670 by the Parisian composers Michel Mauzel (died 1676), Louis Constantin (*c.* 1585–1657), Michel Verdier (dates unknown) and De La Haye (dates unknown). It includes, in addition, music by Guillaume Dumanoir (1615–*c.* 1690), the 'Roi des Violons', who was also the conductor of the *24 Violons*. The music, taken from or modelled on dance music in French court ballets, formed part of *divertissements* at the court of Hesse.

The contents include 25 'Pièces Symphonique', 3 Ballets and 113 dances. As was true in the *Terpsichore*, more than half the dances are courantes with the sarabande next in line—a situation that parallels that of the Chambonnières harpsichord collection. Surprisingly, there is only one gigue and one minuet included.

Of interest is the fact that the allemandes are found among the 'symphonic pieces'—a clear indication, as Ecorcheville points out, that this dance had already lost much of its choreographic character and had, in effect, become a type of 'overture' to the suite. As early as 1636, Mersenne had observed that '. . . one is content today to play it [allemand] on instruments without dancing it . . . if it is not in a Ballet' ('Livre Second des Chants', *Harmonie Universelle*, p. 164).

Example 87 below gives the incipit from a typical allemande found in the Cassel Manuscript. It lacks an upbeat, and its wide melodic profile and dotted rhythms have an affinity with the type of overture that had already been in use to introduce court ballets.

A manuscript copied by Philidor in 1705 and now at Versailles (Ms 168) probably provides a good cross-section of some of the reper-

Example 87
Allemande from the Cassel Ms (after Ecorcheville).

tory of the *Ecurie*. It bears the long and descriptive title: *Partition de Plus-Marches et batteries de tambour tant françoises qu'étrangères avec les airs de fifre et de hautbois à 3 et 4 parties et Plusieurs Marches de Timballes et de Trompettes à cheval avec l'air du Carrousel en 1686. Et les appels et fanfares de troupes pour la chasse.*

Represented in the collection are compositions by some of the best performers and composers in the service of the king. Three members of the Philidor dynasty are included: *viz.*, the copiest himself, André Danican Philidor ('L'aîné'), his brother Jacques ('Le cadet') and his nephew Pierre. In addition, Martin Hotteterre, Delalande and the oboist of the *mousquetaires*, Desjardins.

This is obviously a collection of *pièces d'occasion*, and many of the compositions bear inscriptions that indicate the occasion. For example, the 'Air de Trompettes, Timballes et hautbois' by Lully was composed 'by order of the King for the carrousel of Monseigneur, in the year 1686'. It is a dance suite composed of prelude, minuet, gigue and gavotte. The Prelude is scored *a* 9 (5 trumpets, 4 oboes) although, because of massive doublings, the texture is actually much thinner. In the year 1672 the king also ordered from Lully an 'Air de hautbois' based on the *Folies d'espagne*. That this type of 'occasional' work was not always to the taste of Lully is implied by Philidor's marginal comments regarding the '4ᵉ Air des hautbois fait par M. de Luly'. 'Philidor', he wrote, 'composed the *parties*, M de Luly having wished not to have to do it'.

Two additional sources that include dance music of the seventeenth century are the *Pièces pour le violon à quatre parties* printed by Ballard (Paris, 1665),[9] and the Gustaf Düben collection found today in the University Library at Uppsala (*Instrumental musik i handshrift* 409).[10]

Ballard's edition includes music from the *Ballet du Roy dansé à Fontainebleau* in 1664, several *Branles de Monsieur Brular* that differ considerably from the same titles in the Cassel Manuscript, some independent dances and two short dance suites both in B♭-Major.

Gustaf Düben (1624–90) copied 206 dances from the repertory of the *24 Violons* for performance at the court of Queen Kristina of Sweden (reigned 1644–54). By far the most popular dances in the collection are courantes (75), allemandes (37) and sarabandes (28). About 16 composers are represented, most of whom were active at the courts of Louis XIII and Louis XIV.

An impressive amount of instrumental ensemble and orchestral music is included in the 28 volumes of Marc-Antoine Charpentier's *Meslanges*. Much of this music serves as preludes or overtures to motets, and much has a liturgical function: verses of hymns, symphonies for alternating Mass movements, a *Messe pour plusieurs instruments* and symphonies for consecrations and street processionals.

There is also a category of instrumental secular music composed for the more than 25 stage works that Charpentier wrote for the private *fêtes* of the Duchesse de Guise, for Molière's troupe at the Comédie Française, for the Latin plays of the Jesuit Collège Louis-le-Grand and for the Académie Royale de Musique. In addition, there are a few independent compositions including overtures, marches, minuets, a fanfare for two trumpets, symphonies, Noëls and a *Concert pour quatre parties de violes.*[11]

It is questionable whether or not Charpentier actually composed the *Sonate à huit instruments* that carries his name in ink placed by a later hand on a seventeenth century manuscript (Vm⁷4813). It is an ensemble sonata in part-books that is scored for two flutes, two violins, bass viol, bass violin, harpsichord and theorbo. Internal stylistic evidence, more than the fact that Charpentier never scored for theorbo in the *Meslanges*, casts doubt on the authenticity of the assignation. The *Sonate* includes two *récits*: one for bass viol, the other for bass violin. Although an impressive orchestrator with a refined sense of instrumental colour and sonority, Charpentier almost never indulged in the empty display of virtuosities on solo instruments exhibited by these *récits*.

The independent ensemble and orchestra music of Charpentier is a good marriage of elements from both the Italian and French styles. The continued use of viols in ensemble writing, often in conjunction with violins, is French. So is the conservative writing for the first violins. But the predominantly four-part texture of the orchestral pieces and the exploitation of *concertato* effects are Italian.

The set of compositions used during the Corpus Christi processionals for the pauses at street altars (*reposoirs*) combines French overture, verses of hymns in archaic cantus firmus style and, in two instances, an *Allemande grave*. Here again is documentation of the allemande as a 'symphonic piece' stripped of its choreographic past. Significantly, as Hitchcock points out, there are no titled allemandes among the 110 dances of Charpentier which include minuets, marches, gigues, sarabandes, gavottes, chaconnes, bourrées, loures, galliards, passacailles, passepieds, courantes and canaries.

The 10 ensemble Noëls conceal an artful counterpoint and freshness of harmony that transcend their unpretentious charm. In the setting for violins of 'Or Nous dites Marie' (No. 5), Charpentier juxtaposes two strikingly different harmonizations of the same short melodic phrase. The use of mutes for the lower strings in the second harmonization adds to the contrast (see Example 88).

The *Concert pour quatre parties de violes* is a six-movement ensemble dance suite in the order: prelude I, prelude II, sarabande 'en rondeau', gigue 'angloise', gigue 'françoise' and passacaille. The opening prelude is a throwback to the earlier style of the ensemble

Example 88
Charpentier: *Extract from an ensemble* noel, *'Or Nous dites Marie'* (*after the* Meslanges, *vol.* v).

fantasia, and the second prelude resembles an allemande. The two contrasting gigues foreshadow the *goûts-réunis* of Couperin's *Concerts Royaux*. No figured bass is provided and, due to the careful spacing of parts, none is needed.

Among the most imaginative and apparently popular of the many *Symphonies pour le souper du Roy* are those of Delalande which exist in three manuscript copies (1703, 1727 and 1745). The copy of 1703, made by Philidor for the Comte de Toulouse, includes 10 suites taken in part from the ballets and *divertissements* composed by Delalande between 1682 and 1700. The order of dances appears to be random, and there is no attempt to guard a tonal unity in the suites. The title page helps document the division of labour between the

Grande Bande and the *Petits Violons* in asserting that these symphonies were performed 'ordinairement au souper du Roy' by 'la Troupe des petits violons'.

The copy of 1727 includes 18 suites, again with a random mixture of overture, prelude, titled dances, characteristic dances and free compositions such as 'caprices ou fantaisies'. Included at the end of the volume are four *Symphonies des Noëls* which, according to information found in the manuscript, were 'played in the King's Chapel on Christmas night'.

The third copy of 1745 is a true manuscript *de luxe* bearing the title *Simphonies de M. De La Lande* 'qu'il faisoit éxecuter tous les 15 jours pendant le souper du Louis XIV et Louis XV'. This collection, although based on that of 1727, carefully orders the suites and even numbers the 'souper' for which each suite was performed. It includes some examples of outdoor music 'in which are mixed six Airs de Trompettes from the *concert* given on the Versailles canal' (Suite 7).

Suites six to eight are entitled *Caprices* or *Caprices ou Fantaisies*. These imaginative works are a classic illustration of the Brossard definition of a fantasia as a composition 'created according to the *fantaisie* of the composer'. They are free symphonic pieces divorced from any specific dances; each Caprice has over-all key unity and reflects the sonorities that result from placing solo violin and oboe in apposition with the *tous*.

The seventh suite, 'which the King often asked for', is divided into five movements designated only by tempo indications moving from slow to fast: 1. 'Un peu lent'; 2. 'Doucement'; 3. 'Gratieusement'; 4. 'Gayement'; 5. 'Vivement'. The final Caprice (Suite 8) is made up of a series of 'airs' and includes as the second 'air' a set of free variations. The variations increase in complexity and, contrary to normal procedures, the *tous* sections appear more complex than the solos.

Chapter 20

―»» «««―

Instrumental Ensemble and Orchestral Music of the Early Eighteenth Century

The first half of the eighteenth century saw such a variety of instrumental ensemble and orchestral music in France that exact classification of genres poses a very knotty problem. It was a period of experimentation and a period that witnessed the rapid absorption of elements from the Italian sonata and concerto, by then in co-existence with the traditional French forms of overture and dance. Added to this was the penchant, particularly French, for descriptive or programmatic music which by the eighteenth century had been virtually elevated to an aesthetic dogma. It was, therefore, natural to expect a transfer to independent ensemble or orchestral music of the descriptive symphonies found in the *tragédie lyrique* and in the oratorio and cantata. Even Rousseau, certainly no partisan of French music, deprecates the 'pure *symphonie* in which one seeks only to show off the instruments' (*Dictionnaire*, p. 452). He quotes with obvious approbation the famous words of Fontenelle that had already become a slogan: 'Sonate, que me veux-tu?' ('Sonata, what do you want of me?').

The problem of classification is further confounded by the numerous performance possibilities and the indefinite terminology which fails to differentiate between such contrasting genres as sonata, suite, concerto and symphony. The head spins, and the mind rebels at the mixture of genres found in such titles as *Simphonies contenant six suittes en trio* (Dornel), *Sonade et Suite de Simphonie en Trio* (Couperin), *Concerto de simphonie* (Corrette), *Concerto de violon avec chant* (Mondonville), *Livre de Symphonie qui contient deux Suites* (Mouret) and *Suites de Concert de Simphonie en Trio* (Aubert). These titles are confusing to the modern reader, addicted as he is to the later eighteenth and nineteenth century definitions of 'symphony' or 'concerto'. However, the difficulties are more imagined than actual if we remember that a source as late as the Diderot *Encyclopédie* defines 'symphonie' as 'all instrumental music whether it be compositions designated for instruments, such as sonatas and concertos, or whether

304

it be those works where the instruments are mixed with the voice as in our operas . . .'.

This chapter considers only ensemble music that was designed to be performed by more than one person on a part; that is, there is every indication in the titles or in the *avertissements* that this was desired. At the same time, however, the possibility of a performance by one person on a part must not be ruled out; indeed it is often impossible to tell which mode of performance was desired by the composer.

The next chapter, on the contrary, considers those compositions that are restricted in principle at least to one performer on a part.

It must be emphasized, however, that this large classification is in no way meant to be an air-tight organization in view of the performance practices of the period. In works described in their titles or sub-titles, for example, as having been composed for 'violons, flûtes & hautbois', we may read in the *avertissement* that the entire collection 'can be performed with just one treble and one bass instrument', as in the case with Montéclair's *Sérénade ou Concert* of 1697. At the same time, compositions that would seem to be appropriate for only solo instruments were occasionally performed with a multiple instrumental doubling of the solo lines. Why else would 'M. de L. T.' in his important 'Dissertation sur la Musique Italienne & Françoise', which appeared in the *Mercure galant* of November 1713, have felt it necessary to emphasize that Italian solo violin sonatas 'must only be played by a single violin, which is then free to arch the line and show off its brilliance as much as it pleases; they (the sonatas) would become very confused if the same part were to be performed by several instruments . . .'. This carries a hint of admonition for what was, in all likelihood, a common performance practice. Therefore, it is clear that our classification is artificial and designed only to deal with a bulk of music in some systematic manner.

In order to give greater focus to the music that concerns us in this chapter, we may establish two sub-classifications based on texture and instrumentation.

1. Compositions in the first group are thinly scored (*a 2* or *a 3*) and are designed for small ensemble performance with perhaps more than one instrument on a part. There is usually some latitude of choice in the instrumentation and some use of *concertato* effects between solo instruments and *tous*.

2. Compositions in the second group were conceived for orchestral performance and have predominantly *a 4* texture (at least for the *tous*). They have less latitude in the choice of instruments.

There is also a 'shadow zone' of compositions for small ensemble that derive from collections originally scored for one or two solo instruments. Through the *avertissements* of solo harpsichord collections

(Dieupart, Le Roux, Couperin and others) and of compositions for one or two viols (Marais), we learn that some or, in some cases, all the pieces may be *mises en concert* with a list of suggested instruments supplied. The only problem, it would seem, was 'to know how to make a choice between each of the instruments' (Marais, *Avertissement*, Book III). Because these works derive from solo literature, and, indeed much of the time the solo original is all that we have, they are discussed in the following chapter.

Properly belonging to the first category of ensemble pieces with more than one instrument on a part are the many collections which according to their title pages were composed for violins, flutes and the like. Much of this music is in trio texture which was favoured for instrumental ensembles from the late years of the seventeenth century to the 1730's.

It would be helpful to further subdivide this category into those collections that indicate specific instrumentation and those that merely suggest appropriate instruments. Without a complete survey of each individual piece in any given collection, however, this is untenable. French composers of the period were not bound by what their title pages or subtitles suggest. In Dornel's *Livre de Simphonies*, for example, we read that the six suites were composed for flutes, violins and oboes, yet it is very rare that any specific instrumentation is indicated. In contrast, Montéclair's *Sérénade ou Concert*, whose titles often give specific instrumentation, adds instruments not found in the titles (trumpet, *Tambour de Basque*, etc.).

Among the late seventeenth century works in this first category, we may place the *Pièces en Trio pour les Flûtes, Violons et dessus de Viole* by Marin Marais (Paris, 1692). Included are a total of six suites scored simply for *Dessus* I, *Dessus* II and a *Basse continue* thereby allowing the performer to choose his treble instruments. Each suite is introduced by a prelude, but each is terminated by a different type of composition chosen from a character piece or a dance. The dance components within the six suites are sarabandes, loures, gigues, gavottes, minuets, branles and rigaudons. In addition, there are some 'free' forms such as caprices and fantasias as well as some descriptive pieces ('La Marienne', 'La Bagatelle', etc.). The trios show little evidence of Italian influence and stem more from the note-against-note style of the trios in Lully's operas. Even the fantasias found in five of the six suites are predominantly homophonic after an initial point of imitation. On the other hand, there is rich harmony, and the frequent crossing of voices helps counteract the static rhythmic organization.

At the turn of the century, there are several collections of trios scored for violins, flutes and oboes and conceived of as a type of *Gebrauchsmusik*. Typical of such a collection is Montéclair's *Sérénade ou Concert, Divisé en trois suites pour les Violons, Flûtes &*

Hautbois (Paris, 1697). We are informed that the set includes pieces 'suitable for dancing' and, as mentioned earlier, the entire collection could be reduced to just a treble and bass instrument.

In spite of the vagueness of the subtitle with regard to instrumentation, each suite is cleverly built around a particular instrumental colour and mood. Indeed, the rather thin musical substance of the suites is rendered quite tolerable because of Montéclair's exploitation of marked and sometimes quite sudden contrasts.

The first suite revels in the typically French 'trio des hautbois' contrasting with a *tous*. It includes some trumpet fanfares as well as an amusing two-part fantasia that imitates C-Major fife flourishes. The second suite, subtitled 'Air tendre', is night music filled with the poetry of flutes and violins. An extensive 'Sommeil' with solo sections for violin, bass viol and bass violin frames the suite. Musettes and a 'Tambour de Basque' colour the third suite, 'Air Champêtre".

Similar in style although with less attention paid to contrasts of sonorities are the seven suites included in the *Pièces en Trio pour les Violons, Flûtes et Hautbois* (1700) by Michel de La Barre (1675–1743). Brossard described the composer as 'the most excellent player of the transverse flute in Paris, and the one responsible for creating the vogue for this instrument' (*Catalogue*, p. 352). There is little evidence from the music, however, that La Barre sought to exploit the technical limits of his instrument or, indeed, considered the flute lines, when indicated, as any different from those accorded the violins or oboes.

Louis-Antoine Dornel (1685–1765) brought out three instrumental collections (1709, 1711, 1713) of which the first, a *Livre de Simphonies,* is of some interest. It includes six suites *en trio* for flutes, violins, oboes, 'etc.', as well as a *Sonate en Quatuor*. Perhaps reflecting the background of the organist,[1] Dornel's suites and the sonata give the illusion of being more polyphonic than they actually are. Initial points of imitation are sustained over a longer time span than was normal, and there is some attractive rhythmic counterpoint, but inevitably, the upper voices in approaching a cadence will fall into place in parallel motion. More important is the influence stemming from Corelli. Chains of suspensions, circles of 5ths, series of diatonically harmonized first inversion chords are evident. Unfortunately, Dornel's mediocre melodic gifts rob these procedures of any real character and reduce them to formulae.

Only the Prelude to the sixth suite gives specific instrumentation ('flûtes allemandes et violons'). The suites were printed in part books, but the *Sonate en Quatuor*, found only in the part book labelled 'Basse Continue', was printed in score which may indicate that it is to be performed by solo instruments. It is divided into four sections approximating the SFSF ordering of the Italian church sonata. The third movement is broadly paced and sarabande-like. Its many stops

307

and starts show how Dornel, in common with many of his contemporaries, had not learned how to use, or perhaps chose not to use, the Corelli vocabulary to allow expansion rather than contraction of a musical idea.

François Couperin composed 14 *Concerts* which were performed at Versailles in 1714 and 1715 perhaps to brighten the deepening shadows of Louis xiv's last years. The first four were published in 1722 together with the third book of *Pièces de Clavecin* and bear the title, *Concerts Royaux*; the remaining ten were brought out two years later and constitute the major portion of *Les Goûts réunis*.

The 1722 set is printed on two staves as though originally planned for harpsichord. Rarely is specific instrumentation supplied, but Couperin informs us that the pieces are 'suitable not only for harpsichord, but also for Violin, Flute, Oboe, Viol and Bassoon'. Helpfully, he even supplied the names of his musicians in the 'petits Concerts de Chambre' that took place on Sundays before the king: Duval (violin), Philidor (oboe and bassoon), Alarius (viol) and Dubois (oboe and bassoon).[2]

Mellers' suggestion of 'two stringed instruments, two wind instruments and continuo, the strings and winds playing either together or alternately' provides a practical solution to the problem of the choice of instruments if we remember to seek out the 'affection' of each piece. In seventeenth and eighteenth century France in particular, instrumental colour could be as carefully compartmentalized as the choice of certain dances or the use of certain keys.

A study of the textures of the *Concerts Royaux* coupled with an examination of those few places where specific instrumentation is given strongly suggests the use of some sort of *concertato* principle. The clearest example is in the extended 'Courante à l'italienne' from *Concert* iv. Each of the two sections of the binary dance includes a thickening of texture from *a* 2 to *a* 3. Except for an occasional full-voiced chord at cadence points, the sections in *a* 3 texture are consistently maintained with individual lines clearly differentiated. At the first occurrence of the *a* 3 texture in Part A, Couperin indicated 'viole', perhaps referring to a treble viol for the upper melodic line or, conceivably, for a *concertino* group of solo viols. This being the case, the *a* 2 sections of the dance would then be performed by the full group. The fact that this suggestion of *concertato* performance occurs in a composition 'à l'italienne' is perhaps not fortuitous.

A similar possibility exists in 'Echos' from *Concert* ii with specific solo sections indicated for one 'viole' and one 'clavecin' playing together or 'viole seule' in apposition to the harpsichord. The Prelude to *Concert* iii includes a middle part (*contre partie*) for viol or for 'violin, flute, oboe, etc.' The Prelude and the 'Sarabande Grave' from the same suite contain the thickest texture of any of the *Concerts*. Only in the *contre partie* is the linear writing consistently maintained. The upper and lower staves are continually dividing, suggesting the possibility of more than one instrument on a part.

The four *Concerts* all begin with a prelude, usually of a serious nature and resembling the opening movement of a Corelli church sonata. A series of freely disposed dances follows. These include allemandes, courantes, sarabandes, gigues, minuets, gavottes, chaconnes, rigaudons, and a forlane. French and Italian elements are constantly juxtaposed. In *Concert* ii, the prelude, labelled 'gracieusement', is a French dance; the Allemande 'fuguée', which follows with its bass 'travaillée toujours', is Italian; the 'Air Tendre', with its expressive *port de voix*, *coulés* and cross-relations (see Measure 13 of Part B) is the quintessence of a French air; the 'Air Contrefugué' and the concluding 'Echos' pair national styles in a similar manner.

Over-all, however, the four *Concerts Royaux* are basically French. Much of their source material is rooted in the *Pièces de Clavecin*. Their dissonance comes from French ornamentation and linear clashes rather than from suspensions or sequences of 7th chords. The Sarabandes from *Concerts* iii and iv, with their depth of feeling achieved through a noble melodic line, elegant part writing and strong dissonant clashes, go 'far beyond the normal confines of entertainment music' (Mellers).

The ten *Concerts* (v to xiv) that comprise the greater part of the *Goûts réunis* are numbered as though they were a continuation of the *Concerts Royaux*, but exhibit many differences from the latter. Added to the typical French suite dances that make up most of the movements of the *Concerts Royaux* are many descriptive pieces and independent *symphonies* drawn from a much broader milieu.

Except for certain portions of *Concert* viii, 'Dans le goût théâtral', the texture of these *Concerts* is more consistently *a 2* and the writing, more idiomatic for instruments and somewhat less harpsichordic. The scope and development of these *Concerts* are also greater than in the first group. *Concert* xii and *Concert* xiii are clearly specified for two viols 'or other instruments of the same pitch'. In fact, after stating that the harpsichord or theorbo could be used as accompaniment in *Concert* xii, Couperin recommends two viols 'with nothing more' for the best performance. Perhaps to emphasize this, he eliminates the figured bass after the prelude for the only time in the *Concerts*. Other than for these two *Concerts* and a 'plainte' for viols in *Concert* x, no instrumentation is suggested.

In addition to achieving a 'goût réuni' by the juxtaposition of the two styles in a series of dances, Couperin composed entire *Concerts* to illustrate a certain 'goût'. Thus, *Concert* viii in microcosm contains the *symphonies* usually found in a Lully opera. A fine French overture and a 'Grande Ritournelle' open the *Concert* and are followed by a cross-section of those *airs de danse* that might be found in an operatic *divertissement*. The next *Concert*, entitled 'Ritratto dell'Amore', includes some lively genre pieces ('Le je-ne-sçais quoy', 'L'et Coetera') and a composition called simply 'La Vivacité' which, with its fire, its driving rhythms and its economy of thematic material, is a clear attempt to imitate the closing movement of a Corelli or a Vivaldi violin sonata.

In some compositions, Couperin combined Italian and French styles. The 'Sarabande mesurée' from *Concert* VI, for example, is the only sarabande of the entire collection of *Concerts* that bears the typically Italian metre signature of 3/4 (all the remainder are 3). Its use of triplet figures in the bass line comes dangerously close at times to converting the dance into an Italian sicilienne. French is the profuse ornamentation which results in considerable rhythmic freedom between the parts.

A similar, if somewhat more startling, example is the allemande from *Concert* XI. It begins like one of the 'Allemande-Overture' types in which choreographic origins are lost in a maze of dotted rhythms that give to the piece a true dramatic mien. Suddenly, the dotted rhythms give way to even 16th notes, and we are catapulted into a circle of 5ths with the string figurations typical of pure Corelli—all this within nine short measures.

Could Couperin have entertained second thoughts about the uninhibited nature of his Franco-Italian alliance in this allemande? He followed it immediately with a 'Seconde Allemande, plus légère' which poses no problems. The situation reminds us of the 8th Ordre from the *Pièces de Clavecin* in which the powerfully dramatic allemande, 'La Raphaéle', that introduces the *ordre* is followed by a second allemande, 'L'Ausonières', with the performance direction 'légèrement'.

Concert XIV, which closes the series, is one of Couperin's best realizations of *goûts-réunis*. The musical language seems natural to the composer without the conceit of mimicry or a self-conscious imitation. French ornaments and melodic elegance coalesce with Italian formal direction and a greater sense of development. The whole is cast in the four movement scheme (SFSF) of the Italian sonata. The final movement is a busy 'Fugueté' which, in the manner of many closing movements of Corelli, Vivaldi and Handel sonatas, sacrifices fugal integrity to an over-all vigour and kinetic drive. The fugal process itself is fragmented and even abandoned in the wake of episodic, concerto-like passages that assume considerable importance.

Couperin's *Concerts* stand at the very pinnacle of the chamber music for small ensemble that allows for the greatest latitude in performance possibilities. At the opposite end of the ensemble spectrum are those collections written in the late 1720's and early 1730's that, because of their more 'symphonic' use of specific instruments, inch the small ensemble closer to an orchestral concept and thereby form a transition between our two categories.

Representative of these collections are the *Suites de Symphonies* by Jean-Joseph Mouret and the *Concerts de Symphonies* by Jacques Aubert and Etienne Mangean.

Dating from 1729, Mouret's *Suites* are carefully scored with unusual attention paid to combinations of timbres. The first suite carries the title *Fanfares pour les Trompettes, Violons et Hautbois* and is written for trumpet in D, violins I and II, oboes, bassoon, bass and timpani. Trio texture is maintained throughout, and violins and oboes generally double the upper lines. The suite has four movements, the first of which has achieved great popularity as the 'theme song' of 'Masterpiece Theatre'.

The second suite, *Symphonies pour les Violons, les Hautbois et les Cors de Chasse*, was performed before the king at the Hôtel de Ville (*Mercure*, October 1729), and in Viollier's words is a 'joyeuse musique de table'.[3] It includes six binary dances, three with doubles. The instrumentation, which is clearly indicated, exploits the colour contrast between horns and strings.

The *Suite de Concert de Simphonie en trio pour les Violons, Flûtes et Hautbois* (1730) by Jacques Aubert (1689–1753) includes five suites and is the first item listed by Barry Brook as an 'antecedent' of the French symphony.[4] The preface informs us that these pieces 'may be performed with a large group (*à grand choeur*) like Concertos'.

The *Concert de Symphonie pour les Violons, Flûtes et Hautbois* of 1735 by Etienne Mangean (died 1756) includes two suites with precise instructions concerning the employment of the instruments. In effect, because of this precision we can perhaps hypothesize some of the performance possibilities in the innumerable *Concerts en trio* where little or no information is found regarding exact scoring. Some dances are scored *a 3* for specific soloists; others are labelled 'tous'.

We may consider Aubert's suggestion of performing his *Concerts de Symphonie* 'à grand choeur comme les Concertos' as an appropriate point of departure for our discussion of ensemble music composed for larger instrumental forces. In 1730 Aubert was obviously thinking of 'concerto' in the sense of the original Italian meaning of the word; that is, 'to work or join together' rather than in the sense of the original Latin term (*concertare*) which means 'to compete, to contend'.[5]

In France, the type of concerto that places one instrument or a group of solo instruments 'in competition' with a full group was rather late in appearing as a distinct genre. In his *Dictionnaire*, Rousseau gave both meanings of the word. The first, and more general meaning, is a

'*Simphonie* composed to be performed by an entire orchestra'; for the more particular meaning, Rousseau gave a succinct summary of the *ritornello* principle as applied to a solo instrument and *tutti*.

It is clear that after 1750, the Italian concept of 'symphony' and the generalized definition of 'concerto', given above by Rousseau, merge. Thus, Rousseau, in his 'Concerto' article for the *Encyclopédie*, added that 'as for those [concertos] where all play together (*en choeur*) and where no instrument solos, Italians also call them *Symphonies*'.

As early as 1727 the Italian expatriate Michele Mascitti (1664–1760) gave the first clear models for the Italian concerto in Paris with his *Sonate a Violino solo e Basso e quattro Concerti a sei....* The 'quattro Concerti' were numbered IX to XII and thus considered by the composer as a simple extension of his first eight sonatas. The four concertos, however, are clearly distinct in every way from the sonatas and are genuine *concerti grossi* scored for a concertino of two violins and a 'Basso del Concertino' plus another violin, viola and bass to make up the *ripieno*.

Although they belong in the category of music for small ensemble, the *VI Concertos pour 5 Flûtes traversières ou autres instruments sans basse* (Opus XV) by the prolific Joseph Bodin de Boismortier also appeared in 1727. The subtitle adds the helpful information that the concertos 'may also be played with a Bass', and a figured bass is included in the part book for the *Flauto quinto*. Of interest in the history of the concerto in France is the fact that all the concertos are cast in three movements; three are SFS, and the remainder are FSF. Further, much of the time the music is organized in alternating solo and *tutti* groups. The thematic material is, however, more French than Italian. An occasional theme that begins in the style of a Corelli or Torelli often reaches a cadence point before the forward drive has been consolidated.

In 1728 the *VI Concertos pour les Flûtes, Violons ou Hautbois, avec la Basse Chiffrée pour le Clavecin*, Opus III, by Michel Corrette was printed. These may rightfully be considered the first concertos in France written by a native Frenchman that conform to the typical features of the Italian concerto. Perhaps the conventionalized title of 'Flûtes, Violons ou Hautbois' may be partly responsible for the neglect of these works in their role of the first French *concerti grossi*. As such, this emphasizes the need in French music especially of looking beyond the title into each work itself. All six concertos follow an Allegro-Adagio-Allegro ordering of movements. Each has a clearly indicated *concertino* composed of either two or three 'Flauti e Violoncello obbligato'. Three of the concertos (I, III, V) cast the Allegro in binary form with each section normally repeated; the even-numbered concertos employ some adaptation of the *ritornello* principle systematized over 20 years before in the Opus VIII *Concerti Grossi* of Giuseppe

Torelli (1658–1709), published in 1709. Typical is Concerto II 'con Tre Fluti e Violoncello obbligato' whose opening Allegro has a total of four *tuttis* with the Dominant minor and relative major keys chosen in addition to the Tonic key. The Adagio movement, in typically Corelli fashion, ends on a Phrygian cadence.

For the most productive part of his long life, Corrette was involved in some fashion with the concerto, and although the musical interest is not always commensurate with the imaginative formats, it is curious that these works have been ignored in studies of Baroque instrumental music.[6] The *VI Concerti a sei Strumenti* (Opus XXVI) of 1756 advertises itself by its title as being scored for harpsichord or organ obbligato, three violins, flute, viola and violoncello. The fact that most of the time the first violin doubles the right hand of the keyboard instrument or adds nonmelodic chord outlines, serves to remind us that Corrette's Opus XXV, presumably composed 14 years before the six concertos, comprises *Sonates pour le Clavecin avec accompagnement de violon ou viole*. However, in parts of Concerto III and in much of Concerto VI the keyboard acts as a legitimate obbligato instrument sharing its solo material with the first and second violins. The thin keyboard writing, with its persistent use of the Alberti bass, is much in the character of the *style galant*.

Example 89
Corrette: Extract from Allegro of Concerto VI 'a sei strumenti' (after ed. of 1742).

We learn from the *Avertissement* that, with the exception of Concerto III, all may be performed on the organ 'sans symphonie'. Corrette carefully specifies the organ registration: '. . . one must play the Allegros on the *grand jeu*; the Adagios on the Flutes; and the Solos on the *Cornet de Récit*'.

Corrette also composed a series of concertos in simulated 'champêtre' style (*VI Concertos pour musette ou vielles composés sur les vaudevilles les plus connus*, Opus VIII) and three *Concertos de Noëls* for three treble instruments and bass with material drawn from popular Noëls and even Gregorian themes (*Christe redemptor*, for example). In addition, there are the 25 *Concertos comiques* for various instrumental combinations which range in time from 1732 to 1760 and are examples of 'descriptive concertos.' Many of these works are of a popular nature and some even employ such rustic instruments as musettes and hurdy-gurdies.[7] The concertos seem to have been composed with the theatre in mind and at least one of them, 'L'Allure', was heard at the *Opéra comique* in 1732. For the last of these, 'La Prise de Port-Mahon', Corrette wrote in his *Avertissement*: 'In a *grand concert* it is necessary to add Trumpets and Drums (*Timbales et Tambour*) in order to render the concerto well. The composer will consider it a pleasure to supply the parts for Trumpet and *Timbale*'. Such a work would have surely resembled a *grande symphonie* which, as defined by Rousseau, needed only two additional instrumental parts (normally the *taille* and *quinte*) between the treble and bass instruments. This gives the orchestral music of Corrette some significance as a transition between concerto and symphony in France.

From the above information, it is clear that the role of wind instruments (especially the transverse flute) in the history of the concerto in France must not be underestimated. In about 1735, Jacques-Christophe Naudot (*d.* 1762) introduced the flute concerto to France with his *Six Concertos en sept parties pour une flûte traversière*. The 'sept parties' refers to the accompanying parts of three violins, one viola and two basses. All six concertos are in a FSF movement scheme and all make use of the *ritornello* principle. Boismortier, in ten publications following his Opus XV of 1727, made use of one or more flutes in his concertos, and in the 1730's Corrette and others composed many chamber concertos for flutes with other instruments.

Yet curiously, French composers seemed reluctant to engage in writing concertos in the Italian style. Jacques Aubert's first book of *Concerto à quatre Violons, Violoncelle et Basse Continue*, Opus XVII was not published until seven years after Corrette's Opus III (Aubert's Book II, bearing the same title, was printed in 1739). This is quite a change from the absorption rate of the Italian sonata, for Couperin's first two sonatas date from 1692, and François Duval's solo violin sonatas were published in 1705.

The advance publicity for Aubert's first book appeared in the *Mercure* of November 1734 in which the author, ignorant of the Opus III of Corrette, wrote that Aubert's concertos would be 'the first works of this genre to have left the pen of a Frenchman'. The concertos were printed in six part books: violins I, II, III and IV, violoncello and *basso organo*. All are in the three movement form of the Italian concerto with the middle movement an Aria in three of the concertos and a *gavotta* in those remaining. In two instances (Concertos I and v) the final Allegro is a *minuetto*.

The first violin is given the burden of the solo passages while the remaining violins act as *ripieno* instruments. Although Aubert was conservative in his handling of the solo instrument when compared with his Italian contemporaries, the influence of Torelli (see especially Torelli's Opus VIII) and Corelli is fairly obvious. Mechanical rhythmic pulsations, circles of 5ths and typical Italian violin figurations spring from every page. The opening Allegros generally begin *tutti e forte* with unison passages. The opening *tutti* of Concerto II, indeed, is arranged in two or four measure phrases that repeat exactly, much in the manner of the early Italian symphonies. The music has gestic drive and a wide melodic profile. Its *tutti* themes are constructed in short, contrasting motifs with clearly differentiated rhythms that allow for motivic expansion or contraction in subsequent *tutti* or solo groups.

The only French concerto composer that could seriously rival the Italian school is Jean-Marie Leclair (1697–1764) who was dubbed by Blainville as the 'Corelli of France' (*L'Esprit de l'art musical*, p. 88). Leclair, who had been a violin student of Giovanni Battista Soumis in Turin, was a featured performer at the *Concert Spirituel* between 1728 and 1736 as well as the *Premier Symphonist du Roi*.

Leclair composed two sets of violin concertos, each set including six concertos. The first book, *Concerto a 3 Violini alto e basso, Per organo e violoncello* (Opus VII), was printed in 1736; the second book (Opus X), in 1744. All but two concertos are in the typical concerto format of three movements. Although all were written for a *violino principale*, number three of Opus VII may be performed 'on the transverse flute or oboe'.

The influence of Torelli and Vivaldi is very much in evidence, but here, as compared with Aubert or Corrette, the violin solo is a real challenge to the performer. The second book especially exploits the solo instrument. The finale of Concerto v has a 72-measure solo, and the Allegro of the same concerto reaches the seventh position. Many concertos of both sets include dazzling passages in double stops and difficult arpeggio figures.

As in Vivaldi, some of the Allegro movements suffer from sequential patterns that are too long and too abundant, but in general the thematic material is to the point and adaptable for the greatest motivic concentration. Moreover, in this music there is more than a skilful parroting of Italian models. In essence, the Italianisms contribute to the total architecture and to surface gesture, but the inner core of the music contains the strong personal stamp of Leclair. The composer's harmonic language is bolder than most of his French contemporaries, and some of his key relationships between movements are more adventurous than, for example, those in the concertos of Torelli. The slow middle movements are usually cast in relative keys, but in Concerto v (Book I) in A-Minor, the slow movement, a *sicilienne*, is in F-Major which permitted the composer the luxury of an expressive five-measure modulatory Adagio designed to restore tonal equilibrium. The same concerto has an extended *tutti* section in B flat Major, the key of the Neapolitan, in its opening movement.

Arthur Hutchings has mentioned Leclair's treatment of his motivic material by an almost constant extension and variation technique.[8] At times the solo is clearly a variation of the *tutti*; at times a motivic fragment extracted from the main *tutti* accompanies independent melodic material, thus modestly suggesting the beginnings of the 'obbligato technique' that reached fruition in the symphonies of Joseph Haydn.

The variety with which Leclair approached *tutti* and solo rivalry attracts attention. Some concertos are clearly cast in a *ritornello* form with a constant alternation of *tutti* and solo; others rival Vivaldi in their use of solo interpretation of the *tutti* sections. In the Allegro of Concerto II (Book II), it is the solo that rounds off the main theme (Example 90a); in the aria from Concerto IV (Book II), the solo constantly interrupts the *tutti* to add its own commentary as in Example 90b below.

Example 90
Leclair: Solo penetration of tutti in selected concertos.

The music of Jean-Ferry Rebel (1666–1747) more than that of any other composer highlights the particularly French pre-occupation with both descriptive music and ballet. Jean-Ferry was the most famous member of the Rebel dynasty of musicians who for over 100 years served in the corps of the king's musicians and in the opera. His knowledge of ballet and descriptive *symphonies* was a natural by-product of his close association with the Académie Royale de Musique where in 1700 he entered the orchestra and became its conductor about 17 years later.

Out of this experience, Rebel created the first choreographic and programme symphonies which, if they were not to find issue during the eighteenth century, would serve as isolated monuments to one man's imaginative power and sense of fantasy. The series begins with *Caprice* (1711), scored for five stringed instruments, which was planned as background music for the choreographic skills of Mlle Prévost. Much more impressive is *Les Caractères de la danse*, subtitled 'Fantaisie', of 1715 which perhaps was also created for Mlle Prévost but which later became a popular vehicle for young Mlle Camargo who first danced it 5 May 1726 'with all the vivacity and intelligence that one could expect from a young person of 15 or 16 years' (*Mercure*).

The object of this *Fantaisie* appears to have been to give a summary of the most popular dances of the period. The entire work is a type of suite in which all the dance components are fragmented and telescoped together so as to create one large dance. This device may be observed in a much more modest way as early as the repertory of the *24 Violons* (see Ecorcheville, *Vingt Suites*, II, 235), and Lully made use of it in the first *intermède* of *Le Bourgeois gentilhomme*. It was exploited in particular by such *préramiste* composers as Campra, Bourgeois and Mouret in their *opéras-ballets*.

Table 5 below shows the distribution of the dances of this *Fantaisie* with their key schemes. The shortest dance fragment is an eight-measure courante; the longest, a chaconne of 36 measures. The *Fantaisie* also acknowledges a *goûts réunis* by including two sonata movements written in a much more genuine Italian style than, for example, the French concertos of the 1720's. If examined closely, the second sonata is actually a development and extension of the first one with transitory modulations to the keys of B and E-Minor.

Table 5
Dances of Les Caractères de la Danse *by Rebel*
showing distribution and key schemes (I = D-Major)

Dance:	Prelude /	Courante /	Menuet /	Bourrée /	Chaconne/
Key Scheme:	I – V	I – V	I – V	I – I	I – I
Dance:	Sarabande /	Gigue /	Rigaudon /	Passepied /	
Key Scheme:	i – v	i – i	i – v	i – III	
Dance:	Gavotte /	Sonate /	Loure /	Musette /	Sonate //
Key Scheme:	I – I	I – I	I – V	I – I	vi – I

Only the Chaconne and the Musette are autonomous. The Musette is in binary form with each part repeated. Unfortunately, the score is a *partition réduite* with only a few of the dances giving exact instrumentation.

The *Fantaisie* of 1729 and *Les Plaisirs champêtres* of 1734 are similar choreographic symphonies, their components also being telescoped into one large dance. The *Fantaisie* includes two chaconnes, here again closely related thematically. The final chaconne repeats the first but in a reverse order of sections and with one section eliminated: thus, the A B C of the first chaconne becomes C A in the second. Apparently, this work, too, could be converted into a *grande symphonie*, as we read in the *Avertissement* that the 'Contrebass, trumpets and timpani add much embellishment to this piece'.

Much the most spectacular of all is a veritable symphonic poem called *Les Elémens*, 'simphonie nouvelle', of 1737. According to the *Avertissement*, this *symphonie* was printed in a manner that permits a performance *en concert* by two violins, two flutes and a bass. As is so often the case, however, the whole may be performed on a solo harpsichord or undoubtedly be converted into a *grande symphonie* by the addition of other instruments (which, incidentally, are called for in any case).

The *Avertissement* gives us a capsule version of the programme and the instruments as well as harmonies to be used for specific descriptive ends.

> The introduction to this *Simphonie* ... is Chaos itself, the confusion that reigned between the Elements before the instant when, obeying unchanging laws, they had taken the places assigned to them in the Natural order.
>
> In order to designate each Element in the chaos, I resorted to the most recognized conventions. The Bass expresses the Earth by its slurred notes to be played with a tremolo (*secousses*); the Flutes by their melodic traits ... imitate the course and the murmur of the Water; the Air is painted by the sustained sounds followed by trills played on the *petites flûtes*; finally, the Violins by their liveliness and brilliance represent the action of Fire.
>
> The distinct characteristics of each Element can be recognized, separated or intermingled, in all or in part, and in the diverse repetitions that I have named Chaos (*Cahos*) which mark the efforts of the Elements to extricate themselves one from the other. . . .
>
> I have dared to undertake to join to the idea of the confusion of the Elements that of the confusion of the harmony. I have tried to have heard at first all the sounds mixed together, or rather, all the notes of the Octave united in a single sound. Following this, these notes climb together in unison in an altogether natural progression and, after a dissonance, one hears a perfect chord.

The programme symphony is constructed in two large sections. The first, an introduction labelled 'Cahos', has a total of seven 'cahos' intrusions; all but the initial one are interspersed between airs and dances representing the autonomous Elements. The final 'Cahos' is followed by an 'Air pour l'Amour' for flute and two violins which leads into the second large section titled *Les Elémens*. This section is composed of a random collection of nine airs, dances and descriptive pieces exhibiting a wide range of instrumental scoring. 'L'Eau', for example, is scored for oboes, violins, bassoons and *tambours* whereas the final air is written for flute alone.

Unfortunately, Rebel's fertile imagination is not sustained throughout by a commensurate musical inventiveness. Nonetheless, the Chaos sections are perhaps without precedent in the eighteenth century. Plate IX reproduces the first page of the score and shows the opening chord described above (note figuring of bass). The score directs the timpani to begin at the 16th notes (measure 5) and to continue through the half notes up to the sign). One thinks immediately of the more restrained 'representation of chaos' from Haydn's *The Creation*, but it is not until Beethoven combined all the notes of the same D-Minor scale in the 'chaotic' opening chord of the Presto episode directly before the baritone recitative in the final movement of the Ninth Symphony that we have a sound complex of such descriptive power.

Chapter 21

-》》》 《《《-

The Sonata and Suite
for Solo Instruments

The burden of this chapter is to consider the music composed in France during the Baroque period for a single instrument on each part; that is, every indication of title and *avertissement* suggests this mode of performance. The bulk of this solo instrumental music may be organized by genre into two large categories: the sonata and the suite.

Of all ultramontane importations, the sonata caused the French musical pulse to beat most rapidly, and it was the sonata in company with the cantata that gave the sharpest focus to the confrontation of national styles during the first decades of the eighteenth century.[1]

If we accept Couperin's statement found in the preface to his *Les Goûts réunis* (1724) that the first Italian sonatas appeared in Paris over 30 years before his publication, we arrive at a date sometime before 1694; in fact, Couperin himself, perhaps as early as 1692, wrote his first sonata *en trio* modelled on the trio sonatas of Corelli whose first two *opere* had been in print since 1681 and 1685 respectively.

Corelli sonatas were not printed in France until Foucault's publication of Opus v about 1701,[2] but they surely had been circulated and heard within any of the small Parisian groups dedicated to the performance of Italian music. Michel Corrette in the preface to his treatise *Le Maître de Clavecin pour l'accompagnement* (1753), unequivocally stated that it was at a concert given by Abbé Mathieu, the curé of Saint-André-des-Arts, where the 'trios of Corelli, printed in Rome, appeared for the first time. This new kind of music encouraged all composers to work in a more brilliant style.... All concerts took on a different form; scenes and *symphonies* from opera were replaced by sonatas'.[3]

Lecerf made reference to such a milieu with his resigned observation that there were 'not only professional musicians, but men of quality and Prelates who sing nothing else and have nothing else played in their homes but Italian Pieces and Sonatas' (*Comparaison*, II, p. 54). Brossard remarked that 'All the composers of Paris, above all the

Organists, had at that time (1695), so to speak, the craze to compose *Sonates à la manière Italienne'* (*Catalogue*, p. 544).

In rare agreement both Lecerf and Couperin admitted that the 'novelty and the love of change' (Lecerf), the 'greed of the French for foreign novelties above all else' (Couperin) first stimulated French interest in Italian music, including the sonata. At the turn of the century, the solo sonatas that comprise Corelli's Opus v were considered the most modern and progressive music available in Paris—a position that was eventually usurped by the incredible popularity of Vivaldi's *L'Estro armonico* which between 1715 and about 1750 resulted in a true 'snobisme vivaldien' in the French capital.[4]

Certainly there was snob appeal in the cultivation of a taste for the sonata. After all, had not Louis xiv himself as early as 1682 so thoroughly enjoyed a performance by the Dutch violinist Johann Paul Westhoff (1656–1705) of his solo violin sonata that the king nicknamed the work 'La Guerre' after its programmatic movement?[5] And now 20 years later it was fashionable to declare oneself a partisan of Italian music, safe in the knowledge that arbiters of style such as the Duc d'Orléans made no effort to hide their admiration for this music. It is with heavy sarcasm that Lecerf wrote, 'What joy, what a good opinion a man has of himself who knows something of the fifth opus of Corelli!' (*Comparaison*, iii, p. 201). Foolishly, Lecerf engaged in a diatribe against the 11th sonata of Corelli's Opus v (*Comparaison*, iii, p. 203). He denounced such harmonic practices as, for example, the use of '24 consecutive 7ths in three measures', and what is even more surprising in the light of Corelli's great melodic gifts, he found the melodic line to be 'poverty-stricken, with only scraps of melody'. Perhaps this unconsidered attack was precipitated not only by Abbé Raguenet's allusions to Lecerf's lack of critical acumen, but also out of a frustrated awareness of the extent to which the younger generation of French composers was falling under the influence of the great Italian's music.

This same feeling may help to explain the ambivalence of Titon du Tillet who, after admitting having listened with pleasure to Italian music over a seven year period at the home of the harpsichord virtuosi Mme and Mlle Duhallay, suddenly felt compelled to cry out that as a 'bon François' his loyalty was to Lully, Campra, Destouches, Delalande and Couperin as opposed to Corelli, Gasparini, Scarlatti or Tartini.

An alliance between sonata and dance suite had already been accomplished in the *sonata da camera*, but the vogue for sonatas in France was so great as the eighteenth century progressed that it even invaded the realm of choreographically oriented dance music. We have already seen in the previous chapter the important place accorded an Italianate sonata in Rebel's choreographic fantasy *Les Caractères de la Danse*, of 1715. In 1725, Montéclair brought out a set of *Menuets tant Anciens que Nouveaux* which includes 100 minuets! In his *Avertissement* Montéclair stated that his collection was divided into two parts; the first containing 'graceful and easy Minuets suitable for dancing', whereas the second part includes 'more difficult Minuets in the *goût des Sonates*'. Unfortunately, the major difference seems to lie in Montéclair's neat categories themselves, for the minuets of both parts are practically indistinguishable and totally undistinguished.

It is appropriate that he who was most concerned about the efficacy of a judicious union of French and Italian styles should have composed the first French sonatas 'à la manière italienne'. The first six of François Couperin's nine sonatas *en trio* date from about 1692 to 1695. Conserved in manuscript at the Bibliothèque Nationale (Brossard Collection) are the first four sonatas bearing the titles 'La Pucelle', 'La Visionnaire', 'L'Astrée' and 'La Steinquerque'; the Bibliothèque de Lyon has two others entitled 'La Sultane' and 'La Superbe'. In 1726, Couperin re-cast three of the above sonatas for use in his *Les Nations, Sonades et Suites de Simphonies en Trio*. In a 'Aveu de l'Auteur au Public', Couperin described a subterfuge through which the first French sonata, his 'La Pucelle', had been performed on a concert under the name of a fictitious Italian composer. The ruse worked. The sonata was well received, and Couperin was encouraged to continue composing in the same genre.

The three early sonatas chosen later for inclusion in *Les Nations* were 'La Pucelle', 'La Visionnaire' and 'L'Astrée'. The only important change made by Couperin was to re-title the sonatas in order to conform better with the generic title. Thus, 'La Pucelle', 'La Visionnaire' and 'L'Astrée' became 'La Françoise', 'L'Espagnole' and 'La Piémontoise' respectively. For the bellicose and not too interesting 'La Steinquerque', Couperin substituted a more mature sonata entitled 'L'Impériale'.

Two programmatic sonatas, 'Apothéoses' for Corelli and for Lully, crown Couperin's achievements in this genre. The Corelli 'Apothéose' follows the ten *concerts* of *Les Goûts réunis* (1724), and the Lully 'Apothéose' was published separately in 1725.

In the entire collection of nine trio sonatas there is very little indication of specific instrumentation. Only in the Lully 'Apothéose' did Couperin suggest 'Flutes or Violins' for the 'Plainte' and 'two violins' for the two short airs. Moreover, in the *Avis* for the Lully 'Apothéose', he emphasized that the two 'Apothéoses' as well as *Les Nations* 'may be performed on two Harpsichords as well as on all other instruments'. As was true in the *Concerts Royaux* and the *Goûts réunis*, the latitude for performance possibilities is very great indeed.

In the case of the trio sonatas and the Corelli 'Apothéose', however, Couperin was careful to indicate for the three staves: *premier dessus, deuxième dessus* and *basse d'archet*. The upper two parts are ideal for two violins, and the numerous textual and stylistic references to Corelli strongly suggest that violins were the favoured instruments for performance. The writing, although completely idiomatic and competent for the violin, rarely extends beyond the third position, and no double stops are employed.

On the other hand, the Lully 'Apothéose' is called a 'concert instrumental' and the words 'de Simphonie' are added to the first and second *dessus* designations. The fact that many of the movements in the Lully 'Apothéose' derive from the type of orchestral *symphonies* used in the opera suggests that this *concert* could have been performed with more than one instrument on a part and would, therefore, conform to the collections discussed in the previous chapter.

The four sonatas of *Les Nations*, in Couperin's words, were to 'serve as Preludes or in the manner of introductions' to extended dance suites. Both sonata and suite are grouped together under the generic title of 'Ordre'. Thus on a grander scale than in *Les Goûts réunis*, Couperin placed Italian sonata and French dance suite in apposition and created a 'series of diptychs' that are reminiscent of the Bach violin sonatas and partitas.[6] Yet, in terms of scope and breadth of material, these four sonatas far transcend any 'introductory' role. Most have seven or eight movements ('L'Impériale' has six) whose titles, with the exception of 'airs', only indicate relative tempos.

Each sonata opens with a 'gravement' or a 'grave' movement corresponding to the first movement of an Italian *sonata da chiesa*. Here, as elsewhere, there is interpenetration of national styles. The long-breathed melodies remind us of Corelli or even Handel. The closely knit part writing with much crossing of voices and the chains of suspensions are Italian; but the ornamentation and certain harmonic practices such as the use of the mediant 9th chord with augmented 5th (see, for example, 'La Françoise', measure 11) are French. Only the 'Gravement' of 'L'Impériale' has the steady 8th note bass line, the 'basse travaillée', so typical of Corelli and used here to support constantly intertwining melodies of great lyric sweep. In contrast, the 'Gravement' of 'La Piémontoise', with its expressive use of rests and its basically homophonic texture, resembles an operatic 'lament' more than a sonata movement.

Most of the quick movements, usually titled 'Gayement' or 'Vivement', employ some form of free fugal writing. Most notable is the concluding 'Vivement et marqué' of 'L'Espagnole' which is a skilful cross between a chaconne and a fugue. The chaconne bass, in the minor form of the descending tetrachord, is presented first by the continuo accompanied only by a lively 'Badinage pour le Clavecin, si l'on veut'. Unfortunately, this optional harpsichord part is written out only for the first eight measures, but thereby gives some clues regarding a possible manner of realization. Chaconne merges with fugue as the bass line is transferred to the second violin and becomes subject. The counter-subject is so distinctive and consistently carried out that it is even possible to consider this as a chaconne-double fugue combination.

The most tightly organized of all Couperin's fugal movements is the 'Vivement' that concludes 'L'Impériale'. This is music particularly well suited for the violin with its wide leaps juxtaposed against rapid scale passages. In spite of its length, it never becomes diffused. The authoritative octaves that open its long subject (reproduced in Mellers, p. 117) generate exciting episodes which build to *stretto* passages of a Bach-like concentration.

In most of the quick movements, the bass shares in the melodic material, and in the concluding 'Gayement' of 'La Françoise' it is in perpetual motion, a vortex of swirling 16th notes. The fourth movement of the same sonata ('Gayement') is yet another example of Couperin's ability to expand and develop his material, often in combination with independent motifs that pass in and out of the texture sometimes never to return. This results in a type of free variation in which there is rarely an exact repetition of the initial melodic material.

'L'Impériale' is the only one of the four sonatas of *Les Nations* that does not include one or more 'airs'. The 'airs' are a totally French contribution to the sonatas and are always framed by fast movements; as such, they offer the greatest possible contrast of tempo and style. The simple, symmetrical tunes almost cry out for parody treatment and have much in common with the popular 'brunettes' and 'air tendre' repertory.

In the opinion of this writer, the suites 'introduced' by the sonatas are less interesting musically than the suites of *Les Goûts réunis*. To be sure, the dances are exquisitely fashioned, but it is as though Couperin were summing up the heritage of French dance types with the essence of each dance carefully preserved and labelled for all to see. Nothing ruffles the surface, all is neatly arranged, predictable and quite conservative. Each suite is introduced by an allemande which is followed by two courantes, sarabande, gigue and optional dances with an occasional optional dance inserted between the sarabande and gigue. Most of the allemandes revert to the earlier type in which there is little unity between the two sections.

In these suites one misses the occasional dramatic outbursts of an allemande like 'La Raphaéle' or that of *Ordre* XI of the *Goûts réunis*; one seeks for some sign of the pathos of the 'Sarabande très grave' behind the elegantly shaped melodies of these sarabandes.

Only the chaconnes, the passacailles and the rondeaux capture some of the fantasy and imagination we have come to expect from mature Couperin. Three of the four *ordres* include one chaconne or passacaille, and it is clear that Couperin himself made little distinction between the genres, for he labelled the example from the first *ordre* 'Chaconne ou Passacaille'. Most use techniques borrowed from the large orchestral chaconnes of Lully's operatic *divertissements*. The most extensive is the chaconne of 'L'Impériale' which is clearly organized in a large three-part form with its middle section in the Tonic minor key. All chaconnes show an increased rhythmic activity as the dance progresses, and several include episodes that transfer to a basic SSB texture the effect of couplets that are scored for two flutes with a viola (*haute-contre*) support in the orchestral chaconnes.

Along with the 10 *concerts* of *Les Goûts réunis*, the two 'Apothéoses' climax Couperin's efforts in achieving a synthesis between French and Italian musical styles. *Le Parnasse ou L'Apothéose de Corelli* is subtitled 'Grande Sonade en Trio'. It is divided into seven contrasting movements that bear programmatic titles as well as tempo indications. The 'programme' deals with Corelli's happy welcome by the muses at Mount Parnassus and gives an opportunity for the apposition of Italian 'vivacité', in the scenes of Corelli's 'enthousiasme' (No. 4) and general rejoicing (Nos. 2, 6, 7), and French 'douceur', in the charming pastoral scenes describing Corelli's drinking at the Spring of Hypocrene (No. 3) and sleeping to the accompaniment of a 'Sommeil' (No. 5).

The opening movement is a 'Gravement' representing Corelli 'at the foot of Parnassus asking the Muses to allow him to be received among them'. It is the first movement of an Italian church sonata that exhibits great purity of style. The upper lines have direction and purpose; their melodies combine in wide arches supported by an almost continuous 8th note bass line.

The fugal movements (Nos. 2 and 7) show Couperin's skill in devising subjects that 'work' convincingly in short *stretti* and generate much forward motion. Exciting passage work interpenetrates the fugal texture; fugal procedures are never adhered to consistently throughout, and this may make the movements more effective as pieces of pure chamber music.

Number 3 ('Corelli drinking at the Spring of Hypocrene') is a bucolic 'mood' piece with the hypnotic spell of murmuring waters achieved by the continuous, gentle motion of 8th notes slurred in groups of four. It is a Lullian nature scene infused with Corelli's suspension chains which help sustain the motion by cadence evasion.

Number 5 is a 'Sommeil' and Number 6 ('The Muses awaken Corelli') is a piece of theatre music in which trumpet calls blazon forth Corelli's arrival before Apollo. Unlike real trumpet fanfares with their static harmony, this simulated version is free to range far and wide in its harmonic organization. The short composition begins in D-Major and ends in F♯-Minor after rapid excursions through A-Major and C♯-Minor.

The *concert instrumental* entitled *Apothéose composé à la mémoire immortelle de l'incomparable Monsieur de Lully* is a 'trio sonata' only by virtue of its final section, 'La Paix de Parnasse'. Reversing the procedure used in *Les Nations*, Couperin this time used a series of 12 descriptive pieces and airs to 'introduce' the final movement, a 'Sonade en trio'.

The 12 programmatic pieces that form the bulk of the 'Apothéose' draw heavily for their inspiration from the descriptive *symphonies* of Lully's *tragédie lyrique*. Again, it is a Lully seen through the enlightened eye of Couperin, with all the harmonic resources, colour effects and sense of fantasy used on a scale unknown by the Florentine. The harmonic range of the 12 pieces is in itself much greater than is normally found in a Couperin *ordre*. Flanked by movements in G-Minor and G-Major, the inner portions of the 'Apothéose' are in the keys of B♭, E♭ and C-Minor.

The opening movement ('Lully in the Elysian Fields') is an elegiac, operatic *ritournelle*, its expressiveness enhanced by the sharp dissonances that result naturally from the linear writing. Numbers 3, 4, 5, 6 and 7, entitled 'Flight of Mercury', 'Descent of Apollo', 'Subterranean clamour', 'Plaintes' and 'Rising up of Lully' respectively, are all examples of stage music for which any number of models could be found in the court ballets or *tragédie lyrique* of the *grand siècle*. Indeed, the source for 'Subterranean clamour' is undoubtedly the 'Trembleurs' scene from *Isis* (IV, 1), and the sighs of the two flutes in the 'Plainte' resemble the flute passages in the 'Plainte de Pan' in the same key, also from *Isis* (III, 6).

The actual reunion of styles begins in earnest with Number 10 at which point 'Apollo persuades Lully and Corelli that the reunion of French and Italian taste can only result in the perfection of Music'. The 'reunion' includes an 'Essai en forme d'Ouverture', two airs and the concluding 'Sonade en trio'. In each case 'Lully', 'Corelli' and their Muses are assigned their respective roles on the staves of music with Lully's part always scored in the French violin clef (G on the first line) and Corelli's, on the other hand, in the normal violin clef (G on the second line).

The overture exploits both the dotted rhythms of the French overture and characteristically Italian chains of triplets. The faster middle section unites arpeggio figuration and circles of 5ths with a discreet use of French ornamentation. 'Lully' and 'Corelli', each with his solo violin, play the two short 'airs' taking turns on the 'subject'—a delightful artifice of combining French ornamentation (see especially the chains of *coulés* played by 'Lully') and Italian sequences and continuous 8th note motion.

In the concluding 'Sonade en trio', we are informed that because of complaints by the French Muses, 'One should henceforth say *Sonade*,

Cantade, in speaking their language, just as one says *Ballade, Sérénade,* etc.' Couperin's attempts to appease the 'complaining French Muses' are not as far afield as the obstinate use of French titles in Book II of the solo sonatas of Jean-Baptiste Anet (*c.* 1661–1755) in which 'Allaigre' is substituted for 'Allegro'.

Couperin chose to cap two of his most important chamber works with fine examples of a church sonata and a chamber sonata. The 'Sonade en trio' of the Lully 'Apothéose' is a four-movement church sonata with the tempo designations 'Gravement', 'Vivement', 'Ronde-ment' and 'Vivement'; the final *concert* of *Les Goûts réunis*, if played by one solo instrument and continuo, is in reality a chamber sonata, also organized in the classical four-movement scheme in the order prelude, allemande, sarabande grave and 'fugueté' (see Chapter 20, p. 310.)

The opening 'Gravement' of the 'Apothéose' sonata begins like a French allemande which in itself introduces consecutive and combined passages that best characterize the two 'goûts'. Example 91 below illustrates the extent of the contrast between these passages in which a French 'nature' scene gives way to a forceful Italian statement organized in sequences and practically devoid of ornamentation.

Example 91
Couperin: Extract from Gravement *of the 'Apothéose' sonata (after the ed. of 1725).*

During the period 1692–95 when Couperin was composing his earliest sonatas, Sébastien de Brossard, Elisabeth-Claude Jacquet de La Guerre and Jean-Ferry Rebel were also experimenting with the new genre. Brossard, who in his dictionary gave us one of the first classifications of the sonata into *da chiesa* and *da camera*, was obviously well acquainted with the Italian sonata and, in fact, he had copied the Opus V sonatas of Giovanni Battista Bassani (*c.* 1647–1716) from the second edition of 1688. Brossard composed four sonatas of which two are for violins and an obbligato bass viol and the other two, which were never completed, are for solo violin and continuo. The style is conservative and austere with little ornamentation and reflects the influence of Lully more than Corelli. A clue as to why Brossard, a partisan of Italian music, should compose in such a conservative style is offered by his comments regarding the Bassani sonatas which he described as 'completely charming and excellent and not too difficult to perform, in contrast to (those) of the typical Italians who believe they have not written a *belle Sonate* unless they have filled it with fast movements that are often extravagant, without reason other than their fantasy, and with a perpetual wrangling more suitable for grating one's ears than soothing them.' (*Catalogue*, p. 545.)

Of greater musical merit are the sonatas of Elisabeth-Claude Jacquet de La Guerre,[7] which include a set of six sonatas in manuscript and six that were printed with the *Pièces de Clavecin qui peuvent se jouer sur le Viollon* in 1707.

The manuscript sonatas, loaned or given to Brossard in 1695, comprise two sonatas 'a violino solo e viol da gamba obbligata', with organ or harpsichord continuo, and a set of four trio sonatas. The solo sonatas along with those of Brossard and Rebel are among the first examples of the genre in France.

Both solo and trio sonatas exhibit some progressive features including what may be the first use of double stops in French solo violin music. Interesting shifts of texture also result from the use of the obbligato bass viol which, on occasion, separates from the continuo line and takes on a solo role.

Regarding the printed set of six sonatas, Edith Borroff takes issue with La Laurencie's comment that 'one can hardly understand how the King . . . could feel any surprise in hearing this innocent music'. La Laurencie, objects Miss Borroff, 'does not do de La Guerre justice, for she used strong materials from the modern style of her own day, presenting them with taste and assurance and wielding them into effective forms with a power and style both personal and representative of the best of that remarkable generation of which she was an honoured member'.[8] Based on Borroff's study it is clear that the printed sonatas combine light Italian polyphony and harmonic procedures in the quick movements with French formal ingenuity that ranges from a highly developed French overture (Sonata 4) to long free-form structures that eschew exact repetitions. As in the manuscript sonatas, the solo role of the bass viol at times thickens the *a 2* texture.

The *Recüeil de douze sonates à II et III parties & B.C.* by Jean-Ferry Rebel was published in 1712–13 but dates from about 1695. Brossard owned copies of these sonatas and wrote: 'They are all magnificent; and I have heard them performed many times by the Composer . . .' (*Catalogue*, p. 335). The collection includes seven trio sonatas and five solo sonatas. The writing for the solo instrument is conservative; there are far fewer Italian traits than are found, for example, in the earlier sonatas of Couperin or the sonatas of La Guerre. In fact, Lecerf was so pleased with Rebel's restraint that he singled him out as one composer who 'has the taste and care to temper it [Italian fire] with French wisdom and gentleness, and he has abstained from those frightening and monstrous cadenza passages ('chutes') that so delight the Italians' (*Comparaison*, I, p. 93).

Also published in 1713 was Rebel's *12 Sonates à violon seul mellées de plusieurs récits pour la Viole*. The collection is divided into two parts; the first six sonatas use mostly tempo or descriptive titles, the second six are composed of the typical dances of the French dance suite. More advanced technically than the earlier set of 12 sonatas, this collection makes some use of double stops and tremolo passages, although the music remains mostly in the first three positions. The *récits* for bass viol convert several movements into an *a 3* texture. At times the viol *récit* is no more than an elaboration of the continuo line; at other times it is independent of the continuo and vies with the solo line itself for a dominant position.

The most prolific among the first generation of French sonata composers was François Duval (*c*. 1673–1728) whose seven collections span the years 1704–20. Duval was also the first composer in France to publish sonatas for the violin, and beginning with his Book IV (1708) he was the first French composer of violin sonatas to favour the more common G clef to the French violin clef. His *Premier Livre de Sonates et autres pièces pour le violon et la basse* of 1704 is, in effect, 'the first officially sanctioned acknowledgement of the French taste for such Italianisms' (Newman, p. 365).

French dance measures and descriptive touches of the music blend artfully with more advanced Italian instrumental techniques such as new bowing styles, double stops and passages that go beyond the third position (La Laurencie, I, 117–120).

Undoubtedly, Louis-Nicolas Clérambault and Jean-François Dandrieu were among those organists described by Brossard as having the 'craze' to compose Italianate sonatas. As might be anticipated, the six sonatas by Clérambault (all in manuscript) and the *Livre de Sonates en trio* (1705) by Dandrieu reflect the polyphonic bias of the organist, as do the later collections by Louis-Antoine Dornel.

In the case of Dandrieu, this results from time to time in the use of the violoncello obbligato part as a linear partner in its own right, thereby thickening the texture to *a 4*. Most of Dandrieu's sonatas are church sonatas which often have a short transitional third movement (Adagio or Largo), that in typical Corelli fashion ends in a Phrygian cadence on the Dominant of a minor key. Instead of progressing to the expected Tonic, it moves to the Tonic of the relative major key for the final movement. There is much of Corelli in the trio sonatas of Dandrieu as the example below from the Adagio of Sonata V illustrates.

Example 92
Dandrieu: *Extract from Adagio of Sonata* v *(after ed. of 1705).*

Couperin and Leclair are the two pillars of the Baroque sonata in France. In the generation of composers between these two monumental figures, there were perhaps as many as 35 minor masters (see Newman, p. 367) who were busily engaged in supplying the increasing demand of the French public for sonata literature. In a study of some of the eighteenth century editions of selected composers, one observes certain trends in the composition of sonatas that culminated in the four books of Jean-Marie Leclair.

Among the composers who published collections of violin sonatas before the appearance of Leclair's first book (1723) are Jean-Baptiste Senallié (*c.* 1687–1730), Louis-Antoine Dornel (*c.* 1685–1765), Louis Francoeur 'the elder' (*c.* 1692–1745), François Francoeur 'the younger' (1698–1787), Jacques Aubert (1689–1753) and two Italian composers residing in Paris, Michel Mascitti (*c.* 1664–1760) and Antonio Piani, called 'Desplanes napolitano' (*c.* 1664–1760).

The violinist Mascitti published nine collections of sonatas between 1704 and 1738. In a reversal of the general trend of French composers seeking to absorb the style of the Italian sonata, Mascitti admitted in his *Avertissement* to his Opus II (1706) that 'I have applied myself in some of my Sonatas to reconcile this with *le goût italien'*. Except for a more conspicuous use of double stops, Mascitti's sonatas do not progress technically beyond those of his teacher, Corelli.

The single collection of solo sonatas by Piani published in 1712 is worth noting because of the increased technical difficulties (use of triple stops, for example) and explicit performance directions (the use of ◄ and ►, for instance, to indicate crescendo and diminuendo) (La Laurencie, I, p. 191).[9]

Both Louis Francoeur and his younger brother, François, each of whom composed two books of solo sonatas, advanced the technique of violin writing in France by offering varieties of bowings, use of the first five positions, use of triple and quadruple stops, wide leaps and rapid arpeggio figurations that demand the left-hand thumb on the fingerboard in some instances (see La Laurencie, I, pp. 200 and 259). In the development of a more technically demanding repertory for the solo violin in France, however, Jean-Baptiste Senallié (or Senaillé) is the most important composer between Couperin and Leclair. A violinist himself, who had studied in Modena with Tomasso Antonio Vitali, the son of the great Giovanni Battista, Senallié published 50 solo violin sonatas in five books from 1710 to 1727. The *Mercure* of June, 1738 is explicit in assigning responsibility to Senallié for the greater development of technical violin writing during the 1720's:

> ... he had made a *séjour* in Italy and had absorbed enough of an ultramontane *goût* to blend it artfully with beautiful French melody. The progress made in writing for the violin since (that time) in France is due to him, because he put into the Music passages that were difficult to execute, and ... everybody ... wished to learn how to play them, especially at that time when we had scarcely begun to familiarize ourselves with music that was a little difficult.

> (Quoted by La Laurencie, I, p. 171)

In addition to his elaborate passage work, long and frequent trills, his attainment of the 7th position, and his use of up to 24 notes on a bow (see La Laurencie, I, pp. 178–79), Senallié also enriched the harmonic vocabulary of the violin sonata. Of considerable interest is his use of the type of 'bi-modality' which had intrigued French com-

Example 93
Senallié: Extract from Adagio of Sonata IX from Book IV (after ed. of 1721).

posers since the middle years of the seventeenth century. Leclair, especially in his third and fourth books, carried this technique of the purposeful ambiguity of mode to its highest point, but in passages such as those extracted from the Adagio of Sonata 9 in Senallié's Opus IV (1721), it is clear that Senallié is a most important precursor of Leclair in this practice.

Senallié also experimented with the derivation of thematic material that could be used to unify different movements of the sonata. In the ninth sonata from his Opus III (1716) and the fifth sonata from Opus IV, Senallié appears to have used the device in a systematic manner evolving, in the case of the former work, three movements of the sonata from one basic 'head-motive'.

Example 94
Senallié: Thematic unity in Sonata IX, *Book* III *(after ed. of 1716).*

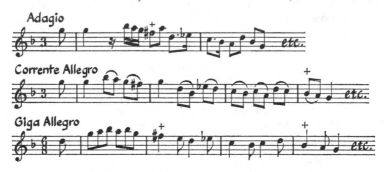

The 49 sonatas for solo violin and continuo, the 25 trio sonatas and the 12 sonatas for two violins *en duo* by Jean-Marie Leclair crown the history of the violin sonata in France. The impressive list of secondary sources all written within the last 20 years attests to the increased awareness of the importance of Leclair as a major Baroque composer of sonatas.[10] The solo violin sonatas are grouped into four books of 12 sonatas each (Book I, Opus I, 1723; Book II, Opus II, *c.* 1728; Book III, Opus V, *c.* 1734; and Book IV, Opus IX, *c.* 1738). The 49th sonata is a posthumous work carrying the opus number of XV and printed in 1767. The majority of the sonatas are cast in the typical SFSF movement scheme. There is no attempt to adhere to any 'chamber' or 'church' distinction. Rather, the sonatas mix elements of both within the same composition. Often the first two movements use only tempo designations, and the final movements (or movement) use dance titles. Such, for example, are the first and third sonatas of Opus IV whose movements appear in the following respective orders: Adagio, Allegro Assai, Andante, Minuetto; and Andante, Allegro, Sarabande, Tambourin. Reflecting the growing popularity of the transverse flute, many

332

sonatas bear the direction 'may be played on the *flûte allemande*'. In fact, Book II carries the subtitle 'Pour le Violon et pour la Flûte Traversière'. In some of the sonatas that are so designated, Leclair added a more difficult part 'pour le violon seul' (see, for example, Sonatas 2 and 7 from Book IV).

There is some evidence that Leclair, like Senallié before him, attempted an over-all unity of some of his sonatas through a free use of a 'head-motive' technique. The clearest example is that of Sonata 12 from Book I in which the two Allegro movements find their genesis in the opening Largo.

Example 95
Leclair: Thematic unity in Sonata XII of Book I (after ed. of 1723).

Leclair is French to the core in the 'beau chant' of such dance movements as the minuets, sarabandes, gavottes, tambourins, musettes and rondeaux. Here and there, he composed some dances with variations. Such is the Sarabande of Sonata 9 of Book I with its Largo theme followed by an Allegro variation, which resembles the old technique of diminution that, in turn, is followed by a closing variation employing the Alberti bass throughout.

Through Soumis and others, Leclair had thoroughly absorbed into his writing for the violin the technical advances made in Italian violin music after Corelli. The *Mercure* of June, 1738 erroneously claimed that Leclair was 'the first Frenchman who, in imitation of the Italians, used double stops . . . he pushed this device so far that the Italians themselves confessed that he was a master of the genre'. As we have seen, Mlle de La Guerre had employed double stops as early as 1695. Leclair did, to be sure, 'push' their use along with triple and quadruple stops to a degree never before realized in France. In addition, he developed the use of double trills in thirds and sixths, a left-hand tremolo, a great variety of bow strokes—all carefully notated (Lemoine recognizes five different combinations of legato, spiccato and detaché in the sonatas)—and by the eighth sonata of Book IV, he had reached the 8th position.

One should remember, however, that in spite of the technical competence required to play these sonatas by Leclair, the virtuoso elements were not used as ends in themselves, and they never compromise the musical integrity of the sonatas. In spite of the number of Allegro or Allegro assai movements, Leclair took pains to emphasize in the *Avertissement* to his *Ouvertures et Sonates en trio* of 1753 that he did not mean by the term 'Allegro' a movement 'which is too fast; it is a gay movement. Those who push the tempo too much, above all in the serious pieces such as the Fugues in 4/4 metre, render the melody trivial....' Also, like Couperin, he insisted on a scrupulous reading of his ornamentation which was written out and symbolized. In the *Avertissement* to Book IV, he commented forcefully: 'One important point, on which I cannot insist too much, is to avoid this confusion of notes that are sometimes added to the melodic and expressive passages but which serve only to disfigure them.'

Preston has convincingly demonstrated that the sophisticated harmonic language of the Leclair sonatas is as important to any style study of the composer as are his advanced violinistic techniques. The use of Augmented 6th chords, Neapolitan 6ths (often with a major 7th added) and Diminished 7ths is frequent after his first book. The latter chord is often used, as in Rameau, to climax a long phrase or to evade a cadence (see, for example, the Adagio of Sonata 10, Book II).

The modulatory schemes are as expansive and original as may be found anywhere in the music of the French Baroque, and Leclair's sensitivity to key contrasts both from one movement to the next and within the same movement is highly developed.

The Adagio movements of the fifth and ninth sonatas of Book IV contain the quintessence of Leclair's refinement of harmony. His greatly expanded harmonic vocabulary parallels that of Rameau and even rivals that of J. S. Bach. In these movements, Leclair appears, as does Bach, isolated from the music of his generation much of which had already succumbed to the short, symmetrical melodies and the slow harmonic rhythm of the *style galant*. The Adagio of the fifth sonata is reproduced in facsimile from the 1738 edition as Plate X; that of the ninth sonata may be found, also in facsimile, at the end of Nutting's article in *The Musical Quarterly* (facing p. 517). The Adagio of the fifth sonata begins in F-Major and cadences in C-Minor in the eighth measure. A new section in A♭-Major follows with transitory modulations to B♭-Minor (measure 13), F-Minor (measure 19), G-Minor (measure 25), and the movement closes with a phrygian cadence on the Dominant of A-Major. These are just the bare harmonic bones, however, and tell us nothing of the poetry of the forceful participation by the bass in close imitation (measures 5–6) or of a continually unfolding melodic line, widely arched and rich in invention that only turns back on itself at the A♭ statement in measure 9.

334

The Adagio of the ninth sonata begins in A-Major with a melodic and harmonic innocence that gradually gives way before the darkening colours of chords borrowed from the Tonic minor key, a remarkable enharmonic modulation to C♯-Minor and the use of triple and quadruple stops. Only the bass line remains undisturbed and, as is so often the case in Bach, its abstract pattern acts to unify the entire movement.

Worlds apart is the opening Adagio of the 12th sonata of Book III reproduced from the 1734 edition as Plate XI. This movement dramatically reveals the extent to which Leclair could make use of decorative arabesques, sweeping *tirades* and double trills, set off by the sharply pointed rhythms of the overture, and a harmonic background that ranges from passages in slow harmonic rhythm to a series of rapid transitory modulations achieved through secondary dominants.

The 12 trio sonatas that comprise Leclair's Opus IV (*c.* 1730) and Opus XIII (1753) are impressive works that should be better known. In Nutting's words, here is Leclair, the 'great craftsman-composer, undistracted by his pursuit of violin virtuosity'.[11] The *Sonates à deux violons sans basse*, Opus III, another work destined for the amateur performer, is superior musically to similar sets by La Barre, Boismortier, Aubert and Guignon. Leclair's combinations of sonorities and his ability to 'orchestrate' (Pincherle) the violins give pleasure to listener and performer alike.

Although outside the scope of this book, such contemporaries and successors of Leclair as Boismortier, Mondonville, Louis-Gabriel Guillemain (1705–70) and Jean-Pierre Guignon (1702–74) all contributed to the later development of the violin sonata in France. Of these composers, Mondonville and Guillemain were the most experimental. In Guillemain's *Amusements pour le Violon seul* (Opus XVIII, 1762), we have the first use in France of sonatas 'senza basso'. Mondonville's *Sonates pour le Violon & B. C.*, Opus I, of 1733 are already technically advanced over most of the sonatas of his contemporaries, and his 'Les Sons harmoniques', *Sonates à Violon seul avec B. C.*, Opus IV, of 1738 constitute the first extensive use of harmonics on the violin ('The same sounds are found on all sorts of instruments. . . . Why should we not use them with the same sensitivity on the violin . . .' *Avertissement*). The harmonics are indicated with a trill sign and are often used in alternation with double stops.

Sonatas for Flute and for Violoncello

'The instruments which are the most popular now in Paris are the harpsichord and the transverse or German flute. The French today play these instruments with an unparalleled *delicatesse*.' So wrote Nemeitz in his *Séjour de* Paris (1727) about 20 years after the publication of Jacques Hotteterre's treatise, *Principes de la Flûte Traversière, ou Flûte d'Allemagne* (Paris, 1707, later editions in 1713, 1720, 1721, 1722, *c.* 1728, 1741 and *c.* 1765). We have seen how Leclair and others had specified the use of the transverse flute as a substitute instrument in certain of their violin sonatas and how Dornel, in 1711, had gathered eight violin sonatas and four flute suites together in one collection.

At this time the transverse flute co-existed with the recorder in much the same way as the bass viol did with the violoncello, but gradually, solo performance on the recorder was restricted more and more to the amateur who could not achieve a high degree of performance skill on the flute. At first much flute repertory indicated in its titles that the music could be performed on the recorder or oboe—this again was a practical means of stimulating a wider dissemination of the music. Later in the century, however, it was evident that the recorder was less in use as a substitute instrument. Thus, in his Opus xxxiv which includes six sonatas for four parts 'différentes et également travaillés' (1731), Boismortier specified 'transverse flutes, violins or other instruments' for the upper parts, but added that the treble part could be played on the recorder 'in case of need'.

Interest in the transverse flute was stimulated by the virtuoso performances by René-Pignon Descoteaux (*c.* 1646–1728), Philibert Rebillé (called Philibert, *c.* 1650–1712) and Michel de la Barre(*c.* 1675–1743) that took place at the court near the turn of the century. These men were all part of the king's musicians (*Chambre* and *Ecurie*) and flutists in the Paris Opéra. The *Mercure de France* of June 1725 reveals that Louis xiv took great pleasure in hearing Philibert and Descoteaux and had them come often to play in his apartments and in the wooded glades of Versailles. Beginning with the appearance of Michel Blavet (1700–68) as flute soloist at the *Concert Spirituel* on 1 October 1726, the flute surpassed the recorder and began to rival the violin as a virtuoso solo instrument.

There is an enormous amount of eighteenth century French literature for the flute beginning with La Barre's *Pièces pour la flûte traversière avec la basse continue* of 1702 and going through the 13 sets of solo or trio sonatas by Jacques-Christophe Naudot (? –1762). It remains a musical *terra incognita*, for, to date, no systematic study with the scope of La Laurencie in his study of the violin repertory has been published.[12]

Between 1702 and 1722, Michel de La Barre brought out several collections of suites and sonatas for flute and continuo, for trio combinations and for two flutes without bass. The personal rapport that could exist between composer and consumer is documented by La Barre's statement in his *Avertissement* for the *Deuxième Livre de Pièces pour la Flûte traversière avec basse continue* (1710). In discussing the total compass of the instrument, La Barre commented that 'there are two or three notes which I believe no one knows (how to produce), and I would not know how to tell him in writing how to perform these notes; But if those who would like to learn would take the trouble to pass by my home . . . it would give me great pleasure, with no obligation to them, to show them how. . . .'

La Barre's *Troisième Livre des Trios pour les Violons, Flûtes et Hautbois* of 1707 includes six trio sonatas for two flutes and continuo which, curiously, are not mentioned by Newman. They are all four-movement sonatas that mix dances (gigues, gavottes, rondeaux) with Italianate preludes. Three of the six sonatas include two fugues (movements 2 and 4) and all but one ends with a fugue. La Barre's 'fugues' are far from academic exercises in the 'learned style' and, except for initial points of imitation, they usually ignore any consistent application of fugal procedures. The final movement of the last sonata is yet another example of a combination 'fugue' and 'gigue'.

La Barre was the first to publish collections of pieces scored for two treble instruments without bass. Between 1709 and 1725 there is a total of 15 suites for two flutes *sans basse*. As is so often the case during this period of wide latitude in performance possibilities, one must beware of categorizing and tabulating on the basis of title alone. Composers and publishers were often so eager to propagate performances and/or sales that their *avertissements* at times belied their titles. The *Avertissement* to La Barre's first book for flute and continuo points out that the accompaniment may be dropped for most of the pieces.

Jacques Hotteterre, 'le Romain', was more influential as a flute virtuoso and writer of instruction manuals than as a composer for his instrument, although Jane Bowers comments on the high musical quality of his works which 'are more consistently imaginative and well-wrought than the works of La Barre'.[13] Of some interest is the little instruction book *L'Art de Préluder sur la Flûte traversière, sur la Flûte à bec, Sur le Haubois, et Autres Instrumens de Dessus*, of 1719, which includes exercises called Preludes along with many musical examples to illustrate various problems of performance. Thirty-two years after his

Example 96
Boismortier: Extract from Allemande of Sonata VI for flute without bass (after ed. of 1725).

337

death, Lully heads the list of composers from whom Hotteterre draws his examples. Lully is cited 32 times while Corelli comes in a poor second with 10 examples.

Joseph Bodin de Boismortier was the most prolific composer of flute music in the first half of the eighteenth century. Bowers lists 48 opus numbers by Boismortier that include parts for flute. He was most influential in establishing the sonata as opposed to the suite as the preferred form for flute music in France. From 1724 to 1733 he composed eight books of sonatas for two flutes without bass. The Opus VI of flute duets of 1725 includes six sonatas and, as the example above from the Allemande of the last sonata shows, it is attractive music idiomatically conceived for the instruments.

The four sets of sonatas for flute and continuo (Opus III, 1724; Opus IX, 1725; Opus XIX, 1727; Opus XLIV, 1733) are among the first of their kind in France. The six sonatas of Opus III are typical of his style. Each is in four movements and each is a *sonata da camera* dominated by French dances (allemendes, courantes, sarabandes, gavottes). The music is superficially elegant and makes few demands on listener or performer. The six sonatas of Opus XCI[14] (1741) are the only examples in France of works composed for flute and obbligato keyboard. Boismortier also left us ten sets of trio sonatas composed between 1724 and 1740 which include parts for at least one flute, and during the decade 1720–30 he published at least 30 concertos that included parts for solo flute and which could be 'reduced' to trio sonatas 'by omitting the *ripieno*'.[15]

Although mainly committed to the concerto (see Chapter 20, pp. 312–314), Michel Corrette in his Opus II followed the lead of Boismortier in composing sonatas (1727) for two flutes without bass. More important for the solo flute literature in France are the sonatas of two performer-composers, Jacques-Christophe Naudot and Michel Blavet. Naudot was less interested in duet sonatas and concentrated instead on pieces for flute and bass of which six books are extant. On the other hand, Blavet's Opus I (1728) contains six sonatas for two flutes without bass followed by two collections (Opus II, 1732; Opus III, 1740) of sonatas for flute and bass. Between 1731 and 1735, Blavet rivalled the popularity of the violinists Leclair and Guignon at the *Concert Spirituel*.

Many other composers contributed to the burgeoning flute literature in France before a decline set in between 1740 and 1750. Chief among these are Pierre-Gabriel Buffardin, Louis de Caix d'Hervelois, Nicolas Chédeville, Andre Chéron, Louis-Gabriel Guillemain, Jacques Louillet, Thomas Lot, J.-J. Cassanéa de Mondonville, Quentin Le Jeune, Clair-Nicolas Roger and Alexandre Villeneuve.

Chapter XV of Michel Corrette's *Méthode théorique et pratique pour apprendre ... le Violoncelle* (1741) is aimed for those who already

'know how to play the Viol and who wish to learn the Violoncello ...
as the majority of those who play the Viol presently have the taste for
playing the Violoncello'. Corrette's treatise appeared two years after
the spectacular success of Martin Berteau (Berthau, Berteaud, ?–1756)
as violoncellist soloist at the *Concert Spirituel* in 1739, and Berteau's
performance followed by ten years the publication of the first sonatas
for violoncello, the Opus XXVI of Boismortier. The title, *Cinq sonates
pour le violoncelle, viole ou basson*, as is so often the case, allows for
multiple performance possibilities. The sonatas are all in the SFSF
tempo scheme and each sonata includes at least one dance movement.
The five sonatas are followed by a concerto for cello, viol or bassoon
which qualifies for the position of the first French solo concerto. Boismortier followed this collection with a second set of five sonatas plus
one trio sonata for cello (Opus L, 1734). Neither collection makes difficult demands on the performer and in spite of a total compass of two
octaves and a fifth, the tessitura rarely requires leaving the first position. Of comparable difficulty are the six sonatas for cello, viol or bassoon by Michel Corrette subtitled 'Les Délices de la solitude' (Opus
XX, *c.* 1733).

Of much greater significance are the six *Sonates pour le violoncelle,
avec la basse continue* by Jean Barrière (1705–1747) first published
in 1733. Indeed, Berteau's performance at the *Concert Spirituel* in
1739, Corrette's method of 1741 and the eventual publication in 1740
of Books I–IV of Barrière's cello sonatas (see Newman, p. 388) did
more than anything else to popularize the cello in France and to doom
the bass viol as a solo instrument in spite of the great prestige of such
virtuosi as Antoine Forqueray (1672–1745) and Louis de Caix
d'Hervelois (1680–1760).

Even a glance at the incipits of the Barrière sonatas[16] reveals that we
are no longer in the realm of works for cello *or* other instruments sharing the same range. Double stops abound and sweeping *tirades* of 32nd
notes found in certain Adagio movements (see, for example, Sonata
No. 5 of Book I) would not be out of place in a Bach cello suite. The
movement scheme in Books I–III is basically SFSF. In Book IV, however, Barrière adopted the three movement scheme of the Italian concerto.

Suites for Viol

La Barre concluded his *Avertissement* to his 1710 set of suites for the
transverse flute with a tribute to Marin Marais: 'I believed that for
the glory of my Flute ... I should follow the example of M. Marais,
who took so much care and trouble to perfect the Viol and who
succeeded so happily in this end.' In like manner we take a backward

glance and conclude this chapter with a discussion of the extensive literature for one, two or three viols by Marais and his followers.[17]

According to Jean Rousseau (dates unknown), 'the first men to excel as performers on the Viol in France were Messieurs Maugard (André Maugars) and Hotman (Nicolas Hotman, died 1663)' (*Traité de la viole*, 1687, p. 23). However, it was Hotman's student, Sainte-Colombe, who was really responsible for developing both the instrument itself and the technique of viol performance in the seventeenth century. Rousseau dedicated his treatise to his teacher, Sainte-Colombe, and informs us that it was Sainte-Colombe who added the seventh string to the instrument, thus extending its range down to low A. The use of the seventh string may be easily observed in Sainte-Colombe's *Concerts à deux Violes*, a manuscript collection now in the Bibliothèque Nationale.[18] There are 67 'concerts', each containing from two to five pieces unified by tonality. They reveal Sainte-Colombe to have been a composer full of fantasy and rich imagination. Dances and character pieces co-exist. The most frequently found titled dances in the *Concerts* are sarabandes (22), gavottes (26) and gigues (20). Surprisingly, there are only 12 minuets and 5 courantes.

In the same year as Rousseau's *Traité de la Viole* (1687), Danoville, another of Sainte-Colombe's students, published his *Traité pour toucher le dessus et basse de violle*. Danoville, like Rousseau, is concerned with hand positions, finger charts and ornamentation and even more than Rousseau with lavishing praise on his teacher, whom he characterized as the 'Orphée de nostre temps'.

The earliest extant music for solo viol in France is by Du Buisson, who composed four suites for bass viol without continuo dating from 1666 (manuscript in Library of Congress). What appears to be the first printed music for solo viol in France preceded by two years the viol tutors by Rousseau and Danoville and by one year the first book of *Pièces à une et à deux Violes* by Marais. These *Pièces de Violles* were composed by Demachy, about whom little is known. This burst of activity in the late 1680's documents Rousseau's observation that 'until recently [the viol] has not been esteemed in France'.

Most important of all the students of Sainte-Colombe was Marin Marais (1656–1728) who was recognized in the eighteenth century as 'an incomparable Parisian violist whose works are known all over Europe' (Johann Gottfried Walther, *Musikalisches Lexicon*, 1732). His compositions for one, two or three viols and continuo number over 550 and are distributed in five books (Book I, 1686; Book II, 1701; Book III, 1711; Book IV, 1717; and Book V, 1725). In 1689 he published a *Basse-Continue des Pièces à une ou à deux Violes* which is actually the continuo part for the first book but which in addition includes 10 new compositions in score rather than in the customary part books.

Each book contains over 100 compositions arranged, as in Couperin, in suites with a mixture of titled dances and descriptive pieces. There are, indeed, some superficial parallels between the Marais of the *Pièces de Violes* and the Couperin of the *Pièces de Clavecin*. Both composers are miniaturists who, at their best, show a sense of fantasy, a freedom of invention disciplined by melodic purity and an unerring sense of rhythmic organization. Both make allowances for different media of performance (Marais sanctioned performances on organ, harpsichord, lute, theorbo, violin, treble viol, transverse flute, recorder, guitar and oboe!—see *Avertissements* to Books II and III). Both Couperin and Marais left extensive *Avertissements* with rather precise information on how they wanted their pieces performed.[19]

From the first book, Marais attempted to balance the many pieces of each suite by including compositions that are relatively easy alongside those of considerable difficulty. It is unlikely that the suites were ever meant to be performed as a unit, but rather that one might pick and choose on the basis of taste or one's technical proficiency. In this respect the suites are more loosely organized than those by Couperin and contain, in general, many more individual numbers. The policy of mixing the difficult with the easy is discreetly expressed by Marais in his *Avertissement* to the first book:

> And because most people have a taste for simple melodies, I have, with this in mind, composed some pieces almost without chords; one will find others where I have used them [chords] to advantage, and several which are entirely filled [with chords] for those who love harmony and who are more advanced.

Marais differs markedly from Couperin in that he makes little conscious effort to achieve anything resembling a 'goûts réunis' in his viol suites. This is not surprising, since the music itself is so wedded to the instrument and so bound to the tradition of virtuoso solo performance in France. It will be remembered that, many years prior to Marais, Maugars discovered that the Italians had already given up solo performance on the viol. Thus, the sources of Marais' suites are the French dance and earlier genres such as the *tombeaux* cultivated by the lutenists and harpsichordists. Included in Book II are two *tombeaux*: one for 'Mons. de Lully' and the other for 'M. de Sainte-Colombe'; Book I has a particularly moving example, the 'Tombeau de M. Meliton'.

Some of the expressive and quasi-improvisatory preludes, especially from Book II, seem to derive from the lute repertory in particular. The same ornaments, the same melodic turns and rhythms are found. As we move through the suites, descriptive and genre pieces come more into view. In the final book, for example, the last suite includes 25 pieces, and only 4 lack descriptive titles. The increase in the number of descriptive pieces from Book I to V is undoubtedly due to the pervading influence of Couperin's *Pièces de Clavecin*, and Marais himself clearly stated in the *Avertissement* to the fifth book that 'since character pieces are received favourably today, I have judged it appropriate to insert several. The different titles will indicate the meaning easily.' The most notorious of these character pieces is the famous 'Le Tableau de l'Opération de la Taille' ('A Presentation of the Gall-Bladder Operation')[20] which includes titles in the score proper such as 'The sight of the equipment', 'Shivering on observing it', 'The descent of the equipment', 'Serious reflections', etc.

The most demanding of all of the books of viol suites is the fourth which Marais divided into three sections: the first, composed of pieces that are 'easy, of a singing nature and with few chords'; the second, aimed for those who are 'advanced on the viol'; and the third consists of pieces for three viols 'which had not been done before in France'. (Yet, see page 291 for contradictory information.)

Section II contains a descriptive suite entitled 'Suitte d'un goût Etranger' with 36 different pieces in several different keys. Included are pieces bearing such titles as 'Le Labyrinth' and 'Allemande la Bizarre'. The former composition includes many different key signatures within the same piece, a series of melodic tritones with sudden shifts of register and a progression through a thorny 'labyrinth' of keys far removed from the home Tonic.

When the quality of Couperin's *Pièces de Violes* (Paris, 1728) is considered, it is regrettable that he did not write more music for this instrument. The two suites that comprise the set are musically superior to the *concerts* from *Les Goûts réunis* written for 'two viols or other instruments of the same pitch' (Nos. 12 and 13). Both suites are scored for two viols; the second viol part is designed as a continuo with harpsichord realization, although there is nothing to prevent the performance of the suites on two unaccompanied viols.

The two suites, of modest dimensions, present many different aspects of the French dance suite. The first, in E-Minor, contains only titled dances following a prelude (allemande, courante, sarabande grave, gavotte, gigue and passacaille); the second, in A-Major, includes no titled dances and, as is true in the final *concert* of *Les Goûts réunis*, it approaches a four-movement sonata (gravement, fuguette, pompe funèbre, 'La Chemise blanche').

The prelude to the first suite is a compendium of French harmonic and melodic practices of the period. It employs dotted rhythms and *tirades*; its short phrases are given amplitude by a melodic contour that includes many expressive intervals; the use of melodic sequence and chromaticism is restrained, and dissonance is achieved mainly through the typical *ports de voix* and *coulés* of French ornamentation with one striking dissonant use of the mediant $\sharp\substack{7 \\ 5 \\ 2}$ chord in measure

33. As we have observed elsewhere in the music of Couperin, features of a particularly strong initial movement occasionally carry over into subsequent movements. Thus in this first viol suite, the Sarabande Grave repeats the descending melodic patterns found in the prelude in dotted notes.

The second suite includes the greatest possible contrast of material; the first two sections resemble the opening movement of an Italian church sonata with a fugal second movement in which both instruments share the melodic material equally. The third movement, a Lullian 'Tombeau', makes its effect through a breadth of melody, rich harmonies achieved by the use of double stops, and a formal clarity resulting from the relatively infrequent use, in Couperin, of a rounded binary form. It is in total contrast to the last movement, 'La Chemise blanche', a humorous descriptive piece that closes the suite in a continuous swirl of rapid 16th note patterns.

As we have observed, in spite of the talents of such students of Marin Marais as his son, Roland-Pierre (*c.* 1680–*c.* 1750), Jacques Morel (born *c.* 1700) and Louis de Caix d'Hervelois (*c.* 1680–*c.* 1760), the voice of the solo viol was stilled in France after the mid-eighteenth century. The adoption by viol composers of fashionable Italian clichés, on the one hand, and a retreat into ever more difficult performance techniques, on the other, pulled post-Marais viol music two ways at the same time and did nothing to stem its decline. This direction may be observed in Book v (1748) of Louis de Caix d'Hervelois' *Pièces à deux Violes* where, for example, *da capo* forms are used within French dance suites.

The two most important members of the Forqueray dynasty are Antoine (*c.* 1671–1745) and his son, Jean-Baptiste-Antoine (1699–1782).[21] Both were virtuoso performers and composers although the *Mercure de France* of 1738 chided them for having written pieces 'so difficult that only he (Forqueray, *père*) and his son can execute them with grace'.[22]

With the exception of a few dances in manuscript, all that remains of the elder Forqueray's production are five suites for viol and continuo published in 1747 by his son. Jean-Baptiste-Antoine sadly conceded that 'the viol, in spite of its advantages, has fallen ino oblivion'. A poignant epitaph for the instrument can be seen in the earnest efforts of the younger Forqueray to perpetuate the musical heritage represented by his father. At the same time as the above publication, he made harpsichord transcriptions of his father's suites adding three pieces of his own to the third suite 'as it did not contain enough pieces'.[23]

Part five

Vocal Chamber Music

Chapter 22

→»-«‹-

The Air de Cour and Related Genres

For almost 200 years the *air de cour* served French composers as a primary source for their vocal music.[1] Lully chose it rather than Italian aria and recitative as a model for the airs and dialogues of his court and comedy ballets and his *tragédies lyriques*; the *récits* of many seventeenth century motets were nourished by it; and in combination with dance measures its influence was even felt in instrumental music where, in the case of the fantasia and organ repertory, it succeeded in initiating important stylistic changes. Its restricted range and generally conservative harmony acted as a deterrent to the adoption of Italian vocal techniques throughout much of the *grand siècle*. Even after the turn of the century its identity was maintained in such collections as the *Airs sérieux et à boire* published by J. B. C. Ballard.

For Lecerf the *air de cour* was the touchstone against which all French vocal writing was to be judged. Predictably, the melodies of many French cantatas with their Italianate vocalises failed the test. 'What has become of *le bon goût*', railed Lecerf, 'Must it too expire under the confused jumble of all these Cantatas? What would the Lamberts, the Boëssets, the Le Camus and the Baptistes say were it possible for them to return to earth only to find French melody so changed, so degraded and so disfigured?' (*Comparaison*, I, p. 302).

The sixteenth century used many different terms such as 'vaudeville', 'air', 'air de cour' and 'chansonette' to designate vocal airs. The first publication actually to bear the title of 'air de cour' was Adrian Le Roy's *Livre d'Airs de Cour* of 1571. In his dedication to the Comtesse de Retz, Le Roy documented the rise of the court air from the popular *vaudeville* and clearly differentiated it from the polyphonic chanson. He described the chansons of Lassus as 'difficult and arduous' in contrast to his 'much lighter little collection of court chansons which were formerly called *voix de ville* and today, *Airs de Cour* ...'. So it was, wrote Levy, that the homophonic and popular genre of the *vaudeville* acquired a new dignity in the guise of the court air.[2] The word 'air' was applied indiscriminately to a polyphonic vocal composition in four or five parts and to its transcription for solo voice and lute. Although more than 500 ensemble airs appeared from 1576 to 1600 there were no subsequent sixteenth century collections for solo voice and lute following that of Le Roy in 1571.

In the early years of the seventeenth century there was a shift in emphasis from a random mixture of many different types of airs in a collection to a clear separation of genres with the *air de cour* gradually severing its ties with the *vaudeville* and becoming more serious and at the same time more *précieux*. Reflecting this change was the poetry chosen for *airs de cour*. The genre was dominated by themes and images drawn from Petrarch and fashioned by Desportes and his followers into a sentimental and *précieux* language. Through the first half of the seventeenth century, the verses of Philippe Desportes were among those most sought after by composers of court airs. In addition, the names of François de Malherbe, Honorat de Racan, Saint-Amant, Théophile de Vau, Jacques Davy Du Perron, Boisrobert, Honoré d'Urfé and Tristan l'Hermite are conspicuous in many *recueils*.

André Verchaly, in comparing the contents of two sets of airs published seven years apart by Jacques Mangeant, documented the increased significance of the *air de cour* as a separate genre.[3] In 1608 in Caen, Mangeant printed three collections of solo airs all bearing the title, *Airs nouveaux, accompagnez des plus belles chansons à dancer.* The publisher in his preface described how youths would often dance to songs were there no instruments available, and it was this observation that occasioned him to solicit appropriate texts for dance songs among his poet friends. The collection then is a mélange of *chansons à danser*, with and without texts, and polyphonic *airs de cour* with only the treble notated. Branles, courantes, voltes, villanelles, pastorales, *airs de ballet*, *chansons à boire* and *airs de cour* are found in a seemingly random selection.

In 1615 Mangeant again published three collections of solo airs. The first volume is almost entirely composed of *airs de cour* extracted from various ensembles and solo collections of the time. These are serious and often elegant melodies showing little trace of their humble origins.[4] In contrast, the second and third volumes include the 'plus belles Chansons de dancer de ce temps' (vol. II) and the 'plus belles Chansons des Comédiens François' (vol. III).

In 1608 Pierre Ballard printed the first book of *Airs de différents autheurs mis en tablature de luth* intabulated by Gabriel Bataille (1575–1630). There are 16 books in this important collection with Bataille responsible for Books I–VI (1615), and Antoine Boësset (1587?–1643), for Books XI–XVI (1643); Books VII and VIII were intabulated by the composers of the airs themselves. In addition to Bataille, the following composers are among the 'différents auteurs' of this set: Pierre Guédron, Guillaume Tessier, Jacques Mauduit, Vincent, Antoine Boësset, J. Thibaut de Courville, Sauvage and Jacques Le Fevre. Other significant collections of court airs 'mis en tablature de luth' are the five books (1624–35) by Etienne Moulinié, Pierre Ballard's eight books of melodies only (1615–28) and the collections of Jean Boyer (1621), Louis de Rigaud (1623), François Richard (1637) and Denis Caignet (1625). The above collections embrace over 1,000 airs for solo voice and lute and include some examples for voice and guitar as well.

Co-existing with court airs 'mis en tablature de luth' were the collections of ensemble airs in four or five parts that in many instances were the original source for the solo airs. Among the most important of the collections of *Airs de cour à quatre et cinq parties* that date from the first half of the seventeenth century are the six books of Guédron (from 1602–20), nine books of Antoine Boësset (1617–42), Books III–V of Moulinié (1635–39, Books I and II are lost) and one book each by Boyer (1619) and Richard (1637).

In general, the ensemble version was printed first and given the signature of the composer. Afterwards, an intabulation for lute and solo voice was made often by someone other than the composer. Some editions were published with solo voice only, and as we move along in the seventeenth century, some airs exist as accompanied monodies or dialogues independent of any known polyphonic source. The melodic shape of the solo air remains fairly close to that of its ensemble original with the exception of rhythmic changes to allow for the numerous *ports de voix* and diminutions which were added sometimes to deepen the expressive content but more often to afford the singer a vehicle for vocal display.

The formal structure of most *airs de cour* is simple. Short stanzas made up of four or six lines are arranged musically in a variety of binary forms with AB, AAB or AA BB being the most common. In earlier collections, the stanzas usually are organized verbally by octosyllables or alexandrines. Bar lines, which in the Le Roy 1571 collection actually mark the isometric divisions, cease to have any metric function in the early seventeenth century. Rather, they were employed to mark the end of each line of poetry. Metre signs, when used, had no metric significance and may be viewed merely as a convenient way of grouping time units; they must never be interpreted as depicting strong or weak metric accents.

Walker divides early seventeenth century *airs de cour* into two distinct rhythmic groups: the first obeys a principle in which text metre is emphasized by notes of a longer duration at caesura points and at the ends of lines; the second group is completely free rhythmically with no discernible metrical plan and often a total disregard for verbal prosody.[5] This distortion of the verbal rhythm was noted by an English publication of *French Court Aires with their Ditties Englished* printed in 1629 by a Ed. Filmer Gent. who wrote in the preface that 'the French when they compose to a ditty in their own Language being led rather by their free Fant'sie of Aire . . . than by any strict and artificiall scanning of the Line, doe often, by disproportion'd Musicall Quantities, invert the naturell Stroke of a Verse . . .' (quoted by Walker, p. 158).

Although cautioning against blaming the influence of the *vers mesuré* for all the ills of text distortion in the early seventeenth century *air de cour*, Walker concedes that application of some of the *vers mesuré* principles was a contributing factor. Its influence may be clearly seen in Example 97 below which also illustrates Walker's first group with point of caesura and the end of the octosyllabic set in longer note values.

Example 97
Influence of vers mesuré *on* air de cour *(after 2ᵉ Livre d'Airs, Bataille, 1609).*

C'est un a - mant, ouvrez la por - te, Il est pleind'a-mour et de foy

Disregard for the natural verbal rhythm of the text is nowhere more evident than in the vogue for diminutions that converted subsequent strophes of the air into true 'doubles'. The results of this practice in which the musician runs roughshod over the poet may be observed in the airs by Boësset and Moulinié with their subsequent couplets 'en diminution' included by Mersenne in his *Harmonie universelle* ('Embellissement de chants', p. 410) in order that 'each might imitate the method of those who teach singing in Paris, & whose exercise and Art consists in knowing how to compose good Melodies & how to create diminutions and embellishments'.[6] In many instances a different composer provided the embellished strophe. According to Bacilly, Henry du Bailly (died 1637) was a specialist 'who dedicated himself entirely to the ornamentation of other men's works, without spending any time whatsoever at original composition'.[7]

Pierre Guédron (1565–1621),[8] who in 1601 succeeded Claude Le Jeune as composer of the *Chambre du Roi*, dominated the early years of seventeenth century *air de cour* production. Although any direct influence of Italian recitative in his airs is minimal, he does, nonetheless, exhibit a genuine feeling for the dramatic representation of the text—a fact which suggests the possibility that he may have been impressed with the court performances of Caccini in 1604 and 1605. Unlike most of his peers, Guédron took care to avoid the distortion of verbal rhythms described above.

Some of his melodies are in the tradition of the popular chanson (see Example 98a below), but his most important contribution was the creation of a supple and convincing melodic style in the *récits* of the court ballets that may be numbered among the first models for French recitative. Example 98b, 'Quel excès de douleur', is a *récit* with no polyphonic original. Its discreet use of 'affective' intervals and its narrow melodic range are typical of Guédron who even in his *récits* held to the strophic tradition of the *air de cour*.

Guédron, and later Antoine Boësset, were the first in France to make a timid use of the basso continuo long before the Ballard 1650 publication of Du Mont's *Cantica sacra* (see Chapter 12, p. 162). Admittedly, Guédron's polyphonic setting of 'Berger, que penses vous faire' (Book III, 1617) contains no more than bass fragments scored 'Pour le luth', but as Verchaly points out they represent the first appearance in France of a continuo here used in support of a dramatic dialogue. Bataille's intabulation of this air in his fourth book represents, then, the first genuine realization of a continuo line in France (Verchaly, *Airs de cour pour voix et luth*, p. xlvi).

This innovation was not seized upon by the conservative French,

Example 98
Melodic style in Guédron.
(*a*) '*Sus sus Bergers*' (*after 5e Livre d'Airs, Guédron, 1620*).
(*b*) '*Quel excès de douleur*' (*after 9e Livre d'Airs, Boësset, 1620*).

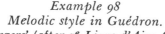

although Boësset from 1620 on has occasional passages in his polyphonic airs scored only 'Pour le luth'. It was not until 13 years later in his seventh book that Boësset included a 'basse continue pour les instruments' for the five-part air 'Mourons Tirsis' (*ibid.*, p. lxiv) and not until 25 years later that the same composer in his ninth book included other ensemble airs with continuo.

François Richard (*c.* 1585–1650), in the dedication to Louis XIII found in his *Airs de cour à quatre parties* (1637), alluded to the pleasure the king took in the music of his Chamber: 'I know that after the sounds of the Trumpets and Drums (of war), that of Lute and voices does not displease you.' Richard is an important forerunner of Lambert and Lully in the development of dialogue airs. The dialogue 'Cloris attends un peu' from the *Airs de cour avec le tablature de luth* (1637) concludes with an 'operatic' duo sung by Tircis and Cloris.

Dialogues could also exist with polyphonic settings of *airs de cour*. The dialogue 'Faut-il mourir sans espérance' by François de Chancy (*c.* 1600–56), Book I (1635) uses a four-part chorus for its refrain and shares its dialogues between soprano and tenor.

Etienne Moulinié and Antoine Boësset are among the most important composers of court airs following Guédron. Unlike Guédron, however, there is little feeling for the dramatic in their airs. Rather, there is a natural facility that created melodies of refined grace and suppleness. As early as 1628, Moulinié was the 'chef de musique' for Louis XIII's brother, Gaston d'Orléans, whose household was one of the most musical in the realm. Gaston had recourse to the king's 24 *Violons*, kept a vocal ensemble of seven or eight singers and by 1643 had already divided his musical estate into 'Chambre' and 'Chapelle' modelled on that of the king. Marolles commented that Gaston had 'the best dancers in France' which possibly accounts for the large number of vocal extracts from court ballets found among the works of Moulinié.

Moulinié's name appears most often in the collections of *airs de cour* printed between 1624 and 1639. There is, however, one book of *Airs à quatre avec la B. C.*, his last known work, that was printed by Ballard in 1668 at which time the composer described himself as 'maistre de la musique des Etats de Languedoc'.

The 16 books of *airs de cour* by Antoine Boësset[9] give us the most complete picture of the development of the genre from Guédron to Michel Lambert. Of all the composers of court airs, Boësset was perhaps the greatest melodist. The thought persists that Guédron was inhibited by the narrow frame of the air and that he would have wished a larger canvas to display his dramatic gifts. Not so with Boësset—the miniature design with all of its limitations, far from having a deleterious effect on the composer, actually seems to have stimulated him to shape and mould exquisite melodies of modest proportions. In addition, in his long career, Boësset became more and more sensitive to the setting of the text. He made less use, for example, of the purely abstract melodic patterns that in earlier collections were often employed indiscriminately with little regard for the text. Even some of the best *récits* of Guédron are marred by such patterns as are illustrated below:

Example 99
Use of abstract melodic patterns in Guédron.

After ten years of silence, Boësset brought out his ninth book of *Airs de cour à quatre et cinq parties*. 'My advancing age', he wrote in the dedication to the king, 'causes me to lose little by little the ardour of youth and diminishes the gaiety necessary for the embellishment of the Airs; thus, I am unable to produce them in as great a number as when I had the force and vigour of my early years.' It is true that these products of Boësset's old age are tinted with a 'gay melancholy' not unlike some of the lute pieces of his contemporaries; at the same time, however, the book contains some of the composer's best efforts. There is a greater melodic amplitude achieved by longer phrases and a more extensive vocal range. There is also an intensity of expression rarely encountered in the *air de cour* which is achieved by a more conspicuous use of affective intervals, a careful placement of rests for dramatic effect and the judicious use of repeated text fragments.

The remarkable change of style reflected in the example below surely owes something to Italian vocal writing, and it is no accident that according to Lecerf the melodies of Boësset were admired by Luigi Rossi. Undoubtedly the person most responsible for orienting the *air de cour* more towards an expressive realization of the text was the singer Pierre de Nyert (c. 1597–1682), friend of La Fontaine, who

Example 100
Melodic intensity in late Boësset (after ed. of 1642).

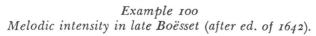

sometime after 1633 studied in Rome. According to Saint-Evremond, Nyert believed that 'in order to render music pleasurable, one should hear Italian airs in the mouth of a Frenchman' (quoted by Prunières, *L'Opéra italien en France*, p. 96). After 1640 Nyert's influence was felt everywhere among composers and performers of French vocal music. He was a favourite singer of Louis XIII and one of the strongest influences on Lambert and above all on Bacilly who, in his *Remarques curieuses sur l'art de bien chanter* (1668), attempted a reform of French singing by systematizing rules of pronunciation, ornamentation, prosody and correct breathing.

Not all were convinced that the salvation of the *air de cour* lay in the 'method' of Nyert or the more intensely personal language of Boësset's ninth book. In fact opposition to the new style was in part responsible for confrontation between Boësset and the Dutch musician-priest Johannes Albertus Bannius.[10] Although only a minor skirmish, it involved some of the most important names in French music and aesthetics of the time, and it stemmed from the same age-old impulses that brought about such a major battle as that between Artusi and Monteverdi at the beginning of the seventeenth century.

Both Bannius and Boësset composed an air on the text 'Me veux-tu voir mourir'. In a letter to Anne Maria van Schuurman, found today in the Bibliothèque Mazarine, Bannius gives a detailed criticism of Boësset's setting with special emphasis on the latter's use of the tritone (actually a diminished 5th) in the opening phrase. Boësset received the support of Mersenne who indeed had been the prime mover behind the 'little harmonic combat' (see Walker, p. 234). In a letter to Huygens Mersenne commented that Boësset had, after all, 'divided the tritone into two minor thirds (see 'voir mourir' in Example 101 below), thereby softening the harshness'. In a conciliatory manner, Descartes wrote to Mersenne in 1640 as follows: 'with regard to the music of M. Ban [Bannius] I believe that it differs from the air of Boësset as the exercises in rhetoric of a student eager to practice all the rules differs from an oration of Cicero' (quoted by Pirro, p. 119).

Bannius had indeed composed his music by employing a 'science très certaine' (Pirro) and had even contrived the key of F without a B flat because that to him expressed 'indignation'. Yet we can tell at a glance that his music is stillborn. His opening phrase is awkward and unconvincing, lacking rapport with the text, whereas, the melody of Boësset is a little masterpiece of musico-dramatic expression.

After the 16th book of Boësset's *Airs de cour avec la tablature de luth* (1643), the use of lute tablature became much less frequent. The basso continuo was substituted with the theorbo preferred as the principal accompanying instrument ('The viol and harpsichord have not the grace and accommodation found in the theorbo', Bacilly). The change from lute tablature to continuo went hand in hand with the

Example 101
Opening phrase of 'Me veux-tu mourir' by Bannius and Boësset.

Me veux – tu voir mourir   Me veux-tu voir mourir

Bannius   *Boësset*

abandonment of the designation 'air de cour'. In the collections of
the second half of the seventeenth century, the simple terms 'air' or
'air sérieux' were used instead.

In a Ms *Recueil de paroles de musique* (B. N. fr. 2208, *c.* 1667),
Perrin has given us a working definition of the 'air' as seen by composers and authors of the period of Louis XIV:

> The Air is organized in a free but serious measure and thus
> is more proper for the expression of love . . . and tender
> emotions. . . . It does not exceed the length of six lines. . . . In
> my opinion, the best are (composed of) *quatrains, cinquains* or
> *sixaines* of irregular lengths. It may be composed in three parts
> (texture), but it succeeds best in two. . . . It may make use of
> *Rondeaux* at the beginning, in the middle, at the end. . . .
> The *Chanson* differs from the Air in that the Air as we have
> said, follows a free measure, and the Chanson (follows a) metre
> regulated by the dance. . . .

Bacilly also created a separate category for those 'short airs . . . such
as Gavottes, Sarabandes and Minuets' and warned that it was always
necessary to 'maintain the metric proportions so as not to alter a
minuet or a sarabande to such an extent that it becomes a song in
free metre, such as is usually implied by the term "air"' (*Remarques
curieuses*, trans. Caswell, p. 49).

The various collections of airs published by Robert Ballard and
later by Jean-Baptiste-Christophe Ballard are among the richest sources
of airs for the second half of the seventeenth century and the early
years of the eighteenth century. Such a collection is the 38 volume
Airs de différents autheurs à deux parties printed and edited by
Robert Ballard between 1658 and 1694. Unfortunately, Ballard identified neither composers nor poets in the above collection. We must
rely on Bacilly's three-part *Recueil des plus beaux vers qui ont esté
mis en chant* in which Bacilly helpfully provided the names of the
'Authors of the Airs as well as of the Words'. The first part of this
important source was published in 1661, and Bacilly attested to the
popularity of the art of singing in France at mid-century: 'The number of those who sing being infinite, there is no one who does not

353

have his favourite *chanson*; And the collection would have little merit if he could not find it here in its proper category.'

The composer most often cited by Bacilly is Michel Lambert followed in order of frequency by Sébastien Le Camus, Louis de Mollier, Antoine Boësset, Bacilly, Moulinié, Jean-Baptiste Boësset, Jean de Cambefort, François Richard, Sablières, Joseph Chabanceau de La Barre and Chambonnières. Of these composers Michel Lambert (*c.* 1610–96) is the most representative composer of airs in the second half of the seventeenth century. He owed his fame as much to his singing and teaching of voice as to his compositions themselves. In the words of Lecerf, the airs of Lambert represented the quintessence of French vocal music and the most important models for Lully. Seen in this light the miniaturist Lambert received larger-than-life treatment from Lecerf:

> After him (Bailly) came Lambert who, in the opinion of all Europe, was the best Master to have appeared for many centuries. His song was so natural, so clear, so graceful that one sensed its charm immediately. . . . There was no one in Paris, French or foreigner, who did not wish to study with him, and he led the way for such a long time that he had a thousand excellent Students. His method spread in a few years to the Provinces. . . . The Opéra of Paris prescribed it.
>
> (*Comparaison*, ii, p. 77.)

Lambert's first collection, dedicated to Nyert, was engraved by Richer in 1660. The vocal technique employed by Lambert and his students may be observed in the 'doubles' provided for each air in this collection. At the same time, this continues the practice of the domination of poet by musician, and it is easy to understand why Lully, as a text-oriented composer, was opposed to this tradition. Collected over many years, the *Airs à une, deux, trois et quatre parties avec la basse continue* of 1689 sums up the art of Michel Lambert. The chronology of these airs is difficult to determine, and it may be that in such airs as 'Ma Bergère est tendre & fidelle' or 'Vos mespris' both constructed over chaconne basses, Lambert was influenced by La Barre or even by his son-in-law. Most airs in the collection begin with a *ritournelle* for two violins and continuo followed by solo and ensemble settings all sharing the same melodic and harmonic materials. Most of Lambert's airs use the short binary structure so typical of the *air de cour*. There are some examples of rounded binary airs (see 'Mes yeux, que vos plaisirs') and airs *en rondeau* (see 'Ah! qui voudra desormais s'engager'). Some borrow the rhythmic organization of sarabandes and minuets and some are organized as dialogues. Certain of his more dramatic airs (see 'Ombre de mon amant')

354

border on recitative and may have had an influence on those who created French opera.

The *Airs à deux parties avec les seconds couplets en diminution* (1669) by the king's organist Joseph Chabanceau de La Barre (1633–78) are more innovative with regard to form than are the airs of Lambert. La Barre, on the other hand, even experimented with the binary format: Part A of 'Quand une âme est bien atteinte', for example, is a passacaille; Part B, a short dramatic scene with tempo changes 'Lentement' and 'Gayement' mirroring the text. The technique of converting the second part of an air into a little 'operatic' scene is also found in 'Ah! je sens que mon coeur' in which text repetition, affective intervals and changes of tempo combine to heighten the dramatic effect of this bucolic quarrel.

La Barre's dramatic techniques stem more from the French tradition than from any Italian influence, yet it is worth noting that the above collection includes an 'Air Italien' some 30 years before Ballard's first *Recueil des meilleurs airs italiens*. The air, 'Sospiri ohimè', contains many indications of expression and occasional archaic madrigalisms such as a 'Presto' over 'ridete' in the phrase 'il mio morir ridete'.

In later collections of *airs sérieux*, dramatic elements based on the dialogues of Richard, La Barre, Lambert and others were expanded, and it was not uncommon to find airs, recitatives and ensembles grouped together to form autonomous dramatic entities. Such is the 'Adieu de Tircis à Climène' by Montéclair found in the Ballard *Recueil d'Airs sérieux et à boire* for the month of October 1695. The musical components of the little scene are as follows: 1. Recitative of Tircis; 2. Air of Climène; 3. Recitative of Tircis; 4. Duo.

It is possible that a systematic study of such air-recitative ensemble complexes, scattered throughout the Ballard collections of the late seventeenth century, would shed more light on the early history of the secular cantata in France.

Many of the collections in the later seventeenth century and early eighteenth century carried the generic labels 'Airs sérieux et à boire' in which the healthy strain of lighter genres—the chansons, *vaudevilles, airs à boire, brunettes* and *airs champêtres*—co-existed with the *airs sérieux*. With their broad base of popular appeal, these types had never really been seriously threatened by the more esoteric and *précieux air de cour* and its progeny, the *air sérieux*. Typical of such collections are the *Brunetes ou Petits airs tendres avec les doubles et la basse continue mêlées de chansons à danser* printed by Ballard in 1703, 1704 and 1711. In one of the few studies of popular vocal genres of the French Baroque, Masson has recognized three main catagories of *brunettes*: 1) those pieces in which both the music and the words are of a popular nature; 2) those pieces in which a more worldly type of poetry

355

is combined with melodies of popular origin; and 3) those pieces in which both the poetry and the music is of a more sophisticated nature.[11] The first category corresponds most closely to the 'chansons a danser'. The second and most important category is closely related to the *vaudeville* and the third category resembles in general the *air sérieux.*

Annual publications of *Airs sérieux et à boire* had been initiated by Ballard in the 1670's. Responding to the unprecedented demand for more airs, Ballard in 1694 began a publication bearing the same title intended to appear at the beginning of every month—a practice which continued for over 30 consecutive years. Ballard also adopted the more progressive use of a full score as opposed to the part books of his earlier collections. Scattered throughout these and similar collections are the illustrious names of such composers as Campra, Charpentier, Couperin, Dandrieu, Dornel, Lully, Mouret, Montéclair, Boismortier, Sicard and Rameau.

The *air à boire* had a great vogue throughout the seventeenth century. Pierre Ballard, beginning in 1627, published several collections of *Chansons pour dancer et pour boire.* The example below with its note-against-note texture, its narrow range, symmetrical phrases and

Example 102
A chanson à boire *from Ballard collection of 1637.*

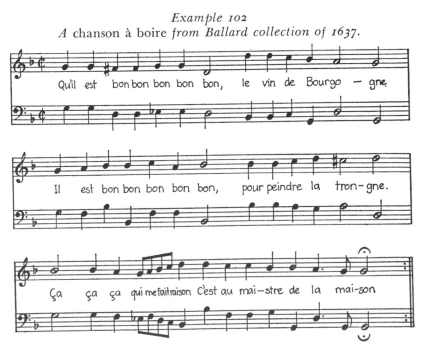

contrasting concluding refrain is taken from the fifth book of 1637. It is altogether typical of the genre in the first half of the century.

Beginning with Bacilly and Sicard, the *airs à boire* became more musically significant. Jean Sicard brought out 17 books of *Airs à boire* between 1666 and 1683. A glance at these collections vindicates the opinions of his peers, many of whom found Sicard the composer 'par excellence' of the Bacchic genre. The range of invention and the variety of musical settings are much greater than one would anticipate. Many are scored for bass voice and two violins and are examples of the 'double continuo' airs found in French opera until Rameau. Some are virtuoso pieces for bass far removed from the naïve simplicity of Example 102. In common with some of the *airs sérieux*, there are even a few *airs à boire* organized as dialogues.

Beginning with Sicard's first 'Advis au Lecteur', there is clear evidence that we are in the presence of a true wit: 'But I confess that I have an extreme passion to divert those indifferent to good taste. . . .' In the third book of 1668, Sicard tells us that he had been advised that year 'to mix in some *Airs Sérieux* among my *Chansons Bachiques*'. One such *air sérieux*, 'Languir', written for soprano, violin ('Si l'on veut') and continuo, is as moving a lament as exists in seventeenth century French music.

Example 103
Sicard: Extracts from 'Languir' (after ed. of 1668).

In the 'Advis' of the fourth book of 1669, Sicard actually blurred the distinctions between his *airs sérieux* and *airs à boire* in stating that 'Among the *Sérieux* there are those that are joyful and demand a fast tempo: there are also among the *Boire* those that demand a *Sérieux* tempo'.

Satire and a raucous humour are apparent in every collection. The duo 'Amis, je suis triste' (Book v, 1670) uses the musical language of an *air tendre* to mourn a broken wine bottle. Amusing is the 'Ne vous estonnez pas' from the same set which, like so many others, is scored for bass voice and two violins. The bass line with its precipitous fall of almost two octaves vividly portrays the meaning of the text.

In addition to the *Airs sérieux et à boire*, Ballard printed many other collections that were made up of related genres. Such are the *Recueil d'airs des comédies modernes* (Book 1, 1706) and above all the *Recueil des meilleurs airs italiens* which were printed from 1699 to 1708. The latter collection, more than any other, reflects the inroads made by Italian vocal music in France at the turn of the century. The last volume of 1708 includes all the previous collections as well for a total of over 115 airs. Most of the airs are really *arie da capo* taken from the *divertissements* of *tragédies lyriques* and *opéras-ballets* with a liberal sprinkling of airs and arias by such Italian composers as Carissimi and Scarlatti; some, although written expressly for such and such a performance of an opera, exist only in this collection.[12]

Chapter 23

⋙⋘

The Cantate Françoise

> *On n'entend parler que de* cantates,
> *on ne voit au coin des rues que des*
> *affiches des* cantates.
>
> (*Dictionnaire de Trévoux*)

The early years of the eighteenth century in France witnessed a brief but rich flowering of the secular cantata.[1] Most of the important collections were composed between 1706 and 1730[2] by which time the genre had already gone out of fashion. It is no accident that 'cantata' and 'sonata' are often coupled together in French sources of the time that describe, sometimes with annoyance, the popularity of these two totally different genres, for the cantata like the sonata was an importation from across the Alps. In the *Mercure* of November 1714, those cantatas and sonatas 'which have inundated all Paris' are blamed squarely for the change in taste that caused Parisian audiences to cool towards Lully's operas. The same journal a year previously had already observed that 'a musician no longer arrives (in Paris) without a sonata or cantata in his pocket'.

French eighteenth century sources are almost unanimous in attributing the birth of the cantata there to the poet Jean-Baptiste Rousseau (1671–1741). Similarly, most eighteenth century writers agree that it was Jean-Baptiste Morin (1677–1745) who, in setting Rousseau's cantata texts to music (1706), was the 'first composer of French Cantatas' (Nemeitz, *Le Séjour de Paris*).

At the same time, there is some evidence that French composers had experimented with cantatas or with at least cantata-like compositions in the previous century. We have mentioned the striking resemblances to the cantata of some of the *airs sérieux* found in late seventeenth century collections. In Perrin's *Oeuvres de Poésie* (1661) and his Ms *Recueil de Paroles de Musique* there are several texts designed for musical settings. Unfortunately, no music for them can be found. The texts are clearly laid out in the format of the cantata, and Perrin took great care to indicate textual divisions into solo, ensemble and chorus—even going so far as to specify the required voices (*dessus, taille,* etc.) for the solo portions. This fact is rendered more tantalizing by the inclusion in the margins of the names of such composers as Moulinié, Boësset, Sablières and Cambert.

Two works by Charpentier dating from the early 1680's must also figure in any pre-history of the French cantata, although since both exist only in manuscript and one is but a fragment, it is difficult to see how they could have had much influence on later composers—a regrettable recurring theme in the evaluation of Charpentier's position in French Baroque music. The first work, 'Coulez, coulez charmans ruisseaux', is identified as a 'Cantate françoise' in an eighteenth century Ms at the Bibliothèque d'Avignon. It is a short fragment of little musical interest for solo voice (tenor), two violins and continuo. The second work, *Orphée descendant aux enfers* (*Méslanges*, vol. 6), is a genuine cantata in the French style.[3] It must have been written for Mlle de Guise and was probably performed at a concert at the Hôtel du Marais. It is scored for three voices, two violins, a recorder, a transverse flute and continuo. The role of Orphée (tenor) may have been

Example 104

Charpentier: *Extract from* Orphée descendant aux enfers (*after the* Meslanges, *vol.* VI).

sung by Charpentier himself. A high point musically is the 'Récit d'Orphée' following the opening *Sinfonia*. It is an accompanied monologue in the tradition of those found in the later operas of Lully but with an Italianate richness of harmony and text painting used to intensify such lines as 'laissez moy descendre aux ombres du trépas!'

There is no mention of any of these seventeenth century 'cantatas' in the many dictionary definitions of the genre in the eighteenth century. In 1703, the cantata for Brossard was still 'an extended composition whose words are in Italian'. It was only in subsequent editions that he offered the information that 'recently French cantatas have been composed which have been very successful'.[4] In his Ms *Mélanges*, Brossard added that 'there is nothing that has been more applauded in France, nothing whose performances have been more generally and widely disseminated than that which we now title *cantate* after the Italian word'. The *Dictionnaire de Trévoux* gives a succinct, clear definition of the eighteenth century French cantata: 'A *cantate* is a piece varied by recitatives, *ariettes* or small airs in contrasting tempos. Ordinarily it is written for solo voice with a continuo, but often two violins or several instruments (are used).'

The most important source, however, to illuminate the early history of the French cantata is Bachelier's *Recueil de Cantates, contenant toutes celles qui se chantent dans les Concerts: pour l'usage des Amateurs de la Musique et de la Poésie* (1728). The *recueil* contains the texts of 99 cantatas including some set by Bernier (24), Clérambault (14), Stuck (11), Morin (7), Bourgeois (2) and Montéclair (12). Texts are by Rousseau, Mennesson, Serré de Rieux, Fuzelier, Thibault and De La Grange; three cantata texts are by the Regent, Philippe d'Orléans.

In the preface, Bachelier acknowledges Jean-Baptiste Rousseau as the first to work in the genre in a manner to satisfy 'les plus délicats' tastes. He quotes in full Rousseau's own description of how he evolved the format of the cantata text:

> The Italians called these short Poems CANTATES, because they are particularly well suited to song. They are ordinarily composed of three Recitatives interspersed with as many *Airs de mouvements*; which fact obliges them to diversify their Strophes whose lines are sometimes long, sometimes short as in the Choruses of the ancient Tragedies and in the majority of the Pindaric Odes. . . . Since I had no other model than that of the Italians who often, as do we in France, sacrifice reason to the convenience of the Musician, I noticed that after composing several (poems), I lost from the verse what was gained by the Music; I wrote nothing of value and was content to amass vain Poetic Phrases, one upon the other, lacking design or liaison with a subject. This is what gave me the idea of creating a form that

would confine these small poems to exact allegorical treatment in which Recitative would furnish the body of the cantata and tuneful Airs, the soul. From among the ancient Fables, I chose those that I deemed most suitable to this design. . . . My plan was successful enough to stimulate many other (poets) to adopt it. Whether or not it is the best plan that one might choose is not for me to determine, because in the case of something new, nothing is as deceiving as a first vogue, & only time can prove its merits & give it its true worth.

Heading up the *Recueil de Cantates* is Rousseau's *Euterpe* set to music by Morin. Its prominent position is defended by Bachelier: 'I believe that he (Morin) is the first to have set Cantatas to Music; for this reason I have chosen *Euterpe*, the first of those composed (by Morin), to put at the head of the *Recueil*.'

Jean-Baptiste Morin, *Maître de Chapelle* for the Regent's daughter, the Abbesse de Chellesse, wrote three books of cantatas most of which are in the form of three recitatives alternating with three airs suggested by Rousseau in the preface quoted above. Morin's *Avis* to his first book of *Cantates françoises à une et deux voix* suggests that at least some of the six cantatas had been widely circulated before the 1706 publication date. In the best tradition of *goûts réunis*, he claimed to have attempted a synthesis between the 'douceur' of French melody and the Italian cantatas' more diversified accompaniments, tempo contrasts and modulations. To increase the range of performance possibilities, Morin added a modest *symphonie* of flute and violin to one cantata (*Enone*), and the final cantata (*Les Amants mécontents*) is for two solo voices. We are assured, however, that the collection may 'easily be performed as a Musique de Chambre' by a single voice, a harpsichord and a bass viol.

Concerning the first book of *Cantates françoises ou Musique de Chambre à voix seule* (date of privilege, 1703) by Bernier, Bachelier wrote: 'I have heard some capable gentlemen from across the Mountains, who before this time were scornful of French Music, admit to admiring *Diane, L'Absence, Les Muses, Les Forges de Lemnos*[5] from the first book of M. Bernier'. As is the case with Morin, the cantatas of Bernier's first book are all in the format of Recit./Air/Recit./Air/Recit./Air. It is impossible to tell from the privilege date whether or not Bernier's cantatas circulated before those of Morin.

In Bernier's third book (no date) two new elements were introduced to the French cantata. 'Le Caffé' (No. 4) makes use of humour in basing its subject matter on an unequal contest between coffee and wine; and *Hipolite et Aricie* (No. 5) includes descriptive *symphonies* borrowed from the lyric stage. The 'storm scene' and the music describing the approach of the sea monster (see below) in *Hipolite* stem more from *préramiste* opera than from the earlier *tragédies lyriques* of Lully. The extract reproduced below from this scene is an accompanied recitative. The dramatic interpolation of rapid violin passages is an adumbration of the similar scene in the more famous *Hippolyte* written almost 30 years later.

Example 105

Bernier: Extract from Hipolite et Aricie *(after Book* III, *n.d.).*

Jean-Baptiste Stuck, called Batistin (*c.* 1680–1755), the German composer born in Florence who arrived in Paris about 1700, was in the service of the Duc d'Orléans to whom he dedicated his first book of *Cantates françoises* (1706). He was partisan to joining together 'le goust de la Musique Italienne avec les Paroles Françoises'. That he succeeded almost too well is implicit in the praise of Bachelier: 'His Cantatas brought him infinite honour; those of his first Book, although the Recitative be not completely in the French manner, were favoured . . . especially his *Philomèle.*'

Philomèle, the first of the set of six cantatas, was organized in the by then familiar alternation of recitatives and airs and includes parts for two violins. The only French element in the final air of *Philomèle* ('Pourquoi plaintive, Philomèle') is the French language itself; the music, a slow *siciliana*, would do credit to Alessandro Scarlatti as the extract below from the introduction reveals.

Example 106
Stuck. *Italian influence in cantata movement (after ed. of 1706).*

Stuck made considerably more use of obbligato instruments than either Morin or Bernier, and he was careful to add the words 'avec symphonie' to each of his collections of cantatas. He wrote for violin, flute and oboe (*Le Calme de la Nuit*, Book I), for violin and obbligato bass viol (*Mars jaloux*, Book II, 1708), and even for trumpet and violins (*Les Festes bolonnoises*, Book IV, 1714).

The *Cantades et ariettes françoises* (1708) by Brunet de Moland is a curious mixture of four long cantatas and six *ariettes*. The *ariettes* are all extensive *da capo* airs of the type often included in the *divertissements* of the contemporary *opéras-ballets*. Typical of the cantatas is *Apollon et Daphné* which opens the collection and includes six recitatives in alternation with as many airs.

In the 12 cantatas that make up her two books of *Cantates françoises sur des sujets tirez de l'écriture*, Elisabeth Jacquet de La Guerre has given us some of the very few examples of sacred cantatas in French Baroque music. All the subjects, for which Houdar de La Motte supplied the texts, are taken from the Old Testament and include such titles as *Esther, Jacob et Rachel, Jonas, Susanne, Judith, Adam, Jephté* and *Samson*. In addition, there are three descriptive cantatas: *Le Passage de la mer rouge, Le Temple rebasti* and *Le Déluge*.

The subject matter itself obviously suggested numerous descriptive *symphonies*: the 'bruits de guerre' (*Le Passage de la mer rouge*), the 'tempestes' (*Jonas*) and the 'sommeils' (*Judith*). Although she adhered in general to Rousseau's format, Mlle de La Guerre was more successful in sustaining mood and intensity in these miniature dramas than in her one *tragédie lyrique, Céphale et Procris* (1694). This is particularly evident in her recitatives which do indeed 'furnish the body' of the cantatas as Rousseau had originally planned. The sudden shift of mode, the highlighting of certain key words and the use of rests for maximum dramatic effect may be observed in the extract from *Jephté* found below.

Example 107
La Guerre: Extract from Jephté *(after ed. of 1711).*

In her secular cantatas, Mlle de La Guerre borrowed freely from the operatic *divertissement* and used all manner of descriptive *symphonies*. This further fragmented the traditional cantata format. In *L'Ile de Délos*, she added a prelude, a 'Muzette', a chaconne and a 'Simphonie de Rossignol & voix' to the normal air-recitative components.

Following the three secular cantatas in this collection is a short recitative and duo in *buffo* style entitled *Le Racommodement comique de Pierrot et de Nicole*. The popularity of the counter-tenor voice was such in early eighteenth century France that Mlle de La Guerre found it necessary to warn performers of this charming little 'scene' against making any substitutions in the voice parts: 'My wish is to have the piece known as I composed it. It is for a Bass and a Soprano; and it would be very difficult to execute it with a counter-tenor without corrupting the harmony' (*Avertissement*).

In the *Avertissement* to his first book of cantatas (1708), André Campra presents us with a 'veritable manifesto' (Barthélemy, *André Campra*, p. 93) for those now committed to the fashionable *goûts réunis*:

Because Cantatas have become *à la mode*, I felt duty bound to heed the solicitations of many persons to give some of my own to the Public. I have tried as much as possible to mix with the *délicatesse* of French Music, the *vivacité* of Italian Music: perhaps those who have completely abandoned the former will not approve of the manner in which I have treated this small Work. I am persuaded as much as anyone concerning the merit of the Italians, but our language will not accommodate certain things in which they excel. Our Music has beauties that they can not avoid admiring and trying to imitate, although these same beauties are neglected by some of our very own French composers. I have attempted above all to conserve the beauty of melody, the expression and our manner of recitative which, in my opinion, is the best. . . .

This 'safe' paragraph was designed to offend no one and at the same time to create a rationale for the several elaborate vocalises found especially in the lively airs in compound metre. These airs, or more accurately *ariettes*, also make use of rapid modulations, another 'Italianism' that had characterized the music of Campra from the days of *L'Europe galante* (1697). Essentially French, in contrast, are the recitatives, the instrumental music and the simple vocal lines of most of the airs constructed in short phrases with a profusion of *coulés* and *ports de voix*.

Each of the six cantatas of Campra's first book contains at least one *ariette* in addition to airs and recitatives. For Campra, at least in 1708, *ariette* and air were not always clearly differentiated. Both are *da capo* structures; both may have introductions and concluding *ritournelles*; and airs, on occasion, may even be longer than *ariettes*. The only general difference seems to be the prevalence of compound metre and a more rapid tempo in the *ariettes*.

The final cantata of Book 1, *Les Femmes*, includes a gentle yet strikingly harmonized 'sommeil' in F♯-Minor used to introduce a *da capo* air, 'Fils de la nuit', based on the same material. Campra's dramatic sense is shown to good advantage in the opening phrase of this 'double continuo' air where there is the sudden drop of a major 7th in the vocal line and the full measure rest following the word 'silence'.

In his second and third books (1714, 1728) Campra conceived of his cantata texts as ideally suited for the composition of miniature dramas. This should come as no surprise when we realize that his librettists, Danchet and Fuzelier, contributed many of the texts. Campra even

Example 108
Campra: Beginning of air 'Fils de la nuit', Les Femmes (after ed. of 1708).

borrowed the common, effective technique so often employed in operatic *divertissements* of fragmenting the dance between parts of recitative. In *La Dispute de l'Amour* (Book II) a bourée is interrupted in the best operatic fashion by such comments as 'Mais, qu'entends-je'. *Enée et Didon* (Book III), a virtual 'cantata opera' with action for two protagonists, opens with a 'tempest' that continues to penetrate the following duo 'Quel bruit soudain', and *La Colère d'Achille* (Book III) includes a vengeance air of some dramatic power.

Contiguous with this exploitation of operatic devices in the late Campra cantatas is the more expansive use of obbligato instruments and a greater sensitivity to contrast afforded by shifts in tonality within the cantata components. *La Colère d'Achille* is scored for strings, solo violin, flutes, oboes and trumpets; *Les Plaisirs de la Campagne* (Book III) for strings and flutes with an independent violoncello line used in the 'Air des Musettes'.

More operatic than those of Campra are the 20 cantatas by Clérambault printed in five books (1710, 1713, 1716, 1720, 1720) and his five cantatas published separately.[6] Bachelier documents the unprecedented renown of Clérambault as a cantata composer in the first 25 years of the eighteenth century:

A Frenchman attending one of our concerts at which some Cantatas of Ms. Batistin & Bernier were performed exclaimed with surprise, Well, now! Messieurs, are you not familiar with Clérambault? What? You do not sing his *Orphée*, his *Médée*, his *Pigmalion*, *Léandre & Héro*, or his *Musette*? These are works of the greatest beauty and there are few that can compare with their grace of melody, their forceful accompaniments and the difficulty of their execution. They answered that they indeed knew these cantatas ... and it was for this reason that they did not profane them through daily use; rather, they reserved them for the most important Holidays & Sundays; and in order to better prepare their performance 'we use those of M. Bernier and Batistin as Exercises'.

The all too rare congruency of composer and genre may be observed in the cantatas of Clérambault. Competent but superficial in his keyboard music, often tentative or merely decorative in the *petits motets* composed for the young ladies of Saint-Cyr, Clérambault in his cantatas wrote with the assurance and self discipline of one to the manner born. The best of these works, composed with equal parts of felicitous grace and dramatic conviction, do indeed constitute a 'repository of neglected masterpieces' (Tunley).

From his first book it is clear that Clérambault discreetly allowed content to determine form, and in so doing he modified and bent the seemingly inflexible cantata format. This is especially evident in the musical structures chosen for the points of greatest dramatic intensity which often occur near the centre of the cantata. In *Abraham* (1715), a sacred cantata published separately and dedicated to Mme de Maintenon, a recitative forms the centre of the action with the appearance of the angel of the Lord who stays the hand of Abraham. In *Orphée* (Book 1), the most admired French cantata of the entire century (see Tunley, *MQ*, p. 319), the key dramatic action in which Orpheus pleads with Pluto for the release of Euridice is rendered musically by two 'ariosi' separated by a contrasting 'air tendre' placed at the centre of the cantata. The first 'arioso', in B-Major ('Monarque redoute'), is scored for soprano, flute and violin with no bass line; the second, in B-Minor, adds the continuo and, through use of harmony, intensifies the pleadings of Orpheus. In employing a mediant $\frac{9}{7}_{\#5}$ chord that never resolves (Example 109a) and a simultaneous cross-relation resulting from a *port de voix* heard against the bass (Example 109b), Cléram-

Example 109
Clérambault: Extracts from Orphée *(after ed. of 1710).*

bault owes nothing to any Italian model; rather, he draws upon the traditional French treatment of dissonance found in the works of Charpentier, Delalande, Couperin and others.

Médée (Book I) includes both a virtuoso type 'vengeance aria' ('Courons à la vengeance'), which draws much from the driving rhythms of the Vivaldi concerto, and a long accompanied monologue ('Cruelle fille des Enfers') which could have been lifted from Lully's *Armide*. Thus, a single mood of dark despair is sustained by means of totally different musical styles.

In *Pirâme et Tisbé* (Book II) the heart of the cantata, where Pyramus discovers Thisbe's blood soaked veil, is a true operatic scene consisting of the following: recitative/'Plainte'/'Prelude' and Monologue/. A final air marked 'gracieusement et gai' wrenches us free of the scene of Pyramus's tragic discovery and subsequent death, and in the best tradition of the Rousseau cantata, leaves us with a maxim in the guise of a gentle reproach to Love: 'Tu refuses tes récompenses aux plus fidelles coeurs.'

La Muse de l'Opéra ou les Caractères lyriques, published separately in 1716, is one of Clérambault's most ambitious cantatas. It offers the listener a neat catalogue of operatic elements. As descriptive *sym-phonies*, it includes an opening prelude, a *tempeste*, a *sommeil* and a *prélude infernal*. Its opening *da capo* air, scored for trumpet, first and second violins, bass violins, bass viols and continuo, describes in turn the approach of Mars ('Au son des Trompettes'), Diane and her court ('Bruit de chasse') and the inevitable shepherd and shepherdess ('Trio des hautbois')—all this within the formal confines of one long *da capo* air!

In the opinion of this writer, the 20 French and 4 Italian cantatas by Montéclair, published in three books (c. 1709, c. 1717, 1728), also constitute a 'repository of neglected masterpieces'. Montéclair's originality is acknowledged by Bachelier who wrote: 'Montéclair through his own particular taste, gives pleasure to those who hear him.' This is guarded praise, however, and Bachelier was obviously not too happy with Montéclair's choice of texts, for he added that they were not 'among the most regular', and he expressed the hope that some poems 'in the taste of M. Rousseau' would fall into Montéclair's hands so that he would have greater success and gain the 'approbation of connoisseurs'.

Like Clérambault, Montéclair borrowed liberally from operatic sources; his cantatas include a *tempête* (*La Mort de Didon*), a *bruit de guerre* (*Le Retour de la Paix*) and a *sommeil* (*La Bergère*). In addition, in one cantata (*Pyrame et Thisbé*), Montéclair appropriated from the oratorio the use of a narrator ('historien').

More than any other composer of cantatas before Rameau, Montéclair gave a prominent role to his obbligato instruments. There are no 'double continuo' airs, and if a bass voice is used there is always an independent bass line. In *Le Triomphe de la Constance* (Book I) and *Ariane et Bacchus* (Book III), there are extensive solo passages for the bass viol which never become the empty display pieces that too often mar the bass viol writing in the cantatas of Rameau (see, for example, the cantata *L'Impatience*).

When we examine the solo airs of such cantatas as *L'Enlèvement d'Orithée* (Book II) or *Tircis et Climène* (Book III), we are reminded that Montéclair was also the author of a treatise on violin playing. In the *air léger* 'Amants tout cède' (*L'Enlèvement*), for example, a solo violin maintains an independent line sharing its motivic material with both vocal melody and bass in a degree of concentration that resembles more an air from a Bach cantata than an air from a *cantate françoise*.

In the *da capo* air 'Fille du ciel!'(*Le Retour de la Paix*, Book II), the persistent use of detached, often quite dissonant chords describes the destructive power of Mars as he overturns the altars of Peace. Momentary relief is afforded only through the brief recitative that makes up Part B of the air.

The entire cantata *Le Retour de la Paix* is an impressive study in contrasts—contrasts of texture, mood, tempo and key. Two violins and a bass viol comment throughout on the struggle between Mars and Peace. They suggest a background of warring strife with fanfare and battle prelude or describe 'gentle Peace', at which time the incisive notes of the harpsichord are stilled.

The longest and most dramatic of Montéclair's cantatas is *Pyrame et Thisbé* (Book II) written for three voices (soprano, counter-tenor and baritone), violin and continuo. It includes four airs, two *ariettes*,[7] ten recitatives and three duos. The cantata was described by Montéclair as follows:

> Although the Following Cantata has many more lines of text than any of the others I have written, I dare to flatter myself that it will not appear too long. I have cut out the repetitions ordinarily found in this type of work, and I have substituted a variety that hopefully will please. It is half Epic, half Dramatic. What is Epic is sung by a baritone who represents the narrator, and what is Dramatic must be performed by a soprano and a counter-tenor who represent the protagonists.

One of the musical high points of the cantata is the first duo between the unfortunate lovers, 'Que d'allarmes!', the opening measures of which are worth quoting in full. The three-fold statement of the fanfare motif with its interval expanded in repetition from a 4th to a 6th is deprived each time of its forward motion by a searing dissonance followed by a delayed resolution every fifth measure.

Example 110
Montéclair: Opening of duo 'Que d'allarmes', Pyrame et Thisbé
(after the Second livre, n.d.).

As David Tunley has observed, Montéclair 'seems to have drawn far closer to the French style than ever before' in his third volume of cantatas (*The Eighteenth-Century French Cantata*, p. 154). Although 19 out of 30 airs are *da capo*, Montéclair treats the Italian form with great originality. In most instances a French type of binary air is incorporated within the large A section. This binary air structure usually conforms to the type discussed in Chapter 5 (p. 56). Montéclair divided the A section of his *da capo* air into three parts. Part I opens with a 'motto' *ritournelle* followed by a vocal statement of the initial motif which is rounded off by a second *ritournelle*. Part II repeats and expands the motif. This section introduces additional text and new motivic material, modulates to a closely related key and closes with a third *ritournelle* that re-establishes the original key. In Part III, the most important musically, Montéclair created from the material of Part II a self-contained unit in the guise of the French binary air mentioned above, thus creating a synthesis between French and Italian formal procedures.[8]

André Cardinal Destouches composed two cantatas, *Oenone* (1716) and *Sémélé* (1719). In both cantatas operatic techniques served Destouches well. The brilliant air 'Volez grands Dieux' from *Oenone* is interrupted by a poignant recitative over a descending chromatic bass line. In *Sémélé* the abrupt change of key from A-Minor to F-Major gives dramatic import to the following 'bruit de tonnerre'.

Colin de Blamont leaves us three books of cantatas. This is music that borrows equally from French and Italian sources. There are dramatic symphonies resembling those in French opera (see the *tempête* from *Didon*, Book I). French monologue airs penetrated by exciting *tirades* for solo instruments are found (see 'C'est ainsi' from *Circé*, Book III). At the same time the *da capo* aria structure dominates and many *ritournelles* make use of the driving rhythms, melodic shapes and harmonic practices of the Italian concerto.

The six extant cantatas by Rameau[9] are all works of his first period and may be seen as 'advanced studies' for his later stage music. In fact, the composer himself cited *Aquilon et Orithie* and *Thétis* in his letter to the librettist Houdar de La Motte (25 October 1727) as a measure of his skill in the composition of recitatives and airs and in the realization of a dramatic musical characterization.

These two cantatas then are probably his first essays in the genre and date, as he stated in the letter, from a dozen years earlier (1715). All the airs of *Aquilon* contain Italianate elements. Brilliant, concerto-like violin obbligati climax in the 'rage aria', 'Servez mes feux'. *Thétis*, however, takes over from *préramiste* opera such descriptive *symphonies* as a *tonnerre* and a 27-measure *orage*. French also is the prelude to *Thétis* modelled on the *grave* section of the French overture.

Les Amants Trahis (not later than 1721) is a rare example in the French Baroque of a comic cantata and contains the earliest suggestions of a style perfected by Rameau in his lyric comedy *Platée*, of 1745. The various musical means used to characterize 'laughing' or 'weeping' although obvious and overworked are, at least, justifiable from the standpoint of the subject matter, and the obbligato bass viol with its rapid Alberti bass patterns and its awkward leaps adds much to the *buffo* character of Damon's airs. How different this is from similar passages in the cantata *L'Impatience* (not later than 1722) that appear to have no function other than to test the skills of the viol player and to generate endless melismas in the vocal line on such stereotyped words as 'chaîne' and 'flamme'.

Orphée (not later than 1721) follows the format of a Rousseau cantata with the addition of a long series of accompanied recitatives inserted abruptly before the last of too many virtuosi *airs gais*. The most effective contrast that results from this dramatic 'centrepiece' of recitatives is that of a conflict of tonalities. We are catapulted without warning from an *air gracieux* in D-Major to a recitative in B♭-Major. All of the following 'action recitatives' now occur in flat keys (B♭-Major, G-Minor, A♭-Major, E♭-Major, C-Minor and D-Minor) until we are just as abruptly returned to G-Major in an *air gai* that closes the work.

The only cantata from which Rameau borrowed in his later work is the dramatic pastoral *Le Berger fidèle* (*c.* 1728): The charming air 'L'Amour qui règne dans votre âme' recurs in the third *entrée* of *Les Fêtes d'Hébé* of 1739. As Girdlestone has observed, this cantata is one of the few by Rameau to include pages where the composer's personal style breaks through the patina of Italianisms and *préramiste* imitations. In the opening recitative the dramatic leap of an augmented 6th in the bass initiates, by means of a diminished 7th chord, a sudden shift of key from the relative major (F) to C-Minor. This is vintage Rameau as is the correct declamation and the intensity of feeling in the elegiac air 'Faut-il qu'Amaryllis perisse?' that follows.

Although they contain some individual numbers of great charm, most of the cantatas of Charles-Hubert Gervais and Laurent Gervais, Philippe Courbois, Thomas-Louis Bourgeois, Boismortier,[10] François Bouvard, Bernard Burette, Nicolas Racot de Grandval and Louis Neron cannot be classed with the best of Bernier, Campra, Clérambault, Montéclair or Rameau. In an attempt to extend the life of the cantata artificially into the later eighteenth century, composers wrote diminutive works bearing the generic title of *cantatille*. Mouret, for example, brought out a collection of nine *cantatilles* (no date) mostly designed for performance at the *Concerts Français* at the Tuilcries. At least two from this set (*Echo* and *Eglé*) date from as early as 1718.

The *cantatilles*, often composed of two or three short airs and as many recitatives, added nothing fresh to the genre, and Rousseau was probably correct in considering them as 'worse than the Cantata' (*Dictionnaire*). They were often tailor-made for specific performers and performances. Thus, *Borée* by Louis Lemaire (privilege date, 1733) was 'sung at the Concert of the Château de Tuileries by Mlle Petit-Pas' (score), and we read at the end of the score of the same composer's *Hébé* that it was a *cantatille* composed for 'M. Jeyliot (Pierre Jelyotte) whose voice is of a great range. The composer has transposed it up a Fourth in order to accommodate Sopranos and Tenors.'

So it was that the cantata lived on in the eighteenth century through the *cantatille* as an anachronistic vehicle of display for vain performers and an exercise in composition suited to the limited talents of minor composers. As such it parallels the fate of the *grand motet* after Delalande and that of the descriptive harpsichord piece after Couperin. The fault lay not so much with the genre or the medium itself, nor even with the fact that the eddies and tides of fickle fashion had isolated it—rather the critical fact was simply that there were no composers of genius as the century progressed, no Rameaus at the height of their creative power, who were sufficiently interested in the cantata to compose examples of enduring musical value.

Epilogue

Chapter 24

>>> <<<

Thoughts on the Performance
of French Baroque Music

Although it is quite possible to insist energetically that the most critical
problems of ornamentation and rhythmic alteration arise in the music
of the *grand siècle*, it is equally true that this music offers the greatest
latitude of any for stylistically valid alternatives in performance. We
do not propose to become embroiled in the seemingly endless polemics
that heat the pages of our scholarly journals regarding 'correct performance' of, for example, a Couperin trill. Rather, it is more appropriate to conclude a general survey of seventeenth and eighteenth century music in France with some general observations on performance
problems connected with this music.

There is interest now in bringing to the music of Couperin, Delalande, Leclair and Rameau some background based on primary
evidence of the performance practices of their time. The current
interest dates from the pioneering work of scholars such as Arnold
Dolmetsch in the first decades of this century. Since the appearance
of his *The Interpretation of the Music of the XVII and XVIII
Centuries Revealed by Contemporary Evidence* in 1915, the bibliography on performance practices has reached monumental proportions.[1]

With almost methodical regularity, composers of keyboard music
from Chambonnières to Balbastre provided a table of 'agréments'
in the prefaces to their *pièces de clavecin* or *pièces d'orgue*. For
over 150 years the tables maintained a fairly high degree of consistency
in the interpretation of named ornaments, if not in the symbols given
to the defined names. Now that many of the tables are available in
secondary sources,[2] it *is* important that present day performers of this

music consult them and note the discrepancies that do exist. In Couperin, for example, the 'tremblement lié' results in a type of built-in rubato that is most effective in pieces of a moderate or slow tempo; this differs, however, from Marchand's interpretation of the same ornament and from the 'cadence appuyée' of Rameau where the preceding note is considered an *appuy* and the actual oscillation begins on the main note.

Example 111
Ornaments from three tables compared.
(a) Couperin. (b) Marchand. (c) Rameau.

Yet we have become over-zealous, perhaps even puritanical in our attempts to apply rules of ornamentation derived from these tables. Undoubtedly the tables were designed to serve as guidelines for the performer and not necessarily as Holy Writ. Their authors might be startled were they to find the quasi-improvisational tone of their keyboard pieces sacrificed to an overly doctrinaire attitude towards ornamentation in our studios and classrooms. The number of twentieth century specialists in the art of Baroque keyboard ornamentation is impressive, to be sure, but often one cannot help feeling a rigidity in their approach that converts *a* correct manner of application to *the* correct manner. It is amusing to contemplate the trauma of a piano teacher armed with Ralph Kirkpatrick's dictum ('It cannot be too emphatically stated that the Bach trill *always begins with the upper note* . . .')[3] and suddenly faced with the problem posed by the trill in the second *Two-Part Invention*: when begun on the upper note, this trill results in exposed parallel octaves.

Current researchers of problems in Baroque interpretation would do well to heed Donington's words that 'no one interpretation of a Baroque ornament can be singled out as alone correct. There is no one right interpretation. There can be varied interpretations which are within the style, and therefore right, as well as others which are outside the style, and therefore wrong.'[4] Also, it is less important that the 'integrity of the French trill (beginning on the upper note) remains intact'[5] than that the performer is immersed in the over-all style of French Baroque music.

In the performance of instrumental ensemble music and opera, the problem of ornamentation is confounded by most composers' perverse insistence upon indicating their ornamentation by a single sign (+). This, of course, presupposed sufficient general information on the part of performers to be able to choose a suitable ornament, often a mordent or trill (the *ports de voix* were usually expressed by notes in small print) within the context.[6]

Couperin's oft-quoted observation that 'We (French composers) write music differently from the way we play it. . . . The Italians, on the other hand, observe the exact value of the notes in composing their music' (*L'Art de toucher le clavecin*) is one of many comments of the period that attest to the importance of rhythmic alteration in performance traditions of French Baroque music.

One common way of achieving a marked rhythmic deviation from the printed page was through the use of unequal notes (*notes inégales*) in place of the notated even-note values.[7] There can be no argument that this widespread practice was sanctioned by the writings of most theorists and composers, and there emerges from the treatises a 'picture remarkable for a high degree of uniformity with respect to (1) the manner of presentation; (2) the rules that determine which notes are to be even, and which are eligible for unevenness; (3) the nature of the inequality; and (4) the exceptions to the rules' (Neumann, *JAMS*, p. 319). The French mania for using *inégales* may be observed in Plate 12. In spite of warnings against their application to pieces in a brisk tempo, an anonymous hand converted the fast, even 16th notes of the famous 'tempête' from Marais' *tragédie lyrique Alcyone* into an orgy of *inégales* in a reduced score which was used as a performance score for an eighteenth century revival and is found today in the Bibliothèque de l'Opéra.

Naturally there are some points of ambiguity in the degree of inequality desired, in its prohibition and in the application of this French practice to music beyond the borders of France. Composers could prohibit inequality by adding dots over the notes, by slurring together more than a pair of notes, or by clear written instructions such as *notes égales, croches égales, marqué, également, martelées* or *détachées*. Somewhat more equivocal are the general prohibitions against using *inégales* in pieces written in a fast tempo, in pieces where the motion is prevailingly conjunct and in such dances as allemandes. The latter pose a particularly sensitive problem. Saint-Lambert, for example, stated that inequality of 8th notes would not occur in allemandes 'because of the slowness of the tempo' (*Les Principes du clavecin*, 1702), yet we recall that certain types of allemandes are closely related to the French overture and would benefit from the use of dotted rhythms. A suggestion that two possible interpretations of

Epilogue

an allemande were acceptable is found in Perrine's *Pièces de luth en musique* (c. 1680) in which two allemandes notated with even notes are followed by versions in dotted rhythms exemplifying the same piece played 'en gigue'.

If the proliferation of rules for and against using *inégales* is confusing to us, we may take comfort from an eighteenth century composer of excellent repute; Montéclair himself admitted that 'It is very difficult to give general principles on the equality or inequality of notes, because it is the character of the Pieces one sings that governs them.' (*Nouvelle méthode pour apprendre la musique*, 1709, p. 15).

In my opinion we should use extreme discretion in applying rules of inequality to music composed outside France unless this music is unmistakably in the 'goût français'. In spite of their thinness of texture and their idealizations of the *style brisé*, the French Suites by Bach, for example, derive as much from Italian sources (note especially the courantes and gigues) as they do from Couperin and Dieupart. It is difficult to justify Dolmetsch's proposal that *inégales* be used in the sarabande from the first suite in D-Minor, for basically they convert Bach's sarabande into a siciliana! (*The Interpretation of the Music of the XVIIth and XVIIIth Centuries*, p. 86).

Rhythmic alterations other than the *notes inégales* often result from the carelessness or, at best, the indifference of many seventeenth and eighteenth century composers towards precise rhythmic notation. This is especially true of dotted rhythms following a rest. Measure four of Example 18 (Chapter 9, p. 114), an excerpt from a 'revised' version of Lully's *Bellérophon*, illustrates this inexactitude; what is obviously meant is the precise vertical alignment of dotted rhythms between all voices which would mean changing the oboe and bassoon parts to conform to that of the strings. A similar problem exists with the group of rapid upbeat notes (*tirades*) found typically in the French overture. No matter how notated, according to Powell, they were played 'as rapidly as possible' (*Rhythmic Freedom ...*, p. 184).

More controversial are the performance practices of double dotting notes (and rests) and rhythmically synchronizing all parts. For many these remain the two most important characteristics of music written 'à la française'. Two diametrically opposed points of view may be found in Dart and Neumann. Dart stated that in performance the 'conventional lengthening of the dotted note and shortening of the complementary note was in a very widespread use over a very great length of time, and ignorance of this fact is one of the great defects of present-day performances of old music'.[8] Neumann claimed that the written double dot was known in France in the second half of the seventeenth century and therefore would have been employed if lengthening were desired; noting that no French treatises of the period

378

mention it, he concluded that the concept of overdotting in performance is 'essentially a legend'.[9]

Whether or not a French overture is performed with double dotted rhythms or with all rhythms 'adjusted so that they fit the shortest one in the piece' (Dart, p. 81) is less vital than that the style of the music itself spring from the kinetic energy of the French dance. Be the rhythms overdotted or played as notated, we have all known performances of the overture to the *Messiah* sadly lacking the crisp, rhythmic incisiveness appropriate to heraldic gesture and in which the initial *Grave* is taken at such a slow pace that the musical impetus falters. Permeated by the all-enveloping sound of the modern symphony orchestra, such a performance too often succeeds in obliterating the music's dance origins—even though it is a French overture. One is immediately reminded of Igor Stravinsky's cogent observation that 'Whether instrumental or vocal, whether sacred or secular, eighteenth century music is, in one sense, *all* dance music.'[10]

Some brief comments on a term of the period are in order. If we understood *le bon goût* in full, its meaning could help resolve some of the controversies described above. It was a musical 'court of last appeal' to which both composer and performer might turn to vindicate their work. It is certain, however, that French aestheticians and philosophers of the eighteenth century were no better equipped to define *le bon goût* than their twentieth century counterparts.[11] 'They speak without cease of *taste*, of good *taste*, of bad *taste*', despaired the author of the article 'Goût' in the *Dictionnaire de Trévoux* adding that 'it is much easier to say what taste is not than what it is'. For Lecerf *le bon goût* was the 'most natural sentiment rectified or confirmed by the best rules'. For Père André (*Essai sur le beau*, 1741) and for the author of the *Dictionnaire de Trévoux* article, it was a sentiment perceived in a 'premier coup d'oeil' which in an instant revealed the nature of things. For Batteux (*Les Beaux-arts réduits à un même principe*, 1746) 'good taste must be satisfied when Nature is well chosen & well imitated by the Arts', yet in the same year Louis Bollioud de Mermet (*De la Corruption du goust*, 1746) wrote that the 'imitation of nature is a road too well travelled, a too common and trivial device'. He added the sensible comment that 'true Taste demands ... that he who performs follows to the letter the intention of the composer'. Boffrand (*Livre d'architecture*, 1745), recognizing that 'every man claims to have it [good taste]' and yet aware that it was only vaguely defined as a 'certain *je ne sais quoi* which pleases', suggested that one could find demonstrations of good taste only in the clearly defined principles of each art taken individually. Rousseau, in the long articles on 'Goût' in his dictionary and in the Diderot *Encyclopédie*, made a valiant effort to bring a more systematic point of view to definitions of taste. He wisely refrained from arguing with what he called each man's *goût particulier* and concentrated on a *goût général* concerning which 'all well-organized men were in agreement'. In Rousseau's opinion it was reasonable that such men with sufficiently sensitive ears and well-trained minds would, upon attending a concert, reach a unanimous opinion on the relative value of the music heard.

We may be amused, annoyed and often stimulated by the dialectical convolutions expressed in the felicitous language of most eighteenth century French writings on good taste. To expect these sources to illuminate the music of a Couperin or a Rameau, however, is a *reductio ad absurdum*. French taste of the period, good or bad, can only be determined from the music itself. Through total immersion in the score, through detailed analysis of the music *qua* music, guided by one's own musical sensibilities and aided by some knowledge of the performance practices of the period, one may grasp the transcendent worth of a *grand motet* by Delalande or a simple Noël setting by Charpentier.

Appendix

-»» ««-

Preparation and Performance of a Seventeenth Century Ballet de Cour: Ballet of the King at the Hôtel de Ville*

In the year 1626 on the 4th day of February, Monsieur de Bailleul, chevalier of Vaitetot-sur-la-mer and of Soisi-sur-Seine, state councillor, judge and magistrate (*Prévôt des marchands*) of the town, reported to the aldermen (*échevins*) at work that the previous day at the Louvre the king had told him that he wished to come dance his ballet at the said Hôtel de Ville and that he wished to honour the said town by this act; to which end he was to give the order for the necessary preparations and to send for all the most beautiful women of high estate to attend. To which he replied to His Majesty that it would be the greatest honour the town had ever received. And forthwith the said magistrate with the said aldermen, king's prosecutor (*procureur du roy*), town clerk (*greffier*) and tax collector (*receveur*) of the town resolved to issue orders for all the said preparations to receive His Majesty there in the most sumptuous and superb manner possible.

And on Sunday the 8th day of the said month of February, the said magistrate together with M. Clement, the town clerk, went to see the king at the Louvre, to whom His Majesty confirmed that he would come dance his said ballet at the said Hôtel de Ville without fail about Shrovetide and that one should send for the beautiful ladies and the townswomen. To which the said magistrate said that this news was already spread far and wide throughout the entire town which rejoiced in the hearing of it.

And on Monday the 9th day of the said month of February, the said magistrate and aldermen initiated the said preparations to receive His

---

* The ballet described was the *Grand Bal de la Douairière de Billebahaut*, found in Lacroix, *Ballets et mascarades de cour*, vol. 3, pp. 151–202. This description is an 'Extract from the registers of the Hôtel de Ville of Paris' found on pp. 568–72 in vol. v of *Histoire de la ville de Paris*, 1725. Vols. I and II of this source were prepared by Michel de Félibien (1666–1719) and vols. III–V by Guy-Alexis Lobineau (1666–1727).

381

Majesty and to this end immediately sent for the master-masons and master-carpenters of the town to make platforms, circles, theatres and amphitheatres in the great hall of the Hôtel de Ville, in order to accommodate the ladies and guests there; they even sought out the advice of M. Franchine.*

They also sent for the town chandler, whom they ordered to have ready a great quantity of white candles, both large and small, to put in the candlesticks and candlelabra which will be on the floors of the great halls, rooms, galleries and offices of the said Hôtel de Ville and on the tables, also to prepare a great quantity of sweetmeats for the refreshment of the king, princes, maskers and others.

They also sent for the town joiner for him to ply his trade wherever necessary, to make all the said candlesticks and candelabra of wood, to have sconces to fix in place in all the rooms, along the stairways and galleries, ready to receive the small white candles.

They likewise sent for the town's captain of artillery whom they ordered to hold the town artillery, cannons and mortar ready for firing when His Majesty arrives to dance the ballet.

And on Tuesday the 17th of the said month of February, one of the gentlemen of the Duc de Nemours came to the Hôtel de Ville to request the gentlemen to send him the town clerk so he might speak with him on behalf of the King about his ballet. And forthwith the said town clerk was conveyed there, to whom the said Sieur de Nemours said that in His Majesty's ballet there were a great number of machines which could not be transported from the Louvre to the Hôtel de Ville, that the town would have to have similar ones promptly made and that to do this it was necessary to apply to a certain sculptor named Bourdin, living in the Hôtel de Nevers, who made the ones for the Louvre. That having been reported by the said town clerk to the said gentlemen of the town, they sent for the said Bourdin who delivered the memorandum of all that was required to them; and among other things there was a great elephant, a camel, two mules, four parrots and other pieces over which Bourdin and the said gentlemen of the town struck a bargain for the sum of nine hundred pounds without the paintings.

There also came to the said Hôtel de Ville the said M. Franchine and M. Morel, who told the said gentlemen that it was necessary to prepare the large hall of the Hôtel de Ville to accommodate the said machines that were the same as those in the Louvre, and to this end carpenters and joiners were promptly ordered to work there. Similarly they sent for the town painter whom they ordered to make the necessary paintings for the theatres, amphitheatres and all else, just as at the Louvre.

* Tomasso Francini, Engineer of the king.

The said gentlemen also sent for the tapestry-maker of the said town whom they ordered to have ready a great quantity of tapestries for adorning the hall where His Majesty would take his refreshment, also for adorning all the rooms, offices and private studies where His Majesty, Monsieur his brother, the Comte de Soissons and other princes and masked lords would retire to warm themselves and change costumes; likewise for the said tapestry-maker to have ready two beautiful canopies—one to be put in the great ballroom, the other, in the hall where refreshments will be served.

They also sent for twenty violinists and wind players who were contracted to play and lead the town guests in dance while awaiting the maskers.

They also sent for the town cooks to prepare the necessary refreshment.

And on Saturday the 21st of the said month of February, the said magistrate and aldermen and town clerk went in the presence of His Majesty so that it might be determined which day he wished to dance his ballet, in order that they could prepare the said refreshments and invite the ladies. To which gentlemen His Majesty announced that it would be the evening of the day of Shrove Tuesday.

Thus the said gentlemen of the town sent word to the cook, Widow Coissier, to prepare banquets of fish instead of meat, which she promised.

And on Sunday the 22nd of the said month, the said gentlemen of the town were at the home of the Duc de Montbazon, town governor, to entreat him to honour the town with his presence in all this solemnity, which he very willingly promised to do.

And on the same day, he, as well as Monsieur du Hallier, Captain of the king's guards, and other lords, members of the ballet, came to dine at the said Hôtel de Ville in order to investigate the said preparations; also the said Monsieur du Hallier with the said gentlemen of the town were taken everywhere to check the doors, entryways, rooms and places of the said Hôtel de Ville to have barriers made at the great door as well as at certain locations in the galleries and at the stairs to keep out the crowds of people; Monsieur du Hallier told the said gentlemen of the town that he had orders from the king to come with his company to the said Hôtel de Ville the day of the ballet, and that in addition he would dispatch two other companies to the Grève*— one composed of his regiment of guards and the other, of Swiss guards— in order to prevent disorders.

On Monday the 23rd of the said month of February, the said machines were brought to the Hôtel de Ville of the said town.

The same day the said gentlemen of the town invited all the most

* Large square in front of the Hôtel de Ville.

beautiful ladies of Paris and those of high rank to come to the said Hôtel de Ville to see the ballet the next day.

The said gentlemen of the town ordered their tavern keeper and steward to have ready an abundance of wine, bread and meat for the said day of Shrove Tuesday for the dinner and supper of the said governor, du Hallier, and other captains, and gentlemen of their retinue, as well as for several of the said guests, and the same even for the said guards of the king's corps and for other companies; and to put wood in the Grève to warm the guards, and similarly to have wood brought into all the rooms and offices to warm the said guests and the maskers when they have arrived and when they will change their costumes.

The said gentlemen of the town also invited the town counsellors and district officers to be present.

It is noteworthy that the said M. Clement, town clerk and concièrge (of the Hôtel de Ville), had the particular charge of securing with good strong timber props the rooms and all places under the halls, the rooms and private studies where the king would be; he was also to have all the chimneys cleaned to avoid fire or other accidents.

Thus by the great care, order and diligence which the said magistrate, aldermen and town clerk exercised, all was perfect and in a state of readiness by Monday evening.

And as much as the said gentlemen of the town had not had the coverings of embroidered satin made, nor the sky nor the other scenery that was necessary to accompany the machines, nor had they the live horse that was supposed to be there, the said gentlemen of the town beseeched His Majesty to order those at the Louvre brought to the said Hôtel de Ville when they were no longer needed at the Louvre; this His Majesty accorded and commanded M. de la Garde, his treasurer, to take care of it.

And on Tuesday the 24th of the said month, Shrove Tuesday, at six o'clock in the morning, there came to the said Hôtel de Ville M. de Coste, ensign of the guards of the king's corps, followed by two adjutants and a number of archers of the corps, who asked the said M. Clement for all the keys of the gates, rooms and offices of the said Hôtel de Ville, which he directly gave them with a tag attached to each key in order to identify it; and the said guards stationed themselves at all the gates and approaches to the said Hôtel de Ville.

And at about 11 o'clock there came the said du Hallier, captain of the guards, followed by a number of archers; and a short time later the said Monsieur de Montbazon; and they all dined at the said Hôtel de Ville with the said magistrate, aldermen, town clerk and tax collector; the king's prosecutor not being there because of his indisposition.

At 3 o'clock in the afternoon two companies of guards came into the Grève, one was French and the other Swiss, with drums sounding.

At 4 o'clock the guests began to arrive, who were seated one after the other in the said great hall by the said Monsieur du Hallier and de la Coste, followed by the archers. And it can be said, and is true, that never has one seen such fine order and lack of confusion due to the care and foresight of the said Monsieur du Hallier.

At 7 o'clock the said governor, du Hallier, and several other gentlemen supped at the said Hôtel de Ville with the said magistrate, aldermen, town clerk and tax collector and a few of the best-known society of the town.

The lords and ladies being placed in the theatres and on the platforms, all the candles were lit and then all the beautiful ladies were observed, who were laden with pearls and diamonds and adorned to advantage.

At 11 o'clock in the evening there came *Madame la première Présidente* (wife of the president of Parlement, always called Premier Président), who was received by the said gentlemen of the town and given the first seat.

At midnight the refreshment of sweetmeats was laid out for the king in the little hall on the side towards the church of Saint-Jean, where they also set out the town's silver service, guarded by four archers; for this refreshment there were brought more than 600 boxes of fine sweetmeats.

Moreover, three large tables were set up for the banquet of fish which, however, was not cooked until the maskers were seen to arrive.

All night long the twenty violinists performed in the said great hall to entertain the guests without anyone's dancing, since the ladies did not wish to leave their seats.

The gentlemen of the town had the care of seeing that the white candles were changed and replaced as they burned down, there being in the said hall thirty-two candelabra in which there were one hundred and twenty-eight candles which were replaced and changed twice during the night, and likewise in the other halls, rooms and offices.

At 4 o'clock in the morning, the maskers began to arrive. The said magistrate, aldermen, king's prosecutor, town clerk and the tax-collector of the town of Paris were dressed in their woollen robes, each of two colours, except the said magistrate who wore a robe of satin in two colours and went before the king, preceded by ten constables also dressed in their robes of two colours and each holding in his hand two lighted white tapers.

And the said gentlemen of the town met the king on the stairs; to whom the said magistrate offered a short discourse on his happy arrival and concerning the honour which the town received this day by his presence. His Majesty apologized for arriving so late, which was not his fault, but rather that of the workmen who had not completed preparations soon enough. His Majesty was led by the said governor, magistrate, aldermen and town clerk into the private study of the said town clerk which had been prepared for His Majesty where he took his wrap and masquerade costume. Monsieur the king's only brother was led into the room of the said town clerk near the said study where the king was. The Comte de Soissons, prince of the blood, was led into the small office which had been prepared for him. The other princes and lords who were members of the *grand ballet*, in the other rooms. The maskers in the large office. The masked musicians and the violinists, in the room of the first gallery; in each of which there was a fire, bread, wine and meats.

The said magistrate, aldermen and town clerk thus dressed in their robes of two colours constantly attended His Majesty until he was ready to dance his ballet.

The said Monsieur du Hallier, just as had been planned, had removed the town violinists who were on the platform and in their place had brought the king's violinists who would play for the ballet.

And at about 5 o'clock in the morning, His Majesty and all the other maskers went into the great hall to dance the ballet. And then the violinists began to play. And while the first maskers made their entrances, His Majesty, Monsieur, and the other princes sat down in the loge of woodwork, which in the ballet was called the town of Clamart and which in actuality represented a tavern, made expressly at the entrance to the hall. After the completion of some entrances, the king came masked and danced with the others. The machines also made their effect. And afterward, the *grand ballet* was danced by the king and twelve other princes and lords, among whom were Monsieur the brother of the king, Monsieur the Comte de Soissons, Monsieur the grand prior, Monsieur the Duc de Longueville, Monsieur the Duc d'Elbery, Monsieur the Comte d'Harcour, Monsieur the Comte de la Roche-guyon, Monsieur de Liancour, Monsieur de Baradas, Monsieur the Comte de Cramail, and Monsieur the Chevalier de Souvray, all dressed very richly.

After the conclusion of the said ballet which had lasted at least three hours, the violinists began to play a branle, and His Majesty unmasked, and the other maskers unmasked, and all the aforementioned each took a lady to dance the said branle, namely His Majesty took *Madame la première présidente*; Monsieur the brother of the king, Madame de Bailleul wife of the said magistrate; Monsieur the Comte afterward, and then the said princes and lords.

The said branle concluded, His Majesty was led by the said gentlemen of the town into the hall where the banquet and refreshments had been prepared; this banquet which consisted of very fine fish, was admired by the king who, standing the whole while, ate of the said banquet for a very long time, being accompanied by the said princes, lords, etc., named above, who likewise ate very much of the said viands; the said gentlemen of the town with the said town clerk being still near His Majesty at the time of the said banquet. And His Majesty having asked to drink, holding his glass in his hand, said out loud, addressing his words to the said magistrate that he was going to drink to him and to the entire town, and turning towards the said aldermen, drank likewise to them; and particularly addressing himself to the said town clerk, afforded him the favour of drinking to him. And when His Majesty had drunk, he ordered that wine be given to the said magistrate, aldermen, and to the said M. Clement, and said that he wished them to drink also to him, which they also did with unparalleled joy. And immediately His Majesty approached the table of sweetmeats which was covered with two large white cloths; these cloths being lifted, His Majesty drawing back, admiring the great number of exquisite sweetmeats which were there, said out loud: *How beautiful it is!* And at the same time His Majesty himself chose three boxes of the said sweetmeats. And forthwith all the said princes and lords and other persons threw themselves upon the said refreshments which were taken, carried away, and dispersed, and half were turned upside down on the floor, from which scene the king took singular pleasure. This done, His Majesty said to the said gentlemen of the town and to the said town clerk that he was very pleased with them and that he thanked them and that he had never seen better organization and had never eaten with greater appetite than he had just done; and wholly dressed in costume as he was when he danced the *grand ballet,* he departed and was led by the said gentlemen of the town and the said town clerk who still wore their robes of two colours, to the main staircase of the said Hôtel de Ville, where it being about 9 o'clock in the morning, the artillery, cannon and mortar of the town began to fire; from which His Majesty took very great pleasure and remained a long time at the top of the said flight of stairs, being seen by all the people in the Grève, which Grève was entirely filled with people who shouted: *Long live the king* with a great acclamation of joy. And the king thanking anew the said gentlemen of the town, entered his carriage to go to the Louvre, Swiss guards walking before him, and drums sounding.

And it is worthy of note that along the streets where the king passed in order to come from the Louvre to the said Hôtel de Ville, there were paper lanterns of sundry colours at each window of all the houses and shops, following the instructions sent throughout the said town by the district officers to this end; just as the said Hôtel de Ville was also filled with them, outside as well as inside, which was very fine to see.

And it cannot be said that the town was ever more honoured by its king than it was by this act for which there was general rejoicing.

And the next day the 26th day of the said month of February 1626, the magistrate, aldermen and town clerk of the said town were at the Louvre to thank the king for the honour which he bestowed upon the town, to whom His Majesty answered that he was very pleased with them and thanked them for it.

The king danced another ballet at the Hôtel de Ville again the 16th of February the following year.* There were fireworks at the Grève set up and executed by Denis Caresme, firework-maker of the town. The king arrived at 3 o'clock in the morning.

* Possibly *Le Sérieux et le Grotesque*. See Lacroix, vol. iii, pp. 298–321.

Bibliography

→»« ←

The sources listed are those cited in the text and those of particular importance in the preparation of this study.

ABBREVIATIONS

AM	*Acta Musicologica*
AfMW	*Archiv für Musikwissenschaft*
CM	*Current Musicology*
GMB	*Geschichte der Musik in Beispielen*
HAM	*Historical Anthology of Music*
HD	*Harvard Dictionary of Music*
JAMS	*Journal of the American Musicological Society*
MD	*Musica Disciplina*
MF	*Die Musikforschung*
MGG	*Die Musik in Geschichte und Gegenwart*
M&L	*Music and Letters*
MM	*Le Mercure musical*
MQ	*The Musical Quarterly*
MR	*The Music Review*
MT	*The Musical Times*
NOHM	*New Oxford History of Music*
PRMA	*Proceedings of the Royal Music Association*
RBdM	*Revue Belge de Musicologie*
RdM	*Revue de musicologie*
RM	*La Revue musicale*
RMC	*La Revue musicale* (ed. Combarieu, 1901–10)
RMI	*Rivista musicale italiana*
SIMG	*Sammelbände der internationalen Musikgesellschaft*
ZfMW	*Zeitschrift für Musikwissenschaft*

Sources before 1800

André, le père Yves-Marie, *Essai sur le Beau*, Paris, 1741.
Aquin de Château-Lyon, Pierre-Louis d', *Siècle littéraire de Louis* xv *ou Lettres sur les hommes célèbres*, 2 vols., Amsterdam, 1753.

Bachelier, I., *Recueil de cantates*, The Hague, 1728.

Bacilly, Bénigne de, *Remarques curieuses sur l'art de bien chanter*, Paris, 1668. Trans. by Austin B. Caswell, Brooklyn, 1968. Reprint of 1679 ed., Geneva, 1971.

Batteux, Charles, *Les Beaux-Arts réduits à un même principe*, Paris, 1746. Reprint of 1773 ed. Geneva, 1971.

Bedos de Celles, Dom François, *L'Art du facteur d'orgues*, 4 vols, Paris, 1766–78. Facsimile ed., Kassel, 1934.

Bérard, Jean-Baptiste Antoine, *L'Art du chant*, Paris, 1755. Facsimile ed., New York, 1967 and Geneva, 1972; trans. by Sidney Murray, New York, 1967.

Bernier, Nicolas, *Principes de composition*, undated MS, trans. by Philip Nelson, Brooklyn, 1964.

Besche, L'Aîné, *Abrégé historique de la ménestrandie*, Versailles, 1774.

Blainville, Charles-Henri de, *L'Esprit de l'art musical ou réflexions sur la musique*, Geneva, 1754. Reprint Geneva, 1975.

Boffrand, Germain, *Le Théâtre de M. Quinault*, Vol. I, Paris, 1715.
Livre d'Architecture, Paris, 1745.

Boileau-Despréaux, Nicolas, 'Réflexions critiques sur quelques passages de Longin', *Oeuvres diverses*, Paris, 1694.

Bollioud de Mermet, Louis de, *De la corruption du goust dans la musique françoise*, Lyon, 1746.

Bonnet, Jacques, *Histoire de la musique et de ses effets*, Paris, 1715. Reprint Geneva, 1969.

Borjon de Scellery, Charles-Emmanuel, *Traité de la musette*, Lyon, 1672. Facsimile ed., Geneva, 1972.

Bourdelot, Pierre and Jacques Bonnet, *Histoire de la musique et de ses effets*, Amsterdam, 1725. Facsimile ed., Graz, 1966.

Brossard, Sébastien de, *Catalogue des livres de musique théorique et pratique ... qui sont dans le cabinet du sieur Seb. de Brossard*, MS, 1724 in B.N. (Res, Vm⁸ 21).
Dictionnaire de musique, Paris, 1701. Facsimile of 1703 ed., Amsterdam, 1964.

Cahusac, Louis de, *La Danse ancienne et moderne*, 3 vols, The Hague, 1754. Facsimile ed., Geneva, 1971.

Callières, François de, *Histoire poétique de la guerre nouvellement déclamée entre les anciens et les modernes*, Paris, 1688.

Chabanon, Michel-Paul, *De la musique considérée en elle-même*, Paris, 1785. Facsimile ed. Geneva, 1969.

Chappuzeau, Samuel, *Le Théâtre françois*, 3 vols., Lyon, 1674.

Chastelleux, François-Jean, *Essai sur l'union de la poésie et de la musique*, Paris, 1765. Facsimile ed. Geneva, 1970.

Compan, Charles, *Dictionnaire de danse*, Paris, 1787.

Corrette, Michel, *L'Ecole d'Orphée: Méthode pour apprendre facilement à jouer du violon ...*, Paris, 1738. Facsimile ed., Geneva, 1973.

L'Art de se perfectionner dans le violon, Paris, 1782. Facsimile ed., Geneva, 1973.

Le Maître de clavecin pour l'accompagnement, Paris, 1753. Facsimile ed., Hildesheim, 1971.

Méthode pour apprendre à jouer de la contrebasse à trois, à quatre, à cinq cordes, Paris, [1781].

Méthode pour apprendre aisément à jouer la flûte traversière, Paris and Lyon, *c.* 1740. Facsimile ed., Hildesheim, 1971. Trans. by Carol R. Farrar in *Michel Corrette and Flute Playing in the Eighteenth Century*, Brooklyn, 1970.

Méthode théorique et pratique pour apprendre en peu de tems le violoncelle dans sa perfection, Paris, 1741. Facsimile ed., Geneva, 1972.

Le Parfait maître à chanter, Paris, 1758.

Couperin, François, *L'Art de toucher le clavecin*, Paris, 1716. Reprint in *Oeuvres completes*, vol. I, trans. and ed. by Anne Linde in French, German and English, Wiesbaden, 1933. Trans. by Margery Halford, London, 1975.

Règles pour l'accompagnement, Ms *c.* 1698, new ed. by Paul Brunold in *Oeuvres complètes*, vol. 1, 1933.

D'Alembert, Jean Le Rond, 'De la liberté de la musique', *Oeuvres complètes*, Vol. I, Paris, 1821–22. Reprint Geneva, 1967.

Danoville, *L'Art de toucher le dessus et basse de violle*, Paris, 1687. Reprint Geneva, 1972.

Denis, Jean, *Traité de l'accord de l'espinette*, Paris, 1650. Facsimile ed., New York, 1969.

Descartes, René, *Musicae compendium*, Utrecht, 1650. Facsimile ed., New York, 1968. Trans. by W. Robert, Rome, 1961.

Dictionnaire universel françois et latin (commonly known as the *Dictionnaire de Trévoux*), 7 vols, Paris, 1743–52.

Dubos, Jean-Baptiste, *Réflexions critiques sur la poésie et sur la peinture*, 2 vols, Paris, 1719. Facsimile of 7th ed., Geneva, 1967.

Durey de Noinville, Jacques-Bernard, *Histoire du théâtre de l'Académie royale de musique en France*, 2nd ed., Paris, 1757. Facsimile ed. Geneva, 1969.

Encyclopédie, ou Dictionnaire raisonné des sciences, des arts et des métiers, ed. Denis Diderot, 35 vols., Paris, 1751–80.

Favart, Charles-Simon, *Théâtre de M. (et Mme.) Favart*, Paris, 1763–72. Reprint Geneva, 1971.

Félibien, André, *Les Divertissemens de Versailles*, Paris, 1676.

Relation de la feste de Versailles du 18e juillet, 1668, Paris, 1668.

Recueil de descriptions de peintures et d'autres ouvrages faits pour le roi, Paris, 1689.

Félibien, Michel de and Guy-Alexis Lobineau, *Histoire de la ville de Paris*, 5 vols, Paris, 1725.

Feuillet, Raoul-Auger, *Chorégraphie ou l'art de décrire la danse par caractères, figures et signes démonstratifs*, 1700. Facsimile ed., New York, 1968. Trans. by John Weaver as *Orchesography*, London, 1906; reprint Farnsborough Hants, 1971.

François, René (pseud. for Etienne Binet), *Essais des merveilles de nature*, Rouen, 1621.

Freillon-Poncein, Jean-Pierre, *La véritable manière d'apprendre à jouer en perfection du hautbois, de la flûte et du flageolet*, Paris, 1700. Facsimile ed., Geneva, 1971.

Furetière, Antoine, *Dictionnaire universel*, The Hague, 1690.

Gantez, Annibal, *L'Entretien des musiciens*, Auxere, 1643; ed. by Thoinan and Claudin, Paris, 1878. Reprinted Geneva, 1971.

Gherardi, Evaristo, *Le Théâtre italien du Gherardi*, Amsterdam, 1721.
    Le Théâtre italien ou le Recueil général de toutes les comédies et scènes françoises jouées par les comédiens italiens du roy, 6 vols., Paris, 1700.

Goldoni, Carlo, *Mémoires de M. Goldoni*, 3 vols., Paris, 1787.

Grimarest, Jean-Léonard le Gallois de, *Traité du récitatif*, Paris, 1707.

Grimm, Melchior, *Lettre de M. Grimm sur Omphale de Destouches*, Paris, 1752.

Hotteterre, Jacques Martin, *Méthode pour la musette*, Paris, 1737. Reprint Geneva, 1977.
    Principes de la flûte traversière . . ., Paris, 1707. Facsimile ed., Geneva, 1973. Trans. by David Lasocki, London, 1968. Trans. by Paul Douglas, New York, 1968.

La Borde, Jean-Benjamin de, *Essai sur la musique ancienne et moderne*, 4 vols, Paris, 1780. Facsimile ed., Paris, 1972.

La Bruyère, Jean de, *Des Ouvrages de l'esprit*, Paris, 1688.

Lacombe, Jacques, *Dictionnaire portatif des beaux-arts*, Paris, 1752.

La Dixmerie, Bricaire de, *Les Deux âges du goût et du génie français*, The Hague, 1769. Reprinted Geneva, 1971.

L'Affilard, Michel, *Principes très-faciles pour bien apprendre la musique*, Paris, 1694. Facsimile ed., Geneva, 1970.

La Fontaine, Jean de, 'Epître à M. de Niert sur l'opéra', *Oeuvres diverses*, Vol. II, *Paris*, 1677. Reprint 1958.

La Vallière, Louis César de La Baume Le Blanc Duc de, *Ballets, opéra et autres ouvrages lyriques*, Paris, 1760. Reprinted, London, 1967.

Le Blanc, Hubert, *Défense de la basse de viole contre les entreprises du violon et les prétensions du violoncel*, Paris, 1740. Reprinted in *RM*, IX, Nov., Dec., Jan., Feb., Mar., June, 1927–28.

Le Brun, Antoine-Louis, *Théâtre lyrique*, Paris, 1712.

Lecerf de la Viéville, Jean Laurent, *Comparaison de la musique italienne et de la musique françoise*, included as vols II–IV of *Histoire de la musique et de ses effets* (Bourdelot and Bonnet), Amsterdam,

1725 and reprint Graz, 1966. Brussels ed. of 1705–06 reprint Geneva, 1972.

Le Gallois, Jean, *Lettre de Mr le Gallois à Mlle Regnault de Solier touchant la musique*, Paris, 1680. Trans. by David Fuller in *Early Music*, IV (1976), pp. 22–26.

Le Sage, Alain and D'Orneval, *Théâtre de la foire ou l'opéra comique*, 10 vols, Paris, 1724–37.

Lister, Dr. Martin, *A Journey to Paris in the Year 1698*, London, 1699.

Loret, Jean, *La Muze historique*, Paris, 1650–65. Reprinted, Paris, 1877–78.

Loulié, Etienne, *Eléments ou principes de musique*, Paris, 1696; trans. by Albert Cohen, Brooklyn, 1965. Facsimile ed. Geneva, 1971.

Mably, Gabriel Bonnot de, *Lettres à Madame la Marquise de P[ompadour] sur l'opéra*, Paris, 1741.

Manoir, Guillaume du, *Le Mariage de la musique avec la danse*, Paris, 1664. Ed. by J. Gallay, Paris, 1870.

Marmontel, Jean-François, '*Eléments de littérature*', Vols. v–x of the *Oeuvres complètes*, Paris, 1787.

Marolles, Michel de, *Mémoires*, Amsterdam, 1645.

Masson, Charles, *Nouveau traité des règles pour la composition de la musique*, Paris, 2nd ed., 1699. Reprint with introduction by Imogene Horsley, New York, 1967.

Mattheson, Johann, *Das neu-eröffnete Orchestre*, Hamburg, 1713.

Maugars, André, *Response faite à un curieux sur le sentiment de la musique d'Italie*, 1639. Reprinted, London, 1965.

Ménestrier, Claude-François, *Des Ballets anciens et modernes selon des règles du théâtre*, Paris, 1682. Facsimile ed., Geneva, 1972.

Remarques pour la conduite des ballets, 1658, reprinted in appendix of Marie Christout, *Le Ballet de cour de Louis XIV*. Paris, 1967.

Des Représentations en musique anciennes et modernes, Paris, 1681. Facsimile ed., Geneva, 1972.

Mersenne, Marin, *Harmonie universelle*, Paris, 1636. Facsimile with annotations of author, Paris, 1963.

Mervesin, Joseph, *Histoire de la poésie françoise*, Paris, 1706.

Millet, Jean, *L'Art de bien chanter*, Lyon, 1666. Facsimile ed. with introduction by A. Cohen, New York, 1973.

Montéclair, Michel Pignolet de, *Méthode facile pour apprendre à jouer du violon*, Paris, 1712.

Nouvelle méthode pour apprendre la musique, Paris, 1709.

Petite méthode pour apprendre la musique aux enfants . . . , Paris, c. 1730. Summarized by M. Pincherle in *MQ*, XXIV (January, 1948), pp. 61–67.

Principes de musique divisez en quatre parties, Paris, 1736. Facsimile ed., Geneva, 1972.

Muffat, Georg, Preface to *Florilegium primum*, Augsburg, 1695. Trans. by O. Strunk, *Source Readings* ..., pp. 442–44.

 Preface to *Florilegium secundum*, Passau, 1698. Trans. by O. Strunk, *Source Readings* ..., pp. 445–47, and Kenneth Cooper and Julius Zsako in 'Georg Muffat's Observations on the Lully Style of Performance', *MQ*, LIII (April, 1967), pp. 220–45.

Nemeitz, Joachim Christoph, *Le Séjour de Paris*, Leiden, 1727.

Nivers, Guillaume Gabriel, *Dissertation sur le chant grégorien*, Paris, 1683.

 Méthode certaine pour apprendre le pleinchant de l'Eglise, Paris, 1698.

 Traité de la composition de musique, Paris, 1667; trans. by Albert Cohen, Brooklyn, 1961.

North Roger, *Memoires of Musick*, 1728, in *Roger North on Music*, ed. John Wilson, London, 1959, pp. 315–59.

Nougaret, Pierre-Jean-Baptiste, *De l'Art du théâtre*, 2 vols., Paris, 1769. Facsimile ed., Geneva. 1971.

Noverre, Jean-Georges, *Lettres sur la danse et sur les ballets*, 1760. Modern ed. by André Levenson, Paris, 1927: trans. by Cyril W. Beaumont, Brooklyn, 1966. Facsimile of 1760 ed., New York, 1967.

Parfaict, Claude and François, *Dictionnaire des théâtres de Paris*, 7 vols, Paris, 1756. Reprint of 1767–70 ed., Geneva, 1971.

 Histoire de l'académie royale de musique, Ms in B.N. (n.a. 6532).

 Mémoires pour servir à l'histoire des spectacles de la foire, 2 vols., Paris, 1743.

Perrault, Charles, *Critique de l'opéra ou examen de la tragédie intitulée 'Alceste ou le Triomphe d'Alcide'*, Paris, 1674.

 Les Hommes illustres qui ont paru en France pendant ce siècle, 2 vols. in 1, Paris, 1696–1700.

 Le Siècle de Louis le Grand, Paris, 1687.

Perrin, Pierre, *Les Oeuvres de poésie de M. Perrin*, Paris, 1661.

 Cantica pro capella regis, Paris, 1665.

 Recueil de paroles de musique (MS, B.N. fr. 2208), c. 1667.

Peyrat, Guillaume du, *Histoire ecclésiastique de la cour ou les antiquitez et recherches de la chapelle et oratoire du roy de France*, Paris, 1645.

Pluche, Noël-Antoine, *Le Spectacle de la nature*, Paris, 1746.

Pure, Michel de, *Idée des spectacles anciens et nouveaux*, Paris, 1668. Facsimile ed., Geneva, 1972.

Raguenet, François, *Parallèle des Italiens et des Français, en ce qui regarde la musique et les opéra*, Paris, 1702. Reprint Geneva, 1976. Trans. as *A Comparison between the French and Italian Musick and Operas*, anon. (J. E. Galliard?), London, 1709. Facsimile ed. with introduction by C. Cudworth, Farnborough, 1968.

 Défense du parallèle des Italiens et des Français, Paris, 1705.

Reprint (with *Parallèle des Italiens . . .*) Geneva, 1976.

Rameau, Jean-Philippe, Complete Theoretical Works projected in 6 vols, ed. by Erwin Jacobi, 1967–

Rameau, Pierre, *Le Maître à danser*, Paris, 1725, trans. by Cyril W. Beaumont, London, 1931.

Recueil général des opéras, ed. J. N. de Francini, 16 vols, Paris, 1703–1745. Reprinted Geneva, 1971.

Rémond de Saint-Mard, 'Réflexions sur l'opéra', in *Oeuvres*, v, Paris, 1749. Reprinted Geneva, 1972.

Riccoboni, Luigi, *Réflexions historiques et critiques sur les différens théâtres de l'Europe*, Paris, 1738. Trans. as *Reflections upon Declamation; or the Art of Speaking in Publick; with an Historical and Critical Account of the Theatres in Europe*, anon., London, 1741.

De Rochemont. *Réflexions d'un patriote sur l'opéra françois et sur l'opéra italien*, Lausanne, 1754.

Rousseau, Jean, *Traité de la viole*, Paris, 1687. Facsimile ed., Amsterdam, 1965. Reprint with introduction by François Lesure, Geneva, 1975.

Méthode claire, certaine et facile, pour apprendre à chanter la musique, Paris, 1683. Reprint of 2nd ed. (Amsterdam, 1710), Geneva, 1976.

Rousseau, Jean-Jacques, *Dictionnaire de musique*, Paris, 1768, and Amsterdam, 2 vols., 1768. Facsimile ed. of Paris ed., Hildesheim and New York, 1969.

Dissertation sur la musique moderne, Paris, 1743.

Lettre sur la musique françoise, Paris, 1753. Trans. by O. Strunk, *Source Readings . . .*, pp. 636–54.

Roy, Pierre-Charles, 'Lettre sur l'opéra', in *Lettres sur quelques écrits de ce tems*, ii, Geneva, 1749.

Saint-Evremond, *Les Opéra, Comedie*, Paris, 1684.

Sur les opéra, in vol. xi of *Oeuvres meslées*, Paris, 1714.

Saint-Hubert, *La Manière de composer et faire réussir les ballets*. Paris, 1641.

Saint-Lambert, Michel de, *Les Principes du clavecin*, Paris, 1702. Facsimile ed., Geneva, 1972.

Nouveau traité de l'accompagnement, Paris, 1707. Fascimile ed., Geneva, 1972.

Sauval, Henri, *Histoire et recherches des antiquités de la ville de Paris*, 3 vols., Paris, 1724. Reprinted Geneva, 1973.

Serré de Rieux, Jean de, *Les Dons des enfants de Latone*, Paris, 1734.

Sonnet, Martin, *Caeremoniale parisiennse ad usum omnium ecclesiarum collegiatarum, parochialium . . . et dioecesis parisiennsis*, Paris, 1662.

Terrasson, Antoine, *Dissertation historique sur la vielle*, Paris, 1741.

Facsimile ed. Amsterdam, 1966.
Titon du Tillet, *Le Parnasse françois*, Paris, 1732 with supplements in 1743, 1755 and 1760. Reprint of 1732–43 ed., Geneva, 1971. Reprint of 1755–60 ed., Geneva, 1977.
Trichet, Pierre, *Traité des instrumens de musique*, c. 1640. Published with introduction by François Lesure, Neuilly-sur-Seine, 1957; also included in *Annales musicologiques*, III (1955) and IV (1956).

Sources after 1800

Alderman, Pauline, 'Anthoine Boësset and the *air de cour*', unpublished Ph.D. dissertation, University of Southern California, 1946.
Aldrich, Putnam, 'The Principal "agréments" of the Seventeenth and Eighteenth Centuries', unpublished Ph.D. dissertation, Harvard, 1942.
Anthony, James R., 'The French Opera-Ballet in the Early Eighteenth Century: Problems of Definition and Classification', *JAMS*, XVIII (1965), pp. 197–206.
'Printed Editions of André Campra's *L'Europe galante*', *MQ*, LVI (January, 1970), pp. 54–73.
'Some Uses of the Dance in the French Opéra-Ballet', *Recherches*, IX (1969), pp. 209–20.
'Thematic Repetition in the Opéra-Ballets of André Campra', *MQ*, LII (April, 1966), pp. 209–20.
Antoine, Adam, *Histoire de la littérature française au* XVIIᵉ *siècle*, 5 vols., Paris, 1949.
Antoine, Michel, *Henry Desmarest*, Paris, 1965.
Apel, Willi, 'Du nouveau sur la musique française pour l'orgue au XVIᵉ siècle', *RM*, XVIII (1937), pp. 96–108.
Geschichte der Orgel- und Klaviermusik bis 1700, Cassel, 1967. Trans. and rev. by Hans Tischler as *History of Keyboard Music to 1700*, Bloomington, 1972.
Appia, Edmond, 'The Violin Sonatas of Leclair', *The Score*, III (June, 1950), pp. 3–19.
Arger, Jane, 'Le Rôle expressif des "agréments" dans l'école française de 1680 à 1760', *RdM*, I–II (1919), pp. 215–26.
Arnold, Franck Thomas, *The Art of Accompaniment from a Thorough-Bass*, London, 1931. Reprint in 2 vols., New York, 1965.
Barber, Clarence, 'The Liturgical Music of Marc-Antoine Charpentier', unpublished Ph.D. dissertation, Harvard, 1955.
'Les Oratorios de Marc-Antoine Charpentier', *Recherches*, III (1963), pp. 90–130.
Bardet, Bernard, 'Les Violons de la musique de chambre sous Louis

xiv, 1634–1715', unpublished thesis, Ecole Nationale des Chartes, 1956.

Barnes, Clifford R., 'Instruments and Instrumental Music at the "Théâtres de la Foire"', *Recherches*, v (1965), pp. 142–68.

'Vocal Music at the "Théâtres de la Foire"', *Recherches*, viii (1968), pp. 141–60.

Le Baroque au théâtre et le théâtralité du Baroque, 2nd session of the Journées internationales d'Etude du Baroque, Montauban, 1967.

'Le Baroque musical', vol. iv of *Les Colloques de Wégimont*, Liège, 1963.

Barthélemy, Maurice, *André Campra*, Paris, 1957.

'Les Divertissements de Jean-Joseph Mouret pour les comédies de Dancourt', *RBdM*, vii (1953), pp. 47–51.

'La Musique dramatique à Versailles de 1660 à 1715', *Bulletin de la Société d'étude du* xviie *siècle*, xxxiv (1957), pp. 7–18.

'L'Orchestre et l'orchestration des oeuvres de Campra', *RM*, numéro spécial 226 (1955), pp. 97–104.

'Théobaldo di Gatti et la tragédie en musique, "Scylla"', *Recherches*, ix (1969), pp. 56–66.

Benoit, Marcelle, *Musiques de cour: Chapelle, Chambre, Ecurie, 1661–1733*, Paris, 1971.

Versailles et les musiciens du roi, 1661–1733, Paris, 1971.

Benoit, Marcelle, and N. Dufourcq, 'A propos des Forquerays', *Recherches*, viii (1968), pp. 229–41.

Bert, Marie, 'La Musique à la maison royale Saint-Louis de Saint-Cyr', *Recherches*, iii (1963), pp. 55–71; iv (1964), pp. 127–31; and v (1965), pp. 91–127.

Bjurstöm, Per, *Giacomo Torelli and Baroque Stage, Design*, 2nd ed., Stockholm, 1961.

Blaze, François-Henri-Joseph (called Castil-Blaze), *L'Académie impériale de musique*, 2 vols., Paris, 1856.

Bloch, Michel-Antoine, 'Les Messes d'Aux-Cousteaux', *Recherches*, iii (1963), pp. 31–40.

Bobillier, Marie, *see* Brenet, Michel.

Bol, Hans, *La Basse de viole du temps de Marin Marais et d'Antoine Forqueray*, Bilthoven, 1973.

Bonfils, Jean, Les Fantaisies instrumentales d'Eustache Du Caurroy', *Recherches*, ii (1961–62), pp. 5–31.

'L'Oeuvre d'orgue de Jehan Titelouze', *Recherches*, v (1965), pp. 5–16.

Bonnet, Georges-Edgar, 'La Naissance de l'opéra-comique en France', *RM*, ii (1921), pp. 231–43.

Borowitz, Albert, 'Lully and the Death of Cambert', *MR*, xxxv (November, 1974), pp. 231–39.

Borrel, Eugène, 'L'Interprétation de l'ancien récitatif français', *RdM*, XII (February, 1931), pp. 13–21.

'L'Interprétation de Lully après Rameau', *RdM*, x (1929), pp. 17–25.

L'Interprétation de la musique française de Lully à la Révolution, Paris, 1934.

Jean-Baptiste Lully, Paris, 1949.

'Notes sur la musique de la Grande Ecurie de 1650 à 1789', *Bulletin de la Société d'étude du XVIIe siècle*, XXXIV (1957), pp. 33–41.

'Notes sur l'orchestration de l'opéra *Jephté* de Montéclair (1733) et de la symphonie des *Elemens* de J. F. Rebel (1737)', *RM*, numéro spécial 226 (1955), pp. 105–16.

Borroff, Edith, 'The Instrumental Style of Jean-Joseph Cassanéa de Mondonville', *Recherches*, VII (1967), pp. 165–204.

'The Instrumental Works of Jean-Joseph Cassanéa de Mondonville', unpublished Ph.D. dissertation, University of Michigan, 1959.

An Introduction to Elisabeth-Claude Jacquet de La Guerre, Brooklyn, 1966.

The Music of the Baroque, Dubuque, 1970.

Böttger, Friedrich, *Die 'Comedie-Ballet' von Molière-Lully*, Berlin, 1931.

Boulay, Laurence, 'Les Cantiques spirituels de Racine, mis en musique au XVIIe siècle', *Bulletin de la Société d'étude du XVIIe siècle*, XXXIV (1957), pp. 79–92.

'La Musique instrumentale de Marin Marais', *RM*, numéro spécial 226 (1955), pp. 61–75.

'Notes sur quatre motets inédits de Michel-Richard Delalande', *Recherches*, I (1960), pp. 77–86.

Bourligneux, Guy, 'Le mystérieux Daniel Danielis', *Recherches*, IV (1964), pp. 146–78.

Bowers, Jane, 'The French Flute from 1700–1760', unpublished Ph.D. dissertation, University of California, Berkeley, 1971.

Boyden, David, 'When is a Concerto not a Concerto?', *MQ*, LIII (April, 1957), pp. 220–32.

Boyer, Ferdinand, 'Giulio Caccini à la cour d'Henri IV', *RM*, VII (October, 1926), pp. 241–50.

Brenet, Michel (pseud. for Marie Bobillier), *Les Concerts en France sous l'ancien régime*, Paris, 1900. Reprinted New York, 1970.

'La Jeunesse de Rameau', *RMI*, IX (1902), pp. 868–93, and x (1903), pp. 62–85, 185–286.

Les Musiciens de la Sainte-Chapelle du Palais, Paris, 1921. Reprinted Geneva, 1973.

La Musique sacrée sous Louis XIV, Paris, 1899.

'Notes sur l'introduction des instruments dans les églises de France', *Riemann Festschrift*, Leipzig, 1909, pp. 277–86.

'Sébastien de Brossard, prêtre, compositeur, écrivain et bibliophile, d'après ses papiers inédits', *Memoires de la Société de l'histoire de Paris et de l'Ile de France*, XXIII (1896), pp. 72–124.

Bricqueville, Eugene de, *Le Livret d'opéra de Lully à Gluck*, Paris, 1888.

Bridgman, Nanie, 'L'Aristocratie française et le ballet de cour', *Cahiers de l'Association Internationale des études français*, XI (1959), pp. 9–21.

Brofsky, Howard, 'Notes on the Early French Concerto', *JAMS*, XIX (Spring, 1966), pp. 87–91.

Brook, Barry, *La Symphonie française dans la seconde moitié du XVIIIe siècle*, Paris, 1962.

Brosset, Jules, *Le grand orgue, les maîtres de chapelle et musiciens du choeur, les organistes de la cathédrale Saint-Louis-de-Blois*, Etampes, 1907. Reprint Geneva, 1972.

Brunold, Paul, *Traité des signes et agréments employés par les clavecinistes français des 17e et 18e siècles*, Nice, 1935.

'Trois livres de pièces de clavecin de J. F. Dandrieu', *RdM*, XIII (1932), pp. 147–51.

Burton, Humphrey, 'Les Académies de musique en France au XVIIIe siècle, *RdM*, XXXVII (December, 1955), pp. 122–47.

Campardon, Emile, *Les Spectacles des foires*, Paris, 1880.

Carlez, Jules, *La Musique à Caen de 1066 à 1848*, Caen, 1876. Reprint Geneva, 1974.

Carmody, Francis J., *Le Répertoire de l'opéra-comique en vaudevilles de 1708 à 1764*, Berkeley, 1933.

Castle, Conan J., 'The Grands Motets of André Campra', unpublished Ph.D. dissertation, University of Michigan, 1962.

Castil-Blaze, *see* Blaze, François-Henri-Joseph.

Caswell, Austin, 'The Development of Seventeenth-Century French Vocal Ornamentation and Its Influence upon Later Baroque Ornamentation Practice', unpublished Ph.D. dissertation, University of Minnesota, 1964.

Cauchie, Maurice, 'La Dynestie Boësset', *RdM*, I–II (1920), pp. 13–26.

Chailley, Jacques, 'Notes sur la famille de Lully', *RdM*, XXXIV (1952) pp. 101–08.

Charnassé, Hélène, 'Contribution à l'étude des grands motets de Pierre Robert', *Recherches*, III (1963), pp. 49–54, and IV (1964), pp. 105–20.

'Contribution à l'étude du récitatif chez l'Abbé Pierre Robert', *Recherches*, I (1960), pp. 61–67.

'Quelques aspects des "ensembles de récits" chez l'Abbé Pierre Robert', *Recherches*, II (1961–62), pp. 61–70.

Chartier, François-Léon, *L'Ancienne chapitre de Notre-Dame de Paris,*

Paris, 1897. Reprinted Geneva, 1971.

Chouquet, Gustave, *Histoire de la musique dramatique en France*, Paris, 1873.

Christout, Marie, *Le Ballet de cour de Louis* xiv, Paris, 1967.

Citron, Pierre, 'Autour des folies françaises', *RM*, numéro spécial 226 (1955), pp. 89–96.

Clercx, Susanne, *Le Baroque et la musique*, Brussels, 1948.

Clerval, J. A., *L'Ancienne maitrise de Notre-Dame de Chartres*, Paris, 1899. Reprinted Geneva, 1972.

Cohen, Albert, 'The Evolution of the Fantasia and Works in Related Styles in the Seventeenth-Century Instrumental Ensemble Music of France and the Low Countries', unpublished Ph.D., Dissertation, New York University, 1958.

  'The *Fantaisie* for Instrumental Ensemble in Seventeenth-Century France', *MQ*, xlviii (1962), pp. 234–43.

  'The Ouvrard–Nicaise Correspondence (1663–93)', *M&L*, lvi (July–October, 1975), pp. 356–63.

  'René Ouvrard (1624–1694) and the Beginnings of French Baroque Theory', *Report of the 11th Congress of the IMS*, Copenhagen, 1972, I, pp. 336–42.

  'A Study of Instrumental Ensemble Practice in Seventeenth-Century France', *Galpin Society Journal*, xv (1962), pp. 1–5.

  'Symposium on Seventeenth-Century Music Theory: France', *Journal of Music Theory*, xvi (1972), pp. 16–35.

Cole, William P., 'The Motets of J. B. Lully', unpublished Ph.D. dissertation, University of Michigan, 1967.

Collins, Michael, 'A Reconsideration of French Over-Dotting', *M&L*, L (January, 1969), pp. 111–23.

Cooper, Martin, *Opéra comique*, New York, 1949.

Cooper, Kenneth, and Julius Zsako, 'Georg Muffat's Observations on the Lully Style of Performance', *MQ*, liii (April, 1967), pp. 220–45.

Cordey, Jean, 'Lulli d'après l'inventaire de ses biens', *RdM*, xxxvii (1955), pp. 78–83.

Crussard, Claude, *Un Musicien français oublié, Marc-Antoine Charpentier*, Paris, 1945.

Cucuel, Georges, *Les Créateurs de l'opéra-comique français*, Paris, 1914.

  'Sources et documents pour servir à l'histoire de l'opéra-comique en France', *L'Année musicale*, iii (1913), pp. 247–82.

Cudworth, C. L., 'Baptist's Vein: French Orchestral Music and its Influence', *PRMA*, lxxxiii (1956–57), pp. 29–47.

Curtis, Alan, 'Unmeasured Preludes in French Baroque Instrumental Music', unpublished Master's thesis, University of Illinois, 1956.

Cyr, Mary, 'On Performing 18th-Century Haute-Contre Roles', *MT*, 118 (April, 1977), pp. 291–95.

Dacier, Emile, 'Les Caractères de la danse: histoire d'un divertissement pendant la première moitie du xviiie siècle', *RM*, v (1905), pp. 324–35, 365–67.

'L'Opéra au xviiie siècle: les premières représentations du *Dardanus* de Rameau', *Revue d'histoire et de critique musicales*, iii (1903), pp. 163–73.

Dart, Thurston, *The Interpretation of Music*, 4th ed., New York, 1967.

Daval, Pierre, *La Musique en France au* xviiie *siècle*, Paris, 1961.

Dean, Robert H., 'The Music of Michele Mascitti (c. 1664–1760): A Neapolitan Violinist in Paris', unpublished Ph.D. dissertation, University of Iowa, 1970.

Demuth, Norman, *French Opera, Its Development to the Revolution*, Sussex, 1963.

Despois, Eugène, *Le Théâtre français sous Louis* xiv, Paris, 1874.

Dictionnaire de la musique, ed. M. Honegger, 4 vols., Paris, 1970–76.

Documents du Minutier Central concernant l'histoire de la musique 1600–1650, 2 vols., ed. Madeleine Jurgens, Paris, 1969 and 1974.

Dolmetsch, Arnold, *The Interpretation of the Music of the* xviith *and* xviiith *Centuries Revealed by Contemporary Evidence*, London, 1915. New ed., London, 1944. Reprint Seattle and London, 1969.

Donington, Robert, *The Interpretation of Early Music*, new version, New York, 1974.

Douglas, Fenner, *The Language of the Classical French Organ*, New Haven, 1969.

'Should Dom Bedos play Lebègue', *The Organ Yearbook*, iv (1973), pp. 101–11.

Ducrot, Ariane, 'Recherches sur Jean-Baptiste Lully (1632–1687) et sur les débats de l'Académie Royale de Musique', unpublished thesis, Ecole des Chartes, 1961.

'Les Représentations de l'Académie Royale de Musique au temps de Louis xiv', *Recherches*, x (1970), pp. 19–55.

Dufourcq, Norbert, 'Les Barricades mystérieuses de François Couperin', *Recherches*, xiii (1973), pp. 23–34.

'Les Chapelles de musique de Saint-Sernin et de Saint-Etienne de Toulouse dans le dernier quart du xviie siècle', *RdM*, xxxix-xl (1957), pp. 36–55.

'Concerts parisiens et associations de symphonistes', *RBdM*, viii (1954), pp. 46–57.

'De l'emploi du temps des organistes parisiens', *RM*, numéro spécial 226 (1955), pp. 35–47.

'Le Disque et l'histoire de la musique', *Recherches*, iii (1963), pp. 207–20.

Jean-Baptiste de Boësset, 1614–1685, Paris, 1962.

'Die klassische französische Musik, Deutschland und die deutsche Musikwissenschaft,' *AfMW*, xxii (1965), pp. 194–207.

Le Livre de l'orgue français, 5 vols., Paris, 1968–.

La Musique d'orgue français de Jehan Titelouze à Jehan Alain, Paris, 1949.

'La Musique religieuse française de 1660 à 1789', *RM*, numéro spécial (1953–1954), pp. 89–110.

'Quelques réflexions sur les ballets et divertissements de Michel Delalande', *Bulletin de la Société d'étude du* xviie *siècle*, xxiv (1957), pp. 58–72.

'Recent Researches into French Organ Building from the Fifteenth to the Seventeenth Century', *Galpin Society Journal*, x (1957), pp. 66–81.

'Retour à Michel-Richard Delalande', *Recherches*, i (1960), pp. 69–75.

Dufourcq, Norbert, and Marcelle Benoit, 'A propos de Nicolas Bernier', *RdM*, xxxix (July, 1957), pp. 78–91.

Durand, Georges, *La Musique de la cathédrale d'Amiens avant la Révolution*, Amiens, 1922. Reprint Geneva, 1972.

Durand, Henri-André, 'Notes sur la diffusion de M.-R. Delalande dans les chapitres provençaux au xviiie siècle', *RdM*, xxxix (1957), pp. 72–73.

Ecorcheville, Jules, *Corneille et la musique*, Paris, 1906.

De Lulli à Rameau 1690–1730: l'esthétique musicale, Paris, 1906. Reprinted Geneva, 1970.

'Lully, gentilhomme et sa descendance', *MM*, vii, no. 5 (1911), pp. 1–19, no. 6, pp. 1–27, no. 7, pp. 36–52.

'Quelques documents sur la musique de la Grande Ecurie du roi', *SIMG*, ii (1900–01), pp. 608–42.

Vingt Suites d'orchestre du xviie *siècle français*, Paris, 1906. Reprinted New York, 1970.

Ellis, Helen Meredith, 'The Dances of J. B. Lully', unpublished Ph.D. dissertation, Stanford University, 1967.

'Inventory of the Dances of Jean-Baptiste Lully', *Recherches*, ix, (1969), pp. 21–55.

'The Sources of Jean-Baptiste Lully's Secular Music', *Recherches*, viii (1968), pp. 89–130.

See also Little, Meredith Ellis.

Encyclopédie de la musique, ed. François Michel, 3 vols., Paris 1958.

Encyclopédie de la musique et dictionnaire du conservatoire, ed. by Albert-Alexandre-Jean Lavignac and Lionel de La Laurencie, 11 vols., Paris, 1913–31.

Encyclopédie des musiques sacrées, ed. Jacques Porte, 4 vols., Paris, 1968–70.

Eppelsheim, Jurgen, *Das Orchester in dem Werken Jean-Baptiste Lullys*, Tutzing, 1961.

Ferguson, Howard, *Keyboard Interpretation*, New York & London, 1975.

Farrar, Carol R., *Michel Corrette and Flute Playing in the Eighteenth Century*, Brooklyn, 1970.

Fleury, Louis, 'The Flute and Flutist in the French Art of the Seventeenth and Eighteenth Centuries', *MQ*, IX (1923), pp. 515–37.

Flood, W. H. Grattan, 'Quelques précisions nouvelles sur Cambert et Grabu à Londres', *RM*, IX (August, 1928), pp. 351–61.

Foster, Donald H., 'Louis-Nicolas Clérambault and his Cantates françaises', unpublished Ph.D. dissertation, University of Michigan, 1967.

   'The Oratorio in Paris in the 18th Century', *AM*, XLVII (January–June, 1975), pp. 67–133.

Fournel, Victor, *Les Contemporains de Molière*, 3 vols., Paris, 1875.

François-Sappey, Brigitte, L'Oeuvre de clavecin de Jean-François Dandrieu, 1682-1738', *Recherches*, XIV (1974), pp. 155–235.

Fuller, David R., 'Accompanied Keyboard Music', *MQ*, LX (1974), pp. 222–45.

   'Eighteenth-Century French Harpsichord Music', unpublished Ph.D. dissertation, Harvard, 1965.

Garros, Madeleine, 'Mme de Maintenon et la musique', *RdM*, Série spéciale no. 1 (January, 1943), pp. 8–17.

Gastoué, Amedée, 'La Musique à Avignon et dans le Comtat du XIVe au XVIIIe siècle', *RMI*, XII (1905), pp. 555–78, 768–77.

Gaudefroy-Demombynes, Jean, *Les Jugements allemands sur la musique française au XVIIIe siècle*, Paris, 1941.

Genest, Emile, *'L'Opéra-comique connu et inconnu*, Paris, 1925.

Geoffroy-Dechaume, Antoine, *Les 'secrets' de la musique ancienne*, Paris, 1964.

Gérold, Théodore, *L'Art du chant en France au XVIIe siècle*, Strasbourg, 1921. Reprinted Geneva, 1971.

Gervais, Françoise, 'La Musique pure au service du drame lyrique chez Rameau', *RM*, numéro spécial 260 (1965), pp. 37–45.

Girdlestone, Cuthbert, *Jean-Philippe Rameau: His Life and Work*, London, 1957; 2nd ed., Paris, 1962.

   La Tragédie en musique considerée comme genre litteraire, 1673–1750, Geneva, 1972.

Goldschmidt, Hugo, *Studien zur Geschichte der italienischen Oper im 17. Jahrhundert*, I, Leipzig, 1901.

Gomart, Charles, *Notes historiques sur la maîtrise de Saint-Quentin et sur les célébrités musicales de cette ville*, Saint-Quentin, 1851. Reprint Geneva, 1972.

Gros, Etienne, 'Les Origines de la tragédie-lyrique et la place des tragédies en machines dans l'évolution du théâtre vers l'opéra', *Revue d'histoire littéraire* (April–June, 1928), pp. 161–93.

   Philippe Quinault, Paris, 1926.

Grout, Donald, 'The Music of the Italian Theatre at Paris, 1682–

1697', *Papers of the AMS*, xx (1941), pp. 158–70.

'The Origins of the Opéra-comique', unpublished Ph.D. dissertation, Harvard, 1939.

'Seventeenth-Century Parodies of French Opera', *MQ*, xxvii (1941), pp. 211–19, 514–26.

A Short History of Opera, 2nd ed.,New York, 1965.

'Some Forerunners of the Lully Opera', *M&L*, xxii (1941), pp. 1–25.

Grove's Dictionary of Music and Musicians, ed. Eric Blom, 9 vols., 5th ed., London, 1954.

Guilcher, Jean-Michel, 'André Lorin et l'invention de l'écriture chorégraphique', *Revue d'histoire du théâtre*, xxi (1969), pp. 256–64.

La Contredanse et les renouvellements de la danse française, Paris, 1969.

Guillet, Pierre, 'Les Livres de clavecin de Christophe Moyreau', *Recherches*, xi (1971), pp. 179–220.

Haas, Robert, *Die Musik des Barocks*, Wildpark-Potsdam, 1929.

Hajdu, John H., 'The Life and Works of Jean Gilles', unpublished Ph.D., dissertation, University of Colorado, 1973.

Hamburger, Paul, 'Ein handschriftliches Klavierbuch aus der ersten Hälfte der 17. Jahrhundert', *ZfMW*, xiii (1930–31), pp. 138–40, 556–58.

Hardouin, Pierre, 'François Roberday (1624–1680)', *RdM*, xlv (July, 1960), pp. 44–62.

Hibberd, Lloyd, 'Mme de Sévigné and the Operas of Lully', *Essays in Musicology: a Birthday Offering for Willi Apel*, Bloomington, 1968, pp. 153–63.

Hilton, Wendy, *Dance and Music of Court and Theatre: The French Noble Style, 1690–1725*, Princeton, 1977.

'A Dance for Kings: The 17th-Century French *Courante*', *Early Music*, v (April, 1977), pp. 161–72.

Histoire de la musique, ed. Roland-Manuel, 2 vols., Paris, 1960.

Hitchcock, H. Wiley, 'The Instrumental Music of Marc-Antoine Charpentier', *MQ*, xlvii (January, 1961), pp. 58–72.

'The Latin Oratorios of Marc-Antoine Charpentier', *MQ*, xli (January, 1955), pp. 41–65.

'The Latin Oratorios of Marc-Antoine Charpentier', unpublished Ph.D. dissertation, University of Michigan, 1954.

'Marc-Antoine Charpentier and the Comédie-Française', *JAMS*, xxiv (Summer 1971), pp. 255–81.

'Problèmes d'édition de la musique de Marc-Antoine Charpentier pour *Le Malade imaginaire*', *RdM*, lviii (1972), pp. 3–15.

Hofman, Shlomo, *L'Oeuvre de clavecin de François Couperin le Grand*, Paris, 1961.

Hutchings, Arthur, *The Baroque Concerto*, London, 1961.
L'Interprétation de la musique française aux xviième *et* xviiième *siècles*, ed. Edith Weber, CNRS, Paris, 1974.
Isherwood, Robert M., *Music in the Service of the King*, Ithaca, 1973.
Jacquot, Albert, *La Musique en Lorraine*, Paris, 1882. Reprint Geneva, 1972.
Jansen, Albert, *Jean-Jacques Rousseau als Musiker*, Berlin, 1884. Reprinted Geneva, 1971.
Jonckbloet, W. J. A., and Land, J. P. N., *Musique et musiciens au* xviie *siècle*, Leyden, 1882.
Kimbell, David R. B., 'The "Amadis" Operas of Destouches and Handel', *M&L*, xlix (1968), pp. 329–46.
Kinney, Gordon J., 'Marin Marais as Editor of His Own Compositions', *Journal of the Viola da Gamba Society of America*, iii (1966), pp. 5–16.
Kirkpatrick, Ralph, 'Eighteenth-century Metronomic Indications', *Papers of the AMS* (1938), pp. 30–50.
Kish, Anne L., 'Jean-Baptiste Senallié: His Life, His Time, and His Music', unpublished Ph.D. dissertation, Bryn Mawr College, 1964.
Lacroix, Paul, *Ballets et mascarades de cour de Henri* iii *à Louis* xiv, 6 vols., Geneva, 1868–70. Reprinted Geneva, 1968.
Lagrave, Henri, *Le Théâtre et le public à Paris de 1715 à 1750*, Paris, 1972.
Lajarte, Théodore, *Bibliothèque musicale du théâtre de l'opéra: catalogue historique, chronologique, anecdotique*, 2 vols., Paris, 1878. Reprinted Geneva, 1971.
La Laurencie, Lionel de, 'André Campra, musicien profane', *L'Année musicale*, iii (1913), pp. 153–205.
Les Créateurs de l'opéra français, Paris, 1920.
'Les Débuts de la musique de chambre en France', *RdM*, xv (1934), pp. 25–34.
'Deux violistes célèbres: Les Forqueray', *Bulletin français de la SIM* (1908), pp. 1251–74, and (1909), pp. 48–60.
L'Ecole française de violon de Lully à Viotti, 3 vols., Paris, 1922–1924. Reprinted Geneva, 1971.
Le Goût musical en France, Paris, 1905. Reprinted Geneva, 1971.
Lully, Paris, 1911. Reprinted New York, 1977.
'Un musicien dramatique du xviie siècle, Pierre Guédron', *RMI*, xxx (1922), pp. 445–72.
'Notes sur la jeunesse d'André Campra', *SIMG*, x (1908–09), pp. 159–258.
'L'Orfeo nell' inferni d'André Campra', *RdM*, ix (1928), pp. 129–33.
'Les Pastorales en musique au xviie siècle en France avant Lully et leur influence sur l'opéra', *International Music Society, 4th Con-*

gress Report (London, 1912), pp. 139–46.

'Quelques documents sur Jean-Philippe Rameau et sa famille', *Bulletin français de la SIM*, III (1907), pp. 541–614.

Rameau, biographie critique, Paris, 1908.

Lancaster, H. Carrington, 'Comedy versus Opera in France 1683–1700', *Essays and Studies in Honor of Carleton Brown* (New York, 1940), pp. 257–63.

Lance, Evelyn B., 'Molière the Musician: A Tercentenary View', *MR*, XXXV (August, 1974), pp. 120–30.

Lancelot, Francine, 'Ecriture de la danse: le système Feuillet', *Revue de la Société d'ethnographie française*, Nouvelle Série I (1971), pp. 29–58.

Lang, Paul Henry, 'The Literary Aspects of the History of Opera in France', unpublished Ph.D. dissertation, Cornell, 1935.

Music in Western Civilization, New York, 1941.

Larousse de la musique, ed. Dufourcq, 2 vols., Paris, 1957.

Launay, Denise, 'A Propos d'une messe de Charles d'Helfer', in *Le 'Baroque' musical*, vol. IV of *Les Colloques de Wégimont*, (Liège, 1963), pp. 177–99.

'La Fantaisie en France jusqu'au milieu du XVIIᵉ siècle', in *La Musique instrumentale de la Renaissance*, ed. Jean Jacquot (Paris, 1955), pp. 327–38.

'Les Motets à double choeur', *RdM*, XL (December, 1957), pp. 173–95.

'La "Paraphrase des pseaumes" de Godeau et ses musiciens', *RdM*, L (1964), pp. 30–75.

Lawrence, William J., 'The French Opera in London: A Riddle of 1686', *Times Literary Supplement* (28 March 1936), p. 268.

Leclerc, Hélène, 'Les Indes galantes (1735–1952)', *Revue d'histoire du théâtre*, V (1953), pp. 259–85.

Lefebvre, Léon, *La Musique et les Beaux-Arts à Lille au XVIIIᵉ siècle*, Lille, 1893. Reprint Geneva, 1973.

Le Moël, Michel, 'La Chapelle de musique sous Henri IV et Louis XIII', *Recherches*, VI (1966), pp. 5–26.

'Les Dernières années de J. Champion de Chambonnières, 1655–1672', *Recherches*, I (1960), pp. 31–46.

'Un foyer d'Italianisme à la fin du XVIIᵉ siècle', *Recherches*, III (1963), pp. 43–48.

Lemoine, Micheline, 'La Technique violonistique de Jean-Marie Leclair', *RM*, 225 (1953–54), pp. 117–43.

Lespinard, Bernadette, 'Henry Madin (1698–1748), sous-maître de la Chapelle royale', *Recherches*, XIV (1974), pp. 236–96, XV (1975), pp. 107–45, and XVI (1976), pp. 9–23.

Lesure, François, 'Un Contrat d'exclusivité entre Nicolas Formé et Ballard, 1638', *RdM*, L (December, 1964), pp. 228–29.

'Marin Marais: sa carrière, sa famille', *RBdM*, VII (1953), pp. 129–36.

L'Opéra classique français (Iconographie musicale, I), Geneva, 1972.

'Les Orchestres populaires à Paris vers la fin du XVIe siècle', *RdM*, XXXVI (July, 1954), pp. 39–54.

'Le Recueil de ballets de Michel Henry', *Les Fêtes de la Renaissance*, I (Paris, 1956), pp. 205–19.

'Die Terpsichore von Michael Praetorius und die Französische Instrumentalmusik unter Heinrich IV', *MF*, V (1952), pp. 7–17.

Levinson, André, 'Notes sur le ballet du XVIIe siècle: les danseurs de Lully', *RM*, VI (January, 1925), pp. 44–55.

Levy, Kenneth, 'Vaudeville, vers mesurés et airs de cour', *Musique et poésie au XVIe siècle* (Paris, 1954), pp. 185–99.

Little, Meredith Ellis, 'The Contribution of Dance Step to Musical Analysis and Performance: *La Bourgogne*', *JAMS*, XXVIII (Spring, 1975), pp. 112–24.

'Dance under Louis IV and XV', *Early Music*, III (October, 1975), pp. 331–40.

See also Ellis, Helen Meredith.

Loewenberg, Alfred, *Annals of Opera*, 2nd ed., Geneva, 1955.

Lote, Georges, 'La Déclamation du vers français à la fin du XVIIe siècle', *Revue de phonétique*, II (1912), pp. 313–63.

Lough, John, *An Introduction to Seventeenth Century France*, London, 1954.

Lowe, Robert, *Marc-Antoine Charpentier et l'opéra de collège*, Paris, 1966.

'Les Représentations en musique dans les collèges de Paris et de Provence, 1632–1757', *Revue d'histoire du théâtre*, III (1950), pp. 120–36.

Le Luth et sa musique, ed. Jean Jacquot, Neuilly-sur-Seine, 1958.

Malignon, Jean, 'Zoroastre et Sarastro', *Recherches*, VI (1966), pp. 144–58.

Maniates, Maria Rika, ' "Sonate, que me veux-tu?" The Enigma of French Musical Aesthetics in the Eighteenth Century', *CM*, no. 9 (1969), pp. 117–40.

Marsan, Jules, *La Pastorale dramatique en France à la fin du XVIe et au commencement du XVIIe siècles*, Paris, 1905. Reprint New York, 1971.

Marx, Joseph, 'The Tone of the Baroque Oboe', *Galpin Society Journal*, IV (1951), pp. 3–19.

Massenheil, Gunther, 'Marc-Antoine Charpentier als Messenkomponist', *Colloquium Amicorum*, ed. Siegfried Kross and Hans Schmidt (Bonn, 1967), pp. 228–38.

Massip, Catherine, *La Vie des musiciens de Paris au temps de Mazarin*

(*1643–1661*), Paris, 1976.

Masson, Chantal, 'Journal du Marquis de Dangeau', *Recherches*, II (1961), pp. 193–223.

Masson, Paul-Marie, 'Le Ballet-heroïque', *RM*, IX (1928), pp. 132–54.

    'Les Brunettes', *SIMG*, XII (1910–11), pp. 347–68.

    'Les Deux versions du *Dardanus* de Rameau', *AM*, XXVI (1954), pp. 36–48.

    '*Les Fêtes vénitiennes* d'André Campra', *RdM*, XVIII (1932), pp. 127–46, 214–26.

    'La "Lettre sur Omphale" (1752)', *RdM*, XXVII (1945), pp. 1–19.

    'Lullistes et Ramistes', *Année musicale*, I (1911), pp. 187–213.

    'Musique italienne et musique française', *RMI*, XIX (1912), pp. 519–45.

    L'Opéra de Rameau, Paris, 1930. Reprinted New York, 1972.

    'Rameau and Wagner', *MQ*, XXV (1939), pp. 446–78.

Mather, Betty Bang, *Interpretation of French music from 1675 to 1775: for Woodwind and Other Performers*, New York, 1973.

McGowan, Margaret M., *L'Art du ballet de cour en France, 1581–1643*, Paris, 1963.

Mélèse, Pierre, *Répertoire analytique des documents contemporains . . . concernant les théâtres à Paris sous Louis XIV*, Paris, 1934.

    Le Théâtre et le public à Paris sous Louis XIV, Paris, 1934.

Mellers, Wilfrid, *François Couperin and the French Classical Tradition*, London, 1950.

Morby, John E., 'Musicians at the Royal Chapel of Versailles, 1683–1792', unpublished Ph.D. dissertation, University of California, Berkeley, 1971.

Mráček, Jaroslav, 'An Unjustly Neglected Source for the Study and Performance of Seventeenth-Century Instrumental Dance Music', *Report of the 11th Congress of the IMS*, Copenhagen, 1972, pp. 563–71.

Musiciens de Paris, 1535–1792 (from the Fichier Laborde of the B.N.), ed. Yolande de Brossard, Paris, 1965.

Die Musik in Geschichte und Gegenwart, ed. Friedrich Blume, 14 vols., Kassel, 1949–68.

La Musique, Les hommes, des instruments, les sources, ed. Dufourcq, 2 vols., Paris, 1965.

Nelson, Philip, 'Nicolas Bernier: a Bibliographic Study', *Studies in Musicology: Essays . . . in Memory of Glen Haydon* (Chapel Hill, 1969), pp. 109–17.

    'Nicolas Bernier: a Resumé of His Work', *Recherches*, I (1960), pp. 93–98.

    'Nicolas Bernier: a Study of the Man and his Music', unpublished Ph.D. dissertation, University of North Carolina, 1958.

Neumann, Frederick, 'Facts and Fiction about Overdotting', *MQ*, LXIII (April, 1977), pp. 155–85.

'The French *inégales*, Quantz and Bach', *JAMS*, xviii (Fall, 1965), pp. 313–58.

'La Note pointée et la soi-disant "manière française"', *RdM*, li (1965), pp. 66–92. Trans. by Raymond Harris and Edmund Shay as 'The Dotted Note and the so-called French Style', *Early Music*, v (July, 1977), pp. 310–24.

Newman, Joyce, 'Formal Structure and Recitative in the *tragédie lyrique* of Jean Baptiste de Lully', unpublished Ph.d. dissertation, University of Michigan, 1974.

Newman, William S., *The Sonata in the Baroque Era*, rev. ed., Chapel Hill, 1966.

New Oxford History of Music, vol. 5 ('Opera and Church Music, 1630–1750'), ed. Anthony Lewis and Nigel Fortune, London, 1975. Vol. 7 ('The Age of Enlightenment, 1745–1790'), ed. Egon Wellesz and Frederick Sternfeld, London, 1973.

Newton, Richard, 'Hommage à Marin Marais', *The Consort* (June, 1952), pp. 12–21.

Notes et références pour servir à une histoire de Michel-Richard Delalande, ed. Norbert Dufourcq and others, Paris, 1957.

Nuitter, *see* Truinet, Charles-Louis-Etienne.

Nutting, Geoffrey, 'Jean-Marie Leclair, 1698–1764', *MQ*, l (October, 1964), pp. 504–14.

Oboussier, Philippe, 'A Couperin Discovery', *MT*, 112 (May, 1971), pp. 429–30.

'Couperin Motets at Tenbury', *PRMA*, xcviii (1971–72), pp. 17–29.

'Lalande's Grands Motets', *MT*, 117 (June, 1976), pp. 483–86.

Oldham, Guy, 'Louis Couperin. A New Source of French Keyboard Music of Mid-Seventeenth-Century', *Recherches*, i (1960), pp. 51–59.

Oliver, Alfred, *The Encyclopedists as Critics of Music*, New York, 1947.

Oliver, Richard, 'Molière's Contribution to the Lyric Stage', *MQ*, xxxiii (July, 1947), pp. 350–64.

Packer, Dorothy S., ' "La Calotte" and the Eighteenth-Century French Vaudeville', *JAMS*, xxiii (Spring, 1970), pp. 61–83.

Paillard, Jean-François, *La Musique française classique*, Paris, 1960.

'Les Premiers concertos français pour instruments à vent', *RM*, numéro spécial 226 (1954–55), pp. 448–51.

Palisca, Claude V., *Baroque Music*, Englewood Cliffs, 1968.

Pierre, Constant, *Histoire du Concert Spirituel*, Paris, 1975.

Pincherle, Marc, *Corelli, His Life, His Work*, trans. Hubert Russell, New York, 1956.

Jean-Marie Leclair, Paris, 1952.

'La Technique du violon chez les premiers sonatistes français (1695–1723)', *Bulletin français de la SIM*, vii (August–September, 1911), pp. 1–32, and (October, 1911), pp. 19–35.

Pirro, André, *Les Clavicinistes*, Paris, 1925.

Descartes et la musique, Paris, 1907.

Populus, Bernard, *L'Ancienne maîtrise de Langres*, Langres, 1939. Reprint Geneva, 1973.

Powell, Newman, 'Rhythmic Freedom in the Performance of French Music from 1650–1735', unpublished Ph D. dissertation, Stanford, 1958.

Précis de musicologie, ed. Jacques Chailley, Paris, 1958.

Preston, Robert E., 'The Forty-Eight Sonatas for Violin and Figured Bass of Jean Marie Leclair, l'aîné', unpublished Ph.D. dissertation, University of Michigan, 1959.

'The Treatment of Harmony in the Violin Sonatas of Jean-Marie Leclair', *Recherches*, III (1963), pp. 131–44.

Prévost, Arthur-Emile, *Histoire de la maîtrise de la cathédrale de Troyes*, Troyes, 1906. Reprint Geneva, 1972.

Prim, Jean, ' "Chant sur le livre" in French Churches in the 18th Century', *JAMS*, XIV (Spring, 1961), pp. 37–49.

Prod'homme, J.G., 'Les Forqueray', *RMI*, X (1903), pp. 670–706.

Pruitt, James 'Bibliographie des oeuvres de Guillaume Gabriel Nivers', *Recherches*, XIII (1973), pp. 133–56.

'The Organ Works of Guillaume Gabriel Nivers (1632–1714), *Recherches*, XIV (1974), pp. 7–81; (1975), pp. 47–90.

Prunières, Henry, 'L'Académie royale de musique et de danse', *RM, VI* (January, 1925), pp. 3–25.

Le Ballet de cour en France avant Benserade et Lully, Paris, 1914.

'Jean de Cambefort, Surintendant de la musique du roi', *L'Année musicale*, II (1912), pp. 205–26.

'La Jeunesse de Lully', *MM*, V (1909), pp. 234–42, 329–53.

'Lecerf de la Viéville et l'esthétique musicale classique au XVIIᵉ siècle', *Bulletin français de la SIM*, IV (1908), pp. 619-54.

Lully, Paris, 1909.

'Lully, fils de meunier', *MM*, VIII (1912), pp. 57–61.

'La Musique de la chambre et de l'écurie sous le règne de François I', *L'Année musicale*, I (1911), pp. 215–51.

'Notes sur l'origine d l'ouverture française', *SIMG*, XII (1910–11), pp. 565–85.

L'Opéra italien en France avant Lulli, Paris, 1913.

'Paolo Lorenzani à la cour de France', *RM, III* (1922), pp. 97–120.

'Les Petits violons de Lully', *L'Echo musical*, V (April, 1920), pp. 118–30.

'Les Premiers ballets de Lully', *RM, XII* (1931), pp. 1–17.

'Recherches sur les années de jeunesse de J. B. Lully', *RMI*, XVII (1910), pp. 646–54.

La Vie illustre et libertine de Jean-Baptiste Lully, Paris, 1929.

Quittard, Henri, 'Les Années de jeunesse de J.-P. Rameau', *Revue d'histoire et de critique musicales*, II (1902), pp. 61–63, 100–14, 152–70, 208–18.

'Un Chanteur compositeur de musique sous Louis XIII: Nicolas Formé', *RMC*, III (1903), pp. 362–67.

Un Musicien en France au XVIIᵉ *siècle: Henry Du Mont*, Paris, 1906. Reprint Geneva, 1973.

'Un Musicien oublié du XVIIᵉ siècle français: G. Bouzignac', *SIMG*, VI (1904–05), pp. 356–417.

'Orphée descendant aux enfers', *RMC*, IV (1904), pp. 495–98.

'La Première comédie française en musique', *Bulletin français de la SIM*, IV (1908), pp. 378–96, 497–537.

Raugel, Félix, 'The Ancient French Organ School', *MQ*, XI (October, 1925), pp. 560–71.

'Une Maîtrise célèbre au grand siècle: la maîtrise de la cathédrale d'Aix-en-Provence', *Bulletin de la Société d'étude du* XVIIᵉ *siècle*, XXI–XXII (1954), pp. 422–32.

'La Musique à la chapelle de Versailles sous Louis XIV, *Bulletin de la Société d'étude du* XVIIᵉ *siècle*, XXXIV (1957), pp. 19–25.

Rave, Wallace, 'Some Manuscripts of French Lute Music, 1630–1700: An Introductory Study', unpublished Ph.D. dissertation, University of Illinois, 1972.

Réau, Louis, *Histoire de la peinture française au* XVIIIᵉ *siècle*, 2 vols., Paris, 1925.

Rebourd, René-Marie, 'Messire Arthus Aux-Cousteaux, maître de musique de la Sainte-Chapelle au Palais', *Bulletin de la Société d'étude du* XVIIᵉ *siècle*, XXI–XXII (1954), pp. 403–17.

Reilly, Edward R., 'Quantz on National Styles in Music', *MQ*, XLIX (April, 1963), pp. 163–87.

Reimann, Margarete, *Untersuchungen zur Formgeschichte der französischen Klavier-Suite*, Regensburg, 1940.

Richards, James E., 'The "Grand Motet" of the Late Baroque in France as Exemplified by Michel-Richard de Lalande', unpublished Ph.D. dissertation, University of Southern California, 1950.

'Structural Principles in the Grands Motets of de Lalande', *JAMS*, XI (1958), pp. 119–27.

Roche, Martine, 'Un Livre du clavecin français de la fin du XVIIᵉ siècle', *Recherches*, VII (1967), pp. 39–73.

Rolland, Romain, *Musiciens d'autrefois*, 4th ed. revised, Paris, 1914.

'Notes sur l'*Orfeo* de Luigi Rossi et sur les musiciens italiens à Paris sous Mazarin', *Revue d'histoire et de critiques musicales*, I (1901), pp. 225–36, 363–71.

Rollin, Monique, 'La Suite pour luth dans l'oeuvre de Charles Mouton', *RM*, numéro spécial 226 (1955), pp. 76–88.

Royer, Louis, *Les Musiciens et la musique à l'ancienne collégiale*

Saint-André de Grenoble du xve *au* xviiie *siècle*, Paris, 1938. Reprint Geneva, 1973.

Royster, Don Lee, 'Pierre Guédron and the *air de cour*', unpublished Ph.D. dissertation, Yale, 1972.

Ruff, L. M., 'M.-A. Charpentier's "Regles de Composition" ', *The Consort,* xxiv (1967), pp. 233–70.

Sadler, Graham, 'Rameau, Piron and the Parisian Fair Theatres', *Soundings,* iv (1974), pp. 13–29.

Sandman, Susan Goertzel, 'The Wind Band at Louis xiv's Court', *Early Music,* v (January, 1977), pp. 27–37

Sceaury, Paul Loubet de, *Musiciens et facteurs d'instruments sous l'ancien régime*, Paris, 1949.

Schmitz, Eugen, *Geschichte der Weltlichen Solokantate*, Wiesbaden, 1955.

Schneider, Herbert, *Die französische Kompositionslehre in der ersten Hälfte des 17. Jahrhunderts*, Tutzing, 1972.

Schwandt, Erich, 'L'Affilard on the French Court Dances', *MQ* (July, 1974), pp. 389–400.

 'L'Affilard's Published "Sketchbooks" ', *MQ,* lxiii (January, 1977), pp. 99–113.

Scott, R. H. F., *Jean-Baptiste Lully*, London, 1973.

Seagrave, Barbara, 'The French Style of Violin Bowing and Phrasing from Lully to Jacques Aubert', unpublished Ph.D. dissertation, Stanford, 1958.

Shaw, Gertrude, 'The Violoncello Sonata Literature in France during the Eighteeenth Century', unpublished Ph.D. dissertation, Catholic University, 1963.

Silin, Charles, *Benserade and his Ballets de Cour*, Baltimore, 1940.

Snyders, Georges, *Le Goût musical en France aux* xviie *et* xviiie *siècles*, Paris, 1968.

Stricker, Remy, *Musique du baroque*, Paris, 1968.

Strunk, Oliver, *Source Readings in Music History*, New York, 1950.

Taitz-Desouches, Danièle, 'Jean Mignon: Maître de Chapelle de Notre Dame', *Recherches,* xiv (1974), pp. 82–153.

Tapié, Victor, *Baroque et classicisme*, Paris, 1957.

Tessier, André, 'La Carrière versaillaise de La Lande', *RdM,* ix (1928), pp. 134–48.

 'Correspondance d'André Cardinal des Touches et du Prince Antoine i^{er} de Monaco', *RM,* vii (1926), pp. 97–114, and viii (1927), pp. 104–17, 209–24.

 Couperin, Paris, 1926.

 'L'Oeuvre de Marin Marais', *Bulletin de la Société de l'histoire de l'art français* (1924), pp. 76–80.

 'Quelques parodies de Couperin', *RdM,* x (1929), pp. 40–44.

 'Robert Cambert à Londres', *RM,* iv (1927), pp. 101–22.

Théâtre des Jésuites, ed. Jean Jacquot, Paris, 1968.

Thoinan, Ernest (pseud. for A. E. Roquet), *Les Hotteterres et les Chédevilles*, Paris, 1894.

Thompson, Clyde H., 'Instrumental Style in Marin Marais's Pièces de Violes', *Recherches*, III (1963), pp. 79–89.

'Marin Marais' Pièces de Violes', *MQ*, XLVI (October, 1960), pp. 482–99.

'The Music of Marin Marais', unpublished Ph.D. dissertation, University of Michigan, 1959.

Tiersot, Julien, 'La Musique des comédies de Molière à la Comédie-Française', *RdM*, III (1922), pp. 20–28.

'François ii Couperin, compositeur de musique réligieuse', *RdM*, III (1922), pp. 101–09.

Tribout de Morembert, H., 'Bodin de Boismortier: Notes sur un musicien lorrain', *RdM*, LIII (1967), pp. 41–52.

Truinet, Charles-Louis-Etienne (pseud. Nuitter) and A. E. Roquet (pseud. Thoinan), *Les Origines de l'opéra français*, Paris, 1886. Reprint Geneva, 1972.

Tunley, David, 'The Cantatas of Louis Nicolas Clérambault, *MQ*, LII (July, 1966), pp. 313–31.

The Eighteenth-Century French Cantata, London, 1974.

'An Embarkment for Cythera—Social and Literary Aspects of the Eighteenth Century French Cantata', *Recherches*, VII, 1967, pp. 103–14.

'The Emergence of the Eighteenth Century French Cantata', *Studies in Music*, I (1967), pp. 67–88.

Underwood, T. Jervis, 'The Works of Jacques-Christophe Naudot', unpublished Ph.D. dissertation, North Texas State University, 1970.

Vanuxem, Macques, 'Les Fêtes théâtrales de Louis XIV et le baroque de *La Finta Pazza* à *Psyché*', *Actes de Journées internationales d'étude du baroque*, 2nd session ('Le Baroque au théâtre et le théâtralité du baroque'), Montauban, 1967.

Verchaly, André, 'A propos des chansonniers de Jacques Mangeant', *Mélanges d'histoire et d'esthétique musicales offerts à Paul-Marie Masson*, vol. 11 (Paris, 1955), pp. 169–77.

'A propos du récit français au début du XVIIe siècle', *Recherches*, XV (1975), pp. 39–46.

'Les Ballets de cour d'après les recueils de musique vocale (1600–1643)', *Cahiers de l'Association internationale des études français*, IX 1957, pp. 198–218.

'Desportes et la musique', *Annales musicologiques*, II (1954), pp. 271–328.

'Gabriel Bataille et son oeuvre personnelle pour chant et luth', *RdM*, XXIX (1947), pp. 1–24.

'La Métrique et le rhythme musical', *Report of the Eighth Congress of the IMS, New York* (1961), pp. 66–74.

'La Musique religieuse française de Titelouze à 1660', *RM*, 222 (1953–54), pp. 77–88.

'Poésie et airs de cour en France jusqu'à 1620', *Musique et poésie au XVIe siècle* (Paris, 1954), pp. 211–23.

'La Poésie française baroque et sa musique (1580–1645)', *Actes des Journées internationales d'étude du baroque*, Montauban (1968), pp. 127–36.

'Un Précurseur de Lully: Pierre Guédron', *Bulletin de la Société d'étude du XVIIe siècle*, XXI–XXII (1954), pp. 383–93.

Viollier, Renée, *Jean-Joseph Mouret, le musicien des grâces*, Paris, 1950. Reprinted Geneva, 1976.

'La Musique à la cour de la Duchesse du Maine', *RM* (1939), pp. 96–105, 133–38.

Vollen, Gene E., 'The French Cantata: a Survey and Thematic Catalogue', unpublished Ph.D. dissertation, North Texas State University, 1970.

Walker, D. P., 'The Influence of *Musique mesurée à l'antique*, Particularly on the *Airs de Cour* of the Early Seventeenth Century', *MD*, II (1948), pp. 141–63.

'Joan Albert Ban and Mersenne's Musical Competition of 1640', *M&L*, LVII (July, 1976), pp. 233–55.

Wild, Nicole, 'Aspects de la musique sous la régence, Les Foires: Naissance de l'opéra-comique', *Recherches*, V (1965), pp. 129–41.

Yates, Frances A., *The French Academies of the Sixteenth Century*, London, 1947.

Zaslaw, Neal, 'The Enigma of the Haute-contre', *MT*, 115 (November, 1974), pp. 939–41.

'Materials for the Life and Works of Jean-Marie Leclair, L'aîné', unpublished Ph.D. dissertation, Columbia University, 1970.

'Mozart's Tempo Conventions', *Report of the 11th Congress of the IMS, Copenhagen* (1972), pp. 728–32.

Notes

-»> «<-

Author's Note

1. In fact, Dufourcq extended 'French classical music' from 1571 to the Revolution in his 'Die klassische französische Musik, Deutschland und die deutsche Musikwissenschaft', *AfMW*, XXII (1965), p. 194. In *La Musique des origines à nos jours* the 'Deuxième Partie' is called 'L'Art classique des XVIIe et XVIIIe siècles' and stretches from Monteverdi through Haydn and Mozart. In 1965 for *La Musique* (pub. Larousse, ed.

Dufourcq), the term 'Préclassicism' is used for French music from 1589 to 1661.
2. This colloquium, which had taken place in 1957, was inconclusive although the opening paper by Suzanne Clercx-Lejeune, on the term 'Baroque' and a history of its use in music, is informative; for a summary of the 'battle of the Baroque', see Andrea della Corte, 'Barocco', *La Musica*, I, pp. 358–67.

Chapter 1

Institutions and Organizations of the Grand Siècle (pp. 9–25)

1. *Le Parnasse françois* (Paris, 1732) by Titon du Tillet (1677–1762) is a rich source of information on the musical life of France for almost a 100 year period. There are three supplements dated 1743, 1755 and 1760 that add names and biographies of those musicians 'taken in death' between the above dates.
2. Quoted by Jules Ecorcheville, *Vingt Suites d'orchestre du XVIIe siècle français*, I, Paris, 1906, p. 26, reprinted N.Y. 1970.
3. Marcelle Benoit's *Versailles et les musiciens du roi, 1661–1733,* Paris, 1971, and her *Musiques de cour: Chapelle, Chambre, Ecurie, 1661–1733,* Paris, 1971, are the most complete studies. For the Royal Chapel see John E. Morby, 'Musicians at the Royal Chapel of Versailles, 1683–1792', unpublished Ph.D. dissertation, University of California, Berkeley, 1971, and Félix Raugel, 'La Musique à la chapelle de Versailles sous Louis

XIV', *Bulletin de la Société d'étude du XVIIe siècle*, XXXIV (1957), pp. 19–25. For the *Ecurie* see Ecorcheville, 'Quelques documents sur la musique de la Grande Ecurie du roi', *SIMG*, II (1900–01), pp. 608–42 and Eugène Borrel, 'Notes sur la musique de la Grande Ecurie de 1650 à 1789', *Bulletin de la Société d'étude du XVIIe siècle*, XXXIV (1957), pp. 33–41.
4. See Henry Prunières, 'La Musique de la chambre et de l'écurie sous le règne de François 1er', *L'Année musicale*, I (1911), p. 218.
5. See François Lesure, 'Les Orchestres populaires à Paris vers la fin du XVIe siècle', *RdM*, XXXVI (July, 1954), pp. 39–54.
6. See 'Jean de La Motte' in index to *Documents du Minutier Central concernant l'histoire de la musique (1600–50)*, ed. Madeleine Jurgens, Paris, 1969. From a selection of 1,751 notarial

documents over a 50 year period, Mlle Jurgens has fashioned a research tool of inestimable value for the first half of the seventeenth century.

7. 'Prunières, 'Les Petits violons de Lully', *L'Echo musical*, v (April, 1920), p. 130. The most complete study of the *24 Violons* is Bernard Bardet's 'Les Violons de la musique de chambre sous Louis XIV, 1634–1715', unpublished thesis, Ecole Nationale des Chartes, 1956.

8. See Ecorcheville, *SIMG*, pp. 608–42, from which much of this section is derived.

9. That some were still attached to the *Ecurie* as late as the period of Louis XIV is suggested by the *Etat de France* for the year 1686 mentioned above in which a 'bande de violons de la grande Ecurie' joined the winds for certain court ceremonies.

10. John Lough, *An Introduction to Seventeenth Century France*, London, 1954, p. 161.

11. See Norbert Dufourcq, 'La Musique française de 1661 à 1764' in *La Musique* I, Paris, 1965, p. 286.

12. From the *Etat de la France* of 1708 quoted by Morby, p. 225.

13. For additional information on the situation at Notre-Dame and Sainte-Chapelle, see François-Léon Chartier, *L'Ancienne chapitre de Notre Dame de Paris*, Paris, 1897, and Michel Brenet [Marie Bobillier], *Les Musiciens de la Sainte-Chapelle du Palais*, Paris, 1921.

14. This journal, an important mirror of official opinion, underwent many changes of title; in addition to the *Mercure*, it was known at various times as the *Mercure de France*, the *Mercure galant*, the *Nouveau Mercure galant*, the *Nouveau Mercure* and the *Mercure français*.

15. Quoted by Paul Lacroix in his *XVIIIe Siècle, institutions, usages et costumes*, 3rd ed., Paris, 1875, p. 335.

16. See Lesure, *RdM*, XXXVI, p. 47. For a study of the *Confrérie* see Paul Loubet de Sceaury, *Musiciens et facteurs d'instruments de musique sous l'ancien régime*, Paris, 1949.

17. Michel de Pure, *Idée des spectacles anciens et nouveaux*, Paris, 1668.

18. *Abrégé historique de la ménes-trandie*, Versailles, 1774. See also N. Dufourcq and M. Benoit, 'Une vieille querelle: organistes et violonistes, luthiers et facteurs d'orgues à Paris à la fin du XVIIe *siècle'*, *L'Orgue*, LXXXIII 1957), pp. 41–47.

19. For a description of other associations of 'symphonists' in Paris, see Dufourcq, 'Concerts Parisiens et Associations de Symphonistes', *RBdM*, VIII (1954), pp. 46–57.

20. All the documents pertinent to the establishment of the Académie Royale de Musique are found in Charles Truinet [Nuitter] and A. E. Roquet [Thoinan], *Les origines de l'opéra français*, Paris, 1886. See also, Norman Demuth, *French Opera, Its Development to the Revolution*, Sussex, 1963, pp. 97–118, which includes a helpful series of appendices with many of the *lettres patentes*; Prunières, 'L'Académie royale de musique et de danse', *RM*, VI (January, 1925), pp. 3–25; Charles Malherbe, preface to the *Oeuvres complètes* of Rameau, vol. VI, Paris, 1900, pp. xvii-xxiii; Ariane Ducrot, 'Les Représentations de l'Académie Royale de Musique au temps de Louis XIV', *Recherches*, X (1970), pp. 19–55; and Henri Lagrave, *Le Théâtre et le public à Paris de 1715 à 1750*, Paris, 1972. For a discussion of the establishment of Académies de Musique outside of Paris, see Humphrey Burton, 'Les Académies de Musique en France au XVIIIe siècle', *RdM* (December 1955), pp. 122–47.

21. Quoted by Paul-Marie Masson in his *L'Opéra de Rameau*, Paris, 1930, p. 117.

22. See Malherbe, *Oeuvres complètes*, p. xxv.

23. Brenet's *Les Concerts en France sous l'ancien régime*, Paris, 1900, remains the classic secondary source for information on French concerts during the seventeenth and eighteenth centuries. On the *Concert Spirituel* see Constant Pierre, *Histoire du Concert Spirituel*, Société Française de Musicologie, Paris, 1975. See also Chapter VII ('Les Concerts privés') and Chapter VIII ('Le Concert Spirituel') in Pierre Daval's *La Musique en France au XVIIIe siècle*, Paris, 1961.

24. See David Tunley, 'Philidor's "Concerts Français"', *M&L*, XLVII (April 1966), pp. 130–34. For a list of works performed at the *Concerts Français* from 1727 to 1733 see *id.*, *The Eighteenth-Century French Cantata*, London 1974, pp. 241–49.

Chapter 2

Ballet de Cour I: from Beaujoyeulx to Lully (pp. 27–38)

1. Important studies of the *ballet de cour* are: Paul Lacroix, *Ballets et mascarades de cour de Henri III à Louis XIV*, 1868–70 (reprinted Geneva, 1968) which includes *livrets* of court ballets from 1581 to 1652; Prunières, *Le Ballet de cour en France avant Benserade et Lully*, Paris, 1914; Margaret M. McGowan, *L'Art du ballet de cour en France, 1581–1643*, Paris, 1963; and Marie Christout, *Le Ballet de cour de Louis XIV, 1643–1672*, Paris 1967. See also, Frances A. Yates, *The French Academies of the Sixteenth Century*, London 1947.

2. From the *Avis* in the 1582 edition of the *Ballet comique*. A facsimile of this edition was printed in Turin, 1965.

3. In *Le Paradis d'Amour*, allegory had the Huguenot bridegroom and his followers sent to hell by the Catholic defenders of Paradise: Charles IX and his brothers. A fateful acting-out of the smouldering hostilities exploded only days later (Aug. 24th) in the Massacre of Saint Bartholomew's Eve. (See Yates, pp. 254–59.)

4. See, e.g., Germain Boffrand, *Le Théâtre de M. Quinault*, Paris, 1715, p. 27.

5. The Parfaict source is the *Histoire de l'Académie royale de musique*, MS. (n.a. 6532) in the Bibliothèque Nationale, p. 10; the original statement is found in vol. III (p. 157) of the edition of Jean-Laurent Lecerf de la Viéville's *Comparaison de la musique italienne et de la musique françoise* which comprises vols. II–IV of Pierre Bourdelot's and Jacques Bonnet's *Histoire de la musique et de ses effets*, Amsterdam, 1725. All subsequent references to Lecerf are from this edition available in facsimile and printed in Graz, 1966.

6. From 'Recueil des Dames' in *Oeuvres complètes* IX, Paris, 1865, p. 669.

7. Later in the Baroque period the term applied as well to passages for solo instruments such as a 'récit de viole'.

8. This informative little treatise may be found in the appendix of Christout, pp. 221–26.

9. Lionel de La Laurencie, *Les Créateurs de l'opéra français*, Paris, 1920, p. 76.

10. See preface to Christout by André Chastel, p. 3.

11. See Lesure, 'Le Recueil de ballets de Michel Henry', *Les Fêtes de la Renaissance* I, Paris 1956, pp. 205–19.

12. The extant music from *Renaud* is printed in the appendix of Prunières' *Le Ballet de cour*. For some reason Prunières did not include Guédron's *récit* 'Pour Armide contente de posséder Renault', found in the seventh book of *Aires de differents autheurs mis en tablature de luth par eux-mesmes* (Paris, Ballard, 1617). For modern transcription of this *récit* see Verchaly, 'A propos du récit français au début du XVIIe siècle', *Recherches*, XV (1975), p. 44.

13. Preface by Ogier to Schelandre's *tragi-comédie*, *Tyr et Sidon*, edition of 1628.

14. See Nanie Bridgman, 'L'Aristocratie française et le ballet de cour', *Cahiers de l'Association internationale des études français*, XI (1959), p. 14.

15. See Prunières, 'Notes sur l'origine de l'ouverture française', *SIMG*, XII (1910–11), pp. 565–85.

16. See 'Les Ballets de cour d'après les recueils de musique vocale (1600–1643)', *Cahiers de l'Association . . .* IX (1957), pp. 198–218.

17. See Charles Silin, *Benserade and his Ballets de Cour*, Baltimore, 1940,

for an analysis of Benserade's contribution to the court ballet.

18. See Prunières, 'Jean de Cambefort, Surintendant de la Musique du Roi',

L'Année musicale II (1912), pp. 205-26.

19. From the Ballard MS of the *Ballet Royal de la Nuit*, Paris 1653, today at the Bibliothèque Mazarine.

Chapter 3

Ballet de Cour II: The Period of Lully (pp. 39-46)

1. Important sources that deal with the life of Lully are: Prunières, *Lully*, Paris, 1909; *id.*, 'La Jeunesse de Lully', *MM*, v (1909), pp. 234-42, 329-53; *id.*, 'Lully, fils de meunier', *MM*, VIII (1912), pp. 57-61; *id.*, *La Vie illustre et libertine de Jean Baptiste Lully*, Paris, 1929; *id.*, prefaces to the *Oeuvres complètes de J.-B. Lully*, Paris, 1930-39; Ecorcheville, 'Lully gentilhomme et sa descendance', *MM*, VII, no. 5 (1911), pp. 1-19, no. 6, pp. 1-27, no. 7, pp. 36-52; La Laurencie, *Lully*, Paris, 1911; Romain Rolland, 'Notes sur Lully', in *Musiciens d'autrefois*, Paris, 1914; and Borrel, *Jean-Baptiste Lully*, Paris, 1949. See also the Lully Numéro spécial Vol. VI (January, 1925) of *RM*.

2. Following are the ballets for which Lully composed part or all of the music: *Ballet de la Nuit* (1653); *Ballet du Temps* (1654); *Ballet des Proverbes* (1654); *entrées* for *Le Nozzi di Peleo e di Theti* (1654); *Ballet des Plaisirs* (1655); *Ballet des Bienvenus* (1655); *Ballet de Psyché* (1656); *Ballet des Galanteries du Temps* (1656); *Ballet de l'Amour malade* (1657); *Ballet des Plaisirs troublés* (1657); *Ballet d'Alcidiane* (1658); *Ballet de le Raillerie* (1659); *entrées* for *Serse* (1660); *Ballet de la Revente des Habits* (before 1661); *Ballet de l'Impatience* (1661); *Ballet des Saisons* (1661); *entrées* for *Ercole amante* (1622); *Ballet des Arts* (1663); *Ballet des Noces de Village* (1663); *Ballet des Amours déguisés* (1664); *Ballet des Plaisirs de l'Ile enchantée* (1664); *Ballet de la Naissance de Vénus* (1665); *Ballet des Gardes* (1665); *Ballet de Créquy* or *Le Triomphe de Bacchus dans les Indes* (1666); *Ballet des Muses* (1666); *Le Carnaval* or *Le Mascarade de Versailles* (1668—later version, 1675); *Les Fêtes de Versailles* and *Intermèdes de George Dandin* (1668); *La Grotte de Versailles*

(1668); *Ballet de Flore* (1669); *Ballet de la Jeunesse* (1669); *Ballet des Jeux pythiens* (1670); *Ballet de Psyché* (second version, 1671); *Ballet des Ballets* (1671); *Le Triomphe de l'Amour* (1681), *Le Temple de la Paix* (1685).

3. Letter of 19 February 1656 from *La Muze historique* (1650-65) reprinted in Paris, 1877-78. *La Muze Historique* is a collection of letters in verse that comment on the newsworthy events of the day. Although poor as poetry, it is rich as a source of information on individuals and musical events.

4. Manfred Bukofzer's assertion that the use of triple metre in the second part of the French overture 'was to become standard practice' and that the overture to *Serse* (1660) is 'perhaps the first example of the fully developed French overture' (*Music in the Baroque Era*, p. 154) is not borne out by the facts. Six of the overtures to Lully's *tragédies lyriques* are constructed with both sections in duple metre.

5. See Prunières, *Oeuvres complètes*, 'Les Ballets', vol. II, p. x.

6. These statistics are drawn from Helen Meredith Ellis, 'Inventory of the Dances of Jean-Baptiste Lully', *Recherches*, IX (1969), pp. 30-31.

7. The same chorus was appropriated by Pascal Collasse, Lully's protégé, in the prologue to his *Ballet des Saisons* (2nd ed., 1700).

8. *Catalogue des livres de musique théorique et pratique . . . qui sont dans le cabinet du Sieur Seb. de Brossard*, 1724, p. 532; this MS catalogue of the great bibliophile's personal library with his valuable annotations is an important source of information on all aspects of seventeenth and early eighteenth-century music in France.

9. See André Levinson, 'Notes sur le

ballet du xviie siècle: Les Danseurs de Lully', *RM*, vi (January, 1925), pp. 44–55.

10. An extract from the prelude may be found in the Lavignac *Encyclopédie* . . . Part ii, vol. iii, p. 1,508.

11. The 'peace' was of short duration. Three years later, Louis xiv embarked on the disastrous war with the Grand Alliance ·that saw Austria, Holland, Spain and England in powerful league against France.

12. See Eugène Despois, *Le Théâtre* *français sous Louis XIV*, Paris 1874, p. 329.

13. See *Le Théâtre des Jésuites*, ed. Jean Jacquot, Paris, 1968; Robert W. Lowe, 'Les Représentations en musique dans les collèges de Paris et de Provence, 1632–1757', *Revue d'histoire du théâtre*, iii (1950), pp. 120–36; and *id., Marc-Antoine Charpentier et l'opéra de collège*, Paris, 1966. The appendix to this study lists all performances at the Collège Louis-le-Grand with or without music from 1579 to 1761.

Chapter 4
Italian Opera in France (pp. 47–53)

1. *L'Opéra italien en France avant Lulli*, Paris, 1913, p. 64.

2. *L'Opéra de Rameau*, p. 27. Neal Zaslaw believes that this first Italian production in the winter of 1645 was the serenata or dramatic cantata *Il Capriccio, ovvero Il giudizio fra la belta e l'affetto*, with music by Marco Marazzoli and text by Francesco Buti. See Zaslaw's review of Catherine Massip's *La Vie des musiciens de Paris au temps de Mazarin* in *MT*, 118 (June, 1977), p. 483.

3. 'Les Fêtes théâtrales de Louis xiv et la Baroque de *La Finta Pazza* à *Psyché*', *Actes des Journées internationales d'étude du baroque*, 2nd session ('Le Baroque au théâtre et le théâtralité du baroque') Montauban, 1967, p. 32.

4. *Oeuvres complètes*, 'Les Ballets', ii, p. xi. On *Orfeo* see also Romain Rolland, *Musiciens d'autrefois*, 4th ed. re-vised, Paris, 1914, pp. 63–100, and Hugo Goldschmidt, *Studien zur Geschichte der italienischen Oper im 17. Jahrhundert*, i, Leipzig, 1901, pp. 295–311.

5. On the completion of the theatre, Gaspard and his sons returned to Modena, but less than two months later Louis xiv recalled them for engineering *divertissements* and *ballets de cour*.

6. The *sommeil* from *L'Orfeo* is in Arnold Schering, *GMB*, pp. 248–49; that from *Les Amants magnifiques*, in the Lully *Oeuvres complètes*, 'Les Comédies-Ballets', iii, pp. 184–87. Cavalli's *Ercole amante* also contains a *sommeil*, 'Dormi, dormi, dormi, O sonno' (ii, 6) found on pp. 27–32 of the Appendix to Prunières' *L'Opéra italien en France avant Lulli*.

7. See Etienne Gros, *Philippe Quinault*, Paris, 1926, p. 591.

Chapter 5
Comédie-Ballet and Related Genres (pp. 54–61)

1. This ostentatious party proved disastrous to Fouquet who was arrested soon afterwards by order of the king. In the words of Victor Tapié, it meant that the king alone could mount such a lavish display. (*Baroque et classicism*, Paris, 1957, p. 105.)

2. The *comédies-ballets* of Molière and Lully are: *L'Impromptu de Versailles* (1663); *Le Mariage forcé* (1664); *Les Plaisirs de l'isle enchantée* (1664); *La Princesse d'Elide* (1664); *L'Amour médecin* (1665); *La Pastorale comique* (1667); *Le Sicilien ou L'Amour peintre*

(1667); *George Dandin ou Le Grand Divertissement royal de Versailles* (1668); *Monsieur de Pourceaugnac* (1669); *Les Amants magnifiques* (1670); and *Le Bourgeois gentilhomme* (1670). In addition, Charpentier collaborated with Molière on comic *intermèdes* for the 1672 revivals of *Le Mariage forcé* and *La Comtesse d'Ascarbagnas* (1672) as well as for the first performance and revivals of *Le Malade imaginaire* (1673, 1674, c. 1686). He also composed music for the 1679 revival of *Le Sicilien* and perhaps for the 1672 revival of *Les Fâcheux*.
3. Compare, e.g., the ballet of the 'Grand Turc Mahomet' in *Le Grand Bal de la Douairière de Billebahaut* with the Turkish ceremony from *Le Bourgeois gentilhomme*.
4. See *Oeuvres complètes*, 'Les Comédies-Ballets', III, pp. 24–27.
5. Out of 214 airs of all types in the four *opéras-ballets* of André Campra, 75 are cast in this form.
6. The term is Masson's. See *L'Opéra de Rameau*, p. 222.
7. See Théodore Gérold, *L'Art du chant en France au XVIIᵉ siècle*, Strasburg 1921, p. 162.
8. See Pluto's air, 'Pur troppo inequali', *Il Pomo d'oro* (I, 3) and 'Herr nun lässest du deinen Deiner' for two violins, bass voice and continuo.
9. A detailed account of Charpentier's music for the French theatre is found in H. Wiley Hitchcock's article 'Marc-Antoine Charpentier and the Comédie-Française', *JAMS*, XXIV (Summer, 1971), pp. 255–81. On Charpentier's music for *Le Malade imaginaire* see Hitchcock, 'Problèmes d'édition de la musique de

Marc-Antoine Charpentier pour *Le Malade imaginaire*', *RdM*, LVIII (1972), pp. 3–15. Hitchcock has edited the music of this *comédie-ballet* in his *Prologues et intermèdes du Malade imaginaire de Molière*, Geneva, 1973.
10. Charles Varlet de La Grange gave a financial record of all spectacles given at the *salles* of the Palais Bourbon, Palais Royal and the Théâtre Guénégard from 1658–85.
11. 'Molière's Contribution to the Lyric Stage', *MQ*, XXXIII (July, 1947), pp. 361–62. See also Evelyn B. Lance, 'Molière the Musician: A Tercentenary View', *MR*, XXXV (August, 1974), pp. 120–30.
12. *Les Contemporains de Molière*, III, Paris 1875, p. xxiv.
13. The 'Théâtre des Machines' of the Tuileries constructed at such a great cost by the Vigarani was only in use for six years.
14. Antoine Adam, *Histoire de la littérature française au XVIIᵉ siècle*, II, Paris 1949, p. 334.
15. *Grand Larousse encyclopédique*, I, Paris 1960, p. 394.
16. See, e.g., the chorus 'Le Monstre est mort', *Cadmus et Hermione*, Prologue, sc. 4.
17. A more highly developed musical characterization of a similar situation occurs in the Prologue to Mouret's *opéra-ballet*, *Les Fêtes de Thalie* (1714). See Chapter 10, p. 138.
18. Etienne Gros, 'Les Origines de la tragédie-lyrique et la place des tragédies en machines dans l'évolution du théâtre vers l'opéra', *Revue d'histoire littéraire* (April–June 1928), p. 174.

Chapter 6
Pastorale (pp. 62–68)

1. *La Pastorale dramatique en France à la fin du XVIᵉ et au commencement du XVIIᵉ siècles*, Paris 1905, pp. 214–15.
2. La Laurencie, 'Les Pastorales en musique au XVIIᵉ siècle en France avant Lully et leur influence sur l'opéra', *International Music Society, 4th Congress Report*, London, 1912, p. 141.

3. 'La Première comédie française en musique', *Bulletin français de la SIM*, IV (April 1908), p. 380.
4. See Chapter 1, footnote 20.
5. See André Tessier, 'Robert Cambert à Londres', *RM*, IV (December 1927), pp. 101–22, and W. H. Grattan Flood, 'Quelques précisions nouvelles sur

Cambert et Grabu à Londres', *RM*, ix (August, 1928), pp. 351–61. The circumstances of Cambert's death are obscure. In his polemical allegory against Lully, *Lettre de Clément Marot à M de xxx touchant sur qui s'est passé à l'arrivée de J.-B. de Lulli sur Champs-Elysées* (1688), Bauderon de Senécé referred to Cambert as a 'furious spirit' who appeared 'still totally disfigured by the wounds 'from his assassination in England'. The fact that no seventeenth or eighteenth century source documents this murder makes one suspect that de

Senécé's account is a fanciful literary conceit.

6. Pierre-Jean-Baptiste Nougaret defined the *pastorale héroïque* as a 'Drama whose subject is more serious than simple and whose dénouement is sometimes tragic' (*De l'art du théâtre*, ii, p. 230, Paris 1769). The following *pastorales héroïques* were performed at the Opéra before Rameau: *Coronis* (Gatti, Beauge 1691) *Issé* (Destouches, La Motte 1697); *Le Pastorale héroïque* (Rebel, La Serre, 1730); and *Endymion* (Blamont, Fontenelle, 1731).

Chapter 7

Tragédie Lyrique I: Dramatic Organization and Vocal Music
(pp. 69–91)

1. Quoted by Prunières in his preface to the *Oeuvres complètes*, 'Opéras', i, n.p.

2. Quoted by Pierre Mélèse, *Répertoire analytique des documents contemporains . . . concernant les théâtres à Paris sous Louis XIV*, Paris, 1934, p. 157.

3. Following are Lully's *tragédies lyriques* (the *livrets* are by Quinault unless otherwise indicated): *Cadmus et Hermione*, 1673; *Alceste*, 1674; *Thésée*, 1675; *Atys*, 1676; *Isis*, 1677; *Psyché*, 1678 (T. Corneille and Fontenelle); *Bellérophon*, 1679 (T. Corneille); *Proserpine*, 1680; *Persée*, 1682; *Phaëton*, 1683; *Amadis de Gaule*, 1684; *Roland*, 1685; *Armide et Renaud*, 1686; *Acis et Galatée*, 1686 (J. G. de Campistron); *Achille et Polyxène*, 1687 (Campistron, only Act I completed by Lully).

4. In France 'Opéra' was used from the beginning to describe a large-scale dramatic work that was sung throughout ('Nos Opéra, que nous appelons des Tragédies en Musique', Lecerf); however, the plural ('Opéras') was not in general use until the late eighteenth century. 'It seems to me', wrote Nougaret, 'that the word Opéra is common enough among us to merit a plural form.' (*De l'art du théâtre*, i, p. 20.)

5. F. W. von Grimm, *Le Petit prophète de Boehmisch-Broda* (1753), trans. Oliver Strunk, *Source Readings in*

Music History, New York 1950, p. 631.

6. For a discussion of the term 'counter tenor' in French Baroque music see Neal Zaslaw, 'The Enigma of the Haute-contre', *MT*, 115 (November, 1974), pp. 939–41, and my response in 'Letters to the Editor', *MT*, 116 (March, 1975), p. 237.

7. However, Racine's son, Louis, insisted that those who believed that his father had made use of a high-flown (*enflée*) and singing manner of declamation on the stage were in error. (Quoted by Georges Lote, 'La Déclamation du vers français à la fin du xviiᵉ siècle', *Revue de phonétique*, ii (1912), p. 321.

8. For a summary of the recitatives, airs and choruses in Lully's operas see Paul-Marie Masson, 'French Opera from Lully to Rameau', *NOHM*, v, London, 1975, pp. 206–22.

9. Trans. by Edward R. Reilly in 'Quantz on National Styles in Music', *MQ*, xlix (April, 1963), p. 173.

10. Renaud's monologue may be found in *The Opera*, i, ed. Hellmuth C. Wolf, Cologne, 1971, pp. 89–93.

11. See Madeleine Garros, 'Mme de Maintenon et la musique', *RdM*, Série spéciale no. 1 (January, 1943), p. 10.

12. See, e.g., Denise Launay's edition of a Charpentier *Te Deum* (Paris, 1969) for 'le Pupitre'.

Chapter 8

Tragédie Lyrique II: Instrumental Music and the Dance (pp. 92–107)

1. Quoted by Jurgen Eppelsheim, *Das Orchester in dem Werken Jean Baptiste Lullys*, Tutzing, 1961, p. 150.

2. Maurice Barthélemy, 'Théobaldo di Gatti et la tragédie en musique, "Scylla"', *Recherches*, IX (1969), p. 62.

3. 'The Tone of the Baroque Oboe', *Gal. Soc. Jour.*, IV (1951), p. 14.

4. The most complete treatment of the dance in the operas and ballets of Lully is found in Helen Meredith Ellis, 'The Dances of J. B. Lully', Unpublished Ph.D. dissertation, Stanford 1967.

5. This statistical summary was adapted from Ellis's informative table in *Recherches*, IX (1969), pp. 30–31.

6. A helpful summary which includes eighteenth century metronome markings is found in Appendix D of Wilfrid Mellers, *François Couperin and the French Classical Tradition*, London, 1950. See also Ralph Kirkpatrick, 'Eighteenth-century Metronomic Indications', *Papers of the AMS* (1938), pp. 30–50, and the useful table of 'Selected 18th Century Metronomic Indications' in Neal Zaslaw, 'Mozart's Tempo Conventions', *Report of the 11th Congress of the IMS*, Copenhagen (1972), pp. 730–31.

7. The performance of the minuet from Rameau's *Hippolyte* (IV, 3) as found in two recordings give dramatic evidence of the importance of looking into eighteenth century discussions of tempo.

In an otherwise excellent interpretation, Anthony Lewis inexplicably chose a 'Don Giovanni minuet' tempo (L'Oiseau-Lyre recording no. 286–7–8). Contrast this with the more lively and appropriate tempo chosen by Roger Desormière in his performance of extracts from *Hippolyte* (L'Oiseau-Lyre recording no. 50034). Zaslaw's table (see footnote 6 above) gives the metronome marking of a minuet as ♩. = 70 from 1717 to 1747 and as ♩. = 53 in 1752.

8. See also the *Menuet de Poitou* to which Louis Couperin added a *double* (found in *HAM*, II, p. 93).

9. For additional information on such systems of notation see Meredith Ellis Little, 'Dance under Louis XIV and XV, *Early Music*, III (October, 1975), pp. 331–40.

10. It is surprising, however, that until recently little work has been done on the relationship between the musical components of the dance (phrase structure, tempo) and the choreography. Important sources which deal with this problem follow: Meredith Ellis Little, 'The Contribution of Dance Step to Musical Analysis and Performance: *La Bourgogne*', *JAMS*, XXVIII (Spring, 1975), pp. 112–24; Wendy Hilton, 'A Dance for Kings: The 17-Century French *Courante*', *Early Music*, V (January, 1977), pp. 27–37; and *id.*, *Dance and Music of Court and Theatre: The French Noble Style 1690–1725*, Princeton Book Co., 1977.

Chapter 9

Tragédie Lyrique III: Between Lully and Rameau (pp. 108–129)

1. See W. L. Lawrence, 'The French Opera in London: A Riddle of 1686', *Times Literary Supplement*, 28 March 1936, p. 268.

2. For information concerning the influence of Lully on Corelli, see Marc

Pincherle, *Corelli, His Life, His Work*, trans. Hubert Russell, New York, 1956, pp. 74–75, 130–31.

3. The above information comes from Alfred Loewenberg, *Annals of Opera*, 2nd ed., Geneva, 1955.

Notes

4. On Lorenzani see Prunières, 'Paolo Lorenzani à la cour de France', *RM*, III (1922), pp. 97–120.

5. See Michel Le Moël, 'Un foyer d'Italianisme a la fin du xviie siècle', *Recherches*, III (1963), pp. 43–48.

6. The *Journal* of the Bibliothèque de l'Opéra is a handwritten, year-by-year account of the performances that took place at the Opéra. In addition to being an important source for determining the number of subsequent performances of any opera, it includes some anecdotal information.

7. The reference is, of course, to the famous passage in a letter of Mme de Sévigné of 1 December 1673 describing a performance or rehearsal of *Alceste* which she and Mme de La Fayette attended.

8. After the deaths of Lully and Quinault, the question of the 'honoraires d'auteurs' was first resolved in principle at the time of the first performance of *L'Europe galante* (1697), when Campra and La Motte refused to accept the paltry fee offered by an economy-minded administration. It remained for the 1713 ordinance, however, to spell out the details.

9. Not surprisingly, a similar situation existed in painting after the death of the court painter, Le Brun (1690). Despite the great popularity of the portrait (the Salon of 1699 included 100 portraits and 150 historical paintings), painters of large historical canvasses remained the 'aristocracy of the brush'. Nattier, therefore, devised the mythological portrait in an attempt to gain more prestige for the art of portraiture. See Louis Réau, *Histoire de la peinture française au XVIIIe siècle*, I, Paris, 1925, p. 64.

10. Théodore de Lajarte, *Bibliothèque musicale du théâtre de l'opéra*, I, Paris, 1878, p. 72.

11. Desmarest left France in 1699, his opera, *Iphigénie en Tauride* unfinished. Campra and his librettist, Danchet, completed the *tragédie lyrique*, which was first performed in 1704. Campra composed the prologue, Act II, scene I, Act IV, scene 2, last three scenes of Act V and several airs.

12. Gustave Chouquet, *Histoire de la musique dramatique en France*, Paris, 1873, p. 127.

13. Robert Haas, *Die Musik des Barocks*, Wildpart-Potsdam, 1929, p. 229.

14. See Borrel, 'Notes sur l'orchestration de l'opéra *Jephté* de Montéclair (1733) et de la symphonie des *Elémens* de J. F. Rebel (1737)', *RM*, Numéro spécial 226 (1955), pp. 105–16; Barthélemy, 'L'Orchestre et l'orchestration des oeuvres de Campra', *Ibid.*, pp. 97–104.

15. See Paul-Marie Masson, 'La "Lettre sur Omphale" (1752)', *RdM*, XXVII (1945), pp. 1–19.

16. The passage is found in Girdlestone, *Jean-Philippe Rameau*, pp. 154–55.

17. Introduction to *Jean-Joseph Mouret, le musicien des grâces*, Paris, 1950.

18. Masson, 'Lullistes et Ramistes', *Année musicale*, I (1911), p. 213.

19. The *tragédies lyriques* are: *Hyppolyte et Aricie* (Pellegrin), 1733; *Castor et Pollux* (Bernard), 1737; *Dardanus* (Le Clerc de la Bruère), 1739; *Zoroastre* (Cahusac), 1749; and *Abaris ou les Boreades* (Cahusac?), never performed. His *opéras-ballets* are: *Les Indes galantes* (Fuzelier), 1735; *Les Fêtes d'Hébé* (Montdorge), 1739; *Les Fêtes de Polymnie* (Cahusac), 1745; *Le Temple de Gloire* (Voltaire), 1745; *Les Fêtes de l'Hymen et l'Amour* (Cahusac) 1747, and *Les Surprises de l'Amour* (Bernard), 1748. His *pastorales héroïques* are: *Zaïs* (Cahusac), 1748; *Naïs* (Cahusac), 1749; *Acante et Céphise* (Marmontel), 1751; and *Daphnis et Eglé* (Collé), 1753. Rameau's operas have been the subject of several important studies, chief of which are: Emile Dacier, 'L'Opéra au xviiie siècle: les premières représentations du *Dardanus* de Rameau', *Revue d'histoire et de critique musicales*, III (1903), pp. 163–73; Françoise Gervais, 'La Musique pure au service du drame lyrique chez Rameau', *RM*, numéro spécial 260 (1965), pp. 37–45; Cuthbert Girdlestone, *Jean-Philippe Rameau: His Life and Work*, London, 1957, 2nd ed., Paris, 1962; Hélène Leclerc, 'Les Indes galantes (1735–1952)', *Revue d'histoire du*

423

théâtre, v (1953), pp. 259–85; Jean Malignon, 'Zoroastre et Sarastro', *Recherches*, vi (1966), pp. 144–58; Paul-Marie Masson, *L'Opéra de Rameau*, Paris, 1930; *id.*, 'Les Deux versions du *Dardanus* de Rameau', *AM*, xxvi (1954), pp. 36–48; *id.*, 'Rameau and Wagner', *MQ*, xxv (1939), pp. 466–78; *id.*, 'French Opera from Lully to Rameau', *NOHM*, v, London, 1975, pp. 240–66.

Chapter 10

Opéra-Ballet (pp. 130–146)

1. The Dauphin, Louis XIV's only son, died in 1711; the king's eldest grandson, the Duc de Bourgogne, his wife and elder son, in 1712.

2. Selected from the extracts found in Chantal Masson's article, 'Journal du Marquis de Dangeau', *Recherches*, ii (1961), pp. 193–223.

3. 'Le Ballet-héroïque', *RM*, ix (1928), p. 133. For the *opéra-ballet*, see also the following: La Laurencie, 'André Campra, musicien profane', *L'Année musicale*, iii (1913), pp. 153–205; Masson, '*Les Fêtes vénitiennes* d'André Campra', *RdM*, xiii (1932), pp. 127–46, 214–26; James R. Anthony, 'The French Opera-Ballet in the Early Eighteenth Century: Problems of Definition and Classification', *JAMS*, xviii (1965), pp. 197–206; *id.*, 'Thematic Repetition in the Opera-Ballets of André Campra', *MQ*, lii (April, 1966), pp. 209–20.

4. The musical sources are the following: Destouches' *Isis* (the *sommeil* from Act iv, sc. 2 and the 'nature scene' from Act v, sc. 1); Lully's *Atys* (the *sommeil* and the *Entrée des Songes funestes* from Act iii, sc. 4); and the famous 'tempête' from Marais' *Alcyone*.

5. In fact, Masson suggested the term 'opéra-ballet héroïque' to distinguish those *ballets héroïques*, which exhibited

the *opéra-ballet's* structure, from the few examples which, although labelled 'ballet héroïque', have a continuous dramatic action. (See *RM*, ix, p. 133.)

6. Max Lütolf has edited *Les Fêtes vénitiennes* for 'Le Pupitre', Paris, 1971.

7. Lavignac, *Encyclopédie*, Partie i, Vol. iii, p. 1383. Unfamiliarity with the 7#5 chord in French music of the period undoubtedly caused Mellers to dismiss it as an 'abstruse dissonance' (*François Couperin*, p. 242), and prompted F. T. Arnold to consider the ♯5 as 'a retarded 6 which is taken unprepared in a very unusual manner' (*The Art of Accompaniment from a Thorough-Bass*, p. 187). At this writing a dissertation by Charles J. Moomaw is in progress dealing with this chord ('The Use of the Augmented Mediant Triad in the Music of the French Baroque', University of Cincinnati).

8. Reprinted by Gregg Press in 1967. See my article, 'Printed Editions of André Campra's *L'Europe galante'*, *MQ*, lvi (January, 1970), pp. 54–73.

9. Lavignac, *Encyclopédie*, Partie i, Vol. iii, p. 1,365.

10. *Les Fêtes vénitiennes* contains two additional 'cantates' found in 'L'Amour saltimbanque', scene 3, and 'Les Serenades et les joueurs', scene 4.

Chapter 11

From Divertissement to Opéra Comique (pp. 147–158)

1. The *grands divertissements de Versailles* are discussed in detail by Robert M. Isherwood in his *Music in the Service of the King*, Ithaca, 1973, pp. 265–80.

2. The anonymity of the composer of *L'Europe galante* was a poorly guarded secret as evidenced by the following extract from a 1697 *chanson*:

Quand notre Archeveque scaura L'Auteur du nouvel Opéra (L'Europe galante) De sa Cathédrale Campra Décampera.

3. *Don Quichotte chez la duchesse* has been edited by Roger Blanchard for 'Le Pupitre', Paris, 1971.
4. Important sources on the history of the *opéra comique* are: Georges Cucuel, *Les Créateurs de l'opéra comique français*, Paris, 1914; *id.*, 'Sources et documents pour servir à l'histoire de l'opéra-comique en France', *L'Année musicale*, III (1913), pp. 247–82; Emile Genest, *L'Opéra-comique connu et inconnu*, Paris, 1925; Emile Campardon, *Les Spectacles des foires*, Paris, 1880; La Laurencie, 'L'Opéra-comique', *Encyclopédie*, ed. Lavignac, Part I, Vol. III, pp. 1,457–89; Francis J. Carmody, *Le Répertoire de l'opéra-comique en vaudevilles de 1708 à 1764*, Berkeley, 1933; Martin Cooper, *Opéra comique*, New York, 1949; *id.*, 'Opera in France', *NOHM*, VII, London, 1973, pp. 200–56; Donald Grout, 'Eighteenth-Century Comic Opera', *A Short History of Opera*, 2nd ed., New York, 1965, pp. 254–59; *id.*, "The Origins of the *Opéra-comique*', unpublished Ph.D. dissertation, Harvard, 1939; Nicole Wild, 'Aspects de la musique sous la régence, Les Foires: Naissance de l'opéra-comique', *Recherches*, V (1965), pp. 129–41; Clifford R. Barnes, 'Instruments and Instrumental Music at the "Théâtres de la Foire"', *Recherches*, V, pp. 142–68; *id.*, 'Vocal Music at the "Théâtres de la Foire"', *Recherches*, VIII (1968), pp. 141–60; and Dorothy S. Packer, ' "La Calotte" and the Eighteenth-Century French Vaudeville', *JAMS*, XXIII (1970), pp. 61–83.
5. The harpsichord piece 'Les Sauvages', from the *Nouvelles Suites de Pièces de clavecin* of about 1728, was adapted from a dance composed by Rameau for one of the Fair Theatre productions of 1725. For additional information on Rameau and the Fair Theatre see Graham Sadler, 'Rameau, Piron and the Parisian Fair Theatres', *Soundings*, IV (1974), pp. 13–29.

Chapter 12

From Du Caurroy to Du Mont (pp. 159–173)

1. These are the chronological boundaries of Denise Launay's *Anthologie du motet latin polyphonique en France*, Vol. 17 of Series I of the Société Française de Musicologie, Paris, 1963. The valuable introduction to this anthology and the same author's 'Les Motets à double choeur', *RdM*, XL (December, 1957), pp. 173–95, and 'Church Music in France (a) 1630–60', *NOHM*, V, London, 1975, pp. 414–37, are among the few sources that deal with the French motet in the early seventeenth century.
2. Modern edition, ed. E. Martin and J. Burold, Paris, 1951.
3. Quoted in W. J. A. Jonckbloet and J. P. N. Land, *Musique et musiciens au* XVIIᵉ *siècle*, Leyden, 1882, p. CCXVII.
4. Quoted by Launay, *RdM*, XL, p. 179.
5. See Launay, 'A Propos d'une messe de Charles d'Helfer', *Le 'Baroque' musical*, Vol. IV of *Les Colloques de Wégimont*, 1963, p. 191.
6. Quoted by Brenet, 'Notes sur l'introduction des instruments dans les églises de France', *Riemann Festschrift*, Leipzig, 1909, p. 283.
7. Quoted by Launay, *Le 'Baroque' musical*, p. 189.
8. On the Masses of Auxcousteaux see Michel-Antoine Bloch, 'Les Messes d'Aux-Cousteaux', *Recherches*, III (1963), pp. 31–40.
9. For a discussion of this Mass see Launay, 'A propos d'une messe de Charles d'Helfer', pp. 177–99.
10. See Lesure, 'Un Contrat d'exclusivité entre Nicolas Formé et Ballard, 1638', *RdM*, L (December, 1964), pp. 228–29.
11. Henri Sauval (1623–76) was an

important French historian whose researches resulted in the invaluable *Histoire et recherches des antiquités de la ville de Paris* which was not published until 1724 by Claude Bernard Rosseau.

12. Henri Quittard, *Un Musicien en France au* xviie *siècle: Henry Du Mont*, Paris, 1906, p. 97. See also André Verchaly, 'La Musique religieuse française de Titelouze à 1660', *RM*, 222 (1953–54), p. 83. For a summary of the arguments on both sides see Norbert Dufourcq, *Jean-Baptiste de Boësset*, Paris, 1962, pp. 57–63.

13. Ms 168 of the Bibliothèque de Tours and the Rés. Vma ms 571 (the Brossard collection) of the Bibliothèque Nationale. Many motets by Bouzignac have been edited by Denise Launay, Bernard Loth and Félix Raugel for the Editions musicales de la Schola Cantorum in their series, 'Oeuvres Françaises du temps de Richelieu et du xviie siècle'. This music deserves a far greater audience than has been accorded it to date.

14. See Quittard, 'Un Musicien oublié du xviie siècle français, G. Bouzignac', *SIMG*, vi (1904–05), pp. 356–417.

15. See Marcel Frémiot, 'L'Ecole provençale', *Encyclopédie des musiques sacrées*, ii, Paris, 1969, pp. 541–52.

16. See Félix Raugel, 'La Maîtrise de la Cathédrale d'Aix-en-Provence', *Bulletin de la Société d'Etude du XVIIe siècle* (1954), pp. 422–32.

17. *La Musique sacrée sous Louis* xiv, Paris, 1899, p. 32.

18. See James Pruitt, 'The Organ Works of Guillaume Gabriel Nivers (1632–1714)', *Recherches*, xiv (1974), p. 38.

19. On Desportes see André Verchaly, 'Desportes et la musique', *Annales musicologiques*, ii (1954), pp. 271–328. Denise Launay has edited settings of Desportes' translations by Du Caurroy, Chastillon, de la Tour, J. Boyer, de Courbes and Signac in her *Anthologie du Psaume français polyphonique, 1610–1663* (Paris, 1974).

Chapter 13
Motet: From Du Mont to Delalande (pp. 174–202)

1. In point of fact, Gobert and Expilly retired in 1669 leaving Du Mont and Robert as the only *sous-maîtres* until their retirement in 1683.

2. Psalm 19:10, 'Domine salvum fac regem: Et exaudi nos in die qua invocaverimus te'. ('Grant victory to the king, O Lord, and answer this day our appeal'.) The *Domine salvum* was a salutation to the king that from the days of Louis XIII was traditionally used as a closing motet for both high and low mass.

3. Madeleine Garros, 'La Musique religieuse en France de 1600 à 1750', *Histoire de la musique*, ed. Roland-Manuel, i, p. 1,598.

4. In actuality the Ballard edition labels them *dessus, haut-contre, haute-taille, basse-taille* and *basse.*

5. See Prunières, 'Les Motets', *Oeuvres complètes*, i, p. v.

6. *Ibid.*, p. vi.

7. Prunières, 'Les Motets', *Oeuvres complètes*, ii, p. v.

8. *Ibid.*

9. See Hélène Charnassé, 'Quelques aspects des "ensembles de récits" chez l'Abbé Pierre Robert', *Recherches*, ii (1961–62), p. 65. Mlle Charnassé has edited two of the Robert *grands motets (Deus noster refugium* and *Quare fremuerunt gentes)* for 'Le Pupitre', Paris, 1969.

10. Collasse remained until 1704 and Minoret until 1714. In 1722, Delalande, in semi-retirement, shared his duties with Campra, Bernier and Gervais.

11. Quoted in Daval, *La Musique en France au XVIIIe siècle*, p. 154.

12. See especially Dufourcq's list of Charpentier recordings in 'Le Disque et l'histoire de la musique', *Recherches*, iii (1963), p. 219. For a recent list of performing editions of the religious music of Charpentier, see Guy-Lambert,

'Charpentier', *Dictionnaire de la Musique*, ed. M. Honegger, Paris, 1970, I, p. 202.

13. See James E. Richards, 'The "Grand Motet" of the Late Baroque in France as exemplified by Michel-Richard de Lalande', unpublished Ph.D. dissertation, University of Southern California, 1950. See also, *id.*, 'Structural Principles in the Grands Motets of de Lalande', *JAMS*, XI (1958), pp. 119–27 and Philippe Oboussier, 'Lalande's Grands Motets', *MT*, 117 (June, 1976), pp. 483–86. There is some hope that Delalande's position as the most important religious composer of the *grand siècle* will soon be recognized. At the present time two dissertations are in progress (Ines Groh, 'Die Motetten von Michel-Richard Delalande', Freiburg; Lionel Sawkins, 'The Sacred Music of Michel-Richard Delalande', Oxford) and Sawkins and Oboussier have edited and performed several of the *grands motets*. For a list of modern editions of Delalande's religious music see Dufourcq, 'Delalande', *Dictionnaire de la musique*, I, p. 264.

14. Volume numbers refer to the Charpentier *Meslanges*.

15. This interesting document was written for the Duc d'Orléans between 1692 and 1698. It is a short treatise on composition appended by an 'Abrégé des règles de l'accompagnement'. The original given to the future Regent has not survived, but there are two copies in the Brossard *Meslanges sur la musique* in the Bibliothèque Nationale.

16. See Dufourcq, *Recherches*, III (1963), p. 214.

17. In the Brossard copy, the copyist described the Augmented 6th chord thus: 'This chord is very plaintive'.

18. From the translation by Philip Nelson, *Principles of Composition*, Brooklyn, 1964, p. 14. Rameau treats this chord as an example of 'chords by supposition with which we may also avoid Cadences while imitating them' (*Traité de l'harmonie*, Chapter 10 of Book II, trans. Philip Gossett, New York, 1971, pp. 88–91.

19. The last volume of the Cauvin Ms is at the Bibliothèque Nationale (Rés. Vmb. Ms. 16). There are also 11 grands motets of Delalande in the Toulouse-Philidor collection at St Michael's College, Tenbury Wells. Certain of these copies (e.g. *Super Flumina*) differ in certain details from the Versailles collection. In addition, five motets and shorter works are in a private collection belonging to M. R. Lutz in Strasburg. For a discussion, see Dufourcq, 'Retour à Michel-Richard Delalande', *Recherches*, I (1960), pp. 69–75; also Laurence Boulay, 'Notes sur quatre motets inédits de Michel-Richard Delalande', *ibid.*, pp. 77–86.

20. There are: *De profundis, Dixit Dominus, Dominus in virtute tua, Exaudi Deus, In convertendo, Lauda Jerusalem, Miserere mei* and *Te Deum*. As noted above, *Exaudi Deus* is not in the printed edition.

Chapter 14

The Motet in the Eighteenth Century (pp. 203–222)

1. For similar descriptions see Benoit, *Versailles et les musiciens du roi*, pp. 46–61.

2. For biographical information on Desmarest see Michel Antoine, *Henry Desmarest*, Paris, 1965, pp. 46–61.

3. He abducted the daughter of the director of taxation for the Senlis district, Mlle de Saint-Gobert, and was exiled from France before the turn of the century.

4. On Jean Gilles see John H. Hajdu, 'The Life and Works of Jean Gilles', unpublished Ph.D. dissertation, University of Colorado, 1973.

5. On the popular music of this area through the eighteenth century see Amédée Gastoué, 'La Musique à Avignon et dans le Comtat du XIVe au XVIIIe siècle', *RMI*, XII (1905), pp. 555–

78 and 768–77.

6. On the music at St. Cyr see Marie Bert, 'La musique à la maison royale Saint-Louis de Saint-Cyr', *Recherches*, III (1963), pp. 55–71; IV 1964), pp. 127–31; and V (1965), pp. 91–127.

7. See Laurence Boulay, 'Les Cantiques spirituels de Racine, mis en musique au xvIIᵉ siècle', *Bulletin de la Société d'étude du xvIIᵉ siècle*, xxxIV (1957), pp. 79–92.

8. Concerning Danielis see Guy Bourligneux, 'Le mystérieux Daniel Danielis', *Recherches* IV (1964), pp. 146–78.

9. Campra's motets are discussed in some detail in La Laurencie, 'Notes sur la jeunesse d'André Campra', *SIMG*, x (1908–09), pp. 159–258; see also, Barthèlemy, *André Campra*, pp. 28–41 and Conan J. Castle, 'The Grands Motets of André Campra', unpublished Ph.D. dissertation, University of Michigan, 1962. The bulk of Campra's motets remain in MS in the B.N. I am indebted to Miss Ann Baker who pointed out the existence of several additional Campra motets in MS that are now in the Bibliothèque Méjanes at Aix-en-Provence.

10. On Bernier see Philip Nelson, 'Nicolas Bernier: a Study of the Man and his Music', unpublished Ph.D. dissertation, University of North Carolina, 1958;

id., 'Nicolas Bernier: A Resumé of his Work', *Recherches*, I (1960), pp. 93–98; and *id.*, 'Nicolas Bernier: A Bibliographic Study', *Studies in Musicology: Essays . . . in Memory of Glen Haydon*, Chapel Hill, 1969, pp. 109–17.

11. The sacred vocal music of Couperin is found in Vols. 11 and 12 of the *Oeuvres complètes de François Couperin*, ed. Maurice Cauchie, Paris, 1932-33. A new edition of the three *Leçons de Ténèbres* edited by Daniel Vidal is included in the 'Le Pupitre' series, Paris, 1968.

The Count de Toulouse-Philidor Collection at St Michael's College, Tenbury Wells, includes 26 'Motets à voix seules, deux et trois parties et symphonies', by Couperin. Surprisingly, these *petits motets*, listed only in the MS supplement to Fellowes' Tenbury catalogue, have only recently been studied (see Philippe Oboussier, 'A Couperin Discovery,' *MT*, 112, May, 1971, pp. 429–30). Nine of them, never before printed, have been edited by Oboussier for 'Le Pupitre' (Paris, 1972).

12. On Madin see Bernadette Lespinard, 'Henry Madin (1698–1748), sous-maître de la Chapelle royale', *Recherches*, xIV (1974), pp. 236–96, and xV (1975), pp. 107–45.

Chapter 15

Mass and Oratorio: the Domain of Marc-Antoine Charpentier
(pp. 223–232)

1. One such exception is the 'Messe à deux choeurs' by Desmarest, copied by Philidor in 1704 and found today at St Michael's College, Tenbury Wells (Ms 118–233).

A checklist of Masses printed in France during the lifetime of the Notre Dame composer Jean Mignon (1640–1710) may be found on pp. 140–47 of Danièle Taitz-Destouches' article 'Jean Mignon: Maître de Chapelle de Notre Dame de Paris', *Recherches*, xIV (1974). For omissions to this list see Edward Higginbottom's review of the 1974 *Re-*

cherches in *M&L*, LVII (July, 1976), p. 328.

2. These are as follows: *Messe à quatre choeurs* (Vol. 16); *Messe pour le Port Royal* (Vol. 22); *Messe pour le Samedy de Pasques* (Vol. 5); *Messe pour M. Mauroy* (Vol. 10); *Messe des Morts à 4 voix* (Vol. 24); *Messe des Morts à 4 voix et simphonie* (Vol. 26); *Messe pour les Trespasses* (Vol. 1); *Messe à 8 voix et 8 violons et flûtes* (Vol. 15); *Messe à quatre voix et instruments* (Vol. 14); *Messe de Minuit pour Noël* (Vol. 25);

Messe pour plusieurs instruments au lieu des orgues (Vol. 1); and *Missa Assumpta est Maria* (Vol. 27).

3. *Un Musicien français oublié, Marc-Antoine Charpentier,* Paris, 1945, pp. 19–20. For additional information on the Masses by Charpentier see Gunther Massenheil, 'Marc-Antoine Charpentier als Messenkomponist', *Colloquium Amicorum,* ed. Siegfried Kross and Hans Schmidt (Bonn, 1967).

4. 'The Liturgical Music of Marc-Antoine Charpentier', unpublished Ph.D. dissertation, Harvard, 1955, p. 83.

5. See Hitchcock's edition of this mass for Concordia (1962) for the Noël tunes and texts.

6. Modern edition prepared by Martin Herman, Colorado College Music Series, Colorado Springs, 1958.

7. For further information on Ouvrard see Albert Cohen, 'René Ouvrard (1624–1694) and the Beginnings of French Baroque Theory', *Report of the 11th Congress of the IMS,* Copenhagen, 1972, II, pp. 336–42, and *id.,* 'The Ouvrard-Nicaise Correspondence (1663–93)', *M&L,* LVI (July-October, 1975), pp. 356–63.

8. 'The Latin Oratorios of Marc-Antoine Charpentier', unpublished Ph.D. dissertation, University of Michigan, 1954, p. 384.

9. We await publication of recent research by Hitchcock first presented at the 1974 annual meeting of the AMS concerning the inappropriateness of the word *oratorio* in describing those works of Charpentier that were performed at Mass as substitutes for motets.

10. Extract in Gunther Massenheil, *Das Oratorium,* ed. K. G. Fellerer, Cologne, 1970, pp. 87–91.

11. Donald H. Foster, 'The Oratorio in Paris in the 18th Century', *AM,* XLVII (January–June, 1975), p. 74.

12. This article neglects to include in its bibliography Hitchcock's important dissertation mentioned above or his article, 'The Latin Oratorios of Marc-Antoine Charpentier', *MQ,* XLI (January, 1955), pp. 41–65, both of which were available before the 1962 date of the *MGG* article. See also Clarence H. Barber, 'Les Oratorios de Marc-Antoine Charpentier', *Recherches,* III, (1963), pp. 90–130.

13. Hitchcock's *MQ* article includes a complete breakdown of all titles and their location in the *Meslanges.*

14. This oratorio is available in an edition prepared by Hitchcock for *Recent Researches in Baroque Music,* Vol. I, New Haven, 1964.

15. The entire scene is included in Carl Parrish, *A Treasury of Early Music,* New York, 1958, pp. 244–52.

Chapter 16
Lute (pp. 233–243)

1. The Centre National de la Recherche Scientifique (CNRS) is publishing much of the extant repertory of seventeenth-century lute music not already in modern editions in their series 'Corpus des luthistes français'. Among the composers listed above, Vaumesnil, Perichon (Perrichon), Mésangeau, Bocquet, Mercure, Bouvier, Belleville, Chancy, Chevalier and Dubuisson have already appeared in this collection.

2. *Le Luth et sa musique,* ed. Jean Jacquot, CNRS, Neuilly-sur-Seine, 1958, p. 164.

3. Her MS treatise *Instruction for the*

Lute that dates from about 1670 is printed in *The Gal. Soc. Jour.,* XI (May, 1958), pp. 33–69.

4. Besard's solo works for lute have been transcribed by André Souris in the CNRS series, Paris, 1969.

5. The *Oeuvres de Nicolas Vallet pour luth seul* have been transcribed by Souris in the CNRS series, Paris, 1970.

6. The *Premier Livre* and the *Deuxième Livre* (1614) by Robert Ballard have been transcribed by André Souris, Sylvie Spycket and Jacques Veyrier for CNRS, Paris, 1963.

7. See Daniel Heartz, 'Le Style instru-

mental dans la musique de la Renaissance', *La Musique instrumentale de la Renaissance*, Paris, 1955, p. 66.

8. *Oeuvres du Vieux Gaultier*, from the CNRS series, 'Corpus des luthists français', Paris 1966.

9. Transcribed and analysed by Souris in *Le Luth et sa musique*, pp. 290–92. All six preludes are in *Oeuvres du Dufaut*, transcribed by Souris in the CNRS series, Paris, 1965.

10. The entire collection may be found in the transcription by André Tessier, published by the Société française de

musicologie, Paris, 1932–33.

11. On Mouton's lute music see Monique Rollin, 'La Suite pour luth dans l'oeuvre de Charles Mouton', *RM*, Numéro spécial 226 (1955), pp. 76–88.

12. Published with an introduction by F. Lesure, Neuilly-sur-Seine, 1957; included also in *Annales musicologiques*, III (1955), pp. 283–387 and IV, pp. 175–248.

13. These books plus additional MS pieces by De Visée have been transcribed by Robert W. Strizich in the 'Le Pupitre' collection, 1969.

Chapter 17
Harpsichord (pp. 244–269)

1. *La Musique instrumentale de la Renaissance*, p. 72.

2. See Paul Hamburger, 'Ein handschriftliches Klavierbuch aus der ersten Hälfte der 17 Jht.', *ZfMW*, XIII (1930–1931), pp. 138–40 and 556–58.

3. Transcribed by André Pirro in *RM*, II (1921), pp. 1–3 of Supplement.

4. *Les Clavecinistes*, Paris, 1925, p. 162. For arguments supporting the concept of a 'common vocabulary' for lute and harpsichord that reflect more a basic style change than an accommodation to a specific instrument, see André Souris, 'Apport du répertoire du luth à l'étude des problèmes d'interprétation' in *L'Interprétation de la musique française aux* XVIIème *et* XVIIIème *siècles*, ed. Edith Weber, Paris, 1974, pp. 107–19.

5. For recent information concerning the French harpsichord see David R. Fuller's review of my *French Baroque Music* in *JAMS*, XXVIII (Summer, 1975), pp. 377–78. See also G. Thibault (Mme de Chambure), 'L'Interprétation, sur les clavecins anciens, de la musique française des XVIIème et XVIIIème siècles', in *L'Interprétation de la musique française* . . ., pp. 197–202.

6. Chambonnières' extant harpsichord music is included in *Oeuvres complètes de Chambonnières*, ed. Paul Brunold and André Tessier, Paris, 1925. Thurston Dart has also edited the *Pièces de clavecin* for L'Oiseau-Lyre, Monaco,

1970. For a facsimile of the 1670 Paris edition, see Broude Bros., New York 1967.

7. See Fuller, *JAMS* (Summer, 1975), p. 383. On Chambonnières' life see Michel Le Moël, 'Les Dernières années de J. Champion de Chambonnières, 1655–1672', *Recherches*, I (1960), pp. 31–46.

8. See the *Oeuvres complètes de Louis Couperin*, ed. Paul Brunold for L'Oiseau-Lyre, Paris, 1936. See also *Pièces de clavecin*, ed. Brunold, and 'revues d'après le Manuscrit Bauyn' by Thurston Dart for L'Oiseau Lyre, Monaco, 1959. A new edition of Couperin's harpsichord music has been edited by Alan Curtis for 'Le Pupitre', Paris, 1970. It includes 6 previously unknown pieces found in the 'Parville MS' now at Berkeley.

9. On the unmeasured prelude see Newman Powell, 'Rhythmic Freedom in the Performance of French Music from 1650–1735', unpublished Ph.D. dissertation, Stanford, 1958, pp. 237–83; Alan Curtis, 'Unmeasured Preludes in French Baroque Instrumental Music', unpublished master's thesis, University of Illinois, 1956; *id.*, preface to 'Le Pupitre' edition; and Howard Ferguson, *Keyboard Interpretation*, New York & London, 1975, pp. 23–28.

10. Edited by Dufourcq, Monaco, 1956.

11. Edited by Marguerete Roesgen-Champion, Paris, 1934 and by Kenneth

Gilbert for 'Le Pupitre', Paris, 1975. Facsimile edition, New York, 1965.

12. D'Anglebert was not the first to transcribe extracts from Lully's operas for keyboard. An anonymous transcription for organ of extracts from *Alceste, Thésée, Atys, Isis* and *Bellérophon* may be seen in a manuscript in the Bibliothèque Nationale (Fonds du Conservatoire, 2094). See Almonte C. Howell, *Nine Seventeenth Century Organ Transcriptions from the Operas of Lully* (Lexington, Kentucky, 1963).

13. On Couperin's 'Folies françoises' see Pierre Citron, 'Autour des folies françaises', *RM*, Numéro spécial 226 (1955), pp. 89–96.

14. Martine Roche, 'Un Livre de clavecin français de la fin du XVIIᵉ siècle', *Recherches*, VII (1967), pp. 39–73.

15. Fuller, *JAMS* (Summer, 1975), p. 378.

16. The only detailed survey of this music from its seventeenth century origins through the many sonatas for 'clavecin ou piano-forte' of the 1780's is David R. Fuller's unpublished Ph.D. dissertation, 'Eighteenth-Century French Harpsichord Music', Harvard, 1965. Hopefully, this dissertation will soon be available in book form.

17. Edited by Paul Brunold, Paris, 1934.

18. See Fuller, 'Accompanied Keyboard Music', *MQ*, LX (1974), pp. 233–34.

19. See introduction to Albert Fuller's edition, *Pieces for Harpsichord* by Gaspard Le Roux, Alpeg Editions, New York, 1956. This introduction contains much valuable information on many aspects of the performance of seventeenth and eighteenth century harpsichord music including ornamentation, fingering, articulation and phrasing as well as comments on the instrument and its registration.

20. *L'Esthétique de J. S. Bach*, Paris, 1907, pp. 430–31.

21. Edited by Thurston Dart, Monaco, 1960.

22. See Boroff, *An Introduction to Elisabeth-Claude Jacquet de la Guerre*, Brooklyn, 1966, p. 115.

23. The most complete discussions of the suites may be found in Mellers, *François Couperin*, pp. 188–233; Margarete Reimann, *Untersuchungen zur Formgeschichte der französischen Klavier-Suite*, Regensburg, 1940, pp. 82–122; and Shlomo Hofman, *L'Oeuvre de clavecin de François Couperin le Grand*, Paris, 1961. The music of the 4 books is in vols 1–4 of the *Oeuvres complètes* and was published in an edition by Brahms and Chrysander (London, 1888). A welcome new edition has been prepared by Kenneth Gilbert for 'Le Pupitre', (Paris, 1969–72). In addition, Sylvia Marlowe has edited selected pieces from each of the 4 books for G. Schirmer (N.Y., 1970). For a discussion of ornamentation and registration in Couperin's harpsichord pieces see Gilbert's prefaces to his 'Le Pupitre' editions, *id.*, 'Le Clavecin français et la registration', in *L'Interprétation de la musique française . . .*, pp. 203–11, and Thurston Dart, 'Quelques précisions sur la notation des pièces de clavecin de François Couperin', *ibid.*, pp. 213–20.

24. There is no reason, in my opinion, to make of this piece a 'technical joke' (with) the continuous suspensions being a mysterious barricade to the basic harmony' (Mellers, p. 358). To use military vocabulary in amorous 'war' between the sexes was a common conceit of the time. In this context, the 'baricades misterieuses' are no more than the mysterious defences employed by the fair sex against male assault. For further information on 'Les Barricades misterieuses' see Dufourcq, 'Les Barricades misterieuses de François Couperin', *Recherches*, XIII (1973), pp. 23–34.

25. See Tessier, 'Quelques parodies de Couperin', *RdM*, X (1929), pp. 40–44.

26. The three *Livres de clavecin* have been edited by P. Aubert and B. François-Sappey, Paris, 1973. See also François-Sappey, 'L'Oeuvre de clavecin de Jean-François Dandrieu, 1682–1738', *Recherches*, XIV (1974), pp. 155–235.

27. Paul Brunold, 'Trois livres de pièces de clavecin de J. F. Dandrieu', *RdM*, XIII (1932), pp. 147–51.

28. Note that the 'La' in proper names need have nothing to do with the sex of the individual portrayed. Often, and certainly in the above case, it should be understood as 'la pièce intitulée. . .'.

29. Edited by Howard Ferguson for 'Le Pupitre', Paris, 1969.

30. Edited by Paul Brunold, Paris, n.d.

31. Erwin R. Jacobi has edited the only completely accurate modern edition of the keyboard music of Rameau (Bärenreiter, 1958).

32. There is no evidence that Rameau was familiar with the sonatas of Scarlatti. His comments in his manual regarding 'Les Cyclopes' indicate that he believed that these kinds of 'batteries' had 'never appeared before'.

33. See Girdlestone, *J. P. Rameau*, pp. 53–54, for a complete listing of these transcriptions.

34. Edited by Marc Pincherle, Paris, 1935. For information on the keyboard music of Mondonville, see Edith Borroff, 'The Instrumental Style of Jean-Joseph Cassanéa de Mondonville', *Recherches*, VII (1967), pp. 165–204, and *id.*, 'The Instrumental Works of Jean-Joseph Cassanéa de Mondonville', unpublished Ph.D. dissertation, University of Michigan, 1959.

35. See Fuller, *MQ*, LX (1974), pp. 239–40.

36. There is a facsimile edition prepared by Pincherle, London, 1966. A modern edition may be found as Vol. II of Borroff's dissertation (see footnote 34).

37. All four books (Book I, *c.* 1744; Book II, *c.* 1748; Book III, *c.* 1758; and Book IV, *c.* 1768) are available in a modern edition by Françoise Petit as part of 'Le Pupitre', Paris, 1967. On the harpsichord music of Moyreau see Pierre Guillet, 'Les Livres de clavecin de Christophe Moyreau', *Recherches*, XI (1971), pp. 179–220.

Chapter 18
Organ Music of the Grand Siècle (pp. 270–287)

1. Titelouze's complete works for organ as well as the works of Raison, Clérambault, Du Mage, Daquin, Gigault, Grigny, Couperin, Boyvin, Dandrieu, Guilain, and Lebègue are found in the ten volumes of the *Archives des maîtres de l'orgue* Paris (1899–1908), ed. Alexandre Guilmant and André Pirro. The Pirro introductions which include the composers' prefaces are invaluable research aids. Selected works by Lebègue, Daquin, Raison, Dornel and others are also included in the collection *Orgue et Liturgie*, ed. by Dufourcq, Raugel and J. de Valois for the Éditions musicales de la Schola Cantorum. On the organ music of Titelouze see Jean Bonfils, 'L'Oeuvre d'orgue de Jehan Titelouze', *Recherches*, V (1965), pp. 5–16.

2. The most helpful glossary of terms in English dealing with the classical French organ may be found in Fenner Douglass, *The Language of the Classical French Organ*, New Haven, 1969, pp. 217–21; Peter Williams, *The European Organ*, London, 1966, pp. 169–203; and William Pruitt, 'The Organ Works of G. G. Nivers', *Recherches*, XIV (1974), especially pp. 68–81. The most complete study of the French organ from 1589 to 1789 is Dufourcq's *Le Livre de l'orgue français* in five volumes ('Les Sources', 'Le Buffet', 'La Facture', 'La Musique', 'Miscellanea'), of which Vol. I, Vol. II, part 1 of Vol. III and Vol. IV have been published in Paris in 1971, 1969, 1975 and 1972 respectively. For a discussion of French organ building in selected locations outside of Paris see *Recherches*, XII (1972), a special number devoted to 'L'Histoire de l'orgue français aux XVIe, XVIIe et XVIIIe siècles'.

3. See Willi Apel, 'Du nouveau sur la musique française pour l'orgue au XVIe siècle', *RM* XVIII (1937), pp. 96–108. These have been transcribed by Jean Bonfils for the 'Le Pupitre' series as *Chansons françaises pour orgue, vers 1550*, Paris, 1968.

4. See Jean Bonfils, 'Les Fantaisies instrumentales d'Eustache Du Caurroy', *Recherches*, II (1961–62), pp. 5–31.

5. See Dufourcq, *La Musique d'orgue français de Jehan Titelouze à Jehan Alain*, Paris, 1949, p. 49.

6. Denis' *Traité de l'accord de l'espin-*

ette, 1650. This informative and chatty work is available in a Da Capo Press reprint of 1969.

7. Edited by André Tessier in *La Petite Maîtrise*, April, 1930.

8. The keyboard music of Du Mont, ed. J. Bonfils, is found in *L'Organiste liturgique*, XIII (1956).

9. Lavignac, *Encyclopédie*, Part II, Vol. II, p. 1,272. All of Richard's known organ works have been collected by Dufourcq in *L'Orgue parisien sous le règne de Louis XIV*, Copenhagen, 1956.

10. See Guy Oldham, 'Louis Couperin. A New Source of French Keyboard Music of the Mid-seventeenth century', *Recherches*, I (1960), pp. 51–59.

11. See Dufourcq, *Le Livre de l'orgue français*, IV, p. 61.

12. An important examination of these 'minor changes' may be found in Fenner Douglass, 'Should Dom Bedos play Lebègue', *The Organ Yearbook*, IV (1973), pp. 101–11.

13. See Dufourcq, 'Recent Researches into French Organ Building from the fifteenth to the seventeenth century', *Gal. Soc. Jour.*, X (1957), pp. 66–81.

14. The word *Jeu* may refer to both single stops (Mersenne's 'jeux simples') and to combinations of stops (Mersenne's 'jeux composés').

15. Williams writes that the '*Tierce en taille* is essentially a melodic registration for the left hand on the Positif under a soft accompaniment on the *Grand Orgue*', *The European Organ*, p. 189.

16. For more detailed information on the specifications and registrations of French classical organs, see Douglass, *The Language of the Classical French Organ*, pp. 78–114.

17. See Dufourcq, 'De l'emploi du temps des organistes parisiens', *RM*, Numéro Spécial 226 (1955), pp. 35–47.

18. Edited by Dufourcq, Paris, 1963. On Nivers' organ music see William Pruitt, 'The Organ Works of G. G. Nivers', *Recherches* XIV (1974), pp. 7–81, and XV (1975), pp. 47–90.

19. Published in a modern edition, *Livre d'orgue* (1667), ed. Dufourcq, Editions of the Schola Cantorum, Paris, 1956.

20. Modern edition by Dufourcq is Vol. 14 of Series I of the Société Française de Musicologie, Paris, 1958.

21. See the preface to Jean Bonfils' edition of the *Livre d'orgue attribué à J. N. Geoffroy* (Paris, 1974). See also N. Dufourcq, *Le Livre de l'orgue français*, IV, pp. 80–83.

22. A 'Trio en passacaille' from the Christe of the Mass in the 12th mode gave Bach the first 4 measures of his great C-Minor Passacaglia.

23. Modern edition by Dufourcq is Vol. 13 of Series I of the Société Française de Musicologie, Paris, 1952.

24. Jean Bonfils has edited two MS collections at the Bibliothèque Nationale (MSS 561/1 and 2) of *Pièces d'orgue du grand Marchand*, Paris, 1974.

Chapter 19

Instrumental Ensemble and Orchestral Music of the Seventeenth Century (pp. 289–303)

1. Brenet's *Les Concerts en France sous l'ancien régime* remains the most complete discussion of concert life in seventeenth and eighteenth century France. See also Constant Pierre, *Histoire du Concert Spirituel*, where all the programs of the *Concert Spirituel* from 1725 to 1790 are recorded (pp. 232–344).

2. See Yates, *The French Academies of the Sixteenth Century*, p. 320.

3. For the first 30 measures of a Jehan Henry fantasy ('Livres des instrumens'), Mersenne includes diminutions 'in order that one may observe the customary manner in which the Violins (24 *Violons*) *diminuer* all sorts of melodies'; this suggests that this practice was

already well established by Lully's time. 4. Trichet even commented that 'formerly one accompanied the bride and groom to the church with the sound of oboes and returned them to their home with the sound of violins'.

5. See Albert Cohen, 'The *Fantaisie* for Instrumental Ensemble in Seventeenth-Century France', *MQ*, XLVIII (1962), p. 234. See Cohen's unpublished Ph.D. dissertation, 'The Evolution of the Fantasia and Works in Related Styles in the Seventeenth-Century Instrumental Ensemble Music of France and the Low Countries', New York Univ., 1958. See also, Launay, 'La Fantaisie en France jusqu'au milieu du XVIIe siècle', *La Musique instrumentale de la Renaissance*, ed. Jean Jacquot, Paris, 1955, pp. 327–38.

6. This fantasia, anonymous in Mersenne, has since been identified as part of a fancy by Alfonso Ferrabosco II. See Cohen, p. 236.

7. Edited by Paul Hooreman for 'Le Pupitre', Paris, 1973.

8. For biographical details, see the index of the *Documents du Minutier Central* and Lesure, 'Die Terpsichore von Michael Praetorius und die Französische Instrumentalmusik unter Heinrich IV', *MF*, V (1952), pp. 7–17.

9. Edited by Martine Roche for the Société Française de Musicologie, Paris, 1971.

10. See Jaroslav Mrácek, 'An Unjustly Neglected Source for the Study and Performance of Seventeenth-Century Instrumental Dance Music', *Report of the 11th Congress of the IMS* (Copenhagen, 1972), pp. 563–71.

11. See Hitchcock, 'The Instrumental Music of Marc-Antoine Charpentier', *MQ*, XLVII (January, 1961), pp. 58–72.

Chapter 20

Instrumental Ensemble and Orchestral Music of the Early Eighteenth Century (pp. 304–319)

1. Dornel was one of six who competed for the position of organist at Ste Madeleine de la Cité. Young Rameau won the competition but chose not to accept the appointment which went to Dornel.

2. See Mellers, *François Couperin*, p. 235. Chap. 10 (pp. 234–71) is a detailed summary of the *Concerts*.

3. *Jean-Joseph Mouret*, p. 208.

4. *La Symphonie française dans la seconde moitié du XVIIIe siècle*, Paris, 1962, p. 45.

5. For a discussion of the etymology of the word 'concerto', see David D.

Boyden, 'When is a Concerto not a Concerto', *MQ*, LIII (April, 1957), pp. 220–32.

6. The composer's name is missing from the index of Palisca's *Baroque Music* and Arthur Hutching's *The Baroque Concerto*, London, 1961.

7. Such composers as Corrette, Boismortier and Naudot wrote many works for such instruments. Typical are the *Six Concertos en quatre parties pour la vièle, musette, flûte traversière, flûte à bec ou hautbois* (Opus 17) of Naudot.

8. *The Baroque Concerto*, p. 315.

Chapter 21

Sonata and Suite for Solo Instruments (pp. 320–343)

1. La Laurencie's *L'Ecole française de Violon de Lully à Viotti*, Paris, 1922–1924, is the most valuable source for a comprehensive style analysis of the violin literature in France of the period.

For a discussion of problems of technique and interpretation, see Marc Pincherle, 'La Technique du violon chez les premiers sonatistes français (1695–1723)', *Bulletin français de la SIM*, VII

(August–September, 1911), pp. 1–32, and (October, 1911), pp. 19–35. In addition, William S. Newman, *The Sonata in the Baroque Era*, rev. ed., Chapel Hill, 1966, includes a two chapter summary of the sonata in France up to 1750 (pp. 352–92). Many important extracts from the prefaces to Couperin's sonata collections are translated into English in this source.

2. See Pincherle, *Corelli, His Life, His Work*, p. 169.

3. Translated by Robert E. Preston in the preface to his edition of the *Sonatas, Op. v*, by Leclair for violin and continuo, New Haven, 1968.

4. The term is Pincherle's. See *Antonio Vivaldi et la musique instrumentale*, Paris, 1948, p. 259.

5. See Newman, *The Sonata in the Baroque Era*, p. 235 and 252.

6. Mellers, *François Couperin*, p. 103. Chapter 6 includes a detailed discussion of the sonatas.

7. See Borroff, *An Introduction to Elisabeth Claude Jacquet de La Guerre*, pp. 87–95 and 135–59.

8. *Ibid.*, 158.

9. In his *Principes de musique* (1736), Montéclair claimed credit for suggesting these symbols to Piani. The interesting passage (p. 88) follows:

> There is no symbol to designate the swelling of a sound (*son enflé*) or the diminishing of a sound (*son diminué*). Because of this, Mr dePlanes (Piani), an Italian, asked me what he could use to indicate this *agrément* in certain passages of his Sonatas. I advised him to use a line that would thicken according to the swelling of the sound and, on the contrary, would become thinner as the sound diminished. He used this innovation with success and as it was my idea, I will make use of it below.

Piani's sonatas have been edited by Barbara Jackson for A-R Editions, Madison, 1975.

10. In addition to La Laurencie and Newman, the sources are: Pincherle, *Jean-Marie Leclair*, Paris, 1952; Neal Zaslaw, 'Materials for the Life and Works of Jean-Marie Leclair, L'aîné',

unpublished Ph.D. dissertation, Columbia University, 1970; Edmond Appia, 'The Violin Sonatas of Leclair', *The Score*, III (June, 1950), pp. 3–19; Micheline Lemoine, 'La Technique violonistique de Jean-Marie Leclair', *RM*, no. 225 (1953–54), pp. 117–43; Geoffrey Nutting, 'Jean-Marie Leclair, 1698–1764', *MQ*, L (October, 1964), pp. 504–14; Robert Preston, 'The Treatment of Harmony in the Violin Sonatas of Jean-Marie Leclair', *Recherches*, III (1963), pp. 131–44; and Preston's preface to his edition of the Op. v violin sonatas is an important source not only for the Leclair sonatas but for the information it includes on performance practices and ornamentation.

11. *MQ*, L (October, 1964), p. 507. Nutting includes an analysis of the D-Minor trio, Op. IV, No. 3.

12. The most complete study to date on French Baroque flute music is Jane Bowers, 'The French Flute from 1700–1760', unpublished Ph.D. dissertation, University of California, Berkeley, 1971; see also Betty Bang Mather, *Interpretation of French Music from 1675 to 1775: for Woodwind and other Performers*, New York, 1973, and Louis Fleury, 'The Flute and Flutists in the French Art of the Seventeenth and Eighteenth Centuries', *MQ*, IX (1923), pp. 515–37.

Jane Bowers has edited La Barre's *Pièces pour flûte et basse* for 'Le Pupitre', Paris, 1976.

13. Bowers, 'The French Flute from 1700–1760', p. 159.

14. Edited by Marc Pincherle for 'Le Pupitre', Paris, 1970.

15. See Jean-François Paillard, 'Les Premiers concertos français pour instruments à vent', *RM*, Numéro spécial 226 (1954–55), p. 146.

16. Found in Gertrude Shaw, 'The Violoncello Sonata Literature in France during the eighteenth Century', unpublished Ph.D. dissertation, Catholic University, 1963.

17. The most complete study of the viol and its music in the French Baroque is Hans Bol, *La Basse de Viole du temps de Marin Marais et d'Antoine Forqueray*, Bilthoven, 1973.

18. *Concerts à deux Violes esgales du*

Sieur de Sainte-Colombe, ed. Paul Hooreman, Paris, 1973.

19. All the *avertissements* from the five books have been translated into English and are included in Gordon J. Kinney, 'Martin Marais as Editor of his own Compositions', *Journal of the Viola da Gamba Society of America*, III (1966), pp. 5–16. For helpful discussions of the viol suites of Marais, see Laurence Boulay, 'La Musique instrumentale de Marin Marais', *RM*, Numéro spécial 226 (1955), pp. 61–75; and Clyde H. Thompson's articles, 'Marin Marais' Pièces de Violes', *MQ*, XLVI (October, 1960), pp. 482–99 and 'Instrumental Style in Marin Marais's Pièces de Viole', *Recherches*, III, pp. 73–89, and his unpublished dissertation, 'The Music of Marin Marais', University of Michigan, 1959. See also André Tessier, 'L'Oeuvre de Marin Marais', *Bulletin de la Société de l'histoire de l'art français* (1924), pp. 76–80; Richard Newton, 'Hommage à Marin Marais', *The Consort* (June, 1952), pp. 12–21; and François Lesure, 'Marin Marais: sa carrière, sa famille', *RBdM*, VII (1953), pp. 129–36.

20. Reprinted in Lavignac, *Encyclopédie*, Partie II, Vol. III, *p.* 1,776.

21. On the Forqueray family see Jacques-Gabriel Prod'homme, 'Les Forqueray', *RMI*, x (1903), pp. 670–706; La Laurencie, 'Deux violistes célèbres: Les Forqueray', *Bulletin français de la SIM* (1908), pp. 1251–74, and (1909), pp. 48–60; M. Benoit and N. Dufourcq, 'A propos des Forquerays', *Recherches*, VIII (1968), pp. 229–41.

22. Quoted by Jean Bonfils, 'Forqueray', *MGG*, IV, col. 564.

23. Edited by Colin Tilney for 'Le Pupitre', Paris, 1970.

Chapter 22

Air de Cour (pp. 345–358)

1. Among the most important references are: Théodore Gérold, *L'Art du chant en France au XVIIe siècle*; Kenneth Levy, 'Vaudeville, vers mesurés et airs de cour', *Musique et poésie au XVIe siècle*, CNRS, Paris, 1954, pp. 185–199; D. P. Walker, 'The Influence of *Musique mesurée à l'antique*, particularly on the *Airs de cour* of the Early Seventeenth Century', *MD*, II (1948), pp. 141–63; André Verchaly, 'Poésie et airs de cour en France jusqu'à 1620', *Musique et poésie au XVIe siècle*, pp. 211–23; id., 'La Métrique et le rythme musical', *Report of the Eighth Congress*, New York, 1961, pp. 66–74; id., 'Air de cour et ballet de cour', *Histoire de la musique*, ed. Roland-Manuel, I, pp. 1,529–60. See also the introductions to La Laurencie and A. Mairy, *Chansons au luth et airs de cour français du XVIe siècle*, Paris, 1934, and Verchaly, *Airs de cour pour voix et luth (1603–1643)*, Vol. 16 of Series I of the Société Française de Musicologie, Paris, 1961.

2. *Musique et poésie*, p. 187.

3. See 'A propos des chansonniers de Jacques Mangeant', *Mélanges d'histoire et d'esthétique musicales offerts à Paul-Marie Masson*, II, Paris, 1955, pp. 169–77.

4. The *airs de cour* of this volume contrast strangely with the title, *Recueil des plus beaux airs accompagnés de chansons à dancer, Ballets, Chansons folâtres & Bachanales, autrement dites Vaudevires*. This may be yet another example of a publisher's mis-representing the contents of his publication for commercial ends.

5. *MD*, II, p. 141.

6. Examples of Boësset's 'N'Esperez plus mes yeux' with a diminution by Bailly and a second one by the composer are taken from Mersenne by Walker, pp. 162–53.

7. Bénigne de Bacilly, *Remarques curieuses sur l'art de bien chanter*, Paris, 1668. Trans. Austin B. Caswell, Brooklyn, 1968, p. 29.

8. On Guédron see Don Lee Royster, 'Pierre Guédron and the *air de cour*, 1600–1620', unpublished Ph.D. disserta-

tion, Yale University, 1972.

9. On Boësset see Pauline Alderman, 'Anthoine Boësset and the *air de cour*', unpublished Ph.D. dissertation, University of Southern California, 1946.

10. Discussed by Pirro in *Descartes et la musique*, Paris, 1907, pp. 114–20, and by D. P. Walker in 'Joan Albert Ban and Mersenne's Musical Competition of 1640', *M&L*, LVII (July, 1976), pp. 233–55. The entire correspondence and musical examples may be found in Jonck-

bloet and Land, *Musiques et musiciens au* XVIIᵉ *siècle*, pp. LXX–XC.

11. Masson, 'Les Brunettes', *SIMG*, XII (1910–1911), pp. 347–68. For additional information on both vocal and instrumental *brunettes* see Erich Schwandt, 'L'Affilard's Published "Sketchbooks"', *MQ*, LXIII (January, 1977), pp. 99–113.

12. Such is the case with Louis Marchand's 'Io provo nel cuore' added to Campra's *L'Europe galante*.

Chapter 23
Cantata (pp. 359–374)

1. Important sources on the history of the cantata in France are: La Laurencie, 'Le Motet et la cantate', Lavignac, *Encyclopédie*, Part 1, vol. III, pp. 1,546–562; Malherbe, preface to *Oeuvres complètes* of Rameau, III, pp. ix–xiv; David Tunley, 'The Emergence of the Eighteenth Century French Cantata', *Studies in Music*, 1 (1967), pp. 67–88; *id.*, 'An Embarkment for Cythera—Social and Literary Aspects of the Eighteenth century French Cantata', *Recherches*, VII (1967), pp. 103–14; *id.*, *The Eighteenth-Century French Cantata*, London, 1974; Gene E. Vollen, 'The French Cantata: a Survey and Thematic Catalogue', unpublished Ph.D. dissertation, North Texas State University, 1970; Launay and Simone Wallon, 'Die französische Kantate', *MGG*, VII, col. 576; and Eugen Schmitz, *Geschichte der Weltlichen Solokantate*, Wiesbaden, 1955, pp. 191–235. For a list of modern performing editions of French cantatas see Tunley's Appendix A(ii) in *The Eighteenth-Century French Cantata*.

2. These are (in chronological order): Jean-Baptiste Morin (3 books, 1706–12); Nicolas Bernier (7 books, 1706[?]–23); Jean-Baptiste Stuck (4 books, 1706–14); Elisabeth Jacquet de La Guerre (2 books, 1708, 1711); André Campra (3 books, 1708–28); Brunet de Moland (1 book, 1708); Louis-Thomas Bourgeois (2 books, 1708, 1718); Michel Pignolet de Montéclair (3 books, 1709–28); Philippe Courbois (1 book, 1710); Louis-Nicolas Clérambault (5 books, 1710–

26); Charles Hubert Gervais (1 book, 1712); André Cardinal Destouches (2 cantatas, 1716, 1719); Jean-Joseph Mouret (1 book, 1718); Nicolas Racot de Grandval (1 book, 1720); Jean-Philippe Rameau (6 extant cantatas, *c.* 1720–27); Colin de Blamont (3 books, 1723–29); Joseph Bodin de Boismortier (2 books, 1724, 1737); Laurent Gervais (2 books, 1727, 1732). Single cantatas and cantatas in MS copies may be found in Tunley's important Appendix A of his *The Eighteenth-Century French Cantata*.

3. See Quittard, 'Orphée descendant aux enfers', *RMC*, IV (1904), pp. 495–498.

4. See Launay, *MGG*, VII, col. 576.

5. *Les Forges de Lemnos* may be found in a modern edition prepared by Tunley as 'Music Series 2' and is a supplement to *Studies in Music*, 1 (1967). *Le Caffé* from Book III is edited by Hinnenthal, Kassel, 1959.

6. For background information and a style study of Clérambault's cantatas, see Tunley, 'The Cantatas of Louis Nicolas Clérambault', *MQ*, LII (July, 1966), pp. 313–31; *id.*, *The Eighteenth-Century French Cantata*, pp. 120–49; Donald H. Foster, 'Louis-Nicolas Clérambault and his Cantates françaises', unpublished Ph.D. dissertation, University of Michigan, 1967. For modern editions, see Tunley, *The Eighteenth-Century French Cantata*, Appendix A(ii).

7. For Montéclair, the ariette was not a

lively *da capo* air in compound metre, but rather a short French binary air with each section repeated.

8. This author and Diran Akmajian have edited Book III of Montéclair's cantatas for A-R Editions, Madison, 1978.

9. See Girdlestone, *J. P. Rameau*,

pp. 65–73, and Malherbe, preface to the *Oeuvres complètes*, III, pp. xv–xxxi. 10. Boismortier's *Acteon* of 1732 may be seen under the title of *Diane et Acteon*, incorrectly attributed to Rameau, in Vol. III of the *Oeuvres complètes*.

Epilogue

Thoughts on the Performance of French Baroque Music (pp. 375–380)

1. Most helpful in compiling a source list for ornamentation are the bibliographies found in the following: Robert Donington, 'Ornaments', *Grove's Dictionary*, 5th ed., VI, p. 448; *id.*, *The Interpretation of Early Music*, New Version, New York, 1974, pp. 679–728; Howard Ferguson, *Style and Interpretation* I, London, 1963, p. 20; *id.*, *Keyboard Interpretation*, New York and London, 1975, pp. 177–79; Georg Dadelson, 'Verzierungen', *MGG*, XIII, col. 1,553–1,556; and Putnam Aldrich, 'Ornamentation', *HD*, 2nd ed., p. 633. Of great value are the bibliographies of primary and secondary sources in the unpublished Ph.D. dissertations of Aldrich ('The Principal "agréments" of the Seventeenth and Eighteenth centuries', Harvard, 1942), Newman Powell ('Rhythmic Freedom in the Performance of French Music from 1650–1735', Stanford, 1958), Barbara Seagrave ('The French Style of Violin Bowing and Phrasing from Lully to Jacques Aubert', Stanford, 1958) and Austin Caswell ('The Development of Seventeenth-Century French Vocal Ornamentation and Its Influence upon Later Baroque Ornamentation Practice', University of Minnesota, 1964).

2. See, e.g., the helpful table of 'Keyboard Ornaments Used in France' in Ferguson, *Keyboard Interpretation*, pp. 138–41, and the 26 tables reproduced in Brunold's *Traité des signes et agréments employés par les clavecinistes français des 17e et 18e siècles*, Nice, 1935.

3. Preface to *The Goldberg Variations*, New York, 1938.

4. From a letter sent to the editor of *M&L*, XLVI (October, 1965), p. 381.

5. Michael Collins, 'Jean Rousseau and

the Integrity of the French Trill', *Abstracts of Papers Read at the 36th Annual Meeting of the American Musicological Society* (1970), p. 40.

6. See Thurston Dart, *The Interpretation of Music*, New York, 1963, p. 85; Brunold, *Traité des signes et agréments*, pp. 25–31; and Preston, preface to Leclair *Sonatas*, p. xxi, for summaries of how to interpret the small cross within different contexts.

7. For a bibliography of sources on the *notes inégales*, see titles under footnote 1. In addition, see Frederick Neumann, 'Inégales', *HD*, 2nd ed., p. 412. Professor Neumann has included a reference list of historical treatises that deal with the *inégales* in his important 'The French Inégales, Quantz, and Bach', *JAMS*, XVIII (1965), pp. 318–19. Neumann's list may be supplemented with additional treatises or prefaces found in Powell's dissertation, pp. 75–146. For a summary of sources from the period that deal with 'inégalité' see Jean Saint-Arroman, 'Les Inégalités', in *L'Interprétation de la musique française* · · ·, pp. 67–86.

8. *The Interpretation of Music*, p. 81. See also Donington, *The Interpretation of early Music*, New Version, pp. 448–51; and Geoffroy-Dechaume, *Les 'secrets' de la musique ancienne*, Paris 1964, p. 37.

9. 'La Note pointée et la soi-disant "manière française"', *RdM*, LI (1965), pp. 66–92. Translated by Raymond Harris and Edmund Shay as 'The Dotted Note and the so-called French Style', *Early Music*, V (July, 1977), pp. 310–24. The battle of the double dot rages unabated. See Michael Collins'

answer to Neumann in his 'A Reconsideration of French Over-Dotting', *M&L, L* (January, 1969), pp. 111–23, and Neumann's response, 'Facts and Fiction about Overdotting', *MQ, LXIII* (April, 1977), pp. 155–85. See also David Fuller, 'Dotting, the "French style" and Frederick Neumann's Counter-Reformation', *Early Music*, v (October, 1977), pp. 517–35.

10. *Exposition and Development*, New York, 1962, p. 128.

11. Following are some modern sources that discuss musical taste in the France of the eighteenth century within the larger concept of aesthetics: Ecorcheville, *De Lulli à Rameau 1690–1730; l'esthé-tique musicale*, Paris, 1906; Prunières, 'Lecerf de la Viéville et l'esthétique musicale classique au xvIIe siècle', *Bulletin français de la SIM*, IV (1908), pp. 619–54; Alfred Oliver, *The Encyclopedists as Critics of Music*, New York, 1947; Gisele Brelet, 'Philosophie et esthétique musicales', *Précis de musicologie*, Paris, 1958, pp. 397–400; Georges Snyders, *Le Goût musical en France aux XVIIe et XVIIIe siècles*, Paris, 1968; and Maria Rika Maniates, ' "Sonate, que me veux-tu?" The Enigma of French Musical Aesthetics in the Eighteenth Century', *CM*, no. 9 (1969), pp. 117–40.

Index